A Treatise on
Political Economy

A Treatise on Political Economy

Jean-Baptiste Say

with a new introduction by
Munir Quddus & Salim Rashid

Transaction Publishers
New Brunswick (U.S.A.) and London (U.K.)

New material this edition copyright © 2001 by Transaction Publishers, New Brunswick, New Jersey. Originally published in 1836 by Grigg & Elliot.

This book is printed on acid-free paper that meets the American National Standard for Permanence of Paper for Printed Library Materials.

Library of Congress Catalog Number: 00-064810
ISBN: 0-7658-0653-3
Printed in the United States of America

Library of Congress Cataloging-in-Publication Data

Say, Jean Baptiste, 1767-1832.
    A treatise on political economy / Jean Baptiste Say ; with a new introduction by Munir Quddus and Salim Rasid.
        p. cm.
    Reprint. Originally published: New York : A.M. Kelly, bookseller, 1971, in series: Reprints of economic classics.
        Includes bibliographical references.
        ISBN 0-7658-0653-3 (pbk. : alk. paper)
        1. Economics I. Title.

HB163 .S26 2000
330.15'3—dc21   00-064810
Translated from the fourth edition of the French, by C.R. Prinsep, with notes by the translator.
Original introduction and additional notes by Clement C. Biddle, LL.D.

CONTENTS.

BOOK I.

OF THE PRODUCTION OF WEALTH.

BOOK II.

OF THE DISTRIBUTION OF WEALTH.

BOOK III.

OF THE CONSUMPTION OF WEALTH.

INTRODUCTION TO THE
TRANSACTION EDITION

JEAN-BAPTISTE SAY AND THE *TREATISE*—A PERSPECTIVE

JEAN-BAPTISTE Say (1767–1832) was one of the most important writers in political economy in France and in Europe in the late eighteenth and early nineteenth centuries.[1] Although primarily an economist with the unique distinction of holding the first professorship of political economy in France, he was a scholar with broad interests. A friend of many important literary and political personalities on the French, European, and American scene, he is widely recognized as a distinguished commentator on political and social events of his time. David Ricardo, Thomas Malthus, Thomas Jefferson and Benjamin Franklin were among those with whom Say corresponded on a variety of issues. He has been described as a revolutionary, an author of scholarly books and popular tracts, a social philosopher, a successful entrepreneur—a remarkable Renaissance man. It has been recently pointed out that Say's life coincided with two great revolutions in human history, the French Revolution which he directly experienced and the Industrial Revolution in England of which he was a keen student. Both of these events greatly influenced his writings and development as a political economist and as a social philosopher. The two great merits in Say's writings were his chosen style of exposition—designed with the average interested citizen in mind—and his zeal for economic education for the masses. Say is one of those who believed that true political economy would be of immeasurable benefit to the common mass of mankind. He was always motivated by a desire to improve the lot of the common man and to make the truths of the new science evident by the experience of ordinary life. Present-day readers of this volume would benefit by these traits in the writings of Say and by the remarkable freshness in some of his ideas even as these approach the two-hundred-year mark. The longevity of Say's book proves that good ideas can successfully bear the imprint of time.

Jean-Baptiste Say was born in Lyons, France in 1767. In 1787 at age twenty, he moved to Paris with his parents. As a part of his education he had traveled to England, learning business and the English language during the two years he lived there. As a young man in Paris, Say worked for an insurance firm and was later associated with a revolutionary group of intellectuals with whom he founded and edited a journal called *Decade Philosophique*. In 1799 he was appointed a member of the *Tribunat* attached to the *Comite' des Finances* created by Napoleon. However, Say along with several members resigned from the *Tribunnat*, protesting Napoleon's dictatorship.[2] Subsequently, he turned down an offer for a high position in the French tax bureaucracy, set up a cotton factory with a partner, and for the next eleven years (1799–1810) devoted himself to entrepreneurship, building his business into a large textile company until he was forced to sell it, Although Say had read Adam Smith's famous book on political economy in an early edition, he purchased his own copy of the fifth edition of the *Wealth of Nations* only in 1789.[3] Say's earlier reading of the *Wealth of Nations* may have been the catalyst for his interest in economics. In 1803 he published the first edition of his book, *A Treatise on Political Economy or The Production, Distribution and Consumption of Wealth* (henceforth, the *Treatise*). Because of the dictatorship, it was difficult for Say, who was unsympathetic to Napoleon, to write and publish freely in France. After the fall of Napoleon, Say was officially sent on a mission to England to find out how far France had fallen behind in the Industrial Revolution sweeping across England. In 1819 he became the first French academic teacher of economics when he began teaching a course on "industrial economics" at the *Conservatoire des Arts et Me'tiers*. In 1830, he was appointed the first professor of political economy at the *College de France* in Paris. Jean-Baptiste Say died in 1832, a much admired man in France and widely known in Europe and America as a talented expositor of Adam Smith and an original contributor to political economy. The history of economics would be different without the contributions of Jean-Baptiste Say.

For the American reader, it might be helpful to know that Say was deeply interested in America. According to his published correspondence with Jefferson, he had seriously contemplated moving to America and building a textile factory near the cotton plantations. He kept in close touch with events in America.[4] Several important Americans, including Benjamin Franklin and Thomas Jefferson, were known to him personally. Like other Frenchmen of his generation, Say was greatly impressed with Benjamin Franklin, and even wrote a short biography which was published as an introduction to the 1974 reprint of the French translation of Franklin's book *Poor Richard's Almanac*.[5]

In 1803, soon after publishing his book, Say sent a copy to President Jefferson. In his letter, he expressed his personal compliments to Jefferson and his deep admiration for the new nation that he hoped would become the light of the world.

> Please accept the homage of my *Treatise in Political Economy* as a mark of my high regard for your personal qualities and the principles that you profess. I hope you may find in it some signs of that enlightened love of liberty and humanity for which right-thinking man so much respect you.

> The happiness enjoyed by your country, and greatly enhanced under your administration, is enough to arouse the envy of the nations of Europe; your prosperity may be the source of theirs. They will see the degree of happiness attainable by a human society that practices common sense in its legislation, economy in its expenditures, and morality in its politics. It will no longer be possible to represent wise counsels as mere impractical theories. (Palmer, 83-84)

Jefferson cordially responded to Say in 1804 with some thoughts on future possibilities of trade and commerce between America and Europe. Ten years later, in 1814, Say sent Jefferson a copy of the second edition of the *Treatise*. In his letter to the retired President, he gave a brief history of the second edition of the book, mentioning the danger of it being suppressed in revolutionary France, and also wrote about his own somewhat exaggerated expectations of the success of the new edition. It was in this letter to Jefferson that Say chose to discuss his plans to emigrate to America.

> Ten years ago I had the honor of receiving your letter of February 1, 1804, acknowledging receipt of the first edition of my *Treatise on Political Economy*...

Moments of leisure in a busy life in the depths of the countryside allowed me to start over and entirely remake my Treatise on Political Economy, and the latest political events have finally removed the obstacles to the printing of my work. It has now just appeared, and to prevent the stopping of its circulation I have put it under the protection of the emperor of Russia....

If you take the trouble to look through it, I flatter myself to think that you will find that I have been able, by a better method, to place Political Economy on such a secure foundation that it will henceforth be counted among the positive sciences. I do not think that it can now face any insoluble difficulty, and the consequences to be drawn from it for improvement of the social art and for human happiness seem to me immense.

... and I will admit that I am thinking seriously of settling there (United States) myself with my wife and four younger children. I will be deterred only by the uncertainty of being able to make a living by using my assets, which are not great, to purchase and develop a tract of land. (Palmer, 84-85)

With the defeat of Napoleon at Waterloo, the political landscape in France changed markedly in 1815. For Say the atmosphere had greatly improved and he cancelled his plans to immigrate to America. The *Treatise*, however, was well received in America, both in the political circles and in academia. The supporters of free trade and the doctrine of *laissez faire* published the first American edition of the English translation of the *Treatise*. The book was also used as a text at Harvard University and was popular with citizens and scholars interested in the subject because the *Treatise* was considered more lucid and understandable than the *Wealth of Nations*.

During Say's life, the *Treatise* went through five editions and was translated into the major European languages, and, belatedly into English in 1821. The first American translation came out in the same year, followed by twenty-eight reprints over sixty years, all in the United States. This alone suggests the considerable impact of the *Treatise* in the United States on the learning and teaching of economics in the nineteenth century, much more so than in England. It was also used as a textbook on economics in Europe. Along with McCulloch's book, the *Treatise* was the dominant textbook in political economy used in American institutions of higher learning. The book also had considerable influence over textbooks on political economy subsequently published in America.[6]

Say was unhappy with the English translation of his book by C. R. Prinsep. There were good reasons for his displeasure, as the editor had not only dropped the introductory chapter but also included notes critical of Say's views, all without giving the author an opportunity to respond. Say wrote to Prinsep politely thanking him for his endeavors but expressed his disappointment with the decision to drop the preamble and with the translator's critical notes.[7] In an occasionally scathing letter, Say wrote a detailed rebuttal to each note on which they disagreed. Say evidently felt the preamble was of significance.

> I know not why you have supposed that a preamble setting forth the purpose of political economy, answering objections raised against it as a field of knowledge, showing its advantages to mankind, and giving a brief history of its progress, should be without interest for readers of a book on this subject. Professors using it as a text in Italy, Germany, Poland, Russia, Sweden, and Holland have not shared in your opinion. (Palmer, 125)

The American editor of *Treatise* was more respectful of the author. Not only was the missing introductory chapter brought back, but also Prinsep's critical notes were deleted. Say wrote to the American editor thanking him for including the introductory chapter. Colonel Clement C. Biddle, a former Federalist, merchant, and writer had published the first American edition of the *Treatise* in 1821 to strengthen the cause of free trade and economic learning in the United States. At the time Ricardo was waging a war against the Corn Laws in England, the United States too was divided on the issue of free trade and the benefits of unencumbered foreign commerce. One group wanted the system of restrictions and prohibitions on foreign trade and the other stood for "the natural course of things"[8] without any artificial support for the manufacturers. The latter group, composed of rice, cotton, and tobacco planters and most of the merchants, was stronger both numerically and in ideas. According to Biddle, Say rigidly pursued the "inductive method of investigation" against the hypothetical method of Ricardo and succeeded in presenting a complete analysis of the simple and general laws on which production, distribution, and consumption of wealth depend. Any sentence or passage in the book inconsistent with the free-trade stand of the editor and his group was "corrected" in the appropriate footnotes. For example, Biddle found Say, like Smith, to be in error in declaring that internal commerce is most advantageous, though foreign trade should not be restrained. Capital, whether in home or in foreign trade, is equally productive, said the editor for if home trade realized a greater profit, capital would leave foreign trade and enter the former.[9]

In the United States, some influential people believed that, with few exceptions, the doctrine of *laissez faire* was true, but the task of fully exploring these exceptions had not yet been adequately performed by the economists. Others agreed with Napoleon's view on economists as "mere systematizers, whose principles were correct in theory, but erroneous in practice."[10] Among those opposed to the views of Classical economists on the merits of free trade were Caleb Cushing, a former Harvard tutor, who published a book in 1825 called *Summary of the Practical Principles of Political Economy.* A self-proclaimed friend of domestic industry, Cushing denounced Adam Smith and Jean-Baptiste Say and regretted the use of the *Treatise* as a textbook at Harvard.[11]

Thomas Jefferson was perhaps the most prominent American statesman of the era who was acquainted with J. B. Say and his work. Jefferson was a friend and correspondent of such leading contemporary figures in the sciences as J. B. Say and Dupont de Nemours. He was well read in the standard literature of political economy and found the new subject useful in formulating and defending his political views.[12] According to Jefferson, the great advantage of the *Treatise* was that it presented the same principles as the *Wealth of Nations* in a "shorter compass and more lucid manner."[13]

According to both Schumpeter and Dorfman, the most popular European book on political economy used as a text in the United States was the *Treatise.* J. B. Say was known to his readers as the French professor with long experience in business and also as the translator of Franklin's *Poor Richard* for distribution among the French poor. Say, who enjoyed the friendship of Jefferson, was closely attuned to the American mind.

The *Treatise* unabashedly praised America, avoided the distinction between "productive" and "unproductive" employment, presented the role of the entrepreneur as the great organizer of industry, treated *laissez faire* as the only sensible economic policy, and, according to some, pretended to teach individuals as well as nations how to get rich. Any reservations on free markets or trade or on the question of unrestrained freedom of acquisition in the *Treatise* were duly answered in footnotes by the American editor for whom the book provided ample ammunition to support his own *laissez faire* views. According to Dorfman, another reason for the popularity of the *Treatise* in America was the fact that a condensed version of the book had been available in America earlier. This elementary condensed version of the book, translated into English and titled *Catechism of Political Economy* or *Familiar Conversations on the Manner in Which Wealth is Produced, Distributed, and Consumed in Society*, had been available in America since 1817 from a reprint by Mathew Carey. A conservative reviewer described it as a convenient compendium for those who love to arrive directly at conclusions.[14]

In his Introduction ("Advertisement") to the 1834 reprint of the sixth edition, Biddle paid high tributes to the author not just for Say's scholarly and public attainments but also because,

His private life was a model of domestic virtues . . . he passed unsullied through all the trials and temptations which have left a stain on every man of feeble virtue among his conspicuous contemporaries. He kept aloof from public life, but was the friend and trusted adviser of some of its brightest ornaments; and few have contributed more, though in private station, to keep alive in the hearts and in the contemplation of men, a lofty standard of public virtue. (Say 1971, v)

Regarding the *Treatise*, Biddle wrote in his Introduction to the first American edition (1832) of the English translation of the fifth edition, "It is unquestionably the most methodical, comprehensive and best digested treatise on the elements of political economy that has yet been presented to the world."

(Say 1880, vi). In the 1834 reprint of the sixth edition, the editor wrote:

> Perhaps the writings of no authors, however great their celebrity may be, are exerting a more powerful and enduring influence on the well-being of the people of Europe and America than those of Adam Smith and John Baptiste Say. (1971, iv)

What are some of the defects in the *Treatise*? Critics of the book have referred to Say's excessive emphasis on the doctrine of *laissez faire*, his optimism with regard to the role of the free markets ignoring the possibility of market failure of any type, and his belittling of the role of the state in supporting free markets and trade. Others have pointed to his confusion between the individual and social point of view, his narrow and jealous criticism of Smith, Malthus and Ricardo,[15] and the semblance of superficiality in his writings.[16]

The American editor, Clement Biddle, did point out that there are a few errors in the work. He, however, remarked that these errors are minor in nature, easily detectable, and would not mislead the reader. He compared the *Treatise* with A. Smith's *Wealth of Nations* only to conclude that in many aspects Say's book is superior. The debates between Say and his English critics, namely Ricardo and Malthus, were discussed mostly in favor of Say. The editor suggested that the superior techniques used by the English writers may have swayed some readers in their favor, but that did not imply that Say's critics were right.

> The mathematical cast given to their reasoning by these writers has captivated and led astray the understandings of intelligent and sagacious readers, and induced them to adopt, as scientific truths, what, when properly investigated and analyzed, are found to be merely specious hypothesis. (1880, viii)

Biddle expressed astonishment that the English editor of the book did not include the introductory chapter. He felt satisfied that this mistake had been rectified in the American edition and that the reader now had access to the most recent edition of the book without the extraneous and provocative comments of the translator.

The *Treatise* was a milestone in Say's career as a political economist. Upon this book rests his reputation as the leading

French economist of his time. Say wrote on economic issues in a number of other forums but kept coming back to this book which he revised many times, incorporating new developments in the field and responding to his critics. The book represents the crown jewel of his contributions as an economist.

What would be a fair and accurate assessment of the significance of the *Treatise* in the intellectual history of economics? We agree with Schumpeter, Haney, and other scholars that in the arena of political economy Say was no Smith or Ricardo; but he was no mere popularizer either. His abilities and contributions to economic science were significant enough to earn him a lasting place in the intellectual history of economics. The history of political economy would have been different without J. B. Say and the *Treatise*.[17]

THE ORGANIZATION AND CONTENT OF THE *TREATISE*

The Augustus M. Kelley Reprints of Economic Classics, 1971 edition of the *Treatise*, on which this reprint is based, has 488 pages, 42 chapters (22+11+9 in that order in the three books) and a 45-page preamble translated by Clement Biddle. An appendix to Part III is also included. The book is divided into three parts. Part I deals with the production of wealth and includes chapters on production and also on what is today considered to be macro and monetary topics. It is in this part of the book, chapter XV to be exact, that the famous Law of Markets is expounded. Part II addresses the distribution of wealth and topics on state revenues from industry, land, and capital. This section also includes topics on customs, commercial policy, trade, and population. Part III deals with the consumption of wealth and the implications of private and public consumption for revenue collection and the economy. The *Treatise* was rightly recognized by reviewers for its original subject classification scheme, namely the arrangement of the chapters into the three broad categories of economic activities—production, distribution, and consumption.

In his Introduction, Say provides an overview of the scope and methodology of political economy, a rapid sketch of the history of the development of economic ideas up to the period when the *Wealth of Nations* was published and the merits of the inductive method of investigation. The 46-page preamble also includes a frontal attack on many of the mercantilist ideas that, despite the efforts of the Physiocrats, were prevalent in France. Lastly, the chapter presents a critique of Adam Smith who Say considered to be the person most qualified to be named the father of the new discipline.

Book I ("On the Production of Wealth") clarifies the definition of wealth, its measurement in terms of value and price and, importantly, a recognition that value arises not from the labor embedded in production but from the intrinsic utility perceived by others who are willing to purchase the product in exchange for other goods. In fact, Say claims to be the first to use the word "utility" to describe "the inherent fitness or capability of certain things to satisfy the various wants of mankind."[18] Therefore, the production of wealth lies not in the creation of new "matter," which man cannot do, but the in creation of utility, which man can do by giving matter another form. Production itself is defined as "the creation, not of matter, but of utility."[19] He goes on to distinguish three forms of industry—agriculture, manufacturing, and commerce. Each is useful in contributing to production of wealth. He emphasizes that more savings and more capital are accumulated from industry and commerce than from agriculture.[20] Thus earlier writers were in error when they suggested that only agriculture produces wealth and industry and commerce only deals in transfer of this wealth.

The capital of a nation is simply the sum of the private capital of its citizens. Are there any limits to wealth creation? Say argued that "it is not nature, but ignorance and bad government, that limit the productive power of industry."[21] He goes on to discuss how specialization increases productivity many fold and contributes to the wealth of a nation. He draws his examples, like Smith, from everyday items that are marvels of modern civilization, items like glass, paper, and razor blades. The first of the three important steps in modern production is knowledge, the second is the application of this knowledge to produce something useful, and the last step in modern production is the application of labor. These three operations are performed by different persons, and this specialization is the key to the prodigious productivity of modern industry.[22] An interesting discussion of trading or "transport over time" or speculation is also included in this chapter. Say very clearly explains why it is an error to confine wealth to raw materials and physical capital.[23] As Smith has demonstrated, wealth consists of raw material, plus the value added.

Chapter XV with the title "On the Demand or Market for Products" discusses what later came to be called the Law of Market or simply Say's law. Nowhere did Say use the phrase "supply creates its own demand," although several passages do imply this. Towards the end of the chapter, Say raises the specter of recession. "Depopulation, misery, and returning barbarism occupy the place of abundance and happiness," whenever "by reason of blunders of the nation or its government, production is stationary, or does not keep pace with consumption, the demand gradually declines."[24] It follows that it is not overproduction that leads to a glut or recession but rather policy mistakes on the part of the government. State intervention and regulations are roundly condemned in chapter XVII: "The grand mischiefs of authoritative interference proceed not from exceptions to established maxims, but from false ideas of the nature of things, and false maxims built upon them."[25] One of the earliest statements on the benefits of the European union is found in the discussion of Napoleon's conquests. Say wrote that by causing a breakdown in commerce between England and other nations, he did a great deal of injury to these lands. He goes on to say that France has greatly benefited as these conquests have brought down the barriers and "the world at large would derive similar benefit from the demolition of those, which insulate, as it were, the various communities, into which the human race is divided."[26]

After the creation of wealth (production) is taken care of in Book I, the next part (Book II) addresses the distribution of wealth. To understand distribution, according to Say, the nature of value and the object of distribution must be first investigated, followed by the laws that regulate the distribution of value once created. Separate chapters are devoted to the distribution of income ("revenue") from industry, from capital, and from land. In addition, a chapter is devoted to income generated from foreign trade ("revenue between nations"). Say discusses at length how population plays a role in economic development and what factors determine the distribution of income between groups within a nation. The important role of property rights (justice of right of property) in the creation of wealth is discussed.

Book III examines issues in the consumption of wealth. Early on, the author discusses how consumption and production are related: "production cannot be afforded without consumption."[27] Somewhat narrowly, consumption is defined as the process of destruction of utility, not that of matter. The national consumption is "the aggregate values consumed within the year by all the individuals and communities."[28] By consumption he means output that is used up and not wealth that helps produce the output. Just as in production, he emphasizes that it is "utility" that is consumed and not matter itself. His remark that a good can be consumed only once shows that he failed to take into consideration "public" goods where many can simultaneously enjoy utility. He did understand the difference between stocks and flows in a national accounting framework (a landed estate cannot be consumed; but its annual production). Say attempted to clarify some of the national income accounting concepts. The annual consumption of a nation is defined as the aggregate values consumed within the year by all the individuals and the communities in the nation. He states that imports should be considered as part of the national product, and exports a part of national consumption (389). In chapter two, he makes a distinction between productive and unproductive consumption. Whereas unproductive consumption results in immediate gratification but no new value, productive consumption requires an exertion of labor and skills (industry). This is the standard distinction between consumption and investment.

Recent scholarship in the history of economic ideas has generally been favorable to the view that Say did make lasting contributions to political economy in a number of areas. These include his writings on the schema of economics, the scope and methodology of economics, utility theory, his emphasis on the central role of the entrepreneur, his discussions on the triad factors of production, his recognition of the importance of the role of economic education and last, but not least, his Law of Markets. Moreover, Say's contribution to economics goes beyond the *Treatise*. He played a significant role as one of the early pioneers in political economy and helped dispel the entrenched populist myths of mercantilism. He was above all an economic educator and a social philosopher deeply concerned with the general welfare of man.

DEFINITION, SCOPE, AND METHODOLOGY

Like other writers of the era, the desire to define the purpose and scope of the new discipline on the part of Say is understandable. The introductory chapter of the *Treatise* discussed why the discipline was called political economy and whether the term was appropriate. In other writings, Say used the term political economy interchangeably with terms such as the economy of society, social economy, and the economy of nations. We are also reminded that political economy is a "moral science" since it is based on human considerations and seeks to improve the welfare of all citizens, rich or poor. It is clear that Say believed that most issues in political economy are multidisciplinary in nature.

In the preamble, Say tackled the definition of political economy. He wrote that most contemporary writers seemed to be confused on how economics relates to politics. Political economy and political science have much in common although they are different sciences. He was somewhat skeptical of the notion that political liberty and democracy are preconditions for economic prosperity:

Wealth, nevertheless, is essentially independent of political organization. Under every form of government, a state whose affairs are well administered may prosper. Nations have risen to opulence under absolute monarchs, and have been ruined by popular councils.[29] (xv)

The secret to wealth creation is good governance, not liberty. In this he would not be politically correct by contemporary standards. However, Say was convinced that only a free and representative government that can assure and protect individual liberty could maintain the most productive economy. Such a state would improve the welfare of all citizens, not just the rich and powerful.

Say made a strong case for distinguishing economics from related fields. His own definition of economics is somewhat novel: "In the science of political economy, agriculture, commerce and manufactures are considered only in relation to the increase or diminution of wealth, and not in reference to their processes of execution" (xvi). He goes on to say, "to acquire a thorough knowledge of the causes and consequences of each phenomenon, the study of political economy is essentially necessary to them all" (xvi).

Say had much to say about the scope and usefulness of this new field of inquiry. He had a vision that the study of political economy would be "useful" to both the rulers and the ordinary citizens. He passionately believed that every citizen should be familiar with the basic principles of political economy. In his opinion, men of business could not succeed without a basic understanding of the principles of political economy and wealth creation. He was concerned with opposition to the new discipline from various quarters. He had expected that the wealthy class, having already achieved success, might choose to oppose the spread of this knowledge among the ordinary citizens. Therefore, he found support from the business community for the young science very encouraging. It reinforced his belief that the new discipline could be beneficial to practical men in both the private and the public sector. For the rulers, politicians, and others involved in policy making, he considered the knowledge of economics indispensable. France, he wrote, had fallen behind its potential for nearly two centuries because of misguided economic policies influenced by the mercantilist school of thought.

Say was critical of the practice of blindly applying the principles of Baconian inductive reasoning to political economy. Theory should not be formulated before gathering appropriate facts. But what are the facts? Science can be "descriptive," simply arranging and discussing the properties found in nature, or it may be "experimental," where the emphasis is on the connection between cause and effect. In this sense, political economy is clearly experimental.

On the Usefulness of Mathematical Methods in Political Economy

Say held strong reservations on the suitability of statistics and mathematics in political economy. A distrust of quantification pervades Say's writings on political economy. He was concerned that mathematics, instead of serving the discipline as a useful tool of analysis, would eventually come to dominate the methodology and scope of political economy. Say is known for his lack of faith in the importance and usefulness of mathematics in political economy. Following Smith's reservations regarding political arithmetic Say wrote: "Dr. Smith accordingly avows, that he puts no great faith in political arithmetic; which is nothing more than the arrangement of numerous statistical data" (xix-xx).

Say's opposition to mathematics and statistics may seem to contradict his fascination with science in general and the inductive method of investigation in particular that permeates his writings. For example, "The excellence of this method consists in only admitting facts carefully observed, and the consequences rigorously deduced from them; thereby effectually excluding those prejudices and authorities which, in every department of literature and science, have so often been interposed between man and truth" (Say 1880, xvii). It is clear that his opposition to statistics and mathematical methods was based on considerations that, although statistics and quantitative methods are helpful in advancing a science, there are dangers in the incorrect and fallacious use of these methods.

Say was convinced that political economy did not need higher mathematics in order for it to evolve into a mature science. The attempts to foist quantitative techniques on eco-

nomics just to gain respectability as a science must be resisted. Say's opposition is noteworthy because he himself frequently noted the importance of maximization as a unifying
principle in economics (Palmer 124, 130). Responding to
those in the hard sciences who looked down upon the
new field of inquiry because of a lack of its mathematical content, he thought that these scholars misunderstood the essentially moral nature of political economy:

> Persons, moreover, distinguished by their attainments in other branches of
> knowledge, but ignorant of the principles of this, are too apt to suppose that
> absolute truth is confined to mathematics and to results of careful observation
> and experiment in physical sciences, imagining that the moral and political
> sciences contain no invariable facts or indisputable truths, and therefore cannot
> be considered as genuine sciences. (xxiv)

What are some of the other reasons for Say's lack of enthusiasm for mathematical tools? Say felt that the moral and subjective natures of many variables in political economy are
such that attempts to quantify or measure them precisely would
be inappropriate. The essentially moral and subjective natures
of economic variables would render the facts and values in-
determinate and therefore, non-quantifiable.

> Political economy like mathematics is based on an abstraction; in mathematics
> one deals in magnitudes, in political economy one deals in values. As
> values are susceptible of increase or decrease they belong to the
> domain of mathematics but as they are subject to the action of the
> faculties, needs and the will of man, they return to the domain of
> morals. And this, by the way, shows how it is superfluous to apply
> the formulae of algebra to the demonstrations of Political Economy.
> No quantity, there, is susceptible of a rigorous evaluation. (Say, quoted
> in Theocharis, 84)

On a different occasion, he wrote:

> All attempts to reduce political economy to mathematical calculations had been
> misleading, for the simple reason that this discipline called upon human will,
> human needs and faculties, which did not provide sufficiently precise data to
> constitute the basis of calculation. (Menard, 528)

Facts are essential to building a science, but Say had little
faith in facts without the benefit of theory.[30] He believed that
political economy should be the foundation of statistics, not

the reverse. The relation between political economy and statistics is discussed at several places: "Between political economy and statistics, there is the same difference as between the science of politics and history" (xix). A complete knowledge of the principles of political economy can be discovered, but statistics being simply a recital of facts can never achieve this. Obviously, this comment is based on nineteenth-century statistics that was largely descriptive in its approach. Menard argued that the three most important French economists of the nineteenth century, Say, Cournot, and Walras, all opposed the use of statistical methods in economics for different reasons.

Say anticipated the possible abuse of data gathering and statistical techniques, a topic that has resurfaced in the contemporary debate on the role of econometrics and mathematical methods:

> there is not an absurd theory or extravagant opinion that has not been supported by an appeal to facts; and it is by facts that public authorities have been so often misled. But a knowledge of facts, without a knowledge of their mutual relations, without being able to show why the one is a cause, and the other a consequence, is really no better than crude information of an office clerk. (xxi)

Decrying attempts to apply higher mathematics to the young discipline of economics, Say argued forcefully that the reality is much too complex for greater precision of the tools of analysis to be productive:

> It would, however, be idle to imagine that greater precision or more steady direction could be given to this study, by the application of mathematics to the solution of its problems. The values with which political economy is concerned, admitting of the application to them of the terms plus and minus, are indeed within the range of mathematical inquiry; but being at the same time subject to the influence of the faculties, the wants and the desires of mankind, they are not susceptible of any rigorous appreciation, and cannot, therefore, furnish any data for absolute calculations. In political as well as in physical science, all that is essential is a knowledge of the connection between causes and their consequences. Neither the phenomenon of the moral or material world are subject to strict arithmetical computation. (xxvi)[31]

On Adam Smith

Students of the history of economic thought know that Say considered himself a disciple of the famous Scotsman whom he quoted profusely and openly honored as the father of the science of political economy. A critic might suggest that Say had a Messianic belief in the value of Adam Smith's writings. Even though he came to be quite critical of many views in the *Wealth of Nations*, these criticisms found little public expression and were always couched in sympathetic terms. A possible explanation is that much in the manner of Francis Horner, Say thought it politically inexpedient to expose the errors of Adam Smith.

The *Treatise* served as a bridge between the writings of Adam Smith and other Classical and Neo-Classical writers. Say recognized Smith as the master who traveled widely in Europe and absorbed the best knowledge in the discipline, which he integrated into his groundbreaking book, the *Wealth of Nations*. This monumental work alone earns for Smith the title of father of the new science of political economy. Say was in complete agreement with most of Smith's ideas and expressed his profuse admiration for these contributions. Indeed, his admiration for Smith's work was considered excessive by some commentators who disparagingly called him a "vulgarizer" or "popularizer" of Smith. On the same grounds, Marx and his followers also dismissed Say as an uncritical apologist for capitalism and free markets. The facts are more complex. Despite Say's great regard for Smith, he was a critical reviewer of the *Wealth of Nations*,[32] attempting to correct some of Smith's errors in the *Treatise*. In his opinion, despite giving birth to a new science and discovering many important laws, Smith's book suffered from several errors. He spent several passages in the introductory chapter discussing the merits as well as the errors in Smith. He believed Smith's presentation and organization of material in the book showed poor judgment and led to a few errors. This perspective was at odds with that of other reviewers who had praised Smith for the gracefulness of his writing. On substantive issues, Smith's theory of value is incorrect. It gave too much significance to labor, ignoring other sources of value such as capital. In the introductory chapter, Smith's book is critically described, "it is not, however, a complete treatise of either sci-

ence, but an irregular mass of curious and original speculations, and of known demonstrated results" (xix). Toward the
end of his career, Say's comments on Smith's book suggest
that his views seem to have solidified over the years:

> ... a work that contained enough truths to constitute a true science, but in
> which perhaps they are brought together with too much confusion, are too
> undigested and too poorly connected with each other to form a homogeneous
> whole and carry complete conviction. (Quoted in Palmer, 154)

In the introductory chapter, Say discusses the intellectual history of economics from the ancient literature to his own time.
He analyzes the contributions to economic ideas of Plato,
Aristotle, and other authors in Western civilization. He
searches for and finds a few precursors to Smith's ideas on
production and other topics, but quickly absolves Smith
for not being copious in his footnotes or generous to his
precursors. The highest praise of Smith's work is paid in the
following passages which clearly indicates the impact of
Baconian ideas:

> Many principles strictly correct had often been advanced prior to the time of
> Dr. Smith; he, however, was the first author who established their truth. Nor is
> this all. He has furnished us, also, with the true method of detecting errors; he
> has applied to political economy the new mode of scientific investigation,
> namely, of not looking for principles abstractedly, but by ascending from facts
> the most constantly observed, to the general laws which govern them. The
> work of Dr. Smith is a succession of demonstrations, which has elevated many
> propositions to the rank of indisputable principles, and plunged a still greater
> number into that imaginary gulf into which extravagant hypotheses and vague
> opinions for a certain period struggle before being forever swallowed up.
> (1971, xxxviii-xxxix)

> In his work, its author demonstrated that wealth was the exchangeable value of
> things; that its extent was proportional to the number of things in our posses-
> sion having value; and that in as much as value could be given or added to
> matter, that wealth could be created and engrafted on things previously desti-
> tute of value, and there be preserved, accumulated or destroyed. (1971, xxxvii)

> Whenever the *Inquiry into the Wealth of Nations* is perused with the attention
> it so well merits, it will be perceived that until the epoch of its publication, the
> science of political economy did not exist. (1971, xxviii)

Say identified and attempted to correct the following errors in
the *Wealth of Nations*:

(1) The labor theory of value. Whereas Smith viewed human labor as the sole source of value, Say considered it more correct to say that the industry of man combines with other agents in nature and capital to produce value. Thus Smith overemphasized labor and underestimated the contribution of capital.

(2) A definition of wealth that includes only values fixed and realized in material substance. Say considered this too narrow, arguing that human talents and acquired skills should also be deemed a part of the wealth of a nation. "Of two individuals equally destitute of fortune, the one in possession of a particular talent is by no means as poor as the other" (xlii).

Points (1) and (2) follow from an important and fundamental divergence between Say and Smith. The purpose of economic activity is to create "utility," not material products. Once established, this serves to demonstrate both (1) and (2).

(3) A limited description of the nature of industrial and commercial production. For example, how do improved communications help spur industrial production?

(4) The role of the entrepreneur was not sufficiently emphasized in the *Wealth of Nations*. Modern scholars see this as an outstanding characteristic of Say.

(5) Smith's theory of distribution leaves much to be desired. Say pointed out that this theory could develop into a whole new branch of inquiry if pursued with rigor.

(6) Yet another contention is with the Smithian treatment of consumption and savings. Smith failed to develop a detailed theory of consumption and should have made a distinction between productive and unproductive consumption. By the former, Say meant spending on capital equipment that arises from savings.

(7) Finally, the plan of the *Wealth of Nations* is critically evaluated, "... the manner in which these doctrines are unfolded, is liable to no less weighty objections" (xliii). Elsewhere Say claimed that Smith's work is destitute of method; the best parts of the research are dispersed in the chapters in an ad hoc manner losing part of their worth, the chapters are organized without much logic making reading a laborious

task; the book is full of long digressions, some of which are interesting to only the English reader; Smith had the opportunity but failed to raise the superstructure of the new science (xlv).

LAISSEZ FAIRE AND THE ADVANTAGES OF FREE MARKETS

Say has been described both as a dogmatic believer in *laissez faire* and as one of its most eloquent exponents. Say wrote "the Healthy state of industry and wealth is the state of absolute liberty, in which each interest is left to take care of itself. The only useful protection authority can afford them is that against fraud and violence."[33] He would be at home with the intellectual scene today where the intellectual pendulum has swung to a general adulation for free markets. According to E. Forget, Say considered the process of haggling ("higgling"), even as the market moves toward equilibrium, to be an indicator of societal disorder, thus indicating Say's interpretation of equilibrium as a normatively desirable concept. The ideal market would adjust instantaneously and smoothly. Say's views on the superiority of the free-market mechanism over other economic systems are consistent with the intellectual winds blowing in our times.

Say wrote that increasing the wealth of nations depended on the role played by scientific progress and enlightenment of the people. He anticipated a continuing industrial revolution similar to what was underway in his time in Europe.

the decline of prejudice has been favorable to the advancement of science, or to a more exact knowledge of the immutable laws of nature; and this improvement in the cultivation of science itself has been favorable to the progress of industry, and industry to national opulence. (xxii)

On many occasions in the *Treatise* and in his other writings, Say held that private property, and free enterprise and the invisible hand are the best guarantee of a productive economy. The state must ensure law and order and property rights through a reliable legal system, but should curtail all other interventions in the economy. He criticized high taxes as being detrimental to free commerce and wealth creation.

One of Say's greatest strengths was that he had the ability to write on conceptual topics in a language that an interested average citizen could understand. Schumpeter and other historians of thought have looked down upon this style as representing a certain lack of rigor in his work. Say's approach to economics is in sharp contrast with present attitudes in the discipline, where many of the best academic economists seem to write only for other economists, largely ignoring legislators, politicians, administrators, and the average citizen. It is important to remember that Say believed economics to be a practical science. There is a crying need today for writers in economics to translate and publish the latest economic research for the benefit of the average citizen.

SAY'S LAW OF MARKETS

The proposition known as the Law of Markets (or simply as Say's law) is one of the most widely known laws in economics. Generally, the law has been translated into the idea that in the long run supply and demand must balance. The more popular expression for the law commonly found in introductory textbooks in economics reads "supply creates its own demand." Although classical economists never stated the Law of Markets in this form, their writings are replete with references to the idea, which they have employed to fend off under-consumptionist views and to argue that deviations from full employment are self-correcting.[34] In the first edition of the *Treatise*, Say used less than four pages to discuss his views on this proposition. However, the proposition came under criticism from the beginning.[35] Over the years, as criticism mounted, Say continued to expand the treatment of the law in successive editions of the book. The chapter discussing this proposition occupies eight pages (132–40) in the 1971 reprint of the American edition. In the first edition of *Treatise*, Say explained the law as follows:

It must be stressed that any commodity whatsoever, as soon as it is brought to the market, offers an outlet to other products for the whole amount of its value. In fact when a manufacturer has produced a commodity, he has an extreme need and wish to sell it, so that its value does not dissolve in his hands. But he is no less willing to get rid of the money he obtained from the sale of the commodity, precisely in order to prevent the value of the money vanishing by remaining idle. Now, one cannot get rid of one's own money except by purchasing some product. Therefore, it is clear that the very production of a commodity immediately opens an outlet to other products. (Quoted in Screpanti and Zamagni, 70)

In the American reprint of the fifth edition, Book I on Production, in chapter XV named "On the Demand Or Market for Products," the equivalent passage reads:

It is worthwhile to remark that a product is no sooner created than it, from that instant, affords a market for other products to the full extent of its value. When the producer has put the finishing hand to his product, he is most anxious to sell it immediately, lest its value should diminish in his hands. Nor is he less anxious to dispose of the money he may get for it; for the value of money is also perishable. But the only way of getting rid of the money is in the purchase of some product or other. Thus, the mere circumstance of creation of one product immediately opens a vent for other products. (135)

There are two critical sentences in the above proof. First,

when a manufacturer has produced a commodity, he has an extreme need and wish to sell it, so that its value does not dissolve in his hands.

Why would the value dissolve so suddenly?—an instance more fitted to fresh fish in a village than to manufacturing. Secondly,

he is no less willing to get rid of the money...in order to prevent the value of the money vanishing.

Unless one is facing hyperinflation, one cannot understand why the value of money should vanish. In any well-functioning economy money is commonly accepted precisely because it is a *store* of value and there should be no desperation to dump it. One cannot but regret that Say's name is known principally today as the author of a law whose initial proof was based on such questionable grounds.

In the same chapter, the following remarks spell out the "Law":

A man who applies his labour to the investing of objects with value by the creation of utility of some sort, cannot expect such value to be appreciated and paid for, unless where other men have the means of purchasing it. Now what do these means consist? Of other values of other products, likewise the fruits of industry, capital, and land. *Which leads us to a conclusion that may at first sight appear paradoxical, namely, that it is production which opens a demand for products.* (emphasis added, 133)

Why then do we have periods of glut and overproduction in markets? Say explained that a glut is possible but it would not invalidate the fundamental proposition that supply creates its own demand in each market.

> But it may be asked, if this is so, how does it happen, that there is at times so great a glut of commodities in the market, and so much difficulty in finding a vent for them? Why cannot one of these superabundant commodities be exchanged for another? I answer that the glut of a particular commodity arises from its having outrun the total demand for it in one or two ways; either because it has been produced in excessive abundance, or because the production of other commodities has fallen short. (135)

John Maynard Keynes in *The General Theory* discussed Say's Law of Markets, giving it added significance as broadly representing what Classical economics stood for. For Keynes, the significance of Say's claim lay in the fact that it was equivalent to the proposition that there is no obstacle to full employment.

> Thus Say's law, that the aggregate demand price of output as a whole is equal to its aggregate supply price for all volumes of output, is equivalent to the proposition that there is no obstacle to full employment. If, however, this is not the true law relating the aggregate demand and supply functions, there is a vitally important chapter of economic theory which remains to be written and without which all discussions concerning the volume of aggregate employment are futile. (26)

Malthus said that Say's law,

> ...appears to me to be the most directly opposed to just theory, and the most uniformly contradicted by experience. (363–64)

Insufficiency of demand was part of Malthus's own explanation for unemployment. Unlike Malthus, most Classical writers, including Say, did not recognize the possibility or dangers of overproduction leading to increasing unemployment and depressions. Schumpeter and others have found Keynes's objections to the Law of Markets somewhat contrived:

it would have been more natural (for Keynes) not to object to this p.
... just as we do not object to the law of gravitation on ground that th.
does not fall into the sun, but to say simply that the operation of Say's l.
though it states a tendency correctly, is impeded by certain facts. (Schumpeter,
624)

Schumpeter himself treated Say and his contributions to economic thought generously. Say made several original contributions to economics besides the Law of Markets. It is somewhat unfortunate that the controversy surrounding this law has overshadowed Say's other contributions.

ON THE ENTREPRENEUR

Historical dictionaries for both French and English affirm that J. B. Say was the first to use "entrepreneur" in its modern sense.[36] In the tradition of Cantillon, Say was the first economist to assign to the entrepreneur, as distinct from the capitalist, a distinct role in the schema of the economic process. Say was also unique among economists of his generation (and even today) in that for several years he was in business for himself and took part in activities that he and other economists analyzed. He was no armchair scholar writing from a comfortable position in academia. For ten years, he had struggled every day to produce profits and in the process created employment and development for the local economy. Say believed from his own entrepreneurial experience that the task of the entrepreneur is to combine the factors of production into a business firm. The entrepreneur assembles what the three factors of production can contribute. The entrepreneur then launches and manages an enterprise by combining the productive factors of capital, knowledge, and labor, some of which he may own. This analysis is considered by most writers to be a significant step beyond what Adam Smith and Cantillon had written on the role of the entrepreneur. Say criticized Smith for failing to make a distinction between "profits of the entrepreneur" and the "profits of stock" or the return on capital. According to some critics, Say had failed to move much beyond this contribution.

He did realize, to some extent, that a greatly improved theory of the economic process might be derived by making the entrepreneur in the analytic schema what he is in capitalist reality, the pivot on which everything turns. But he failed to realize that the phrase "combining factors," when applied to a going concern, denotes little more than routine management; and that the task of combining factors becomes a distinctive one only when applied not to the current administration of a going concern but to the organization of a new one. In any case, however, he turned a popular notion into a scientific tool. (Schumpeter, 555)

However, to his credit, Say was well ahead of his contemporary writers in England on the role and importance of the "entrepreneur," bringing into use a term which has found a permanent place in economics. His carefully thought out queries for Jefferson about the cost and availability of the factors of production in America are indicative of his sharp entrepreneurial mind. Say's pioneering thoughts are well appreciated in Hebert and Link (1982).

A Concluding Note

Jean-Baptiste Say is known today as an early French writer in political economy who popularized the writings of Adam Smith, authored the Law of Markets (known as Say's law) and was the first to coin the term "entrepreneur." Readers of this book will find out that he was much more. Say is without doubt one of the luminaries of classical economics. In a sense, he single-handedly revived the study of political economy from its decline after the Physiocrats and kept it alive during a difficult period of oppressive dictatorship that was opposed to liberal ideas. Say had a missionary belief that society will be best served if the principles of political economy are widely disseminated and understood by the citizenry. He did much for the economic education of the average citizen. A contribution for which Say has justly received credit for was his definition of the subject and organization of its subject matter in the *Treatise*. He divided his book into three major parts, production, distribution, and consumption of wealth. This arrangement to some degree continues to guide authors of economic textbooks to this day. He derived the idea of this organization of the subject matter from the notion that national income can conveniently be studied in the form of rent, wages, and profits to distinguish the three factors of production—

land or natural agents, labor, and capital. His treatment of the role of the entrepreneur as a contributor to production different from that of either the manager or the capitalist is the most advanced for his times. His emphasis on the superiority of the inductive method of research following the natural sciences, and yet the healthy skepticism he maintained towards exaggerated borrowings of mathematics in economics, must also be appreciated.

Say's belief in economics as an "experimental science" meant that he wanted a subject based on experience. In the final analysis, only a subject that touched people's everyday experience would be of benefit to the common man. It was his commitment to this touchstone that led him to indignantly reject the idea that Irish absentee landlords were not detrimental to the Irish economy. It may have lain behind his final decision to consider his case for Say's law a definitional one (Sowell, 141) as well as his suspicion of introducing mathematical methods into economics. His Law of Markets has been controversial, perhaps generating more intellectual heat than light over the years. His exposition and application of the supply and demand framework were remarkably mature for his time. So were his contributions to theory of value where he gave greater significance to utility than Smith, Ricardo, or Malthus. His definition of utility as the inherent capability of products to satisfy human wants from which value originates goes well beyond Adam Smith. He also made a distinction between saving and unproductive consumption. Finally, the role played by the *Treatise* in spreading liberal economic ideas and especially the policy of *laissez faire* and free trade in France, the rest of Europe, and in the newly independent United States must also be appreciated. Say was perhaps the first true business economist. One suspects he would have liked nothing better than to have his *Treatise* attract entrepreneurs, managers, and other non-specialist readers to economics since he believed economics to have immense promise to enhance the welfare of individuals and nations. Given the emphasis on capitalism, free markets, and unrestricted global trade, this reprint of Jean-Baptiste Say's great classic could not have been more timely.[37]

NOTES

1. For Schumpeter, in the 1790-1870 period, besides Cournot, there were only two first-ranked French writers in political economy to mention—J. B. Say and de Sismondi (Schumpeter, 491).
2. According to Mr. Fonblanque, editor of the London Political Examiner, Say was actually expelled from the *Tribunat* for having independent opinions. He was thus both courted and persecuted by Napoleon. P. v.
3. Forget 1993, 122.
4. Palmer, 83-89.
5. Ibid, 11.
6. The success of Treatise as a textbook in the United States and Europe was taken by some critics to reinforce the view that Say was at best a popularizer of A. Smith's ideas (Schumpeter, 491).
7. Palmer, 125-26.
8.   Dorfman, 389.
9. Ibid., 389, 390.
10.   Ibid., 390.
11. Ibid., 391.
12. Dorfman., 434.
13. Ibid., 513, 514.
14. Ibid., 514.
15. Haney, 358.
16. Schumpeter, 491,492.
17. Haney, 358.
18. Book I, 62.
19. Ibid., 62.
20. Ibid., 66.
21. Ibid., 77.
22. Adam Smith's example of a pin factory is mentioned in this context. Ibid., 92
23. "Nor can I discover any sound reason, why the talent of a painter should be deemed productive, and not the talent of the musician." Ibid., Book I. chapter XIII, 120.
24. Ibid., 140.
25. Ibid., 143.
26. Book I., 167.
27. Ibid., 387.
28. Ibid., 389.
29. A stronger statement in favor of good governance will be hard to find in the early economic literature. However, this remark should not be construed to indicate support to dictatorship. Say has a record of opposition to dictatorship at considerable personal risks.
30. See Forget (1994), 137 for additional discussion on this.
31. In a footnote to this passage he uses the analogy of the flow of blood in the human body from medicine. The flow of blood is dependent on so many unknown variables that attempts to estimate its speed have defied all attempts at calculation. Similarly, human wants and desires are not amenable to precise calculations.
32. For a good discussion of how Smith's influence on Say, see Forget (1993)
33. Book I, 168.
34. Blaug, 160.
35. Before Say, the Physiocrats also had used this proposition to attack the Mercantilist position of underconsumption. Quesnay reportedly wrote "all that is bought is sold, and all that is sold is bought." See Blaug, 29.
36. Palmer, 70.
37. Our advice to the reader: After you have read the Treatise, if your appetite for Say's ideas is still not satisfied, you can peruse the recent scholarship

on this very modern French author in the works of R.R. Palmer and E. Forget among others. The former is an especially important contribution in that it fills an important gap for the English-speaking reader by presenting in English for the first time many of Say's previously unpublished economic writings and correspondence.

References

Baumol, William. 1977. "Say's (At Least) Eight Laws, or What Say May Really Have Meant." Economica 145–62.

Blaug, Mark. 1983. Economic Theory in Retrospect, 3rd edition. Cambridge: Cambridge University Press.

Colander, David. 1998. Macroeconomics, An Annotated Instructor's Edition. Irwin-McGraw Hill.

Dorfman, Joseph. 1966. The Economic Man in American Civilization, Volumes 1, 2, Reprints in Economic Classics. New York: Augusta M. Kelley.

Forget, E. 1997. "The Market for Virtue: Jean-Baptiste Say on Women in the Economy and Society." Feminist Economics Volume 3, No. 1 (spring): 95–111.

Forget, E. 1994. "Disequilibrium Trade as a Metaphor for Social Disorder in the Work of Jean-Baptiste Say." History of Political Economy Volume 26, Supplement: 135–148.

Forget, E. 1993. "J. B. Say and Adam Smith: An Essay in the Transmission of Ideas." The Canadian Journal of Economics Volume 26, No. 1 (February): 121–33.

Haney, Lewis H. 1968. History of Economic Thought, fourth and enlarged edition. New York: Macmillan.

Hebert, R. F., and A. N. Link. 1982. The Entrepreneur. New York: Praeger.

Henderson, David R (editor). 1993. The Fortune Encyclopedia of Economics. Warner Books.

Keynes, John Maynard. 1964. The General Theory of Employment, Interest and Money, First Harbinger Edition. New York: Harvest Book.

Mankiw, N. Gregory. 1998. Principles of Macroeconomics. Dryden Press, .

Menard, Claude. 1980. "Three Forms of Resistance to Statistics: Say, Cournot, Walras." History of Political Economy Volume 12, No. 4.

O'Brien, Denis, P. 1988. "Classical Reassessments," in William O. Thweatt (editor), Classical Political Economy: A Survey of Recent Literature. Boston: Kluwer Academic Publishers.

Palmer, R. R. 1997. J. B. Say: An Economist in Troubled Times; Selected and Translated. Princeton: Princeton University Press.

Schumpeter, Joseph A. 1994. History of Economic Analysis. Oxford: Oxford University Press.

Screpanti, Ernesto, and Stefano Zamagni. 1995. An Outline of the History of Economic Thought, trans. by David Field. Oxford: Clarendon Press.

Smith, A. 1976. An Inquiry Into the Nature and the Causes of The Wealth of Nations. Chicago: University of Chicago Press.

Sowell, T. 1972. Say's Law: A Historical Analysis. Princeton University Press.

Thweatt, W. 1979. "Early Formulations of Say's Law." Quarterly Review of Economics and Business, Volume 19, No. 4: 79–96.

PREFACE TO THE SIXTH EDITION

A NEW edition of this translation of the popular treatise of M. Say having been called for, the five previous American editions being entirely out of print, the editor has endeavoured to render the work more deserving of the favour it has received, by subjecting every part of it to a careful revision. As the translation of Mr. Prinsep was made in the year 1821, from an earlier edition of the original treatise, namely, the fourth, which had not received the last corrections and improvements of the author, wherever an essential principle had been involved in obscurity, or an error had crept in, which had been subsequently cleared up and removed, the American editor has, in this impression, reconciled the language of the text and notes to the fifth improved edition, published in 1826, the last which M. Say lived to give to the world. It has not, however, been deemed necessary to extend these alterations in the translation any further than to the correction of such discrepancies and errors as are here alluded to; and the editor has not ventured to recast the translation, as given by Mr. Prinsep, merely with a view to accommodate its phraseology, in point of neatness of expression or diction, to the last touches of the author. The translation of Mr. Prinsep, the editor must again be permitted to observe, has been executed with sufficient fidelity, and with considerable spirit and elegance; and in his opinion it could not be much improved by even remoulding it after the last edition. The translation of the introduction, given by the present editor, has received various verbal corrections; and such alterations and additions as were introduced by the author into his fifth edition, will now be found translated.

It is, moreover, proper to state, that at the suggestion of the American proprietors and publishers of this edition of the work, the French moneys, weights and measures, throughout the text and notes, have been converted into the current coins, weights and measures of the United States; when the context strictly required it by a rigorous reduction, and when merely assumed as a politico-arithmetical illustration, by a simple approximation to a nearly equivalent quantity of our own coins, weights or measures. This has been done to render the work as extensively useful as possible, and will, no doubt, make the author's general principles and reasonings more easily comprehended, as well as more readily remembered, by the American student of political economy.

Many new notes, it will be seen, have been added by the American editor, in further illustration or correction of those portions of the text which still required elucidation. The statistical data now incorporated in these notes, have been brought down to the most recent period, both in this country and in Europe. No pains have been spared in getting access to authentic channels of information, and the American editor trusts that the present edition will be found much improved throughout.

The death of M. Say took place, in Paris, during the third week of November, 1832, on which occasion, according to the statements in the French journals, such funeral honours were paid to his memory as are due to eminent personages, and Odilon-Barrot, de Sacy, de Laborde, Blanqui, and Charles Dupin, his distinguished countrymen and admirers, pronounced discourses at the interment in the cemetery of Père Lachaise.

The account of his decease, here subjoined, is taken from the London Political Examiner of the 25th of November, 1832, and is from the pen of its able editor, Mr. Fonblanque, one of the most powerful political writers in England. Mr. Fonblanque, it appears, was the personal friend, as well as the warm admirer, of the genius and writings of M. Say, and was well qualified to appreciate his high intellectual endowments, his profound knowledge and political wisdom, his manly independence, his mild yet dignified consistency of character, and above all, his rare and shining private virtues. There hardly could be a more interesting and instructive task assigned to the philosophical biographer, than a faithful portraiture of the life and labours of this illustrious man, which were so ardently and efficiently devoted to the advancement of the happiness and prosperity of his fellow-men. Perhaps the writings of no authors, however great their celebrity may be, are exerting a more powerful and enduring influence on the well-being of the people of Europe and America, than those of Adam Smith, and John Baptiste Say.

" France has this week lost another of her most distinguished writers and citizens, the celebrated political economist, M. Say. The invaluable branch of knowledge to which the greatest of his intellectual exertions were devoted, is indebted to him, amongst others, for those great and all-pervading truths which have elevated it to the rank of a science; and to him, far more than to any others, for its popularization and diffusion. Nor was M. Say a *mere* political economist; else had he been necessarily a bad one. He knew that a subject so ' immersed in matter,' (to use the fine expression of Lord Bacon,) as a nation's prosperity, must be looked at on many sides, in order to be seen rightly even on one. M. Say was one of the most accomplished minds of his age and country. Though he had given his chief attention to one particular aspect of human affairs, all their aspects were interesting to him; not one was excluded from his survey.   His private life was a model of the domestic virtues.   From the time when, with Chamfort and Ginguené, he founded the *Decade Philosophique*, the first work which attempted to revive literary and scientific pursuits during the storms of the French Revolution—alike when courted by Napoleon, and when persecuted by him (he was expelled from the *Tribunat* for presuming to have an independent opinion); unchanged equally during the sixteen years of the Bourbons, and the two of Louis Philippe—he passed unsullied through all the trials and temptations which have left a stain on every man of feeble virtue among his conspicuous contemporaries.   He kept aloof from public life, but was the friend and trusted adviser of some of its brightest ornaments; and few have contributed more, though in a private station, to keep alive in the hearts and in the contemplation of men, a lofty standard of public virtue.   If this feeble testimony, from one not wholly unknown to him, should meet the eye of any one who loved him, may it, in so far as such things can, afford that comfort under the loss, which can be derived from the knowledge that others know and feel all its irreparableness!"

C. C. B.

PHILADELPHIA, *December*, 1834.

PREFACE TO THE FIFTH EDITION

No work upon political economy, since the publication of Dr. Adam Smith's profound and original Inquiry into the Nature and Causes of the Wealth of Nations, has attracted such general attention, and received such distinguished marks of approbation from competent judges, as the "Traite D'Economie Politique," of M. Say. It was first printed in Paris in the year 1803; and, subsequently, has passed through five large editions, that have received various corrections and improvements from the author. Translations of the work have been made into the German, Spanish, Italian, and other languages; and it has been adopted as a text-book in all the universities of the continent of Europe, in which this new but essential branch of liberal education is now taught. The four former American editions of this translation have also been introduced into many of the most respectable of our own seminaries of learning.

It is unquestionably the most methodical, comprehensive and best digested treatise on the elements of political economy, that has yet been presented to the world. It exhibits a clear and systematical view of all the solid and important doctrines of this very extensive and difficult science, unfolded in their proper order and connexion. In the establishment of his principles, the author's reasonings, with but few exceptions, are logical and accurate, delivered with distinctness and perspicuity, and generally supported by the fullest and most satisfactory illustrations. A rigid adherence to the inductive method of investigation, in the prosecution of almost every part of his inquiry, has enabled M. Say to effect a nearly complete analysis of the numerous and complicated phenomena of wealth, and to enunciate and establish, with all the evidence of demonstration, the simple and general laws on which its production, distribution, and consumption depend. The few slight and inconsiderable errors into which the author has fallen, do not affect the general soundness and consistency of his text, although, it is true, they are blemishes that thus far darken and disfigure it. But these are of rare occurrence, and the false conclusions involved in them may be easily detected and refuted by recurrence to the fundamental principles of the work, with which they manifestly are at variance, and contradict.

The foundation of the science of political economy was firmly laid, and the only successful method of conducting our inquiries in it pointed out and exemplified by the illustrious author of the Wealth of Nations; a number of its leading doctrines were also developed and explained by other eminent writers on the continent of Europe, who, about the same time, were engaged in investigating the nature and causes of social riches. But neither the scientific genius and penetrating sagacity of the former, nor the profound acuteness and extensive research of many of the latter, enabled them to obtain a complete discovery of all the actual phenomena of wealth, and thus to effect an entire solution of the most abstruse and difficult problems in political economy; those, namely, which demonstrate the true theory of value, and unfold the real sources of production. Aided, however, by the valuable materials collected and arranged by the labours of his distinguished predecessors, here referred to, and proceeding in the same path, our author, with the closeness and minutenes of attention due to this important study, has succeeded in examining under all their aspects, the general facts which the ground-work of the science presents, and by rejecting and excluding the accidental circumstances connected with them, has thus established its ultimate laws or principles.

Accordingly, by pursuing the inductive method of investigation, M. Say, in the most strict and philosophical manner, has deduced the true nature of value, traced up its origin, and presented a clear and accurate explanation of its theory. His definition of wealth, therefore, is more precise and correct than that of any of his predecessors in this inquiry. The agency of human industry, which Dr. Adam Smith, not with the strictest propriety, denominated labour, the important operation of natural powers, especially land, and the functions of capital, as well as the relative services of these three instruments, and the modes in which they all concur in the business of production, were first distinctly and fully pointed out and illustrated by our author. In this way he successfully unfolded the manner in which production is carried on, and imparts value to the products of agriculture, manufactures, and commerce. By, also, distinguishing reproductive from unproductive consumption, M. Say has exhibited the exact nature of capital, and its consequent important agency in production, and thus has shown why economy is a source of national wealth. Such are this author's peculiar and original speculations, the fruits of deep and patient meditation on the phenomena observed. The elementary principles derived from them, with others previously ascertained, he has combined into one harmonious, consistent, and beautiful system.

But a few of these solid and well-established positions have been criticised and objected to as inconclusive and inadmissible, by Mr. Ricardo and by Mr. Malthus, two of the ablest and most distinguished political economists among our author's contemporaries. Other doctrines in relation to the nature and origin of value have been advanced by them, and with so much plausibility too, that some of the most acute reasoners of the present day have not been sufficiently on their guard against the fallacies involved in them. The mathematical cast given to their reasonings by these writers, has captivated and led astray the understandings of intelligent and sagacious readers, and induced them to adopt, as scientific truths, what, when properly investigated and analyzed, are found to be merely specious hypotheses. Hence it is that a theory of value, purely gratuitous, has been extolled in one of the principal literary journals of Great Britain, as being " no less logical and conclusive than it was profound and important." Our author, accordingly, deemed it necessary to examine the arguments brought forward in support of these views of his opponents, in order to test their soundness and accuracy, and to submit his own principles to a further review, that he might become satisfied that the conclusions he had deduced from them had not been in any manner invalidated.

In the notes appended by M. Say to' the French translation of Mr. Ricardo's Principles of Political Economy and Taxation, the reader will find what the editor deems a masterly and conclusive refutation of the theoretical errors of this author. M. Say's strictures upon the twentieth chapter of the work, entitled, " Value and Riches, their Distinctive Properties," are in his opinion decisive and unanswerable. The fallacies contained in Mr. Ricardo's theory of value, which, the editor thinks, may be traced to an anxiety to give consistency to the loose and inaccurate proposition of Dr. Adam Smith, that exchangeable value is entirely derived from human labour, are there fully exposed, and his whole train of reasoning, in connection with it, shown to rest upon an unwarrantable assumption. It must, however, be conceded that Mr. Ricardo was an intrepid and uncompromising reasoner, who always proceeded in the most direct and fearless manner from his premises to the conclusion. But not uniting with the strongest powers of reasoning, a capacity for analytical subtilty, he sometimes did not perceive verbal ambiguities in the formation of his premises, and transitions in the signification of his terms in the conduct of his argument, which, in these instances, vitiated his conclusions. The fundamental errors into which he has fallen, accordingly, do not arise from any want of strictness in his deductions, but from undue generalizations and perversions of language. In M. Say's Letters to Mr. Malthus, which have been translated by Mr. Richter, the points at issue between these two eminent political economists are discussed in the most luminous, impartial, and satisfactory manner; and by all candid and unprejudiced critics must be considered as bringing the controversy to a close.

It is not his intention, nor would it be proper on this occasion, for the editor to enter further into the merits of the controversial writings of our author. Any dispassionate inquirer, who will take the pains carefully to review the whole ground in dispute, will, he thinks, find that the disquisitions referred to contain a triumphant vindication of such of the author's general principles as had been assailed by his ingenious opponents. Whenever the study of the science of political economy shall be more generally cultivated as an essential branch of early education, most of the abstruse questions involved in the controversies which now divide the writers on this subject will be brought to a conclusion; the accession of useful knowledge it will occasion will more effectually eradicate the prejudices which have given birth to these disputes and misconceptions, than any direct argumentative refutation.

The great merits of this treatise on political economy are now beginning to be well known and properly estimated by that class of readers who take a deep interest in the progress of a science, which "aims at the improvement of society," as Dugald Stewart so truly remarks, "not by delineating plans of new constitutions, but by enlightening the policy of actual legislators;" a science, therefore, with the right understanding of whose principles, the welfare and happiness of mankind are intimately connected.

In alluding to this admirable work of M. Say, Mr. Ricardo remarks, "that its author not only was the first, or among the first, of continental writers, who justly appreciated and applied the principles of Smith, and who has done more than all other continental writers taken together, to recommend the principles of that enlightened and beneficial system to the nations of Europe; but who has succeeded in placing the science in a more logical, and more instructive order; and has enriched it by several discussions, original, accurate, and profound."

The English public has for some time been in possession of the present excellent translation of this treatise by Mr. Prinsep; the first edition of which was published in London in the spring of 1821. It is executed with spirit, elegance, and general fidelity, and is a performance, in every respect, worthy of the original. It is here given to the American reader without any material alteration.

In various notes which the English translator has thought proper to subjoin to his edition of the text, he has wasted much ingenuity in endeavouring to overthrow some of the author's leading principles, which, notwithstanding these attacks, are as fixed and immutable as the truths which constitute their basis. Had Mr. Prinsep more thoroughly studied M. Say's profound theoretical views on the subject of value, and had he, also, made himself acquainted, which it nowhere appears that he has done, with the powerful and victorious defence of these doctrines, contained in the notes on Mr. Ricardo's work, and in the letters to Mr. Malthus, already referred to, he perhaps might have discovered, that they are the ultimate generalizations of facts, which, agreeably to the most legitimate rules of philosophizing, the author was entitled to lay down as general laws or principles. At all events, Mr. Prinsep should not have ventured upon an attack on these first principles of the science of political economy, without this previous examination.

Such, therefore, of these notes of the English translator as are in opposition to the well-established elements of the science, and have no other support than the hypothesis of Mr. Ricardo and Mr. Malthus, have been entirely omitted; the American editor not deeming himself under any obligation to give currency to errors, which would perpetually interrupt and distract the attention of the reader in a most abstruse and difficult inquiry. Other notes of the translator, which contain interesting and valuable illustrations of other general principles of the work, drawn from the actual state of Great Britain and her colonies, have been retained in this edition, as appropriate and useful. The translator's remarks on the pernicious character and tendency of the restrictive and prohibitive policy, are particularly worthy of regard, confirming as they most fully do, on this subject, all the important conclusions of the author. The folly of attempting, either by extraordinary encouragements, to attract towards some branches of production a larger share of capital and industry than would be naturally employed in them, or by uncommon restraints forcibly to divert from others a portion of the capital and industry that would otherwise be invested in them, is at last beginning to be understood.

The restrictive system, or that which by means of legislative enactments endeavours to give a particular direction to national capital and industry, derived its whole support from the assumption of positions now generally admitted to be gratuitous and unfounded, namely, that in trade whatever is gained by one nation must necessarily be lost by another, that wealth consists exclusively of the precious metals, and consequently, that in all sales of commodities, the great object should be to obtain returns in gold and silver. In Europe these erroneous opinions have now, for some time, been relinquished by political economists of all the various schools, some of whom yet differ and dispute respecting a few of the more recondite and ultimate elements of the science. In the whole range of inquiry in political economy, perhaps there is not a single proposition better established, or one that has obtained a more universal sanction from its enlightened cultivators in every country, than the liberal doctrine, that the most active, general, and profitable employments are given to the industry and capital of every people, by allowing to their direction and application the most perfect freedom, compatible with the security of property. This fundamental position of political economy, and the various principles that flow from it as corollaries, were first systematically developed, explained, and taught by the great father of the science, Dr. Adam Smith; although glimpses of the same important truth had previously, and about the same time, reached the minds of a few eminent individuals in other parts of the world. " The most effectual plan for advancing a people to greatness," says Dr. Smith, " is to maintain that order of things which nature pointed out; by allowing every man, as long as he observes the rules of justice, to pursue his own interest in his own way, and to bring both his industry and his capital into the freest competition with those of his fellow-citizens." Animated by a like desire to promote the improvement and happiness of mankind, with that which actuated the author of the Wealth of Nations, the most profound inquiries among his successors embraced his enlarged and benevolent views, as the only certain means of increasing the general prosperity, and eloquently maintained and enforced them. The doctrines of the freedom of trade and the rights of industry, were vindicated and taught by all the distinguished British political economists; namely, by Dugald Stewart, Ricardo, Malthus, Torrens, Horner, Huskisson, Lauderdale, Bentham, Mills, Craig, Lowe, Tooke, Senior, Bowring, M'Culloch, and Whatley; and, on the continent of Europe, by authors as celebrated, by Say, Droz, Sismondi, Storch, Garnier, Destutt-Tracy, Ganilh, Jovellanos, Sartorius, Queypo, Leider, Von Schlozer, Kraus, Weber, Muller, Scarbeck, Pechio, and Gioja.

"Under a system of perfectly free commerce," says Mr. Ricardo, "each country naturally devotes its capital and labour to such employments as are most beneficial to each. This pursuit of individual advantage is admirably connected with the universal good of the whole. By stimulating industry, by rewarding ingenuity, and by using most efficaciously the powers bestowed by nature, it distributes labour most effectively and most economically: while by increasing the general mass of productions, it diffuses general benefit, and binds together by one common tie of interest and intercourse, the universal society of nations throughout the civilized world. It is this principle which determines that wine shall be made in France and Portugal, that corn shall be grown in America and Poland, and that hardware and other goods shall be manufactured in England."

Our own celebrated countryman, Franklin, too, with a sagacity and force which always characterized his intellect, maintained and exemplified in his " Essay on the Principles of Trade," what he therein repeatedly called "the great principle of freedom in trade." Even before the appearance of the Wealth of Nations, he had with almost intuition anticipated some of the most profound conclusions of the science of political economy, which other inquirers had arrived at only after a patient and laborious analysis of its phenomena. The new and generous commercial policy is not more beholden for support and currency to the arguments and illustrations of any of its early expositors, than to the clear and vigorous pen of the highly gifted American philosopher. "The expressions, *Laissez nous faire*, and *pas trop gouverner*," which, to use the language of DUGALD STEWART, the highest of all authorities, "comprise in a few words two of the most important lessons of political wisdom, are indebted chiefly for their extensive circulation, to the short and luminous comments of Franklin, which had so extraordinary an influence on public opinion, both in the Old and New World." Nevertheless, strange as it may seem, by a perversion or misconception of a few of his incidental opinions, the name of the first of practical statesmen has been invoked, and its authority employed among us, in aid of a system of restraints and prohibitions on commerce, which it was the chief aim of his politico-economical writings to refute and condemn, as alike repugnant to sound theory and destructive to national prosperity. Whenever American statesmen and legislators shall have as clear and steady per-

ceptions as Franklin of the truth and wisdom of the doctrine of commc./
cial freedom, we may expect that our national and state codes will no
longer exhibit so many traces of that empirical spirit of tampering regulation which, instead of invigorating and quickening the development of
national wealth, only cramps and retards its natural growth. " Where
should we expect," says M. Say, in a letter to the editor, " sound doctrine to be better received than amongst a nation that supports and illustrates the value of free principles, by the most striking examples. The
old states of Europe are cankered with prejudices and bad habits; it is
America who will teach them the height of prosperity which may be
reached when governments follow the counsels of reason, and do not
cost too much."

The preliminary discourse has been translated by the American editor,
and in his editions of the work restored to its place. The editor must
confess that he is at a loss to account for the omission by the English
translator of so material a part of the author's treatise as this introduction to his whole inquiry. In itself it is a performance of uncommon
merit, has immediate reference to, and sheds much light over, the general views unfolded in the body of the work. The nature and object of
the science of political economy, the only certain method of conducting
any of our inquiries in it with success, and the causes which have hitherto so much retarded its advancement, are all considered and pointed out
with great clearness and ability. The author has also connected with it
a highly interesting and instructive historical sketch of the progress of
this science during the last and present century, interspersed with numerous judicious and acute criticisms upon the writings and opinions
of his predecessors. Moreover, this discourse, throughout every part,
is deeply philosophical, and well calculated to prepare the reader for the
study on which he is about to enter. The editor has, therefore, he trusts,
performed an acceptable service in putting the American student in possession of so important a part of the original work.*

Notes have also been subjoined by the American editor, for the purpose of marking a few inconsiderable errors and inconsistencies into
which the author has inadvertently fallen, and of supplying an occasional
illustration, drawn from other authors, of such passages of the text
as seemed to require further elucidation or correction.

C. C. B.

PHILADELPHIA, *April*, 1832.

---

* The following extract of a letter from M. Say, to the American editor, it may not
be improper to subjoin, as it contains the author's opinion of the value he attaches to
the preliminary discourse.

"Your translation and restoration of the preliminary discourse adds, in my eyes, a
new value to your edition. It could only have been from a narrow calculation of the
English publisher, that it was omitted in Mr. Prinsep's translation. Ought that portion
of the work to be deemed unuseful, whose aim is to unfold the real object of the science,
to present a rapid sketch of its history, and to point out the only true method of investigating it with success? Mr. George Pryme, professor of political economy in the
university of Cambridge, in England, makes this very discourse the principal topic of
several of his first lectures."

INTRODUCTION.

A SCIENCE only advances with certainty, when the plan of inquiry and the object of our researches have been clearly defined; otherwise a small number of truths are loosely laid hold of, without their connexion being perceived, and numerous errors, without being enabled to detect their fallacy.

For a long time the science of *politics*, in strictness limited to the investigation of the principles which lay the foundation of the social order, was confounded with *political economy*, which unfolds the manner in which wealth is produced, distributed, and consumed. Wealth, nevertheless, is essentially independent of political organization. Under every form of government, a state, whose affairs are well administered, may prosper. Nations have risen to opulence under absolute monarchs, and have been ruined by popular councils. If political liberty is more favourable to he development of wealth, it is indirectly, in the same manner that it is more favourable to general education.

In confounding in the same researches the essential elements of good government with the principles on which the growth of wealth, either public or private, depends, it is by no means surprising that authors should have involved these subjects in obscurity, instead of elucidating them. Stewart, who has entitled his first chapter "Of the Government of Mankind," is liable to this reproach; the sect of "Economists" of the last century, throughout all their writings, and J. J. Rousseau, in the article "Political Economy" in the Encyclopedie, lie under the same imputation.

Since the time of Adam Smith, it appears to me, these two very distinct inquiries have been uniformly separated; the term *political economy** being now confined to the science which treats of wealth, and that of *politics*, to desig-

---

* From οικος a house, and νομος a law; *economy*, the law which regulates the household. *Household*, according to the Greeks, comprehending all the goods in possession of the family; and *political*, from πόλις, *civitas*, extending its application to society or the nation at large.

Political economy is the best expression that can be used to designate the science discussed in the following treatise, which is not the investigation of *natural wealth*, or that which nature supplies us with gratuitously and without limitation, but of *social wealth* exclusively, which is founded on exchange and the recognition of the right of property, both social regulations.

nate the relations existing between a government and its people, and the relations of different states to each other.

The wide range taken into the field of pure politics, whilst investigating the subject of political economy, seemed to furnish a much stronger reason for including in the same inquiry agriculture, commerce and the arts, the true sources of wealth, and upon which laws have but an accidental and indirect influence. Thence what interminable digressions! If, for example, commerce constitutes a branch of political economy, all the various kinds of commerce form a part; and as a consequence, maritime commerce, navigation, geography—where shall we stop? All human knowledge is connected. Accordingly, it is necessary to ascertain the points of contact, or the articulations by which the different branches are united; by this means, a more exact knowledge will be obtained of whatever is peculiar to each, and where they run into one another.

In the science of political economy, agriculture, commerce and manufactures are considered only in relation to the increase or diminution of wealth, and not in reference to their processes of execution. This science indicates the cases in which commerce is truly productive, where whatever is gained by one is lost by another, and where it is profitable to all; it also teaches us to appreciate its several processes, but simply in their results, at which it stops. Besides this knowledge, the merchant must also understand the processes of his art. He must be acquainted with the commodities in which he deals, their qualities and defects, the countries from which they are derived, their markets, the means of their transportation, the values to be given for them in exchange, and the method of keeping accounts.

The same remark is applicable to the agriculturist, to the manufacturer, and to the practical man of business; to acquire a thorough knowledge of the causes and consequences of each phenomenon, the study of political economy is essentially necessary to them all; and to become expert in his particular pursuit, each one must add thereto a knowledge of its processes. These different subjects of investigation were not, however, confounded by Dr. Smith; but neither he, nor the writers who succeeded him, have guarded themselves against another source of confusion, here important to be noticed, inasmuch as the developments resulting from it, may not be altogether unuseful in the progress of knowledge in general, as well as in the prosecution of our own particular inquiry.

In political economy, as in natural philosophy, and in every other study, systems have been formed before facts have been established; the place of the latter being supplied by purely gratuitous assertions. More recently, the inductive method of philosophizing, which, since the time of Bacon, has so much contributed to the advancement of every other science, has been applied to the conduct of our researches in this. The excellence of this method consists in only admitting facts carefully observed, and the consequences rigorously deduced from them; thereby effectually excluding those prejudices and authorities which, in every department of literature and science, have so often been interposed between man and truth. But, is the whole extent of the meaning of the term, *facts*, so often made use of, perfectly understood?

It appears to me, that this word at once designates *objects that exist, and events that take place;* thus presenting two classes of *facts:* it is, for example, one fact, that such an object exists; another fact, that such an event takes place in such a manner. *Objects that exist,* in order to serve as the basis of certain reasoning, must be seen exactly as they are, under every point of view, with all their qualities. Otherwise, whilst supposing ourselves to be reasoning respecting the same thing, we may, under the same name, be treating of two different things.

The second class of *facts,* namely, *events that take place,* consists of the phenomena exhibited, when we observe the manner in which things take place. It is, for instance, a fact, that metals, when exposed to a certain degree of heat, become fluid.

The manner in which things exist and take place, constitutes what is called *the nature of things;* and a careful observation of the nature of things is the sole foundation of all truth.

Hence, a twofold classification of sciences; namely, those which may be styled *descriptive,* which arrange and accurately designate the properties of certain objects, as botany and natural history; and those which may be styled *experimental,* which unfold the reciprocal action of sub-

stances on each other, or in other words, the connexion
between cause and effect, as chemistry and natural philosophy. Both departments are founded on facts, and constitute an equally solid and useful portion of knowledge.
Political economy belongs to the latter; in showing the
manner in which events take place in relation to wealth,
it forms a part of experimental science.*

But *facts that take place* may be considered in two points
of view; either as *general* or *constant*, or as *particular* or
variable. General *facts* are the results of the nature of
things in all analogous cases; *particular facts* as truly result from the nature of things, but they are the result of
several operations modified by each other in a particular
case. The former are not less incontrovertible than the
latter, even when apparently they contradict each other.
In natural philosophy, it is a general fact, that heavy bodies fall to the earth; the water in a fountain, nevertheless, rises above it. The particular fact of the fountain is
a result wherein the laws of equilibrium are combined with
those of gravity, but without destroying them.

In our present inquiry, the knowledge of these two
classes of facts, namely, of *objects that exist* and of *events
that take place*, embraces two distinct sciences, political
economy and statistics.

Political economy, from facts always carefully observed,
makes known to us the nature of wealth; from the knowledge of its nature deduces the means of its creation, unfolds the order of its distribution, and the phenomena attending its destruction. It is, in other words, an exposition of the *general facts* observed in relation to this subject. With respect to wealth, it is a knowledge of effects
and of their causes. It shows what facts are constantly
conjoined with; so that one is always the sequence of the
other. But it does not resort for any further explanations
to hypothesis: from the nature of particular events their
concatenations must be perceived; the science must conduct us from one link to another, so that every intelligent

---

* Experimental science, in order to establish why events take place in a certain manner, or to be able to assign a particular cause for a particular effect, to a certain extent
must be descriptive. Astronomy, in order to explain the eclipses of the sun, must demonstrate the opacity of the moon. Political economy, in like manner, in order to
show that money is a means of the production of wealth, but not the end, must exhibit
its true nature.

understanding may clearly comprehend in what manner the chain is united. It is this which constitutes the excellence of the modern method of philosophizing.

Statistics exhibit the amount of production and of consumption of a particular country, at a designated period; its population, military force, wealth, and whatever else is susceptible of valuation. It is a description in detail.

Between political economy and statistics there is the same difference as between the science of politics and history.

The study of statistics may gratify curiosity, but it can never be productive of advantage when it does not indicate the origin and consequences of the facts it has collected; and by indicating their origin and consequences, it at once becomes the science of political economy. This doubtless is the reason why these two distinct sciences have hitherto been confounded. The celebrated work of Dr. Adam Smith can only be considered as an immethodical assemblage of the soundest principles of political economy, supported by luminous illustrations; of highly ingenious researches in statistics, blended with instructive reflections; it is not, however, a complete treatise of either science, but an irregular mass of curious and original speculations, and of known demonstrated truths.

A perfect knowledge of the principles of political economy may be obtained, inasmuch as all the general facts which compose this science may be discovered. In statistics this never can be the case; this latter science, like history, being a recital of facts, more or less uncertain, and necessarily incomplete. Of the statistics of former periods and distant countries, only detached and very imperfect accounts can be furnished. With respect to the present time, there are few persons who unite the qualifications of good observers with a situation favourable for accurate observation. The inaccuracy of the statements we are compelled to have recourse to, the restless suspicions of particular governments, and even of individuals, their ill-will and indifference, present obstacles often insurmountable, notwithstanding the toil and care of inquirers to collect minute details with exactness; and which, after all, when in their possession, are only true for an instant. Dr. Smith accordingly avows, that he puts no great faith in political arithmetic; which is nothing more than the arrangement of numerous statistical data.

Political economy, on the other hand, whenever the principles which constitute its basis are the rigorous deductions of undeniable general facts, rests upon an immoveable foundation. General facts undoubtedly are founded upon the observation of particular facts; but upon such particular facts as have been selected from those most carefully observed, best established, and witnessed by ourselves. When the results of these facts have uniformly been the same, the cause of their having been so satisfactorily demonstrated, and the exceptions to them even confirming other principles equally well established, we are authorised to give them as ultimate general facts, and to submit them with confidence to the examination of all competent inquirers, who may be again desirous of subjecting them to experiment. A new particular fact, when insulated, and the connexion between its antecedents and consequents not established by reasoning, is not sufficient to shake our confidence in a general fact; for who can say that some unknown circumstance has not produced the difference noticed in their several results? A light feather is seen to mount in the air, and sometimes remain there for a long time before it falls back to the ground. Would it not, nevertheless, be erroneous to conclude that this feather is not affected by the universal law of gravitation? In political economy it is a general fact, that the interest of money rises in proportion to the risk run by the lender of not being repaid. Shall it be inferred that this principle is false, from having seen money lent at a low rate of interest upon hazardous occasions? The lender may have been ignorant of the risk, gratitude or fear may have induced sacrifices, and the general law, disturbed in this particular case, will resume its entire force the moment the causes of its interruption have ceased to operate. Finally, how small a number of particular facts are completely examined, and how few among them are observed under all their aspects? And in supposing them well examined, well observed, and well described, how many of them either prove nothing, or directly the reverse of what is intended to be established by them.

Hence, there is not an absurd theory, or an extravagant

opinion that has not been supported by an appeal to facts;*
and it is by facts also that public authorities have been so
often misled. But a knowledge of facts, without a knowledge of their mutual relations, without being able to show
why the one is a cause, and the other a consequence, is
really no better than the crude information of an office-
clerk, of whom the most intelligent seldom becomes acquainted with more than one particular series, which only
enables him to examine a question in a single point of view.
Nothing can be more idle than the opposition of *theory*
to *practice!* What is theory, if it be not a knowledge of
the laws which connect effects with their causes, or facts
with facts? And who can be better acquainted with facts
than the theorist who surveys them under all their aspects,
and comprehends their relation to each other? And what
is practice† without theory, but the employment of means
without knowing how or why they act? In any investigation, to treat dissimilar cases as if they were analogous,
is but a dangerous kind of empiricism, leading to conclusions never foreseen.

Hence it is, that after having seen the exclusive or restrictive system of commerce, a system founded on the
opinion that one nation can only gain what another loses,
almost universally adopted throughout Europe after the
revival of arts and letters; after having seen taxation
without intermission perpetually increasing, and in some
countries extending itself to a most enormous amount;
and after having seen these same countries become more
opulent, more populous, and more powerful, than at the
time they carried on an unrestricted trade, and were almost
entirely exempt from public burdens, the generality of mankind have concluded that national wealth and power were
attributable to the restraints imposed on the application
of industry, and to the taxes levied from the incomes of
individuals. Shallow thinkers have even pretended that
this opinion was founded on facts, and that every different
one was the offspring of a wild and disordered imagination.

* In France, the minister of the interior, in his *exposé* of 1813, a most disastrous period, when foreign commerce was destroyed, and the national resources of every description rapidly declining, boasted of having proved by indubitable *calculations*, that the
country was in a higher state of prosperity than it ever before had been.
† By the term *practice*, is not here meant the manual skill which enables the artificer
or clerk to execute with greater celerity and precision whatever he performs daily, and
which constitutes his peculiar talent; but the method pursued in superintending and
administering public or private affairs.

It is, however, on the contrary, evident that the supporters of the opposite opinion embraced a wider circle of
facts, and understood them much better than their opponents. The very remarkable impulse given, during the
middle ages, to the industry of the free states of Italy and
of the Hanse towns of the north of Europe, the spectacle
of riches it exhibited in both, the shock of opinions occasioned by the crusades, the progress of the arts and
sciences, the improvement of navigation and consequent
discovery of the route to India, and of the continent of
America, as well as a succession of other less important
events, were all known to them as the true causes of the
increased opulence of the most ingenious nations on the
globe. And although they were aware that this activity
had received successive checks, they at the same time knew
that it had been freed from more oppressive obstacles. In
consequence of the authority of the feudal lords and barons
declining, the intercourse between the different provinces
and states could no longer be interrupted; roads became
improved, travelling more secure, and laws less arbitrary;
the enfranchised towns, becoming immediately dependent
upon the crown, found the sovereign interested in their
advancement; and this enfranchisement, which the natural
course of things and the progress of civilization had extended to the country, secured to every class of producers
the fruits of their industry. In every part of Europe personal freedom became more generally respected; if not
from a more improved organization of political society,
at least from the influence of public sentiment. Certain
prejudices, such as branding with the odious name of
usury all loans upon interest, and attaching the importance
of nobility to idleness, had begun to decline. Nor is this
all. Enlightened individuals have not only remarked the
influence of these, but of many other analogous facts; it
has been perceived by them, that the decline of prejudices
has been favourable to the advancement of science, or to
a more exact knowledge of the immutable laws of nature;
that this improvement in the cultivation of science has
itself been favourable to the progress of industry, and industry to national opulence. From such an induction of
facts they have been enabled to conclude, with much
greater certainty than the unthinking multitude, that

although many modern states in the midst of taxation and restrictions have risen to opulence and power, it is not owing to these restraints on the natural course of human affairs, but in spite of such powerful causes of discouragement. The prosperity of the same countries would have been much greater, had they been governed by a more liberal and enlightened policy.*

To obtain a knowledge of the truth, it is not then so necessary to be acquainted with a great number of facts, as with such as are essential, and have a direct and immediate influence ; and, above all, to examine them under all their aspects, to be enabled to deduce from them just conclusions, and be assured that the consequences ascribed to them do not in reality proceed from other causes. Every other knowledge of facts, like the erudition of an almanac, is a mere compilation from which nothing results. And it may be remarked, that this sort of information is peculiar to men of clear memories and clouded judgments; men who declaim against the best established doctrines, the fruits of the most enlarged experience and profoundest reasoning ; and whilst inveighing against system, whenever their own routine is departed from, are precisely those most under its influence, and who defend it with stubborn folly, fearful rather of being convinced, than desirous of arriving at certainty.

Thus, if from all the phenomena of production, as well as from the experience of the most extensive commerce, you demonstrate that a free intercourse between nations is reciprocally advantageous, and that the mode found to be most beneficial to individuals transacting business with foreigners, must be equally so to nations, men of contracted views and high presumption will accuse you of system. Ask them for their reasons, and they will immediately talk to you of the balance of trade; will tell you, it is clear that a nation must be ruined by exchanging its money for

---

* Hence it is that nations seldom derive any benefit from the lessons of experience. To profit by them, the community at large must be enabled to seize the connexion between causes and their consequences; which at once supposes a very high degree of intelligence and a rare capacity for reflection. Whenever mankind shall be in a situation to profit by experience, they will no longer require her lessons ; plain sound sense will then be sufficient. This is one reason of our being subject to the necessity of constant control. All that a people can desire is that laws conducive to the general interest of society should be enacted and carried into effect ; a problem which different political constitutions more or less imperfectly solve.

merchandise—in itself a system. Some will assert that circulation enriches a state, and that a sum of money, by passing through twenty different hands, is equivalent to twenty times its own value; others, that luxury is favourable to industry, and economy ruinous to every branch of commerce—both mere systems; and all will appeal to facts in support of these opinions, like the shepherd, who, upon the faith of his eyes, affirmed that the sun, which he saw rise in the morning and set in the evening, during the day traversed the whole extent of the heavens, treating as an idle dream the laws of the planetary world.

Persons, moreover, distinguished by their attainments in other branches of knowledge, but ignorant of the principles of this, are too apt to suppose that absolute truth is confined to the mathematics and to the results of careful observation and experiment in the physical sciences; imagining that the moral and political sciences contain no invariable facts or indisputable truths, and therefore cannot be considered as genuine sciences, but merely hypothetical systems, more or less ingenious, but purely arbitrary. The opinion of this class of philosophers is founded upon the want of agreement among the writers who have investigated these subjects, and from the wild absurdities taught by some of them. But what science has been free from extravagant hypotheses? How many years have elapsed since those most advanced have been altogether disengaged from system? On the contrary, do we not still see men of perverted understandings attacking the best established positions? Forty years have not elapsed since water, so essential to our very existence, and the atmosphere in which we perpetually breathe, have been accurately analyzed. The experiments and demonstrations, nevertheless, upon which this doctrine is founded, are continually assailed; although repeated a thousand times in different countries by the most acute and cautious experimenters. A want of agreement exists in relation to a description of facts much more simple and obvious than the most part of those in moral and political science. Are not natural philosophy, chemistry, botany, mineralogy, and physiology, still fields of controversy, in which opinions are combated with as much violence and asperity as in political economy? The same facts are, indeed, observed by both parties, but are classed and explained differently by each; and it is worthy of remark, that in these contests genuine philosophers are not arrayed against pretenders. Leibnitz and Newton, Linnæus and Jussieu, Priestley and Lavoisier, Desaussure and Dolomieu, were all men of uncommon genius, who, however, did not agree in their philosophical systems. But have not the sciences they taught an existence, notwithstanding these disagreements?*

In like manner, the general facts constituting the sciences of politics and morals, exist independently of all controversy. Hence the advantage enjoyed by every one who, from distinct and accurate observation, can establish the existence of these general facts, demonstrate their connexion, and deduce their consequences. They as certainly proceed from the nature of things as the laws of the material world. We do not imagine them; they are results disclosed to us by judicious observation and analysis. Sovereigns, as well as their subjects, must bow to their authority, and never can violate them with impunity.

General facts, or, if you please, the general laws which facts follow, are styled *principles*, whenever it relates to their application; that is to say, the moment we avail ourselves of them in order to ascertain the rule of action of

---

* "The controversies," says Col. Torrens, in his 'Essay on the Production of Wealth,' published in 1821, "which at present exist amongst the most celebrated masters of political economy, have been brought forward by a lively and ingenious author as an objection against the study of the science. A similar objection might have been urged, in a certain stage of its progress, against every branch of human knowledge. A few years ago, when the brilliant discoveries in chemistry began to supersede the ancient doctrine of phlogiston, controversies, analogous to those which now exist amongst political economists, divided the professors of natural knowledge; and Dr. Priestley, like Mr. Malthus, appeared as the pertinacious champion of the theories which the facts established by himself had so largely contributed to overthrow. In the progress of the human mind, a period of controversy amongst the cultivators of any branch of science must necessarily precede the period of their unanimity. But this, instead of furnishing a reason for abandoning the pursuits of science, while its first principles remain in uncertainty, should stimulate us to prosecute our studies with more ardour and perseverance until upon every question within the compass of the human faculties, doubt is removed and certainty attained. With respect to political economy, the period of controversy is passing away, and that of unanimity rapidly approaching. Twenty years hence there will scarcely exist a doubt respecting any of its fundamental principles."

And in the preface of the third edition of his 'Essay on the External Corn Trade,' published in 1826, Col. Torrens makes these further remarks: "On a former occasion, the author ventured to predict, that at no distant period, controversy amongst the professors of political economy would cease, and unanimity prevail, respecting the fundamental principles of the science. He thinks he can already perceive the unequivocal signs of the approaching fulfilment of this prediction. Since it was hazarded, two works have appeared, each of which, in its own peculiar line, is eminently calculated to correct the errors which previously prevailed. These publications are, 'A Critical Dissertation on the Nature, Causes, and Measures of Value, by an anonymous author;' and 'Thoughts and Details on High and Low Prices, by Mr. Tooke.'"—AMERICAN EDITOR.

3 D

any combination of circumstances presented to us. A knowledge of principles furnishes the only certain means of uniformly conducting any inquiry with success.

Political economy, in the same manner as the exact sciences, is composed of a few fundamental principles, and of a great number of corollaries or conclusions, drawn from these principles. It is essential, therefore, for the advancement of this science that these principles should be strictly deduced from observation; the number of conclusions to be drawn from them may afterwards be either multiplied or diminished at the discretion of the inquirer, according to the object he proposes. To enumerate all their consequences, and give their proper explanations, would be a work of stupendous magnitude, and necessarily incomplete. Besides, the more this science shall become improved, and its influence extended, the less occasion will there be to deduce consequences from its principles, as these will spontaneously present themselves to every eye; and being within the reach of all, their application will be readily made. A treatise on political economy will then be confined to the enunciation of a few general principles, not requiring even the support of proofs or illustrations; because these will be but the expression of what every one will know, arranged in a form convenient for comprehending them, as well in their whole scope as in their relation to each other.

It would, however, be idle to imagine that greater precision, or a more steady direction could be given to this study, by the application of mathematics to the solution of its problems. The *values* with which political economy is concerned, admitting of the application to them of the terms *plus* and *minus*, are indeed within the range of mathematical inquiry; but being at the same time subject to the influence of the faculties, the wants and the desires of mankind, they are not susceptible of any rigorous appreciation, and cannot, therefore, furnish any *data* for absolute calculations. In political as well as in physical science, all that is essential is a knowledge of the connexion between causes and their consequences. Neither the phenomena of the moral or material world are subject to strict arithmetical computation.*

---

* We may, for example, know that for any given year the price of wine will infallibly

These considerations respecting the nature and object of political economy, and the best method of obtaining a

depend upon the quantity to be sold, compared with the extent of the demand. But if we are desirous of submitting these two data to mathematical calculation, their ultimate elements must be decomposed before we can become thoroughly acquainted with them, or can, with any degree of precision, distinguish the separate influence of each. Hence, it is not only necessary to determine what will be the product of the succeeding vintage, while yet exposed to the vicissitudes of the weather, but the quality it will possess, the quantity remaining on hand of the preceding vintage, the amount of capital that will be at the disposal of the dealers, and require them, more or less expeditiously, to get back their advances. We must also ascertain the opinion that may be entertained as to the possibility of exporting the article, which will altogether depend upon our impressions as to the stability of the laws and government, that vary from day to day, and respecting which no two individuals exactly agree. All these data, and probably many others besides, must be accurately appreciated, solely to determine the *quantity* to be put in *circulation;* itself but one of the elements of *price.* To determine the *quantity* to be *demanded,* the price at which the commodity can be sold must already be known, as the demand for it will increase in proportion to its cheapness; we must also know the former stock on hand, and the tastes and means of the consumers, as various as their persons. Their ability to purchase will vary according to the more or less prosperous condition of industry in general, and of their own in particular; their wants will vary also in the ratio of the additional means at their command of substituting one liquor for another, such as beer, cider, &c. I suppress an infinite number of less important considerations, more or less affecting the solution of the problem; for I question whether any individual, really accustomed to the application of mathematical analysis, would even venture to attempt this, not only on account of the numerous data, but in consequence of the difficulty of characterizing them with any thing like precision, and of combining their separate influences. Such persons as have pretended to do it, have not been able to enunciate these questions into analytical language, without divesting them of their natural complication, by means of simplifications, and arbitrary suppressions, of which the consequences, not properly estimated, always essentially change the condition of the problem, and pervert all its results; so that no other inference can be deduced from such calculations than from formula arbitrarily assumed. Thus, instead of recognizing in their conclusions that harmonious agreement which constitutes the peculiar character of rigorous geometrical investigation, by whatever method they may have been obtained, we only perceive vague and uncertain inferences, whose differences are often equal to the quantities sought to be determined. What course is then to be pursued by a judicious inquirer in the elucidation of a subject so much involved? The same which would be pursued by him, under circumstances equally difficult, which decide the greater part of the actions of his life. He will examine the immediate elements of the proposed problem, and after having ascertained them with certainty, (which in political economy can be effected,) will approximately value their mutual influences with the intuitive quickness of an enlightened understanding, itself only an instrument by means of which the mean result of a crowd of probabilities can be estimated, but never calculated with exactness.

Cabanis, in describing the revolutions in the science of medicine, makes a remark perfectly analogous to this. 'The vital phenomena,' says he, 'depend upon so many unknown springs, held together under such various circumstances, which observation vainly attempts to appreciate, that these problems, from not being stated with all their conditions, absolutely defy calculation. Hence whenever writers on mechanics have endeavoured to subject the laws of life to their method, they have furnished the scientific world with a remarkable spectacle, well entitled to our most serious consideration. The terms they employed were correct, the process of reasoning strictly logical, and, nevertheless, all the results were erroneous. Further, although the language and the method of employing it were the same among all the calculators, each of them obtained distinct and different results; and it is by the application of this method of investigation to subjects to which it is altogether inapplicable, that systems the most whimsical, fallacious, and contradictory, have been maintained.'

D'Alembert, in his treatise on Hydrodynamics, acknowledges that the velocity of the blood in its passage through the vessels entirely resists every kind of calculation. Senebier made a similar observation in his *Essai sur l'Art d'observer,* (vol. 1, page 81.)

Whatever has been said by able teachers and judicious philosophers, in relation to our conclusions in natural science, is much more applicable to moral; and points out

thorough knowledge of its principles, will supply us with the means of appreciating the efforts hitherto made towards the advancement of this science.

The literature of the ancients, their legislation, their public treaties, and their administration of the conquered provinces, all proclaim their utter ignorance of the nature and origin of wealth, of the manner in which it is distributed, and of the effects of its consumption. They knew, what has always been known wherever the right of property has been sanctioned by laws, that riches are increased by economy, and diminished by extravagance. Xenophon extols order, activity, and intelligence, as certain means of obtaining prosperity; but without deducing these maxims from any general law, or without being able to show the connexion between causes and their consequences. He advises the Athenians to protect commerce, and to receive strangers with kindness; yet so little was he aware to what extent this advice would be proper, that, upon another occasion, he expresses doubts whether commerce be really profitable to the republic.

Plato and Aristotle, it is true, notice some invariable relations between the different modes of production, and the results obtained from them. Plato sketches with tolerable fidelity,* the effects of the separation of social employments; but it is simply with a view to illustrate man's social character and the necessity he is in, from his multifarious wants, of uniting in extensive societies in which each individual may be exclusively occupied with one species of production. His view is entirely a political one; and he has deduced from it no other conclusion.

In his treatise on Politics, Aristotle goes farther. He distinguishes natural from artificial production. He styles natural, whatever creates those objects of consumption required by a family, or, at most, whatever is obtained by exchanges in kind. No other advantage, according to him, is derived from real production; artificial gain he condemns. Besides, he does not support these opinions by any reasoning founded upon accurate observation.

the cause of our always being misled in political economy, whenever we have subjected its phenomena to mathematical calculation. In such case it becomes the most dangerous of all abstractions.

* Republic, Book II.

From the manner in which he expresses himself in relation to the effect of savings and loans on interest, it is evident that he knew nothing of the nature and employment of capital.

What can we expect from nations still less advanced in civilization than the Greeks? We may recollect that a law of Egypt obliged the son to adopt the profession of his father. This, in certain cases, was to require the creation of a greater quantity of products than the particular state of society called for; to oblige an individual, in order to obey the law, to ruin himself, and to continue the exercise of his productive functions, whether in possession of capital or not; which is altogether absurd.* The Romans, in treating every branch of industry, except agriculture (and we know not why,) with contempt, betray the same ignorance. Their pecuniary transactions must be numbered amongst their most unskilful operations.

The moderns, even after having freed themselves from the barbarism of the middle ages, have not for a very long time been more advanced. We shall have occasion to notice the stupidity of a multitude of laws relating to the Jews, to the interest of money, and to money itself. Henry IV. granted to his favourites and mistresses, as favours *which cost him nothing*, the permission to practise a thousand petty extortions, and to collect for their own benefit, from various branches of commerce, as many petty taxes. He authorized the count of Soissons to levy a duty of fifteen sous upon every bale of merchandise which should be exported from the kingdom.†

In every branch of knowledge, example has preceded precept. The fortunate enterprises of the Portuguese and Spaniards during the fifteenth century, the active industry of Venice, Genoa, Florence, Pisa, the provinces of Flanders, and the free cities of Germany at this same epoch, gradually directed the attention of some philosophers to the theory of wealth.

These inquiries, like almost every other in the arts and sciences, after the revival of letters, originated in Italy.

---

* When we find almost every historian, from Herodotus to Bossuet, boasting of this and other similar laws, it will be seen how important it is that all who undertake to write history should have some knowledge of the science of political economy.

† See Sully's Memoirs, Book XVI.

3*

As far back as the sixteenth century, *Botero* was engaged in investigating the real sources of public prosperity. In the year 1613, *Antonio Serra* composed a treatise, in which he particularly noticed the productive power of industry; but the title of his work sufficiently indicates its errors. Wealth, according to his hypothesis, consisted only of gold and silver.* *Davanzati* wrote upon money and upon exchange; and at the beginning of the eighteenth century, fifty years before the time of Quesnay, *Bandini* of Sienna had shown, both from reasoning and experience, that there never had been a scarcity of food, except in those countries where the government had itself interfered to supply the people. *Belloni*, a banker at Rome, in the year 1750, published a dissertation on commerce, evincing his intimate acquaintance with the nature of money and exchanges, although at the same time infected with the theory of the balance of trade. His labours were rewarded by the Pope with the title of marquess. *Carli*, before Dr. Smith, demonstrated that the balance of trade neither taught nor proved any thing. *Algarotti*, whose writings on other subjects Voltaire has made known, wrote also upon the science of political economy; and the little he has left exhibits the accuracy and extent of his knowledge, as well as his acuteness. He confines himself so strictly to facts, and so uniformly founds his speculations on the nature of things, that although he did not get possession of the proof of his principles, and of their relation to each other, he has, nevertheless, guarded himself against every thing like hypothesis and system. In 1764, *Genovesi* commenced a course of public lectures on political economy, in the chair founded at Naples by the care of the highly esteemed and learned *Intieri*. In consequence of this example, other professorships of political economy were afterwards established at Milan, and more recently in most of the universities in Germany and Russia.

In 1750, the abbé *Galiani*, so well known since from his connexion with many of the French philosophers, and by his Dialogues on the Corn Trade, although at that time a very young man, published a Treatise on Money, which discovered such uncommon talents and information, as to

---

* *Breve Trattato delle cause che possono far abondare li regni d'oro et d'argento dove non sono miniere.*

induce a belief that he had been assisted in the composition of his work by the abbé *Intieri* and the Marquess of *Rinuccini*. Its merits, however, appear to be of a description similar to those the author's writings always afterwards displayed; genius united with erudition, carefulness in uniformly ascending to the nature of things; and an animated and elegant style.

One of the most striking peculiarities of this work, is its containing some of the rudiments of the doctrine of Adam Smith; among others, that labour is the sole creator of the value of things or of wealth;* a principle although not rigorously true, as will be made manifest in the course of this work, but which, pushed to its ultimate consequences, would have put *Galiani* in the way of discovering and completely unfolding the phenomena of production. Dr. Smith, who was about the same time a professor in the university of Glasgow, and then taught this doctrine, which has since acquired so much celebrity, in all probability had no knowledge of a work in the Italian language, published at Naples by a young man then hardly known, and whom he has never quoted. But even had he known it, a truth cannot with so much propriety be said to belong to its fortunate discoverer, as to the inquirer who first proves that it must be so, and demonstrates its consequences. Although the existence of universal gravitation had been previously conjectured by Kepler and Pascal, the discovery does not the less belong to Newton.†

---

* "Entro ora a dire della factica, la quale, non solo in tute le opere que sono intiera mente dell' arte come le pitture, sculture, intagli, etc., ma anchi in molti corpi, come sono i minerali, i sassi, le piante spontanee delle selve, etc., é l'unica che dà valore alla cosa. La quantità della materia non per altro coopera in questi corpi al valore se non parché aumenta o sema la fatica." (GALIANI, della Moneta. Lib. I, cap. 2.)

"In relation to labour I will remark, that not only in productions which are entirely the work of art, as in painting, sculpture, engraving, etc., but likewise in productions of nature, as on metals, minerals, and plants, their value is entirely derived from the labour bestowed on their creation. The quantity of matter affects the value of things only so far as it requires more or less labour."

In the same chapter Galiani also remarks, that man, that is to say his labour, is the only correct measure of value. This, also, according to Dr. Smith, is a principle; although considered by me as an error.

† This same Galiani remarks, in the same work, that whatever is gained by some, must necessarily be lost by others; in this way proving, that a very ingenious writer may not even know how to deduce the most simple conclusions, and may pass by the truth without perceiving it. For, if wealth can be *created* by labour, there may then be a new description of wealth in the world, not taken from anybody. Indeed, this author, in his Dialogues on the Corn Trade, published in France a long time afterwards, has himself, in a very peculiar manner, pronounced his own condemnation. "A truth," he observes, "which is brought to light by pure accident, like a mushroom in a mea-

In Spain, *Alvarez Osorio*, and *Martinez-de-mata*, have delivered discourses on political economy, the publication of which we owe to the enlightened patriotism of *Campomanes.* *Moncada, Navarette, Ustaritz, Ward,* and *Ulloa,* have, written on the same subject. These esteemed authors, like those of Italy, entertained many sound views, verified various important facts, and supplied a number of laborious calculations; but from their inability to establish them upon fundamental principles of the science, which were not then known, they have often been mistaken both as to the end as well as the means of prosecuting this study; amidst a variety of useless disquisitions, have only cast an uncertain and deceptive light.*

In France, the science of political economy, at first, was only considered in its application to public finances. *Sully* remarks correctly enough, that agriculture and commerce are the two teats of the state; but from a vague and indistinct conception of the truth. The same observation may be applied to *Vauban*, a man of a sound practical mind, and although in the army, a philosopher and friend of peace, who, deeply afflicted with the misery into which his country had been plunged by the vain-glory of Louis XIV., proposed a more equitable assessment of the taxes, as a means of alleviating the public burdens.

Under the influence of the regent, opinions became unsettled; bank-notes, supposed to be an inexhaustible source of wealth, were only the means of swallowing up capital, of expending what had never been earned, and of making a bankruptcy of all debts. Moderation and economy were turned into ridicule. The courtiers of the prince, either by persuasion or corruption, encouraged him in every species of extravagance. At this period, the maxim that a state is enriched by luxury was reduced to system. All the talents and wit of the day were exerted in gravely maintaining such a paradox in prose, or in embellishing it with the more attractive charms of poetry.

dow, is of no value; we cannot make use of it, if we are ignorant of its origin and consequences; or how and by what chain of reasoning it is derived."

* From my own inability of judging of the merits of such of these writers whose works have not been translated, I have availed myself of the opinions of one of the translators of this Treatise into the Spanish language, *Don Jose Queypo*, an individual alike distinguished by his abilities and patriotism, whose remarks I have only copied.

The dissipation of the national treasures was really supposed to merit the public gratitude. The ignorance of
first principles, with the debauchery and licentiousness of
the duke of Orleans, conspired to effect the ruin of the
kingdom. During the long peace maintained by cardinal
Fleury, France recovered a little; the insignificant administration of this weak minister at least proving, that
the ruler of a nation may achieve much good by abstaining from the commission of evil.

The steadily increasing progress of different branches
of industry, the advancement of the sciences, whose influence upon wealth we shall have occasion hereafter to
notice, and the direction of public opinion, at length estimating national prosperity as being of some importance,
caused the science of political economy to enter into the
contemplation of a great number of writers. Its true
principles were not then known; but since, according to
the observation of Fontenelle, our condition is such, that
we are not permitted at once to arrive at the truth, but
must previously pass through various species of errors
and various grades of follies, ought these false steps to be
considered as altogether useless, which have taught us to
advance with more steadiness and certainty?

Montesquieu, who was desirous of considering laws in all
their relations, inquired into their influence on national
wealth. The nature and origin of wealth he should first
have ascertained; of which, however, he did not form any
opinion. We are, nevertheless, indebted to this distinguished author for the first philosophical examination of
the principles of legislation; and, in this point of view,
he, perhaps, may be considered as the master of the
English writers, who are so generally esteemed as being
ours; just in the same manner as Voltaire has been the
master of their best historians, who now furnish us with
models worthy of imitation.

About the middle of the eighteenth century, certain
principles in relation to the origin of wealth, advanced by
Doctor *Quesnay*, made a great number of proselytes. The
enthusiastic admiration manifested by these persons for
the founder of their doctrines, the scrupulous exactness
with which they have uniformly since followed the same

E

dogmas, and the energy and zeal they displayed in maintaining them, have caused them to be considered as a sect,
which has received the name of *economists*. Instead of
first observing the nature of things, or the manner in
which they take place, of classifying these observations,
and deducing from them general propositions, they commenced by laying down certain abstract general propositions, which they styled axioms, from supposing them to
contain inherent evidence of their own truth. They then
endeavoured to accommodate the particular facts to them,
and to infer from them their 'laws; thus involving themselves in the defence of maxims evidently at variance with
common sense and universal experience,* as will appear
hereafter in various parts of this work. Their opponents
had not themselves formed any more correct views of the
subjects in controversy. With considerable learning and
talents on both sides, they were either wrong or right by
chance. Points were contested that should have been
conceded, and opinions, unquestionably false, acquiesced
in; in short, they combated in the clouds. *Voltaire*, who
so well knew how to detect the ridiculous, wherever it
was to be found, in his *Homme aux quarante ecus*, satirised
the system of the economists; yet, in exposing the tire-
some trash of *Mercer de la Riviere*, and the absurdities
contained in *Mirabeau's L'ami des Hommes*, he was himself unable to point out the errors of either.

The economists, by promulgating some important truths,
directing a more general attention to objects of public
utility, and by exciting discussions, which, although at
that time of no advantage, subsequently led to more accurate investigations, have unquestionably done much
good.† In representing agricultural industry as productive of wealth, they were not deceived; and, perhaps, the
necessity they were in of unfolding the nature of production, caused the further examination of this important phenomenon, which conducted their successors to its entire

---

* When they maintain, for example, that a fall in the price of food is a public calamity.

† Among the discussions they provoked, we must not forget the entertaining Dialogues on the Corn Trade, by the abbé *Galiani*, in which the science of political economy is treated in the humorous manner of Tristram Shandy. An important truth is
asserted, and when the author is called upon for its proof, he replies with some ingenious
pleasantry.

development. On the other hand, the labours of the economists have been attended with serious evils; the many useful maxims they decried, their sectarian spirit, the dogmatical and abstract language of the greater part of their writings, and the tone of inspiration pervading them, gave currency to the opinion, that all who were engaged in such studies were but idle dreamers, whose theories, at best only gratifying literary curiosity, were wholly inapplicable in practice.*

No one, however, has ever denied that the writings of the economists have uniformly been favourable to the strictest morality, and to the liberty which every human being ought to possess, of disposing of his person, fortune, and talents, according to the bent of his inclination; without which, indeed, individual happiness and national prosperity are but empty and unmeaning sounds. These opinions alone entitle their authors to universal gratitude and esteem. I do not, moreover, believe that a dishonest man or bad citizen can be found among their number.

This doubtless is the reason why, since the year 1760, almost all the French writers of any celebrity on subjects connected with political economy, without absolutely being enrolled under the banners of the economists, have, nevertheless, been influenced by their opinions. *Raynal, Condorcet*, and many others, will be found among this number. *Condillac* may also be enumerated among them, notwithstanding his endeavours to found a system of his own in relation to a subject which he did not understand. Many useful hints may be collected from amidst the ingenious

---

* The belief that moral and political science is founded upon chimerical theories, arises chiefly from our almost continually confounding *questions of right* with *matters of fact*. Of what consequence, for instance, is the question so long agitated in the writings of the economists, whether the sovereign power in a country is, or is not, the co-proprietor of the soil? The fact is, that in every country the government takes, or in the shape of taxes the people are compelled to furnish it with, a part of the revenue drawn from real estate. Here then is a fact, and an important one; the consequence of certain facts, which we can trace up, as the cause of other facts (such as the rise in the price of commodities) to which we are led with certainty. *Questions of right* are always more or less matters of opinion; *matters of fact*, on the contrary, are susceptible of proof and demonstration. The former exercise but little influence over the fortunes of mankind; while the latter, inasmuch as facts grow out of each other, are deeply interesting to them; and, as it is of importance to us that some results should take place in preference to others, it is, therefore, essential to ascertain the means by which these may be obtained. The Social Contract of J. J. Rousseau, from being almost entirely founded upon questions of right, has thereby become, what I feel no hesitation in avowing, a work of at least but little practical utility.

trifling, of his work ;* but, like the economists, he almost
invariably founds a principle upon some gratuitous assumption.
Now, an hypothesis may indeed be resorted to, in
order to exemplify and elucidate the correctness of an
author's general reasoning, but never can be sufficient to
establish a fundamental truth. Political economy has only
become a science since it has been confined to the results
of inductive investigation.

Turgot was himself too good a citizen, not sincerely to
esteem as good citizens as the economists ; and accordingly,
when in power, he deemed it advantageous to countenance
them. The economists, in their turn, found their
account in passing off so enlightened an individual and
minister of state as one of their adepts ; the opinions of
Turgot, however, were not borrowed from their school,
but derived from the nature of things ; and although on
many important points of doctrine he may have been deceived,
the measures of his administration, either planned
or executed, are amongst the most brilliant ever conceived
by any statesman. There cannot, therefore, be a stronger
proof of the incapacity of his sovereign, than his inability
to appreciate such exertions, or if capable of appreciating
them, in not knowing how to afford them support.

The economists not only exercised a particular sway
over French writers, but also had a very remarkable influence
over many Italian authors, who even went beyond
them. *Beccaria,* in a course of public lectures at Milan,†
first analysed the true functions of productive capital.
The Count de *Verri,* the countryman and friend of Beccaria,
and worthy of being so, both a man of business and an
accomplished scholar, in his *Meditazione sull' Economia
politica,* published in 1771, approached nearer than any
other writer, before Dr. Smith, to the real laws which
regulate the production and consumption of wealth. *Filangieri,*
whose treatise on political and economical laws
was not given to the public until the year 1780, appears
not to have been acquainted with the work of Dr. Smith,

---

* *Du Commerce et du Gouvernement considérés l'un relativement à l'autre.*

† See the syllabus of his lectures, which was printed for the first time in the year 1804,
in the valuable collection published at Milan by *Pietro Custodi,* under the title of *Scrittori
classici italiani di economia politica.* It was unknown to me until after the publication
of the first edition of this work in 1803.

published four years before. The principles de Verri laid down are followed by Filangieri, and even received from him a more complete development; but although guided by the torch of analysis and deduction, he did not proceed from the most fortunate premises to the immediate consequences which confirm them, at the same time that they exhibit their application and utility.

But none of these inquiries could lead to any important result. How, indeed, was it possible to become acquainted with the causes of national prosperity, when no clear or distinct notions had been formed respecting the nature of wealth itself? The object of our investigations must be thoroughly perceived before the means of attaining it are sought after. In the year 1776, *Adam Smith*, educated in that school in Scotland which has produced so many scholars, historians, and philosophers, of the highest celebrity, published his *Inquiry into the Nature and Causes of the Wealth of Nations*. In this work, its author demonstrated that wealth was the exchangeable value of things; that its extent was proportional to the number of things in our possession having value; and that inasmuch as value could be given or added to matter, that wealth could be created and engrafted on things previously destitute of value, and there be preserved, accumulated, or destroyed.*

In inquiring into the origin of value, Dr. Smith found it to be derived from the labour of man, which he ought to have denominated *industry*, from its being a more comprehensive and significant term than *labour*. From this fruitful demonstration he deduced numerous and important conclusions respecting the causes which, from checking the development of the productive powers of labour, are prejudicial to the growth of wealth; and as they are

---

* During the same year that Dr. Smith's work appeared, and immediately before its publication, *Browne Dignan* published in London, written in the French language, his *Essai sur les principes de l'Economie publique*, containing the following remarkable passage: " The class of reproducers includes all who, uniting their labour to that of the vegetative power of the soil, or modifying the productions of nature in the processes of their several arts, create in some sort a *new value*, of which the sum total forms what is called the *annual reproduction*."

This striking passage, in which reproduction is more clearly characterised than in any part of Dr. Smith's writings, did not lead its author to any important conclusions, but merely gave birth to a few scattered hints. A want of connexion in his views, and of precision in his terms, have rendered his Essay so vague and obscure, that no instruction whatever can be derived from it.

4

rigorous deductions from an indisputable principle, they
have only been assailed by individuals, either too careless
to have thoroughly understood the principle, or of such
perverted understandings as to be wholly incapable of
seizing the connexion or relation between any two ideas.
Whenever the Inquiry into the Wealth of Nations is
perused with the attention it so well merits, it will be perceived that until the epoch of its publication, the science
of political economy did not exist.

From this period, gold and silver coins were considered
as only constituting a portion, and but a small portion,
of national wealth; a portion the less important, because
less susceptible of increase, and because their uses can
be more easily supplied than those of many other articles
equally valuable; and hence it results that a community,
as well as its individual members, are in no way interested
in obtaining metallic money beyond the extent of this
limited demand.

These views, we conceive, first enabled Dr. Smith to
ascertain, in their whole extent, the true functions of
money, and the applications of them, which he made to
bank-notes and paper money, are of the utmost importance in practice.   They afforded him the means of demonstrating, that productive capital does not consist of a
sum of money, but in the value of the objects made use
of in production.   He arranged and analyzed the elements of which productive capital is composed, and
pointed out their true functions.*

Many principles strictly correct had often been advanced prior to the time of Dr. Smith;† he, however, was
the first author who established their truth.   Nor is this

---

* This difficult and abstruse subject has not, perhaps, been treated by Dr. Smith with
sufficient method and perspicuity. Owing to this circumstance, his intelligent and acute
countryman, lord Lauderdale, has composed an entire treatise, in order to prove that
his lordship had completely failed in comprehending this part of the Wealth of Nations.

† In the article *Grains*, in the Encyclopedie, *Quesnay* had remarked, that " commodities *which can be sold*, ought always to be considered without distinction, either as
pecuniary or real wealth, applicable to the purposes of whoever may make use of it."
This, in reality, is Dr. Smith's *exchangeable value*. *De Verri* had observed, (chapter
3,) that *reproduction was nothing more than the reproduction of value*, and that *the value
of things constituted wealth*. Galiani, as has been already noticed, had said, that *labour
was the source of all value;* but Dr. Smith, nevertheless, made these views his own by
exhibiting, as we see, their connexion with all the other important phenomena, and in
demonstrating them even by their consequences.

all. He has furnished us, also, with the true method of detecting errors; he has applied to political economy the new mode of scientific investigation, namely, of not looking for principles abstractedly, but by ascending from facts the most constantly observed, to the general laws which govern them. As every fact may be said to have a particular cause, it is in the spirit of system to determine the cause; it is in the spirit of analysis, to be solicitous to know *why* a particular cause has produced this effect, in order to be satisfied that it could not have been produced by any other cause. The work of Dr. Smith is a succession of demonstrations, which has elevated many propositions to the rank of indisputable principles, and plunged a still greater number into that imaginary gulph, into which extravagant hypotheses and vague opinions for a certain period struggle, before being forever swallowed up.

It has been said that Dr. Smith was under heavy obligations to *Stewart*,* an author whom he has not once quoted, even for the purpose of refuting him. I cannot perceive in what these obligations consist. In the conception of his subject, Dr. Smith displays the elevation and comprehensiveness of his views, whilst the researches of Stewart exhibit but a narrow and insignificant scope. Stewart has supported a system already maintained by Colbert, adopted afterwards by all the French writers on commerce, and steadily followed by most European governments; a system which considers national wealth as depending, not upon the sum total of its productions, but upon the amount of its sales to foreign countries. One of the most important portions of Dr. Smith's work is devoted to the refutation of this theory. If he has not particularly refuted Stewart, it is from the latter not being considered by him as the father of his school, and from having deemed it of more importance to overthrow an opinion, then universally received, than to confute the doctrines of an author, which in themselves contained nothing peculiar.

The economists have also pretended, that Dr. Smith

---

* Sir James Stewart, author of a Treatise on Political Economy.

was under obligations to them. But to what do such pretensions amount? A man of genius is indebted to everything around him; to the scattered lights which he has concentrated, to the errors which he has overthrown, and even to the enemies by whom he has been assailed; inasmuch as they all contribute to the formation of his opinions. But when out of these materials he afterwards embodies enlarged views, useful to his contemporaries and posterity, it rather behoves us to acknowledge the extent of our own obligations, than to reproach him with what he has been supplied by others. Moreover, Dr. Smith has not been backward in acknowledging the advantages he had derived from his intercourse with the most enlightened men in France, and from his intimate correspondence with his friend and countryman *Hume*, whose essays on political economy, as well as on various other subjects, contain so many just views.

After having shown, as fully as so rapid a sketch will permit, the improvement which the science of political economy owes to Dr. Smith, it will not, perhaps, be useless to indicate, in as summary a manner, some of the points on which he has erred, and others which he has left to be elucidated.

To the labour of man alone he ascribes the power of producing values. This is an error. A more exact analysis demonstrates, as will be seen in the course of this work, that all values are derived from the operation of labour, or rather from the industry of man, combined with the operation of those agents which nature and capital furnish him. Dr. Smith did not, therefore, obtain a thorough knowledge of the most important phenomenon in production; this has led him into some erroneous conclusions, such, for instance, as attributing a gigantic influence to the division of labour, or rather to the separation of employments. This influence, however, is by no means inappreciable or even inconsiderable; but the greatest wonders of this description, are not so much owing to any peculiar property in human labour, as to the use we make of the powers of nature. His ignorance of this principle precluded him from establishing the true theory of machinery in relation to the production of wealth.

The phenomena of production being now better known than they were in the time of Dr. Smith, have enabled his successors to distinguish, and to assign the difference found to exist, between a real and a relative rise in prices;* a difference which furnishes the solution of numerous problems, otherwise wholly inexplicable. Such, for example, as the following: *Does a tax, or any other impost, by enhancing the price of commodities, increase the amount of wealth?† The income of the producer arising from the cost of production, why is not this income impaired by a diminution in the cost of production?* Now it is the power of resolving these abstruse problems which, nevertheless, constitutes the science of political economy.‡

By the exclusive restriction of the term *wealth* to values fixed and realized in material substances, Dr. Smith has

---

* See Chapter third, Book second.

† Dr. Smith has, in a satisfactory manner, established the difference between the real and nominal prices of things, that is to say, between the quantity of real values which must be given to obtain a commodity, and the name which is given to the sum of these values. The difference here alluded to, arises from a more perfect analysis, in which the real price itself is decomposed.

‡ It is not, for example, until after the manner in which production takes place is thoroughly understood, that we can say how far the circulation of money and commodities has contributed towards it, and consequently what circulation is useful, and what is not; otherwise, we should only talk nonsense, as is daily done, respecting the utility of a quick circulation. My being obliged to furnish a chapter on this subject (Book I, Chap. 16.) must be attributed to the inconsiderable advancement made in the science of political economy, and to the consequent necessity of directing our attention to some of its more simple applications. The same remark is applicable to the twentieth chapter, in the same book, on the subject of *temporary and permanent emigration, considered in reference to national wealth.* Any person, however, well acquainted with the principles of this science, would find no difficulty in arriving at the same conclusions. The time is not distant when not only writers on finance, but on history and geography, will be required to possess a knowledge of at least the fundamental principles of political economy. A modern treatise on Universal Geography, (vol. 2, page 602,) a work in other respects denoting extensive research and information, contains the following passage: "The number of inhabitants of a country is the basis of every good system of finance; the more numerous is its population, the greater height will its commerce and manufactures attain; and the extent of its military force be in proportion to the amount of its population." Unfortunately, every one of these positions may be erroneous. National revenue, necessarily consisting either of the income of the public property, or of the contributions, in the shape of taxes, drawn from the incomes of individuals, does not depend upon the number, but upon the wealth, and above all, upon the incomes of the people. Now, an indigent multitude has the fewer contributions to yield, the more mouths it has to feed. It is not the numerical population of a state, but the capital and genius of its inhabitants, that most conduce to the advancement of its commerce; these benefit population much more than they are benefited by it. Finally, the number of troops a government can maintain depends still less upon the extent of its population than upon its revenues; and it has been already seen that revenue is not dependent upon population.

narrowed the boundary of this science. He should, also, have included under its values which, although immaterial, are not less real, such as natural or acquired talents. Of two individuals equally destitute of fortune, the one in possession of a particular talent is by no means so poor as the other. Whoever has acquired a particular talent at the expense of an annual sacrifice, enjoys an accumulated capital; a description of wealth, notwithstanding its immateriality, so little imaginary, that, in the shape of professional services, it is daily exchanged for gold and silver.

Dr. Smith, who with so much sagacity unfolds the manner in which production takes place, and the peculiar circumstances accompanying it in agriculture and the arts, on the subject of commercial production presents us with only obscure and indistinct notions. He, accordingly, was unable to point out with precision, the reason why, and the extent to which, facilities of communication are conducive to production.

He did not subject to a rigid analysis the different operations comprehended under the general name of industry, or as he calls it, of labour, and, therefore, could not appreciate the peculiar importance of each in the business of production.

His work does not furnish a satisfactory or well connected account of the manner in which wealth is distributed in society; a branch of political economy, it may be remarked, opening an almost new field for cultivation. The too imperfect views of economical writers respecting the production of wealth precluded them from forming any accurate notions in relation to its distribution.*

Finally, although the phenomena of the consumption of wealth are but the counterpart of its production, and although Dr. Smith's doctrine leads to its correct examination, he did not himself develope it; which precluded him from establishing numerous important truths. Thus, by not characterizing the two different kinds of consumption, namely, unproductive and reproductive, he does not

---

* Witness *Turgot's Reflections sur la formation et la distribution des richesses*, in which he has introduced various views on both these subjects, either entirely erroneous, or very imperfect.

satisfactorily demonstrate, that the consumption of values
saved and accumulated in order to form capital, is as perfect as the consumption of values which are dissipated.
The better we become acquainted with political economy,
the more correctly shall we appreciate the importance of
the improvements this science has received from him, as
well as those he left to be accomplished.*

Such are the principal imperfections of the Inquiry into
the Nature and Causes of the Wealth of Nations, in relation to its fundamental doctrines. The plan of the work,
or, in other words, the manner in which these doctrines
are unfolded, is liable to no less weighty objections.

In many places the author is deficient in perspicuity,
and the work almost throughout is destitute of method.
To understand him thoroughly, it is necessary to accus-
tom one's self to collect and digest his views; a labour,
at least in respect to some passages, he has placed beyond
the reach of most readers; indeed, so much so, that persons otherwise enlightened, professing both to comprehend
and admire his doctrines, have written on subjects he has
discussed, namely, on taxes and bank-notes as supple-
mentary to money, without having understood any part
of his theory on these points, which, nevertheless, forms
one of the most beautiful portions of his Inquiry.

His fundamental principles, too, are not established in
the chapters assigned to their development. Many of
them will be found scattered through the two excellent
refutations of the *exclusive* or *mercantile system* and *the
system of the economists,* but in no other part of the work.
The principles relating to the real and nominal prices of
things, are introduced into a dissertation on the value of
the precious metals during the course of the last four centuries; and the author's opinions on the subject of money
are contained in the chapter on commercial treaties.

Dr. Smith's long digressions, have, moreover, with great
propriety, been much censured. An historical account
of a particular law or institution as a collection of facts,
is in itself, doubtless, highly interesting; but in a work
devoted to the support and illustration of general princi-

---

* Many other points of doctrine, besides those here noticed, have been either overlooked, or but imperfectly analyzed by Dr. Smith.

ples, particular facts not exclusively applicable to these ends, can only unnecessarily overload the attention. His sketch of the progress of opulence in the different nations of Europe after the fall of the Roman empire, is but a magnificent digression. The same remark is applicable to the highly ingenious disquisition on public education, replete as it is with erudition and the soundest philosophy, at the same time that it abounds with valuable instruction.

Sometimes these dissertations have but a very remote connexion with his subject. In treating of public expenditures, he has gone into a very curious history of the various modes in which war was carried on by different nations at different epochs; in this manner accounting for military successes which have had so decided an influence on the civilization of many parts of the earth. These long digressions at times, also, are devoid of interest to every other people but the English. Of this description is the long statement of the advantages Great Britain would derive from the admission of all of her colonies into the right of representation in parliament.

The excellence of a literary composition as much depends upon what it does not, as upon what it does contain. So many details, although in themselves useful, unnecessarily encumber a work designed to unfold the principles of political economy. Bacon made us sensible of the emptiness of the Aristotelian philosophy; Smith, in like manner, caused us to perceive the fallaciousness of all the previous systems of political economy; but the latter no more raised the superstructure of this science, than the former created logic. To both, however, our obligations are sufficiently great, for having deprived their successors of the deplorable possibility of proceeding, for any length of time, with success on an improper route.*

---

* Since the time of Dr. Smith, both in England and France, a variety of publications on political economy have made their appearance; some of considerable length, but seldom containing anything worthy of preservation. The greater part of them are of a controversial character, in which the principles of the science are merely laid down for the purpose of maintaining a favourite hypothesis; but from which, nevertheless, many important facts, and even sound principles, when they coincide with the views of their authors, may be collected. The "*Essai sur les finances de la Grand-Bretagne,*" by *Gentz,* and apology for Mr. Pitt's system of finance, is of this description; so also is *Thornton's Inquiry into the nature and effects of paper credit,* written with a view to justify the suspension of cash payments by the bank of England; as well as a great number of other works on the same subject, and in relation to the corn laws.

We are, however, not yet in possession of an establish-ed text-book on the science of political economy, in which the fruits of an enlarged and accurate observation are re-ferred to general principles, that can be admitted by every reflecting mind; a work in which these results are so complete and well arranged as to afford to each other mutual support, and that may everywhere, and at all times, be studied with advantage. To prepare myself for attempting so useful a task, I have thought it necessary attentively to peruse what had been previously written on the same subject, and afterwards to forget it; to study these authors, that I might profit by the experience of so many competent inquirers who have preceded me; to endeavour to obliterate their impressions, not to be mis-led by any system; and at all times be enabled freely to consult the nature and course of things, as actually exist-ing in society. Having no particular hypothesis to sup-port, I have been simply desirous of unfolding the manner in which wealth is produced, distributed, and consumed. A knowledge of these facts could only be acquired by observing them. It is the result of these observations, within the reach of every inquirer, that are here given. The correctness of the general conclusions I have deduced from them, every one can judge of.

It was but reasonable to expect from the lights of the age, and from that method of philosophizing which has so powerfully contributed to the advancement of other sci-ences, that I might at all times be able to ascend to the nature of things, and never lay down an abstract princi-ple that was not immediately applicable in practice; so that, always compared with well established facts, any one could easily find its confirmation by at the same time discovering its utility.

Nor is this all. Solid general principles, previously laid down, must be noticed, and briefly but clearly proved; those which had not been laid down must be established, and the whole so combined, as to satisfy every one that no material omission has taken place, nor any fundamental point been overlooked. The science must be stript of many false opinions; but this labour must be confined to such errors as are generally received, and to authors of acknowledged reputation. For what injury can an obscure writer or a discredited dogma effect? The utmost precision must be given to the phraseology we employ, so as to prevent the same word from ever being understood in two different senses; and all problems be reduced to their simplest elements, in order to facilitate the detection of any errors, and above all, of our own. In fine, the doctrines of the science must be conveyed in such a popular* form, that every man of sound understanding may be enabled to comprehend them in their whole scope of consequences, and apply their principles to all the various circumstances of life.

The position maintained in this work, that the value of things is the measure of wealth, has been especially objected to. This, perhaps, has been my fault; I should have taken care not to be misunderstood. The only satisfactory reply I can make to the objection, is to endeavour to give more perspicuity to this doctrine. I must, therefore, apologize to the owners of the former editions, for the numerous corrections I have made in the present. It became my duty in treating of a subject of such essential importance to the general welfare, to give it all the perfection within my reach.

Since the publications of the former editions of this work, various authors, some of whom enjoy a well merited celebrity,† have given to the world new treatises on political economy. It is not my province, either to pronounce upon the general character of these productions, or to decide whether they do, or do not, contain a full, clear, and well digested exposition of the fundamental principles of this science. This much I can with sincerity say, that many of these works contain truths and illustrations well calculated greatly to advance the science, and from the

---

* By a *popular treatise*, I do not mean a treatise for the use of persons who neither know how to read, nor to make any use of it. By this expression, I mean a treatise not exclusively addressed to professional or scientific cultivators of this particular branch of knowledge, but one calculated to be read by every intelligent and useful member of society.

† *Ricardo, Sismondi*, and others. The fair sex begin also to perceive that they had done themselves injustice, in supposing that they were unequal to a branch of study destined to exercise so benign an influence over domestic happiness. In England, a lady (Mrs. *Marcet*) has published a work, *Conversations on Political Economy*," since translated into French, in which the soundest principles are explained in a familiar and pleasing style.

perusal of which I have derived important benefit. But, in common with every other inquirer, I am entitled to remark how far some of their principles, which at first sight appear to be plausible, are contradicted by a more cautious and rigid induction of facts.

It is, perhaps, a well founded objection to Mr. Ricardo, that he sometimes reasons upon abstract principles to which he gives too great a generalization. When once fixed in an hypothesis which cannot be assailed, from its being founded upon observations not called in question, he pushes his reasonings to their remotest consequences, without comparing their results with those of actual experience. In this respect resembling a philosophical mechanician, who, from undoubted proofs drawn from the nature of the lever, would demonstrate the impossibility of the vaults daily executed by dancers on the stage. And how does this happen? The reasoning proceeds in a straight line; but a vital force, often unperceived, and always inappreciable, makes the facts differ very far from our calculation. From that instant nothing in the author's work is represented as it really occurs in nature. It is not sufficient to set out from facts; they must be brought together, steadily pursued, and the consequences drawn from them constantly compared with the effects observed. The science of political economy, to be of practical utility, should not teach, what *must necessarily* take place, if even deduced by legitimate reasoning, and from undoubted premises; it must show, in what manner that which in reality does take place, is the consequence of other facts equally certain. It must discover the chain which binds them together, and always, from observation, establish the existence of the two links at their point of connexion.

With respect to the wild or antiquated theories, so often produced, or reproduced by authors who possess neither sufficiently extensive nor well digested information to entitle them to form a sound judgment, the most effectual method of refuting them is to display the true doctrines of the science with still greater clearness, and to leave to time the care of disseminating them. We, otherwise, should be involved in interminable controversies, affording no instruction to the enlightened part of society, and inducing the uninformed to believe that nothing is susceptible of proof, inasmuch as everything is made the subject of argument and disputation.

Disputants, infected with every kind of prejudice, have, with a sort of doctorial confidence, remarked, that both nations and individuals sufficiently well understand how to improve their fortunes without any knowledge of the nature of wealth, and that this knowledge is in itself a purely speculative and useless inquiry. This is but saying that we know perfectly well how to live and breathe, without any knowledge of anatomy and physiology, and that these sciences are, therefore, superfluous. Such a proposition would not be tenable ; but what should we say if it were maintained, and by a class of doctors, too, who, whilst decrying the science of medicine, should themselves subject you to a treatment founded upon antiquated empiricism and the most absurd prejudices ; who, rejecting all regular and systematic instruction, in spite of your remonstrances, should perform upon your own body the most bloody experiments ; and whose orders should be enforced with the weight and solemnity of laws, and, finally, carried into execution by a host of clerks and soldiers ?

In support of antiquated errors, it has also been said, " that there surely must be some foundations for opinions, so generally embraced by all mankind ; and that we ourselves ought rather to call in question the observations and reasonings which overturn what has been hitherto so uniformly maintained and acquiesced in by so many individuals, distinguished alike by their wisdom and benevolence." Such reasoning, it must be acknowledged, should make a profound impression on our minds, and even cast some doubts on the most incontrovertible positions, had we not alternately seen the falsest hypotheses now universally recognized as such, everywhere received and taught during a long succession of ages. It is yet but a very little time, since the rudest as well as the most refined nations, and all mankind, from the unlettered peasant to the enlightened philosopher, believed in the existence of but four material elements. No human being had even dreamt of disputing the doctrine, which is nevertheless false ; insomuch that a tyro in natural philosophy, who should at present consider earth, air, fire, and water, as distinct elements, would be disgraced.* How many other opinions, as universally prevailing and as much respected, will in like manner pass away. There is something epidemical in the opinions of mankind; they are subject to be attacked by moral maladies which infect the whole species. Periods at length arrive when, like the plague, the disease wears itself out and loses all its malignity; but it still has required time. The entrails of the victims were consulted at Rome three hundred years after Cicero had remarked, that the two augurs could no longer examine them without laughter.

The contemplation of this excessive fluctuation of opinions must not, however, inspire us with a belief that nothing is to be admitted as certain, and thus induce us to yield up to universal scepticism. Facts repeatedly observed by individuals in a situation to examine them under all their aspects, when once well established and accurately described, can no longer be considered as mere opinions, but must be received as absolute truths. When it was demonstrated that all bodies are expanded by heat, this truth could no longer be called in question. Moral and political science present truths equally indisputable, but of more difficult solution. In these sciences, every individual considers himself not only as being entitled to make discoveries, but as being also authorized to pronounce upon the discoveries of others; yet how few persons acquire competent knowledge, and views sufficiently enlarged, to become assured that the subject upon which they thus venture to pronounce judgment is thoroughly understood by them in all its bearings. In society, one is astonished to find the most abstruse questions as quickly decided as if every circumstance, which, in any way, could and ought to affect the decision, were known. What

---

* Every branch of knowledge, even the most important, is but of very recent origin. The celebrated writer on agriculture, Arthur Young, after having bestowed uncommon pains in the collection of all the observations that had been made in relation to soils, one of the most important parts of this science, and which teaches us by what succession of crops the earth may be, at all times, and with the greatest success, cultivated, remarked, that he could not find that anything had been written on this subject prior to the year 1768. Other arts, not less essential to the happiness and prosperity of society, are still also in their infancy

would be said of a party passing rapidly in front of a
large castle, that should undertake to give an account of
every thing that is going on within?

Certain individuals, whose minds have never caught a
glimpse of a more improved state of society, boldly affirm
that it could not exist; they acquiesce in established evils,
and console themselves for their existence by remarking,
that they could not possibly be otherwise; in this respect
reminding us of that emperor of Japan who thought he
would have suffocated himself with laughter, upon being
told that the Dutch had no king. The Iroquois were at a
loss to conceive how wars could be carried on with success, if prisoners were not to be burnt.

Although, to all appearance, many European nations
may be in a flourishing condition, and some of them annually expend from one to two hundred millions of dollars
solely for the support of the government, it must not
thence be inferred that their situation leaves nothing to be
desired. A rich Sybarite, residing according to his inclination, either at his castle in the country, or in his palace
in the metropolis, in both, at an enormous expense, par-
taking of every luxury that sensuality can devise, transporting himself with the utmost rapidity and comfort in
whatever direction new pleasures invite him, engrossing
the industry and talents of a multitude of retainers and
servants, and killing a dozen horses to gratify a whim,
may be of opinion that things go on sufficiently well, and
that the science of political economy is not susceptible of
any further improvement. But in countries said to be in
a flourishing condition, how many human beings can be
enumerated, in a situation to partake of such enjoyments?
One out of a hundred thousand at most; and out of a
thousand, perhaps not one who may be permitted to enjoy
what is called a comfortable independence. The haggard-
ness of poverty is everywhere seen contrasted with the
sleekness of wealth, the extorted labour of some compen-
sating for the idleness of others, wretched hovels by the
side of stately colonnades, the rags of indigence blended
with the ensigns of opulence; in a word, the most useless
profusion in the midst of the most urgent wants.

Persons, who under a vicious order of things have obtained a competent share of social enjoyments, are never in want of arguments to justify to the eye of reason such a state of society; for what may not admit of apology when exhibited in but one point of view? If the same individuals were to-morrow required to cast anew the lots assigning them a place in society, they would find many things to object to.

Accordingly, opinions in political economy are not only maintained by vanity, the most universal of human infirmities, but by self-interest, unquestionably not less so; and which, without our knowledge, and in spite of ourselves, exercises a powerful influence over our mode of thinking. Hence the sharp and sour intolerance by which truth has been so often alarmed and obliged to retire; or which, when she is armed with courage, encompasses her with disgrace, and sometimes with persecution. Knowledge is at present so very generally diffused, that a philosopher may assert, without the risk of contradiction, that the laws of nature are the same in a world and in an atom; but a statesman who should venture to affirm, that there is a perfect analogy between the finances of a nation and those of an individual, and that the same principles of economy should regulate the management of the affairs of both, would have to encounter the clamours of various classes of society, and to refute ten or a dozen different systems.

Nor is this all. Writers are found who possess the lamentable facility of composing articles for journals, pamphlets, and even whole volumes, upon subjects, which, according to their own confession, they do not understand. And what is the consequence? The science is involved in the clouds of their own minds, and that is rendered obscure which was becoming clear. Such is the indifference of the public, that they rather prefer trusting to assertions than be at the trouble of investigating them. Sometimes, moreover, a display of figures and calculations imposes upon them; as if numerical calculations alone could prove any thing, and as if any rule could be laid down, from which an inference could be drawn without the aid of sound reasoning.

These are among the causes which have retarded the progress of political economy.

Everything, however, announces that this beautiful, and above all, useful science, is spreading itself with increasing rapidity. Since it has been perceived that it does not rest upon hypothesis, but is founded upon observation and experience, its importance has been felt. It is now taught wherever knowledge is cherished. In the universities of Germany, of Scotland, of Spain, of Italy, and of the north of Europe, professorships of political economy are already established. Hereafter this science will be taught in them, with all the advantages of a regular and systematic study. Whilst the university of Oxford proceeds in her old and beaten track,* within a few years that of Cambridge has established a chair for the purpose of imparting instruction in this new science. Courses of lectures are delivered in Geneva and various other places; and the merchants of Barcelona have, at their own expense, founded a professorship on political economy. It is now considered as forming an essential part of the education of princes; and those who are called to that high distinction ought to blush at being ignorant of its principles. The emperor of Russia has desired his brothers, the grand dukes Nicholas† and Michael, to pursue a course of study on this subject under the direction of M. Storch. Finally, the government of France has done itself lasting honour by establishing in this kingdom, under the sanction of public authority, the first professorship of political economy.

When the youths who are now students shall be scattered through all the various classes of society, and elevated to the principal posts under government, public affairs will be conducted in a much better manner than they hitherto have been. Princes as well as people, becoming more enlightened as to their true interests, will perceive that these interests are not at variance with each

---

* In the year 1826, a professorship of political economy was founded at the university of Oxford, and a highly able and instructive course of lectures has since been delivered before that university, by Nassau William Senior, A. M., the first professor of political economy. We have rarely read a more masterly and entertaining performance than the professor's discussion of the mercantile theory of wealth, which occupies three of his lectures.   AMERICAN EDITOR.

† The present Emperor Nicholas.

other; which on the one side will naturally induce less oppression, and on the other beget more confidence.

At present, authors who venture to write upon politics, history, and *à fortiori* upon finance, commerce, and the arts, without any previous knowledge of the principles of political economy, only produce works of temporary success, that do not succeed in fixing public attention.

But what has chiefly contributed to the advancement of political economy, is the grave posture of affairs in the civilized world during the last thirty years. The expenses of governments have risen to a scandalous height; the appeals which they have been obliged to make to their subjects, in order to relieve their exigencies, have disclosed to them their own importance. A concurrence of public sentiment, or at least the semblance of it, has been almost everywhere called for, if not brought about. The enormous contributions drawn from the people, under pretexts more or less specious, not even having been found sufficient, recourse has been had to loans; and to obtain credit, it became necessary for governments to disclose their wants as well as their resources. Accordingly, the publicity of the national accounts, and the necessity of vindicating to the world the acts of the administration, have in the science of politics produced a moral revolution, whose course can no longer be impeded.

The disorders and calamities incident to the same period, have also produced some important experiments. The abuse of paper money, commercial and other restrictions, have made us feel the ultimate effects of almost all excesses. And the sudden overthrow of the most imposing bulwarks of society, the gigantic invasions, the destruction of old governments and the creation of new, the formation of rising empires in another hemisphere, the colonies that have become independent, the general impulse given to the human mind, so favourable to the development of all its faculties, and the great expectations and the great mistakes, have all undoubtedly very much enlarged our views; at first operating upon men of calm observation and reflection, and subsequently upon all mankind.

It is to the facility of tracing the links in the chain of causes and effects that we must ascribe the great improvement in the kindred branches of moral and political science; and hence it is, when once the manner in which political and economical facts bear upon each other is well understood, that we are enabled to decide what course of conduct will be most advantageous in any given situation. Thus, for example, to get rid of mendicity, that will not be done which only tends to multiply paupers; and, in order to procure abundance, the only measures calculated to prevent it will not be adopted. The certain road to national prosperity and happiness being known, it can and will be chosen.

For a long time it was thought that the science of political economy could only possibly be useful to the very limited number of persons engaged in the administration of public affairs. It is undoubtedly of importance that men in public life should be more enlightened than others; in private life, the mistakes of individuals can never ruin but a small number of families, whilst those of princes and ministers spread desolation over a whole country. But, is it possible for princes and ministers to be enlightened, when private individuals are not so? This is a question that merits consideration. It is in the middling classes of society, equally secure from the intoxication of power, and the compulsory labour of indigence, in which are found moderate fortunes, leisure united with habits of industry, the free intercourse of friendship, a taste for literature, and the ability to travel, that knowledge originates, and is disseminated amongst the highest and lowest orders of the people. For these latter classes, not having the leisure necessary for meditation, only adopt truths when presented to them in the form of axioms, requiring no further demonstration.

And although a monarch and his principal ministers should be well acquainted with the principles upon which national prosperity is founded, of what advantage would this knowledge be to them, if throughout all the different departments of administration, their measures were not supported by men capable of comprehending and enforcing them? The prosperity of a city or province is sometimes dependent upon the official acts of a single individual; and the head of a subordinate department of government, by provoking an important decision, often exercises an influence even superior to that of the legislator himself. In countries blessed with a representative form of government, each citizen is under a much greater obligation to make himself acquainted with the principles of political economy; for there every man is called upon to deliberate upon public affairs.

Finally, in supposing that every person in any way connected with government, from the highest to the lowest, could be well acquainted with these principles, without the nation at large being so, which is wholly improbable, what resistance would not the execution of their wisest plans experience? What obstacles would they not encounter in the prejudices of those even who should most favour their measures?

A nation, in order to enjoy the advantages of a good system of political economy, must not only possess statesmen capable of adopting the best plans, but the population must be in a situation to admit of their application.*

It is also the way of avoiding doubts and perpetual changes of principles, which prevent our profiting even from whatever may be good in a bad system. A steady and consistent policy is an essential element of national prosperity; thus England has become more opulent and powerful than would seem to comport with her territorial extent, by an uniform and steadfast adherence to a system, even in many respects objectionable to her, of monopolizing the maritime commerce of other nations. But to follow for any length of time the same route, it is necessary to be able to choose one not altogether bad; unforeseen and insurmountable difficulties would otherwise have

---

* I here suppose the higher orders of society to be actuated by a sincere desire to promote the public good. When this feeling, however, does not exist, when the government is faithless and corrupt, it is of still greater importance that the people should become acquainted with the real state of things, and comprehend their true interests. Otherwise, they suffer without knowing to what causes their distresses ought to be attributed; or indeed, by attributing them to erroneous causes, the views of the public are distracted, their efforts disunited, and individuals, thus deprived of general support, fail in resolution, and despotism is strengthened; or what is still worse, where the people are so badly governed as to become desperate, they listen to pernicious counsels, and exchange a vicious order of things for one still worse.

to be encountered, which would oblige us to change our course, without even the reproach of versatility.

It is, perhaps, to this cause we must attribute the evils which, for two centuries, have tormented France; a period during which she was within reach of that state of high prosperity she was invited to by the fertility of her soil, her geographical position, and the genius of her inhabitants. With no fixed opinions in relation to the causes of public prosperity, the nation, like a ship without chart or compass, was driven about by the caprice of the winds and the folly of the pilot, alike ignorant of the place of her departure or destination.* A consistent policy in France would have extended its influence over many successive administrations; and the vessel of the state would at least not have been in danger of being wrecked, or exposed to the awkward manœuvres by which she has so much suffered.

Versatility is attended with such ruinous consequences, that it is impossible to pass even from a bad to a good system without serious inconvenience. The exclusive and restrictive system is without doubt vastly injurious to the development of industry, and to the progress of national wealth; nevertheless, the establishments which this policy has created could not be suddenly suppressed, without causing great distress.† A more favourable state of things can only be brought about, without any inconvenience, by the gradual adoption of measures introduced with infinite skill and care. A traveller whose limbs have been frozen in traversing the Arctic regions, can only be preserved from the dangers of a too sudden cure, and restored to entire health, by the most cautious and imperceptible remedies.

The soundest principles are not at all times applicable. The essential object is to know them, and then such as are applicable or desirable can be adopted. There can

---

* In how many instances have not great pains been taken, and considerable capital expended, to increase the evils mankind have been desirous of shunning! How many regulations are just so far carried into execution as to produce all the injury restrictions possibly can effect, and, at the same time, just as far violated as to retain all the inconveniences arising from their infringement!

† This arises from our not being able, without serious losses, to displace the capital and talents, which, owing to an erroneous system, have received a faulty direction.

be no doubt that a new community, which in every instance should consult them, would rapidly reach the highest pitch of opulence; but every nation may, nevertheless, in many respects violate them, and yet attain a satisfactory state of prosperity. The powerful action of the vital principle causes the human body to grow and thrive in spite of the accidents and excesses of youth, or of the wounds which have been inflicted on it. Absolute perfection, beyond which all is evil, and produces only evil, is nowhere found; evil is everywhere mixed with good. When the former preponderates, society declines; when the latter, it advances with more or less rapidity in the road of prosperity. Nothing, therefore, ought to discourage our efforts towards the acquisition and dissemination of sound principles. The least step taken towards the attainment of this knowledge is immediately productive of some good, and ultimately will yield the happiest fruits.

If, for the interest of the state, it is important that individuals should know what are the true principles of political economy, who will venture to maintain that the same knowledge will be useless to them in the management of their own private concerns? That money is readily earned without any knowledge of the nature or origin of wealth, I admit. For that purpose, a very simple calculation, within the reach of the rudest peasant, is all that is necessary: *such an article will, including every expense, cost me so much; I shall sell it for so much, and, therefore, shall gain so much.* Nevertheless, accurate ideas respecting the nature and growth of wealth, unquestionably afford us many advantages in forming a sound judgment of enterprises in which we are interested, either as principals or as parties. They enable us to foresee what these enterprises will require, and what will be their results; to devise the means of their success, and to establish our exclusive claims to them; to select the most secure investments, from anticipating the effects of loans and other public measures; to cultivate the earth to advantage, from accurately adjusting actual advances with probable returns; to become acquainted with the general wants of society, and thus be enabled to make choice of a profession; and to discern the symptoms of national prosperity or decline.

The opinion that the study of the science of political economy is calculated to be useful to statesmen only, fallacious as it is, has been attended with other disadvantages. Almost all the authors on this subject, until the time of Dr. Adam Smith, had imagined that their principal object was to enlighten the public authorities; and as they were far from agreeing among themselves, inasmuch as the facts, and their connexion and consequences, were but imperfectly known to them, and entirely overlooked by the multitude, it is by no means surprising that they should have been regarded as visionary dreamers in relation to the public good. Hence the contempt which men in power always affect towards everything like first principles.

But since the rigorous method of philosophizing, which in every other branch of knowledge leads to truth, has been applied to the investigation of facts, and to the reasonings founded on them, and the science of political economy has been thus confined to a simple exposition of whatever takes place in relation to wealth, it no longer attempts to offer counsel to public authorities. Should they, however, be desirous of ascertaining the good or evil consequences likely to result from any favourite project, they may consult this science, exactly as they would consult hydraulics upon the construction of a pump or sluice. All that can be required from political economy is to furnish governments with a correct representation of the nature of things, and the general laws necessarily resulting from it. Perhaps, until such views be more generally diffused, it may also be required, to point out to them some of the applications of its principles. Should these be despised or neglected, the governments themselves, as well as the people, will be the sufferers. The husbandman who sows tares can never expect to reap wheat.

Certainly, if political economy discloses the sources of wealth, points out the means of rendering it more abundant, and teaches the art of daily obtaining a still greater amount without ever exhausting it; if it demonstrates, that the population of a country may, at the same time, be more numerous and better supplied with the necessaries of life ; if it satisfactorily proves that the interest of the rich and poor, and of different nations, are not opposed to each other, and that all rivalships are mere folly ; and if from all these demonstrations it necessarily results, that a multitude of evils supposed to be without remedy, may not only be reckoned curable, but even easy to cure, and that we need not suffer from them any longer than we are willing so to do ; it must be acknowledged that there are few studies of greater importance, or more deserving the attention of an elevated and benevolent mind.

Time is the great teacher, and nothing can supply its operation. It alone can fully demonstrate the advantages to be derived from a knowledge of political economy in the general principles of legislation and government. On the one hand, the custom which condemns so many men of sense, at the same time that they admit the principles of this science, to speak and act as if they were wholly ignorant of them,* and on the other, the resistance, which individual as well as general interests, imperfectly understood, oppose to many of these principles, exhibit nothing that ought either to surprise or alarm individuals animated with a desire of promoting the general welfare. The philosophy of Newton, which, during a period of fifty years was unanimously rejected in France, is now taught in all its schools. Ultimately it will be perceived, that there are studies of still greater importance than this, if estimated by their influence on the happiness and prosperity of mankind.

Still how unenlightened and ignorant are the very na-

---

* "They would wish, so to express myself, that I might be able to demonstrate that my proofs are conclusive, and that they are not wrong in submitting to them. The soundness of my reasoning has produced a momentary conviction ; but they afterwards feel the habitual influence of their former opinions return with undiminished authority, although without any adequate cause, as in the case of the apparent increase in the diameter of the moon at the horizon. They would wish to be freed by me from these troublesome relapses, of whose delusiveness they are sensible, but which nevertheless importune them. In a word, they are desirous that I should be enabled to effect by reason what time alone can accomplish ; which is impossible. Every cause has an effect peculiar to itself. Reason may convince, opinions carry us along, and illusions perplex us ; but time alone, and the frequent repetition of the same acts, can produce that state of calmness and ease which we call habit. Hence it is, that all new opinions are such a length of time in spreading themselves. If an innovator has ever had immediate success, it is only from having discovered and promulgated opinions already floating in every mind." DESTUTT-TRACY, *Logique*, chap. 8.

tions we term civilized! Survey entire provinces of proud Europe; interrogate a hundred, a thousand, or even ten thousand individuals, and of this whole number, you will hardly, perhaps, find two embued with the slightest tincture of the improved science of which the present age so much boasts. This general ignorance of recondite truths is by no means so remarkable as an utter unacquaintance with the simplest rudiments of knowledge applicable to the situation and circumstances of every one. How rare, also, are the qualifications necessary for one's own instruction, and how few persons are solely capable of observing what daily happens, and of questioning whatever they do not understand!

The highest branches of knowledge are then very far from having yielded to society all the advantages to be expected from them, and without which they would be mere curious speculations. Perhaps their perfect application is reserved for the nineteenth century. In moral as well as in physical science, inquirers of superior minds will appear, who, after having extended their theoretical views, will disclose methods of placing important truths within the reach of the humblest capacities. In the ordinary occurrences of life, instead of then being guided by the false lights of a transcendental philosophy, mankind will be governed by the maxims of common sense. Opinions will not rest on gratuitous assumptions, but be the result of an accurate observation of the nature of things. Thus, habitually and naturally ascending to the source of all truth, we shall not suffer ourselves to be imposed upon by empty sounds, or submit to the guidance of erroneous impressions. Corruption, deprived of the weapons of empiricism, will lose her principal strength, and no longer be able to obtain triumphs, calamitous to honest men, and disastrous to nations.

BOOK I.

OF THE PRODUCTION OF WEALTH.

CHAPTER I.

OF WHAT IS TO BE UNDERSTOOD BY THE TERM, PRODUCTION.

IF we take the pains to inquire what that is, which mankind in a social state of existence denominate wealth, we shall find the term employed to designate an indefinite quantity of objects bearing inherent value, as of land, of metal, of coin, of grain, of stuffs, of commodities of every description. When they further extend its signification to landed securities, bills, notes of hand, and the like, it is evidently because they contain obligations to deliver things possessed of inherent value. In point of fact, wealth can only exist where there are things possessed of real and intrinsic value.

Wealth is proportionate to the quantum of that value; great, when the aggregate of component value is great; small, when that aggregate is small.

The value of a specific article is always vague and arbitrary, so long as it remains unacknowledged. Its owner is not a jot the richer, by setting a higher ratio upon it in his own estimation. But the moment that other persons are willing, for the purpose of obtaining it, to give in exchange a certain quantity of other articles, likewise bearing value, the one may then be said to be worth, or to be of equal value with, the other.

The quantity of money, which is readily parted with to obtain a thing, is called its *price*. *Current price*, at a given time and place, is that price which the owner is sure of obtaining for a thing, if he is inclined to part with it.*

The knowledge of the real nature of wealth, thus defined, of the difficulties that must be surmounted in its attainment, of the course and order of its distribution amongst the members of society, of the

---

* The numerous and difficult points arising out of the confusion of *positive* and *relative* value are discussed in different parts of this work; particularly in the leading chapters of Book II. Not to perplex the attention of the reader, I confine myself here to so much as is absolutely necessary to comprehend the phenomenon of the production of wealth.

uses to which it may be applied, and, further, of the consequences resulting respectively from these several circumstances, constitutes that branch of science now entitled Political Economy.

The value that mankind attach to objects originates in the use it can make of them. Some afford sustenance; others serve for clothing; some defend them from the inclemencies of the season, as houses; others gratify their taste, or, at all events, their vanity, both of which are species of wants: of this class are all mere ornaments and decorations. It is universally true, that, when men attribute value to any thing, it is in consideration of its useful properties; what is good for nothing they set no price upon.* To this inherent fitness or capability of certain things to satisfy the various wants of mankind, I shall take leave to affix the name of utility. And I will go on to say, that, to create objects which have any kind of utility, is to create wealth; for the utility of things is the ground-work of their value, and their value constitutes wealth.

Objects, however, cannot be created by human means; nor is the mass of matter, of which this globe consists, capable of increase or diminution. All that man can do is, to re-produce existing materials under another form, which may give them an utility they did not before possess, or merely enlarge one they may have before presented. So that, in fact, there is a creation, not of matter, but of utility; and this I call *production of wealth*.

In this sense, then, the word production must be understood in political economy, and throughout the whole course of the present work. Production is the creation, not of matter, but of utility. It is not to be estimated by the length, the bulk, or the weight of the product, but by the utility it presents.

Although price is the measure of the value of things, and their value the measure of their utility, it would be absurd to draw the inference, that, by forcibly raising their price, their utility can be augmented. Exchangeable value, or price, is an index of the recognised utility of a thing, so long only as human dealings are exempt from every influence but that of the identical utility: in like manner as a barometer denotes the weight of the atmosphere, only while the mercury is submitted to the exclusive action of atmospheric gravity.

In fact, when one man sells any product to another, he sells him the utility vested in that product; the buyer buys it only for the sake of its utility, of the use he can make of it. If, by any cause whatever, the buyer is obliged to pay more than the value to himself of

---

* It would be out of place here to examine, whether or no the value mankind attach to a thing be always proportionate to its actual utility. The accuracy of the estimate must depend upon the comparative judgment, intelligence, habits, and prejudices of those who make it. True morality, and the clear perception of their real interests, lead mankind to the just appreciation of benefits. Political economy takes this appreciation as it finds it—as one of the *data* of its reasonings; leaving to the moralist and the practical man, the several duties of enlightening and of guiding their fellow-creatures, as well in this, as in other particulars of human conduct.

that utility, he pays for value that has no existence, and consequently which he does not receive.*

This is precisely the case, when authority grants to a particular class of merchants the exclusive privilege of carrying on a certain branch of trade, the India trade for instance; the price of Indian imports is thereby raised, without any accession to their utility or intrinsic value. This excess of price is nothing more or less than so much money transferred from the pockets of the consumers into those of the privileged traders, whereby the latter are enriched exactly as much as the former are unnecessarily impoverished. In like manner, when a government imposes on wine a tax, which raises to 15 cents the bottle what would otherwise be sold for 10 cents, what does it else, but transfer 5 cents per bottle from the hands of the producers or the consumers of wine to those of the tax-gatherer?† The particular commodity is here only the means resorted to for getting at the tax-payer with more or less convenience; and its current value is composed of two ingredients, viz. 1. Its real value originating in its utility: 2. The value of the tax that the government thinks fit to exact, for permitting its manufacture, transport, or consumption.

Wherefore, there is no actual production of wealth, without a creation or augmentation of utility. Let us see in what manner this utility is to be produced.

CHAPTER II.

OF THE DIFFERENT KINDS OF INDUSTRY, AND THE MODE IN WHICH THEY CONCUR IN PRODUCTION.

Some items of human consumption are the spontaneous gifts of nature, and require no exertion of man for their production; as air, water, and light, under certain circumstances. These are destitute of exchangeable value; because the want of them is never felt, others being equally provided with them as ourselves. Being neither procurable by production, nor destructible by consumption, they come not within the province of political economy.

But there are abundance of others equally indispensable to our existence and to our happiness, which man would never enjoy at all, did not his industry awaken, assist, or complete the operations of

---

* This position will hereafter be further illustrated. For the present it is enough to know, that, whatever be the state of society, current prices approximate to the real value of things, in proportion to the liberty of production and mutual dealing.

† It will be shown in Book III. of this work, what proportion of the tax is paid by the producer, and what by the consumer.

nature. Such are most of the articles which serve for his food, raiment and lodging.

When that industry is limited to the bare collection of natural products, it is called *agricultural industry*, or simply *agriculture*.

When it is employed in severing, compounding, or fashioning the products of nature, so as to fit them to the satisfaction of our various wants, it is called *manufacturing industry*.*

When it is employed in placing within our reach objects of want which would otherwise be beyond reach, it is called *commercial industry*, or simply *commerce*.

It is solely by means of industry that mankind can be furnished, in any degree of abundance, with actual necessaries, and with that variety of other objects, the use of which, though not altogether indispensable, yet marks the distinction between a civilized community and a tribe of savages. Nature, left entirely to itself, would provide a very scanty subsistence to a small number of human beings. Fertile but desert tracts have been found inadequate to the bare nourishment of a few wretches, cast upon them by the chances of shipwreck: while the presence of industry often exhibits the spectacle of a dense population plentifully supplied upon the most ungrateful soil.

The term *products* is applied to things that industry furnishes to mankind.

A particular product is rarely the fruit of one branch of industry exclusively. A table is a joint product of agricultural industry, which has felled the tree whereof it is made, and of manufacturing industry, which has given it form. Europe is indebted for its coffee to the agricultural industry, which has planted and cultivated the bean in Arabia or elsewhere, and to the commercial industry, which hands it over to the consumer.

These three branches of industry, which may at pleasure be again infinitely subdivided, are uniform in their mode of contributing to the act of production. They all either confer an utility on a substance that possessed none before, or increase one which it already possessed. The husbandman who sows a grain of wheat that yields twenty-fold, does not gain this product from nothing: he avails himself of a powerful agent; that is to say, of Nature, and merely directs an operation, whereby different substances previously scattered throughout the elements of earth, air, and water, are converted into the form of grains of wheat.

Gall-nuts, sulphate of iron, and gum-arabic, are substances existing separately in nature. The joint industry of the merchant and manufacturer brings them together, and from their compound derives the black liquid, applied to the transmission of useful science. This joint operation of the merchant and manufacturer is analogous to that

---

* Since matter can only be modified, compounded, or separated, by means either mechanical or chemical, all branches of manufacturing industry may be subdivided into the mechanical and the chemical arts, according to the predominance of the one or the other in their several processes.

of the husbandman, who chooses his object and effects its attainment by precisely the same kind of means as the other two.

No human being has the faculty of originally creating matter, which is more than nature itself can do. But any one may avail himself of the agents offered him by nature, to invest matter with utility. In fact, industry is nothing more or less than the human employment of natural agents; the most perfect product of labour, the one that derives nearly its whole value from its workmanship, is probably the result of the action of steel, a natural product upon some substance or other, likewise a natural product.*

Through ignorance of this principle, the economists of the 18th century, though many enlightened writers were to be reckoned amongst them, were betrayed into the most serious errors. They allowed no industry to be productive, but that which procured the raw materials; as the industry of the husbandman, the fisherman and the miner; not adverting to the distinction, that wealth consists, not in matter, but in the value of matter; because matter without value is no item of wealth; otherwise water, flint-stones, and dust of the roads, would be wealth. Wherefore, if the value of matter constitutes wealth, wealth is to be created by the annexation of value. Practically, the man who has in his warehouse a quintal of wool worked up into fine cloths, is richer than one who has the same quantity of wool in packs.

To this position the economists replied, that the additional value communicated to a product by manufacture, was no more than equivalent to the value consumed by the manufacturer during the process; for, said they, the competition of manufactures prevents their ever raising the price beyond the bare amount of their own expenditure and consumption; wherefore their labour adds nothing to the total wealth of the community, because their wants on the one side destroy as much as their industry produces on the other.†

---

* *Alagrotti* in his *Opuscula*, by way of exemplifying the prodigious addition of the value given to an object by industry, adduces the spiral springs that check the balance-wheels of watches. A pound weight of pig-iron costs the operative manufacturer about five cents. This is worked up into steel, of which is made the little spring that moves the balance-wheel of a watch. Each of these springs weighs but the tenth part of a grain; and when completed, may be sold as high as three dollars, so that out of a pound of iron, allowing something for the loss of metal, 80,000 of these springs may be made, and a substance of five cents value be wrought into a value of 240,000 dollars.

† *Mercier de la Riviere*, in his work entitled "*Ordre Naturel des Sociétés Politiques*," tom. ii. p. 255, while labouring to prove, that manufacturing labour is barren and unproductive, makes use of an argument, which I think it may be of some service to refute, because it has been often repeated in different shapes, and some of them specious enough. He says, "that if the unreal products of industry are considered as realities, it is a necessary inference, that an useless multiplication of workmanship is a multiplication of wealth." But because human labour is productive of value, when it has an useful result, it by no means follows, that it is productive of value, when its result is either useless or injurious. All labour is not productive; but such only as adds a real value to any substance or thing. And the futility of this argument of the economists is put

But it should have been previously demonstrated by those who made use of this argument, that the value, consumed by mechanics and artizans, must of necessity barely equal the value produced by them, which is not the fact; for it is unquestionable, that more savings are made, and more capital accumulated from the profits of trade and manufacture, than from those of agriculture.(1).

Besides, even admitting that the profits of manufacturing industry are consumed in the satisfaction of the necessary wants of the manufacturers and their families, that circumstance does not prevent them being positive acquisitions of wealth. For unless they were so, they could not satisfy their wants: the profits of the land-owner and agriculturist are allowed to be items of positive wealth; yet they are equally consumed in the maintenance of those classes.

Commercial, in like manner as manufacturing industry, concurs in production, by augmenting the value of a product by its transport from one place to another. A quintal of Brazil cotton has acquired greater utility, and therefore larger value, by the time it reaches a warehouse in Europe, than it possessed in one at Pernambuco. The transport is a modification that the trader gives to the commodity, whereby he adapts to our use what was not before available; which modification is equally useful, complex and uncertain in the result, as any it derives from the other two branches of industry. He avails himself of the natural properties of the timber and the metals used in the construction of his ships, of the hemp whereof his rigging is composed, of the wind that fills his sails, of all the natural agents brought to concur in his purpose, with precisely the same view and the same result, and in the same manner too, as the agriculturist avails himself of the earth, the rain, and the atmosphere.*

---

beyond all question by the circumstance, that it may be equally employed against their own system and that of their opponents. They may be told, "You admit the industry of the cultivator to be productive; therefore he has only to plough and sow his fields ten times a year to increase his productiveness tenfold," which is absurd.

* *Genovesi*, who lectured on political economy at Naples, defines commerce to be "the exchange of superfluities for necessaries." He gives as his reason, that in every transaction of exchange, the article received appears to each of the contracting parties more necessary than that given. This is a far-fetched notion, which I think myself called on to notice, because it has obtained considerable currency. It would be difficult to prove, that a poor labourer, who goes to the

---

(1) [Our author, in here asserting, "that more savings are made, and more capital accumulated from the profits of trade and manufacture, than from those of agriculture," has fallen into an error, which it is proper to notice. In the absence of prohibitions and restraints, the profits of agriculture, manufactures and commerce, will all be on an equality, or always nearly approaching towards it; for any material difference will cause a diversion of capital and industry to the more productive channel, and by that means restore the equilibrium. In overthrowing the hypothesis of the economists, the author has inadvertently, for a moment, lost sight of his own general principles, which so clearly establish the equality of profits in all the different branches of industry.]

AMERICAN EDITOR.

Thus, when Raynal says of commerce, as contrasted with agriculture and the arts, that "it produces nothing of itself," he shows himself to have had no just conception of the phenomenon of production. In this instance Raynal has fallen into the same error with regard to commerce, as the economists made respecting both commerce and manufacture. They pronounced agriculture to be the sole channel of production; Raynal refers production to the two channels of agriculture and manufacture: his position is nearer the truth than the other, but still is erroneous.

Condillac also is confused in his endeavour to explain the mode in which commerce produces. He pretends that, because all commodities cost to the seller less than the buyer, they derive an increase of value from the mere act of transfer from one hand to another. But this is not so; for, since a sale is nothing else but an act of barter, in which one kind of goods, silver for example, is received in lieu of another kind of goods, the loss which either of the parties dealing should sustain on one article would be equivalent to the profit he would make on the other, and there would be to the community no production of value whatsoever.* When Spanish wine is bought at Paris, equal value is really given for equal value: the silver paid, and the wine received, are worth one the other; but the wine had not the same value before its export from Alicant: its value has really increased in the hands of the trader, by the circumstance of transport, and not by the circumstance, or at the moment, of exchange.

---

alehouse on a Sunday, exchanges there his superfluity for a necessary. In all fair traffic, there occurs a mutual exchange of two things, which are worth one the other, at the time and place of exchange. Commercial production, that is to say, the value added by commerce to the things exchanged, is not operated by the act of exchange, but by the commercial operations that precede it.

The Count *de Verri* is the only writer within my knowledge, who has explained the true principle and ground-work of commerce. In the year 1771, he thus expresses himself: "Commerce is in fact nothing more than the transport of goods from one place to another." (*Meditazioni sulla economia politica,* § 4.) The celebrated Adam Smith himself appears to have had no very clear idea of commercial production. He merely discards the opinion, that there is any production of value in the act of exchange.

* This circumstance has escaped the attention of Sismondi, or he would not have said, "The trader places himself between the producer and the consumer, to benefit them both at once, making his charge for that benefit upon both." (*Nouveaux Principes d'Economie Pol.* Liv. ii. ch. 8). He would make it appear as if the trader subsisted wholly upon the value produced by the agriculturist and the manufacturer; whereas he is maintained by the real value he himself communicates to commodities by giving them an additional modification, an useful property. It is this very notion that stirs up the popular indignation against the dealers in grain.

L. Say, of Nantes, has fallen into the same mistake (*Principales Causes de la Richesse,* &c. p. 110). By way of demonstrating the value conferred by commerce to be unreal, he alleges it to be absorbed by the charges of transport. By this incidental process of reasoning, the economist concluded manufacture to be unproductive; not perceiving, that in these very charges consists the revenue of the commercial and manufacturing producers; and that it is in this way that the values raised by production at large are distributed amongst the several producers.

The seller does not play the rogue, nor the buyer the fool; and Condillac has no grounds for his position, that "if men always exchanged equal value for equal value, there would be no profit to be made by the traders."*

In some particular cases the two other branches of industry produce in a manner analogous to commerce, *viz.* by giving a value to things to which they actually communicate no new quality, but that of approximation to the consumer. Of this description is the industry of miners. The coal or metal may exist in the earth, in a perfect state, but unpossessed of value. The miner extracts them thence, and this operation gives them a value, by fitting them for the use of mankind. So also of the herring fishery. Whether in or out of the sea, the fish is the same; but under the latter circumstances, it has acquired an utility, a value, it did not before possess.†

Examples might be infinitely multiplied, and would all bear as close an affinity, as those natural objects, which the naturalist classifies only to facilitate their description.

This fundamental error of the economists, in which I have shown that their adversaries in some measure participated, led them to the strangest conclusions. According to their theory, the traders and manufacturers, being unable to add an iota to the general stock of wealth, live entirely at the expense of the sole producers, that is to say, the proprietors and cultivators of the land. Whatever new value they may communicate to things, they at the same time consume an equivalent product, furnished by the real producers: manufacturing and commercial nations, therefore, subsist wholly upon the wages they receive from their agricultural customers; in proof of which position, they alleged that Colbert ruined France by his protection of manufactures, &c.‡

The truth is, that, in whatever class of industry a person is engaged, he subsists upon the profit he derives from the additional

---

* See his work entitled, "*Le Commerce et le Gouvernment considérés relativement l'un a l'autre.*" 1re. *partie, ch.* 6.

† We may consider as agents of the same class of industry, the cultivator of the land, the breeder of cattle, the woodcutter, the fisherman that takes fish he has been at no pains in breeding, and the miner who, from the bowels of the earth, extracts metal, stone, or combustibles, that nature has placed there in a perfect state; and, to avoid multiplicity of denominations, the whole of these occupations may be called by the name of agricultural industry, because the superficial cultivation of the earth, is the chief and most important of all. Terms are of little consequence, when the ideas are clear and definite. The wine-grower, who himself expresses the juice of his grapes, performs a mechanical operation, that partakes more of manufacture than agriculture. But it matters little whether he be classed as a manufacturer or agriculturist; provided that it be clearly comprehended in what manner his industry adds to the value of the product. If we wish to give separate consideration to every possible manner of giving value to things, industry may be infinitely subdivided. If it be the object to generalize to the utmost, it may be treated as one and the same; for every branch of it will resolve itself into this: the employment of natural substances

value, or portion of value, no matter in what ratio, which his agency attaches to the product he is at work upon. The total value of products serves in this way to pay the profits of those occupied in production. The wants of mankind are supplied and satisfied out of the *gross* values produced and created, and not out of the *net* values only.

A nation, or a class of a nation, engaged in manufacturing or commercial industry, is not a whit more or less in the pay of another, than one employed in agriculture. The value created by one branch is of the same nature as that created by others. Two equal values are worth one the other, although perhaps the fruit of different branches of industry: and when Poland barters its staple product, wheat, for the staple commodity of Holland, East and West India produce, Holland is no more in the pay or service of Poland, than Poland is of Holland.

Nay, Poland herself, which exports at the rate of ten millions of wheat annually, and therefore, according to the economists, takes the sure road to national wealth, is, notwithstanding, poor and depopulated: and why?—Because she confines her industry to agriculture, though she might be at the same time a commercial and manufacturing state. Instead of keeping Holland in her pay, she may with more propriety be said to receive wages from the latter, for the raising of ten millions of wheat, per annum. Nor is she a jot less dependent than the nations that buy wheat of her: for she has just as much desire to sell to them, as they have to buy of her.*

Moreover, it is not true that Colbert ruined France. On the contrary, the fact is that France, under Colbert's administration, emerged from the distress that two regencies and a weak reign had involved her in. She was, indeed, afterwards ruined again; but for this second calamity, she may thank the pageantry and the wars of Louis XIV. Nay, the very prodigality of that prince is an undeniable evidence of the vast resources that Colbert had placed at his disposal. It must, however, be admitted that those resources would have been still more ample, if he had but given the same protection to agriculture, as to the other branches of industry.

Thus it is evident, that the means of enlarging and multiplying wealth within the reach of every community are much less confined than the economists imagined. A nation, by their account, was unable to produce annually any values beyond the net annual produce of its lands; to which fund alone recourse could be had for the support not only of the proprietary and the idler, but likewise of the merchant, the manufacturer, and the mechanic, as well as for the total consumption of the government. Whereas we have just seen that the annual produce of a nation is composed, not of the mere net pro-

---

* We shall find in the sequel, that, if any one nation can be said to be in the service of another, it is that which is the most dependent; and that the most dependent nations are, not those which have a scarcity of land, but those which have a scarcity of capital.

duce of its agriculture, but of the gross produce of its agriculture, commerce, and manufacture united. For, in fact, is not the sum total, that is to say, the aggregate of the gross product raised by the nation, disposable for its consumption? Is value produced less an item of wealth, because it must needs be consumed? And does not value itself originate in this very applicability to consumption.

The English writer, Stewart, who may be looked upon as the leading advocate of the exclusive system, the system founded on the maxim, that the wealth of one set of men is derived from the impoverishment of another, is himself no less mistaken in asserting, that, "when once a stop is put to external commerce, the stock of internal wealth cannot be augmented."* Wealth, it seems, can come only from abroad; but abroad, where does it come from? from abroad also. So that in tracing it from abroad to abroad, we must necessarily, in the end, exhaust every source, till at last we are compelled to look for it beyond the limits of our own planet, which is absurd.

Forbonnais,† too, builds his prohibitory system on this glaring fallacy; and to speak freely, on this fallacy are founded the exclusive systems of all the short-sighted merchants, and all the governments of Europe and of the world. They all take it for granted, that what one individual gains must needs be lost to another; that what is gained by one country is inevitably lost to another: as if the possessions of abundance of individuals and of communities could not be multiplied, without the robbery of somebody or other. If one man or set of men, could only be enriched at others' expense, how could the whole number of individuals, of whom a state is composed, be richer at one period than at another, as they now confessedly are in France, England, Holland, and Germany, compared with what they were formerly? How is it, that nations are in our days more opulent, and their wants better supplied in every respect, than they were in the seventeenth century? Whence can they have derived that portion of their present wealth, which then had no existence? Is it from the mines of the new continent? They had already advanced in wealth before the discovery of America. Besides, what is that which these mines have furnished? Metallic wealth or value. But all the other values which those nations now possess, beyond what they did in the middle ages, whence are they derived? Is it not clear, that these can be no other than created values?

We must conclude, then, that wealth, which consists in the value that human industry, in aid and furtherance of natural agents, communicates to things, is susceptible of creation and destruction, of increase and diminution, within the limits of each nation and independently of external agency, according to the method it adopts to bring about those effects. An important truth, which ought to teach

---

* Essay on Political Economy, b. ii. c. 26.
† *Elemens de Commerce.*

mankind, that the objects of rational desire are within their reach, provided they have the will and intelligence to employ the true means of obtaining them. Those means it is the purpose of this work to investigate and unfold.

CHAPTER III.

OF THE NATURE OF CAPITAL, AND THE MODE IN WHICH IT CONCURS IN THE BUSINESS OF PRODUCTION.

As we advance in the investigation of the processes of industry. we cannot fail to perceive, that mere unassisted industry is insufficient to invest things with value. The human agent of industry must, besides, be provided with pre-existing products; without which his agency, however skilful and intelligent, would never be put in motion. These pre-existing requisites are,

1. The tools and implements of the several arts. The husbandman could do nothing without his spade and mattock, the weaver without his loom, or the mariner without his ship.

2. The products necessary for the subsistence of the industrious agent, as long as he is occupied in completing his share of the work or production. This outlay of his subsistence is, indeed, in the long run, replaced by the product he is occupied upon, or the price he will receive for it; but he is obliged continually to make the advance.

3. The raw materials, which are to be converted into finished products by the means of his industry. These materials, it is true, are often the gratuitous offerings of nature, but they are much more generally the products of antecedent industry, as in the case of seed-corn supplied by agriculture, metals, the fruit of the labour of the miner and smelter, drugs brought by the merchant perhaps from the extremities of the globe. The value of all these must be found in advance by the industrious agent that works them up.

The value of all these items constitutes what is denominated productive capital.

Under this head of productive capital must likewise be classed the value of all erections and improvements upon real or landed property, which increase its annual produce, as well as that of the farming live and dead stock, that operates as machinery in aid of human industry.

Another item of productive capital, is money, whenever it is employed to facilitate the interchange of products, without which production could never make any progress. Money distributed through the whole mechanism of human industry, like the oil that greases the wheels of complex machinery, gives the requisite ease and facility to its movements. But gold and silver are not productive unless employed by industry: they are like the oil in a machine remaining in a state of inaction. And so also of all other tools and implements of human industry.

It would evidently be a great mistake to suppose that the capital of a community consists solely of its money. The merchant, the manufacturer, the cultivator, commonly have the least considerable portion of the value composing their capital invested in the form of money; nay, the more active their concern is, the smaller is their relative proportion of their capital so vested to the residue. The funds of the merchant are placed out in goods on their transit by land or water, or warehoused in different directions: the capital of the manufacturer chiefly consists of the raw material in different stages of progress, of tools, implements, and necessaries for his workmen: while that of the cultivator is vested in farming buildings, live stock, fences and enclosures. They all studiously avoid burthening themselves with more money than is sufficient for current use.

What is true of one, two, three, or four individuals, is true of society in the aggregate. The capital of a nation is made up of the sum total of private capitals; and, in proportion as a nation is prosperous and industrious, in the same proportion is that part of its capital, vested in the shape of money, trifling compared to the amount of the gross national capital. Neckar estimates the circulating medium in France, in the year 1784, at about 440 millions of dollars, and there are reasons for believing his estimate exaggerated; but this is not the time to state them. However, if account be taken of all the works, enclosures, live stock, utensils, machines, ships, commodities, and provisions of all sorts belonging to the French people or their government in any part of the world; and, if to these be added the furniture, decorations, jewellery, plate, and other items of luxury or convenience, whereof they were possessed, at the same period, it will be found that 440 millions of circulating medium was a mere trifle compared to the aggregate of these united values.*

Beeke estimates the total capital of Great Britain at 2300 millions sterling,† (equal to more than 11,000 millions of dollars.) The total amount of her circulating specie, before the establishment of her present paper money, was never reckoned by the highest estimates at more than 47 millions sterling;‡ that is to say, about 1-50th of her capital. Smith reckoned it at no more than 18 millions, which could not be the 1-127th part. (1).

---

* Arthur Young, in his "*Journey in France*," in spite of the unfavourable view he gives of French Agriculture, estimates the total capital employed in that kingdom, in that branch of industry alone, at more than 2200 millions of dollars; and states his belief, that the capital of Great Britain, similarly employed, is in the proportion of two to one.

† *Observations on the produce of the income-tax.*

‡ Pitt, who is supposed to have overrated the quantity of specie, states the gold at forty-four-millions; and Price estimates the silver at three millions, making a total of forty-seven millions.

(1) [The following summary recapitulation of the value of property in Great Britain and Ireland, in the year 1833, is extracted from "Table XVI. GENERAL

Capital in the hands of a national government forms a part of the gross national capital.

We shall see, by-and-by, how capital, which is subject to a continual wear and consumption in the process of production, is continually replaced by the very operation of production; or rather, how its value, when destroyed under one form, re-appears under another. At present it is enough to have a distinct conception, that, without it, industry could produce nothing. Capital must work, as it were, in concert with industry; and this concurrence is what I call *the productive agency of capital*.

ESTIMATE of the PUBLIC and PRIVATE Property of ENGLAND and WALES, SCOTLAND and IRELAND, (1833)," from "PEBRER on the TAXATION, DEBT, CAPITAL, RESOURCES, &c. of the whole BRITISH EMPIRE," a work of the highest authority, published in London, April, 1833.

SUMMARY RECAPITULATION.

AGGREGATE VALUE OF PROPERTY IN GREAT BRITAIN AND IRELAND.

Productive Private Property,		£2,995,000,000
Unproductive do.		580,700,000
		3,575,700,000
Public Property,		103,800,000
	Total,	£3,679,500,000
Equal to dollars,		17,661,600,000

ENGLAND AND WALES:

Productive Private Property,	£2,054,600,000	
Unproductive do.	374,300,000	
		2,428,900,000

SCOTLAND:

Productive Private Property,	318,300,000	
Unproductive do.	51,100,000	
		369,400,000

IRELAND:

Productive Private Property,	622,100,000	
Unproductive do.	116,400,000	
		738,500,000
Do. do. in Great Britain and Ireland,		38,900,000

Public Property in England and Wales,	42,000,000	
Do. in Scotland,	3,900,000	
Do. in Ireland,	11,900,000	
Do. in common to Great Britain and Ireland, as the Navy, Military, and Ordnance Stores, &c.	46,000,000	
		103,800,000
	Grand Total,	£3,679,500,000
Equal to dollars,		17,661,600,000

AMERICAN EDITOR.

CHAPTER IV.

ON NATURAL AGENTS THAT ASSIST IN THE PRODUCTION OF WEALTH, AND
SPECIALLY OF LAND.

INDEPENDENTLY of the aid that industry receives from capital,
that is to say, from products of her own previous creation, towards
the creation of still further products, she avails herself of the agency
and powers of a variety of agents not of her own creation, but offered
spontaneously by nature: and from the co-operation of these natural
agents derives a portion of the utility she communicates to things.

Thus, when a field is ploughed and sown, besides the science and
the labour employed in this operation, besides the pre-created values
brought into use, the values, for instance, of the plough, the harrow,
the seed-corn, the food and clothing consumed by labourers during
the process of production, there is a process performed by the soil,
the air, the rain, and the sun, wherein mankind bears no part, but
which nevertheless concurs in the creation of the new product that
will be acquired at the season of harvest. This process I call the
productive agency of natural agents.

The term *natural agents* is here employed in a very extensive
sense; comprising not merely inanimate bodies, whose agency operates to the creation of value, but likewise the laws of the physical
world, as gravitation, which makes the weight of a clock descend;
magnetism, which points the needle of the compass: the elasticity of
steel; the gravity of the atmosphere; the property of heat to discharge itself by ignition, &c. &c.

The productive faculty of capital is often so interwoven with that
of natural agents, that it is difficult, or perhaps impossible, to assign,
with accuracy, their respective shares in the business of production.
A hot-house for the raising of exotic plants, a meadow fertilized by
judicious irrigation, owe the greater part of their productive powers
to works and erections, the effect of antecedent production, which
form a part of the capital devoted to the furtherance of actual and
present production. The same may be said of land newly cleared
and brought into cultivation; of farm-buildings; of enclosures; and
of all other permanent ameliorations of a landed estate. These
values are items of capital, though it be no longer possible to sever
them from the soil they are attached to.*

In the employment of machinery, which wonderfully augments
the productive power of man, the product obtained is due partly to
the value of the capital vested in the machine, and partly to the

---

* It is for the proprietor of the land and of the capital respectively, when the
ownership is in different persons, to settle between them the respective value
and efficacy of the agency of these two productive agents. The world at large
may be content to comprehend, without taking the trouble of measuring, their
respective shares in the production of wealth.

agency of natural powers. Suppose a tread-mill,* worked by ten men, to be used in place of a wind-mill, the product of the mill might be considered as the fruit of the productive agency of a capital consisting of the value of the machine, and of the labour of ten men employed in turning the wheel. If the tread-mill be supplanted by sails, it is evident that the wind, a natural agent, does the work of ten human beings.

In this instance, the absence of the natural agent might be remedied, by the employment of another power; but there are many cases, in which the agency of nature could not possibly be dispensed with, and is yet equally positive and real; for example, the vegetative power of the soil, the vital principle which concurs in the production of the animals domesticated to our use. A flock of sheep is the joint result of the owner's and shepherd's care, and the capital advanced in fodder, shelter, and shearing, and of the action of the organs and viscera with which nature has furnished these animals.

Thus nature is commonly the fellow-labourer of man and his instruments; a fellowship advantageous to him in proportion as he succeeds in dispensing with his own personal agency, and that of his capital, and in throwing upon nature a larger part of the burthen of production.

Smith has taken infinite pains to explain, how it happens that civilized communities enjoy so great an abundance of products, in comparison with nations less polished, and in spite of the swarm of idlers and unproductive labourers that is to be met with in society. He has traced the source of that abundance to the division of labour;† and it cannot be doubted, that the productive power of industry is wonderfully enhanced by that division, as we shall hereafter see by following his steps; but this circumstance alone is not sufficient to explain a phenomenon, that will no longer surprise, if we consider the power of the natural agents that industry and civilization set at work for our advantage.

Smith admits that human intelligence, and the knowledge of the laws of nature, enable mankind to turn the resources she offers to better account: but he goes on to attribute to the division of labour this very degree of intelligence and knowledge: and he is right to a certain degree; for a man, by the exclusive pursuit of a single art or science, has ampler means of accelerating its progress towards perfection. But, when once the system of nature is discovered, the production resulting from the discovery, is no longer the product of the inventor's industry. The man who first discovered the property of fire to soften metals, was not the actual creator of the utility this process adds to smelted ore. That utility results from the physical

---

* A wheel in the form of a drum, turned by men walking inside, (roue a marchre.)

† Take his own words: "It is the great multiplication of the productions of all the different arts, in consequence of the division of labour, which occasions, in a well-governed society, that universal opulence, which extends itself to the lowest ranks of the people." Wealth of Nations, b. i. c. 1.

action of fire, in concurrence, it is true, with the labour and capital of those who employ the process. But are there no processes that mankind owes the knowledge of to pure accident? or that are so self-evident, as to have required no skill to discover? When a tree, a natural product, is felled, is society put into possession of no greater produce than that of the mere labour of the woodman?

From this error Smith has drawn the false conclusion, that all values produced represent pre-exerted human labour or industry, either recent or remote; or, in other words, that wealth is nothing more than labour accumulated; from which position he infers a second consequence equally erroneous, *viz.* that labour is the sole measure of wealth, or of value produced.

This system is obviously in direct opposition to that of the economists of the eighteenth century, who, on the contrary, maintained that labour produces no value without consuming an equivalent; that, consequently, it leaves no surplus, no net produce; and that nothing but the earth produces gratuitous value,—therefore nothing else can yield net produce. Each of these positions has been reduced to system; I only cite them to warn the student of the dangerous consequences of an error in the outset,* and to bring the science back to the simple observation of facts. Now facts demonstrate, that values produced are referable to the agency and concurrence of industry, of capital,† and of natural agents, whereof the chief, though by no means the only one, is land capable of cultivation; and that no other but these three sources can produce value, or add to human wealth.

---

* Amongst other dangerous consequences of the system of the economists, is the notable one of substituting a land-tax in lieu of all other taxation; in the certainty, that this tax would affect all produced value whatever. Upon a contrary principle, and in pursuance of the maxims laid down by Smith, the net produce of land and of capital ought to be exempted from taxation altogether, if with him we take for granted, that they produce nothing spontaneously; but this would be as unjust on the opposite side.

† Although Smith has admitted the productive power of land, he has disregarded the completely analogous power of capital. A machine, an oil-mill for example, which employs a capital of 4000 dollars, and gives an annual net return of 200 dollars, after paying all expenses, gives a product quite as substantial as that of a real estate, that cost 4000 dollars, and brings an annual rent or net produce of 200 dollars, all charges deducted. Smith maintains, that a mill which has cost 4000 dollars, represents labour to that amount, bestowed at sundry times upon the different parts of its fabric; therefore, that the net produce of the mill is the net produce of that precedent labour. But he is mistaken: granting for argument sake, the value of the mill itself to be the value of this previous labour; yet the value daily produced by the mill is a new value altogether; just the same as the rent of a landed estate is a totally different value from the value of the estate itself, and may be consumed, without at all affecting the value of the estate. If capital contained in itself no productive faculty, independent of that of the labour which created it, how is it possible, that capital could furnish a revenue in perpetuity, independent of the profit of the industry that employed it? The labour that created the capital would receive wages after it ceased to operate—would have interminable value; which is absurd. It will be seen by-and-by, that these notions have not been mere matter of speculation.

Of natural agents, some are susceptible of appropriation, that is to say of becoming the property of an occupant, as a field, a current of water; others can not be appropriated, but remain liable to public use, as the wind, the sea, free navigable streams, the physical or chemical action of bodies one upon another, &c. &c.

We shall by-and-by have an opportunity of convincing ourselves, that this alternative, of productive agents being or not being susceptible of appropriation, is highly favourable to the progress of wealth. Natural agents, like land, which are susceptible of appropriation, would not produce nearly so much, were not the proprietors certain of exclusively gathering their produce, and able to vest in them, with full confidence, the capital which so much enlarges their productiveness. On the other hand, the indefinite latitude allowed to industry to occupy at will the unappropriated natural agents, opens a boundless prospect to the extension of her agency and production. It is not nature, but ignorance and bad government, that limit the productive powers of industry.

Such of the natural agents as are susceptible of appropriation, form an item of productive means; for they do not yield their concurrence without equivalent; which equivalent, as we shall see in the proper place, forms an item of the revenues of the appropriators. At present we must be content to investigate the productive operation of natural agents of every description, whether already known, or hereafter to be discovered.

CHAPTER V.

ON THE MODE IN WHICH INDUSTRY, CAPITAL, AND NATURAL AGENTS
UNITE IN PRODUCTION.

We have seen how industry, capital, and natural agents concur in production, each in its respective department; and we have likewise seen that these three sources are indispensable to the creation of products. It is not, however, absolutely necessary that they should all belong to the same individual.

An industrious person may lend his industry to another possessed of capital and land only.

The landholder may lend his estate to a person possessing capital and industry only.

Whether the thing lent be industry, capital, or land, inasmuch as all three concur in the creation of value, their use also bears value, and is commonly paid for.

The price paid for the loan of industry is called *wages*.
The price paid for the loan of capital is called *interest*.
And that paid for the loan of land is called *rent*.

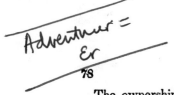

The ownership of land, capital, and industry is sometimes united in the same hands. A man who cultivates his own garden at his own expense, is at once the possessor of land, capital, and industry, and exclusively enjoys the profits of proprietor, capitalist, and labourer.

The knife-grinder's craft requires no occupancy of land; he carries his stock in trade upon his shoulders, and his skill and industry at his fingers' ends; being at the same time adventurer, (*a*) capitalist, and labourer.

It is seldom that we meet with adventurers in industry so poor, as not to own at least a share of the capital embarked in their concern. Even the common labourer generally advances some portion; the bricklayer comes with his trowel in his hand; the journeyman tailor is provided with his thimble and needles; all are clothed better or worse; and though it be true, that their clothing must be found out of their wages, still they find it themselves in advance.

Where the land is not exclusive property, as is the case with some stone-quarries, with public rivers and seas to which industry resorts for fish, pearls, coral, &c., products may be obtained by industry and capital only.

Industry and capital are likewise competent to produce by themselves, when that industry is employed upon products of foreign growth, procurable by capital only; as in the European manufacture of cotton and many other articles. So that every class of manufacture is competent to raise products, provided there be industry and capital exerted. The presence of land is not absolutely necessary, unless perhaps the area whereon the work is done, and which is commonly rented, may be thought to come under this description, as in extreme strictness it certainly must. However, if the ground where the business of industry is carried on, be reckoned as land used, it must at least be admitted, that, with aid of a large capital, an immense manufacturing concern may be conducted upon a very trifling spot of ground. Whence this conclusion may be drawn, that national industry is limited, not by territorial extent, but by extent of capital.

A stocking manufacturer with a capital say of 4000 dollars, may keep in constant work ten stocking frames. If he manages to double his capital he can employ twenty; that is to say, he may buy ten more frames, pay double ground-rent, purchase double the quantity of silk or cotton to be wrought into stockings, and make the requisite advances to double the number of workmen, &c. &c.

But that portion of agricultural industry, devoted to the tillage of

---

(*a*) The term *entrepreneur* is difficult to render in English; the corresponding word, *undertaker*, being already appropriated to a limited sense. It signifies the master-manufacturer in manufacture, the farmer in agriculture, and the merchant in commerce; and generally in all three branches, the person who takes upon himself the immediate responsibility, risk, and conduct of a concern of industry, whether upon his own or a borrowed capital. For want of a better word, it will be rendered into English by the term *adventurer*.   T.

land, is, in the course of nature, limited by extent of surface. Neither individuals nor communities can extend or fertilize their territory, beyond what the nature of things permits; but they have unlimited power of enlarging their capital, and consequently, of setting at work a larger body of industry, and thus of multiplying their products; in other words, their wealth.

There have been instances of people, like the Genevese, who with a territory that has not produced the twentieth part of the necessaries of life, have yet contrived to live in affluence. The natives of the barren glens of Jura are in easy circumstances because many mechanical arts are there practised. In the 13th century, the world beheld the republic of Venice, ere it held a foot of land in Italy, derive wealth enough from its commerce to possess itself of Dalmatia, together with most of the Greek isles, and even the capital of the Greek empire. The extent and fertility of a nation's territory depend a good deal upon its fortunate position. Whereas the power of its industry and capital depends upon its own good management; for it is always competent to improve the one and augment the other.

Nations deficient in capital, labour under great disadvantage in the sale of their produce; being unable to sell at long credit, or to grant time or accommodation to their home or foreign customers. If the deficiency be very great indeed, they may be unable even to make the advance of the raw material and their own industry. This accounts for the necessity, in the Indian and Russian trade, of remitting the purchase-money six months or sometimes a year in advance, before the time when an order for goods can be executed. These nations must be highly favoured in other respects, or they never could make considerable sales in the face of such a disadvantage.

Having informed ourselves of the method in which the three great agents of production, industry, capital and natural agents, concur in the creation of products, that is to say, of things applicable to the uses of mankind, let us proceed to analyze more minutely the particular operation of each. The inquiry is important, inasmuch as it leads imperceptibly to the knowledge of what is more and what is less favourable to production, the true source of individual affluence, as well as national power.

CHAPTER VI.

OF OPERATIONS ALIKE COMMON TO ALL BRANCHES OF INDUSTRY.

IF we examine closely the workings of human industry, it will be found, that, to whatever object it be applied, it consists of three distinct operations.

The first step towards the attainment of any specific product, is the study of the laws and course of nature regarding that product. A lock could never have been constructed without a previous knowledge of the properties of iron, the method of extracting from the mine and refining the ore, as well as of mollifying and fashioning the metal.

The next step is the application of this knowledge to an useful purpose: for instance, the conclusion, or conviction, that a particular form, communicated to the metal, will furnish the means of closing a door to all the wards, except to the possessor of the key.

The last step is the execution of the manual labour, suggested and pointed out by the two former operations; as, for instance, the forging, filing, and putting together of the different component parts of the lock.

These three operations are seldom performed by one and the same person. It commonly happens, that one man studies the laws and conduct of nature; that is to say, the philosopher, or man of science, of whose knowledge another avails himself to create useful products, being either agriculturist, manufacturer, or trader; while the third supplies the executive exertion, under the direction of the former two; which third person is the operative workman or labourer.

All products whatever will be found, on analysis, to derive existence from these three operations.

Take the example of a sack of wheat, or a pipe of wine. The first stage towards the attainment of either of these products was, the discovery by the natural philosopher or geologist, (a) of the conduct and course of nature in the production of the grain or the grape; the proper season and soil for sowing or planting; and the care requisite to bring the herb or plant to maturity. The tenant, if not the proprietor himself, must afterward have applied this knowledge to his own particular object, brought together the means requisite to the creation of an useful product, and removed the obstacles in the way of its creation. Finally, the labourer must have turned up the soil, sown the seed, or pruned and bound up the vine. These three distinct operations were indispensable to the complete production of the product, corn or wine.

Or take the example of a product of external commerce; such as indigo. The science of the geographer, the traveller, the astronomer, brings us acquainted with the spot where it is to be met with, and the means of crossing the seas to get at it. The merchant equips his vessels, and sends them in quest of the commodity; and the mariner and land-carrier perform the mechanical part of this production.

But, loooking at the substance, indigo, as a mere primary material of a further or secondary product, of blue cloth for instance; we all

---

(a) *Agronome:* I am not aware of any corresponding English term, denoting the student in that branch of geology conversant with the properties of the surface of the earth; in other words, the scientific agriculturist.　　　　T know that the chemist is first applied to for information, as to the nature of the substance, the method of dissolving it, and mordants requisite for fixing the colour; the means of perfecting the process of dyeing are then collected by the master manufacturer, under whose orders the labourer executes the manual part of the process.

Industry is, in all cases, divisible into theory, application, and execution. Nor can it approximate to perfection in any nation, till that nation excel in all three branches. A people, that is deficient in one or other of them cannot acquire products, which are and must be the result of all three. And thus we may learn to appreciate the vast utility of many sciences, which, at first sight, appear to be the objects of mere curiosity and speculation.*

The negroes of the coast of Africa are possessed of considerable ingenuity, and excel in all athletic exercises and handicraft occupations; but they seem greatly deficient in the two previous operations of industry. Wherefore, they are under the necessity of purchasing from Europe the stuffs, arms, and ornaments, they stand in need of. Their country yields so few products, notwithstanding its natural fertility, that the slave traders are obliged to lay in their stock of provisions beforehand, to feed the slaves during the voyage.†

In qualities favourable to industry, the moderns have greatly surpassed the ancients, and the Europeans outstrip all the other nations of the globe. The meanest inhabitant of an European town enjoys innumerable comforts unattainable to the sovereign of a savage tribe. The single article, glass, that admits light into his apartment, and, at the same time, excludes the inclemency of the weather, is the beautiful result of observation and science, accumulated and perfected during a long course of ages. To obtain this luxury, it was necessary previously to know what kind of sand was convertible into a substance possessing extension, solidity, and transparency; as well as by the compound of what ingredients, and by what degree of heat, the substance was obtainable: to ascertain, besides, the best form of furnace. The very wood-work, that supports the roof of a glass-house, requires, in its construction, the most extensive knowledge of the strength of timber, and the means of employing it to advantage.

Nor was the mere knowledge of these matters sufficient; for that knowledge might possibly have lain dormant in the memory of one or two persons, or in the pages of literature. It was further requi-

* Besides the direct impulse, given by science to progressive industry, and which indeed is indispensable to its success, it affords an indirect assistance, by the gradual removal of prejudice; and by teaching mankind to rely more upon their own exertions, than on the aid of superhuman power. Ignorance is the inseparable concomitant of practical habits, of that slavery of custom which stands in the way of all improvement; it is ignorance that imputes to a supernatural cause the ravages of an epidemical disease, which might perhaps be easily prevented or eradicated, and makes mankind recur to superstitious observances, when precaution, or the application of the remedy, is all that is wanted. Sciences, like facts, are linked together by a chain of general connexion, and yield one another mutual support and corroboration.

† See *Œuvres de Poivre*, p. 77, 78.

site, that a manufacturer should have been found, possessed of the
means of reducing the knowledge into practice; who should have
at first made himself master of all that was known of that particular branch of industry, and afterwards have accumulated, or
procured the requisite capital, collected artificers and labourers, and
assigned to each his respective occupation.

Finally, the work must have been completed by the manual skill
of the workmen employed; some in constructing the buildings and
furnaces, some in keeping up the fire, mixing up the ingredients,
blowing, cutting, rolling out, fitting and fixing the pane of glass.
The utility and beauty of the resulting product, are inconceivable to
those who have never beheld this admirable creation of human industry. By means of industry, the vilest materials have been invested with the highest degree of utility. The very rags and refuse
of wearing apparel have been transformed into the white and thin
sheets, that convey from one end of the globe to the other, the requisitions of commerce and the particulars of art; that serve as the
depositories of the conceptions of genius, and the vehicles of human
experience from one age to another; to them we look for the evidence of our properties; to them we entrust the most noble and
amiable sentiments of the heart, and by them we awaken corresponding feelings in the breasts of our fellow-creatures. The extraordinary facilities for the communication of human intelligence which
paper affords, entitles it to be considered as one of the products that
have been most efficacious in ameliorating the condition of mankind.
Fortunate, indeed, would it have been, had an engine so powerful
never have been made the vehicle of falsehood, or the instrument
of tyranny!

It is worth while to remark, that the knowledge of the man of
science, indispensable as it is to the development of industry, circulates with ease and rapidity from one nation to all the rest. And
men of science have themselves an interest in its diffusion; for upon
that diffusion they rest their hopes of fortune, and, what is more
prized by them, of reputation too. For this reason, a nation, in
which science is but little cultivated, may nevertheless carry its industry to a very great length, by taking advantage of the information
derivable from abroad. But there is no way of dispensing with the
other two operations of industry, the art of applying the knowledge
of man to the supply of his wants, and the skill of execution. These
qualities are of advantage to none but their possessors; so that a
 country well stocked with intelligent merchants, manufacturers, and
agriculturists has more powerful means of attaining prosperity, than
one devoted chiefly to the pursuit of the arts and sciences. At the
period of the revival of literature in Italy, Bologna was the seat of
science; but wealth was centred in Florence, Genoa, and Venice.

In our days, the enormous wealth of Britain is less owing to her
own advances in scientific acquirements, high as she ranks in that
department, than to the wonderful practical skill of her adventurers
in the useful application of knowledge, and the superiority of her

workmen in rapid and masterly execution. The national pride, that the English are often charged with, does not prevent their accommodating themselves with wonderful facility to the tastes of their customers and the consumers of their produce. They supply with hats both the north and the south, because they have learnt to make them light for the one market, and warm and thick for the other. Whereas the nation that makes but of one pattern, must be content with the home market only.

The English labourer seconds the master manufacturer; he is commonly patient and laborious, and does not willingly send out an article from his hands, without giving it the utmost possible precision and perfection; not that he bestows more time upon it, but that he gives it more of his care, attention and diligence, than the workmen of most other nations.

There is no people, however, that need despair of acquiring the qualities requisite to the perfection of their industry. It is but 150 years since England herself had made so little progress, that she purchased nearly all her woollens from Belgium; and it is not more than 80 years since Germany supplied with cotton goods the very nation, that now manufactures them for the whole world.*

I have said that the cultivator, the manufacturer, the trader, make it their business to turn to profit the knowledge already acquired, and apply it to the satisfaction of human wants. I ought further to add, that they have need of knowledge of another kind, which can only be gained in the practical pursuit of their respective occupations, and may be called their technical skill. The most scientific naturalist, with all his superior information, would probably succeed much worse than his tenant, in the attempt to improve his own land. A first-rate mechanist would most likely spin very indifferently without having served his apprenticeship, though admirably skilled in the construction of the cotton-machinery. In the arts there is a certain sort of perfection, that results only from repeated trials, sometimes successful and sometimes the contrary. So that science alone is not sufficient to ensure the progress, without the aid of experiment, which is always attended with more or less of risk, and does not always indemnify the adventurer, whose profit, even when successful, is moderated by competition; although society at large receives the accession of a new product, or, what amounts to the same thing, of an abatement in the price of an old one.

In agriculture, experiments usually cost the rent of the soil for a year or more, over and above the labour and the capital engaged in them.

---

*The cotton manufacture did not exist in England in the 17th century. In 1705, we see by the returns of the English customs, that the raw cotton manufactured in that country then amounted to no more than 1,170,880 pounds weight. In 1785, the quantity imported was 6,706,000 lbs.; but in 1790 it had got up to 25,941,000 lbs., and in 1817 to as much as 131,951,000 lbs., for the English market and for re-exportation. The quantity of cotton imported in 1831, into the United Kingdoms, was 288,708,453 lbs.

Experiment (Risk)

In manufacture, experiment is hazarded on safer grounds of calculation, capital engaged for a much shorter period, and if success ensue, the adventurer rewarded by a longer period of exclusive advantage, because his process is less open to observation. In some places, too, the exclusive advantage is protected by patents of invention. For all which reasons, the progress of manufacturing is generally more rapid and more diversified than that of agricultural industry.

Adventurer
↓
Tea

In commercial industry, the risk of experiment would be greater than in the other two branches, if the costs of the adventure had no auxiliary and concurrent object. But it is usually in the course of a regular trade, that a merchant hazards the introduction of a virgin commodity of foreign growth into an untried market. In this manner it was that the Dutch, about the middle of the seventeenth century, while prosecuting their commerce with China, with no very sanguine expectation, made experiment of a small assortment of dried leaves, from which the Chinese were in the habit of preparing their favourite beverage. Thus commenced the tea-trade, which now occasions the annual transport of more than 45 millions of pounds weight, that are sold in Europe for a sum of more than 80,000,000 of dollars.*

*IE

In some cases of very rare occurrence, boldness is nearly certain of success. When the Europeans had recently discovered the passage round the Cape of Good Hope and the continent of America, their world was suddenly expanded to the East and West; and such was the infinity of new objects of desire in two hemispheres, whereof one was not at all, and the other but very imperfectly known before, that an adventurer had only to make the voyage, and was sure of selling his returns to great advantage.

*Risk bearing
→ π*

In all but such extraordinary cases it is perhaps prudent to defray the charges of experiments in industry, not out of the capital engaged in the regular and approved channels of production, but out of the revenue that individuals have to dispose of at pleasure, without fear of impairing their fortune. The whims and caprices that divert to an useful end the leisure and revenue which most men devote to mere amusement, or perhaps to something worse, cannot be too highly encouraged. I can conceive no more noble employment of wealth and talent. A rich and philanthropic individual may, in this way, be the means of conferring upon the industrious classes, and upon the consumers at large, in other words, upon the mass of mankind, a benefit far beyond the mere value of what he actually disburses, perhaps beyond the whole amount of his fortune, however princely it may be. Who will attempt to calculate the value conferred on mankind by the unknown inventor of the plough?†

A government, that knows and practises its duties, and has large resources at its disposal, does not abandon to individuals the whole

---

* *Voyage Commerciel et Politique aux Indes Orientales, par M. Felix Renouard de Sainte Croix.*

† Thanks to the art of Printing, the names of the benefactors of mankind will henceforward be lastingly recorded; and if I mistake not, with more veneration

glory and merit of invention and discovery in the field of industry. The charges of experiment, when defrayed by the government, are not subtracted from the national capital, but from the national revenue; for taxation never does, or, at least, never ought to touch any thing beyond the revenue of individuals. The portion of them so spent is scarcely felt at all, because the burthen is divided among innumerable contributors; and, the advantages resulting from success being a common benefit to all, it is by no means inequitable that the sacrifices, by which they are obtained, should fall on the community at large.

CHAPTER VII.

OF THE LABOUR OF MANKIND, OF NATURE, AND OF MACHINERY RESPECTIVELY.

By the term *labour* I shall designate that continuous action, exerted to perform any one of the operations of industry, or a part only of one of those operations.

Labour, upon whichever of those operations it be bestowed, is productive, because it concurs in the creation of a product. Thus the labour of the philosopher, whether experimental or literary, is productive; the labour of the adventurer or master-manufacturer is productive, although he perform no actual manual work; the labour of every operative workman is productive, from the common day-labourer in agriculture, to the pilot that governs the motion of a ship.

Labour of an unproductive kind, that is to say, such as does not contribute to the raising of the products of some branch of industry or other, is seldom undertaken voluntarily; for labour, under the definition above given, implies trouble, and trouble so bestowed could yield no compensation or resulting benefit: wherefore, it would be mere folly or waste in the person bestowing it. When trouble is directed to the stripping another person of the goods in his possession by means of fraud or violence, what was before mere extravagance and folly, degenerates to absolute criminality; and there results no production, but only a forcible transfer of wealth from one individual to another.

Man, as we have already seen, obliges natural agents, and even

---

than those which derive lustre from the deplorable exploits of military prowess. Among these will be preserved the names of *Olivier de Serres*, the father of French agriculture; the first who established an experimental farm; of *Duhamel*, of *Malsherbes*, to whom France is indebted for many vegetables now naturalized in her soil and climate: of *Lavoisier*, whose new system of chemistry has effected a still more important revolution in the arts; and of the numerous scientific travellers of modern times; for travels, with an useful object, may be regarded as adventures in the field of industry.

the products of his own previous industry, to work in concert with him in the business of production. There will, therefore, be no difficulty in comprehending the terms *labour* or *productive service* of nature, and *labour* or *productive service* of capital.

The labour performed by natural agents, and that executed by pre-existent products, to which we have given the name of capital, are closely analogous, and are perpetually confounded one with the other: for the tools and machines which form a principal item of capital, are commonly but expedients more or less ingenious, for turning natural powers to account. The steam engine is but a complicated method of taking advantage of the alternation of the elasticity of water reduced to vapour, and of the weight of the atmosphere. So that, in point of fact, a steam engine employs more productive agency, than the agency of the capital embarked in it: for that machine is an expedient for forcing into the service of man a variety of natural agents, whose gratuitous aid may perhaps infinitely exceed in value the interest of the capital invested in the machine.

It is in this light that all machinery must be regarded, from the simplest to the most complicated instrument, from a common file to the most expensive and complex apparatus. Tools are but simple machines, and machines but complicated tools, whereby we enlarge the limited powers of our hands and fingers; and both are, in many respects, mere means of obtaining the co-operation of natural agents.* Their obvious effect is to make less labour requisite for the raising the same quantity of produce, or, what comes exactly to the same thing, to obtain a larger produce from the same quantity of human labour.—And this is the grand object and the acme of industry.

Whenever a new machine, or a new and more expeditious process is substituted in the place of human labour previously in activity, part of the industrious human agents, whose service is thus ingeniously dispensed with, must needs be thrown out of employ. Whence many objections have been raised against the use of machinery, which has been often obstructed by popular violence, and sometimes by the act of authority itself.

To give any chance of wise conduct in such cases, it is necessary beforehand to acquire a clear notion of the economical effect resulting from the introduction of machinery.

A new machine supplants a portion of human labour, but does not diminish the amount of the product; if it did, it would be absurd to adopt it. When water-carriers are relieved in the supply of a city by any kind of hydraulic engine, the inhabitants are equally well supplied with water. The revenue of the district is at least as great, but it takes a different direction. That of the water-carriers is reduced, while that of the mechanists and capitalists, who furnish

---

* Generalization may at pleasure be carried still further; a landed estate may be considered as a vast machine for the production of grain, which is refitted and kept in repair by cultivation: or a flock of sheep as a machine for the raising of mutton or wool.

the funds, is increased.   But, if the superior abundance of the product and the inferior charges of its production, lower its exchangeable value, the revenue of the consumers is benefited; for to them every saving of expenditure is so much gain.

This new direction of revenue, however advantageous to the community at large, as we shall presently see, is always attended with some painful circumstances.   For the distress of a capitalist, when his funds are unprofitably engaged or in a state of inactivity, is nothing to that of an industrious population deprived of the means of subsistence.

Inasmuch as machinery produces that evil, it is clearly objectionable.   But there are circumstances that commonly accompany its introduction, and wonderfully reduce the mischiefs, while at the same time they give full play to the benefits of the innovation. For,

1. New machines are slowly constructed, and still more slowly brought into use; so as to give time for those who are interested, to take their measures, and for the public administration to provide a remedy.*

2. Machines cannot be constructed without considerable labour, which gives occupation to the hands they throw out of employ. For instance, the supply of a city with water by conduits gives increased occupation to carpenters, masons, smiths, paviours, &c. in the construction of the works, the laying down the main and branch pipes, &c. &c.

3. The condition of consumers at large, and consequently, amongst them, of the class of labourers affected by the innovation, is improved by the reduced value of the product that class was occupied upon.

Besides, it would be vain to attempt to avoid the transient evil, consequential upon the invention of a new machine, by prohibiting its employment. If beneficial, it is or will be introduced somewhere or other; its products will be cheaper than those of labour conducted on the old principle; and sooner or later that cheapness will run away with the consumption and demand.   Had the cotton spinners on the old principle, who destroyed the spinning-jennies on their introduction into Normandy, in 1789, succeeded in their object, France must have abandoned the cotton manufacture; every body would have bought the foreign article, or used some substitute; and the spinners of Normandy, who, in the end, most of them, found employment in the new establishments, would have been yet worse off for employment.

---

* Without having recourse to local or temporary restrictions on the use of new methods or machinery, which are invasions of the property of the inventors or fabricators, a benevolent administration can make provision for the employment of supplanted or inactive labour in the construction of works of public utility at the public expense, as of canals, roads, churches, or the like; in extended colonization; in the transfer of population from one spot to another.   Employment is the more readily found for the hands thrown out of work by machinery, because they are commonly already inured to labour.

So much for the immediate effect of the introduction of machinery. The ultimate effect is wholly in its favour.

Indeed if by its means man makes a conquest of nature, and compels the powers of nature and the properties of natural agents to work for his use and advantage, the gain is too obvious to need illustration. There must always be an increase of product, or a diminution in the cost of production. If the sale-price of a product do not fall, the acquisition redounds to the profit of the producer; and that without any loss to the consumer. If it do fall, the consumer is benefited to the whole amount of the fall, without any loss to the producer.

The multiplication of a product commonly reduces its price, that reduction extends its consumption; and so its production, though become more rapid, nevertheless gives employment to more hands than before. It is beyond question, that the manufacture of cotton now occupies more hands in England, France, and Germany, than it did before the introduction of the machinery that has abridged and perfected this branch of manufacture in so remarkable a degree.

Another striking example of a similar effect is presented by the machine used to multiply with rapidity the copies of a literary performance,—I mean the printing press.

Setting aside all consideration of the prodigious impulse given by the art of printing to the progress of human knowledge and civilization, I will speak of it merely as a manufacture, and in an economical point of view. When printing was first brought into use, a multitude of copyists were of course immediately deprived of occupation; for it may be fairly reckoned, that one journeyman printer does the business of two hundred copyists. We may, therefore, conclude, that 199 out of 200 were thrown out of work. What followed? Why, in a little time, the greater facility of reading printed than written books, the low price to which books fell, the stimulus this invention gave to authorship, whether devoted to amusement or instruction, the combination, in short, of all these causes, operated so effectually as to set at work, in a very little time, more journeymen printers than there were formerly copyists. And if we could now calculate with precision, besides the number of journeymen printers, the total number of other industrious people that the press finds occupation for, whether as type-founders and moulders, paper-makers, carriers, compositors, bookbinders, booksellers, and the like, we should probably find, that the number of persons occupied in the manufacture of books is now 100 times what it was before the art of printing was invented.

It may be allowable to add, that viewing human labour and machinery in the aggregate, in the supposition of the extreme case, viz. that machinery should be brought to supersede human labour altogether, yet the numbers of mankind would not be thinned; for the sum total of products would be the same, and there would probably be less suffering to the poorer and labouring classes to be apprehended; for in that case the momentary fluctuations, that distress the different branches of industry, would principally affect machinery, which, and not human labour, would be paralyzed; and machinery cannot die of hunger; it can only cease to yield profit to its employers, who are generally farther removed from want than mere labourers.

But however great may be the advantages, which the adventurers in industry, and even the operative classes, may ultimately derive from the employment of improved machinery, the great gain accrues to the consumers, which is always the most important class, because it is the most numerous; because it comprehends every description of producers whatever; and because the welfare of this class, wherein all others are comprised, constitutes the general well-being and prosperity of a nation.* I repeat, that it is the consumers who draw the greatest benefit from machinery; for though the inventor may indeed for some years enjoy the exclusive advantage of his invention, which it is highly just and proper he should, yet there is no instance of a secret remaining long undivulged. Nothing can long escape publicity, least of all what people have a personal interest in discovering, especially if the secret be necessarily confided to the discretion of a number of persons employed in constructing or in working the machine. The product is thenceforward cheapened by competition to the full extent of the saving in the cost of production; and thenceforward begins the full advantage to the consumer.—The grinding of corn is probably not more profitable to the miller now than formerly; but it costs infinitely less to the consumer.

Nor is cheapness the sole benefit that the consumer reaps from the introduction of more expeditious processes: he generally gains in addition the greater perfection of the product. Painters could undoubtedly execute with the brush or pencil the designs that ornament our printed calicoes and furniture papers, but the copperplates and rollers employed for that purpose give a regularity of pattern, and uniformity of colour, which the most skilful artist could never equal.

The close pursuit of this inquiry through all the arts of industry would show, that the advantage of machinery is not limited to the bare substitution of it for human labour, but that, in fact, it gives a positive new product, inasmuch as it gives a degree of perfection before unknown. The flatting-mill and the die execute products, that the utmost skill and attention of the human hand could never accomplish.

In fine, machinery does still more; it multiplies products with which it has no immediate connexion. Without taking the trouble to reflect, one perhaps would scarcely imagine that the plough, the harrow, and other similar machines, whose origin is lost in the night

* Paradoxical as it may appear, it is nevertheless true, that the labouring class is of all others the most interested in promoting the economy of human labour; for that is the class which benefits the most by the general cheapness, and suffers most from the general dearness of commodities.

of ages, have powerfully contributed to procure for mankind, besides the absolute necessaries of life, a vast number of the superfluities they now enjoy, whereof they would otherwise never have had any conception. Yet, if the different dressings the soil requires could be no otherwise given, than by the spade, the hoe, and other such simple and tardy expedients, if we were unable to make available in agricultural production those domestic animals, that, in the eye of political economy, are but a kind of machines, it is most likely that the whole mass of human labour, now applicable to the arts of industry, would be occupied in raising the bare necessary subsistence of the actual population. Thus, the plough has been instrumental in releasing a number of hands for the prosecution of the arts, even of the most frivolous kind; and what is of more importance, for the cultivation of the intellectual faculties.

The ancients were unacquainted with water or wind-mills. In their time, the wheat their bread was made of, was pounded by the labour of the hand: so that perhaps no less than twenty individuals were occupied in pounding as much wheat as one mill can grind.* Now a single miller, or two at the most, is enough to feed and superintend a mill. By the aid, then, of this ingenious piece of mechanism, two persons are as productive as twenty were in the days of Cæsar. Wherefore, in every one of our mills, we make the wind, or a current of water, do the work of eighteen persons; which eighteen extra persons are just as well provided with subsistence; for the mill has in no respect diminished the general produce of the community: and whose exertions may be directed to the creation of new products, to be given by them in exchange for the produce of the mill; thereby augmenting the general wealth of the community.†

CHAPTER VIII.

OF THE ADVANTAGES AND DISADVANTAGES RESULTING FROM DIVISION OF LABOUR, AND OF THE EXTENT TO WHICH IT MAY BE CARRIED.

We have already observed that the several operations, the combination of which forms but one branch of industry, are not in general undertaken or performed by the same person; for they commonly

---

* Homer tells us, in the Odyssey, b. xx., that twelve women were daily employed in grinding corn for the family consumption of Ulysses, whose establishment is not represented as larger than that of a private gentleman of fortune of modern days.

† Since the publication of the third edition of this work, M. de Sismondi has published his *Nouveaux Principes d'Economie Politique.* This valuable writer seems to have been impressed with an exaggerated notion of the transient evils,

require different kinds of talent; and the labour requisite to each is enough to take up a man's whole time and attention. Nay, in some instances, a single one of these operations is split again into smaller subdivisions, each of them sufficient for one person's exclusive occupation.

Thus, the study of nature is shared amongst the chemist, the botanist, the astronomer, and many other classes of students in philosophy.

Thus, too, in the application of human knowledge to the satisfaction of human wants, in manufacturing industry, for instance, we find different classes of manufacturers employed exclusively in the fabric of woollens, pottery, furniture, cottons, &c. &c.

Finally, in the executive part of each of the three branches of industry, there are often as many different classes of workmen as there are different kinds of work. To make the cloth of a coat, there must have been set to work the several classes of spinners, weavers, dressers, shearers, dyers, and many other classes of labourers, each of whom is constantly and exclusively occupied upon one operation.

The celebrated Adam Smith was the first to point out the immense increase of production, and the superior perfection of products referable to this division of labour.* He has cited among other

---

and a faint one of the permanent benefits of machinery, and to be utterly unacquainted with those principles of the science, which place those benefits beyond controversy. (a)

* *Beccaria*, in a public course of lectures on political economy, delivered at Milan in the year 1769, and before the publication of Smith's work, had remarked the favourable influence of the division of labour upon the multiplication of products. These are his words: " *Ciascuno prova coll' esperienza, che, applicando la mano e l'ingegne sempre allo stesso genere di opere e di prodotti, egli piu facilli, piu abondanti e migliori ne travo i resultati, di quello, che se ciascuno isolatamente le cose tutte a se necessarie soltanto facesse: onde altri pascono le pecore, altri ne cardano le lane, altri le tessonoe : chi coltiva biade, chi ne fa il pane : chi veste, chi fabrica agli agricoltorie la voranti ; crescendo e concatenandosi le arti, e dividendosi in tal maniera, per la commune e privata utilità gli nomini in varie classi e condizioni.*" " We all know, by personal experience, that, by the continual application of the corporeal and intellectual faculties to one peculiar kind of work or product, we can obtain the product with more ease, and in greater abundance and perfection, than if each were to depend upon his own exertions for all the objects of his wants. For this reason, one man feeds sheep, a second cards the wool, and a third weaves it : one man cultivates wheat, another makes bread, another makes clothing or lodging for the cultivators and mechanics : this multiplication and concatenation of the arts, and division of mankind into a variety of classes and conditions, operating to promote both public and private welfare."

However, I have given Smith the credit of originality in his ideas of the division of labour; first, because, in all probability, he had published his opinions from his chair of professor of philosophy at Glasgow before Beccaria, as it is

---

(a) Our author, in his recent argument with Malthus, upon the subject of the excess of manufacturing power and produce, appears to me to have completely vindicated his own positions against the attacks of Sismondi and Malthus ; and to have exposed the fallacy of the appalling doctrine, that the powers of human industry can ever be too great and too productive.—*Vide Letters à M. Malthus.*

examples, the manufacture of pins. The workmen occupied in this manufacture execute each but one part of a pin. One draws the wire, another cuts it, a third sharpens the points. The head of a pin alone requires two or three distinct operations, each performed by a different individual. By means of this division, an ill-appointed establishment, with but ten labourers employed, could make 48,000 pins per day, by Smith's account. Whereas, if each person were obliged to finish off the pins one by one, going through every operation successively from first to last, each would probably make but 20 per day, and the ten workmen would produce in the whole but 200, in lieu of 48,000.

Smith attributes this prodigious difference to three causes:

1. The improved dexterity, corporeal and intellectual, acquired by frequent repetition of one simple operation. In some fabrics the rapidity with which some of the operations are performed exceeds what the human hand could, by those who had never seen them, be supposed capable of acquiring.

2. The saving of the time which is commonly lost in passing from one species of work to another, and in the change of place, position, and tools. The attention, which is always slowly transferred, has no occasion to transport itself and settle upon a new object.

3. The invention of a great number of machines, which facilitate and abridge labour in all its departments. For the division of labour naturally limits each operation to an extremely simple task, and one that is incessantly repeated; which is precisely what machinery may most easily be made to perform.

Besides, men soonest discover the methods of arriving at a particular end, when the end is approximate, and their attention exclu-

---

well known he did the principles that form the ground-work of his book; but chiefly because he has the merit of having deduced from them the most important conclusions. (1)

(1) [*All* the fundamental doctrines contained in the Inquiry into the Wealth of Nations, were comprehended in Dr. Smith's course of political lectures, delivered at Glasgow as early as the year 1752; "at a period surely," says DUGALD STEWART, "when there existed no French (and he might have added, nor Italian) performance on the subject, that could be of much use to him in guiding his researches." A short manuscript, drawn up by Dr. Smith in the year 1755, fully establishes his exclusive claim to the most important opinions detailed in his treatise on the Wealth of Nations, which did not appear until the beginning of the year 1776. "A great part of the opinions enumerated in this paper, (he observes,) is treated of at length in some lectures which I have still by me (1755,) and which were written in the hand of a clerk who left my service six years ago. They have all of them been the constant subject of my lectures, since I first taught Mr. Craigie's class, the first winter I spent in Glasgow, down to this day, without any considerable variation.—They had all of them been the subject of lectures which I read in Edinburgh the winter before I left it, and I can adduce innumerable witnesses, both from that place and from this, who will ascertain them sufficiently to be mine." Vide Mr. Stewart's Account of the Life and Writings of Adam Smith, LL. D. read before the Royal Society of Edinburgh, January 21 and March 18, 1793.]

AMERICAN EDITOR.

sively directed to it. Discoveries, even in the walk of philosophy, are for the most part referable, in their origin, to the subdivision of labour; because it is this subdivision that enables men to devote themselves to the exclusive pursuit of one branch of knowledge; which exclusive devotion has wonderfully favoured their advancement.*

Thus the knowledge or theory necessary to the advancement of commercial industry for instance, attains a far greater degree of perfection, when different persons engage in the several studies; one of geography, with the view of ascertaining the respective position and products of different countries; another of politics, with a view to inform himself of their national laws and manners, and the advantages and disadvantages of commercial intercourse with them; a third of geometry and mechanics, by way of determining the preferable form of the ships, carriages, and machinery of all kinds, that must be employed; a fourth of astronomy and natural philosophy, for the purposes of navigation, &c. &c.

Thus, too, the application of knowledge in the same department of commercial industry will obviously arrive at a higher degree of perfection, when divided amongst the several branches of internal, Mediterranean, East and West Indian, American, wholesale and retail, &c. &c.

Moreover, such a division is no obstacle to the combination of operations not altogether incompatible, more especially if they aid and assist each other. There is no occasion for two different merchants to conduct, one the trade of import for home consumption, and the other the trade of export of home products; because these operations, far from clashing, mutually facilitate and assist each other. (a)

The division of labour cheapens products, by raising a greater quantity at the same or less charge of production. Competition soon obliges the producer to lower the price to the whole amount of the saving effected; so that he derives much less benefit than the consumer; and every obstacle the latter throws in the way of that division is an injury to himself.

---

* But though many important discoveries in the arts have originated in division of labour, we must not refer to that source the actual products that have resulted, and will to eternity result, from those discoveries. The increased product must flow from the productive power of natural agents, no matter what may have been the occasion of our first becoming acquainted with the means of employing those agents. *Vide supra*, Chap. IV.

(a) The combination of operations which at first sight appears to be distinct, is far more practicable in what our author calls the branch of application, than in either the theoretical or the executive branch. A general merchant, by means of clerks and brokers, will combine a vast variety of different commercial operations, and yet prosper. Why? Because his own peculiar task is that of superintendence of commercial dealings; which superintendence may be extended over a greater surface of dealing without incongruity, being on a closer inspection, but a repetition of the same operation. 57CT.

Should a tailor try to make his own shoes as well as his coat, he would infallibly ruin himself.* We see every day people acting as their own merchants, to avoid paying a regular trader the ordinary profit of his business; to use their own expression, with the view of pocketing that profit themselves. But this is an erroneous calculation; for this division of labour enables the regular dealer to execute the business for them much cheaper than they can do it themselves. Let them reckon up the trouble it costs them, the loss of time, the money thrown away in extra charges, which is always proportionally more in small than in large operations, and see if all these together do not amount to more than the two or three per cent. that might be saved on every paltry item of consumption; even supposing them not to be deprived of what little advantage they might expect, by the avarice of the cultivator or manufacturer they would have to deal directly with, who will of course impose, if he can, upon their inexperience.

It is no advantage, even to the cultivator or manufacturer himself, except under very particular circumstances, to intrude upon the province of the merchant, and endeavonr to deal directly with the consumer without his intervention. He would only divert his attention from his ordinary occupation, and lose time that might be far better employed in his own peculiar line; besides being under the necessity of keeping up an establishment of people, horses, carriages, &c. the expenses of which would far exceed the merchant's profit, reduced as it always must be by competition.

The advantages accruing from division of labour can be enjoyed in respect of particular kinds of products only; and not in them, until their consumption has exceeded a certain point of extension. Ten workmen can make 48,000 pins in a day; but would hardly do so, unless where there was a daily consumption of pins to that amount; for, to arrive at this degree of division of labour, one workman must be wholly and exclusively occupied in sharpening the points, while the rest are severally engaged, each in a different part of the process. If there be a daily demand for no more than 24,000, he must needs lose half his day's work, or change his occupation, in which case, the division of labour will be less extensive and complete.

For this reason, divisions of labour cannot be carried to the extreme limit, except in products capable of distant transport and the consequent increase of consumption; or where manufacture is carried on amidst a dense population, offering an extensive local consumption. For the same reason, too, many kinds of work, the products of which are destined to instantaneous consumption, are executed by the same individual, in places where the population is limited. In a small town or village, the same person is often barber, surgeon, doctor,

* The low price of sugar in China is probably occasioned, in part, by the circumstance of the grower leaving to a separate class the extraction of the sugar from the cane. This operation is performed by itinerant sugar pressers, who go from house to house, offering their services, and provided with an extremely simple apparatus. *Vide* Macartney's Embassy, vol. iv. p. 198.

and apothecary; while in a populous city, and there only, these are not merely separate and distinct occupations, but some of them are again subdivided into several branches; that of the surgeon, for instance, is split into the several occupations of dentist, oculist, accoucher, &c.; each of which practitioners, by confining his practice to a single branch of this extensive art, acquires a degree of skill, which, but for this division, he could never attain.

The same circumstance applies equally to commercial industry. Take the village grocer; the consumption of his groceries is so limited, as to oblige him to be at the same time haberdasher, stationer, innkeeper, and who knows what, perhaps even news-writer and publisher; whereas in large cities, not only grocery at large, but even the sale of a single article of grocery, is a great commercial concern. At Paris, London, and Amsterdam, there are shops, where nothing else is sold but the single article tea, oil or vinegar; and it is natural to suppose that such shops have a much better assortment of the single article, than those dealing in many different commodities at once. Thus, in a rich and populous country, the carrier, the wholesale, the intermediate, and the retail dealer conduct each a separate branch of commercial industry, and conduct it with greater perfection as well as greater economy. Yet they all benefit by this economy; and that they do so, if the explanations already given are not convincing, experience bears irrefragable testimony; for consumers always buy cheapest where commercial industry is the most subdivided. *Ceteris paribus*, a commodity brought from the same distance is sold cheaper at a large town or fair, than in a village or hamlet.

The limited consumption of hamlets and villages, besides obliging dealers to combine many elsewhere distinct occupations, prevents many articles from finding a regular sale at all seasons. Some are not presented for sale at all, except on market or fair days; on such days the whole week's or perhaps year's consumption is laid in. On all other days, the dealer either travels elsewhere with his wares, or finds some other kind of occupation. In a very rich and very populous district, the consumption is so great, as to make the sale of one article only, quite as much as a trader can manage, though he devote every day in the week to the business. Fairs and markets are expedients of an early stage of national prosperity; the trade by caravans is a still earlier stage of international commerce; but even these expedients are far better than none at all.*

---

* The country markets of France not only exhibit extreme inertness in particular channels of consumption; but a very cursory observation is sufficient to show, that the sale of products in them is very limited, and the quality of what are sold very inferior. Besides the local products of the district, one sees nothing there, except a few tools, woollens, linens, and cottons of the most inferior quality. In a more advanced stage of prosperity, one would find some few objects of gratification of wants peculiar to a more refined state of existence: some articles of furniture combining convenience and elegance of form; woollens of some variety of fineness and pattern; articles of food of a more expensive kind, whe-

From the necessity of the existence of a very extended consumption, before division of labour can be carried to its extreme point, it follows, that such division can never be introduced in the manufacture of products, which, from their high price, are placed within the reach of few purchasers. In jewellery, especially of the better kinds, it is practised in a very limited degree; and such division being, as we have seen, one cause of the invention and application of ingenious processes, it is not surprising that such processes are least often met with in the preparation of products of highly finished workmanship. In visiting the workshop of a lapidary, one is often dazzled with the costliness of the materials, and the skill and patience of the workman; but it is only in the grand manufactories of articles of universal consumption, that one is astonished with the display of ingenuity employed to give additional expedition and perfection to the product. In looking at an article of jewellery, it is easy to form an idea of the tools and processes, by means of which it has been executed; whereas few people, on viewing a common stay-lace, would suppose it had been made by a horse or a current of water, which is actually the case.

Of the three branches of industry, agriculture is the one that admits division of labour in the least degree. It is impossible to collect any great number of cultivators on the same spot, to use their joint exertions in the raising of one and the same product. The soil they work upon is extended over the whole surface of the globe, and obliges them to work at considerable distance from each other. Besides, agriculture does not allow of one person being continually employed in the same operation. One man cannot be all the year ploughing or digging, any more than another can find constant occupation in gathering in the crop. Moreover, it is very rarely that the whole of one's land can be devoted to the same kind of cultivation, or that the same kind of cultivation can be continued on the same spot for many successive years. The land would be exhausted; and, supposing the cultivation of the whole property to be uniform, yet even then, the preparing and dressing of the whole ground, and the getting in of the whole of the crops, would come on at the same time, and the labourers be unoccupied at other periods of the year.*

---

ther on account of their preparation or the distance they may have been brought from; a few works of instruction or tasteful amusement; a few books besides mere almanacs and prayer-books. In a still more advanced stage, the consumption of all these things would be constant and extensive enough to support regular and well-stocked shops in all these different lines. Of this degree of wealth examples are to be found in Europe, particularly in parts of England, Holland, and Germany.

* It is not common to meet with such large concerns in agriculture, as in the branches of commerce and manufacture. A farmer or proprietor seldom undertakes more than four or five hundred acres; and his concern, in point of capital and amount of produce, does not exceed that of a middling tradesman, or manufacturer. This difference is attributable to many concurrent causes; chiefly to the extensive area this branch of industry requires; to the bulky nature of the

Moreover, the nature of his occupation and of agricultural products makes it highly convenient for the cultivator to raise his own vegetables, fruit, and cattle, and even to manufacture part of the tools and utensils employed in his house-keeping; though in the other channels of industry, these items of consumption give exclusive occupation to a number of distinct classes.

Where concerns of industry are carried on in manufactories, in which one and the same master manufacturer conducts the product through all its stages, he can never establish any great subdivision of the various operations, without great command of capital. For such division requires larger advances of wages, of raw materials, and of tools and implements. Where eighteen workmen manufacture but twenty pins each per day, that is to say, in all 360 pins, weighing scarcely an ounce of metal, the daily advance of an ounce of fresh metal is enough to keep them in regular work. But if, in consequence of division of labour, these same eighteen persons can be brought, as we know they can, to produce 86,400 pins, the daily supply of raw material requisite for their regular employ will be 240 ounces weight of metal; consequently a much more considerable advance will be called for. If we further take into calculation, that there is an interval of probably a month or more, from the purchase of the metal by the manufacturer to the period of his reimbursement by the sale of his pins, we shall find that he must necessarily have at all times on hand, in different stages of progressive manufacture, 30 times 240 ounces of metal; in other words, the portion of his capital vested in raw material alone will amount to the value of 450 lbs. of metal. In addition to which, it must be observed, that the division of labour cannot be effected without the aid of various implements and machines, that form themselves an important item of capital. Thus, in poor countries, we frequently find a product carried through all its stages, from first to last, by one and the same workman, from mere want of the capital requisite for a judicious division of the different operations.

We must not however suppose, that, to effect this division of labour, it is necessary the capital should be placed all in the hands of a single adventurer, or the business conducted all within the walls of one grand establishment. A pair of boots undergoes a variety of processes, whereof all are not executed by the bootmaker alone; the grazier, the tanner, the currier, all others, who immediately or remotely furnish any substance or tool used in the making of boots, contribute to the raising of the product; and though there is a very considerable subdivision of labour in the making of this article, the

produce, and consequently difficulty of collecting it at one point from the distant parts of the farm, or sending it to very remote markets; to the nature of the business itself, which is not susceptible of any regular and uniform system, and requires in the adventurer a succession of temporary expedients and directions, suggested by the difference of culture, of manuring and dressings, and the variety of each labourer's occupations, according to the seasons, the change of weather, &c.

greater part of the joint and concurrent producers may have very little command of capital.

Having detailed the advantages of the subdivision of the various occupations of industry, and the extent to which it may be carried, the view of the subject would be incomplete, were we to omit noticing, on the other hand, the inconveniences that inseparably attend it.

A man, whose whole life is devoted to the execution of a single operation, will most assuredly acquire the faculty of executing it better and quicker than others; but he will, at the same time, be rendered less fit for every other occupation, corporeal or intellectual; his other faculties will be gradually blunted or extinguished; and the man, as an individual, will degenerate in consequence. To have never done any thing but make the eighteenth part of a pin, is a sorry account for a human being to give of his existence. Nor is it to be imagined that this degeneracy from the dignity of human nature is confined to the labourer, that plies all his life at the file or the hammer; men, whose professional duties call into play the finest faculties of the mind, are subject to similar degradation. This division of occupations has given rise to the profession of attorneys, whose sole business it is to appear in the courts of justice instead of the principals, and to follow up the different steps of the process on their behalf. These legal practitioners are, confessedly, seldom deficient in technical skill and ability; yet it is not uncommon to meet with men, even of eminence in this profession, wholly ignorant of the most simple processes of the manufactures they every day make use of; who, if they were set to work to mend the simplest article of their furniture, would scarcely know how to begin, and could probably not drive a nail, without exciting the risibility of every carpenter's awkward apprentice; and if placed in a situation of a greater emergency, called upon, for instance, to save a drowning friend, or to rescue a fellow-townsman from a hostile attack, would be in a truly distressing perplexity; whereas a rough peasant, inhabiting a semi-barbarous district, would probably extricate himself from a similar situation with honour.

With regard to the labouring class, the incapacity for any other than a single occupation, renders the condition of mere labourers more hard and wearisome, as well as less profitable. They have less means of enforcing their own rights to an equitable portion of the gross value of the product. The workman, that carries about with him the whole implements of his trade, can change his locality at pleasure, and earn his subsistence wherever he pleases: in the other case, he is a mere adjective, without individual capacity, independence, or substantive importance, when separated from his fellow-labourers, and obliged to accept whatever terms his employer thinks fit to impose.

On the whole, we may conclude, that division of labour is a skilful mode of employing human agency, that it consequently multiplies the productions of society; in other words, the powers and the enjoyments of mankind; but that it in some degree degrades the faculties of man in his individual capacity. (a) (1)

CHAPTER IX.

OF THE DIFFERENT METHODS OF EMPLOYING COMMERCIAL INDUSTRY, AND THE MODE IN WHICH THEY CONCUR IN PRODUCTION.

COMMODITIES are not all to be had in all places indifferently. The immediate products of the earth depend upon the local varieties of soil and climate; and even the products of industry are met with only in such places as are most favourable to their production.

Whence it follows that, where products, whether of industry or of the earth, do not grow naturally, they can not be introduced or produced in a perfect state, and fit for consumption, without undergoing a certain modification; that is to say, that of transport or conveyance.

This transfer gives occupation to what has been called commercial industry.

External commerce consists of the supply of the home market with foreign, and of foreign markets with home products.*

Wholesale commerce is the buying of large quantities and re-selling to inferior dealers.

Retail commerce is the buying of wholesale dealers, and re-selling to consumers.

---

*Products that are bought to be re-sold, are called *merchandise;* and merchandise bought for consumption is denominated *commodities.* (b)

(a) This consideration makes it peculiarly incumbent upon the government of a manufacturing nation to diffuse the benefits of early education, and thus prevent the degeneration from being intellectual as well as corporeal.   T.

(b) This distinction has been discarded in the translation, for the sake of simplification; the general term products being sufficiently intelligible and specific.   T.

---

(1) ["The extensive propagation of light and refinement," says DUGALD STEWART, "arising from the influence of the press, aided by the spirit of commerce, seems to be the remedy to be provided by nature against the fatal effects which would otherwise be produced, by the subdivision of labour accompanying the progress of the mechanical arts: nor is any thing wanting to make the remedy effectual, but wise institutions to facilitate general instruction, and to adapt the education of individuals to the stations they are to occupy. The mind of the artist, which, from the limited sphere of his activity, would sink below the level of the peasant or the savage, might receive in infancy the means of intellectual enjoyment and the seeds of moral improvement; and even the insipid uniformity of his professional engagements, by presenting no object to awaken his ingenuity or to distract his attention, might leave him at liberty to employ his faculties on subjects more interesting to himself, and more extensively useful to others."]

AMERICAN EDITOR.

The commerce of money or specie is conducted by the banker, who receives or pays on account of other people, or gives bills, orders, or letters of credit, payable elsewhere than at the place where they are given. This is sometimes called the banking trade. (a)

The broker brings buyers and sellers together.

The persons engaged in these several branches are all agents of commercial industry, whose agency tends to approximate products to the hands of the ultimate consumer. The agency of the retailer of an ounce of pepper is quite as indispensable to the consumer, as that of the merchant, who despatches his vessel to the Moluccas for a cargo; and the only reason why these different functions are not both performed by one and the same individual is, because they can be executed with more economy and convenience by two. To enter minutely into an examination of the limits and practices of these various departments of commercial industry, would be to write a treatise on commerce.* All we have to do in this work is, to inquire in what manner and degree they influence the production of values.

In Book II., we shall see how the actual demand for a product originating in its utility, is limited by the amount of the cost of production, and upon what principle its relative value is determined in each particular place. At present it is sufficient for the clear conception of commercial production, to consider the value of a product as a given quantity or *datum*. Thus, without examining the reason why oil of olives is worth at Marseilles thirty, and at Paris forty *sous* per lb., I shall content myself with simply stating, that whoever effects the transport of that article from Marseilles to Paris, thereby increases its value to the amount of ten *sous* per lb. Nor is it to be supposed, that its intrinsic value has received no accession by the transit. The value has positively augmented. The intrinsic value of silver is greater at Paris than at Lima; and the cases are precisely similar.

In fact, the transport of products can not be effected without the concurrence of a variety of means, which have each an intrinsic value of their own, and of which the actual transport itself, in the literal and confined sense of the term, is commonly not the most chargeable. There must be one commercial establishment at the

---

* A complete treatise on commerce is still a desideratum in literature, notwithstanding the labours of *Melon* and *Forbonnais*, for hitherto the principles and consequences of commerce have been little understood. (1)

(a) The banker's business is not confined to dealings in metal, coined or uncoined, but is extended to dealings in paper-money, and dealings in credit, as we shall see when we come to the chapter upon money, *infra*.   T.

---

(1) The Society for the Diffusion of Useful Knowledge, in London, in 1833, published a Treatise on Commerce, by J. R. M'Culloch, Esq. the eminent political economist, in which the grand principles, practice and history of Commerce, are unfolded and explained with great ability. It is a work that should be read by every well-educated merchant.

AMERICAN EDITOR.

place where the products are collected; another at the place it is transported to; besides package and warehousing.

There must be an advance of capital equivalent to the value transported. Moreover, there are agents, insurers, and brokers, to be paid. All these are really productive occupations, since, without their agency, the consumer can never enjoy the product; and supposing their remuneration to be reduced by competition to the lowest rate possible, he can be in no way cheaper supplied.

In commercial, as well as manufacturing industry, the discovery of a more economical or more expeditious process, the more skilful employment of natural agents, the substitution, for instance, of a canal in place of a road, or the removal of a difficulty interposed by nature or by human institutions, reduces the cost of production, and procures a gain to the consumer, without any consequent loss to the producer, who can lower his price without prejudice to himself, because his own outlay and advance are likewise reduced.

The same principles govern both external and internal commerce. The merchant that exports silks to Germany or to Russia, and sells at Petersburg for 40 cents per yard, stuffs that have cost but 30 cents at Lyons, creates a value of 10 cents per yard. If the same merchant brings a return cargo of peltry from Russia, and sells at Havre for 240 dollars what cost him at Riga but 200 dollars, or a value equivalent to 200 dollars, there will be a new value of 40 dollars, created and shared amongst the different agents engaged in this production of value, whatever nation they may belong to, and whatever be the relative importance of their respective productive agency, from the first-rate merchant to the ticket-porter inclusive.* And by this creation of value, the wealth of the French nation is enriched to the amount of all the gains of French industry and of French capital, in the course of this production; and the Russian nation to the amount of those of Russian industry and Russian capital. Nay, perhaps a third nation, independent both of France and of Russia, may get the whole profit accruing from the mutual commercial intercourse between these nations; and yet neither of them loses any thing, if their industry and capital have other equally lucrative employments at home. The very circumstance of the existence of an active external commerce, no matter what agents it be conducted by, is a very powerful stimulus to internal industry. The Chinese, who abandon the whole of their external commerce to other nations, must nevertheless raise an enormous gross product, otherwise they could never support, as they do, a population twice as large as that of all Europe, upon a surface of nearly equal extent. A shop-keeper in good business is quite as well off as a pedlar that travels the country with his wares on his back.† Commercial jealousy is, after all, nothing but prejudice: it is a wild fruit, that will drop of itself when it has arrived at maturity.

---

* The ordinary proportions of this division will be explained, *infrà*, Book II. Chap. 7.

† It has been often asked, Why not combine commercial with agricultural and

The external commerce of all countries is inconsiderable, compared with the internal. To convince ourselves of the truth of this position, it will be sufficient to take note at all numerous or even sumptuous entertainments, how very small is the proportion of values of foreign growth, in comparison with those of home production; especially, if we take into the account, as we ought to do, the value of buildings and habitations, which is necessarily of home production.* (a)

The internal commerce of a country, though, from its minute ramification, it is less obvious and striking, besides being the most considerable, is likewise the most advantageous. (1) For both the remittances and returns of this commerce are necessarily home products. It sets in motion a double production, and the profits of it are not participated with foreigners. For this reason, roads, canals, bridges, the abolition of internal duties, (b) tolls, duties on transit, (c) which are in effect tolls, every measure, in short, which promotes internal circulation, is favourable to national wealth.

---

manufacturing productions? Why, for the same reason that makes a wholesale cotton spinner, if he have a surplus of time and capital, more apt to extend his spinning concern, than to employ his labour and capital in the working up of his own filiature into muslin and printed calicoes.

* It would be impossible to estimate the proportion with any tolerable accuracy, even in countries where calculations of this kind are most in vogue. Indeed, the attempt would be a sad waste of time. To say the truth, statistical statements are of little real utility; for, be their accuracy ever so well assured, they can only be correct for the moment. The only knowledge really useful is, the knowledge of general principles and laws, that is to say, the knowledge of the connexion between cause and effect, which alone can safely teach us what measures it is best to adopt in every possible emergency. The sole use of statistics in political economy is, to supply examples and illustrations of general principles. They can never be the basis of principles, which are grounded upon the nature of things; whereas statistics, in the most improved state, are only an index of their quantity.

(a) This position may be correct or not, according to circumstances. The national wants must always, in the long run, be supplied by the national industry and exertions: but what is there to prevent a nation from exchanging the larger portion of its domestic products for the products of other nations? The people of Tyre probably consumed more products of external than of domestic industry, although indeed those external must have been purchased with domestic products. Tyre, it is true, was rather a city than a nation. Holland resembled her in many particulars. The observation applies to every community, the chief part of whose production is, the modification of external products.   T.

 (b) Douanes.   (c) Octrois.

---

(1) [The author has here, in common with Dr. Smith, fallen into an error. Capital, whether employed in the home or foreign trade, is equally productive. If, for example, the home trade realized greater profits than foreign commerce, every cent of capital employed in the latter would, in a very little time, be withdrawn from so comparatively disadvantageous an investment. Capital will flow into the foreign, instead of the home trade, only because it will thereby yield a larger profit. The internal commerce of a country cannot therefore be said to be "the most advantageous."]   AMERICAN EDITOR.

There is a further branch of commerce, called the trade of speculation, which consists in the purchase of goods at one time, to be re-sold in the same place and condition at another time, when they are expected to be dearer. Even this trade is productive; its utility consists in the employment of capital, warehouses, care in the preservation, in short, human industry in the withdrawing from circulation a commodity depressed in value by temporary superabundance, and thereby reduced in price below the charges of production, so as to discourage its production, with the design and purpose of restoring it to circulation when it shall become more scarce, and when its price shall be raised above the natural price, the charges of production, so as to throw a loss upon the consumers. The evident operation of this kind of trade is, to transport commodities in respect of time, instead of locality. If it prove an unprofitable or losing concern, it is a sign that it was useless in the particular instance, and that the commodity was not redundant at the time of purchase, and scarce at the time of re-sale. This operation has also been denominated, with much propriety, the trade of reserve. (a) Where it is directed to the buying up of the whole of an article, for the sake of exacting an exorbitant monopoly price, it is called *forestalling*, which is happily difficult, in proportion as the national commerce is extensive, and, consequently, the commodities in circulation both abundant and various.

The carrying trade, as Smith calls it, consists in the purchase of goods in one foreign market for re-sale in another foreign market. This branch of industry is beneficial not only to the merchant that practises it, but also to the two nations between whom it is practised; and that for reasons which have been explained while treating of external commerce. The carrying trade is but little suited to nations possessed of small capital, whereof the whole is wanted to give activity to internal industry, which is always entitled to the preference. The Dutch carry it on in ordinary times with advantage, because their population and capital are both redundant. (b) The French, in peace time, have carried on a lucrative carrying trade between the different ports of the Levant; because adventurers could procure advances of capital on better terms in France than in the Levant, and were perhaps less exposed to the oppression of the detestable government of that country. They have since been supplanted by other nations, whose possession of the carrying trade is so far from being an injury to the subjects of the Porte, that it actually keeps alive the little remaining industry of its territories. Some governments, less wise in this particular than the Turkish, have interdicted their carrying trade to foreign adventurers. If the native traders can carry on the

---

(a) *Commerce de reserve.* There is no corresponding term in English; it is intelligible enough.

(b) The carrying trade of Holland is now almost extinct. In fact, whether or no it be suited to a given nation at a given time, depends upon a great variety of circumstances. The advantage of the neutral character gave a very large proportion of it for some years to the American Union, though notoriously deficient in capital for the purposes of internal cultivation.   T.

transport to greater profit than foreigners, there is no occasion to exclude the latter; and, if it can be conducted cheaper by foreigners, their exclusion is a voluntary sacrifice of the profit of employing them. An example will serve to elucidate this position. The freight of hemp from Riga to Havre costs a Dutch skipper, say 7 dollars per ton. It must be taken for granted, that no other but the Dutchman can carry it so cheap. He makes a tender to the French government, which is a consumer of Russian hemp, to provide tonnage at 8 dollars per ton, thereby obviously securing to himself a profit of 1 dollar per ton. Suppose then, that the French government, with a view to favour the national shipping, prefers to employ French tonnage, which can not be navigated for less than 10 dollars per ton, or 11 dollars, allowing the same profit to the ship-owner—What is the consequence? The government will be out of pocket 3 dollars per ton, for the mere purpose of giving a profit of 1 dollar to the national ship-owners. And, as none but the individuals of the nation contribute towards the national expenditure, this operation will have cost to one class of Frenchmen 3 dollars for the purpose of giving to another class of Frenchmen a profit of 1 dollar only. However the numbers may vary, the result must be similar; for there is but one fair way of stating the account.

It is hardly necessary to caution the reader, that I have throughout been considering maritime industry solely in its relation to national wealth. Its influence upon national security is another thing. The art of navigation is an expedient of war, as well as of commerce. The working of a vessel is a military manœuvre; and the nation containing the larger proportion of seamen, is, therefore, *ceteris paribus*, the more powerful in a military point of view; consequently, political and military considerations have always interfered with national views of commerce, in matters of navigation; and England, in passing her celebrated Navigation Act, interdicting her carrying trade to all vessels, the owners and at least three-fourths of the crews whereof were not British subjects, had in view, not so much the profits of the carrying trade, as the increase of her own military marine, and the diminution of that of the other powers, especially of Holland, which then enjoyed an immense carrying trade, and was the chief object of English jealousy.

Nor can it be denied, that these views may actuate a wise national administration; assuming always, that it is an advantage to one nation to domineer over others. But these political dogmas are fast growing obsolete. Policy will some day or other be held to consist in coveting the pre-eminence of merit rather than of force. The love of domination never attains more than a factitious elevation, that is sure to make enemies of all its neighbours. It is this that engenders national debt, internal abuse, tyranny and revolution; while the sense of mutual interest begets international kindness, extends the sphere of useful intercourse, and leads to a prosperity, permanent, because it is natural. (1)

(1) [The operation of the British Navigation-acts, like all other restrictive regulations, has been prejudicial to the growth of national wealth, without, at the same time, having contributed in any degree to the establishment of the naval

CHAPTER X.

OF THE TRANSFORMATIONS UNDERGONE BY CAPITAL IN THE PROGRESS OF PRODUCTION.

WE have seen above (Chap. III.) of what the productive capital of a nation consists, and to what uses it is applicable. So much it was necessary to specify, in enumerating the various means of production. We now come to consider and examine, what becomes of capital in the progress of production, and how it is perpetuated and increased.

To avoid fatiguing the reader with abstract speculation, I shall begin with giving examples, which I shall take from every day's experience and observation. The general principles will follow of themselves, and the reader will immediately see their applicability to all other cases, which he may have occasion to pronounce a judgment upon.

When the land-owner is himself the cultivator, he must possess a capital over and above the value of his land; that is to say, value to some amount or other consisting, in the first place, of clearance of the ground, together with works and erections thereon, which may at pleasure be looked upon as part of the value of the estate, but which

---

preponderance of Great Britain. " If it can be made to appear," says a highly distinguished political economist, " that the greater wealth which we should, in the absence of these laws, have possessed, would have supplied a revenue adequate to the maintenance of an equal number of seamen in the navy, it would follow that we are no gainers by these acts; and if it further appear that this additional revenue would have been equal to the maintenance of twice or three times as many seamen, *it would be clear that we are losers by them.* It is acknowledged by many of the advocates for these laws, that their tendency has not been to increase the national revenue, but in some degree the reverse.

" Our national preponderance," says, we believe, Mr. Horner, "rests on a very different basis. Our national energy and wealth originate in our freedom, and in that security of property which is its happy consequence. The number of our seamen in merchant shipping is owing to the spirit and capital of our traders, and to our great extent of coast. The magnitude of our navy is due neither to navigation-acts, nor to colonial monopolies, but to the resources of an industrious country.

" How different are the ideas suggested by such observations, from the narrow theories of those who trace our naval superiority to the operation of a few acts of Parliament! They remind us of the technical philosophy of the judge, who gravely ascribed the lamentable prevalence of duelling, not to the violence of human passions, but to a misapprehension of the law of the land! Besides, our naval greatness, as it is well remarked by Dr. Smith, was conspicuous before our navigation laws were framed. It existed then, as it had done before, and has done since, in a degree commensurate with our commerce, and with the extent of our national prosperity. These circumstances, and not navigation laws, will be found the regulators of naval power in all countries. They determine its extent among the Dutch, to whom, even in the season of their greatest strength, navigation laws were entirely unknown." Vide Edinburgh Review, vol. xiv. page 95.]

AMERICAN EDITOR.

vertheless, the result of previous human exertion, and an ac-
ʌ to the original value of the land.*

ıs portion of his capital is little subject to wear and tear; trifling
sional repairs will preserve it entire. If the cultivator obtain
from the annual produce wherewithal to effect these repairs, this
item of capital is thereby preservable in perpetuity.

Ploughs, and other farming implements and utensils, together
with the animals employed in tillage, form another item of the cultivator's capital, and an article of much quicker consumption, which,
however, may in like manner be kept up and renovated, as occasion
may require, at the expense of the annual produce of the concern,
and thus be maintained at its full original amount.

Finally, he must have stores of various kinds; seeds for his ground,
provisions, fodder for his cattle, and food as well as money for his
labourers' wages, &c.† Observe, that this branch of capital is totally
decomposed once in the course of the year, at least; and sometimes
three or four times over. The money, grain and provisions of every description disappear altogether; but so it must necessarily be,
and yet not an atom of the capital is lost, if the cultivator, after
abstracting from the produce a fair allowance for the productive
service of his land (rent) for the productive service of the capital
embarked (interest) and for the productive service of the personal
labour that has set the whole in motion (wages), contrive to make the
annual produce replace the outlay of money, seed, live stock, &c.,
even to the article of manure, so as to put himself in possession of a
value equal to what he started with the preceding year.

Thus we find, that capital may yet be kept up, though almost
every part of it have undergone some change, and many parts be
completely annihilated; for, indeed, capital consists not in this or
that commodity or substance, but in its value.

Nor is it difficult to conceive, that if the estate be sufficiently
extensive, and managed with order, economy, and intelligence, the
profits of the cultivator may enable him to lay by a surplus, after
replacing the entire value of his capital, and defraying the expenses
of himself and family. The mode of disposing of this surplus is of
the utmost importance to the community, and will be treated of in
the next chapter. All that is at present necessary is, to impress a

* Arthur Young, in his *View of the Agriculture of France*, makes no estimate
of this item of capital permanently vested in the land of France within its old
limits; but merely reckons it to be less than the capital so vested in England, in
the proportion of 36 *livres tournois* per English acre. So that, in the very moderate supposition, that half as much capital is vested in permanent amelioration of
the land in France as in England, the capital so vested in Old France, reckoned
at 7 dollars per acre, would amount, upon 131 millions of acres, to 817 millions
of dollars for this item of French capital alone.

† The same writer (Young) estimates, that in France, these two last items of
capital, viz. implements, beasts of husbandry, stores of provisions, &c. may be
set down at 9 dollars per acre, one acre with another; making an aggregate of
1179 millions of dollars; which, added to the former estimate, shows a total of
1996 millions of dollars, capital engaged in the agricultural industry of Old
France. He estimates the same items of capital in England at twice as much
per acre.

clear conviction, that the value of capital, though consumed, is not yet destroyed, wherever it has been consumed in such way as to re-produce itself; and that a concern may go on forever, and annually render a new product with the same capital, although that capital be in a perpetual course of consumption.

After tracing capital through its various transformations in the department of agriculture, it will be easy to follow its transformations in the other two departments of manufacture and commerce.

In manufacture, as well as agriculture, there are some branches of capital that last for years; buildings and fixtures for instance, machinery and some kinds of tools; others, on the contrary, lose their form entirely; the oil and pot-ash used by soap-makers cease to be oil and pot-ash when they assume the form of soap. In the same manner, the drugs employed in dyeing indigo cease to be Brazil wood or annatto, as the case may be, and are incorporated with the fabric they are employed in colouring. And so of the wages and maintenance of the labourers.

In commerce, almost the whole capital undergoes complete transmutation, and many items of it several times in the course of a year. A merchant exchanges his specie for woollens or jewellery, which is one change of form. He ships them for Turkey, and on the voyage, some more of his money is converted into the wages of the crew. The cargo arrives at Constantinople, where he sells the investment to the wholesale dealers, who pay him in bills upon Smyrna, which is a second metamorphosis; the capital embarked is now in the shape of bills, which he makes use of in the purchase of cotton at Smyrna; a third transformation. The cotton is shipped for France and sold there, which completes the fourth change of form; thus reproducing the capital, most probably with profit, under its original shape of French coin.

It is obvious, that the objects capable of acting the part of capital are innumerable. If, at any given period, one wishes to know what the capital of a nation consisted of, it would be found composed of an infinity of objects, commodities and substances, of which it would be impossible to guess the aggregate value with any tolerable accuracy, and of which some are situated many thousand leagues from its frontiers. At the same time, it appears that the most insignificant and perishable articles are a part, and often a very important part, too, of the national capital; that although the items of capital are in a continual course of consumption and decomposition, it by no means follows, that the capital itself is destroyed and consumed, provided that its value be preserved in some other shape; consequently, that the introduction or import of the vilest and most perishable commodities may be just as profitable as that of the most costly and durable — gold or silver; that, in fact, the former, are more profitable the instant they are more sought after; that the producers themselves are the only competent judges of the transformation, export, and import, of these various matters and commodities;

and that every government which interferes, every system calculated
to influence production, can only do mischief.

There are concerns, in which the capital is completely renovated,
and the work of production begun afresh, several times in the year.
An operation of manufacture, that can be perfected and the product
sold in three months, will admit of the capital being turned to
account annually four times. It may be supposed that the profit
each time is less than when the capital is turned but once in twelve
months. Were it otherwise, there would be four times the profit
gained; an advantage that would soon attract an overflow of capital
in this particular channel, and lower the profit by competition. On
the other hand, products that it requires more than a year to perfect,
such as leather, must, over and above the original capital, yield the
profits of more than one year; otherwise, who could undertake to
raise them?

In the trade of Europe with China and the East Indies, the capital embarked is two or three years before its return. Nor is it necessary in commerce or in manufacture, any more than in agriculture, which has been cited as an example, that the capital should be
realized in the form of money, to be entirely replaced. Merchants
and manufacturers, for the most part, realize in this way the whole
of their capital but once in their lives, and that is when they wind
up and leave off business. Yet they are at no loss to discover at any
time whether their capital be enlarged or diminished, by referring to
the inventory of their assets for the time being.

The capital employed on a productive operation is always a mere
advance made for payment of productive services, and reimbursed
by the value of their resulting product.

The miner extracts the ore from the bowels of the earth; the
iron-founder pays him for it. Here ends the miner's production,
which is paid for by an advance out of the capital of the iron-founder. This latter next smelts the ore, refines and makes it into steel,
which he sells to the cutler: thus is the production of the founder
paid, and his advance reimbursed by a second advance on the part
of the cutler, made in the price for the steel. This again the cutler
works up into razor-blades, the price for which replaces his advance
of capital, and at the same time pays for his productive agency.

It is manifest, then, that the value of the ultimate product, razor-
blades, has been sufficient to replace all the capital successively employed in its production, and, at the same time, to pay for the production itself; or rather, that the successive advances of capital have
paid for the productive services, and the price of the product has
reimbursed those advances; which is precisely the same thing as if
the aggregate or gross value of the product had gone immediately
to defray the charges of its production.

CHAPTER XI.

OF THE FORMATION AND MULTIPLICATION OF CAPITAL.

In the foregoing chapter, I have shown how productive capital, though kept, during the progress of production, in a continual state of employment, and subject to perpetual change and wear, is yet ultimately reproduced in full value, when the business of production is at an end. Since, then, wealth consists in the value of matter or substance, not in the substance or matter itself, I trust my readers have clearly comprehended, that the productive capital employed, notwithstanding its frequent transmutations, is all the while the same capital.

It will be conceived with equal facility, that, inasmuch as the value produced has replaced the value consumed, that produced value may be equal, inferior, or superior in amount, to the value consumed, according to circumstances. If equal, the capital has been merely replaced and kept up; if inferior, the capital has been encroached upon; but if superior, there has been an actual increase and accession of capital. This is precisely the point to which we traced the cultivator, cited by way of an example in the preceding chapter. We supposed him, after the complete re-establishment of his capital, so as to put him in a condition to begin the new year's cultivation with equal means at his disposal, to have netted a surplus produce beyond his consumption of some value or other; say of 1000 dollars.

Now, let us observe the various methods, in which he may dispose of his surplus of 1000 dollars; for simple as the matter may appear to be, there is no point upon which more error has prevailed, or which has greater influence upon the condition of mankind.

Whatever kind of produce this surplus, which we have valued at 1000 dollars, may consist of, the owner may exchange it for gold or silver specie, and bury it in the earth till he wants it again. Does the national capital suffer a loss of 1000 dollars by this operation? Certainly not; for we have just seen, that the value of that capital was before completely replaced. Has any one been injured to that amount? By no means; for he has neither robbed nor cheated any body, and has received no value whatever, without giving an equivalent. It may be said, perhaps, he has given wheat in exchange for the dollars he has thus buried, which wheat was very soon consumed; yet the 1000 dollars still continue withdrawn from the capital of the community. But I trust it will be recollected, that wheat, as well as silver or gold, may compose a part of the national capital; indeed, we have seen that national capital must necessarily consist, in a great measure, of wheat and such like substances, liable to either partial or total consumption, without any diminution of capital thereupon; for, in short, that reproduction completely replaces the value consumed, including the profits of the producers, whose productive agency is part of the value consumed. Wherefore, the instant that the cultivator has fully replaced his capital, and begins again with the same means as before, the 1000 dollars may be thrown into the sea without reducing the national capital.

But let us trace the disposal of this surplus of 1000 dollars to every imaginable destination. Suppose, for instance, that instead of being buried, they have been spent by the cultivator upon an elegant entertainment. In this case, this whole value has been destroyed in an afternoon; a sumptuous feast, a ball, and fireworks, will have swallowed up the whole. The value thus destroyed exists no longer in the community : it no longer forms an item in the aggregate of wealth; for those persons, into whose hands the identical pieces of silver have come, have given an equivalent in wines, refreshments, eatables, gunpowder, &c., all which values are reduced to nothing; the gross national capital, however, is no more diminished in this case than in the former. A surplus value had been produced; and this surplus is all that has been destroyed, so that things remain just as they were.

Again, suppose these 1000 dollars to have been spent in the purchase of furniture, plate, or linen. Still there is no reduction of national productive capital; although it must be allowed there is no accession; for in this case, nothing more is gained than the additional comforts the cultivator and his family derive from the newly purchased moveables.

Fourthly and lastly, suppose the cultivator to add this excess of 1000 dollars to his productive capital, that is to say, to re-employ it in increasing the productive powers of his farm as circumstances may require, in the purchase of more beasts of husbandry, or the hire and support of more labourers; and in consequence, at the end of the year, to gather produce enough to replace the full value of the 1000 dollars, with a profit, in such manner, as to make them capable of yielding a fresh product the year after, and so on every year to eternity. It is then, and then only, that the productive capital of the community is really augmented to that extent.

It must on no account be overlooked, that, in one way or other, a saving such as that we have been speaking of, whether expended productively or unproductively, still is in all cases expended and consumed; and this is a truth, that must remove a notion extremely false, though very much in vogue—namely, that saving limits and injures consumption. No act of saving subtracts in the least from consumption, provided the thing saved be re-invested or restored to productive employment. On the contrary, it gives rise to a consumption perpetually renovated and recurring; whereas there is no repetition of an unproductive consumption. (a)

_____

(a) On the subject of saving, *Sismondi,* and after him our own Malthus, have adopted a different opinion. According to them, the powers of production have already outrun the desire and the ability to consume; consequently, every thing that tends to reduce that desire is injurious, because it is already too inert for the interests of production. Wherefore, inasmuch as the desire of accumulation

It must be observed, too, that the form in which the value saved is so saved and re-employed productively, makes no essential difference. The saving is made with more or less advantage, according to the circumstances and intelligence of the person making it. Nor is there any reason why this portion of capital should not have been accumulated, without ever having for a moment assumed the form of specie. It may be that an actual product of the farm has been saved and resown or planted, without having undergone any transmutation ; perhaps the wood, that might have been used as firing to warm superfluous apartments, may have been converted into palings or other carpenter's work ; and what was cut down in the first instance as an item of revenue, be so employed, as to become an item of capital.

Now, the *only* way of augmenting the productive capital of individuals, as well as the aggregate productive capital of the community, is by this process of saving ; in other words, of re-employing in production more products created than have been consumed in their creation. Productive capital cannot be accumulated by the mere scraping together of values without consuming them ; nor any otherwise, than by withdrawing them from unproductive, and devoting them to reproductive consumption. There is nothing odious in the real picture of the accumulation of capital ; we shall presently see its happy consequences.

---

is the direct opposite of that of consumption, it must of necessity be injurious in the highest degree. On these principles, it might be proved without difficulty, that the prodigality of public authority, war, or the poor law of England, is a national benefit: for all of them stimulate consumption. Indeed they leave their readers to draw this inevitable conclusion ; for they maintain in plain terms, that the enlargement of the productive powers of man, by the use of machinery or otherwise, makes the existence of unproductive consumers a matter, not of mere possibility or probability, but of actual necessity and expedience. (*Vide Sismondi, Nouv. Prin.* liv. ii. c. 3. and liv. iv. c. 4. Malthus, *Prin. of Pol. Econ.*) These maxims would justify the prodigality of Louis XIV. of France, and of the Pitt system of England. But fortunately they are erroneous ; and if the contrary principles laid down by our author here and *infrà*, Chap. XV., needed further illustration or support, they have been rendered still more clear and convincing by his recent *Lettres à* M. Malthus.—It is true, that the enlargement of productive power naturally leads to the multiplication of unproductive consumers: why ? because the desire of barren consumption, instead of being inert, is always active in the human breast. But that multiplication is not necessary ; for the consumer may be made a producer, if not of material, at least of immaterial products, which latter are capable of infinitely more multiplication and variety, as well as of more general diffusion than material products. While this field remains open, a national administration never need despair of finding occupation for the human labour supplanted by machinery. And what is the parsimony of modern days ? It is not the hoarding of coin or other valuables, which, though as our author observes, it subtracts nothing from the national capital, is yet a social mischief, because it suspends the utility of an existing product, or at any rate, prevents it from yielding the human gratification, which its barren consumption would afford. The accumulations of the miser are now either vested in reproduction which is beneficial, or in the ownership of the sources of production, land, &c. &c. which it matters not to public wealth who may be possessed of, or in the incumbrances of those sources, mortgages, national funds, &c. &c., which are but portions of that ownership, and to which the same observation applies. T.

The form under which national capital is accumulated, is commonly determined by the respective geographical position, the moral character, and the peculiar wants of each nation. The accumulations of a society in its early stages consist, for the most part, of buildings, implements of husbandry, live stock, improvements of land; those of a manufacturing people chiefly of raw materials, or such as are still in the hands of its workmen, in a more or less finished state; and in some part, of the necessary manufacturing tools and machinery. In a nation devoted to commerce, capital is mostly accumulated in the form of wrought or unwrought goods, that have been bought by the merchant for the purpose of re-sale.

A nation that at the same time directs its energies to all three branches of industry, namely, agriculture, manufactures, and commerce, has a capital compounded of all three different forms of production; of that amazing quantity of stores of every kind, that we find civilized society actually possessed of; and which, by the intelligent use that is made of them, are constantly renovated, or even increased, in spite of their enormous consumption, provided that the industry of the community produces more than is destroyed by its consumption.

I do not mean to say, that each nation has produced and laid by the identical article that composes its actual capital. Values, in some shape or other, have been produced and laid by; and these, through various transmutations, have assumed the form most convenient for the time being. A bushel of wheat saved will feed a mason as well as a worker in embroidery. In the one case, the bushel of wheat will be reproduced in the shape of the masonry of a house; in the other, under that of a laced suit.

Every adventurer in industry, that has a capital of his own embarked in it, has ready means of employing his saving productively; if engaged in husbandry, he buys fresh parcels of land; or, by judicious outlays and improvements, augments the productive powers of what already belongs to him; if in trade, he buys and sells a greater quantity of merchandise. Capitalists have nearly the same advantage: they invest their whole savings in the same manner as their former capital is invested, and increase it *pro tanto*, or look out for new ways of investment, which they are at no loss to discover; for the moment they are known to be possessed of loose funds, they seldom have to wait for propositions for the employment of them; whereas the proprietors of lands let out to farm, and individuals that live upon fixed income, or the wages of their personal labour, have not equal facility in the advantageous disposal of their savings, and can seldom invest them till they amount to a good round sum. Many savings are therefore consumed, that might otherwise have swelled the capitals of individuals, and consequently of the nation at large. Banks and associations, whose object is to receive, collect, and turn to profit the small savings of individuals, are consequently very favourable to the multiplication of capital, whenever they are perfectly secure.

The increase of capital is naturally slow of progress: for it can never take place without actual production of value, and the creation of value is the work of time and labour, besides other ingredients.* Since the producers are compelled to consume values all the while they are engaged in the creation of fresh ones, the utmost they can accumulate, that is to say, add to reproductive capital, is the value they produce beyond what they consume; and the sum of this surplus is all the additional wealth that the public or individuals can acquire. The more values are saved and reproductively employed in the year, the more rapid is the national progress towards prosperity. Its capital is swelled, a larger quantity of industry is set in motion, and saving becomes more and more practicable, because the additional capital and industry are additional means of production.

Every saving or increase of capital lays the groundwork of a perpetual annual profit, not only to the saver himself, but likewise to all those whose industry is set in motion by this item of new capital. It is for this reason that the celebrated Adam Smith likens the frugal man, who enlarges his productive capital but in a solitary instance, to the founder of an almshouse for the perpetual support of a body of labouring persons upon the fruits of their own labour; and on the other hand, compares the prodigal that encroaches upon his capital, to the roguish steward that should squander the funds of a charitable institution, and leave destitute, not merely those that derived present subsistence from it, but likewise all who might derive it hereafter. He pronounces, without reserve, every prodigal to be a public pest, and every careful and frugal person to be a benefactor of society.†

It is fortunate, that self-interest is always on the watch to preserve the capital of individuals; and that capital can at no time be withdrawn from productive employment, without a proportionate loss of revenue.

Smith is of opinion, that, in every country, the profusion and ignorance of individuals and of the public authorities, is more than compensated by the prevalent frugality of the people at large, and by

---

* The savings of a rich contractor, of a swindler or cheat, of a royal favourite, saturated with grants, pensions, and unmerited emoluments, are actual accumulations of capital, and are sometimes made with facility enough. But the values thus amassed by a privileged few, are, in reality, the product of the labour, capital, and land, of numbers, who might themselves have made the saving, and turned it to their own account, but for the spoliation of injustice, fraud, or violence.

† Wealth of Nations, b. ii. c. 3. Lord Lauderdale, in a work entitled, "Enquiry into the Nature and Origin of Public Wealth," has proved, to his own conviction, in opposition to Smith, that the accumulation of capital is adverse to the increase of wealth: grounding his argument on the position that such accumulation withdraws from circulation values which would be serviceable to industry. But this position is untenable. Neither productive capital, nor the additions made to it, are withdrawn from circulation: otherwise they would remain inactive, and yield no profit whatever. On the contrary, the adventurer in industry, who makes use of it, employs, disposes of, and wholly consumes it, but in a way that reproduces it, and that with profit. I have noted this error of his lordship, because it has been made the basis of other works on political economy, which abound in false conclusions, having set out on this false principle.

their careful atttention to their own interests.* At least it seems undeniable, that almost all the nations of Europe are at this moment advancing in opulence; which could not be the case, unless each of them, taken in the aggregate, produced more than it consumed unproductively.† Even the revolutions of modern times appear to have been rather favourable than otherwise to the progress of opulence; for they are no longer, as in ancient days, followed by continued hostile invasion, or universal and protracted pillage; whereas, on the other hand, they have commonly overthrown the barriers of prejudice, and opened a wider field for talent and enterprise. But it is still a question, whether this frugality, which Smith gives individuals credit for, be not, in the most numerous classes of society, a forced consequence of a vicious political organization. Is it true, that those classes receive their fair proportion of the gross produce, in return for their productive exertions? How many individuals live in constant penury, in the countries considered as the most wealthy! How many families are there, both in town and country, whose whole existence is a succession of privations; who, with every thing around them to awaken their desires, are reduced to the satisfaction of the very lowest wants, as if they lived in an age of the grossest barbarism and national poverty!

Thus I am forced to infer, that, though unquestionably there is an annual saving of produce in almost all the nations of Europe, this saving is extorted much more commonly from urgent and natural wants, than from the consumption of superfluities, to which policy and humanity would hope to trace it. Whence arises a strong suspicion of some radical defect in the policy and internal economical systems of most of their governments.

Again, Smith thinks that the moderns are indebted for their comparative opulence, rather to the prevalence of individual frugality,

---

* *Wealth of Nations*, b. ii. c. 3.

† Except during the continuance of ruinous wars, or excessive public extravagance, such as occured in France under the domination of Napoleon. It cannot be doubted, that, at that disastrous period of her history, even in the moments of her most brilliant military successes, the amount of capital dilapidated exceeded the aggregate of savings. Requisitions and the havoc of war, in addition to the compulsory expenditure of individuals, and the pressure of exorbitant taxation, must unquestionably have destroyed more values than the exertions of individual economy could devote to reproductive investment. This sovereign, wholly ignorant of political economy himself, and consequently affecting to despise its suggestions, encouraged his courtiers, like himself, to squander the enormous revenues derived from his favour, in the apprehension that wealth might make them independent. (1)

---

(1) [We are told by Dr. Bowring and Mr. Villiers, in their valuable report on the Commercial Relations between France and Great Britain, published during the present year (1834), that the best authorities agree in declaring that the national riches of France were greatly diminished by the Imperial Régime, and, probably, a much larger amount was sacrificed in increased prices and diminished trade than was lost by the more direct operation of Napoleon's policy.]
AMERICAN EDITOR.

than to the enlargement of productive power. I admit, that some absurd kinds of profusion are more rare now-a-days than formerly;* but it should be recollected, that such profusion can never be practised, except by a very small number of persons; and if we take the pains to consider how widely the enjoyment of a more abundant and varied consumption is diffused, particularly among the middle classes of society, I think it will be found, that consumption and frugality have increased both together; for they are by no means incompatible. How many concerns are there in every branch of industry, that, in times of prosperity, yield enough produce to the adventurers to enable them to enlarge both their expenses and their savings? What is true of one particular concern, may possibly be true of the national production in the aggregate. The wealth of France was progressively increasing during the first forty years of the reign of Louis XIV., in spite of the profusion, public and private, that the splendour of the court occasioned. The stimulus given to production by Colbert, multiplied her resources faster than the court squandered them. Some people supposed, that this very prodigality was the cause of their multiplication; the gross fallacy of which notion is demonstrated by the circumstance, that after the death of that minister, the extravagancies of the court continuing at the same rate, and the progress of production being unable to keep pace with them, the kingdom was reduced to an alarming state of exhaustion. The close of that reign was the most gloomy that can be imagined.

After the death of Louis XIV., the public and private expenditure of France have been still further increasing;† and to me it ap-

---

* It is not, however, to be supposed, that the internal economy of ancient and of modern states is so widely different as some may be led to imagine. There is a striking similarity between the rise and fall of the opulent cities of Tyre, Carthage, and Alexandria, and those of the Venetian, Florentine, Genoese, and Dutch republics. The same cause must ever be attended with the same effect. We read of the wonderful riches of Crœsus, king of Lydia, even before his conquest of some neighbouring states: whence we may infer, that the Lydians were an industrious and frugal people; for a king can draw his resources solely from his subjects. The dry study of political economy would lead to this inference; but it happens to be also confirmed by the historical testimony of Justin, who calls the Lydians a people once powerful in the resources of industry; (*gens industriâ quandam potens;*) and gives a notion of their enterprising character, when he tells us that Cyrus did not complete their subjugation, until he had habituated them to indolence, gaming and debauchery. (*Jussique cauponias, et ludicras artes et lenocinia exercere.*) It is clear, therefore, that they must have before been possessed of the opposite qualities. Had Crœsus not taken a turn for pomp and military renown, he would probably have remained a powerful monarch, instead of ending his days in misfortune. The art of connecting cause with effect, and the study of political economy, are probably as conducive to the personal welfare of kings, as to that of their subjects.

† This increase of expenditure has not been altogether nominal, and consequentially upon the reduction in the standard of the silver coinage of France; a greater quantity and variety of products were consumed, and those of a better and more expensive quality. And though refined silver is now intrinsically worth nearly as much as in the days of Louis XIV., since the same weight of silver is given for the same quantity of wheat; yet the same ranks of society now actually expend more silver in weight as well as in denomination.

pears indisputable, that her national wealth has advanced likewise: Smith himself admits that it did; and what is true of France is so of most of the other states of Europe in some degree or other.

Turgot* falls in with Smith's opinion. He expresses his belief, that frugality is more generally prevalent now than in former times, and gives the following reasons: that, in most European countries, the interest of money was, on the average, lower than it had ever before been, a clear proof of the greater abundance of capital; therefore, that greater frugality must have been exerted in the accumulation of that capital than at any former period; and, certainly, the low rate of interest proves the existence of more abundant capital; but it proves nothing with regard to the manner of its acquirement; in fact, it may have been acquired just as well by enlarged production as by greater frugality, as I have just been demonstrating.

However, I am far from denying, that in many particulars, the moderns have improved the art of saving as well as that of producing. A man is not easily satisfied with less gratifications than he has been accustomed to: but there are many which he has learnt to procure at a cheaper rate. For instance, what can be more beautiful than the coloured furniture papers that adorn the walls of our apartments, combining the grace of design with the freshness of colouring? Formerly, many of those classes of society that now make use of paper hangings, were content with whitewashed walls, or a coarse ill-executed tapestry, infinitely dearer than the modern paperings. By the recent discovery of the efficacy of sulphuric acid in destroying the mucilaginous articles of vegetable oils, they have been rendered serviceable in lamps on the Argand principle of a double current of air, which before could only be lighted with fish oil, twice or thrice as dear. This discovery has of itself placed the use of those lamps, and the fine light they give, within reach of almost every class.†

For this improvement in frugality, we are indebted to the advances of industry, which has, on the one hand, discovered a greater number of economical processes; and, on the other, everywhere solicited the loan of capital, and tempted the holders of it, great or small, by better terms and greater security. In times when little industry existed, capital, being unprofitable, was seldom in any other shape than that of a hoard of specie locked up in a strong box, or buried in the earth as a reserve against emergency: however considerable in amount, it yielded no sort of benefit whatever, being in fact little else than a mere precautionary deposit, great or small. But the moment that this hoard was found capable of yielding a profit proportionate to its magnitude, its possessor had a double motive for increasing it, and that not of remote or precautionary, but of actual,

* *Reflex sur la Form. et la Distrib. des Rich.* § 81.

† It is to be feared, that taxation will ultimately deprive the consumer of the advantage of such improvements. The increase of the internal taxes (*droits réunis*), of the stamps on patents, of the taxes and impediments affecting the internal transport of commodities, have already brought the price of these vegetable oils almost to a par with the article they had so beneficially supplanted.

immediate benefit; since the profit yielded by the capital might, without the least diminution of it, be consumed and procure additional gratifications. Thenceforward it became an object of greater and more general solicitude than before, in those that had none to create, and in those that had one to augment, productive capital; and a capital bearing interest began to be regarded as a property equally lucrative, and sometimes equally substantial with land yielding rent. To such as regard the accumulation of capital as an evil, insomuch as it tends to aggravate the inequality of human fortune, I would suggest, that, if accumulation has a constant tendency to the multiplying of large fortunes, the course of nature has an equal tendency to divide them again. A man, whose life has been spent in augmenting his own capital and that of his country, must die at last, and the succession rarely devolves upon a sole heir or legatee, except where the national laws sanction entails and the right of primogeniture. In countries exempt from the baneful influence of such institutions, where nature is left to its own free and beneficent action, wealth is naturally diffused by subdivision through all the ramifications of the social tree, carrying health and life to the furthest extremities.* The total capital of the nation is enlarged at the same time that the capital of individuals is subdivided.

Thus, the growing wealth of an individual, when honestly acquired and reproductively employed, far from being viewed with jealous eyes, ought to be hailed as a source of general prosperity. I say honestly acquired, because a fortune amassed by rapine or extortion is no addition to the national stock; it is rather a portion of capital transferred from the hands of one man, where it already existed, to those of another, who has exerted no productive industry. On the contrary, it is but too common, that wealth ill-gotten is ill-spent also.

The faculty of amassing capital, or, in other words, value, I apprehend to be one cause of the vast superiority of man over the brute creation. Capital, taken in the aggregate, is a powerful engine consigned to the use of man alone. He can direct towards any one channel of employment the successive accumulations of many generations. Other animals can command, at most, no more than their

---

* It is to be regretted that people should be so little attentive to merit in their testamentary dispositions. There is always a degree of discredit thrown upon the memory of a testator, by his bounty to an unworthy object; and, on the contrary, nothing endears him more to the survivors than a bequest dictated by public spirit, or the love of private virtue. The foundation of a hospital, of an establishment for the education of the poor, of a perpetual premium for good actions, or a bequest to a writer of eminent merit, extends the influence of the wealthy beyond the limits of mortality, and enrols his name in the records of honour. (a)

(a) This laudable ambition is always proportionate to the wealth, the civil liberty, and the intelligence of a nation. In England, scarcely a year passes over our heads without more than one instance of useful and extensive munificence. The bequests to the elder Pitt, to Wilberforce, and other public men, the frequent foundations and enlargements of institutions of relief or education, reflect equal honour on the character of the nation, and the memory of the individuals. T.

respective individual accumulations, scraped together in the course of a few days, or a season at the utmost, which can never amount to any thing considerable: so that, granting them a degree of intelligence they do not seem possessed of, that intelligence would yet remain ineffectual, for want of the materials to set it in motion.

Moreover, it may be remarked, that the powers of man, resulting from the faculty of amassing capital, are absolutely indefinable; because there is no assignable limit to the capital he may accumulate, with the aid of time, industry, and frugality.

CHAPTER XII.

OF UNPRODUCTIVE CAPITAL

WE have seen above, that values once produced may be devoted, either to the satisfaction of the wants of those who have acquired them, or to a further act of production. They may also be withdrawn both from unproductive consumption and from reproductive employment, and remain buried or concealed.

The owner of values, in so disposing of them, not only deprives himself of the self-gratification he might have derived from their consumption, but also of the advantage he might draw from the productive agency of the value hoarded. He furthermore withholds from industry the profits it might make by the employment of that value.

Amongst abundance of other causes of the misery and weakness of the countries subjected to the Ottoman dominion, it cannot be doubted, that one of the principal is, the vast quantity of capital remaining in a state of inactivity. The general distrust and uncertainty of the future induce people of every rank, from the peasant to the pacha, to withdraw a part of their property from the greedy eyes of power: and value can never be invisible, without being inactive. This misfortune is common to all countries, where the government is arbitrary, though in different degrees proportionate to the severity of despotism. For the same reason, during the violence of political convulsions, there is always a sensible contraction of capital, a stagnation of industry, a disappearance of profit, and a general depression while the alarm continues: and, on the contrary, an instantaneous energy and activity highly favourable to public prosperity, upon the re-establishment of confidence. The saints and madonnas of superstitious nations, the splendid pageantry and richly decorated idols of Asiatic worship, gave life to no agricultural or manufacturing enterprise. The riches of the fane and the time lost in adoration would really purchase the blessings that barren prayers can never extort from the object of idolatry. There is a great deal of inert capital in countries, where the national habits lead to the extended use of the precious metals in furniture, clothes, and decorations. The silly admiration bestowed by the lower orders on the display of such idle and unproductive finery, is hostile to their own interests. For the opulent individual, who vests 20,000 dollars, in gilding, plate, and the splendour of his establishment, has it not to lay out at interest, and withdraws it from the support of industry of any kind. The nation loses the annual revenue of so much capital, and the annual profit of the industry it might have kept in activity.

Hitherto we have been considering that kind of value only, which is capable, after its creation, of being, as it were, incorporated with matter, and preserved for a longer or shorter period. But all the values producible by human industry, have not this quality. Some there are, which must have reality, because they are in high estimation, and purchased by the exchange of costly and durable products, which nevertheless have themselves no durability, but perish the moment of their production. This class of values I shall define in the ensuing chapter, and denominate *immaterial* products.*

CHAPTER XIII.

OF IMMATERIAL PRODUCTS, OR VALUES CONSUMED AT THE MOMENT OF PRODUCTION.

A physician goes to visit a sick person, observes the symptoms of disease, prescribes a remedy, and takes his leave without depositing any product, that the invalid or his family can transfer to a third person, or even keep for the consumption of a future day.

Has the industry of the physician been unproductive? Who can for a moment suppose so? The patient's life has been saved perhaps. Was this product incapable of becoming an object of barter? By no means; the physician's advice has been exchanged for his fee; but the want of this advice ceased the moment it was given. The act of giving was its production, of hearing its consumption, and the consumption and production were simultaneous.

This is what I call an immaterial product.

The industry of a musician or an actor yields a product of the same kind: it gives one an amusement, a pleasure one can not possibly retain or preserve for future consumption, or as the object of barter for other enjoyments. This pleasure has its price, it is true:

---

* It was my first intention to call these *perishable* products, but this term would be equally applicable to products of a material kind. *Intransferable* would be equally incorrect, for this class of products does pass from the producer to the consumer. The word *transient* does not exclude all idea of duration whatever, neither does the word *momentary*.

but it has no further existence, except perhaps in the memory, and no exchangeable value, after the instant of its production.

Smith will not allow the name of products to the results of these branches of industry. Labour so bestowed he calls unproductive; an error he was led into by his definition of wealth, which he defines to consist of things bearing a value capable of being preserved, instead of extending the name to all things bearing exchangeable value: consequently, excluding products consumed as soon as created. The industry of the physician, however, as well as that of the public functionary, the advocate or the judge, which are all of them of the same class, satisfies wants of so essential a nature, that without those professions no society could exist. Are not, then, the fruits of their labour real? They are so far so, as to be purchased at the price of other and material products, which Smith allows to be wealth; and by the repetition of this kind of barter, the producers of immaterial products acquire fortunes.*

To descend to items of pure amusement, it cannot be denied, that the representation of a good comedy gives as solid a pleasure as a box of comfits, or a discharge of fire-works, which are products, even within Smith's definition. Nor can I discover any sound reason, why the talent of the painter should be deemed productive, and not the talent of the musician.†

Smith himself has exposed the error of the economist in confining the term, wealth, to the mere value of the raw material contained in each product; he advanced a great step in political economy, by demonstrating wealth to consist of the raw material, *plus* the value added to it by industry; but, having gone so far as to promote to the rank of wealth an abstract commodity, *value*, why reckon it as nothing, however real and exchangeable, when not incorporated in matter? This is the more surprising, because he went so far as to treat of labour, abstracted from the matter wherein it is employed; to examine the causes which operate upon and influence its value; and even to propose that value as the safest and least variable measure of all other values.‡

The nature of immaterial products makes it impossible ever to accumulate them, so as to render them a part of the national capital. A people containing a host of musicians, priests, and public functionaries might be abundantly amused, well versed in religious doctrines, and admirably governed; but that is all. Its capital would receive no direct accession from the total labour of all these individuals, though industrious enough in their respective vocations, because their products would be consumed as fast as produced.

---

* Wherefore *de Verri* is wrong in asserting, that the occupations of the sovereign, the magistrate, the soldier, and the priest, do not fall within the cognizance of political economy. (*Meditazioni sulla Economia Politica,* § 24.)

† This error has already been pointed out by *M. Germain Garnier*, in the notes to his French translation of Smith.

‡ Some writers, who have probably taken but a cursory view of the positions here laid down, still persist in setting down the producers of immaterial products

Consequently, nothing is gained on the score of public prosperity, by ingeniously creating an unnatural demand for the labour of any of these professions; the labour diverted into that channel of production can not be increased, without increasing the consumption also. If this consumption yield a gratification, then indeed we may console ourselves for the sacrifice; but when that consumption is itself an evil, it must be confessed the system which causes it is deplorable enough.

This occurs in practice, whenever legislation is too complicated. The study of the law, becoming more intricate and tedious, occupies more persons, whose labour must likewise be better paid. What does society gain by this? Are the respective rights of its members better protected? Undoubtedly not: the intricacy of law, on the contrary, holds out a great encouragement to fraud, by multiplying the chances of evasion, and very rarely adds to the solidity of title or of right. The only advantage is, the greater frequency and duration of suits. The same reasoning applies to superfluous offices in the public administration. To create an office for the administration of what ought to be left to itself, is to do an injury to the subject in the first instance, and make him pay for it afterwards as if it were a benefit.*

Wherefore it is impossible to admit the inference of† M. Garnier, that because the labour of physicians, lawyers, and the like, is productive, therefore a nation gains as much by the multiplication of that class of labour as of any other. This would be the same as bestowing upon a material product more manual labour than is necessary for its completion. The labour productive of immaterial products, like every other labour, is productive so far only as it augments the utility, and thereby the value of a product: beyond this point it is a purely unproductive exertion. To render the laws intricate purposely to give lawyers full business in expounding them, would be equally absurd, as to spread a disease that doctors may find practice.

Immaterial products are the fruit of human industry, in which term we have comprised every kind of productive labour. It is not so easy to understand how they can at the same time be the fruit of capital. Yet these products are for the most part the result of some talent or other, which always implies previous study; and no study can take place without advances of capital.

Before the advice of the physician can be given or taken, the phy-

---

amongst the unproductive labourers. But it is vain to struggle against the nature of things. Those at all conversant with the science of political economy, are compelled to yield involuntary homage to its principles. Thus *Sismondi*, after having spoken of the values expended in the wages of unproductive labourers, goes on to say, " *Ce sont des Consummations rapides qui suivent immediatement la production,*" *Nouv. Princ.* tom. ii. p. 203; admitting a production by those he had pronounced to be unproductive!

* What, then, are we to think of those who assert in substance, if not in words, that such a formality or such a tax is productive of one benefit at least, namely, the maintenance of such or such an establishment of clerks and officers?

† *Traduction de Smith, note* 20.

sician or his relations must first have defrayed the charges of an education of many years' duration : he must have subsisted while a student; professors must have been paid; books purchased; journeys perhaps have been performed ; all which implies the disbursement of a capital previously accumulated.* So likewise the lawyer's opinion, the musician's song, &c. are products, that can never be raised without the concurrence of industry and capital. Even the ability of the public functionary is an accumulated capital. It requires the same kind of outlay, for the education of a civil or military engineer, as for that of a physician. Indeed we may take it for granted, that the funds expended in the training of a young man for the public service, are found by experience to be a fair investment of capital, and that labour of this description is well paid; for we find more applicants than offices in almost every branch of administration, even in countries where offices are unnecessarily multiplied.

The industry productive of immaterial products will be found to go through exactly the same process, as, in the analysis made in the beginning of this work, we have shown to be followed by industry in general. This may be illustrated by an example. Before an ordinary song can be executed, the arts of the composer and the practical musician must have been regular and distinct callings; and the best mode of acquiring skill in them must have been discovered ; this is the department of the man of science, or theorist. The application of this mode and of this art, has been left to the composer and singer, who have calculated, the one in composing his tune, the others in the execution of it, that it would afford a pleasure, to which the audience would attach some value or other. Finally, the execution is the concluding operation of industry.

There are, however, some immaterial products, with respect to which the two first operations are so extremely trifling, that one may almost account them as nothing. Of this description is the service of a menial domestic. The art of service is little or nothing, and the application of that art is made by the employer; so that nothing is left to the servant, but the executive business of service, which is the last and lowest of industrious operations.

It necessarily follows, that, in this class of industry, and some few others practised by the lowest ranks of society, that of the porter for instance, or of the prostitute, &c. &c.: the charge of training being little or nothing, the products may be looked upon not only as the fruits of very coarse and primitive industry, but likewise as products, to the creation of which capital has contributed nothing; for I can not think the expense of these agents' subsistence from infancy, till the age of emancipation from parental care, can be considered as a

* I will not here anticipate the investigation of the profits of industry and capital, but confine myself to observe, *en passant*, that capital is thrown away upon the physician, and his fees improperly limited, unless, besides the recompense of his actual labour and talent, (which latter is a natural agent gratuitously given to him,) they defray the interest of the capital expended in his education, and not the common rate of interest, but calculated at the rate of an annuity.

capital, the interest of which is paid by the subsequent profits. I shall give my reasons for this opinion when I come to speak of wages.*

The pleasures one enjoys at the price of any kind of personal exertion, are immaterial products, consumed at the instant of production by the very person that has created them. Of this description are the pleasures derived from arts studied solely for self-amusement. In learning music, a man devotes to that study some small capital, some time and personal labour; all which together are the price paid for the pleasure of singing a new air or taking part in a concert.

Gaming, dancing, and field-sports, are labours of the same kind. The amusement derived from them is instantly consumed by the persons who have performed them. When a man executes a painting, or makes any article of smith's or joiner's work for his amusement, he at the same time creates a durable product or value, and an immaterial product, viz. his personal amusement.†

In speaking of capital, we have seen, that part of it is devoted to the production of material products, and part remains wholly unproductive. There is also a further part productive of utility or pleasure, which, can, therefore, be reckoned as a portion neither of the capital engaged in the production of material objects, nor of that absolutely inactive. Under this head may be comprised dwelling-houses, furniture and decorations, that are an addition to the mere pleasures of life. The utility they afford is an immaterial product.

When a young couple sets up house-keeping for the first time, the plate they provide themselves with cannot be considered as absolutely inactive capital, for it is in constant domestic use; nor can it be reckoned as capital engaged in the raising of material products; for it leads to the production of no one object capable of being reserved for future consumption; neither is it an object of annual consumption, for it may last, perhaps, for their joint lives, and be handed down to their children; but it is capital productive of utility and pleasure. Indeed, it is so much value accumulated or in other words withdrawn from reproductive consumption; consequently, yielding neither profit nor interest, but productive of some degree of benefit or utility, which is gradually consumed and incapable of being realised, yet it is possessed of real and positive value, since it is occa-

---

* The wages of the mere labourer are limited to the bare necessaries of life, without which his agency cannot be continued and renewed; there is no surplus for the interest on capital. But the subsistence of his children, until old enough to earn their livelihood, is comprised in the necessaries of the labourer.

† An indolent and inert people is always little addicted to amusements result-ing from the exercise of personal faculties. Labour is attended with so much pain to them, as very few pleasures are intense enough to repay. The Turks think us mad to find pleasure in the violent motions of the dance; without reflecting, that it causes to us infinitely less fatigue than to themselves. They prefer pleasures prepared by the fatigue of others. There is, perhaps, as much industry expended on pleasures in Turkey as with us; but it is exerted in general by slaves, who do not participate in the product.

sionally the object of purchase: as in the instance of the rent of a house or the hire of furniture, and the like.

Although it be a sad mistake of personal interest to vest the smallest particle of capital in a manner wholly unproductive, it is by no means so to lay out, in a way productive of utility or amusement, so much as may be not disproportionate to the circumstances of the individual. There is a regular gradation of the ratio of capital so vested by individuals respectively, from the rude furniture of the poor man's hovel, up to the costly ornaments and dazzling jewels of the wealthy. When a nation is rich, the poorest family in it possesses a capital of this kind, not indeed of any great amount, but still enough to satisfy moderate and limited desires. The prevalence of general wealth in a community is more strongly indicated by meeting universally with some useful and agreeable household conveniences in the dwellings of the inferior ranks, than by the splendid palaces and costly magnificence of a few favourites of fortune, or by the casual display of diamonds and finery we sometimes see brought together in a large city, where the whole wealth of the place is often exhibited at one view, at a fête or a theatre of public resort; but which, after all, are a mere trifle, compared with the aggregate value of the household articles of a great people.

The component items of a capital producing bare utility or amusement, are liable to wear and tear, though in a very slight degree; and if that wear and tear be not made good out of the savings of annual revenue, there is a gradual dissipation and reduction of capital.

This remark may appear trifling; yet how many people think they are living upon their revenue, when they are at the same time partially consuming their capital! Suppose, for instance, a man is the proprietor of the house he lives in; if the house be calculated to last 100 years, and have cost 20,000 dollars in the building, it costs the proprietor or his heirs 200 dollars per annum, exclusive of the interest upon the original cost, otherwise the whole capital will be extinguished, or nearly so, by the end of 100 years. The same reasoning is applicable to every other item of capital devoted to the production of utility or pleasure; to a sideboard, a jewel, every imaginable object, in short, that comes under the same denomination.

And, *vice versâ*, when annual revenue, arising from whatever source, is encroached upon for the purpose of enlarging the capital devoted to the production of useful or agreeable objects, there is an actual increase of capital and of fortune, though none of revenue.

Capital of this class, like all other capital, without exception, is formed by the partial accumulations of annual products. There is no other way of acquiring capital, but by personal accumulation, or by succession to accumulation of others. Wherefore, the reader is referred on this head to Chap. XI, where I have treated of the accumulation of capital.

A public edifice, a bridge, a highway, are savings or accumulations of revenue, devoted to the formation of a capital, whose returns are an immaterial product consumed by the public at large. If the construction of a bridge or highway, added to the purchase of the ground it stands upon, have cost 200,000 dollars, the use the public makes of it may be estimated to cost 10,000 dollars per annum.*

There are some immaterial products, towards which the land is a principal contributor. Such is the pleasure derived from a park or pleasure-garden. The pleasure is afforded by the continual and daily agency of the natural object, and is consumed as fast as produced. A ground yielding pleasure must, therefore, not be confounded with ground lying waste or in fallow. Wherein again appears the analogy of land to capital, of which, as we have seen, some part is productive of immaterial products, and some part is altogether inactive.

Gardens and pleasure-grounds have generally cost some expense in embellishment; in which case, capital and land unite their agency to yield an immaterial product.

Some pleasure-grounds yield likewise timber and pasturage: these are productive of both classes of products. The old-fashioned gardens in France yielded no material product; those of modern times are somewhat improved in this particular, and would be more so, if culinary herbs and fruit-trees were oftener introduced. Doubtless, it would be harsh to find fault with a proprietor in easy circumstances, for appropriating part of his freehold to the mere purpose of amusement. The delightful moments he there passes with his family around him, the wholesome exercise he takes, the spirits he inhales, are among the most valuable and substantial blessings of life. By all means then let him lay out on the ground as he likes, and give full scope to his taste, or even caprice; but if caprice can be directed to an useful end, if he can derive profit without abridging enjoyment, his garden will have additional merit, and present a two-fold source of delight to the eye of the statesman and the philosopher.

I have seen some few gardens possessed of this double faculty of production; whence, although the lime, horse-chestnut and sycamore trees, and others of the ornamental kind, were by no means excluded, any more than the lawns and parterres; yet at the same time the fruit-trees, decked in the bloom of vernal promise, or weighed down by the maturity of autumnal wealth, added a variety and richness of colouring to the other local beauties. The advantages of distance and position were attended to without violating the convenience of division and inclosure. The beds and borders, planted with vegetables, were not provokingly straight, regular, or uniform,

---

* If it entail a further charge of 300 dollars for annual repairs and maintenance, the public consumption of pleasure or utility may be set down at 10,200 dollars per annum. This is the only way of taking the account, with a view to compare the advantage derived by the payers of public taxes, with the sacrifices imposed on them for the acquisition of such conveniences. In the case put above, the public will be a gainer, if the outlay of 10,200 dollars have effected an annual saving in the charge of national production, or, what is the same thing, an annual increase of the national product, of still larger amount. In the contrary supposition, the national administration will have led the nation into a losing concern.

but harmonised with the undulations of the surface, and of vegetation of larger growth; and the walks were so disposed as to serve both for pleasure and cultivation. Every thing was arranged with a view to ornament, even to the vine-trelliced well for filling the watering pots. The whole, in short, was so ordered, as if designed to impress the conviction, that utility and beauty are by no means incompatible, and that pleasure may grow up by the side of wealth.

A whole country may, in like manner, grow rich even upon its ornamental possessions. Were trees planted wherever they could thrive without injury to other products,* besides the accession of beauty and salubrity, and the additional moisture attracted by the multiplication of timber-trees, the value of the timber alone would, in a country of much extent, amount to something considerable.

There is this advantage, in the cultivation of timber-trees, that they require no human industry beyond the first planting, after which nature is the sole agent of their production. But it is not enough merely to plant, we must check the desire of cutting down, until the weak and slender stalk, gradually imbibing the juices of the earth and atmosphere, shall, without the hand of cultivation, have acquired bulk and solidity, and spread its lofty foliage to the heavens.† The best that man can do for it is, to forget it for some years; and even where it yields no annual product, it will recompense his forbearance when arrived at maturity, by an ample supply of firing, and of timber for the carpenter, the joiner, and the wheel-wright.

In all ages, the love of trees and their cultivation has been strongly recommended by the best writers. The historian of Cyrus records, among his chief titles to renown, the merit of having planted all Asia Minor. In the United States, upon the birth of a daughter, the cultivator plants a little wood, to grow up with her, and to be her portion on the day of marriage. (1) Sully, whose views of policy were extremely enlightened, enriched most of the provinces of France with the plantation he directed. I have seen several, to which public gratitude still affixes his name; and they remind me of the saying of Addison, who was wont to exclaim, whenever he saw a plantation, "A useful man has passed this way."

---

* In many countries, an exaggerated notion seems to prevail, of the damage done by timber-trees, to other products of the soil; yet it should seem, that they rather enhance than diminish the revenue of the landholder; for we find those countries most productive, that are the best clothed with timber: witness Normandy, England, Belgium and Lombardy.

† The leaves of trees absorb the carbonic-acid gas floating in the atmosphere we breathe, and which is so injurious to respiration. When this gas is superabundant, it brings on *asphyxia*, and occasions death. On the contrary, vegetation increases the proportion of oxygen, which is the gas most favourable to respiration and to health. *Ceteris paribus*, those towns are the healthiest, which have the most open spaces covered with trees. It would be well to plant all our spacious quays.

---

(1) The American cultivator might be said, with much greater semblance of truth, on the birth of a daughter, to cut down "a little wood," instead of planting one. AMERICAN EDITOR.

As yet we have been taken up with the consideration of the agents essential to production; without whose agency mankind would have no other subsistence or enjoyment, than the scanty and limited supply that nature affords spontaneously. We first investigated the mode in which these agents, each in its respective department, and all in concert, co-operate in the work of production, and have afterwards examined in detail the individual action of each, for the further elucidation of the subject. We must now proceed to examine the intrinsic and accidental causes, which act upon production, and clog or facilitate the exertion of productive agents.

CHAPTER XIV.

OF THE RIGHT OF PROPERTY.

It is the province of speculative philosophy to trace the origin of the right of property; of legislation to regulate its transfer; and of political science to devise the surest means of protecting that right. Political economy recognises the right of property solely as the most powerful of all encouragements to the multiplication of wealth, and is satisfied with its actual stability, without inquiring about its origin or its safeguards. In fact, the legal inviolability of property is obviously a mere mockery, where the sovereign power is unable to make the laws respected, where it either practises robbery itself,* or is impotent to repress it in others; or where possession is rendered perpetually insecure, by the intricacy of legislative enactments, and the subtleties of technical nicety. Nor can property be said to exist, where it is not matter of reality as well as of right. Then, and then only, can the sources of production, namely, land, capital, and industry, attain their utmost degree of fecundity. (1)

---

* The strength of an individual is so little, when opposed to that of the government he lives under, that the subject can have no security against the exactions and abuses of authority, except in those countries where the guardianship of the laws is entrusted to the all-searching vigilance of a free press, and their violation checked by an efficient national representation.

---

(1) Although, according to our author, it is the province of speculative philosophy to trace the origin of property, the existence of which, in all politico-economical inquiries, is assumed as the foundation of national wealth, it may not here be improper to introduce a few observations on the *Right of Property*, illustrating its historical origin, and pointing out its true character. Most writers on natural law, among whom may be named Grotius, Puffendorff, Barbeyrac, and Locke, ascribe, in general, the origin of property to priority of occupancy, and have much perplexed themselves in attempting to prove how this act should give an exclusive right of individual enjoyment to what was previously held in common. Blackstone, although he does not enter into the dispute about the manner, as has

There are some truths so completely self-evident, that demonstration is quite superfluous. This is one of that number. For who will attempt to deny, that the certainty of enjoying the fruits of one's

been remarked, in which occupancy conveys a right of property, expresses no doubt about its having this effect, independent of positive institutions.

Later writers on jurisprudence have adopted other theories on the subject of property, which being altogether unsatisfactory, we will not notice, except to remark that the most refined and ingenious speculations, although equally inconclusive, respecting the nature and origin of property, are those of Lord Kames, in the Essay on Property, in his Historical Law Tracts.

DUGALD STEWART, however, is the first inquirer who has taught us to think and reason with accuracy on this subject, and it is to his observations on the *Right of Property*, contained in the supplement to the chapter, "Of Justice," in his work on the "Philosophy of the Active and Moral Powers of Man," that we must refer the reader who is desirous of possessing just and unanswerable arguments for the true foundations on which property rests. We must here content ourselves with extracting a few passages, which will exhibit this illustrious philosopher's views of the origin of the acquisition of property, which he traces to *two* distinct sources.

"It is necessary," says Stewart, "to distinguish carefully the complete right of property, which is founded on labour, from the transient right of possession which is acquired by mere priority of occupancy; thus, before the appropriation of land, if any individual had occupied a particular spot, for repose or shade, it would have been *unjust* to deprive him of possession of it. This, however, was only a transient right. The spot of ground would again become *common*, the moment the occupier had left it; that is, the *right* of possession would remain no longer than the *act* of possession. Cicero illustrates this happily by the similitude of a theatre. 'Quemadmodum theatrum, cum commune sit, recte tamen dici *potest* ejus esse cum locum quem quisque occuparit.' The general conclusions which I deduce are these:—1. That in every state of society labour, wherever it is exerted, is understood to found a right of property. 2. That, according to natural law, labour is the *only* original way of acquiring property. 3. That, according to natural law, mere occupancy founds only a right of possession; and that, whenever it founds a complete right of property, it owes its force to positive institutions."

After premising these leading propositions, he proceeds with what he terms a slight historical sketch of the different systems respecting the origin of property, from which we have only room to copy the following passage, which, however, contains this eminent author's views of the *right of property, as recognised by the law of nature;* and the *right of property, as created by the municipal regulations,* and demonstrating the futility of the attempts hitherto made to resolve all the different phenomena into *one general principle.*

"In such a state of things as that with which we are connected, the right of property must be understood to derive its origin from *two* distinct sources; the one is, that natural sentiment of the mind which establishes a moral connexion between labour and an exclusive enjoyment of the fruits of it; the other is the municipal institutions of the country where we live. These institutions everywhere take rise partly from ideas of natural justice and partly (perhaps chiefly) from ideas of supposed utility,—two principles which, when properly understood, are, I believe, always in harmony with each other, and which it ought to be the great aim of every legislator to reconcile to the utmost of his power. Among those questions, however, which fall under the cognizance of positive laws, there are many on which natural justice is entirely silent, and which, of consequence, may be discussed on principles of *utility* solely. Such are most of the questions concerning the regulation of the succession to a man's property after his death; of some of which it perhaps may be found that the determination ought to vary with the circumstances of the society, and which have certainly, *in fact*, been frequently determined by the caprice of the legislator, or by some principle ulti-

land, capital and labour, is the most powerful inducement to render them productive? Or who is dull enough to doubt, that no one knows so well as the proprietor how to make the best use of his property? Yet how often in practice is that inviolability of property disregarded, which, in theory, is allowed by all to be so immensely advantageous? How often is it broken in upon for the most insignificant purposes; and its violation, that should naturally excite indignation, justified upon the most flimsy pretexts? So few persons are there who have a lively sense of any but a direct injury, or, with the most lively feelings, have firmness enough to act up to their sentiments! There is no security of property, where a despotic authority can possess itself of the property of the subject against his consent. Neither is there such security, where the consent is merely nominal and delusive. In England, the taxes are imposed by the national representation; if, then, the minister be in the possession of an absolute majority, whether by means of electioneering influence, or by the overwhelming patronage foolishly placed at his disposal, taxation would no longer be in reality imposed by the national representatives; the body bearing that name would, in effect, be the representatives of the minister; and the people of England would be forcibly subjected to the severest privations, to further projects that possibly might be every way injurious to them.*

It is to be observed that the right of property is equally invaded, by obstructing the free employment of the means of production, as by violently depriving the proprietor of the product of his land, capital, or industry: for the right of property, as defined by jurists, is the right of use or even abuse. Thus, landed property is violated by arbitrarily prescribing tillage or plantation; or by interdicting particular modes of cultivation; the property of the capitalist is violated, by prohibiting particular ways of employing it; for instance, by interdicting large purchases of corn, directing all bullion to be carried to the mint, forbidding the proprietor to build on his own soil, or prescribing the form and requisites of the building. It is a further violation of the capitalist's property to prohibit any kind of industry, or to load it with duties amounting to prohibition, after he has once embarked his capital in that way. It is manifest, that a prohibition upon sugar would annihilate most of the capital of the sugar refiners, vested in furnaces, utensils, &c. &c. †

The property a man has in his own industry, is violated, whenever

---

mately resolvable into an accidental association of ideas. Indeed, various cases may be supposed in which it is not only useful, but necessary, that a rule should be fixed; while, at the same time, *neither* justice nor utility seem to be much interested in the particular decision."—AMERICAN EDITOR.

* Adam Smith has asserted, that the security afforded to property by the laws of England has more than counteracted the repeated faults and blunders of its government. It may be doubted, whether he would now adhere to that opinion.

† It would be vain to say to him, why not employ your works in some other way? Probably, neither the spot nor the works of a refinery could be otherwise employed without enormous loss.

he is forbidden the free exercise of his faculties and talents, except insomuch as they would interfere with the rights of third parties. A similar violation is committed when a man's labour is put in requisition for one purpose, though designed by himself for another; as when an artisan or trader is forced into the military life, whether permanently or merely for the occasion.

I am well aware, that the importance of maintaining social order, whereon the security of property depends, takes precedence of property itself; for which very reason, nothing short of the necessity of defending that order from manifest danger can authorise these or similar violations of individual right. And this it is which impresses upon the proprietors the necessity of requiring, in the constitution of the body politic, some guarantee or other, that the public service shall never be made a mask to the passions and ambition of those in power.

Thus taxation, when not intended as an engine of national depression and misery, must be proved indispensable to the existence of social order; every step it takes beyond these limits, is an actual spoliation; for taxation, even where levied by national consent, is a violation of property; since no values can be levied, but upon the produce of the land, capital, and industry of individuals.

But there are some extremely rare cases, where interference between the owner and his property is even beneficial to production itself. For example, in all countries that admit the detestable right of slavery, a right standing in hostility to all others, it is found expedient to limit the master's power over his slave. (a) Thus also, if a

---

* The industrious faculties are, of all kinds of property, the least questionable; being derived directly either from nature, or from personal assiduity. The property in them is of higher pretensions than that of the land, which may generally be traced up to an act of spoliation; for it is hardly possible to show an instance, in which its ownership has been legitimately transmitted from the first occupancy. It ranks higher than the right of the capitalist also; for even taking it for granted, that this latter has been acquired without any spoliation whatever, and by the gradual accumulations of ages, yet the succession to it could not have been established without the aid of legislation, which aid may have been granted on conditions. Yet, sacred as the property in the faculties of industry is, it is constantly infringed upon, not only in the flagrant abuse of personal slavery, but in many other points of more frequent occurrence.

A government is guilty of an invasion upon it, when it appropriates to itself a particular branch of industry, the business of exchange and brokerage for example; or when it sells the exclusive privilege of conducting it. It is still a greater violation to authorize a *gendarme*, commissary of police, or judge, to arrest and detain individuals at discretion, on the plea of public safety or security to the constituted authorities; thus depriving the individual of the fair and reasonable certainty of having his time and faculties at his own disposal, and of being able to complete what he may begin upon. What robber or despoiler could commit a more atrocious act of invasion upon the public security, certain as he is of being speedily put down, and counteracted by private as well as public opposition?

(a) This is merely an instance of the necessity of counteracting one poison by another. T.

society stand in urgent need of timber for the shipwright or carpenter, it must reconcile itself to some regulations respecting the felling of private woods;* or the fear of losing the veins of mineral that intersect the soil, may sometimes oblige a government to work the mines itself. It may be readily conceived, that, even if there were no restraints upon mining, want of skill, the impatience of avarice, or the insufficiency of capital, might induce a proprietor to exhaust the superficial, which are commonly the poorest loads, and occasion the loss of superior depth and quality. (1) Sometimes a vein of mineral passes through the ground of many proprietors, but is accessible only in one spot. In this case, the obstinacy of a refractory proprietor must be disregarded, and the prosecution of the works be compulsory; though, after all, I will not undertake to affirm, that it would not be more advisable on the whole to respect his rights, or that the possession of a few additional mines is not too dearly purchased by this infringement upon the inviolability of property.

Lastly, public safety sometimes imperiously requires the sacrifice of private property; but that sacrifice is a violation, notwithstanding an indemnity given in such cases. For the right of property implies the free disposition of one's own; and its sacrifice, however fully indemnified, is a forced disposition.

When public authority is not itself a spoliator, it procures to the nation the greatest of all blessings, protection from spoliation by others. Without this protection of each individual by the united force of the whole community, it is impossible to conceive any considerable development of the productive powers of man, of land, and of capital; or even to conceive the existence of capital at all; for it is nothing more than accumulated value, operating under the safeguard of authority. This is the reason why no nation has ever arrived at any degree of opulence, that has not been subject to a regular government. Civilized nations are indebted to political organization for the innumerable and infinitely various productions, that satisfy their infinite wants, as well as for the fine arts and the opportunities of leisure that accumulation affords, without which the

---

* Probably, also, were it not for maritime wars, originating, sometimes in puerile vanity, and sometimes in national errors of self-interest, commerce would be the best purveyor of timber for ship-building; so that, in reality, the abuse of the interference of public authority, in respect to the growth of private timber, is only a consequence of a previous abuse of a more destructive and less excusable character.

---

(1) [If no one knows so well as the proprietor, how to make the best use of his property, as our author has just remarked, what advantage can result to society from the interference, in any case, of public authority, with the rights of individuals in the business of production. Nothing but the absolute maintenance of the social order should ever be permitted, for an instant, to violate the sacred right of private property. Quite as specious, though equally unsound reasons may be assigned for imposing restraints upon a variety of other employments besides mining.] AMERICAN EDITOR.

faculties of the mind could never be cultivated, or man by their means attain the full dignity, whereof his nature is susceptible.

The poor man, that can call nothing his own, is equally interested with the rich in upholding the inviolability of property. His personal services would not be available, without the aid of accumulations previously made and protected. Every obstruction to, or dissipation of these accumulations, is a material injury to his means of gaining a livelihood; and the ruin and spoliation of the higher is as certainly followed by the misery and degradation of the lower classes. A confused notion of the advantages of this right of property has been equally conducive with the personal interest of the wealthy, to make all civilized communities pursue and punish every invasion of property as a crime. The study of political economy is admirably calculated to justify and confirm this act of legislation; inasmuch as it explains why the happy effects, resulting from the right of property, are more striking in proportion as that right is well guarded by political institutions.

CHAPTER XV.

OF THE DEMAND OR MARKET FOR PRODUCTS.

It is common to hear adventurers in the different channels of industry assert, that their difficulty lies not in the production, but in the disposal of commodities; that products would always be abundant, if there were but a ready demand, or market for them. When the demand for their commodities is slow, difficult, and productive of little advantage, they pronounce money to be scarce; the grand object of their desire is, a consumption brisk enough to quicken sales and keep up prices. But ask them what peculiar causes and circumstances facilitate the demand for their products, and you will soon perceive that most of them have extremely vague notions of these matters; that their observation of facts is imperfect, and their explanation still more so; that they treat doubtful points as matter of certainty, often pray for what is directly opposite to their interests, and importunately solicit from authority a protection of the most mischievous tendency.

To enable us to form clear and correct practical notions in regard to markets for the products of industry, we must carefully analyse the best established and most certain facts, and apply to them the inferences we have already deduced from a similar way of proceeding; and thus perhaps we may arrive at new and important truths, that may serve to enlighten the views of the agents of industry, and to give confidence to the measures of governments anxious to afford them encouragement.

A man who applies his labour to the investing of objects with value by the creation of utility of some sort, can not expect such a value to be appreciated and paid for, unless where other men have the means of purchasing it. Now, of what do these means consist? Of other values of other products, likewise the fruits of industry, capital, and land. Which leads us to a conclusion that may at first sight appear paradoxical, namely, that it is production which opens a demand for products.

Should a tradesman say, " I do not want other products for my woollens, I want money," there could be little difficulty in convincing him that his customers could not pay him in money, without having first procured it by the sale of some other commodities of their own. " Yonder farmer," he may be told, " will buy your woollens, if his crops be good, and will buy more or less according to their abundance or scantiness ; he can buy none at all, if his crops fail altogether. Neither can you buy his wool nor his corn yourself, unless you contrive to get woollens or some other article to buy withal. You say, you only want money ; I say, you want other commodities, and not money. For what, in point of fact, do you want the money ? Is it not for the purchase of raw materials or stock for your trade, or victuals for your support ?* Wherefore, it is products that you want, and not money. The silver coin you will have received on the sale of your own products, and given in the purchase of those of other people, will the next moment execute the same office between other contracting parties, and so from one to another to infinity ; just as a public vehicle successively transports objects one after another. If you can not find a ready sale for your commodity, will you say, it is merely for want of a vehicle to transport it ? For, after all, money is but the agent of the transfer of values. Its whole utility has consisted in conveying to your hands the value of the commodities, which your customer has sold, for the purpose of buying again from you ; and the very next purchase you make, it will again convey to a third person the value of the products you may have sold to others. So that you will have bought, and every body must buy, the objects of want or desire, each with the value of his respective products transformed into money for the moment only. Otherwise, how could it be possible that there should now be bought and sold in France five or six times as many commodities, as in the miserable reign of Charles VI. ? Is it not obvious, that five or six times as many commodities must have been produced, and that they must have served to purchase one or the other ?"

Thus, to say that sales are dull, owing to the scarcity of money, is to mistake the means for the cause ; an error that proceeds from the circumstance, that almost all produce is in the first instance

---

* Even when money is obtained with a view to hoard or bury it, the ultimate object is always to employ it in a purchase of some kind. The heir of the lucky finder uses it in that way, if the miser do not ; for money, as money, has no other use than to buy with.

exchanged for money, before it is ultimately converted into other produce: and the commodity, which recurs so repeatedly in use, appears to vulgar apprehensions the most important of commodities, and the end and object of all transactions, whereas it is only the medium. Sales cannot be said to be dull because money is scarce, but because other products are so. There is always money enough to conduct the circulation and mutual interchange of other values, when those values really exist. Should the increase of traffic require more money to facilitate it, the want is easily supplied, and is a strong indication of prosperity—a proof that a great abundance of values has been created, which it is wished to exchange for other values. In such cases, merchants know well enough how to find substitutes for the product serving as the medium of exchange or money:* and money itself soon pours in, for this reason, that all produce naturally gravitates to that place where it is most in demand. It is a good sign when the business is too great for the money; just in the same way as it is a good sign when the goods are too plentiful for the warehouses.

When a superabundant article can find no vent, the scarcity of money has so little to do with the obstruction of its sale, that the sellers would gladly receive its value in goods for their own consumption at the current price of the day: they would not ask for money, or have any occasion for that product, since the only use they could make of it would be to convert it forthwith into articles of their own consumption.†

This observation is applicable to all cases, where there is a supply of commodities or of services in the market. They will universally find the most extensive demand in those places, where the most of values are produced; because in no other places are the sole means of purchase created, that is, values. Money performs but a momentary function in this double exchange; and when the transaction is finally closed, it will always be found, that one kind of commodity has been exchanged for another.

It is worth while to remark, that a product is no sooner created, than it, from that instant, affords a market for other products to the full extent of its own value. When the producer has put the finishing hand to his product, he is most anxious to sell it immediately, lest its value should diminish in his hands. Nor is he less anxious to dispose of the money he may get for it; for the value of money is also perishable. But the only way of getting rid of money is in the purchase of some product or other. Thus, the mere circum-

---

* By bills at sight, or after date, bank-notes, running-credits, write-offs, &c. as at London and Amsterdam.

† I speak here of their aggregate consumption, whether unproductive and designed to satisfy the personal wants of themselves and their families, or expended in the sustenance of reproductive industry. The woollen or cotton manufacturer operates a two-fold consumption of wool and cotton: 1. For his personal wear. 2. For the supply of his manufacture; but, be the purpose of his consumption what it may, whether personal gratification or reproduction, he must needs buy what he consumes with what he produces.

stance of the creation of one product immediately opens a vent for other products.

For this reason, a good harvest is favourable, not only to the agriculturist, but likewise to the dealers in all commodities generally. The greater the crop, the larger are the purchases of the growers. A bad harvest, on the contrary, hurts the sale of commodities at large. And so it is also with the products of manufacture and commerce. The success of one branch of commerce supplies more ample means of purchase, and consequently opens a market for the products of all the other branches; on the other hand, the stagnation of one channel of manufacture, or of commerce, is felt in all the rest.

But it may be asked, if this be so, how does it happen, that there is at times so great a glut of commodities in the market, and so much difficulty in finding a vent for them? Why cannot one of these superabundant commodities be exchanged for another? I answer that the glut of a particular commodity arises from its having outrun the total demand for it in one or two ways; either because it has been produced in excessive abundance, or because the production of other commodities has fallen short.

It is because the production of some commodities has declined, that other commodities are superabundant. To use a more hackneyed phrase, people have bought less, because they have made less profit;* and they have made less profit for one or two causes; either they have found difficulties in the employment of their productive means, or these means have themselves been deficient.

It is observable, moreover, that precisely at the same time that one commodity makes a loss, another commodity is making excessive profit.† And, since such profits must operate as a powerful stimulus to the cultivation of that particular kind of products, there must needs be some violent means, or some extraordinary cause, a political or natural convulsion, or the avarice or ignorance of authority, to perpetuate this scarcity on the one hand, and consequent glut on the other. No sooner is the cause of this political disease removed, than the means of production feel a natural impulse towards the vacant channels, the replenishment of which restores activity to all the others. One kind of production would seldom outstrip every other, and its products be disproportionately cheapened, were production left entirely free.‡

---

* Individual profits must, in every description of production, from the general merchant to the common artisan, be derived from the participation in the values produced. The ratio of that participation will form the subject of Book II., *infrà*.

† The reader may easily apply these maxims to any time or country he is acquainted with. We have had a striking instance in France during the years 1811, 1812, and 1813; when the high prices of colonial produce of wheat, and other articles, went hand-in-hand with the low price of many others that could find no advantageous market.

‡ These considerations have hitherto been almost wholly overlooked, though forming the basis of correct conclusions in matters of commerce, and of its regulation by the national authority. The right course where it has, by good luck,

Should a producer imagine, that many other classes, yielding no material products, are his customers and consumers equally with the classes that raise themselves a product of their own; as, for example, public functionaries, physicians, lawyers, churchmen, &c., and thence infer, that there is a class of demand other than that of the actual producers, he would but expose the shallowness and superficiality of his ideas. A priest goes to a shop to buy a gown or a surplice; he takes the value, that is to make the purchase, in the form of money. Whence had he that money? From some tax-gatherer who has taken it from a tax-payer. But whence did this latter derive it? From the value he has himself produced. This value, first produced by the tax-payer, and afterwards turned into money, and given to the priest for his salary, has enabled him to make the purchase. The priest stands in the place of the producer, who might himself

---

been pursued, appears to have been selected by accident, or, at most, by a confused idea of its propriety, without either self-conviction, or the ability to convince other people.

Sismondi, who seems not to have very well understood the principles laid down in this and the three first chapters of Book II. of this work, instances the immense quantity of manufactured products with which England has of late inundated the markets of other nations, as a proof, that it is impossible for industry to be too productive. (*Nouv. Prin.* liv. iv. c. 4.) But the glut thus occasioned proves nothing more than the feebleness of production in those countries that have been thus glutted with English manufactures. Did Brazil produce wherewithal to purchase the English goods exported thither, those goods would not glut her market. Were England to admit the import of the products of the United States, she would find a better market for her own in those States. The English government, by the exorbitance of its taxation upon import and consumption, virtually interdicts to its subjects many kinds of importation, thus obliging the merchant to offer to foreign countries a higher price for those articles, whose import is practicable, as sugar, coffee, gold, silver, &c. for the price of the precious metals to them is enhanced by the low price of their commodities, which accounts for the ruinous returns of their commerce. I would not be understood to maintain in this chapter, that one product can not be raised in too great abundance, in relation to all others; but merely that nothing is more favourable to the demand of one product, than the supply of another; that the import of English manufactures into Brazil would cease to be excessive and be rapidly absorbed, did Brazil produce on her side returns sufficiently ample; to which end it would be necessary that the legislative bodies of either country should consent, the one to free production, the other to free importation. In Brazil every thing is grasped by monopoly, and property is not exempt from the invasion of the government. In England, the heavy duties are a serious obstruction to the foreign commerce of the nation, inasmuch as they circumscribe the choice of returns. I happen myself to know of a most valuable and scientific collection of natural history, which could not be imported from Brazil into England by reason of the exorbitant duties. (*a*)

(*a*) The views of *Sismondi*, in this particular, have been since adopted by our own Malthus, and those of our author by Ricardo. This difference of opinion has given rise to an interesting discussion between our author and Malthus, to whom he has recently addressed a correspondence on this and other parts of the science. Were any thing wanting to confirm the arguments of this chapter, it would be supplied by a reference to his *Lettre* 1, *à M. Malthus*. *Sismondi* has vainly attempted to answer Ricardo, but has made no mention of his original antagonist. *Vide Annales de Legislation*, No. 1. art. 3. Geneve, 1820. T.

have laid the value of his product on his own account, in the purchase, perhaps, not of a gown or surplice, but of some other more
serviceable product. The consumption of the particular product, the
gown or surplice, has but supplanted that of some other product. It
is quite impossible that the purchase of one product can be affected,
otherwise than by the value of another.*

From this important truth may be deduced the following important
conclusions :—

1. That, in every community the more numerous are the producers, and the more various their productions, the more prompt,
numerous, and extensive are the markets for those productions; and,
by a natural consequence, the more profitable are they to the producers; for price rises with the demand. But this advantage is to be
derived from real production alone, and not from a forced circulation
of products; for a value once created is not augmented in its passage
from one hand to another, nor by being seized and expended by the
government, instead of by an individual. The man, that lives upon
the productions of other people, originates no demand for those productions; he merely puts himself in the place of the producer, to
the great injury of production, as we shall presently see.

2. That each individual is interested in the general prosperity of
all, and that the success of one branch of industry promotes that of
all the others. In fact, whatever profession or line of business a
man may devote himself to, he is the better paid and the more
readily finds employment, in proportion as he sees others thriving
equally around him. A man of talent, that scarcely vegetates in a
retrograde state of society, would find a thousand ways of turning
his faculties to account in a thriving community that could afford to
employ and reward his ability. A merchant established in a rich
and populous town, sells to a much larger amount than one who sets
up in a poor district, with a population sunk in indolence and apathy.
What could an active manufacturer, or an intelligent merchant, do
in a small deserted and semi-barbarous town in a remote corner of
Poland or Westphalia? Though in no fear of a competitor, he could
sell but little, because little was produced; whilst at Paris, Amsterdam, or London, in spite of the competition of a hundred dealers in
his own line, he might do business on the largest scale. The reason
is obvious: he is surrounded with people who produce largely in an
infinity of ways, and who make purchases, each with his respective
products, that is to say, with the money arising from the sale of
what he may have produced.

This is the true source of the gains made by the towns' people out
of the country people, and again by the latter out of the former; both

---

* The capitalist, in spending the interest of his capital, spends his portion of the
products raised by the employment of that capital. The general rules that regulate the ratio he receives will be investigated in Book II., *infrà*. Should he ever
spend the principal, still he consumes products only; for capital consists of products, devoted indeed to reproductive, but susceptible of unproductive consumption; to which it is in fact consigned whenever it is wasted or dilapidated.

of them have wherewith to buy more largely, the more amply they themselves produce. A city, standing in the centre of a rich surrounding country, feels no want of rich and numerous customers; and, on the other hand, the vicinity of an opulent city gives additional value to the produce of the country. The division of nations into agricultural, manufacturing, and commercial, is idle enough. For the success of a people in agriculture is a stimulus to its manufacturing and commercial prosperity; and the flourishing condition of its manufacture and commerce reflects a benefit upon its agriculture also.*

The position of a nation, in respect of its neighbours, is analogous to the relation of one of its provinces to the others, or of the country to the town; it has an interest in their prosperity, being sure to profit by their opulence. The government of the United States, therefore, acted most wisely, in their attempt, about the year 1802, to civilize their savage neighbours, the Creek Indians. The design was to introduce habits of industry amongst them, and make them producers capable of carrying on a barter trade with the States of the Union; for there is nothing to be got by dealing with a people that have nothing to pay. It is useful and honourable to mankind, that one nation among so many should conduct itself uniformly upon liberal principles. The brilliant results of this enlightened policy will demonstrate, that the systems and theories really destructive and fallacious, are the exclusive and jealous maxims acted upon by the old European governments, and by them most impudently styled *practical truths,* for no other reason, as it would seem, than because they have the misfortune to put them in practice. The United States will have the honour of proving experimentally, that true policy goes hand-in-hand with moderation and humanity.†

---

* A productive establishment on a large scale is sure to animate the industry of the whole neighbourhood. " In Mexico," says Humboldt, " the best cultivated tract, and that which brings to the recollection of the traveller the most beautiful part of French scenery, is the level country extending from Salamanca as far as Silao, Guanaxuato, and Villa de Leon, and encircling the richest mines of the known world. Wherever the veins of precious metal have been discovered and worked, even in the most desert part of the Cordilleras, and in the most barren and insulated spots, the working of the mines, instead of interrupting the business of superficial cultivation, has given it more than usual activity. The opening of a considerable vein is sure to be followed by the immediate erection of a town; farming concerns are established in the vicinity; and the spot so lately insulated in the midst of wild and desert mountains, is soon brought into contact with the tracts before in tillage." *Essai pol. sur. la Nouv. Espagne.*

† It is only by the recent advances of political economy, that these most important truths have been made manifest, not to vulgar apprehension alone, but even to the most distinguished and enlightened observers. We read in Voltaire that "such is the lot of humanity, that the patriotic desire for one's country's grandeur, is but a wish for the humiliation of one's neighbours;——that it is clearly impossible for one country to gain, except by the loss of another." (*Dict. Phil. Art. Patrie.*) By a continuation of the same false reasoning, he goes on to declare, that a thorough citizen of the world cannot wish his country to be greater or less, richer or poorer. It is true, that he would not desire her to extend the limits of her dominion, because, in so doing, she might endanger her own

3. From this fruitful principle, we may draw this further conclusion, that it is no injury to the internal or national industry and production to buy and import commodities from abroad; for nothing can be bought from strangers, except with native products, which find a vent in this external traffic. Should it be objected, that this foreign produce may have been bought with specie, I answer, specie is not always a native product, but must have been bought itself with the products of native industry; so that, whether the foreign articles be paid for in specie or in home products, the vent for national industry is the same in both cases.*

4. The same principle leads to the conclusion, that the encouragement of mere consumption is no benefit to commerce; for the difficulty lies in supplying the means, not in stimulating the desire of consumption; and we have seen that production alone, furnishes those means. Thus, it is the aim of good government to stimulate production, of bad government to encourage consumption.

For the same reason that the creation of a new product is the opening of a new market for other products, the consumption or destruction of a product is the stoppage of a vent for them. This is no evil where the end of the product has been answered by its destruction, which end is the satisfying of some human want, or the creation of some new product designed for such a satisfaction. Indeed, if the nation be in a thriving condition, the gross national re-production exceeds the gross consumption. The consumed products have fulfilled their office, as it is natural and fitting they should; the consumption, however, has opened no new market, but just the reverse.†

Having once arrived at the clear conviction, that the general demand for products is brisk in proportion to the activity of production, we need not trouble ourselves much to inquire towards what channel of industry production may be most advantageously directed. The products created give rise to various degrees of demand, according to the wants, the manners, the comparative capital, industry, and

---

well-being; but he will desire her to progress in wealth, for her progressive prosperity promotes that of all other nations.

* This effect has been sensibly experienced in Brazil of late years. The large imports of European commodities, which the freedom of navigation directed to the markets of Brazil, has been so favourable to its native productions and commerce, that Brazilian products never found so good a sale. So there is an instance of a national benefit arising from importation. By the way, it might have perhaps been better for Brazil if the prices of her products and the profits of her producers had risen more slowly and gradually; for exorbitant prices never lead to the establishment of a permanent commercial intercourse; it is better to gain by the multiplication of one's own products than by their increased price.

† If the barren consumption of a product be of itself adverse to re-production, and a diminution *pro tanto* of the existing demand or vent for produce, how shall we designate that degree of insanity, which would induce a government deliberately to burn and destroy the imports of foreign products, and thus to annihilate the sole advantage accruing from unproductive consumption, that is to say, the gratification of the wants of the consumer?

natural resources of each country; the article most in request,
owing to the competition of buyers, yields the best interest of money
to the capitalist, the largest profits to the adventurer, and the best
wages to the labourer; and the agency of their respective services
is naturally attracted by these advantages towards those particular
channels.

In a community, city, province, or nation, that produces abundantly, and adds every moment to the sum of its products, almost all
the branches of commerce, manufacture, and generally of industry,
yield handsome profits, because the demand is great, and because
there is always a large quantity of products in the market, ready to
bid for new productive services. And, *vice versâ*, wherever, by
reason of the blunders of the nation or its government, production is
stationary, or does not keep pace with consumption, the demand
gradually declines, the value of the product is less than the charges
of its production; no productive exertion is properly rewarded; profits and wages decrease; the employment of capital becomes less
advantageous and more hazardous; it is consumed piecemeal, not
through extravagance, but through necessity, and because the sources
of profit are dried up.* The labouring classes experience a want of
work; families before in tolerable circumstances, are more cramped
and confined; and those before in difficulties are left altogether destitute. Depopulation, misery, and returning barbarism, occupy the
place of abundance and happiness.

Such are the concomitants of declining production, which are
only to be remedied by frugality, intelligence, activity, and freedom.

CHAPTER XVI.

OF THE BENEFITS RESULTING FROM THE QUICK CIRCULATION OF
MONEY AND COMMODITIES.

It is common to hear people descant upon the benefits of an active
circulation; that is to say, of numerous and rapid sales. It is material to appreciate them correctly.

The values engaged in actual production cannot be realized and
employed in production again, until arrived at the last stage of completion, and sold to the consumer. The sooner a product is finished
and sold, the sooner also can the portion of capital vested in it be
applied to the business of fresh production. The capital being
engaged a shorter time, there is less interest payable to the capi-

---

* Consumption of this kind gives no encouragement to future production, but
devours products already in existence. No additional demand can be created,
until there be new products raised; there is only an exchange of one product for
another. Neither can one branch of industry suffer without affecting the rest.

talist; there is a saving in the charges of production; it is, therefore, an advantage, that the successive operations performed in the course of production should be rapidly executed.

By way of illustrating the effects of this activity of circulation, let us trace them in the instance of a piece of printed calico.*

A Lisbon trader imports the cotton from Brazil. It is his interest that his factors in America be expeditious in making purchases and remitting cargoes, and likewise, that he meet no delay in selling his cotton to a French merchant; because he thereby gets his returns the sooner, and can sooner recommence a new and equally lucrative operation. So far, it is Portugal that benefits by the increased activity of circulation; the subsequent advantage is on the side of France. If the French merchant keep the Brazil cotton but a short time in his warehouse, before he sells it to the cotton-spinner, if the spinner after spinning sell it immediately to the weaver, if the weaver dispose of it forthwith to the calico printer, and he in his turn sell it without much delay to the retail dealer, from whom it quickly passes to the consumer, this rapid circulation will have occupied for a shorter period the capital embarked by these respective producers; less interest of capital will have been incurred; consequently the prime cost of the article will be lower, and the capital will have been the sooner disengaged and applicable to fresh operations.

All these different purchases and sales, with many others that, for brevity's sake, I have not noticed, were indispensable before the Brazil cotton could be worn in the shape of printed calicoes. They are so many productive fashions given to this product; and the more rapidly they may have been given, the more benefit will have been derived from the production. But, if the same commodity be merely sold several times over in a year in the same place, without undergoing any fresh modification, this circulation would be a loss instead of a gain, and would increase instead of reducing the prime cost to the consumer. A capital must be employed in buying and re-selling, and interest paid for its use, to say nothing of the probable wear and tear of the commodity.

Thus, jobbing in merchandise necessarily causes a loss, either to the jobber, if the price be not raised by the transaction, or to the consumer, if it be raised.†

The activity of circulation is at the utmost pitch to which it can be carried with advantage, when the product passes into the hands

---

* The term circulation, as well as many others employed in the science of political economy, is daily made use of at random, even by persons that pride themselves upon their precision. "The more equally circulation is diffused," says *La Harpe*, in one of his works, "the less indigence is to be found in the community." With great deference to the learned academician, what possible meaning can the word circulation have in this passage?

† The trade of speculation, as we have before observed, (*suprà*, Chap. IX.) is sometimes of use in withdrawing an article from circulation, when its price is so low as to discourage the producer, and restoring it to circulation, when that price is unnaturally raised upon the consumer.

of a new productive agent the instant it is fit to receive a new modification, and is ultimately handed over to the consumer, the instant it has received the last finish. All kind of activity and bustle not tending to this end, far from giving additional activity to circulation, is an impediment to the course of production—an obstacle to circulation by all means to be avoided.

With respect to the rapidity of production arising from the more skilful direction of industry, it is an increase of rapidity not in circulation, but in productive energy. The advantage is analogous; it abridges the amount of capital employed.

I have made no distinction between the circulation of goods and of money, because there really is none. While a sum of money lies idle in a merchant's coffers, it is an inactive portion of his capital, precisely of the same nature as that part of his capital which is lying in his warehouse in the shape of goods ready for sale.

The best stimulus of useful circulation is, the natural wish of all classes, especially the producers themselves, to incur the least possible amount of interest upon the capital embarked in their respective undertakings. Circulation is much more apt to be interrupted by the obstacles thrown in its way, than by the want of proper encouragement. Its greatest obstructions are, wars, embargoes, oppressive duties, the dangers and difficulties of transportation. It flags in times of alarm and uncertainty, when social order is threatened, and all undertakings are hazardous. It flags, too, under the general dread of arbitrary exactions, when every one tries to conceal the extent of his ability. Finally, it flags in times of jobbing and speculation, when the sudden fluctuations caused by gambling in produce, make people look for a profit from every variation of mere relative price: goods are then held back in expectation of a rise, and money in the prospect of a fall; and, in the interim, both these capitals remain inactive and useless to production. Under such circumstances, there is no circulation, but of such products as cannot be kept without danger of deterioration; as fruits, vegetables, grain, and all articles that spoil in the keeping. With regard to them, it is thought wiser to incur the loss of present sale, whatever it be, than to risk considerable or total loss. If the national money be deteriorated, it becomes an object to get rid of it in any way, and exchange it for commodities. This was one of the causes of the prodigious circulation that took place during the progressive depreciation of the French *assignats*. Everybody was anxious to find some employment for a paper currency, whose value was hourly depreciating; it was only taken to be re-invested immediately, and one might have supposed it burnt the fingers it passed through. On that occasion, men plunged into business, of which they were utterly ignorant; manufactures were established, houses repaired and furnished, no expense was spared even in pleasure; until at length all the value each individual possessed in *assignats* was finally consumed, invested or lost altogether.

CHAPTER XVII.

OF THE EFFECT OF GOVERNMENT REGULATIONS INTENDED TO INFLUENCE PRODUCTION.

STRICTLY speaking, there is no act of government but what has some influence upon production. I shall confine myself in this chapter to such as are avowedly aimed at the exertion of such influence; reserving the effects of the monetary system, of loans, and of taxes, to be treated of in distinct chapters.

The object of governments, in their attempts to influence production, is, either to prescribe the raising of particular kinds of produce which they judge more advantageous than others, or to prescribe methods of production, which they imagine preferable to other methods. The effects of this two-fold attempt upon national wealth will be investigated in the two first sections of this chapter; in the remaining two, I shall apply the same principles to the particular cases of privileged companies, and of the corn-trade, both on account of their vast importance, and for the purpose of further explaining and illustrating the principles. We shall see, by the way, what reasons and circumstances will require or justify a deviation from general principles. The grand mischiefs of authoritative interference proceed not from occasional exceptions to established maxims, but from false ideas of the nature of things, and the false maxims built upon them. It is then that mischief is done by wholesale, and evil pursued upon system; for it is well to beware, that no set of men are more bigoted to system, than those who boast that they go upon none.*

SECTION I.

Effect of Regulations prescribing the Nature of Products.

The natural wants of society, and its circumstances for the time being, occasion a more or less lively demand for particular kinds of products. Consequently, in these branches of production, productive services are somewhat better paid than in the rest; that is to say, the profits upon land, capital and labour, devoted to those branches of production, are somewhat larger. This additional profit naturally

---

* The greatest sticklers for adhering to practical notions, set out with the assertion of general principles: they begin, for instance, with saying, that no one can dispute the position, that one individual can gain only what another loses, and one nation profit only by the sacrifices of another. What is this but system? and one so unsound, that its abettors, instead of possessing more practical knowledge than other people, show their utter ignorance of many facts, the acquaintance with which is indispensable to the formation of a correct judgment. No man, who understands the real nature of production, and sees how new wealth may be, and is daily created, would attempt to advance so gross an absurdity.

attracts producers, and thus the nature of the products is always regulated by the wants of society.   We have seen in a preceding chapter (XV.,) that these wants are more ample in proportion to the sum of gross production, and that society in the aggregate is a larger purchaser, in proportion to its means of purchasing.

When authority throws itself in the way of this natural course of things, and says, the product you are about to create, that which yields the greatest profit, and is consequently the most in request, is by no means the most suitable to your circumstances, you must undertake some other, it evidently directs a portion of the productive energies of the nation towards an object of less desire, at the expense of another of more urgent desire.

In France, about the year 1794, there were some persons persecuted, and even brought to the scaffold, for having converted cornland into pasturage.   Yet the moment these unhappy people found it more profitable to feed cattle than to grow corn, one might have been sure that society stood more in need of cattle than of corn, and that greater value could be produced in one way than in the other.

But, said the public authorities, the value produced is of less importance than the nature of the product, and we would rather have you raise 10 dollars worth of grain than 20 dollars worth of butcher's meat.   In this they betrayed their ignorance of this simple truth, that the greatest product is always the best; and that an estate, which should produce in butcher's meat wherewith to purchase twice as much wheat as could have been raised upon it, produces, in reality, twice as much wheat as if it had been sowed with grain; since wheat to twice the amount is to be got for its product. This way of getting wheat, they will tell you, does not increase its total quantity.   True, unless it be introduced from abroad; but nevertheless, this article must at the time be relatively more plentiful than butcher's meat, because the product of two acres of wheat is given for that of one acre of pasture.*   And, if wheat be sufficiently scarce, and in sufficient request to make tillage more profitable than grazing, legislative interference is superfluous altogether; for self-interest will make the producer turn his attention to the former.

The only question then is, which is the most likely to know what kind of cultivation yields the largest returns, the cultivator or the government; and we may fairly take it for granted, that the cultivator, residing on the spot, making it the object of constant study and inquiry, and more interested in success than anybody, is better informed in this respect than the government.

---

* At the disastrous period in question, there was no actual want of wheat; the growers merely felt a disinclination to sell for paper money.   Wheat was sold for real value at a very reasonable rate ; and, though a hundred thousand acres of pasture land had been converted into arable, the disinclination to exchange wheat for a discredited paper-money would not have been a jot reduced.

Should it be insisted upon in argument, that the cultivator knows only the price-current of the day, and does not, like the government, provide for the future wants of the people, it may be answered, that one of the talents of a producer, and a talent his own interest obliges him assiduously to cultivate, is not the mere knowledge, but the foreknowledge, of human wants.*

An evil of the same description was occasioned, when, at another period, the proprietors were compelled to cultivate beet-root, or woad in lieu of grain: indeed, we may observe, *en passant*, that it is always a bad speculation to attempt raising the products of the torrid, under the sun of the temperate latitudes. The saccharine and colouring juices, raised on the European soils, with all the forcing in the world, are very inferior in quantity and quality to those that grow in profusion in other climates;† while, on the other hand, those soils yield abundance of grain and fruits too bulky and heavy to be imported from a distance. In condemning our lands to the growth of products ill suited to them, instead of those they are better calculated for, and, consequently, buying very dear what we might have cheap enough, if we would consent to receive them from places where they are produced with advantage, we are ourselves the victims of our own absurdity. It is the very *acme* of skill, to turn the powers of nature to best account, and the height of madness to contend against them; which is in fact wasting part of our strength, in destroying those powers she designed for our aid.

Again, it is laid down as a maxim, that it is better to buy products dear, when the price remains in the country, than to get them cheap from foreign growers. On this point I must refer my readers to that analysis of production which we have just gone through. It will there be seen, that products are not to be obtained without some sacrifice,—without the consumption of commodities and productive services in some ratio or other, the value of which is in this way as completely lost to the community, as if it were to be exported.‡

* Of course, in extraordinary cases, like that of a siege or a blockade, ordinary rules of conduct must be disregarded. However irksome the necessity, violent obstructions to the natural course of human affairs must be removed by counteracting violence; poison is in dangerous cases resorted to as a medicine; but these remedies require extreme care and skill in the application.

† *M. de Humboldt* has remarked, that seven square leagues of land in a tropical climate, can furnish as much sugar as the utmost consumption of France, in its best days, has ever required.

‡ In the sequel of this chapter, it will be shown, that values exported give precisely the same encouragement to domestic industry, as if they are consumed at home. In the instance just cited, suppose that wine had been grown instead of the sugar of beet-root, or the blue dye of woad, the domestic and agricultural industry of the nation would have been quite as much encouraged. And, since the product would have been more congenial to the climate, the wine produced from the same land would have procured a larger quantity of colonial sugar and indigo through the channel of commerce, even if conducted by neutrals or enemies. The colonial sugar and indigo would have been equally the product of our own land, though first assuming the shape of wine; only the same space of land would have produced them in superior quantity and quality. And the encouragement to domestic industry would be the same, or rather would be

I can hardly suppose any government will be bold enough to object, that it is indifferent about the profit, which might be derived from a more advantageous production, because it would fall to the lot of individuals. The worst governments, those which set up their own interest in the most direct opposition to that of their subjects, have by this time learnt, that the revenues of individuals are the regenerating source of public revenue; and that, even under despotic and military sway, where taxation is mere organized spoliation, the subjects can pay only what they have themselves acquired.

The maxims we have been applying to agriculture are equally applicable to manufacture. Sometimes a government entertains a notion, that the manufacture of a native raw material is better for the national industry, than the manufacture of a foreign raw material. It is in conformity to this notion, that we have seen instances of preference given to the woollen and linen above the cotton manufacture. By this conduct we contrive, as far as in us lies, to limit the bounty of nature, which pours forth in different climates a variety of materials adapted to our innumerable wants. Whenever human efforts succeed in attaching to these gifts of nature a value, that is to say, a degree of utility, whether by their import, or by any modification we may subject them to, a useful act is performed, and an item added to national wealth. The sacrifice we make to foreigners in procuring the raw material is not a whit more to be regretted, than the sacrifice of advances and consumption, that must be made in every branch of production, before we can get a new product. Personal interest is, in all cases, the best judge of the extent of the sacrifice, and of the indemnity we may expect for it; and, although this guide may sometimes mislead us, it is the safest in the long-run, as well as the least costly.*

But personal interest is no longer a safe criterion, if individual

---

greater; because a product of superior value would reward more amply the agency of the land, capital, and industry, engaged in the production.

* One is obliged every moment to turn round and combat objections, that never could have been started, if the science of political economy had been more widely diffused. It will here, for instance, in all probability, be said,—granting that the sacrifice made in the purchase of the raw flax for manufacture, and that made in the purchase of cotton, is to the manufacturer or merchant equal in the one case and the other,—still, in the one case, the amount of the sacrifice is expended and consumed in the nation itself, and conduces to the national advantage; in the other, the whole advantage goes to the foreign grower. I answer, the advantage goes to the nation in either case; for the foreign raw material, cotton, cannot be purchased, except with a domestic product, which must be bought of the national grower before the merchant can go to market; whether flax or any thing else, it must be some value of domestic creation. Why may he not buy with money? Money itself must have been originally purchased with some other product, which must have employed domestic industry, as much as the growth of flax. Turn it which way you will, it comes to the same thing in the end. Wealth can only be acquired by the production of value, or lost by its consumption; and, putting absolute robbery out of the question, the whole consumption of a nation must always be supplied from its internal resources, its land, capital, and industry, even that portion of it which falls upon external objects.

interests are not left to counteract and control each other. If one individual, or one class, can call in the aid of authority to ward off the effects of competition, it acquires a privilege to the prejudice and at the cost of the whole community; it can then make sure of profits not altogether due to the productive services rendered, but composed in part of an actual tax upon consumers for its private profit; which tax it commonly shares with the authority that thus unjustly lends its support.

The legislative body has great difficulty in resisting the importunate demands for this kind of privileges; the applicants are the producers that are to benefit thereby, who can represent, with much plausibility, that their own gains are a gain to the industrious classes, and to the nation at large, their workmen and themselves being members of the industrious classes, and of the nation.*

When the cotton manufacture was first introduced in France, all the merchants of Amiens, Rheims, Beauvais, &c. joined in loud remonstrances, and represented, that the industry of these towns was annihilated. Yet they do not appear less industrious or rich than they were fifty years ago; while the opulence of Rouen and all Normandy has been wonderfully increased by the new fabric.

The outcry was infinitely greater, when printed calicoes first came into fashion; all the chambers of commerce were up in arms; meetings, discussions everywhere took place; memorials and deputations poured in from every quarter, and great sums were spent in the opposition. Rouen now stood forward to represent the misery about to assail her, and painted, in moving colours, "old men, women, and children, rendered destitute; the best cultivated lands in the kingdom lying waste, and the whole of a rich and beautiful province depopulated." The city of Tours urged the lamentations of the deputies of the whole kingdom, and foretold "a commotion that would shake the frame of social order itself." Lyons could not view in silence a project "which filled all her manufactories with alarm." Never on so important an occasion had Paris presented itself at the foot of a throne, "watered with the tears of commerce." Amiens viewed the introduction of printed calicoes as the gulf that must inevitably swallow up all the manufactures of the kingdom. The memorial of that city, drawn up at a joint meeting of the three corporations, and signed unanimously, ended in these terms: "To conclude, it is enough for the eternal prohibition of the use of printed calicoes, that the whole kingdom is chilled with horror at the news of their proposed toleration. *Vox populi vox dei.*"

Hear what Roland de la Platiere, who had the presentation of these remonstrances in quality of inspector-general of manufactures, says on this subject, "Is there a single individual at the present

---

* No one cries out against them, because very few know who it is that pays the gains of the monopolist. The real sufferers, the consumers themselves, often feel the pressure, without being aware of the cause of it, and are the first to abuse the enlightened individuals, who are really advocating their interests.

moment, who is mad enough to deny, that the fabric of printed calicoes employs an immense number of hands, what with the dressing
of cotton, the spinning, weaving, bleaching, and printing? This
article has improved the art of dyeing in a few years, more than all
the other manufactures together have done in a century."

I must beg my readers to pause a moment, and reflect, what firmness and extensive information respecting the sources of public prosperity were necessary to uphold an administration against so general
a clamour, supported, amongst the principal agents of authority, by
other motives, besides that of public utility.

Though governments have too often presumed upon their power
to benefit the general wealth, by prescribing to agriculture and
manufacture the raising of particular products, they have interfered
much more particularly in the concerns of commerce, especially of
external commerce. These bad consequences have resulted from a
general system, distinguished by the name of the *exclusive* or *mercantile system*, which attributes the profits of a nation to what is
technically called *a favourable balance of trade*. Before we enter
upon the investigation of the real effect of regulations, intended to
secure to a nation this balance in its favour, it may be as well to
form some notion of what it really is, and what is its professed
object; which I shall attempt in the following

DIGRESSION,

UPON WHAT IS CALLED THE BALANCE OF TRADE.

The comparison a nation makes between the value of its exports
to, and that of its imports from, foreign countries, forms what is
called the balance of its trade. If it have exported more commodities than it has imported, it is taken for granted that the nation has
to receive the difference in gold and silver; and the balance of trade
is then said to be in its favour; and when the case is reversed, the
balance is said to be against it.

The exclusive system proceeds upon these maxims: 1. That the
commerce of a nation is advantageous, in proportion as its exports
exceed its imports, and as there is a larger cash balance receivable
in specie, or in the precious metals: 2. That by means of duties,
prohibitions, and bounties, the government can make that balance
more in favour of, or less against, the nation.

These two maxims must be analysed minutely in the first place;
then, let us see what is the course of practice.

When a merchant sends goods abroad, he causes them to be there
sold, and receives, by the hands of his foreign correspondents, the
price of his goods, in the money of the country. If he expects to
make a profit upon the return cargo, he causes that price to be laid
out in foreign produce, and remitted home to him. The operation
is with little variation the same, when he begins at the other end;
that is to say, by making purchases abroad, which he pays for by

remitting domestic products thither. These operations are not always executed on account of the same merchant. It sometimes happens that the trader, who undertakes the outward, will not undertake the homeward adventure. In that case he draws bills payable after date, or upon sight, upon his correspondents, by whom the goods have been sold; these bills he sells or negotiates, to somebody, who sends them to the place they are drawn upon, where they are made use of in the purchase of fresh goods, which the last mentioned person imports himself.*

In both cases, one value is exported, another value is imported in return ; but we have not to stop to inquire, if any part of the value either exported or imported consisted of the precious metals. It may reasonably be assumed, that merchants, when left the free choice of what goods they will speculate in, will prefer those that offer the largest profit ; that is to say, those which will bear the greatest value when they arrive at the place of destination. For example, a French merchant has consigned brandies to England, and has to receive from England for such his consignment, 1000*l.* sterling : he naturally sits down to calculate the difference between what he will receive, if he import his 1000*l.* in the shape of the precious metals, and what he will receive, if he import that sum in the shape of cotton manufactures.†

* What has been said of one trader, may be said equally of two—three,—in short, of all the traders in the nation. As far as concerns the balance of commerce, the operations of the whole will resolve themselves into what I have just stated. Individual losses may occur on either side, from the folly or knavery of some few of the traders engaged ; but we may take it for granted, that they will, on the average, be inconsiderable, in comparison with the total of business done ; at all events, the losses on the one side will commonly balance those on the other.

It is of very little importance to our purpose to inquire, by whom the charge of transport is borne: usually, the English trader pays the freight of the goods he buys, and imports from France, and the French trader does the same upon his purchases from England ; both of them look for the reimbursement of this outlay to the value added to the articles by the circumstance of transport.

† It may be well here to point out a manifest blunder of some partisans of the exclusive system. They look upon nothing that a nation receives from abroad as a national gain, except what is received in the form of specie ; which is in effect, to maintain, that a hatter who sells a hat for 5 dollars gains the whole 5 dollars, because he receives it in specie. But this cannot be ; money, like other things, is itself a commodity. A French merchant consigns to England, brandies to the amount of 20,000 *fr.*: his commodity was equivalent in France to that sum in specie ; if it sell in England for 1000*l.* sterling, and that sum remitted in gold or silver be worth 24,000 *fr.* there is a gain of 4000 *fr.* only, although France has received 24,000 *fr.* in specie. And, should the merchant lay out his 1000*l.* sterling in cotton goods, and be able to sell them in France for 28,000 *fr.* there would then be a gain to the importer and to the nation of 8000 *fr.*, although no specie whatever had been brought into the country. In short, the gain is precisely the excess of the value received above the value given for it, whatever be the form in which the import is made.

It is curious enough, that the more lucrative external commerce is, the greater must be the excess of the import above the export ; and that the very thing, which the partisans of the exclusive system deprecate as a calamity, is of all

If the merchant find it more advantageous to get his returns in goods than in specie, and if it be admitted, that he knows his own interest better than anybody else, the sole point left for discussion is, whether returns in specie, though less advantageous to the merchant, may not be better for the nation, than returns of any other article: whether, in short, it be desirable in a national point of view, that the precious metals should abound, in preference to any other commodity.

What are the functions of the precious metals in the community? If shaped into trinkets or plate, they serve for personal ornament, for the splendour of our domestic establishments, or for a variety of domestic purposes; they are converted into watch-cases, spoons, forks, dishes, coffee-pots; or rolled out into leaves for the embellishment of picture frames, book-binding, and the like; in which case, they form part of that portion of the capital of the community, which yields no interest, but is devoted to the production of utility or pleasure. It is doubtless an advantage to the nation, that the material, whereof this portion of its capital consists, should be cheap and abundant. The enjoyment they afford in these various ways is then obtained at a lower rate, and is more widely diffused. There are many establishments on a moderate scale, which, but for the discovery of America, would have been unable to make the show of plate that is now seen upon their tables. But this advantage must not be over-rated; there are other utilities of a much higher order. The

---

things to be desired. I will explain why. When there has been an export of 10, and an import in return of 11 millions, there is in the nation a value of 1 million more than before the interchange. And, in spite of the specious statements of the balance of commerce, this must almost always be so, otherwise the traders would gain nothing. In fact, the value of the export is estimated at its value before shipment, which is increased by the time it reaches its destination: with this augmented value the return is purchased, which also receives a like accession of value by the transport. The value of this import is estimated at the time of entry. Thus, the result is the presence of a value equal to that exported, *plus* the gains outward and homeward. Wherefore, in a thriving country, the value of the total imports should always exceed that of the exports. What then are we to think of the Report of the French Minister of the Interior of 1813, who makes the total exports to have been 383 millions of *francs*, and the total imports, exclusive of specie, but 350 millions; a statement upon which he felicitates a nation, as the most favourable that had ever been presented. Whereas, this balance shows, on the contrary, what everybody felt and knew, that the commerce of France was then making immense losses, in consequence of the blunders of her administration, and the total ignorance of the first principles of political economy.

In a tract upon the kingdom of Navarre in Spain, (*Annales des Voyages*, tom. i. p. 312,) I find it stated, that, on the comparison of the value of the exports with that of the imports of that kingdom, there is found to be an annual excess of the former above the latter of 120,000 dollars. Upon which the author very sagely observes, "that if there be one truth more indisputable than another, it is this, that a nation which is growing rich cannot be importing more than it is exporting, for then its capital must diminish perceptibly. And, since Navarre is in a state of gradual improvement, as appears from the advance of population and comfort, it is clear,"—that I know nothing about the matter, he might have added;—" for I am citing an established fact to give the lie to an indisputable principle." We are every day witnessing contradictions of the same kind.

window-glass, that keeps out the inclemency of the weather, is of much more importance to our comfort, than any species of plate whatsoever; yet no one has ever thought of encouraging its import or production by special favour or exemptions.

The other utility of the precious metals is, to act as the material of money, that is to say, of that portion of the national capital, which is employed in facilitating the interchange of existing values between one individual and another. For this purpose, is it any advantage that the material selected should be abundant and cheap? Is a nation, that is more amply provided with that material, richer than one which is more scantily supplied?

I must here take leave to anticipate a position, established in Chap. XXI. of this book, wherein the subject of money is considered, namely, that the total business of national exchange and circulation, requires a given quantity of the commodity, money, of some amount or other. There is in France a daily sale of so much wheat, cattle, fuel, property movable and immovable, which sale requires the daily intervention of a given value in the form of money, because every commodity is first converted into money, as a step towards its further conversion into other objects of desire. Now, whatever be the relative abundance or scarcity of the article money, since a given *quantum* is requisite for the business of circulation, the money must of course advance in value, as it declines in quantity, and decline in value as it advances in quantity. Suppose the money of France to amount now to 3000 millions of *francs*,* and that by some event, no matter what, it be reduced to 1500 millions; the 1500 millions will be quite as valuable as the 3000 millions. The demands of circulation require the agency of an actual value of 3000 millions; that is to say, a value equivalent to 2000 millions of pounds of sugar, (taking sugar at 30 *sous* per lb.) or to 180 millions of *hectolitres* of wheat (taking wheat at 20 *fr.* the *hectolitre*). Whatever be the weight or bulk of the material, whereof it is made, the total value of the national money will still remain at that point; though in the latter case, that material will be twice as valuable as in the former. An ounce of silver will buy eight instead of four lbs. of sugar, and so of all other commodities; and the 1500 millions of coin will be equivalent to the former 3000. But the nation will be neither richer nor poorer than before. A man who goes to market with a less quantity of coin, will be able to buy with it the same quantity of commodities. A nation that has chosen gold for the material of its money, is equally rich with one that has made choice of silver, though the volume of its money be much less. Should silver become fifteen times as scarce as at present, that is to say, as scarce as gold now is, an ounce of silver would perform the same functions, in the character of money, as an ounce of gold now does; and we should be equally rich in money. Or, should it fall to a par with copper, we should not be a

---

* 564 millions of dollars.

iot the richer in the article of money; we should merely be encumbered with a more bulky medium of circulation.

On the score, then, of the other utilities of the precious metals, and on that score only, their abundance makes a nation richer, because it extends the sphere of those utilities, and diffuses their use. In the character of money, that abundance no wise contributes to national enrichment;* but the habits of the vulgar lead them to pronounce an individual rich, in proportion to the quantity of money he is possessed of; and this notion has been extended to national wealth, which is made up of the aggregate of individuals' wealth. Wealth, however, as before observed, consists, not in the matter or substance, but in the value of that matter or substance. A money of large, is worth no more than a money of small volume; neither is a money of small, of less value than one of large volume. Value, in the form of commodities, is equivalent to value to the same amount in the form of money.

It may be asked, why, then, is money so generally preferred to commodities, when the value on both sides is equal? This requires a little explanation. When I come to treat of money, it will be shown, that the coined metal of equal value commands a preference, because it insures to the holder the attainment of the objects of desire by means of one exchange instead of two. He is not, like the holder of any other commodity, obliged, in the first instance, to exchange his own commodity, money, for the purpose of obtaining, by a second exchange, the object of his desire; one act of exchange suffices; and this it is, combined with the extreme facility of apportionment, afforded by graduated denominations of the coin, which renders it so useful in exchanges of value. Every individual, who has an exchange to make, becomes a consumer of the commodity, money; that is to say, every individual in the community; which accounts for the universal preference of money to commodities at large, where the value is equal.

---

* It is a necessary inference from these positions, that a nation gains in wealth by the partial export of its specie, because the residue is of equal value to the total previous amount, and the nation receives an equivalent for the portion exported. How is this to be accounted for? By the peculiar property of money to exhibit its utility in the exercise, not of its physical or material qualities, but those of its value alone. A less quantity of bread will less satisfy the cravings of hunger; but a less quantity of money may possess an equal amount of utility; for its value augments with the diminution of its volume, and its value is the sole ground of its employment.

Whence it is evident, that governments should shape their course in the opposite direction to that pursued at present, and encourage, instead of discouraging, the export of specie. And so they assuredly will, when they shall understand their business better: or rather, they will attempt neither the one nor the other, for it is impossible that any considerable portion of the national specie can leave the country, without raising the value of the residue. And when it is raised, less of it is given in exchange for commodities, which are then low in price, so as to make it advantageous again to import specie and export commodities, by which action and reaction the quantity of the precious metals is, in spite of all regulations, kept pretty nearly at the amount required by the wants of the nation.

But this superiority of money, in the interchange between individuals, does not extend to that between nation and nation. In the latter, money, and, *à fortiori*, bullion, lose all the advantage of their peculiar character, as money, and are dealt with as mere commodities. The merchant, who has remittances to make from abroad, looks ·at nothing but the gain to be made on those remittances, and treats the precious metals as a commodity he can dispose of with more or less benefit. In his eyes, an exchange more or less is no object; for it is his business to negotiate exchanges, so as to get a profit upon them. An ordinary person might prefer to receive money instead of goods, because it is an article, whose value he is better acquainted with: but a merchant, who is apprised of the prices current in most of the markets of the world, knows how to appreciate the value he receives in return, whatever shape it may appear under.

An individual may be under the necessity of liquidating, for the purpose of giving a new direction to his capital, or of partition, or the like. A nation is never obliged to do so. This liquidation is effected with the circulating money of the nation, which it occupies only for the time; the same money going almost immediately to operate another act of liquidation or of exchange.

We have seen above (Chap. XV.) that the abundance of specie is not even necessary for the national facilitation of exchanges and sales; for that buyers really buy with products,—each with his respective portion of the products he has concurred in creating: that with this he buys money, which serves but to buy some further product; and that, in this operation, money affords but a temporary convenience; like the vehicles employed to convey to market the produce of a farm, and to bring back the articles that have been purchased with the produce. Whatever amount of money may have been employed in the purchase of liquidation, it has passed for as much as it was taken for: and, at the close of the transaction, the individual is neither richer nor poorer. The loss or profit arises out of the nature of the transaction itself, and has no reference to the medium employed in the course of it.

In no one way do the causes, that influence individual preference of money to commodities, operate upon international commerce. When the nation has a smaller stock than its necessities require, its value within the nation is raised, and foreign and native merchants are equally interested in the importation of more: when it is redundant, its relative value to commodities at large is reduced, and it becomes advantageous to export to that spot, where its command of commodities may be greater than at home. To retain it by compulsory measures, is to force individuals to keep what is a burthen to them.*

---

* No one but an entire stranger to these matters would here be inclined to object, that money can never be burthensome, and is always disposed of easily enough. So it may be, indeed, by such as are content to throw its value away altogether, or at least, to make a disadvantageous exchange. A confectioner

And here I might, perhaps, now dismiss the subject of the balance of trade; but such is the prevailing ignorance on this topic, and so novel are the views I have been taking, even to persons of the better classes, to writers and statesmen of the purest intentions and well informed on other points, that it may be worth while to put the reader on his guard against some fallacies which are often set up in opposition to liberal principles, and are unfortunately the groundwork of the prevailing policy of most of the European States. I shall uniformly reduce the objections to the simplest terms possible, that their weight may be the more easily estimated.

It is said, that, by increasing the currency through the means of a favourable balance of trade, the total capital of a nation is augmented; and, on the contrary, by diminishing it, that capital is reduced. But it must be always kept in mind, that capital consists, not of so much silver or gold, but of the values devoted to reproductive consumption, which values necessarily assume an infinite variety of successive forms. When it is intended to vest a given capital in any concern, or to place it out at interest, the first step is undoubtedly to realize the amount, by converting * into ready money the different

---

may give away his sugar-plums, or eat them himself; but in that case he loses the value of them. It should be observed, that the abundance of specie is compatible with national misery; for the money, that goes to buy bread, must have been bought itself with other products. And, when production has to contend with adverse circumstances, individuals are in great distress for money, not because that article is scarce, which oftentimes it is not, but because the creation of the products, wherewith it is procurable, can not be effected with advantage.

* A merchant's leger for two successive years may show him richer in the end of the second, than at the end of the first, although possessed of a smaller amount of specie. Suppose the first year's amount to stand thus:—

	Dollars.
Ground and buildings	8000
Machinery and movables	4000
Stock in hand	3000
Balance of good credits	1000
Cash	4000
Total	20,000

And the second year's thus:—

	Dollars.
Ground and buildings	8000
Machinery and movables	5000
Stock in hand	6000
Balance of good credits	2000
Cash	1000
Total	22,000

Exhibiting an increase of 2000 dollars, although his cash be reduced to one quarter of the former amount.

A similar account, differing only in the ratios of the different items, might be made out for the whole of the individuals in the community, who would then be evidently richer, though possessed of much less specie or cash.

values one has at command. The value of the capital, thus assuming the transient form of money, is quickly transmuted by one exchange after another into buildings, works, and perishable substances requisite for the projected enterprise. The ready money employed for the occasion passes again into other hands, for the purpose of facilitating fresh exchanges, as soon as it has accomplished its momentary duty; in like manner as do many other substances, the shape of which this capital successively assumes. So that the value of capital is neither lost nor impaired by parting with its value, whatever material shape it happens to be under, provided that we part with it in a way that ensures its renovation.

Suppose a French dealer in foreign commodities to consign to a foreign country a capital of 10,000 dollars in specie for the purchase of cotton; when his cotton arrives, he possesses 20,000 dollars value in cotton instead of specie, putting his profit out of the question for the moment. Has anybody lost this amount of specie? Certainly not: the adventurer has come honestly by it. A cotton manufacturer gives cash for the cargo; is he the loser of the price? No, surely: on the contrary, the article in his hands will increase to twice its value, so as to leave him a profit, after repaying all his advances. If no individual capitalist has lost the 20,000 dollars exported, how can the nation have lost them? The loss will fall on the consumer, they will tell you: in fact, all the cotton goods bought and consumed will be so much positive loss; but the same consumers might have consumed linens or woollens of exactly the same value, without one dollar of the 20,000 being sent out of the country, and yet there would equally be a loss or consumption to that amount of value. The loss of value we are now speaking of is not occasioned by the export, but by the consumption, which might have taken place without any export whatever. I may, therefore, say, with the strictest truth, that the export of the specie has caused no loss at all to the nation.

It has been urged, with much confidence, that, had the export of 20,000 dollars never been made, France would remain in possession of that additional value; in fact, that the nation has lost the amount twice over; first, by the act of export; secondly, by that of consumption: whereas, the consumption of an indigenous product would have entailed a single loss only. But I answer as before, that the export of specie has occasioned no loss; that it was balanced by equivalent value imported; and that it is so certain, that nothing has been lost except the 20,000 dollars worth of imported commodities, that I defy any one to point out any other losers than the consumers of those commodities. If there has been no loser, it is clear there can have been no loss.

Would you put a stop to the emigration of capital? It is not to be prevented by keeping the specie in the country. A man resolved to transfer his capital elsewhere can do it just as effectually by the consignment of goods, whose export is permitted.* So much the bet-

---

* The transfer of capital by bills on foreign countries, comes precisely to the

ter, we may be told; for our manufacturers will benefit by the exports. True; but their value exists no longer in the nation, since they bring back no return wherewith to make new purchases; there has been a transfer of so much capital from amongst you, to give activity not to your own, but to some other nation's industry. This is a real ground of apprehension. Capital naturally flows to those places that hold out security and lucrative employment, and gradually retires from countries offering no such advantages: but it may easily enough retire, without being ever converted into specie.

If the export of specie causes no diminution of national capital, provided it be followed by a corresponding return, on the other hand, its import brings no accession of capital. For, in reality, before specie can be imported, it must have been purchased by an equivalent value exported for that purpose.

On this point it has been alleged, that by sending abroad goods instead of specie, a demand is created for goods, and the producers enabled to make a profit upon their production. I answer, that, even when specie is sent abroad, that specie must have been first obtained by the export of some indigenous product; for, we may rest assured, that the foreign owner of it did not give it to the French importer for nothing; and France had nothing to offer in the first instance but her domestic products. If the supply of the precious metals in the country be more than sufficient for the wants of the country, it is a fitter object of export than another commodity; and, if more of the specie be exported than the excess of the supply above the demand for the purposes of circulation, we may calculate with certainty, that, since the value of specie must have been necessarily raised by the exportation, other specie will be imported to replace what has been withdrawn; for the purchase of which last, home products must have been sent abroad, which will have yielded a profit to the home producers. In a word, every value sent out of France, for the purchase of foreign returns for the French market, may be resolved into a product of domestic industry, given either first or last, for France has nothing else to procure them with.

Again, it has been argued, that it is better to export consumable articles, as, for instance, manufactures, and to keep at home those products not liable to consumption, or, at least, not to quick consumption, such as specie. Yet objects of quick consumption, if more in demand, are more profitable to keep than objects of slower consumption. It would often be doing a producer a very poor service, to make him substitute a quantity of commodities of slow consumption, for an equal portion of his capital of more rapid consumption. If an ironmaster were to contract for the delivery to him of a quantity of coal at a day certain, and when the day came the coal could not be procurable, and he should be offered the value in money in its stead, it would be somewhat difficult to convince him of the

same thing. It is a mere substitute in the place of the individual making the export of commodities, who transfers his right to receive their proceeds, the value of which remains abroad.

service done him by the delivery of money; which is an object of much slower consumption than the coal he contracted for. Should a dyer send an order for dying woods from abroad, it would be a positive injury to send him gold, on the plea, that, with equal value, it has the advantage of greater durability. He had no occasion for a durable article whatever; what he wanted was a substance, which, though decomposed in his vats, would quickly re-appear in the colours of his stuffs.*

If it were no advantage to import any but the most durable items of productive capital, there are other very durable objects, such as stone or iron, that ought to share in our partiality with silver and gold. But the point of real importance is, the durability, not of any particular substance, but of the value of capital. Now the value of capital is perpetuated, notwithstanding the repeated change of the material shape in which it is vested. Nay, it cannot yield either interest or profit, unless that shape be continually varied. To confine it to the single shape of money would be to condemn it to remain unproductive.

But I will go a step further, and, having shown that there is no advantage in importing gold and silver more than any other article of merchandise, I will assert, that, supposing it were desirable to have the balance of trade always in our favour, yet it is morally impossible it should be so.

Gold and silver are like all the other substances that, in the aggregate, compose national wealth; they are useful to the community no longer than while they do not exceed the national demand for them. Any such excess must make the sellers more numerous than the buyers; consequently must depress the price in proportion, and thus create a powerful inducement to buy in the home market, in the expectation of making a profit upon the export. This may be illustrated by an example.

Suppose for a moment the internal traffic and national wealth of a given country to be such as to require the constant employ of a thousand carriages of different kinds. Suppose, too, that, by some peculiar system of commerce, we should succeed in getting more carriages annually imported, than were annually destroyed by wear and tear; so that, at the year's end, there should be 1500 instead of 1000; is it not obvious, that there would be in that case 500 lying by in the repositories quite useless, and that the owners of them, rather than suffer their value to lie dormant, would undersell each other, and even smuggle them abroad if it were practicable, in the hope of turning them to better account? In vain would the govern-

---

* In Book III., which treats of consumption, it will be seen, that the slower kinds of unproductive consumption are preferable to the more rapid ones. But, in the reproductive branch, the more rapid are the better; because, the more quickly the reproduction is effected, the less charge of interest is incurred, and the oftener the same capital can repeat its productive agency. The rapidity of consumption, moreover, does not affect external products in particular; its disadvantages are equal, whether the product be of home or foreign growth.

ment conclude commercial treaties for the encouragement of their import: in vain would it expend its efforts in stimulating the export of other commodities, for the purpose of getting returns in the shape of carriages; the more the public authorities favoured the import, the more anxious would individuals be to export.

As it is with carriages, so is it with specie likewise. The demand is limited; it can form but a part of the aggregate wealth of the nation. That wealth can not possibly consist entirely of specie; for other things are requisite besides specie. The extent of the demand for that peculiar article is proportionate to the general wealth; in the same manner, as a greater number of carriages is wanted in a rich than in a poor country. Whatever brilliant or solid qualities the precious metals may possess, their value depends upon the use made of them, and that use is limited. Like carriages, they have a value peculiar to them; a value that diminishes in proportion to the increase of their relative plenty, in comparison with the objects of exchange, and increases in proportion to their relative scarcity.

One is told, that every thing may be procured with gold or silver. True; but upon what terms? The terms are less advantageous, when these metals are forcibly multiplied beyond the demand; hence their strong tendency to emigration under such circumstances. The export of silver from Spain was prohibited; yet Spain supplied all Europe with it. In 1812, the paper money of England having rendered superfluous all the gold money of that country, and made that metal too abundant for its other remaining uses, its relative value fell, and her guineas emigrated to France, in spite of the ease with which the coasts of an island may be guarded, and of the denunciation of capital punishment against the exporters.

To what good purpose, then, do governments labour to turn the balance of commerce in favour of their respective nations? To none whatever; unless, perhaps, to exhibit the show of financial advantages, unsupported by fact or experience.* How can maxims so clear, so agreeable to plain common sense, and to facts attested by all who have made commerce their study, have yet been rejected in practice by all the ruling powers of Europe,† nay, even have been

---

* The returns of British commerce from the commencement of the 18th century down to the establishment of the existing paper money of that nation, show a regular annual excess, more or less received by Great Britain in the shape of specie, amounting altogether to the enormous total of 347 millions sterling (more than 1600 millions of dollars.) If to this be added the specie already in Great Britain at the outset, England ought to have possessed a circulating medium of very near 400 millions sterling. How happens it, then, that the most exaggerated ministerial calculations have never given a larger total of specie than 47 millions, even at the period of its greatest abundance? *Vide Suprà*, Chap. III.

† All of them have acted under the conviction, 1. That the precious metals are the only desirable kind of wealth, whereas they perform but a secondary part in its production: 2. That they have it in their power to cause their regular influx by compulsory measures. The example of England (*Vide note preceding*,) will show the little success of the experiment. The pre-eminent wealth of that nation, then, is derived from some other cause than the favourable bal-

attacked by a number of writers, that have evinced both genius and information on other subjects? To speak the truth, it is because the first principles of political economy are as yet but little known; because ingenious systems and reasonings have been built upon hollow foundations, and taken advantage of, on the one hand, by interested rulers, who employ prohibition as a weapon of offence or an instrument of revenue; and, on the other, by the personal avarice of merchants and manufacturers, who have a private interest in exclusive measures, and take but little pains to inquire, whether their profits arise from actual production, or from a simultaneous loss thrown upon other classes of the community.

A determination to maintain a favourable balance of trade, that is to say, to export goods and receive returns of specie, is, in fact, a determination to have no foreign trade at all; for the nation, with whom the trade is to be carried on, can only give in exchange what it has to give. If one party will receive nothing but the precious metals, the other party may come to a similar resolution; and, when both parties require the same commodity, there is no possibility of any exchange. Were it practicable to monopolize the precious metals, there are few nations in the world that would not be cut off from all hope of mutual commercial relations. If one country afford to another what the latter wants in exchange, what more would she have? or in what respect would gold be preferable? for what else can it be wanted, than as the means of subsequently purchasing the objects of desire?

The day will come, sooner or later, when people will wonder at the necessity of taking all this trouble to expose the folly of a system, so childish and absurd, and yet so often enforced at the point of the bayonet.(1)

[END OF THE DIGRESSION UPON THE BALANCE OF TRADE.]

---

ance of her commerce. But what other cause? Why from the immensity of her production. But to what does she owe that immensity? To the frugality exerted in the accumulation of individual capital; to the national turn for industry and practical application; to the security of person and property, the facility of internal circulation, and freedom of individual agency, which, limited and fettered as it is, is yet, on the whole, superior to that of the other European states.

(1) In a note, here inserted, in the earlier editions of this work, the American editor referred to the laudable exertions made by Mr. Huskisson, with the support of Mr. Canning and other then prominent members of the British government, to expose the impolicy and injustice of restrictions and prohibitions on commerce, and to the success of some of their measures to relieve the industry of the country from the shackles imposed in a less enlightened age. We also then quoted the observations of the Edinburgh Review, "that Mr. Huskisson, in particular, against whom every species of ribald abuse had been cast, had done more to improve the commercial policy of England during the short period that he was President of the Board of Trade, than all the ministers who had preceded him for the last hundred years. And it ought to be remembered to his honour, that the measures he suggested, and the odium thence arising, were not proposed and incurred by him in the view of serving any party purpose, but solely

To resume our subject.—We have seen, that the very advantages aimed at by the means of a favourable balance of trade, are altogether illusory; and that, supposing them real, it is impossible for a nation permanently to enjoy them. It remains to be shown, what is the actual operation of regulations framed with this object in view.

By the absolute exclusion of specific manufactures of foreign fabric, a government establishes a monopoly in favour of the home producers of these articles, and in prejudice of the home consumers; that is to say, those classes of the nation which produce them, being entitled to their exclusive sale, can raise their prices above the natural rate; while the home consumers, being unable to purchase elsewhere, are compelled to pay for them unnaturally dear.* If the

---

* Ricardo, in his *Essay on the Principles of Political Economy and Taxation*, published in 1817, has justly remarked on this passage, that a government can not, by prohibition, elevate a product beyond its natural rate of price: for in that case, the home producers would betake themselves in greater numbers to its production, and, by competition, reduce the profits upon it to the general level. To make myself better understood, I must therefore explain, that, by natural rate of price, I mean the lowest rate at which a commodity is procurable, whether by commerce or other branch of industry. If commerical can procure it cheaper than manufacturing industry, and the government take upon itself to compel its production by the way of manufacture, it then imposes upon the nation a more chargeable mode of procurement. Thus, it wrongs the consumer, without giving to the domestic producer a profit, equivalent to the extra charge upon the consumer; for competition soon brings that profit down to the ordinary level of profit, and the monopoly is thereby rendered nugatory. So that, although Ricardo is thus far correct in his criticism, he only shows the measure I am reprobating to be more mischievous; inasmuch as it augments the natural difficulties in the way of the satisfaction of human wants, without any counteracting benefit to any class or any individual whatever.

---

because he believed, and most justly, that these measures were sound in principle, and calculated to promote the real and lasting interests of his country."

Since that time all the successive administrations in England, both Tory and Whig, have at least uniformly recognized the soundness of the doctrines of free trade, and some of them, by various important commercial enactments, have given a still wider application to these beneficial truths; and such, too, has been the effect of their liberal measures upon the state of opinion and of legislation throughout Great Britain, that both in and out of parliament, a most gratifying change has taken place. Commercial questions everywhere now occupy a large share of attention, are discussed with the greatest ability and acuteness in almost all the public journals, and must therefore lead to the emancipation of commerce from the fetters which have so long and so perniciously bound it.

In France, however, and other countries which might be named, the state of knowledge, and the state of opinion, are not yet in favour of liberal commercial views. "For thirty years," we are told by the English Commissioners, Messrs. Villiers and Bowring, "nearly every law passed on Custom House matters had been intended either to establish or to consolidate the system of protection and prohibition. Under the encouragement of the legislature, much capital has been invested in the establishment and extension of protected manufactures, whose now tottering and uncertain position (the natural and necessary consequence of the system itself) has made their proprietors most feelingly alive to any change which might affect them."

American Editor.

articles be not wholly prohibited, but merely saddled with an import duty, the home producer can then increase their price by the whole amount of the duty, and the consumer will have to pay the differ- ence. For example, if an import duty of 20 cents per dozen be laid upon earthenware plates worth 60 cents per dozen, the importer, whatever country he may belong to, must charge the consumer 30 cents; and the home manufacturer of that commodity is enabled to ask 80 cents per dozen of his customers for plates of the same qual- ity; which he could not do without the intervention of the duty; because the consumer could get the same article for 60 cents: thus, a premium to the whole extent of the duty is given to the home manufacturer out of the consumer's pocket.

Should any one maintain, that the advantage of producing at home counterbalances the hardship of paying dearer for almost every arti- cle; that our own capital and labour are engaged in the production, and the profits pocketed by our own fellow-citizens; my answer is, that the foreign commodities we might import are not to be had gratis: that we must purchase them with values of home production, which would have given equal employment to our industry and capital; for we must never lose sight of this maxim, that products are always bought ultimately with products. It is most for our ad- vantage to employ our productive powers, not in those branches in which foreigners excel us, but in those which we excel in ourselves; and with the product to purchase of others. The opposite course would be just as absurd, as if a man should wish to make his own coats and shoes. What would the world say, if, at the door of every house an import duty were laid upon coats and shoes, for the lauda- ble purpose of compelling the inmates to make them for themselves? Would not people say with justice, Let us follow each his own pur- suits, and buy what we want with what we produce, or, which comes to the same thing, with what we get for our products. The system would be precisely the same, only carried to a ridiculous extreme.

Well may it be a matter of wonder, that every nation should manifest such anxiety to obtain prohibitory regulations, if it be true that it can profit nothing by them; and lead one to suppose the two cases not parallel, because we do not find individual householders solicitous to obtain the same privilege. But the sole difference is this, that individuals are independent and consistent beings, actuated by no contrariety of will, and more interested in their character of consumers of coats and shoes to buy them cheap, than as manufac- turers to sell unnaturally dear.

Who, then, are the classes of the community so importunate for prohibitions or heavy import duties? The producers of the par- ticular commodity, that applies for protection from competition, not the consumers of that commodity. The public interest is their plea; but self-interest is evidently their object. Well, but, say these gentry, are they not the same thing? are not our gains national gains? no means: whatever profit is acquired in this manner, is so much taken out of the pockets of a neighbour and fellow-citizen. and, if the excess of charge thrown upon consumers by the monopoly could be correctly computed, it would be found, that the loss of the consumer exceeds the gain of the monopolist. Here, then, individual and public interest are in direct opposition to each other; and, since public interest is understood by the enlightened few alone, is it at all surprising, that the prohibitive system should find so many partisans and so few opponents?

There is in general far too little attention paid to the serious mischief of raising prices upon the consumers. The evil is not apparent to cursory observation, because it operates piecemeal, and is felt in a very slight degree on every purchase or act of consumption: but it is really most serious, on account of its constant recurrence and universal pressure. The whole fortune of every consumer is affected by every fluctuation of price in the articles of his consumption; the cheaper they are, the richer he is, and *vice versâ*. If a single article rise in price, he is so much the more poor in respect of that article; if all rise together, he is poorer in respect to the whole. And, since the whole nation is comprehended in the class of the consumers, the whole nation must in that case be the poorer. Besides which, it is crippled in the extension of the variety of its enjoyments, and prevented from obtaining products whereof it stands in need, in exchange for those wherewith it might procure them. It is of no use to assert, that, when prices are raised, what one gains another loses. For the position is not true, except in the case of monopolies; nor even to the full extent with regard to them; for the monopolist never profits to the full amount of the loss to the consumers. If the rise be occasioned by taxation or import-duty under any shape whatever, the producer gains nothing by the increase of price, but just the reverse, as we shall see by and by (Book III. Chapter VII.:) so that, in fact, he is no richer in his capacity of producer, though poorer in his quality of consumer. This is one of the most effective causes of national impoverishment, or at least one of the most powerful checks to the progress of national wealth.

For this reason, it may be perceived, that it is an absurd distinction to view with more jealousy the import of foreign objects of barren consumption, than that of raw materials for home manufacture. Whether the products consumed be of domestic or of foreign growth, a portion of wealth is destroyed in the act of consumption, and a proportionate inroad made into the wealth of the community. But that inroad is the result of the act of consumption, not of the act of dealing with the foreigner; and the resulting stimulus to national production, is the same in either case. For, wherewith was the purchase of the foreign product made? either with a domestic product or with money, which must itself have been procured with a domestic product. In buying of a foreigner, the nation really does no more than send abroad a domestic product in lieu of consuming it at home, and consume in its place the foreign product received in exchange. The individual consumer himself, probably, does not conduct this operation; commerce conducts it for him. No one country can buy of another, except with its own domestic products.

In defence of import duties it is often urged, "that when the interest of money is lower abroad than at home, the foreign has an advantage over the home producer, which must be met by a countervailing duty." The low rate of interest is, to the foreign producer, an advantage, analogous to that of the superior quality of his land. It tends to cheapen the products he raises; and it is reasonable enough that our domestic consumers should take the benefit of that cheapness. The same motive will operate here, that leads us rather to import sugar and indigo from tropical climates, than to raise them in our own.

"But capital is necessary in every branch of production: so that the foreigner, who can procure it at a lower rate of interest, has the same advantage in respect to every product; and, if the free importation be permitted, he will have an advantage over all classes of home producers." Tell me, then, how his products are to be paid for. "Why, in specie, and there lies the mischief." And how is the specie to be got to pay for them? "All the nation has, will go in that way; and when it is exhausted national misery will be complete." So then it is admitted, that before arriving at this extremity, the constant efflux of specie will gradually render it more scarce at home, and more abundant abroad; wherefore, it will gradually rise 1, 2, 3, per cent higher in value at home than abroad; which is fully sufficient to turn the tide, and make specie flow inwards faster than it flowed outwards. But it will not do so without some returns; and of what can the returns be made, but of products of the land, or the commerce of the nation? For there is no possible means of purchasing from foreign nations, otherwise than with the products of the national land and commerce; and it is better to buy of them what they can produce cheaper than ourselves, because we may rest assured, that they must take in payment what we can produce cheaper than they. This they must do, else there must be an end of all interchange.

Again, it is affirmed, and what absurd positions have not been advanced to involve these questions in obscurity? that, since almost all the nation are at the same time consumers and producers, they gain by prohibition and monopoly as much in the one capacity as they lose in the other; that the producer, who gets a monopoly-profit upon the object of his own production, is, on the other hand, the sufferer by a similar profit upon the objects of his consumption; and thus that the nation is made up of rogues and fools, who are a match for each other. It is worth remarking, that every body thinks himself more rogue than fool; for, although all are consumers as well as producers, the enormous profits made upon a single article are much more striking, than reiterated minute losses upon the numberless items of consumption. If an import duty be laid upon calicoes, the additional annual charge to each person of moderate fortune, may, perhaps, not exceed 2½ dollars or 3 dollars at most; and probably he does not very well comprehend the nature of the loss, or feel it much, though repeated in some degree or other upon every thing he consumes; whereas, possibly, this consumer is himself a manufacturer, say a hat-maker; and should a duty be laid upon the import of foreign hats, he will immediately see that it will raise the price of his own hats, and probably increase his annual profits by several thousand dollars. It is this delusion that makes private interest so warm an advocate for prohibitory measures, even where the whole community loses more by them as consumers, than it gains as producers.

But, even in this point of view, the exclusive system is pregnant with injustice. It is impossible that every class of production should profit by the exclusive system, supposing it to be universal, which, in point of fact, it never is in practice, though possibly it may be in law or intention. Some articles can never, from the nature of things, be derived from abroad; fresh fish, for instance, or horned cattle; as to them, therefore, import duties would be inoperative in raising the price. The same may be said of masons and carpenters' work, and of the numberless callings necessarily carried on within the community; as those of shopmen, clerks, carriers, retail dealers, and many others. The producers of immaterial products, public functionaries, and fundholders, lie under the same disability. These classes can none of them be invested with a monopoly by means of import duties, though they are subjected to the hardship of many monopolies granted in that way to other classes of producers.*

Besides, the profits of monopoly are not equitably divided amongst the different classes even of those that concur in the production of the commodity, which is the subject of monopoly. If the master-adventurers, whether in agriculture, manufacture, or commerce, have the consumers at their mercy, their labourers and subordinate productive agents are still more exposed to their extortion, for reasons that will be explained in Book II. So that these latter classes participate in the loss with consumers at large, but get no share of the unnatural gains of their superiors.

Prohibitory measures, besides affecting the pockets of the consumers, often subject them to severe privations. I am ashamed to

---

* There is a sort of malicious satisfaction in the discovery, that those who impose these restrictions are usually among the severest sufferers. Sometimes they attempt to indemnify themselves by a further act of injustice; the public functionaries augment their own salaries, if they have the keeping of the public purse. At other times they abolish a monopoly, when they find it press peculiarly on themselves. In 1599, the manufacturers of Tours petitioned Henry IV. to prohibit the import of gold and silver silk stuffs, which had previously been entirely of foreign fabric. They cajoled the government by the statement, that they could furnish the whole consumption of France with that article. The king granted their request, with his characteristic facility; but the consumers, who were chiefly the courtiers and people of condition, were loud in their remonstrances at the consequent advance of price; and the edict was revoked in six months. *Memoires de Sully*, liv. ii.

say, that, within these few years, we have had the hat-makers of Marseilles petitioning for the prohibition of the import of foreign straw or chip hats, on the plea that they injured the sale of their own felt hats;* a measure that would have deprived the country people and labourers in husbandry, who are so much exposed to the sun, of a light, a cool, and cheap covering, admirably adapted to their wants, the use of which it was highly desirable to extend and encourage.

In pursuit of what it mistakes for profound policy, or to gratify feelings it supposes to be laudable, a government will sometimes prohibit or divert the course of a particular trade, and thereby do irreparable mischief to the productive powers of the nation. When Philip II. became master of Portugal, and forbade all intercourse between his new subjects and the Dutch, whom he detested, what was the consequence? The Dutch, who before resorted to Lisbon for the manufactures of India, of which they took off an immense quantity, finding this avenue closed against their industry, went straight to India for what they wanted, and, in the end, drove out the Portuguese from that quarter; and, what was meant as the deadly blow of inveterate hatred, turned out the main source of their aggrandizement. "Commerce," says Fenelon, "is like the native springs of the rock, which often cease to flow altogether, if it be attempted to alter their course."†

Such are the principal evils of impediments thrown in the way of import, which are carried to the extreme point by absolute prohibition. There have, indeed, been instances of nations that have thriven under such a system; but then it was, because the causes of national prosperity were more powerful than the causes of national impoverishment. Nations resemble the human frame, which contains a vital principle, that incessantly labours to repair the inroads of excess and dissipation upon its health and constitution. Nature is active in closing the wounds and healing the bruises inflicted by our own awkwardness and intemperance. In like manner, states maintain themselves, nay, often increase in prosperity, in spite of the infinite injuries of every description, which friends as well as enemies inflict upon them. And it is worth remarking, that the most industrious nations are those, which are the most subjected to such outrage, because none others could survive them. The cry is then "our system must be the true one, for the national prosperity is advancing." Whereas, were we to take an enlarged view of the circumstances, that, for the last three centuries, have combined to develope the power and faculties of man; to survey with the eye of intelligence

---

* *Bulletin de la Societé d'Encouragement pour l'Industrie Nationale, No. 4.*

† The national convention of France prohibited the import of raw hides from Spain, on the plea that they injured the trade in those of France; not observing, that the self-same hides went back to Spain in a tanned state. The tanneries of France being obliged to procure the raw article at too dear a rate, were quickly abandoned; and the manufacture was transferred to Spain, along with great part of the capital, and many of the hands employed. It is next to impossible for a government, not only to do any good to national production by its interference, but even to avoid doing mischief.

the progress of navigation and discovery, of invention in every branch of art and science; to take account of the variety of useful animals and vegetables that have been transplanted from one hemisphere to the other, and to give a due attention to the vast augmentation and increased scope both of science and of its practical applications, that we are daily witnesses of, we could not resist the conviction, that our actual prosperity is nothing to what it might have been; that it is engaged in a perpetual struggle against the obstacles and impediments thrown into its way; and that, even in those parts of the world where mankind is deemed the most enlightened, a great part of their time and exertions are occupied in destroying instead of multiplying their resources, in despoiling instead of assisting each other; and all for want of correct knowledge and information respecting their real interests.*

But, to return to the subject, we have just been examining, the nature of the injury that a community suffers by difficulties thrown in the way of the introduction of foreign commodities. The mischief occasioned to the country that produces the prohibited article, is of the same kind and description; it is prevented from turning its capital and industry to the best account. But it is not to be supposed that the foreign nation can by this means be utterly ruined and stripped of all resource, as Napoleon seemed to imagine, when he excluded the products of Britain from the markets of the continent. To say nothing of the impossibility of effecting a complete and actual blockade of a whole country, opposed as it must be by the universal motive of self-interest, the utmost effect of it can only be to drive its production into a different channel. A nation is always competent to the purchase and consumption of the whole of its own products, for products are always bought with other products. Do you think it possible to prevent England from producing value to the amount of a million, by preventing her export of woollens to that amount? You are much mistaken if you do. England will employ the same capital and the same manual labour in the preparation of ardent spirits, by the distillation of grain or other domestic products, that were before occupied in the manufacture of woollens for the French market, and she will then no longer bring her woollens to be bartered for French brandies. A country, in one way or other, direct or indirect, always consumes the values it produces, and can consume nothing more. If it cannot exchange its products with its neighbours, it is compelled to produce values of such kinds only as it can consume at home. This is the utmost effect of prohibitions; both parties are worse provided, and neither is at all the richer.

---

* It is not my design to insinuate by this, that it is desirable that all minds should be imbued with all kinds of knowledge; but that every one should have just and correct notions of that, in which he is more immediately concerned. Nor is the general and complete diffusion of information requisite for the beneficial ends of science. The good resulting from it is proportionate to the extent of its progress: and the welfare of nations differs in degree, according to the correctness of their ideas upon those points, which most intimately concern them respectively.

Napoleon, doubtless, occasioned much injury, both to England and to the continent, by cramping their mutual relations of commerce as far as he possibly could. But, on the other hand, he did the continent of Europe the involuntary service of facilitating the communication between its different parts, by the universality of dominion, which his ambition had well-nigh achieved. The frontier duties between Holland, Belgium, part of Germany, Italy, and France, were demolished; and those of the other powers, with the exception of England, were far from oppressive. We may form some estimate of the benefit thence resulting to commerce, from the discontent and stagnation that have ensued upon the establishment of the present system of lining the frontier of each state with a triple guard of *douaniers*. All the continental states so guarded have, indeed, preserved their former means of production; but that production has been made less advantageous.

It cannot be denied, that France has gained prodigiously by the suppression of the provincial barriers and custom-houses, consequent upon her political revolution. Europe had, in like manner, gained by the partial removal of the international barriers between its different political states; and the world at large would derive similar benefit from the demolition of those, which insulate, as it were, the various communities, into which the human race is divided.

I have omitted to mention other very serious evils of the exclusive system; as, for instance, the creation of a new class of crime, that of smuggling; whereby an action, wholly innocent in itself, is made legally criminal: and persons, who are actually labouring for the general welfare, are subjected to punishment.

Smith admits of two circumstances, that, in his opinion, will justify a government in resorting to import-duties:—1. When a particular branch of industry is necessary to the public security, and the external supply cannot be safely reckoned upon. On this account a government may very wisely prohibit the import of gun-powder, if such prohibition be necessary to set the powder-mills at home in activity; for it is better to pay somewhat dear for so essential an article, than to run the risk of being unprovided in the hour of need.* 2. Where a similar commodity of home produce is already saddled with a duty. The foreign article, if wholly exempt from duty, would in this case have an actual privilege; so that a duty imposed has not the effect of destroying, but of restoring the natural equilibrium and relative position of the different branches of production.

Indeed, it is impossible to find any reasonable ground for exempting the production of values by the channel of external commerce from the same pressure of taxation that weighs upon the production effected in those of agriculture and manufacture. Taxation is, doubt-

---

* There is no great weight in this plea of justification. For experience has shown, that saltpetre is stored against the moment of need, in the largest quantity, when it is most an article of habitual import. Yet the legislature of France has saddled it with duties amounting to prohibition.

less, an evil, and one which should be reduced to the lowest possible
degree; but when once a given amount of taxation is admitted to be
necessary, it is but common justice to lay it equally on all three
branches of industry. The error I wish to expose to reprobation is
the notion that taxes of this kind are favourable to production. A
tax can never be favourable to the public welfare, except by the
good use that is made of its proceeds.

These points should never be lost sight of in the framing of commercial treaties, which are really good for nothing but to protect
industry and capital, diverted into improper channels by the blunders
of legislation. These it would be far wiser to remedy than to perpetuate. The healthy state of industry and wealth is the state of
absolute liberty, in which each interest is left to take care of itself.
The only useful protection authority can afford them is that against
fraud or violence. Taxes and restrictive measures never can be a
benefit: they are at the best a necessary evil; to suppose them useful
to the subjects at large, is to mistake the foundation of national prosperity, and to set at naught the principles of political economy.

Import duties and prohibitions have often been resorted to as a
means of retaliation: " Your government throws impediments in the
way of the introduction of our national products: are not we, then,
justified in equally impeding the introduction of yours ?" This is
the favourite plea, and the basis of most commercial treaties; but
people mistake their object: granting that nations have a right to do
one another as much mischief as possible, which, by the way, I can
hardly admit; I am not here disputing their rights, but discussing
their interests.

Undoubtedly, a nation that excludes you from all commercial
intercourse with her, does you an injury;—robs you, as far as in her
lies, of the benefits of external commerce; if, therefore, by the dread
of retaliation, you can induce her to abandon her exclusive measures,
there is no question about the expediency of such retaliation, as a
matter of mere policy. But it must not be forgotten that retaliation
hurts yourself as well as your rival; that it operates, not defensively
against her selfish measures, but offensively against yourself, in the
first instance, for the purpose of indirectly attacking her. The only
point in question is this, what degree of vengeance you are animated
by, and how much will you consent to throw away upon its gratification.* I will not undertake to enumerate all the evils arising from
treaties of commerce, or to apply the principles enforced throughout

---

* The transatlantic colonies, that have within these few years thrown off their
colonial dependence, amongst others, the provinces of La Plata, and St. Domingo
or Haiti, have opened their ports to foreigners, without any demand of reciprocity,
and are more rich and prosperous than they ever were under the operation of the
exclusive system. We are told that the trade and prosperity of Cuba have
doubled since its ports have been opened to the flags of all nations, by a concurrence of imperious circumstances, and in violation of the system of the mother-
country. The elder states of Europe go on like wrong-headed farmers, in a
bigoted attachment to their old prejudices and methods, while they have examples of the good effects of an improved system all around them.

this work to all the clauses and provisions usually contained in them. I will confine myself to the remark, that almost every modern treaty of commerce has had for its basis the imaginary advantage and possibility of the liquidation of a favourable balance of trade by an import of specie. If these turn out to be chimerical, whatever advantage may have resulted from such treaties must be wholly referred to the additional freedom and facility of international communication obtained by them, and not at all to their restrictive clauses or provisoes, unless either of the contracting parties has availed itself of its superior power, to exact conditions savouring of a tributary character; as England has done in relation to Portugal. In such case, it is mere exaction and spoliation.(1)

(1) Mr. Villiers and Dr. Bowring, in their very valuable report on the commercial relations between France and Great Britain, presented to both Houses of Parliament, during the present year, (1834,) in remarking upon the disappointments which had been experienced from treaties of commerce between France and Great Britain, point out the true causes of the failure of these arrangements, however usefully they were intended ; and as it is of importance in other countries to guard against a recurrence to similar experiments which might present a formidable barrier against any permanent or solid change to a more liberal international intercourse, we cannot do better, in this place, than to copy their excellent observations on this head.

" These arrangements, however usefully intended, were productive of so much inconvenience and suffering from the sudden shifting of capital, as to induce an unwillingness to await patiently for their ultimate but somewhat remote advantages. Every treaty of commercial change must, it is certain, affect some interest or other, and by these treaties, particularly the treaty of 1786, so many interests were suddenly and severely affected, that they were enabled, by combining together, to overthrow all the expectations of future good which would have inevitably followed the removal of restrictions and prohibitions."

" It may also be observed, that treaties of commerce are generally agreements for mutual preferences ; and in so far, are encroachments upon sound commercial principles. They are intended to benefit the contracting parties by common intercourse, to the exclusion (and consequently to the detriment) of other nations. They ordinarily propose exclusive advantages, which, if they open some channels of commercial profit, necessarily close others, and prevent the negotiating nations from availing themselves of the improvements or accommodating themselves to the changes which the fluctuations of agriculture, manufactures, or trade demand. The Methuen treaty, for example, bound Great Britain to take the produce of a particular country at diminished duties, whatever superior advantages any other country might chance to offer; while Portugal was, at the same time, compelled to receive the manufactures of England, whether or not she might have supplied herself more profitably elsewhere. A treaty, therefore, with France, proffering reciprocal advantages, that is to say, giving to France peculiar privileges in the English market, or obtaining peculiar privileges for England in the markets of France, did not appear to offer any prospect of permanent utility; but, if it were possible that each country should, for itself, and, with a special view to its own interests, remove those impediments to intercourse which had grown out of hostile feelings or erroneous calculations, and by comparing the facts which each government was enabled to furnish for the elucidation of the inquiry, each should find that it could safely and judiciously prepare for more extended transactions; if, in a word, it could be shown that each possessed sources of wealth which might be made productive to the other, while they lost nothing of their productiveness to the nation that possessed them, we believed that, in selecting such topics for our examination, and such objects for their result, we were best discharging the duty which had devolved on us." AMERICAN EDITOR.

Again, I would observe, that the offer of peculiar advantages by one nation to another, in the way of a treaty of commerce, if not an act of hostility, is at least one of extreme odium in the eyes of other nations. For the concession to one can only be rendered effectual by refusal to others. Hence the germ of discord and of war, with all its mischiefs. It is infinitely more simple, and I hope to have shown, more profitable also, to treat all nations as friends, and impose no higher duties on the introduction of their products, than what are necessary to place them on the same footing as those of domestic growth.

Yet, notwithstanding all the mischiefs resulting from the exclusion of foreign products, which I have been depicting, it would be an act of unquestionable rashness suddenly to change even so ruinous a policy. Disease is not to be eradicated in a moment; it requires nursing and management to dispense even national benefits. Monopolies are an abuse, but an abuse in which enormous capital is vested, and numberless industrious agents employed, which deserve to be treated with consideration; for this mass of capital and industry cannot all at once find a more advantageous channel of national production. Perhaps the cure of all the partial distresses that must follow the downfall of that colossal monster in politics, the exclusive system, would be as much as the talent of any single statesman could accomplish; yet when one considers calmly the wrongs it entails when it is established, and the distresses consequent upon its overthrow, we are insensibly led to the reflection, that, if it be so difficult to set shackled industry at liberty again, with what caution ought we not to receive any proposition for enslaving her!

But governments have not been content with checking the import of foreign products. In the firm conviction, that national prosperity consists in selling without buying, and blind to the utter impossibility of the thing, they have gone beyond the mere imposition of a tax or fine upon purchasing of foreigners, and have in many instances offered rewards in the shape of bounties for selling to them.

This expedient has been employed to an extraordinary degree by the British government, which until recently always evinced the greatest anxiety to enlarge the market for British commercial and manufactured produce.* It is obvious, that a merchant, who re-

---

* The political circumstances of England, during the late war, and her practice of supporting and subsidizing military operations on the continent, furnished her with a more plausible excuse for attempting to export, in the shape of manufactured produce, those values, which she thus expended without return. But she had no need to be at any expense for that purpose. Had England charged a seignorage upon the coinage of gold and silver, as she ought to have done, she needed not to have given herself any trouble about the form of the values she exported to meet her foreign subsidies and expenditure: guineas would themselves have been an object of manufacture.(a)

(a) So they were without the imposition of a seignorage, which, however, should have been charged. But England had no occasion to give bounties with a view to facilitate her foreign expenditure. The discount of her bills was a

ceives a bounty upon export, can, without personal loss, afford to sell his goods in a foreign market at a lower rate than prime cost. In the pithy language of Smith, " We cannot force foreigners to buy the goods of our own workmen, as we may our own countrymen; the next best expedient, it has been thought, therefore, is to pay them for buying."

In fact, if a particular commodity, by the time it has reached the French market, costs the English exporter 20 dollars, his trouble, &c. included, and the same commodity could be bought in France at the same or a less rate, there is nothing to give him exclusive possession of the market. But if the British government pays a bounty of 2 dollars upon the export, and thereby enables him to lower his demand from 20 to 18 dollars, he may safely reckon upon a preference. Yet what is this but a free gift of two dollars from the British government to the French consumer? It may be conceived, that the merchant has no objection to this mode of dealing; for his profits are the same as if the French consumer paid the full value, or cost price, of the commodity. The British nation is the loser in this transaction, in the ratio of 10 per cent. upon the French consumption; and France remits in return a value of but 18 for what has cost 20 dollars.

When a bounty is paid, not at the moment of export, but at the commencement of productive creation, the home consumer participates with the foreigner in the advantage of the bounty; for, in that case, the article can be sold below cost price in the home as well as in the foreign market. And if, as is sometimes the case, the producer pockets the bounty, and yet keeps up the price of the commodity, the bounty is then a present of the government to the producer, over and above the ordinary profits of his industry.

When, by the means of a bounty, a product is raised either for home or foreign consumption, which would not have been raised without one, the effect is, an injurious production, one that costs more than it is worth. Suppose an article, when completely finished off, to be saleable for 5 dollars and no more, but its prime cost, including of course the profits of productive industry, to amount to 6 dollars, it is quite clear that nobody will volunteer the production, for fear of a loss of 1 dollar. But, if the government, with a view to encourage this branch of industry, be willing to defray this loss— in other words, if it offer a bounty of 1 dollar to the producer, the production can then go on, and the public revenue, that is to say, the nation at large, will be a loser of 1 dollar. And this is precisely the kind of advantage that a nation gains by encouraging a branch

---

sufficient premium to the manufacturer; and, where that expenditure was large, greatly exceeded either drawbacks or bounties. Had specie been directly procurable, perhaps it might have saved something to the government, in the reduced profit payable to the merchants upon a mere complex operation. But the merchants must have made their profit upon bullion. The sole difference occasioned by the absurdity of gratuitous coinage was, the expense incurred in that coinage; but the imposition of a seignorage would neither have promoted the import of bullion, nor facilitated its transport to the scene of expenditure. T.

of production which cannot support itself: it is in fact urging the prosecution of a losing concern, the produce of which is exchanged, not for other produce, but for the bounty given by the state.

Wherever there is any thing to be made by a particular employment of industry, it wants no encouragement; where there is nothing to be made, it deserves none. There is no truth in the argument, that perhaps the state may gain, though individuals cannot; for how can the state gain, except through the medium of individuals? Perhaps it may be said, that the state receives more in duties than it pays in bounties; but suppose it does, it merely receives with one hand and pays with the other: let the duties be lowered to the whole amount of the bounty, and production will stand precisely where it did before, with this difference in its favour, viz. that the state will save the whole charge of management of the bounties, and part of that of the duties.

Though bounties are chargeable, and a dead loss to the gross national wealth, there are cases in which it is politic to incur that loss;(1) as when a particular product is necessary to public security, and must be had at any rate, however extravagant. Louis XIV., with a view to restore the marine of France, granted a bounty of 1 dollar per ton upon every ship fitted out in France. His object was to train up sailors. So likewise when the bounty is the mere refunding of a duty previously exacted. The bounty paid by Great Britain upon the export of refined sugar is nothing more than the reimbursement of the import duties upon muscovado and molasses.

Perhaps, too, it may be wise in a government to grant a premium on a particular product, which, though it make a loss in the outset, holds out a fair prospect of profit in a few years' time. Smith thinks otherwise: hear what he says on the subject. "No regulation of commerce can increase the quantity of industry in any society, beyond what its capital can maintain. It can only divert a part of it into a direction, into which it might not otherwise have gone; and it is by no means certain, that this artificial direction is likely to be more advantageous to the society, than that into which it would have gone of its own accord. The statesman, who should attempt to direct private people in what manner they ought to employ their capitals, would not only load himself with a most unnecessary attention, but assume an authority, which could safely be

(1) We already have had occasion to remark (note 1, page 104) that there can be few or no cases in which it would ever be politic to incur a loss by the payment of bounties, even with the expectation of insuring the production of objects necessary to the public safety. For the end aimed at never can be attained by such means. The naval preponderance of England, as we before observed, was not owing to any act of parliament, but can satisfactorily be traced to those causes we have mentioned in the note referred to. Holland, besides, rose to the highest point of European maritime power, without any navigation laws, or bounties to her shipping; and France, it must be remembered, notwithstanding the famous Ordonnance in 1664, of Louis XIV., "to engage builders and merchants to construct French vessels," never obtained the so much desired superiority in ships and in seamen.　　　　　　　AMERICAN EDITOR.

trusted, not only to no single person, but to no council or senate whatever; and which would nowhere be so dangerous, as in the hands of a man who had folly and presumption enough to fancy himself fit to exercise it. Though for want of such regulations, the society should never acquire the proposed manufacture, it would not upon that account necessarily be the poorer in any one period of its duration. In every period of its duration, its whole capital and industry might still have been employed, though upon different objects, in the manner that was most advantageous at the time."*

And Smith is certainly right in the main; though perhaps there are circumstances that may form exceptions to the general rule, that every one is the best judge how to employ his industry and capital. Smith wrote at a period and in a country, where personal interest is well understood, and where any profitable mode of investing capital and industry is not likely to be long overlooked. But every nation is not so far advanced in intelligence. How many countries are there, where many of the best employments of capital are altogether excluded by prejudices that the government alone can remove! How many cities and provinces, where certain established investments of capital have prevailed from time immemorial! In one place, every body invests in landed property, in another, in houses, and in others still, in public offices or national funds. Every unusual application of the power of capital is, in such places, contemplated with distrust or disdain; so that partiality shown to a profitable mode of employing industry or capital may possibly be productive of national advantage.

Moreover, a new channel of industry may ruin an unsupported speculator, though capable of yielding enormous profit, when the labourers shall have acquired practice, and the novelty has once been overcome. France at present contains the most beautiful manufactures of silk and of woollen in the world, and is probably indebted for them to the wise encouragement of Colbert's administration. He advanced to the manufacturers 2000 *fr.* for every loom at work; and, by the way, this species of encouragement has a very peculiar advantage. In ordinary cases, whatever the government levies upon the product of individual exertion is wholly lost to future production; but, in this instance, a part was employed in reproduction; a portion of individual revenues was thrown into the aggregate productive capital of the nation. This was a degree of wisdom one could hardly have expected, even from personal self-interest.† (1)

---

* *Wealth of Nations*, book iv. c. 2.

† I am far from equally approving all the encouragements of this kind held out by this minister; particularly the sums lavished on several establishments of pure ostentation, which, like that of the Gobelin tapestry, have constantly cost more than they have produced.

---

(1) Our author, here, has permitted, although with some slight qualification, an observation to escape from his pen, in direct contradiction with his own general principles, and which, therefore, it is necessary to point out and refute. "France," he remarks, in speaking of her manufactures of silk and woollen, "is

It would be out of place here to inquire, how wide a field bounties open to peculation, partiality, and the whole tribe of abuses incident to the management of public affairs. The most enlightened

---

probably indebted for them to the wise encouragement of Colbert's administration." What is this but admitting that beneficial consequences to manufactures necessarily flow from a protecting system? Now, this we deny, and, in support of this denial, fortunately can at present invoke the highest authority. In the report on the commercial relations between France and Great Britain, which we cannot too often refer to in support of sound principles, Mr. Villiers and Dr. Bowring, both on this point, and regarding the merits and character of Colbert's administration, supply us with the following admirable strictures, which we have great satisfaction in presenting to our readers. They will be found to contain a complete answer to the gratuitous assumption of M. Say, of the wisdom herein displayed by Colbert "by this species of encouragement" to manufactures.

"France thus became the country which adopted and still exhibits the consequences of a protecting system on a large scale. Its introduction may be traced, or rather its extension as far as possible, to Colbert, a minister to whose name and administration a great portion of applause has been given, but whose system of encouragement was based on a complete ignorance of the true principles of commercial legislation. How small an amount of manufacturing prosperity Colbert produced, and how great an amount of agricultural, commercial, and manufacturing wealth he either destroyed or checked in its natural progress, will be obvious to any observer who looks at the immense natural resources and the active intelligence of France. It may be safely asserted, that the whole of the bounties by which he induced adventurers to enter into remote speculations, as well as the excessive duties which he imposed on cheaper foreign articles, were almost uncompensated sacrifices; while, on the other hand, of the manufactures which he transplanted into France, and which he protected by the exclusion of rival productions, scarcely one took permanent root; and of those which still exist, and which he intended to support, there is perhaps none which would not have been more prosperous and extensive, but for those regulations with which his zeal encumbered the early march of manufacturing industry. The popularity in France of Colbert's commercial legislation, and the erroneous deductions drawn from the consequences of his interference, have produced a most prejudicial effect on the minds of a large portion of the French public. Colbert's system was a vain attempt to force capital in new directions. Thus, in order to compel the establishment of a trade with the West Indies, he made the French people pay a premium of thirty francs upon every ton of goods exported, and of fifty francs for every ton of goods imported, independently of other encouragements. In the same spirit, he incited manufacturing settlers, by large rewards, to establish themselves in different parts of France, and boasted of his having set up more than 40,000 looms, whose produce was protected by legal enactments; and no one was found to estimate the counterbalance of loss, while the most flattering pictures were drawn of enormous gain. He began in miscalculation; he brought the most despotic interference to support his errors; and, if their consequences be faithfully traced, they will be found little creditable to his own sagacity, while greatly ruinous to the nation for whose benefit they were intended. The French Revolution broke down many of the absurd and pernicious regulations which Colbert had introduced, but the vestiges of others remain; and although they have become habitual, they interfere with improvement, and give superiority to countries where the action of industry and capital is unfettered."

"Having stated thus much, it would be unjust to withhold from Colbert the credit to which he is entitled for the admirable order he established in the finances, the efforts which he made to improve, in many particulars, the system of taxation, and his opposition to the inconsiderate plan of funding adopted by Louvois. The commercial and maritime legislation of France owes to him

statesman is often obliged to abandon a scheme of evident public utility, by the unavoidable defects and abuses in the execution. Among these, one of the most frequent and prominent is, the risk of paying a premium, or granting a favour to the pretensions, not of merit, but of importunity.   In other respects, I have no fault to find with the honours, or even pecuniary rewards publicly given to artists or mechanics, in recompense of some extraordinary achievement of genius or address.   Rewards of this kind excite emulation, and enlarge the stock of general knowledge, without diverting industry or capital from their most beneficial channels.   Besides, they cost nothing in comparison of bounties of another description.   The bounty on the export of wheat has, by Smith's account, cost England in some years as much as a million and a half of dollars.   I do not believe that the British or any other government ever spent the fiftieth part of that sum upon agriculture in any one year.

SECTION II.

Of the Effect of Regulations fixing the Manner of Production.

The interference of the public authority, with regard to the details of agricultural production, has generally been of a beneficial kind. The impossibility of intermeddling in the minute and various details of agriculture, the vast number of agents it occupies, often widely separated in locality and pursuits, from the largest farming concerns to the little garden of the cottager, the small value of the produce in comparison with its volume, are so many obstacles that nature has placed in the way of authoritative restraint and interference.   All governments, that have pretended to the least regard for the public

---

the compilation of the ordonnance of 1681, a body of maritime law unrivalled to this moment."

As there is, also, another error, in the same paragraph, we must be allowed briefly to notice it.   By advancing to the manufacturers 2000 francs for every loom at work, our author thinks Colbert displayed a degree of wisdom hardly to be expected, inasmuch, as in this instance, "a part of the advance would be employed in reproduction," whereas, according to him, "in ordinary cases, whatever the government levies upon the products of individual exertion is wholly lost to future production."   Now, nothing can be more clear, than that the tax levied, for the payment of this advance, is a pure loss to the tax-paying people, and with this peculiar aggravation, that a large class of the tax-payers are not even the consumers of the "encouraged" product.   Nor is it exactly true, that in "ordinary cases whatever the government levies is wholly lost to future production," for whether the tax be advanced for every loom at work, or for the work of the looms themselves, is precisely the same thing; and, as to the destination of the tax, a portion of it is quite as likely to be employed in reproduction in the latter as in the former case.   Finally, where the tax is simply an "encouragement" to the products, the amount of it will be limited by the effective demand for them, whereas, when the advance is made for every loom at work, there is no such limit to a useless tax.

AMERICAN EDITOR.

welfare, have consequently confined themselves to the granting of premiums and encouragements, and to the diffusion of knowledge which has often contributed largely to the progress of this art. The veterinary college of Alfort, the experimental farm of Ramboullet, the introduction of the Merino breed, are real benefits to the agriculture of France, the enlargement and perfection of which she owes to the providence of the different rulers that her political troubles have successively brought into power.

A national administration that guards with vigilance the facility of communication and the quiet prosecution of the labours of husbandry, or punishes acts of culpable negligence, as the destroying of caterpillars* and other noxious insects, does a service analogous to the preservation of civil order and of property, without which production must cease altogether.

The regulations relative to the felling of trees in France, however indispensable for the preservation of their growth, at least in many of their provisions, appear in others rather to operate as a discouragement of that branch of cultivation, which, though particularly adapted to certain soils and sites, and conducive to the attraction of atmospheric moisture, yet seems to be daily on the decline.

But there is no branch of industry that has suffered so much from the officious interference of authority in its details, as that of manufacture.

Much of that interference has been directed towards limiting the number of producers, either by confining them to one trade exclusively, or by exacting specific terms, on which they shall carry on their business. This system gave rise to the establishment of chartered companies and incorporated trades. The effect is always the same, whatever be the means employed. An exclusive privilege, a species of monopoly, is created, which the consumer pays for, and of which the privileged persons derive all the benefit. The monopolists can prosecute their plans of self-interest with so much the more ease and concert, because they have legal meetings and a regular organization. At such meetings, the prosperity of the corporation is mistaken for that of commerce and of the nation at large; and the last thing considered is, whether the proposed advantages be the result of actual new production, or merely a transfer from one pocket to another, from the consumers to the privileged producers. This is the true reason why those engaged in any particular branch of trade are so anxious to have themselves made the subject of regula-

---

* Under the old *régime* of the canton of Berne, every proprietor of land was required to furnish, in the proper season of the year, so many bushels of cockchafers, in proportion to the extent of his property. The rich landholders were in the habit of buying their contingents from the poorest sort of people, who made it their business to collect them, and did it so effectually, that the district was ultimately cleared of them. But the extreme difficulty, that even the most provident government meets with in doing good by its interference in the business of production, may be judged of by a fact of which I am credibly assured, viz. that this act of paternal care gave rise to the singular fraud of transporting these insects in sacks from the Savoy side of the Leman lake into the *Pays de Vaud.*

tion; and the public authorities are commonly, on their part, very ready to indulge them in what offers so fair an opportunity of raising a revenue.

Moreover, arbitrary regulations are extremely flattering to the vanity of men in power, as giving them an air of wisdom and foresight, and confirming their authority, which seems to derive additional importance from the frequency of its exercise.   There is, perhaps, at this time, no country in Europe where a man is free to dispose of his industry and capital in what manner he pleases; in most places he cannot even change his occupation or place of residence at pleasure.   It is not enough for a man to have the necessary qualifications of ability and inclination to become a manufacturer or dealer in the woollen or silk line, in spirits or calicoes; he must besides have served his time, or been admitted to the freedom of the craft.*   Freedoms and apprenticeships are likewise expedients of police, not of that wholesome branch of police, whose object is the maintenance of public and private security, and which is neither costly nor vexatious; but of that sort of police which bad governments employ to preserve or extend their personal authority at any expense.   By the dispensation of honorary or pecuniary advantages, authority can generally influence the chiefs and superiors it has appointed to the corporations, who think to earn those honours and emoluments by their subservience to the power that confers them.   These are the ready tools for the management of the body at large, and volunteer to denounce the individuals, whose firmness may be formidable, and report those whose servility may be reckoned upon, and all under the pretext of public good.   Official harangues and public addresses are never wanting in plausible reasons for the continuance of old restrictions on liberty of action, or for the establishment of new ones; for there is no cause so bad as to be without some argument or other in its favour.

The chief advantage, and the one most relied upon, is, the insurance of a more perfect execution of the products raised for consumption, and of a superiority in them highly favourable to the national commerce, and calculated to secure the continued demand of foreigners.   But does this advantage result from the system in question?   What security is there that the corporate body itself will always be composed of men not merely of integrity, but of scrupulous delicacy, such as would never be disposed to take in either their own countrymen or foreigners?   We are told that this system facilitates the enforcement of regulations for the warranty and verification of the quality of products; but are not such regulations illusory in practice,

---

* When industry made its first start in the middle ages, and the mercantile classes were exposed to the rapacity of a grasping and ignorant nobility, incorporated trades and crafts were useful in extending to individual industry the protection of the association at large.   Their utility has ceased altogether of late years: for governments have, in our days, been either too enlightened to encroach upon the sources of financial prosperity, or too powerful to stand in awe of such associations.

even under the corporate system? and, supposing them absolutely necessary, is there no more simple way of enforcing them?

Neither will the length of apprenticeship be a better guarantee of the perfection of the work; the only thing to be depended upon for that perfection is the skill of the workman, and that is best attained by paying him in proportion to his superiority. " To teach any young man," says Smith, " in the completest manner how to apply the instruments, and how to construct the machines of the common mechanic trades, cannot well require the lessons of more than a few weeks, perhaps those of a few days might be sufficient. The dexterity of hand, indeed, even in common trades, cannot be acquired without much practice and experience, but a young man would practise with much more diligence and attention, if from the beginning he wrought as a journeyman, being paid in proportion to the little work which he could execute, and paying in his turn for the materials which he might sometimes spoil through awkwardness and inexperience."*

Were apprentices bound out a year later, and the interval spent in schools conducted on the plan of mutual instruction, I can hardly think the products would be worse executed; and, beyond all doubt, the labouring class would be advanced a stage in civilization.

Were apprenticeships a sure means of obtaining a greater perfection of products, those of Spain would be as good as those of Britain. It was not before incorporated trades and compulsory apprenticeships had been abolished in France, that she attained that superiority of execution she has now to boast of.

Perhaps there is no one mechanic art nearly so difficult as that of the gardener or field labourer; yet this is almost the only one that has nowhere been subjected to apprenticeship. Are vegetables and fruits produced in less abundance or perfection? Were cultivators a corporate body, I suppose it would soon be asserted, that highflavoured peaches and white-heart lettuces could not be raised without a code of some hundred well penned-articles.

After all, regulations of this nature, even admitting their utility, must be nugatory as soon as evasion is allowed; now it is notorious that there is no manufacturing towns where money will not purchase exemption. So that they are more than merely useless as a warranty of quality; inasmuch as they are the engine of the most odious injustice and extortion.

In support of these opinions, the advocates for the corporate system appeal to the example of Great Britain, where industry is well known to be greatly shackled, and yet manufactures prosper. But in this they expose their ignorance of the real causes of that prosperity. " These causes," Smith tells us, " seem to be the general liberty of trade, which, notwithstanding some restraints, is at least equal, perhaps superior, to what it is in any other country; the liberty of exporting, duty free, almost all sorts of goods, which are the produce of domestic industry, to almost any foreign country;

---

* *Wealth of Nations*, book i. c. 10.

and, what perhaps is of still greater importance, the unbounded liberty of transporting them from any one part of our own country to any other, without being obliged to give any account to any public office, without being liable to question or examination of any kind," &c.* Add to these, the complete inviolability of all property whatever, either by public or private attack, the enormous capital accumulated by her industry and frugality, and lastly, the habitual exercise of attention and judgment, to which her population is trained from the earliest years; and there is no need of looking farther for the causes of the manufacturing prosperity of Britain.

Those who cite her example in justification of their desire to enthral the exertions of industry, are not perhaps aware that the most thriving towns in that kingdom, those on which her character for manufacturing pre-eminence is mainly built, are the very places where there are no incorporations of crafts and trades; Manchester, Birmingham, and Liverpool,† were mere villages a century or two ago, but now rank in point of wealth and population next to London, and much before York, Canterbury, and even Bristol, cities of the greatest antiquity and privileges, and the capitals of her most thriving provinces, but still subjected to the shackles of these Gothic institutions. "The town and parish of Halifax," says Sir John Nickols,‡ a writer of acknowledged local information, "has, within these forty years, seen the number of its inhabitants quadrupled; whilst many other towns, subjected to corporations, have experienced a sensible diminution of theirs. Houses situated within the precincts of the city of London hardly find tenants, and numbers of them remain empty; whilst Westminster, Southwark, and the other suburbs are continually increasing. These suburbs are free, whilst London supports within itself four-score and twelve exclusive companies of all kinds, of which we may see the members annually adorn, with a silly pageantry, the tumultuous triumphal procession of the Lord Mayor."

The prodigious manufacturing activity of some of the suburbs of Paris is notorious; of the Faubourg St. Antoine, in particular, where industry enjoyed many exemptions. Some products were made nowhere else. How happened it, that without apprenticeships, or the necessity of being free of the craft, the manufacturer acquired a greater degree of skill, than in the rest of the city, which was subject to those institutions that are held up as so indispensable? For a very simple reason: because self-interest is the best of all instructors.

An example or two will serve better than all reasoning in the world, to show the impediments thrown in the way of the develop-

---

* *Wealth of Nations*, book iv. c. 7.   † *Baert.* vol. 1. p. 107.

‡ *Remarks on the Advantages and Disadvantages of France and of Great Britain*, 12mo. 1754, § 4, p. 142. (*a*)

(*a*) This work was originally published in French in 1752, with great success, under the fictitious name of Sir John Nickols, and is supposed to have been the production of a foreigner employed about the court of Versailles. It contains many judicious remarks upon the internal policy of Britain. T.

ment of industry by incorporations of trades and crafts. Argand, the inventor of the lamps that go by his name, and yield, at the same expense, triple the amount of light, was dragged before the *Parlement de Paris*, by the company of tinmen, locksmiths, ironmongers, and journeymen farriers, who claimed the exclusive right of making lamps.* *Lenoir*, the celebrated Parisian philosophical and mathematical instrument maker, had set up a small furnace for the convenience of working the metals used in his business. The syndics of the founders' company came in person to demolish it; and he was obliged to apply to the king for protection. Thus was talent dependent upon court favour. The manufacture of japanned hardware was altogether excluded from France until the era of the revolution, by the circumstance of its requiring the skill and implements of many different trades, and the necessity of being admitted to the freedom of them all, before an individual could carry it on. It would be easy to fill a volume with the recapitulation of the disheartening vexations that personal industry had to encounter in the city of Paris alone, under the corporate system; and another with that of the successful efforts made, since that system was abolished by the revolution.

For the same reason that the free suburb of a chartered town, or a free town in the midst of a country embarrassed by the officiousness of a meddling government, will exhibit an unusual degree of prosperity, a nation that enjoys the freedom of industry, in the midst of others following the corporate system, would probably reap similar advantages. Those have thriven the most, that have been the least shackled by the observance of formalities, provided, of course, that individuals be secured from the exactions of power, the chicanery of law, and the attempts of dishonesty or violence. Sully, whose whole life was spent in the study and practice of measures for improving the prosperity of France, entertained this opinion.† In his memoirs, he notices the multiplicity of useless laws and ordinances, as a direct barrier to the national progress.‡

---

* " Why not get himself made free of the company?" say those who are ever ready to palliate or justify official abuse. The corporation, which had the control over admissions, was itself interested in thwarting a dangerous competitor. Besides, why compel the ingenious inventor to waste in a personal canvass, that time which would be so much more profitably occupied in his calling !

† Liv. xix.

‡ *Colbert's* early education in the counting-house of the Messrs. *Mascrani*, of Lyons, a very considerable mercantile establishment, very early imbued him with the principles of the manufacturers. Commerce and manufacture thrived prodigiously under his powerful and judicious patronage; but, though he liberated them from abundance of oppression, he was himself hardly sparing enough of ordinances and regulations; he encouraged manufactures at the expense of agriculture, and saddled the people at large with the extraordinary profits of monopolists. We cannot shut our eyes to the fact, that to this system, acted upon ever since the days of *Colbert*, France owed the striking inequalities of private fortune, the overgrown wealth of some, and the superlative misery of others; the contrast of a few splendid establishments of industry, with a wide waste of poverty and degradation. This is no ideal picture, but one of sad reality, which the study of principles will help us to explain.

It may, perhaps, be alleged, that, were all occupations quite free, a large proportion of those who engaged in them would fall a sacrifice to the eagerness of competition. Possibly they might, in some few instances, although it is not very likely there should be a great excess of candidates in a line, that held out but little prospect of gain; yet, admitting the casual occurrence of this evil, it would be of infinitely less magnitude, than permanently keeping up the prices of produce at a rate that must limit its consumption, and abridge the power of purchasing in the great body of consumers.

If the measures of authority, levelled against the free disposition of each man's respective talents and capital, are criminal in the eye of sound policy, it is still more difficult to justify them upon the principles of natural right. " The patrimony of a poor man," says the author of the Wealth of Nations, " lies in the strength and dexterity of his hands : and to hinder him from employing this strength and dexterity in what manner he thinks proper, without injury to his neighbour, is a plain violation of his most sacred property."

However, as society is possessed of a natural right to regulate the exercise of any class of industry, that without regulation might prejudice the rest of the community, physicians, surgeons, and apothecaries, are with perfect justice subjected to an examination into their professional ability. The lives of their fellow-citizens are dependent upon their skill, and a test of that skill may fairly be established; but it does not seem advisable to limit the number of practitioners nor the plan of their education. Society has no interest further than to ascertain their qualification.

On the same grounds, regulation is useful and proper, when aimed at the prevention of fraud or contrivance, manifestly injurious to other kinds of production, or to the public safety, and not at prescribing the nature of the products and the methods of fabrication. Thus, a manufacturer must not be allowed to advertise his goods to the public as of better than their actual quality : the home consumer is entitled to the public protection against such a breach of faith; and so, indeed, is the mercantile character of the nation, which must suffer in the estimation and demand of foreign customers from such practices. And this is an exception to the general rule, that the best of all guarantees is the personal interest of the manufacturer. For, possibly, when about to give up business, he may find it answer to increase his profit by a breach of faith, and sacrifice a future object he is about to relinquish for a present benefit. A fraud of this kind ruined the French cloths in the Levant market, about the year 1783; since when the German and British have entirely supplanted them.* We may go still further. An article often derives a value from the name, or from the place of its manufacture. When we judge from long experience, that cloths of such a denomination, and

---

* The loss of this trade has been erroneously imputed to the liberty of commerce, consequent upon the revolution. But *Felix Beaujour*, in his *Tableau du Commerce de la Grèce*, has shown that it must be referred to an earlier period, when restrictions were still in force.

made at such a place, will be of a certain breadth and substance, it is a fraud to fabricate, under the same name and at the same place, a commodity of inferior substance and quality to the ordinary standard, and thus to send it into the world under a false certificate.

Hence we may form an opinion of the extent to which government may carry its interference with benefit. The correspondence with the sample of conditions, express or implied, must be rigidly enforced, and government should meddle with production no further. I would wish to impress upon my readers, that the mere interference is itself an evil, even where it is of use :* first, because it harasses and distresses individuals; and, secondly, because it costs money, either to the nation, if it be defrayed by government, that is to say, charged upon the public purse, or to the consumer, if it be charged upon the specific article; in the latter case, the charge must of course enhance the price, thereby laying an additional tax upon the home consumer, and *pro tanto* discouraging the foreign demand.

If interference be an evil, a paternal government will be most sparing of its exercise. It will not trouble itself about the certification of such commodities, as the purchaser must understand better than itself; or of such as cannot well be certified by its agents; for, unfortunately, a government must always reckon upon the negligence, incapacity, and misconduct of its retainers. But some articles may well admit of certification; as gold and silver, the standard of which can only be ascertained by a complex operation of chemistry, which few purchasers know how to execute, and which, if they did, would cost them infinitely more than it can be executed for by the government in their stead.

In Great Britain, the individual inventor of a new product or of a new process may obtain the exclusive right to it, by obtaining what is called a patent. While the patent remains in force, the absence of competitors enables him to raise his price far above the ordinary return of his outlay with interest, and the wages of his own industry. Thus he receives a premium from the government, charged upon the consumers of the new article; and this premium is often very large, as may be supposed in a country so immediately productive as Great Britain, where there are consequently abundance of affluent individuals, ever on the look-out for some new object of enjoyment. Some years ago a man invented a spiral or worm spring for insertion between the leather braces of carriages, to ease their motion, and made his fortune by the patent for so trifling an invention.

Privileges of this kind no one can reasonably object to; for they neither interfere with, nor cramp any branch of industry, previously in operation. Moreover, the expense incurred is purely voluntary; and those who choose to incur it, are not obliged to renounce the satisfaction of any previous wants, either of necessity or of amusement.

---

* "Every restraint, imposed by legislation, upon the freedom of human action must inevitably extinguish a portion of the energies of the community, and abridge its annual product."—*Verri. Refl. sur l'Econ. Pol. c.* 12.

However, as it is the duty of every government to aim at the constant amelioration of its subjects' condition, it cannot deprive other producers to eternity of the right to employ part of their industry and capital in this particular channel, which perhaps they might sooner or later have themselves discovered, or preclude the consumer for a very long period from the advantages of a competition-price. Foreign nations being out of its jurisdiction, would of course grant no privilege to the inventor, and would, therefore, in this particular, during the operation of the patent, be better off than the nation where the invention originated.

France* has imitated the wise example of England, in assigning a limit to the duration of these patent rights, after which the invention is free for all the world to avail themselves of. It is also provided, that, if the process be capable of concealment, it shall be divulged at the expiration of the term. And the patentee, who in this case, it may be supposed, could do without the patent, has this advantage: that if his secret be discovered by any body in the interim, it cannot be made available till the expiration of the term.

Nor is it at all necessary that the government should inquire into the novelty or utility of the invention; for, if it be useless, so much the worse for the inventor, and, if it be already known, every body is competent to plead and prove that fact, and the previous right of the public; so that the only sufferer is the inventor, who has been at the expense of a patent for nothing. Thus the public is no loser by this species of encouragement, but, on the contrary, may derive prodigious advantage.

The regulations tending to direct either the object or the method of production, which have been above observed upon, by no means comprise all the measures adopted by different nations with those views. Indeed, were I to specify them all, my catalogue would soon be incomplete; for new ones are every day brought into practice. The great point is, to lay down certain principles, that may enable us beforehand to judge of their consequences. But there are two other branches of commerce, that have been the subject of more than usual regulation, and are, therefore, worthy of more special investigation. I shall devote the two succeeding sections to their exclusive examination.

SECTION III.

Of Privileged Trading Companies.

A government sometimes grants to individual merchants, and much oftener to trading companies, the exclusive privilege of buying and selling specific articles, tobacco for example; or of trafficking with a particular country, as with India.

---

* *Vide* the laws dated 7th Jan. and 25th May, 1791, and 20th Sept. 1792. Also the *arret* of the government, dated 5 Vandemaire, an. ix.

The privileged traders, being thus exempted from all competition by the exertion of the public authority, can raise their prices above the level that could be maintained under the operation of a free trade. This unnatural ratio of price is sometimes fixed by the government itself, which thus assigns a limit to the partiality it exercises towards the producers, and the injustice it practises upon the consumers: otherwise, the avarice of the privileged company would be bounded only by the dread of losing more by the reduction of the gross amount of its sales, in consequence of increased prices, than it would gain by their unnatural elevation. At all events, the consumer pays for the commodity more than its worth; and government generally contrives to share in the profits of the monopoly.

It has been said, for the most ruinous expedient is sure to find some plausible argument or other to support it, that the commerce with certain nations requires precautionary measures, which privileged companies only can enforce. At one time the plea is, that forts must be built, and marine establishments kept up; as if in truth it were worth while to traffic sword in hand, or an army were necessary to protect plain dealing; or as if the state did not already maintain at great charge a military force for the protection of its subjects! At another, that diplomatic address is indispensable. The Chinese, for instance, are a people so bigoted to form and prone to suspicion— so entirely independent of other nations, by reason of their remote position, the extent of their territory, and the peculiar character of their wants, that is a matter of special and precarious favour to be allowed to deal with them. We must, therefore, elect either to go without their teas, silks, and nankeens, or be content to submit to precautions, which can alone insure the continuance of the trade; for the dealings of individuals might endanger the continuance of that good humour, without which the mutual intercourse of the two nations would be at an end.

But, let me ask, is it so certain that the agents of a company, who are too apt to presume upon the support of the military power, either of the nation or at least of the company,—is it quite certain, that such agents are more likely to keep alive an amicable feeling than private traders, in whom more deference to local institutions might be expected, and who would have an immediate interest in keeping clear of any misunderstanding that should endanger both their persons and their property?*

But, supposing the worst that could happen, and granting, for argument's sake, that the trade with China can not be conducted otherwise than by a privileged company, does it follow, that without one we must needs give up the taste for Chinese productions?

---

* This has been exemplified in the commercial relations of the United States with China. The American traders conduct themselves at Canton with more discretion, and are regarded by the Chinese authorities with less jealousy than the agents of the English company. The Portuguese, for upwards of a century, carried on the trade with the Eastern seas, without the intervention of a company, and with greater success than any of their contemporaries.

Certainly not. The trade in Chinese goods will always exist, for this plain reason, that it suits both parties, the Chinese and their customers. But shall we not pay dearer for those goods? There is no ground for thinking so. Three-fourths of the European states have never sent a single ship to China, and yet are abundantly supplied with teas, with silks, and with nankeens, and that too at a very cheap rate.

There is another argument of more general application, and still more frequently urged; viz. that a company, having the exclusive trade of any given country, is exempt from the effects of competition, and, therefore, buys at a less price. But, in the first place, it is not true that the exclusive privilege exempts from the effect of competition: the only competition it removes, is that of the national traders, which would be of the utmost benefit to the nation; but it excludes neither the competition of foreign companies, nor of foreign private traders. In the next place, there are many articles that would not rise in price in consequence of the competition, which some people affect to be alarmed at, though in truth it is a mere bugbear.

Suppose Marseilles, Bordeaux, L'Orient, were all to fit out vessels to bring tea from China, we have no reason to believe that all their ventures together would import more tea into France, than France could consume or dispose of. All we have to fear is, that they should not import enough. Now, if they were to import no more than other merchants would have imported for them, the demand for tea in China will have been just the same in both cases; consequently, the commodity will not have become more scare there. Our merchants would hardly have to pay dearer for it, unless the price should rise in China itself; and what sensible effect could the purchases of a few merchants of France have upon the price of an article consumed in China itself, to one hundred times the amount of the whole consumption of Europe?

But, granting that European competition would operate to raise the price of some commodities in the eastern market, is that a sufficient motive for excepting the trade to that part of the world from the general rules that are acted upon in all other branches of commerce? Are we to invest an exclusive company with the sole conduct of the import or export trade between Germany and France, for the sole purpose of getting our cottons and woollens from Germany at a cheaper rate? If the commerce of the East were put upon the same footing as foreign trade in general, the price of any one article of its produce could never long remain much above the cost of production in Asia; for the rise of price would operate as a stimulus to increased production, and the competition of sellers would soon be on a par with that of purchasers.

But, admitting the advantage of buying cheap to be as substantial as it is represented, the nation at large has a right to participate in that cheapness; the home consumers ought to buy cheap as well as the company. Whereas in practice it is just the reverse, and, for a

very simple reason: the company is not exempt from competition as
a purchaser, for other nations are its competitors: but as a seller,it is
exempt; for the rest of the nation can buy the articles it deals in nowhere else, the import by foreigners being wholly prohibited. It
asks its own price, and can command the market, especially if it be
attentive to keep the market always understocked, as the English
call it; that is, if the supply be just so far short of the demand, as to
keep alive the competition of purchasers.*

In this manner, trading companies not only extort exorbitant
profits from the consumer, but moreover saddle him with all the
fraud and mismanagement inseparable from the conduct of these
unwieldy bodies, with their cumbrous organisation of directors and
factors without end, dispersed from one extremity of the globe to the
other. The only check to the gross abuses of these privileged
bodies is the smuggling or contraband trade, which, in this point of
view, may lay claim to some degree of utility.

This analysis brings us to the point in question; are the gains of
the privileged company, national gains? Undoubtedly not; for they
are wholly taken from the pockets of the nation itself. The whole
excess of value, paid by the consumer, beyond the rate at which free
trade could afford the article, is not a value produced, but so much
existing value presented by the government to the trader at the consumer's expense. It will probably be urged, that it must at least be
admitted, that this profit remains and is spent at home. Granted:
but by whom is it spent? that is the point. Should one member of
a family possess himself of the whole family income, dress himself
in fine clothes, and devour the best of every thing, what consolation
would it be to the rest of the family, were he to say, what signifies
it whether you or I spend the money? the income spent is the same,
so it can make no difference.

The exclusive as well as excessive profits of monopoly would soon
glut the privileged companies with wealth, could they depend upon
the good management of their concerns; but the cupidity of agents,
the long pendency of distant adventures, the difficulty of bringing
factors abroad to account, and the incapacity of those interested, are
causes of ruin in constant activity. Long and delicate operations of
commerce require superior exertion and intelligence in the parties
interested. And how can such qualities be expected in shareholders,
amounting sometimes to several hundreds, all of them having other
matters of more personal importance to look after?†

Such are the consequences of privileges granted to trading compa-

---

* It is well known, that, when the Dutch were in possession of the Moluccas,
they were in the habit of burning part of the spices they produced, for the sake
of keeping up the price in Europe.

† The answer of *La Bourdonnais* to one of the directors of the French East
India Company, who asked how it was, that he had managed his own interests
so much better than those of the company, will long be remembered:—"Because," said he, "I manage my own affairs according to the dictates of my own
judgment, but am obliged to follow your instructions in regard to those of the
company."

nies: and these consequences, it must be observed, are in the nature of things inseparable; circumstances may reduce their efficacy, but can never remove them altogether. The English East India Company has met with more success than the three or four French ones that at different times made the experiment.* This company is sovereign as well as merchant; and we know, by experience, that the most detestable governments may last for several generations; witness that of the Mamelukes in Egypt. (1)

There are some minor evils also incident to commercial privileges. The grant of exclusive rights frequently exiles from a country a branch of industry and a portion of capital that would readily have taken root there, but are compelled to settle abroad. Towards the close of the reign of Louis XIV. the French East India Company, being unable to support itself, notwithstanding its exclusive rights, transferred the exercise of its privileges to some speculators at St. Malo, in consideration of a small share in their profits. The trade began to revive under the influence of this comparative liberty, and would, on the expiration of the company's charter, in 1714, have been as active as the then melancholy condition of France would have permitted: but the company petitioned for a renewal, and obtained one, pending the ventures of some private traders. Soon afterwards, a vessel of St. Malo, commanded by a Breton of the name of Lamerville, appeared upon the French coast, on its return from the East Indies, but was refused permission to enter the harbour, on the plea, that it was in contravention of the company's rights. Consequently, he was compelled to prosecute his voyage to the nearest port in Belgium, and carried his vessel into Ostend, where he disposed of the cargo. The governor of the Low Countries, hearing of the enormous profits he had made, proposed to the captain a second voyage, with a squadron to be fitted out for the express purpose; and Lamerville afterwards performed many simi-

---

* The first French East India Company was established in the reign of Henry IV. A. D. 1604, at the instance of a Fleming of the name of *Gerard Leroi.* It met with no success.

---

(1) The commercial monopoly of the English East India Company was finally abolished by three acts of Parliament, passed during the year 1833, namely, chapters 85, 93, and 101 of the 3d and 4th William IV. The first is entitled, an act for effecting an arrangement with the East India Company, and for the better government of His Majesty's Indian territories, till the 30th day of April, 1854; the second, an act to regulate the trade of China and India; and the third, an act to provide for the collection and management of duties on tea.

By these acts the trade with both China and India is thrown open, for the first time, to British enterprise and capital, and British subjects are also permitted to take up their residence in these countries. It is needless to point out the vast importance of these enactments, and the great advantages that must result from them, not only to British subjects, but to the whole commercial world. The resources of regions of rich countries that have hitherto lain dormant will now be called into activity, and the general wealth of the country, and its capacity of absorbing foreign commodities, immensely increased.

AMERICAN EDITOR.

lar voyages for different employers, and laid the foundation of the Ostend Company.*

Thus, the French consumer must necessarily have suffered by this monopoly: and so, in fact, he did. But, at any rate, it will be supposed, the company must have benefited. Just the contrary: the company was itself ruined; in spite of the monopoly of tobacco, the lotteries, and other subsidiary grants bestowed on them by the government.† "In short," says Voltaire,‡ "all that remained to France in the East was the regret of having, in the course of forty years, squandered enormous sums, to bolster up a company that never made a six-pence profit, never made any dividend from the resources of its commerce, either to its share-holders or creditors; and supported its establishments in India, solely by the underhand practice of pillage and extortion upon the natives."

The only case in which the establishment of an exclusive company is justifiable, is, when there is no other way of commencing a new trade with distant or barbarous nations. In that case, the charter is a kind of patent of invention, and confers an advantage, commensurate to the extraordinary risk and expense of the first experiment. The consumers have no reason to complain of the dearness of products, which, but for the grant of the charter, they would either not have enjoyed at all, or have enjoyed at a still dearer rate. But such grants should, like patents, be limited to such duration only, as will repay and fully indemnify the adventurers for the advances and risk incurred. Any thing further is a mere free gift to the company, at the expense of the nation at large, who have a natural right to get what they want wherever they can, and at the lowest possible price.

What has been said with respect to commercial is equally applicable to manufacturing privileges. The reason why governments are so easily entrapped into measures of this kind is, partly because they see a statement of large profits, and do not trouble themselves to inquire whence they are derived; and partly because this apparent profit is easily reduced to numerical calculation, no matter whether wrong or right, correct or incorrect; whereas the loss and mischief resulting to the nation are infinitely subdivided amongst the members of the community, and operate after all in a very indirect, complex, and general way, so as to escape and defy calculation. Some writers maintain arithmetic to be the only sure guide in political economy; for my part, I see so many detestable systems built upon arithmetical statements, that I am rather inclined to regard that science as the instrument of national calamity.

---

* Taylor's *Letters on India.*

† *Raynal. Hist. phil. et polit, des Establ. des Européens, dans les deux Indes,* liv. iv. § 19.

‡ *Siècle de Louis XV.*

Of regulations affecting the Corn Trade.

It would seem that the general principles, which govern the commerce of all other commodities, should be equally applicable to the commerce of grain. But grain, or whatever else may happen to be the staple article of human subsistence to any people, deserves more particular notice.

It is universally found, that the numbers of mankind increase, in proportion to the supply of subsistence. The abundance and cheapness of provisions are favourable to the advance of population; their scarcity is productive of the opposite effect;* but neither cause operates so rapidly as the annual succession of crops. The crop of one year may, perhaps, exceed or fall short of the usual average, by as much as one-fifth or one-fourth; but a country, that, like France, has thirty millions of inhabitants one year, cannot have thirty-six millions the next; nor could its population be reduced to twenty-four millions in the space of one year, without the most dreadful degree of suffering. Therefore it is the law of nature, that the population shall one year be superabundantly supplied with subsistence, and another year be subjected to scarcity in some degree or other of intensity.

And so, indeed, it is with all other objects of consumption; but, as the most of them are not absolutely indispensable to existence, the temporary privation of them amounts not to the absolute extinction of life. The high price of a product, which has wholly or partially failed at home, is a powerful stimulus to commerce to import it from a greater distance and at a greater expense. But it is unsafe to leave wholly to the providence of individuals the care of supplying an article of such absolute necessity: the delay of which, but for a few days, may be a national calamity; the transport of which exceeds the ordinary means of commerce; and whose weight and bulk would make its distant transport, especially by land, double or triple its average price. If the foreign supply of corn be relied upon, it may happen to be scarce and dear in the exporting and importing country at the same moment. The government of the exporting country may prohibit the export, or a maritime war may interrupt the transport. But the article is one the nation cannot do without; or even wait for a few days longer. Delay is death to a part of the population at least.

For the purpose of equalizing the average consumption to the average crop, each family ought literally to lay by, in years of plenty, for the deficiency of years of scarcity. But such providence cannot be reckoned upon in the bulk of the population. A great majority, to say nothing of their utter want of foresight, are destitute of the means of keeping such a store in reserve sometimes several years

---

* *Vide infrà.* Book II. chap. 11.

together; neither have they the accommodations for housing it, or the means of taking it along with them on a casual change of abode.

Can speculative commerce be depended upon for this reserve against a deficiency? At first sight it might appear that it could, that self-interest would be an adequate motive; for the difference of the price of corn in years of abundance and those of scarcity is very great. But the recurrence of the oscillation is too irregular in distance of time, and too infrequent also, to give rise to a regular traffic, or one that can be repeated at pleasure. The purchase of the grain, the number and size of the storehouses, require a very large advance of capital and a heavy arrear of interest: it is an article that must be repeatedly shifted and turned, and is much exposed to fraud and damage, as well as to popular violence. All these are to be covered by a profit of rare occurrence. Wherefore, it is possible, that the article may not hold out sufficient temptation to the speculator, although this would be the most commendable kind of speculation, being framed upon the principle of buying from the producer when he is eager to sell, and selling to the consumer when he finds it difficult to purchase.

In default of the individual providence of the consumer, and of speculative accumulation and reserve, neither of which it would seem can be safely depended upon, can the public authority, as representing the aggregate interest, undertake the charge of providing against a scarcity with any prospect of success? I am aware, that, in a few very limited communities, blessed with a very economical government, like some of the Swiss cantons, public granaries for storing a casual surplus have answered the purpose well enough. But I should pronounce them impracticable in large and populous countries. The advance of capital and its accruing interest would affect the government in the same manner as private speculators, and even in a greater degree; for there are few governments, that can borrow on such low terms as individuals in good credit. The difficulties of managing a commercial concern, of buying, storing, and re-selling to so large an extent, would be still more insuperable. Turgot, in his letters on the commerce of grain, has clearly proved, that, in matters of this kind, a government never can expect to be served at a reasonable rate; all its agents having an interest in swelling its expenditure, and none of them in curtailing. It would be utterly impossible to answer for the tolerable conduct of a business left to the discretion of agents without any adequate control, whose actions are, for the most part, governed by the superior dignitaries of the state, who seldom have either the knowledge or condescension requisite for such details. A sudden panic in the public authorities might prematurely empty the granaries; a political measure, or a war, divert their contents to quite a different destination.

Generally speaking, it appears that there is no safe dependence for a reserve of supply against a season of scarcity, unless the business be confided to the discretionary management of mercantile houses of the first capital, credit, and intelligence, willing to undertake the purchase, and the filling and replenishment of the granaries upon certain stipulated terms, and with the prospect of such advantages, as may fairly recompense them for all their trouble. The operation would then be safe and effectual, for the contractors would give security for due performance; and it would also be cheaper executed in this way than in any other. Different establishments might be contracted with for the different cities of note; and these being thus supplied in times of scarcity from the stores in reserve, would no longer drain the country of the subsistence destined to the agricultural population. (*a*)

Public stores and granaries are after all but auxiliary and temporary expedients of supply. The most abundant and advantageous supply will always be that furnished by the utmost freedom of commerce, whose duties in respect to grain consist chiefly in transporting the produce from the farmyard to the principal markets, and thence in smaller quantities from the markets of the districts where it is superabundant to those of others that may be scantily supplied; or in exporting when cheap, and importing when dear.

Popular prejudice and ignorance have universally regarded with an evil eye those concerned in the corn-trade; nor have the depositories of national authority been always exempt from similar illiberality. The main charge against them is, that they buy up corn with the express purpose of raising its price, or at least of making an unreasonable profit upon the purchase and re-sale, which is in effect so much gratuitous loss to the producer and consumer.

First, I would ask, what is meant by this charge? If it be meant to accuse the dealers of buying in plentiful seasons, when corn is cheap, and laying by in reserve against seasons of scarcity, we have just seen that this is a most beneficial operation, and the sole means of accommodating the supply of so precarious an article to the regularity of an unceasing demand. Large stores of grain laid in at a low price contribute powerfully to place the subsistence of the population beyond risk of failure, and deserve not only the protection, but the encouragement of the public authorities. But, if it be meant to charge the corn-dealers with buying up on a rising market and on the approach of scarcity, and thereby enhancing the scarcity and the price, although I admit that this operation has not the same

(*a*) It is singular, that, after the very careful revision which this section has undergone in the last edition, this paragraph should have been suffered to stand. Indeed, one would almost suspect that our author had left it rather in compliment to the popular notions of his own country, than from personal conviction of the propriety of the measure he suggests; which is impugned by the whole context of the remaining part of the section. The best security against famine is, the total absence of all official interference whatever, whether permanent or temporary, as the example of Great Britain will testify. There the government has at all times abstained from taking a personal part in the supply either of town or country, and has limited its interference to the mere export and import, which have only been cramped and impeded by ill-advised operations. Another important ground of security is, the variety of the national food. Upon this our author has observed.—*Vide, infrà.* T.

recommendation of utility, and that the consumer is saddled with the additional cost of the operation without any direct equivalent benefit, for in this instance the deficiency of one year is not made good by the hoarded surplus of a preceding one; yet I cannot think it has ever been attended with any very alarming or fatal consequences. Corn is a commodity of most extended production; and its price cannot be arbitrarily raised, without disarming the competition of an infinity of sellers, and without an extent of dealing and of agency scarcely practicable to individuals. It is, besides, a most cumbersome and inconvenient article in comparison with its price, and, consequently, most expensive and troublesome in the carriage and warehousing. A store of any considerable value can not escape observation.* And its liability to damage or decay often makes sales compulsory, and exposes the larger speculators to immense loss.

Speculative monopoly is, therefore, extremely difficult, and little to be dreaded. The kind of engrossment most prejudicial, as well as most difficult of prevention, is that practised by the domestic prudence of individuals in apprehension of a scarcity. Some, from excess of precaution, lay by rather more than they want; while farmers, farming proprietors, millers, and bakers, who habitually keep a stock on hand, take care somewhat to swell that stock, in the idea that they shall sell to a profit whatever surplus there may be; and the infinite number of these petty acts of engrossment makes them greatly exceed, in the aggregate, all the united efforts of speculation.

But what if it should turn out, after all, that even the selfish and odious views of such speculators are productive of some good? When corn is cheap, it is consumed with less providence and frugality, and used as food for the domestic animals. The distant prospect of scarcity, or even a slight rise of price, is insufficient to check this improvidence betimes. If the great holders shut up their stores, however, the consequent anticipation of a rise of price immediately puts the public on their guard, and awakens the particular frugality and care of the little consumers, of whom the great mass of consumption is composed. Ingenuity is set at work to find a substitute for the scarce article of food, and not a particle is wasted. Thus, the avarice of one part of mankind operates as a salutary check upon the improvidence of the rest; and, when the stock withheld at length appears in the market, its quantity tends to lower the price in favour of the consumer.

With regard to the tribute which the dealer is supposed to exact from both producer and consumer, it is a charge that will attach with equal justice upon every branch of commerce whatsoever. There would be some meaning in it, could products reach the hands of the consumer without any advance of capital, without warehouses, trou-

---

* *Lamarre*, who was a great advocate for the interference of authority in these matters, and was commissioned by the government, in the scarcities of the years 1699—1709, to discover all concealed hoards, and bring to light the monopolists, frankly confesses, that he was not able to make seizure of so much as 100 quarters altogether.—*Traitè de la Police, Supplement au tome* 11.

ble, combination, or any kind of difficulty.   But, so long as difficulties shall exist, nobody will be able to surmount them so cheaply, as those who make it their special business.   Legislation should take an enlarged view of commerce in the aggregate, small and great; it will find its agents busied in traversing the whole surface of the territory, watching every fluctuation of demand and supply, adjusting the casual or local deficiency of price to meet the charges of production and excess of price above the capacity of consumption.   Is it to the cultivator, to the consumer, or to the public administration that we can safely look for so beneficial and powerful an agency? Extend, if you please, the facility of intercourse, and particularly the capacities of internal navigation, which alone is suited to the transport of a commodity so cumbrous and bulky as grain; vigilantly watch over the personal security of the trader; and then leave him to follow his own track.   Commerce cannot make good the failure of the crop; but it can distribute whatever there may be to distribute, in the manner best suited to the wants of the community, as well as to the interests of production.   And doubtless it was for this reason that Smith pronounced the labour of the corn dealer to be favourable to the production of corn, in the next degree to that of the cultivator himself.

The prevalence of erroneous views of the production and commerce of articles of human subsistence, has led to a world of mischievous and contradictory laws, regulations, and ordinances, in all countries, suggested by the exigency of the moment, and often extorted by popular importunity.   The danger and odium thus heaped upon the dealers in grain have frequently thrown the business into the hands of inferior persons, qualified neither by information nor ability for the business; and the usual consequence has followed; namely, that the same traffic has been carried on in secret, at far greater expense to the consumers; the dealers to whom it was abandoned being of course obliged to pay themselves for all the risk and inconvenience of the occupation.

Whenever a maximum of price has been affixed to grain, it has immediately been withdrawn or concealed.   The next step was to compel the farmers to bring their grain to market, and prohibit the private sales.   These violations of property, with all their usual accompaniments of inquisitorial search, personal violence, and injustice, have never afforded any considerable resource to the government employing them.   In polity as well as morality, the grand secret is, not to constrain the actions, but to awaken the inclinations of mankind.   Markets are not to be supplied by the terror of the bayonet or the sabre.*

When the national government attempts to supply the population

---

* The French minister of the interior, in his report, presented in December, 1817, admits that the markets were never so ill supplied as immediately after the decree of May 4, 1812, prohibiting all sales out of open market. The consumers crowded thither, having nowhere else to resort to; while the farmers, being obliged to sell below the current price, pretended to have nothing for sale.

by becoming itself a dealer, it is sure to fail in satisfying the national wants itself, and at the same time to extinguish all the resources that freedom of commerce would offer; for nobody else will knowingly embark in a losing trade, though the government may.

During the scarcity prevalent throughout many parts of France, in the year 1775, the municipalities of Lyons and some other towns attempted to relieve the wants of the inhabitants, by buying up corn in the country, and re-selling it at a loss in the towns. To defray the expense of this operation, they at the same time obtained an increase of the *octroi* or tolls upon goods entering their gates. The scarcity grew worse and worse, for a very obvious reason; the ordinary dealers naturally abandoned markets where goods were sold below the cost price, and which they could not resort to without paying extra toll upon entry.*

The more necessary an article is, the more dangerous it is to reduce its price below the natural level. An accidental dearness of corn, though doubtless a most unwelcome occurrence, is commonly brought about by causes out of all human power to remove.† There is no wisdom in heaping one calamity upon another, and passing bad laws because there has been a bad season.

Governments have met with no better success in the matter of importation, than in the conduct of internal commerce. The enormous sacrifices made by the *commune* of Paris and the general government, to provision the metropolis in the winter of 1816–17 with grain imported from abroad, did not protect the consumer from an exorbitant advance in the price of bread, which was besides deficient both in weight and quality; and the supply was found inadequate after all.‡

---

* In all ages and in all places this effect will follow. The Emperor Julian, A. D. 362, caused to be sold at Antioch 420,000 *modii* of wheat imported from Chalsis and Egypt for the purpose, at a price lower than the average of the market; the supplies of private commerce were immediately stopped in consequence, and the famine was aggravated. *Vide* Gibbon, c. 24. The principles of political economy are eternal and immutable; but one nation is acquainted with them, and another not.

The metropolis of the Roman empire was always destitute of subsistence, when the government withheld the gratuitous largesses of grain drawn from a tributary world; and these very largesses were the real cause of the scarcity felt and complained of.

† One of the most frequent causes of famine is, indeed, of human creation, and that is war, which both interrupts production, and wastes existing products. This cause is, therefore, within human control; but we can hardly expect it to be effectually exerted, until governments shall entertain more accurate notions of their own, as well as of the national interests; and nations be weaned of the puerility of attaching sentiments of admiration and glory to perils encountered without necessity or reason.

‡ It is mere mockery to talk of the paternal care, solicitude, or beneficence of government, which are never of any avail, either to extend the powers of authority, or to diminish the suffering of the people. The solicitude of the government can never be doubted; a sense of intense personal interest will always *guide* it to the conservation of social order, by which it is sure to be the principal gainer. And its beneficence can have little merit; for it can exert none, but at the expense of its subjects.

On the subject of bounties on import, it is hardly necessary to touch. The most effectual bounty is the high price of the article in the country where the scarcity occurs, amounting sometimes to as much as 200 or 300 per cent. If this be not sufficient to tempt the importer, I know of no adequate inducement that the government could hold out to him.

Nations would be less subject to famine, were they to employ a greater variety of aliments. When the whole population depends upon a single product for subsistence, the misery of a scarcity is extreme. A deficiency of corn in France is as bad as one of rice in Hindostan. When their diet consists of many articles, as butcher's meat, poultry, esculent roots, vegetables, fruits, fish, &c., according to local circumstances, the supply is less precarious; for these articles seldom fail all at a time.*

Scarcity would also be of less frequent occurrence, if more attention were paid to the dissemination and perfection of the art of preserving, at a cheap rate, such kinds of food, as are offered in superabundance at particular seasons and places; fish, for instance; their periodical excess might in this way be made to serve for times of scarcity. A perfect freedom of international maritime intercourse would enable the inhabitants of the temperate latitudes to partake cheaply of those productions, that nature pours forth in such profusion under a tropical sun.† I know not how far it would be possible to preserve and transport the fruit of the banana; but the expe-

---

* Custom, the tyrant of weak minds, and of such, unfortunately, is the great mass of mankind, and of the lower classes in particular, is always a formidable opponent to the introduction of a new article of food. I have observed in some provinces of France, a decided distaste for the paste prepared in the Italian method, although a most nutritious substance, and well calculated for keeping the flour sound and good. Probably, nothing but the frequent recurrence of scarcity during the political agitations of the nation could have extended the cultivation and consumption of the potatoe, so as to have made it a staple article of food in many districts. The appetite for that vegetable would be still more general, were a little more attention bestowed upon preserving and ameliorating the species, and the practice of raising it from the seed rather than the root more strictly observed.

† *Humboldt* tells us, in his *Essai pol. sur la Nouvelle Espagne*, c. ix. that an equal area of land in that country will produce *bananas*, potatoes, and wheat, in the following proportions of weight:—

	Kilogrammes.
Bananas	106,000
Potatoes	2,400
Wheat	800

The product of bananas is, therefore, in weight, 133 times that of wheat, and 44 times that of potatoes. But a large deduction must be made for the aqueous particles of the banana.

A *demi-hectare* of fertile land in Mexico, by proper cultivation of the larger species of banana, may be made to feed more than 50 individuals; whereas the same extent of surface in Europe, supposing it to yield eight-fold, will give an annual product of no more than 576 *kils.* of wheat flour, which is not enough for the sustenance of two persons. It is natural that Europeans, on their first arrival in a tropical region, should be surprised at the very limited extent of cultivated ground, encircling the crowded cabins of the native population.

riment has in a great measure succeeded with respect to the sugar-cane, which furnishes, in a thousand shapes, an agreeable and wholesome article of diet, and is produced so abundantly by all parts of the world, lying within 38° of latitude, that, but for our present absurd legislative provisions, it might be had much cheaper than butcher's meat, and for the same price as many indigenous fruits and vegetables.*

To return to the corn-trade, I must protest against the indiscriminate and universal application of the arguments I have adduced to show the benefits of liberty. Nothing is more dangerous in practice, than an obstinate, unbending adherence to system, particularly in its application to the wants and errors of mankind. The wiser course is, to approximate invariably to the standard of sound and acknowledged principles, to lead towards them by the never-failing influence of gradual and insensible attraction. It is well to fix beforehand a maximum of price beyond which exportation of grain shall either be prohibited, or subjected to heavy duties; for, as smuggling cannot be prevented entirely, it is better that those who are resolved to practise it should pay the insurance of the risk to the state than to individuals.

We have hitherto regarded the inflated price of grain as the only evil to be apprehended. But England, in 1815, was alarmed by a prospect of an opposite evil; viz. that its price would be reduced too low by the influx of foreign grain. The production of this article is, like that of every other, much more costly in England than in the neighbouring states, owing to a variety of causes, which it is immaterial here to explain; amongst others, chiefly to the exorbitance of her taxation. Foreign grain could be sold in England at two-thirds of its cost price to the English grower. It, therefore, became a most important question, whether it were better to permit the free importation, and thus, by exposing the home producer to a ruinous competition with the foreign grower, to render him incapable of paying his rent and taxes, to divert him from the cultivation of wheat altogether, and place England in a state of dependence for subsistence upon foreign, perhaps hostile nations; or, by excluding foreign grain from her market, to give a monopoly to the home producer, at the expense of the consumer, thereby augmenting the difficulty of subsistence to the labouring classes, and, by the advanced price of the necessaries of life, indirectly raising that of all the manufactured produce of the country, and proportionately disabling it to sustain the competition of other nations.

This great question has given rise to the most animated contest both of the tongue and the pen; and the obstinate contention of two parties, each of which had much of justice on its side, leaves the by-

---

* The same author informs us, that, in St. Domingo, a superficial square of 3403 toises, is reckoned at an average capable of producing 10,000 lbs. weight of sugar; and that the total consumption of that commodity in France, taking it at the fair average of 20,000,000 *kils.* might be raised upon a superficial area of seven square leagues.

standers to infer, that neither has chosen to notice the grand cause of mischief; that is to say, the necessity of supporting the arrogant pretensions of England to universal influence and dominion, by sacrifices out of all proportion to her territorial extent. At all events, the great acuteness and intelligence, displayed by the combatants on either side, have thrown new light upon the interference of authority in the business of the supply of grain, and have tended to strengthen the conclusion in favour of commercial liberty.

The substance of the argument of the prohibitionists may be reduced to this; that it is expedient to encourage domestic agriculture, even at the expense of the consumer, to avoid the risk of starvation by external means; which is seriously to be apprehended on two occasions in particular; first, when the power or influence of a belligerent is able to intercept or check the import, which might become necessary; secondly, when the corn-growing countries themselves experience a scarcity, and are obliged to retain the whole of their crops for their own subsistence.*

It was replied by the partisans of free-trade, that if England were to become a regular and constant importer of grain, not one, but many foreign countries would grow into a habit of supplying her: the raising of corn for her market in Poland, Spain, Barbary, and North America, would be more extensively practised, and the sale of their produce would become equally indispensable to them, as the purchase would be to England: that even Bonaparte, the most bitter enemy England had ever encountered, had taken her money for the license to export corn: that crops never fail at the same time all over the world; and that an extensive commerce of grain would lead to the formation of large stores and depôts, which will offer the best possible security against the recurrence of scarcity; and that, accordingly, as they asserted, there are no countries less subject to that calamity, or even to violent fluctuations of price, than those that grow no corn at all; for which they cited the example of Holland and other nations similarly circumstanced.†

However, it cannot be disputed that, even in countries best able to reckon on commercial supply, there are many serious inconveniences to be apprehended from the ruin of internal tillage. Subsistence is the primary want of a nation, and it is neither prudent nor safe to become dependent upon distant supply. Admitting that laws, which, for the protection of the agricultural prohibit the import of grain to the prejudice of the manufacturing interest, are both unjust and impolitic, it should be recollected that, on the other hand, excessive taxation, loans, overgrown establishments, civil, military, or diplomatic, are equally impolitic and unjust, and fall more heavily upon agriculture than upon manufacture. Perhaps one abuse may make another necessary, to restore the equilibrium of production,

---

* Malthus.—*Inquiry into the Nature and Progress of Rent. Grounds of an Opinion,* &c. *on Foreign Corn.*

† Ricardo.—*Essay on the Influence of the Low Price of Corn,* &c.

otherwise industry would abandon one branch, and take exclusively
to another, to the evident peril of the existence of society. (1)

(1) The question of a free trade in corn is itself of such magnitude and importance, that it would not be practicable to discuss it within the compass of a
note. As our author, however, has in this paragraph intimated at least doubts of
the superior advantages of entire freedom in the trade in grain, and even speaks
of the "many serious inconveniences to be apprehended from the ruin of internal
tillage," and deems it "neither prudent nor safe to become dependent upon distant supply," it would not be proper to withhold from the reader some notice of
the labours of the more recent political economists and practical inquirers, who
have poured a flood of light over this whole inquiry, and satisfactorily demonstrated the entire inexpediency, as well as injustice, of restrictions and prohibitions on the importation of foreign corn.

The first work to which we refer, is the "Essay on the External Corn Trade,
by R. Torrens, Esq. M. P. F. R. S., fourth edition, London, 1827." It is entitled
to distinguished notice, as a profound and masterly investigation of the principles
relating to the trade in grain, and explains the manner in which restrictive and
prohibitive laws on this subject have contributed to create revulsions and embar-
rassments, from which England has experienced so much suffering in her commerce and manufactures. The doctrines unfolded by Colonel Torrens, in relation
to the foreign trade in corn, have been sanctioned and confirmed by the authority
of all the principal writers on political economy, who have of late directed their
attention to the same important topic. He condemns these laws as unwise, unjust,
and wholly inexpedient.

Next in order we name Mr. James Mill, the author of the "Elements of
Political Economy," and the "History of British India." In a pamphlet, which
he published in London, in 1823, entitled an "Essay on the Impolicy of a Bounty
on the Exportation of Grain, and on the Principles which ought to regulate the
Commerce of Grain," he has given a most able examination of these questions.
He notices most of the arguments urged in favour of restrictions and prohibitions
in the corn trade, and successfully combats them. He, moreover, presents many
new and luminous views, and discusses the whole subject with a fairness and
candour that cannot fail to produce conviction in any unprejudiced mind.

Among the numerous works, to which this important subject has given birth in
England, none has awakened more attention, or had a more extensive circulation
than the "Catechism on the Corn Laws, by T. Perronet Thompson, of Queen's
College, Cambridge." It was first published in 1827, and we believe has now
passed through ten editions. The author has given a candid and complete exhibition of the fallacies that, from time to time, have been advanced by any writer
or journalist of celebrity in support of the English corn laws, and has annexed
to them respectively the most triumphant and conclusive answers. No point at
issue in the controversy has been left untouched, and every objection to the freedom of trade in grain, we think, removed.

We must not omit to mention the "Address to the Landowners of England
on the Corn Laws, by Viscount Milton, (now Earl Fitzwilliam,) published in
London in 1832." This is an appeal by Lord Fitzwilliam to his fellow proprietors, for he is said to be one of the largest landowners in England, against the
course they are pursuing on this great question, and beseeching them, by every
consideration of their country's peace and welfare, to consent to the abolition of
what he so satisfactorily proves to be a vicious system. Passing over the anti-
commercial character of the corn laws and their effects upon the expenses of
government, he confines himself to exposing the pernicious consequences which
a high price of corn produces upon the population at large, and upon the operations of industrious capitalists, abridging the comforts of the former, frustrating
the exertions of the latter, and not even promoting the welfare of the agriculturists themselves. The impartial review this author has taken of the controversy,
the careful manner in which he has sifted the arguments on either side, and the

CHAPTER XVIII.

OF THE EFFECT UPON NATIONAL WEALTH, RESULTING FROM THE PRODUCTIVE
EFFORTS OF PUBLIC AUTHORITY.

THERE can be no production of new value, consequently no increase of wealth, where the product of a productive concern does not exceed the cost of production.* Thus, whether government or individuals be the adventurers in the losing concern, it is equally ruinous to the nation, and there is so much less value in the country.

It is of no avail to pretend, that, although the government be a loser, its agents, the industrious people, or the workmen it employs, have made a profit. If the concern cannot support itself and pay its own way, the receipt must fall short of the outlay, and the difference fall upon those, who supply the expenditure of the state; that is to say, the tax-payers.†

* It must not be forgotten, that the consumption of the value of the productive agency, exerted in the course of production, is quite as real as that of the raw material. And under this term, productive agency, I comprise that of capital as well as of human beings.

† This is equally true, when the government speculates with its own private or peculiar funds, as with the produce of the national lands; for whatever is thus expended might have gone towards alleviating the public burthens.

known bias of the order to which he belongs in favour of the corn laws, must convince every dispassionate and honest inquirer, that the same process which changed his opinions must change theirs. Years may elapse in England, from the undue influence of the landed aristocracy in legislation, before these restrictive laws can be repealed; but the force of truth is too great to be resisted very long, and must ultimately prevail.

The last writer we shall refer to is William Jacobs, Esquire, F. R. S., the author of the "Tracts relating to the Corn Trade and Corn Laws: including the Second Report ordered to be printed by the two Houses of Parliament," published in London, in 1828. Mr. Jacobs has peculiar claims to the reader's attention on this subject. He has been for many years devoted to the examination of the corn trade, is the Comptroller of Corn Returns, and, from his great knowledge and experience, was selected by the English Board of Trade to proceed to the continent, and there carefully examine the actual condition of the agriculture and trade in corn of the principal grain-growing countries in the North of Europe. This work contains the results of his observations and laborious researches, and is entirely a practical view of the past and present state of the trade in corn, supported by a variety of curious and entirely authentic documents. In this place it would be impracticable to give any detailed account of its great merits as a statistical view of the subject; and this is not its only excellence. From the comprehensive and careful survey the author took of the actual condition of agriculture and trade in corn, in Europe, he became thoroughly satisfied of the inexpediency of the corn laws, and declares it to be his deliberate conviction that the fair and honest trade of speculation in corn should be by law restored, as the only means by which the due price between the producer and consumer can be equitably adjusted; and he adds, that the destruction of this trade has been the chief cause of the depression of the agricultural proprietors both in England and on the continent of Europe.

AMERICAN EDITOR.

The manufacture of Gobelin tapestry, carried on by the government of France, consumes a large quantity of wool, silk, and dyeing-drugs; furthermore, it consumes the rent of the ground and buildings, as well as the wages of workmen employed; all which should be reimbursed by the product, which they are very far from being. This establishment, instead of a source of wealth to the nation at large, for the government is fully aware of the loss to itself, is, on the contrary, a source of perpetual impoverishment. The annual loss to the nation is the whole excess of the annual consumption of the concern, including wages, which are one item of consumption, above the annual product. The same may be said of the manufacture of porcelain at Sevres, and I fear of all manufacturing concerns carried on upon account of governments.

We are told, that this is a necessary sacrifice; that otherwise the sovereign would be unprovided with objects of royal bounty and of royal splendour. This is no place to inquire how far the munificence of the monarch and the splendour of his palaces contribute to the good government of the people. I take for granted that these things are necessary; yet, admitting them to be so, there is no reason why the national sacrifices, requisite to support this magnificence and liberality, should be aggravated by the losses incurred by a misdirection of the public means. A nation had much better buy outright what it thinks proper to bestow; it would probably obtain for less money an object full as precious; for individuals can always undersell the government.*

There is a further evil attending the productive efforts of the government; they counteract the individual industry, not of those it deals with, for they take good care to be no losers, but of its competitors in production. The state is too formidable a rival in agriculture, manufacture, and commerce; it has too much wealth and power at command, and too little care of its own interest. It can submit to the loss of selling below prime cost; it can consume, produce, or monopolize in very little time so large a quantity of products, as violently to derange the relative prices of commodities: and every violent fluctuation of price is calamitous. The producer calculates upon the probable value of his product when ready for market; nothing discourages him so much, as a fluctuation that defies all calculation. The loss he suffers is equally unmerited, as the accidental gains that may be thrown into his hands. His unmerited gains, if any there be, are so much extra charge upon the consumer.

There are some concerns, I know, which the government must of necessity keep in its own hands. The building of ships of war can-

---

* The same may be observed of commercial enterprises undertaken by the public authority. During the scarcity of 1816–17, the French government bought up corn in foreign markets; the price of corn rose to an exorbitant rate in the home market, and the government resold at a very high rate, although somewhat below the average of the market. Individual traders would have found this a very profitable venture; but the government was out of pocket 21 millions of francs and upwards.—*Rapport au Roi du* 24 *Dec.* 1818.

not safely be left to individuals; nor, perhaps, the manufacture of gunpowder. However, in France, cannon, muskets, caissons, and tumbrils are bought of private makers, and seemingly with benefit. Perhaps the same system might be further extended. A government must act by deputy, by the intermediate agency of a set of people, whose interest is in direct opposition to its own; and they will of course attend to their own in preference. If it be so circumstanced as to be invariably cheated in its bargains, there is no need to multiply the opportunities of fraud, by engaging itself in production and adventure; that is to say, embarking in concerns, that must infinitely multiply the occasions of bargaining with individuals.

But, although the public can scarcely be itself a successful producer; it can at any rate give a powerful stimulus to individual productive energy, by well-planned, well-conducted, and well-supported public works, particularly roads, canals, and harbours.

Facility of communication assists production, exactly in the same way as the machinery, that multiplies manufactured products, and abridges the labour of production. It is a means of furnishing the same product at less expense, which has exactly the same effect, as raising a greater product with the same expense. If we take into account the immense quantity of goods conveyed upon the roads of a rich and populous empire, from the commonest vegetables brought daily to market, up to the rarest imported luxuries poured into its harbours from every part of the globe, and thence diffused, by means of land-carriage, over the whole face of the territory, we shall readily perceive the inestimable economy of good roads in the charges of production. The saving in carriage amounts to the whole value the article has derived gratuitously from nature, if, without good roads, it could not be had at all. Were it possible to transplant from the mountain to the plain the beautiful forests that flourish and rot neglected upon the inaccessible sides of the Alps and Pyrenees, the value of these forests would be an entirely new creation of value to mankind, a clear gain of revenue both to the landholder and the consumer also.

Academies, libraries, public schools, and museums, founded by enlightened governments, contribute to the creation of wealth, by the further discovery of truth, and the diffusion of what was known before; thus empowering the superior agents and directors of production, to extend the application of human science to the supply of human wants.* So likewise of travels, or voyages of discovery, undertaken at the public charge; the consequences of which have of late years been rendered particularly brilliant, by the extraordinary merit of those who have devoted themselves to such pursuits.

It is observable, too, that the sacrifices made for the enlargement of human knowledge, or merely for its conservation, should not be reprobated, though directed to objects of no immediate or apparent utility. The sciences have an universal chain of connexion. One

---

* *Supra*, Chap. 6.

which seems purely speculative must advance a step, before another of great and obvious practical utility can be promoted. Besides, it is impossible to say what useful properties may lie dormant in an object of mere curiosity. When the Dutchman, Otto Guericke, struck out the first sparks of electricity, who would have supposed they would have enabled Franklin to direct the lightning, and divert it from our edifices; an exploit apparently so far beyond the powers of man?

But of all the means, by which a government can stimulate production, there is none so powerful as the perfect security of person and property, especially from the aggressions of arbitrary power.* This security is of itself a source of public prosperity, that more than counteracts all the restrictions hitherto invented for checking its progress. Restrictions compress the elasticity of production; but want of security destroys it altogether. (a)   To convince ourselves of this fact, it is sufficient to compare the nations of western Europe with those subject to the Ottoman power.   Look at most parts of Africa, Arabia, Persia, and Asia Minor, once so thickly strown with flourishing cities, whereof, as Montesquieu remarks, no trace now remains but in the pages of Strabo.   The inhabitants are pillaged alike by bandits and pachas; wealth and population have vanished; and the thinly scattered remnant are miserable objects of want and wretchedness.   Survey Europe on the other hand; and, though she is still far short of the prosperity she might attain, most of her kingdoms are in a thriving condition, in spite of taxes and restrictions innumerable; for the simple reason, that persons and property are there pretty generally safe from violence and arbitrary exaction.

There is one expedient by which a government may give its subjects a momentary accession of wealth, that I have hitherto omitted to mention. I mean the robbery from another nation of all its moveable property, and bringing home the spoil, or the imposition of enormous tributes upon its growing produce. This was the mode practised by the Romans in the latter periods of the republic, and under the earliest emperors. This is an expedient of the same

---

* Smith, in his recapitulation of the real causes of the prosperity of Great Britain, places at the head of the list, "That equal and impartial administration of justice, which renders the rights of the meanest British subject respectable to the greatest; and which, by securing to every man the fruits of his own industry, gives the greatest and most effectual encouragement to every sort of industry."—*Wealth of Nations*, b. iv. c. 7.—*Poivre*, who was a great traveller, tells us, that he never saw a country really prosperous, which did not enjoy the freedom of industry as well as security of person and property.

(a) This security is in fact the main duty of all government. Were it not for the imperfections of human nature—the propensity of mankind to vice—society might exist without government, for no man would injure another. It is to protect one against the vices of another that the forms and institutions of society are established or supported; thus arming individual right with the aggregate of social strength. But the same moral imperfections which drive mankind into the bonds of society, undermine and vitiate its institutions. The very engine erected to protect, is directed to the injury and spoliation of individuals, and becomes occasionally more dangerous than individual wrong. T.

nature, as the acquirement of wealth by individual acts of illegal violence or fraud. There is no actual production, but a mere appropriation of the products of others. I mention this method of acquiring wealth, once for all, without meaning to recommend it as either safe or honourable. Had the Romans followed the contrary system with equal perseverance, had they studied to spread civilization among their savage neighbours, and to establish a friendly intercourse that might have engendered reciprocal wants, the Roman power would probably have existed to this day.

CHAPTER XIX.

OF COLONIES AND THEIR PRODUCTS.

Colonies are settlements formed in distant countries by an elder nation, called the mother-country. When the latter wishes to enlarge its intercourse with a country, already populous and civilized, whose territory it has, therefore, no hopes of getting into its own possession, it commonly contents itself with the establishment of a factory or mercantile residence, where its factors may trade, in conformity with the local regulations, as the Europeans have done in China and Japan. When colonies shake off their dependence upon the mother country, they become substantive and independent states.

It is common for nations to colonize, when their population becomes crowded in its ancient territorial limits; and when particular classes of society are exposed to the persecution of the rest. These appear to have been the only motives for colonization among the ancients; the moderns have been actuated by other views. The vast improvements in navigation have opened new channels to their enterprise, and discovered countries before unknown; they have found their way to another hemisphere, and to the most inhospitable climates, not with the intention of there fixing themselves and their posterity, but to obtain valuable articles of commerce, and return to their native countries, enriched with the fruits of a forced, but yet very extensive production.

It is worth while to note this difference of motive, which has made so marked a difference in the consequences of the two systems of colonization. I am strongly tempted to call one the colonial system of the ancients, and the other the colonial system of the moderns; although there have been many colonies in modern times established on the ancient plan, of which those of North America are the most distinguished. (a)

(a) The distinction of the two systems is more imaginary than real. Most of the early establishments of the Europeans in the West were made with the view

The production of colonies, formed upon the ancient system, is inconsiderable at the commencement; but increases with great rapidity. The colonists choose for their country of adoption a spot where the soil is fertile, the climate genial, or the position advantageous for commercial purposes. The land is generally quite fresh, whether it have been the scene of a dense population long since extinguished, or merely the range of roving tribes, too small in number and strength to exhaust the productive qualities of the soil.

Families transplanted from a civilized to an entirely new country, carry with them theoretical and practical knowledge, which is one of the chief elements of productive industry: they carry likewise habits of industry, calculated to set these elements in activity, as well as the habit of subordination, so essential to the preservation of social order; they commonly take with them some little capital also, not in money, but in tools and stock of different kinds: moreover, they have no landlord to share the produce of a virgin soil, far exceeding in extent what they are able to bring into cultivation for years to come. To these causes of rapid prosperity, should, perhaps, be superadded the chief cause of all, the natural desire of mankind to better their condition, and to render as comfortable as possible the mode of life they have adopted.

The rapid increase of products in colonies, founded upon this plan, would have been still more striking, if the colonists had carried with them a larger capital; but, as we have already observed, it is not the families favoured by fortune that emigrate; those who have the command of a sufficient capital to procure a comfortable existence in their native country, the scene of their halcyon days of infancy, will rarely be tempted to renounce habits, friends, and relations, to embark in what must always be attended with hazard, and encounter the inseparable hardships of a primitive establishment. This accounts for the scarcity of capital in newly-settled colonies; and is one reason why it bears so high a rate of interest there.

In point of fact, capital is of much more rapid accumulation in new colonies than in countries long civilized. It would seem as if the colonists, in abandoning their native country, leave behind them part of their vicious propensities; they certainly carry with them little of that fondness for show, that costs so dear in Europe, and brings so poor a return. No qualities, but those of utility, are in estimation in the country they are going to; and consumption is limited to objects of rational desire, which is sooner satisfied than artificial wants. The towns are few and small; the life of agriculturists, which they must necessarily adopt, is of all others the most

---

of absolute migration. The French at St. Domingo, the English at Barbadoes, the Spaniards almost universally, settled without the intention of returning home. The introduction of negro labour was an after-thought. Slavery was an established practice in all the ancient world, and colonies either made prize of the indigenes, or imported slaves from abroad, as soon as they were rich enough to buy them. T.

economical; finally, their industry is proportionately more productive, and requires a smaller capital to work upon.

The character of the colonial government usually accords with that of individuals; it is active in the execution of its duties, sparing of expense, and careful to avoid quarrels; thus there are few taxes, sometimes none at all; and, since the government takes little or nothing from the revenues of the subject, his ability to multiply his savings, and consequently to enlarge his productive capital, is very great. With very little capital to begin upon, the annual produce of the colony very soon exceeds its consumption. Hence, the astonishingly rapid progress in its wealth and population; for human labour becomes dear in proportion to the accumulation of capital, and it is a well-known maxim, that population always increases according to the demand.*

With these *data*, there is no difficulty in explaining the causes of the rapid advance of such colonies. Among the ancients we find that Ephesus and Miletus in Asia Minor, Tarentum and Crotona in Italy, Syracuse and Agrigentum in Sicily, very soon surpassed the parent cities in wealth and consequence. The English colonies in North America, which bear the closest resemblance of any in our times to those of ancient Greece, present a picture of prosperity less striking perhaps, but quite as deserving of notice, and still in the attitude of advance.

It is the invariable practice of colonies founded upon this plan, and without any thoughts of returning home, to provide themselves an independent government; and even where the mother-country reserves the right of legislation, that right will sooner or later be dissolved by the operation of natural causes, and matters be brought to that footing, on which justice and regard to its real interest should have prompted her to put them originally.

But, to proceed to the colonies formed upon the colonial system of the moderns; the founders of them were for the most part adventurers, whose object was, not to settle in an adopted country, but rapidly to amass a fortune, and return to enjoy it in their former homes.†

The early adventurers of this stamp found ample gratification of their extravagant rapacity, first in the cluster of the Antilles, in Mexico and Peru, and subsequently in Brazil and in the Eastern Indies. After exhausting the resources previously accumulated by the aborigines, they were compelled to direct their industry towards discovering the mines of these new countries, and to turn to account the no less valuable produce of their agriculture. Successive swarms of new colonists poured in from time to time, animated for the most

---

* Vide *infrà*, under the head of Population, Book II. c. 11.

† There have been many exceptions in North America and elsewhere. The colonies of Spain and Portugal in the New World were of an ambiguous character. Some of the colonists contemplated a return: others went to establish themselves and their posterity; but the whole plan of them has been subverted, since the commencement of the struggle for emancipation.

part with some hope of return, with the desire, not of living in affluence upon the land they cultivated, and leaving behind them a contented posterity and a spotless name, but of making inordinate gain to be afterwards enjoyed elsewhere : this motive led them to adopt a system of compulsory cultivation, of which negro slavery was the principal instrument.

But let me ask, in what manner does slavery operate upon production? Is the labour of the slave less costly than that of the free labourer? This is an important inquiry, originating in the influence of the modern system of colonization upon the multiplication of wealth.

Stewart, Turgot, and Smith, all agree in thinking, that the labour of the slave is dearer and less productive than that of the freeman. Their arguments amount to this : a man, that neither works nor consumes on his own account, works as little and consumes as much as he can : he has no interest in the exertion of that degree of care and intelligence, which alone can insure success : his life is shortened by excessive labour, and his master must replace it at great expense : besides, the free workman looks after his own support ; but that of the slave must be attended to by the master ; and, as it is impossible for the master to do it so economically as the free workman, the labour of the slave must cost him dearer.*

This position has been controverted by the following calculation : The annual expense of a negro in the West Indies, upon the plantations most humanely administered, does not exceed 60 dollars : add the interest of his prime cost, say at ten per cent., for it is a life interest ; the average price of a negro is about 400 dollars, so that, allowing 40 dollars for the annual interest, the whole expense of a negro to his owner is but 100 dollars per annum, (a) a sum, doubtless, much inferior to the charge of free labour in that part of the world. An ordinary free labourer may earn there from a dollar to a dollar and a half per day, or even more. Taking the medium of a dollar and a quarter, and reckoning about 300 working days in the year, the annual wages will amount to 375 instead of 100 dollars.†

---

* Stewart (Sir Jas.) *Inquiry into the Prin. of Pol. Econ.* book ii. c. 607. Turgot. *Reflections sur la Formation et la Distribution des Richesses,* § 23. Smith. *Wealth of Nations,* book i. c. 8 ; book iii. c. 2.

† It should be observed here, that the free labourers, who are so much better paid, are commonly engaged in occupations which, though less laborious, require a greater degree of intelligence and personal skill. Tailors and watchmakers are generally free men. And the mere existence of slavery itself enhances the price of free field labour by driving all competition out of the market.

(a) In this calculation no account has been taken of the housing of the negro, the tools and implements supplied to him, or the clothing furnished by the master ; neither does our author seem to make any allowance for the probable increase of agricultural production, which free negro labour might afford. Free European labour would doubtless be far more expensive, were it practicable. The interest of money is also estimated far too low, and the infant and the aged must be provided for by the master. T.

Common sense will tell us, that the consumption of a slave must be less than that of a free workman. The master cares not if his slave enjoy life, provided he do but live; a pair of trowsers and a jacket are the whole wardrobe of the negro: his lodging a bare hut, and his food the manioc root, to which kind masters now and then add a little dried fish. A population of free workmen, taken one with another, has women, children, and invalids to support: the ties of consanguinity, friendship, love, and gratitude, all contribute to multiply consumption; whereas, the slave-owner is often relieved by the effects of fatigue from the maintenance of the veteran: the tender age and sex enjoy little exemption from labour; and even the soft impulse of sexual attraction is subject to the avaricious calculations of the master.

What is the motive which operates in every man's breast to counteract the impulse towards the gratification of his wants and appetites? Doubtless, the providential care of the future. Human wants and appetites have a tendency to extend—frugality to reduce consumption; and it is easy to conceive, that these opposite motives, working in the mind of the same individual, help to counteract each other. But, where there are master and slave, the balance must needs incline to the side of frugality; the wants and appetites operate upon the weaker party, and the motive of frugality upon the stronger. It is a well-known fact, that the net produce of an estate in St. Domingo cleared off the whole purchase-money in six years; whereas in Europe the net produce seldom exceeds the one twenty-fifth or one thirtieth of the purchase-money, and sometimes falls far short even of that. Smith, himself, elsewhere tells us, that the planters of the English islands admit that the rum and molasses will defray the whole expenses of a sugar plantation, leaving the total produce of sugar as net proceeds: which, as he justly observes, is much the same as if our farmers were to pay their rent and expenses with the straw only, and to make a clear profit of all the grain. Now I ask, how many products are there that exceed the expenses of production in the same degree? (a)

Indeed, this very exorbitance of profit shows, that the industry of the master is paid out of all proportion with that of the slave. To the consumer it makes no difference. One of the productive classes benefits by the depression of the rest; and that would be all, were it not that the vicious system of production, resulting from this derangement, opposes the introduction of a better plan of industry. The slave and the master are both degraded beings, incapable of approximating to the perfection of industry, and, by their contagion, degrading the industry of the free man, who has no slaves at his

---

(a) What reference can this inequality have to the relative position of the proprietor and the different productive agents one to another? It is a mere question of difference of interest of capital. Capital in the West Indies brings a return very different, in its ratio, to rent or the profit of land, from what it yields in Europe. Land, the source of production, sells cheap, because of the greater unhealthiness of climate, insecurity of tenure, abundance, &c. &c. T.

command. For labour can never be honourable, or even respectable, where it is executed by an inferior caste. The forced and unnatural superiority of the master over the slave, is exhibited in the affectation of lordly indolence and inactivity : and the faculties of mind are debased in an equal degree; the place of intelligence is usurped by violence and brutality.

I have been told by travellers of veracity and observation, that they consider all progress in the arts in Brazil and other settlements of America as utterly hopeless, while slavery shall continue to be tolerated. Those states of the North American Union, which have proscribed slavery, are making the largest strides towards national prosperity. The inhabitants of the slave states of Georgia and Carolina raise the best cotton in the world, but cannot work it up. During the last war with England, they were obliged to send it over land to New-York to be spun into yarn. The same cotton is sent back at a vast expense to be consumed at the place of its original growth in a manufactured state. (*a*) This is a just retribution for the toleration of a practice, by which one part of mankind is made to labour, and subjected to the severest privation, for the benefit of another. Policy is in this point in accordance with humanity. (*b*)

It remains yet to be explained, what are the consequences of the commercial intercourse between the colony and the mother country, in regard to production; always taking it for granted, that the colony continues in a state of dependence, for the moment it shakes off the yoke, it has nothing colonial but its origin, and stands in relation to the mother-country, on exactly the same footing as any other nation on the globe.

The parent state, with a view to secure to the products of its own soil and industry the market of colonial consumption, generally prohibits the colonists from purchasing European commodities from any one else, which enables her own merchants to sell their goods in the colony for somewhat more than they are currently worth. This is a benefit conferred on the subjects of the parent state at the expense of the colonists, who are likewise its subjects. Considering the mother-country and the colony to be integral parts of one and the same state, the profit and loss balance each other; and this restriction is nugatory, except inasmuch as it entails the charge of an

(*a*) So it is now from Hindostan, where labour is free and most abundant. Cotton will flow towards machinery, which has become too powerful for the competition of human labour, even where it is the cheapest. That is, therefore, not the effect of the toleration of slavery in those states. T.

(*b*) Therefore our author has come to this correct conclusion, his reasoning is neither logical nor satisfactory ; indeed, the whole of this important subject is dismissed with a precipitation little suited to its importance. There are two motives of human industry, the hope of enjoyment, and the fear of suffering. The slave is actuated principally by the latter, the free agent by the former. Neither of these motives should have been thus cursorily adverted to in the analysis of actual production, but have been fairly set forth in the outset, immediately after the detail of the sources of production; being both of them the *stimuli* which give activity to those sources. After all that our author and others have done, much yet remains for the organization of the science. T.

establishment of custom or excise officers; and thus increases the national expenditure.

While, on the one hand, the colonists are obliged to buy of the mother-country, they are, on the other, compelled to sell their colonial produce exclusively to its merchants, who thus obtain an extra advantage without any creation of value, at the expense, likewise, of the colonists, by the enjoyment of an exclusive privilege, and of exemption from competition. Here, too, the profit and loss destroy each other nationally, but not individually; what a merchant of Havre or Bordeaux gains in this way is substantial profit; but it is taken from the pockets of one or more subjects of the same state, who had equal right to have their interest attended to. It is true, indeed, that the colonists are indemnified in another way; viz. either by the miseries of the slave population, as we have already explained; or by the privations of the inhabitants of the mother-country, as I am about to show.

So completely is the whole system built upon compulsions, restriction, and monopoly, that these very domestic consumers are compelled to buy what colonial articles of consumption they require exclusively from the national colonies; every other colony, and all the rest of the world, being denied the liberty of importing colonial* produce, or subjected to the payment of a heavy fine, in the shape of an import duty.

It would seem that the home-consumer should at any rate derive an obvious benefit, in the price of colonial produce, from his exclusive right of purchasing of the colonists. But even this unjust preference is denied him; for, as soon as the produce arrives in Europe, the home-merchant is allowed to re-export and sell it where he chooses, and particularly to those nations that have no colonies of their own; so that, after all, the planter is deprived of the competition of buyers, although the home-consumer is made to suffer its full effect.

All these losses fall chiefly upon the class of home-consumers, a class of all others the most important in point of number, and deserving of attention on account of the wide diffusion of the evils of any vicious system affecting it, as well as the functions it performs in every part of the social machine, and the taxes it contributes to the public purse, wherein consists the power of the government. They may be divided into two parts; whereof the one is absorbed in the superfluous charges of raising the colonial produce, which might be got cheaper elsewhere;† this is a dead loss

---

* Or equinoctial; the term is applied to the ordinary products of equinoctial latitudes.

† *Poivre*, a writer of great information and probity, assures us, that white sugar of the best quality is sold in Cochin-China, at the rate of about 3 dollars per quintal of the country, which is little more than two cents per pound, and that more than 80 millions of pounds are thence exported annually to China at that rate. Adding 300 per cent. for the charges and profits of trade, which is a most liberal allowance, the sugar of Cochin-China might, under a free trade, be sold in France at from 8 to 9 cents a pound.

to the consumer, without gain to any body. The other part, which is also paid by the consumer, goes to make the fortunes of West-Indian planters and merchants. The wealth thus acquired is the produce of a real tax upon the people, although, being centred in few hands, it is apt to dazzle the eyes, and be mistaken for wealth of colonial and commercial acquisition. And it is for the protection of this imaginary advantage, that almost all the wars of the eighteenth century have been undertaken, and that the European states have thought themselves obliged to keep up, at a vast expense, civil and judicial, as well as marine and military, establishments, at the opposite extremities of the globe.*

When Poivre was appointed governor of the Isle of France, the colony had not been planted more than 50 years; yet he calculated it to have then cost France no less than 12 millions of dollars; to be a source of regular and large out-going; and to bring her no return of any kind whatsoever.† It is true, that the money spent on the defence of that settlement had the further object of upholding our other possessions in the East Indies; but, when we find that these latter were still more expensive both to the government and to the proprietors of the two companies, old and new, it is impossible to deny, that all we gained by keeping the Mauritius at this enormous expense was, the opportunity of a further waste in Bengal and on the coast of Coromandel.

The same observations will apply to such of our possessions in other parts of the world, as were of no importance, but in a military point of view. Should it be pretended, that these stations are kept up at a great sacrifice, not with the object of gain, but to extend and affirm the power of the mother-country, it might yet be asked, why maintain them at such a loss, since this power has no other object but the preservation of the colonies, which turn out to be themselves a losing concern? ‡

That England has benefited immensely by the loss of her North

---

The English already derive from Asia a considerable quantity both of sugar and indigo, at a cheaper rate than those of the West Indies. And, doubtless, if the Europeans were to plant independent and industrious colonies along the northern coast of Africa, the culture of equinoctial products there would rapidly gain ground, and supply Europe in greater abundance at a still cheaper rate.

* Arthur Young, in 1789, estimated the annual charge entailed on France, by the possession of St. Domingo, at 9 millions of dollars. He has gone into detail to prove, that, if the sums spent on her colonies for 25 years only had been devoted to the improvement of any one of her own provinces, she would have acquired an annual addition of 24 millions of dollars, net revenue, consisting of actual products, without loss to any body. *Vide* his *Journey in France.*

† *Œuvres de Poivre*, p. 209. In this estimate he takes no account of the charge of the military and marine establishment of France herself, of which a part should be set down to the colony.

‡ *Vide* the works of Benjamin Franklin, vol. ii. p. 50, for the opinion of that celebrated man, who had so much experience in these matters. I find it stated in the *Travels* of Lord Valentia that the Cape of Good Hope, in 1802, cost England an excess of from 1,000,000 to 1,200,000 dollars per annum above its own revenue.

American colonies, is a fact no one has attempted to deny.* Yet she spent the incredible sum of 335,000,000 dollars in attempting to retain possession; a monstrous error in policy indeed; for she might have enjoyed the same benefits, that is to say, have emancipated her colonies, without expending a sixpence; besides saving a profusion of gallant blood, and gaining credit for generosity, in the eyes of Europe and posterity.†

The blunders committed by the ministers of George III., during the whole course of the first American war, in which, indeed, they were unhappily abetted, by the corruption of the parliament and the pride of the nation, were imitated by Napoleon, in his attempt to reduce the revolted negroes of St. Domingo. Nothing but its distance and maritime position prevented that scheme from proving equally disastrous with the war of Spain. Yet, comparatively, the independence of that fine island might have been made equally productive of commercial benefit to France, as that of America had been to England. It is high time to drop our absurd lamentations for the loss of our colonies, considered as a source of national prosperity. For, in the first place, France now enjoys a greater degree of prosperity, than while she retained her colonies; witness the increase of her population. Before the revolution, her revenues could maintain but twenty-five millions of people: they now support thirty-two millions and a half, (1831) (1). In the second place, the first princi-

* " Bristol was one of the chief *entrepots* of North American commerce. Her principal merchants and inhabitants joined in a most energetic representation to parliament, that their city would be infallibly ruined by the acknowledgment of American independence; adding, that their port would be so deserted, as not to be worth the charge of keeping up. Notwithstanding their representations, peace became a matter of necessity, and the dreaded separation was consented to. Ten years had scarcely elapsed after this event, when the same worthy persons petitioned the parliament for leave to enlarge and deepen the port, which, instead of being deserted, as they had apprehended, was incapable of receiving the influx of additional shipping, that the commerce of independent America had given birth to." *De Levis, Lettres Chinoises.*

† These remarks are not altogether applicable to the British dependencies in the East; because there the nation is rather a conqueror than a colonist, having the domination over thirty-two millions of inhabitants, and the absolute disposal of the revenue levied upon them. But the clear national profits derived from the acquisition is by no means so considerable, as may be generally supposed; for the charges of administration and protection must be deducted. Colquhoun, in his *Treatise on the Wealth, Power, and Resources of the British Empire*, which gives an exaggerated picture of them, states the total revenue of the sovereign company, at 18,051,478l. sterling; and its expenditure at 16,984,271l.; leaving a surplus of 1,067,207l.

In all probability were India in a state of national independence, the commerce between her and Great Britain would increase so much, as to produce to the latter an additional revenue, larger than the amount of that surplus, to say nothing of the increase of individual profits.

(1) The population of France, notwithstanding the interruption to industry, and the drains occasioned by the long wars, has increased since the commencement of the Revolution. According to calculations made by the National Assembly in 1791, France contained 26,363,074 inhabitants, and in 1831 it contained

ples of political economy will teach us, that the loss of colonies by no means implies a loss of the trade with them. Wherewith did France before buy the colonial products? with her own domestic products to be sure. Has she not since continued to buy them in the same way, though sometimes of a neutral, or even an enemy?

I admit, that the ignorance and vices of her rulers for the time being have made her pay for those products much dearer than she need have done; but now that she buys them at the natural price, (exclusive, of course, of the import duties,) and pays for them as before with her domestic products, in what way is she a loser? Political convulsions have given a new direction to commerce; the import of sugar and coffee is no longer confined to Nantes and Bordeaux; and those cities have suffered in consequence. But, as France now consumes at least as much of those articles as she ever did, all, that has not come by the way of Nantes or Bordeaux, must needs have found its way in some other channel. France can not have bought in any other way, than as of old, with the products of her own land, capital, and industry; for, excepting robbery and piracy, one nation has no other means of buying of another. Indeed, France might have benefited largely by the trade which has supplanted her own colonial commerce, had not old prejudices and erroneous notions constantly opposed the natural current of human affairs.

Perhaps it may be argued, that the colonies furnish commodities which are nowhere else to be had. The nation, therefore, that should have no share of territories so highly favoured by nature, would lie at the mercy of the nation that should first get possession; for the monopoly of purchasing the colonial produce would enable her to exact her own price from her less fortunate neighbour. Now it is proved beyond all doubt, that what we erroneously call colonial produce, grows everywhere within the tropics, where the soil is adapted to its cultivation. The spices of the Moluccas are found to answer at Cayenne, and probably by this time in many other places; and no monopoly was ever more complete, than the trade of the Dutch in that commodity. They had sole possession of the only spice islands, and allowed nobody else to approach them. Has Europe been in any want of spices, or has she bought them for their weight in gold? Have we any reason to regret the not having devoted two hundred years of war, fought a score of naval battles, and sacrificed some hundreds of millions, and the lives of half a million of our fellow-creatures, for the paltry object of getting our pepper and cloves cheaper by some two or three *sous* a pound? And this example, it is worth while to observe, is the most favourable one for the colonial system, that could possibly be selected. One can hardly imagine the possibility of monopolizing sugar, a staple product of most parts of Asia, Africa, and America, so completely as

32,560,000 within the same limits. The annual increase is about 200,000 individuals. (*Vide Annuaire pour l'An* 1834.) AMERICAN EDITOR.

the Dutch did the spice trade; yet has this very trade been snatched
from the avaricious grasp of the monopolist nation, almost without
firing a shot.

The ancients, by their system of colonization, made themselves
friends all over the known world; the moderns have sought to make
subjects, and therefore have made enemies. Governors, deputed by
the mother-country, feel not the slightest interest in the diffusion of
happiness and real wealth amongst a people, with whom they do not
propose to spend their lives, to sink into privacy and retirement, or
to conciliate popularity. They know their consideration in the
mother-country will depend upon the fortune they return with, not
upon their behaviour in office. Add to this the large discretionary
power, that must unavoidably be vested in the deputed rulers of
distant possessions, and there will be every ingredient towards the
composition of a truly detestable government.

It is to be feared, that men in power, like the rest of mankind,
are too little disposed to moderation, too slow in their intellectual
progress, embarrassed as it is at every step by the unceasing
manœuvres of innumerable retainers, civil, military, financial, and
commercial; all impelled, by interested motives, to present things
in false colours, and involve the simplest questions in obscurity, to
allow any reasonable hope of accelerating the downfall of a system,
which for the last three or four hundred years must have wonderfully abridged the inestimable benefits, that mankind at large, in all
the five great divisions of the globe,* have, or ought to have derived
from the rapid progress of discovery, and the prodigious impulse
given to human industry since the commencement of the sixteenth
century. The silent advances of intelligence, and the irresistible
tide of human affairs, will alone effect its subversion.

CHAPTER XX.

OF TEMPORARY AND PERMANENT EMIGRATION, CONSIDERED IN REFERENCE TO NATIONAL WEALTH.

WHEN a traveller arrives in France, and there spends 2000 dollars, it must not be supposed that the whole sum is clear profit to
France. The traveller expends it in exchange for the values he
consumes: the effect is just the same, as if he had remained abroad
and sent to France for what he wanted, instead of coming and consuming it here; and is precisely similar to that of international com-

---

* The vast continent of New Holland, with its surrounding islands, is now
generally considered by geographers as a distinct portion of the globe, under the
denomination of Australia or Australasia, which has been given to it on account
of its position exclusively within the southern hemisphere.

merce, in which the profit made is not the whole or principal value received, but a larger or smaller per centage upon that principal, according to the circumstances.

The matter has not hitherto been viewed in this light. In the firm conviction of this maxim, that metal money was the only item of real wealth, people imagined, that, if a foreigner came amongst them with 2000 dollars in his pocket, it was so much clear profit to the nation; as if the tailor that clothes him, the jeweller that furnishes him with trinkets, the victualler that feeds him, gave him no values in exchange for his specie, but made a profit equal to the total of their respective charges. All that the nation gains is the profit upon its dealings with him, and upon what he purchases: and this is by no means contemptible, for every extension of commerce is a proportionate advantage;* but it is well to know its real amount, that we may not be betrayed into the folly of purchasing it too dearly. An eminent writer upon commercial topics, tells us, that theatrical exhibitions cannot be too grand, too splendid, or too numerous; for that they are a kind of traffic wherein France receives all and pays nothing; a proposition which is the very reverse of truth; for France pays, that is to say, loses, the whole expense of the exhibition, which is productive of nothing but barren amusement, and leaves no value whatever to replace what has been consumed on it. Fêtes of this description may be very pleasant things as affording amusement, but must make a ridiculous figure as a speculation of profit and loss. What would people think of a tradesman, that was to give a ball in his shop, hire performers, and hand refreshments about, with a view to benefit in his business? Besides, it may be reasonably doubted, whether a fête or exhibition of the most splendid kind, does in reality occasion any considerable influx of foreigners. Such an influx would be much more powerfully attracted by commerce, or by rich fragments of antiquity, or by master-pieces of art nowhere else to be seen, or by superiority of climate, or by the properties of medicinal waters, or, most of all, by the desire of visiting the scenes of memorable events, and of learning a language of extensive acceptation. I am strongly inclined to believe, that the enjoyment of a few empty pleasures of vanity has never attracted much company from any great distance. People may go a few leagues to a ball or entertainment, but will seldom make a journey for the purpose. It is extremely improbable, that the vast number of Germans, English, and Italians, who visit the capital of France in time of peace, are actuated solely by the desire

---

* A strange country has some advantages over the traveller, and its dealings with him may be considered as lucrative; for his ignorance of the language and of prices, and often a spice of vanity, make him pay for most of the objects of his consumption above the current rate. Besides, the public sights and exhibitions, which he there pays for seeing, are expenses already incurred by the nation, which he nowise aggravates by his presence. But these advantages, though real and positive, are very limited in amount, and must not be over-rated.

of seeing the French opera at Paris. That city has fortunately many worthier objects of general curiosity. In Spain, the bull-fights are considered very curious and attractive; yet I cannot think many Frenchmen have gone all the way to Madrid to witness that diversion. Foreigners, that have already come into the country on other accounts, are, indeed, frequent spectators of such exhibitions; but it was not solely with this object that they first set out upon their journey. (a)

The vaunted fêtes of Louis XIV. had a still more mischievous tendency. The sums spent upon them were not supplied by foreigners, but by French provincial visiters, who often spent in a week, as much as would have maintained their families at home for a year. So that France was two ways a loser; first, of the sums expended by the monarch, which had been levied on the subjects at large; secondly, of all that was spent by individuals. The sum total of the consumption was thrown away, that a few tradesmen of the metropolis might make their profits upon it; which they would equally have done, had their industry and capital taken a more beneficial direction.

A stranger, that comes into a country to settle there, and brings his fortune along with him, is a substantial acquisition to the nation. There is in this case an accession of two sources of wealth, industry and capital: an accession of full as much value, as the acquirement

(a) This has become a matter of some interest to England, whose unproductive capitalists and proprietors have absolutely overwhelmed the society of France and a great part of Italy, where they consume an immense revenue, derived from Britain by the export of her manufactures without any return. Thus their native country is, *pro tanto*, a producer without being a consumer— the scene of exertion but not of enjoyment. This circumstance, although nowise prejudicial to her productive powers, is extremely so to the comfort and enjoyment and content of her population; for there are few enjoyments so personal and selfish, as not to be diffused in some degree or other at the moment and place of consumption. Besides, the presence of the proprietor is always a benefit, especially in Great Britain, where so many public duties are gratuitously performed. Ireland suffers in a worse degree; her gentry are attracted by England as well as the continent; and the consequences have long been matter of regret and complaint. Though it might be impolitic to check the efflux by authoritative measures, it should at least not be directly encouraged and stimulated, as it really is, by the financial system, which the English ministry so obstinately persevere in. Almost the whole of the taxation is thrown immediately upon consumption; whilst the permanent sources of production and the clear rent they yield to the idle proprietor are left untouched. The proprietor has, therefore, an obvious interest in effecting his consumption where it is least burthened with taxation; that is to say, anywhere but in England. His property is protected gratuitously, and the charge of its protection defrayed by the productive classes, who thus are compelled to pay for the security of other people's property as well as their own, and are themselves unable to imitate their unproductive countrymen, by running away from domestic taxation. A more unjust and discouraging system could not have been devised. Its evils are daily increasing, and threaten the most serious diminution of the national resources. But the ministers neither see the mischief themselves, nor will listen to the warnings of others. Many of them, indeed, have an interest in perpetuating an exemption, by which they benefit personally. T.

of a proportionate extension of territory; to say nothing of what is gained in a moral estimate, if the emigrant bring with him private virtue and attachment to the place of his adoption. "When Frederick William came into the regency," says the royal historian of the house of Brandenburgh, "there was in the country no manufacture of hats, of stockings, of serge, or woollen stuff of any kind. All these commodities were derived from French industry. The French emigrants introduced amongst us the making of broadcloths, baizes and lighter woollens, of caps, of stockings wove in the frame, of hats, of beaver and felt, as well as dyeing in all its branches. Some refugees of that nation established themselves in trade, and retailed the products of their industrious countrymen. Berlin soon could boast of its goldsmiths, jewellers, watch-makers, and carvers; those of the emigrants, that settled in the low country, introduced the cultivation of tobacco, and of garden fruits and vegetables, and by their exertions converted the sandy tract in the environs into capital kitchen-garden grounds."

This emigration of industry, capital, and local attachment, is no less a dead and total loss to the country thus abandoned, than it is a clear gain to the country affording an asylum. It was justly observed by Christina, queen of Sweden, upon the revocation of the edict of Nantes, that Louis XIV. had used his right hand to cut off his left.

Nor can the calamity be prevented by any measures of legal coercion. A fellow-citizen cannot be forcibly retained, unless he be absolutely incarcerated; still less can he be prevented from exporting his movable property, if he be so inclined. For, putting out of the question the channel of contraband, which can never be closed altogether, he may convert his effects into goods, whose export is tolerated or even encouraged, and consign, or cause them to be consigned, to some correspondent abroad. This export is a real outgoing of value; but how is it possible for government to ascertain, that it is intended to be followed by no return?*

The best mode of retaining and attracting mankind is, to treat them with justice and benevolence; to protect every one in the enjoyment of the rights he regards with the highest reverence; to allow the free disposition of person and property, the liberty of continuing or changing his residence, of speaking, reading, and writing in perfect security.

Having thus investigated the means of production, and pointed out the circumstances, that render their agency more or less prolific,

---

* In 1790, when the new authorities of France indemnified the holders of suppressed offices in paper-money, these discarded functionaries for the most part converted their *assignats* into specie, or other commodities of equal value, which they took or sent out of the country. The consequent national loss to France was nearly as great, as if they had received their indemnities in cash; for its paper representative had not then suffered any material depreciation. Even when the individual remains himself in the country, he can not be prevented from transferring his fortune thence, if he be determined on so doing.

it would be endless, as well as foreign to my subject, to attempt a general review of all the various products that compose the wealth of mankind: such a task would furnish materials for many distinct treatises. But there is one amongst these products, the uses and nature of which are very imperfectly known, although the knowledge of them would throw much light upon the matter now under discussion: for which reason I have determined, before the conclusion of this part of my work, to give a separate consideration to the product *money,* which acts so prominent a part in the business of production, in the character of the principal agent of exchange and transfer.

CHAPTER XXI.

OF THE NATURE AND USES OF MONEY.

SECTION I.

General Remarks.

IN a society ever so little advanced in civilization, no single individual produces all that is necessary to satisfy his own wants; and it is rarely that an individual, by his single exertion, creates even any single product; but even if he does, his wants are not limited to that single article; they are numerous and various, and he must, therefore, procure all other objects of his personal consumption, by exchanging the overplus of the single product he himself creates beyond his own wants, for such other products as he stands in need of. And, by the way, it is observable, that, since individual producers, in every line, keep for their own use but a very small part of their own products; the gardener, of the vegetables he raises, the baker, of the bread he bakes, the shoemaker, of the shoes he makes, and so of all others; the great bulk, nay, almost the whole of the products of every community, arrive at consumption by the medium of exchange.

This is the reason, why it has been erroneously concluded, that exchange and transfer are the basis and origin of the production of wealth, and of commerce in particular; whereas they are only secondary and accessory circumstances; inasmuch as, were each family to raise the whole of the objects of its own consumption, as we see practised in some instances in the back settlements of the United States, society might continue to exist, without a single act of exchange or transfer. I make this remark, merely with a view to correctness of first principles, without any design to detract from the importance of exchange and transfer to the progressive advancement of production; indeed, I set out with the position, that they are indispensable in an advanced stage of civilization.

Admitting, then, the necessity of interchange, let us pause a moment, and consider, what infinite confusion and difficulty must arise to all the different component members of society, who are for the most part producers of but a single article, or two or three at the utmost, but of whom even the poorest is a consumer of a vast number of different products; I say, what difficulty must ensue, were every one obliged to exchange his own products specifically for those he may want; and were the whole of this process carried on by a barter in kind. The hungry cutler must offer the baker his knives for bread; perhaps, the baker has knives enough, but wants a coat; he is willing to purchase one of the tailor with his bread, but the tailor wants not bread, but butcher's meat; and so on to infinity.

By way of getting over this difficulty, the cutler, finding he cannot persuade the baker to take an article he does not want, will use his best endeavours to have a commodity to offer, which the baker will be able readily to exchange again for whatever he may happen to need. If there exist in the society any specific commodity that is in general request, not merely on account of its inherent utility, but likewise on account of the readiness with which it is received in exchange for the necessary articles of consumption, and the facility of proportionate subdivision, that commodity is precisely what the cutler will try to barter his knives for; because he has learnt from experience, that its possession will procure him without any difficulty, by a second act of exchange, bread or any other article he may wish for.

Now, money is precisely that commodity.

The two qualities, that give a general preference of value, in the shape of the current money of the country, to the same amount of value in any other shape, are :—

1. The aptitude, in the character of an intermedial object of exchange, to help all who have any exchange or any purchase to make, that is to say, every member of the community, towards the specific object of desire. The general confidence, that money is a commodity acceptable to every body, inspires the assurance of being able, by one act of exchange only, to procure the immediate object of desire, whatever it may be; whereas, the possessor of any other commodity can never be sure that it will be acceptable to the possessor of that particular object of desire.

2. The capability of subdivision and precise apportionment to the amount of the intended purchase; which capability is a recommendation to all who have purchases to make; in other words, to every member of the community. Every one is, therefore, anxious to barter for money the product whereof he holds a superfluity, and which is commonly that he himself produces; because, in addition to the other quality above stated, he feels sure of being able to buy with its value in that shape as small or as large a portion of cor-

responding value, as he may require; and because he may buy, whenever, and wherever he pleases, such objects as he may desire to have in lieu of the product he has sold originally.

In a very advanced stage of civilization, when individual wants have become various and numerous, and productive operations very much subdivided, exchanges become a matter of more urgent necessity, as well as much more frequent and more complicated; and personal consumption and barter in kind becomes less practicable. For instance, if a man makes not the whole knife, but the handle of it only, as in fact is the case in towns where cutlery is conducted on a large scale, he does not produce any thing that he can turn to account; for what could he do with the handle without the blade? He can not himself consume the smallest part of his own product, but must unavoidably exchange the whole of it for the necessaries or conveniences of life, for bread, meat, linen, &c. But neither baker, butcher, nor weaver, can ever stand in need of an article, that is fit for nobody but the finishing cutler, who can not himself give either bread or meat in exchange; because he produces neither; and who must, therefore, give some one commodity, that, by the custom of the country, may be expected to pass currently in exchange for most others.

Thus, money is the more requisite, the more civilized a nation is, and the further it has carried the division of labour. (a) Yet history contains precedents of considerable states, in which the use of any specific article, as money, was utterly unknown; as we are told it was among the Mexicans at the time of the discovery. We are informed, that, just about the period of their conquest by the Spanish adventurers, they were beginning to employ *grains of cacao* as money, in the smaller transactions of commerce.*

I have referred to custom, and not to the authority of government, the choice of the particular article that is to act as money in preference to every other: for though a government may coin what it pleases to call crowns, it does not oblige the subject to give his goods in exchange for these crowns, at least not where property is at all respected. Nor is it the mere impression, that makes people consent to take this coin in exchange for other products. Money passes current like any other commodity; and people may at liberty barter one article for another in kind, or for gold in bars, or silver bullion. The sole reason why a man elects to receive the coin in preference to every other article, is, because he has learnt from ex-

---

* *Raynal, Hist. phil. et pol.* lib. vi.

(a) The utility of money is intense, in the compound ratio of the division of labour and the variety of individual consumption. A sugar colony in the West Indies, though highly productive in proportion to its population, requires little money to facilitate the transfer of the produce; because the bulk of the population, the negroes, have very little variety of consumption : they are fed, clothed, &c. in the wholesale, and in the plainest and most uniform manner. Yet, possibly, the division both of agricultural and manufacturing labour on each plantation may be carried to considerable length. T.

perience, that it is preferred by those whose products he has occasion to purchase. Crown pieces derive their circulation as money from no other authority than this spontaneous preference: and if there were the least ground for supposing, that any other commodity, as wheat, for instance, would pass more currently in exchange for what they calculate upon wanting themselves, people would not give their goods for crown pieces, but would demand wheat, which would then be invested with all the properties of money. And this has occurred occasionally in practice, where the authorized or government money has consisted of paper destitute of credit or public confidence.

Custom, therefore, and not the mandate of authority, designates the specific product that shall pass exclusively as money, whether crown pieces or any other commodity whatever.*

The more frequent recurrence of the exchange of every individual product for the commodity, money, than for any other product, has attached particular names to this transaction; thus, to receive money in exchange is called, *selling*, and to give it, *buying*.

In this way originated the use of money. These positions are by no means purely speculative; for on them must all arguments, and laws, and regulations, on the subject of money, be grounded. A system built upon any other foundation can possess neither beauty nor solidity, and must fail to fulfil the object of its construction.

With the view of throwing the utmost possible light upon the essential properties of money, and the principal contingencies it is subject to, I shall treat of these particulars in separate sections, and endeavour to enable such as may give me their attention, to follow with ease the chain of connexion, notwithstanding that classification; and themselves to arrange in one comprehensive view the whole play of the mechanism, and the causes of that derangement, which human folly or misfortune may occasionally effect.

Section II.

Of the Material of Money.

If, as it would appear by the reasoning in the preceding section, money be employed as a mere intermedial object of exchange be-

---

* When the intercourse between the Europeans and the negroes of the river Gambia first commenced, the commodity most in request with them was iron, for the purposes of war and of tillage. Iron, therefore, became the standard of comparison of value. In a little time, it became a mere nominal standard in their mercantile dealings; and a *bar* of tobacco consisting of 20 or 30 leaves of that herb, was given for a *bar* of rum consisting of four or five pints, according to the abundance or scarcity of the article. In such a state of society, each product successively performs the functions of money in reference to all other products; which leaves the community subject to all the inconveniences of barter in kind, the chief of which is, the inability to offer any one article in general request and acceptation, and capable of ready apportionment in amount to other commodities at large. *Vide* Travels of Mungo Park, vol. i. c. 2.

tween an object in possession and the object of desire, the choice of its material is of no great importance. Money is not desired as an object of food, of household use, or of personal covering, but for the purpose of re-sale, as it were, and re-exchange for some object of utility, after having been originally received in exchange for one such already. Money is, therefore, not an object of consumption; it passes through the hands without sensible diminution or injury; and may perform its office equally well, whether its material be gold or silver, leather or paper.

Yet, to enable it to execute its functions, it must of necessity be possessed of inherent and positive value; for no man will be content to resign an object possessed of value, in exchange for another of less value, or of none at all.

There are some other less essential requisites, which add to its efficiency. A material, wherein these are not combined, is unfit for the purpose, and cannot hope to engross its functions either generally or permanently.

We are told by Homer, that the armour of Diomede had cost nine oxen. A warrior, that wished to arm himself at half the price, must have been puzzled to pay four oxen and a half. Wherefore, the article employed as money must be capable of being readily and without injury apportioned to the different objects of desire, and subdivided in such manner, as to admit of exchanges of the exact amount required.

Again, we read, that in Abyssinia, they make use of salt for money. If the same custom prevailed in France, a man must take a mountain of salt to market to pay for his weekly provisions. Wherefore, the commodity employed as money must not be so abundant, as to make it necessary to transfer a large quantity, on each recurring act of exchange.

At Newfoundland, it is said, that dried cod performs the office of money, and Smith makes mention of a village in Scotland, where nails are made use of for that purpose.* Besides many other inconveniences, that substances of this nature are subject to, there is this grand objection, that the quantity may be enlarged almost at pleasure, and in a very short space of time, and thereby a vast fluctuation effected in their relative value. But who would readily accept in exchange an article, that might, perhaps, in a few moments, lose the half or three-fourths of its value? Wherefore, the commodity employed as money must be of such difficult acquisition, as to ensure those who take it, from the danger of sudden depreciation.

In the Maldive islands, and in some parts of India and Africa, shells, called *cowries*, are employed as money, although they have no intrinsic value, except that they serve for ornament to some rude tribes. This kind of money would never do for nations that carry on trade with many parts of the globe; a medium of exchange of such very limited circulation would offer insuperable objections. It

---

* *Wealth of Nations,* book i. c. 4.

is natural for people to receive most willingly in exchange that article, which is the most universally received in like manner by other
people in their turn.

We need not, then, be surprised, that almost all the commercial
nations of the world should have selected metal to perform the office
of money; when once the more industrious and commercial communities had declared their choice, all the rest had an evident inducement to follow their example.

At times, when the metals now most abundantly produced were
yet rare, people were content to make use of them for the purpose.
The legal currency of Lacedæmon was of iron; that of the early
Romans, of copper. In proportion as those metals were extracted
from the earth in greater quantity, they became liable to the objection above stated in respect to all products of too little comparative*
value; and it is long since the precious metals, that is to say, gold
and silver, have been almost universally adopted. To this use they
are particularly applicable:

1. As being divisible into extremely minute portions, and capable
of re-union, without any sensible loss of weight or value; so that
the quantity may be easily apportioned to the value of the article of
purchase.

2. The precious metals have a sameness of quality all over the
world. One grain of pure gold is exactly similar to another, whether it came from the mines of Europe or America, or from the
sands of Africa. Time, weather, and damp, have no power to alter
the quality: the relative weight of any specific portion, therefore,
determines at once its relative quality and value to every other
portion: two grains of gold are worth exactly twice as much as one.

3. Gold and silver, especially with the mixture of alloy, that they
admit of, are hard enough to resist very considerable friction, and
are therefore fitted for rapid circulation, though, indeed, in this respect, they are inferior to many kinds of precious stones.

4. Their rarity and consequent dearness are not so great that the
quantity of gold or of silver, equivalent to the generality of goods,
is too minute for ordinary perception; nor, on the other hand, are
they so abundant and cheap, as to make a large value amount to a
great weight. It is possible, that in progress of time, they may become liable to objection on this score; especially if new and rich
veins of ore should be discovered: and then mankind must have
recourse to platina, or some other yet unknown metal, for the purpose of currency.

Lastly, gold and silver are capable of receiving a stamp or impression, certifying the weight of the piece, and the degree of its purity.

---

* The money of Lacedæmon is a proof of the position, that public authority
is incompetent of itself to give currency to its money. The laws of Lycurgus
directed the money to be made of iron, purposely to prevent its being easily
hoarded, or transferred in large quantities; but they were inoperative, because
they went to defeat these, the principal purposes of money. Yet no legislator
was ever more rigidly obeyed than Lycurgus.

Although the precious metals used for money have generally some mixture of baser metal, generally of copper, by way of alloy, the value of the baser metal, thus incorporated, is reckoned for nothing. Not that the alloy is itself destitute of value; but because the operation of disuniting it from the purer metal would cost more than it would be worth, after it was extracted. For this reason a piece of coined gold or silver, mixed with alloy, is estimated by the quantity of precious metal only contained in it.*

---

* The present silver coin of France contains one part copper to nine parts fine silver; the relative value of copper to silver being as 1 to 60, or thereabouts. So that the copper contained in the whole silver coinage, amounts to about $\frac{1}{600}$ of the total value of the silver coin, or 1 *cent* in 6 *fr.* Supposing it were attempted to disengage the copper, it would not pay the expenses of the process of separation; to say nothing of the value of the impression that must be destroyed. Wherefore, it is reckoned for nothing in the valuation of the coin. A piece of 5 *fr.* presents the idea of the $22\frac{1}{2}$ *grammes* of fine silver contained in it, though actually weighing 25 *gr.* inclusive of the alloy. (1)

---

(1) The values of the gold, silver, and copper coins of the United States, were first regulated by the act of Congress of the 2d of April, 1792, establishing the mint. By that act, the eagle contained 247.5 grains of pure gold and 22.5 grains of alloy, making together 270 grains of standard gold; and the half eagle and the quarter eagle, their respective fractional proportions of the same metals. By the act of Congress of the 30th of June, 1834, this standard has been debased, and the weight of the gold coins reduced: the eagle now contains 232 grains of pure gold and 26 grains of alloy, making together 258 grains of standard gold; and the half eagle and the quarter eagle are reduced in like proportions. By the act of 1792, the standard of gold was eleven-twelfths of pure gold to one-twelfth of alloy, or 22 carats fine. By the act of the present year, the relative fineness or number of carats has been reduced to about 21.58, equivalent to a debasement of about 1.9 per cent.; and the actual quantity of pure metal in the coin has been diminished more than 6.25 per cent.—(6.262626+). The alloy of standard gold is composed of silver and copper, not exceeding one half silver.

In the silver coins of the United States, no change has been made, since the act of 1792, which regulated their value. The dollar, by that act, is made the unit, of the same value as the Spanish milled dollar then current. The dollar of the United States contains 371.25 grains of pure silver and 416 grains of standard silver; the half dollar 185.625 grains of pure silver and 208 grains of standard silver; the quarter dollar 92.8125 grains of pure silver and 104 grains of standard silver; the dime 37.125 grains of pure silver and 41.6 grains of standard silver; and the half dime 18.5625 grains of pure silver and 20.8 grains of standard silver. The standard of silver is 1485 parts of fine to 179 parts alloy; accordingly, 1485 parts in 1664 parts of the entire weight of the silver coins are of pure silver, and the remaining 179 parts of alloy. The alloy of standard silver is wholly composed of copper.

The copper coins of the United States are the cent and the half cent; the weight of which, since the act of 1792, has been twice reduced. By the act of 1792, the cent contained 264 grains, and the half cent 132 grains, of copper, and the cent was fixed at the value of the hundredth part of the dollar, or unit. By an act of the 14th of January, 1793, the cent was reduced to 208 grains, and the half cent to 104 grains, of copper; and by an act of the 3d of March, 1795, the President was authorized by proclamation, and accordingly, on the 26th of January, 1796, reduced the cent to 168 grains, and the half cent to 84 grains of copper, their present weight. The proportional mint value of gold to silver, by the act of 1792, was as 1 of pure gold to 15 of pure silver; and by the act of

SECTION III.

Of the Accession of Value a Commodity receives by being Vested with the Character of Money.

From the foregoing sections it will appear, that money is indebted for its currency, not to the authority of the government, but to its being a commodity bearing a peculiar and intrinsic value. But its preference, as an object of exchange, to all other commodities of equivalent value, is owing to its characteristic properties as money; and to the peculiar advantage it derives from its employment in that character; namely, the advantage of being in universal use and request. The whole population, from the lowest degree of poverty to the highest of wealth, must effect exchanges, must buy the objects of want; must be consumers of money; or, in other words, must obtain possession of the commodity, that acts as the medium of exchange, the commodity generally admitted to be best suited, and most frequently employed for that purpose. A man that has any other commodity, jewels, for instance, to offer in exchange for the necessaries or luxuries he may have occasion for, cannot get those necessaries or luxuries by the process of exchange, until he has found a consumer for his jewels; nor can he even then be sure, that such a consumer will be able to give him, in return, the very identical article he may want: whereas, a man, with money in his pocket, is quite certain, that it will be acceptable to the person, of whom he would buy any thing; because that person will, in turn, be himself obliged to become a purchaser in like manner.* With the commodity, money, he can obtain all he wants by a single act of exchange only, called a purchase; whereas, with all others two acts at least are necessary; a sale and a purchase. This is the sum total of its advantages in the character of money: but it must be obvious to every body, that the preference, thus shown it as money, is a consequence of its actual use as such.

I must here observe, that the adoption of any specific commodity to serve as money, considerably augments its intrinsic value, or value as an article of commerce. A new use being discovered for the commodity, it unavoidably becomes more in request; the employment of a great part, the half or perhaps three-fourths of the whole stock of it on hand, in this new way cannot fail to render the whole more scarce and dear. (*a*)

---

* The other property of money, the capability of subdivision, and apportionment of the value parted with, must not be lost sight of: by it the jeweller is enabled to exchange a minute portion of his precious commodity for the smallest item of his household expenditure.

(*a*) This point has been well observed upon by *Turgot. Refl. sur la Form. et Distrib. des Rich.*

---

the present year the proportional mint value of gold to silver is as 1 of pure gold to 16.002112+ of pure silver.   AMERICAN EDITOR.

Were the actually existing stock of silver and gold applied to no other use than the fabrication of plate or ornament, the quantity would be abundant and much cheaper than it is at present; that is to say, whenever they were exchanged for other commodities, more of them would be given or received in proportion to the value obtained in exchange. But a large portion of these metals being destined to act as money, and exclusively occupied in that way, there is less remaining to be manufactured into jewellery and plate, and the scarcity of course adds to the value. On the other hand, if they were never used in plate or jewellery, there would be more of them applicable to the purpose of money, and money would grow cheaper, that is to say, more of it would be necessary to purchase an equal quantity of goods. The employment of the precious metals in manufacture makes them scarcer and dearer as money; in like manner as their employment as money makes them scarcer and dearer in manufacture.*

Hence it naturally follows, that these metals being, by reason of their employment as money, raised to such a price, as precludes their so general use in the form of plate and jewellery, it is in consequence found less convenient to use them in that form. The luxury costs more than it is worth. Thus, massive gold plate has gone completely out of fashion, particularly in those countries, where the activity of commerce, and the rapid progress of wealth, make gold in great demand for the purposes of money. The richest individuals content themselves with gilt plate, that is to say, plate covered with a very thin coat of gold; solid gold is used only in smaller articles of manufacture, and those in which the value of the workmanship exceeds that of the metal. In England, plate is made very light, and people of affluence often content themselves with silver-plated goods. The ostentation of displaying a large service of that metal costs the interest of a considerable capital.

The increase of the value of metals is, generally speaking, attended with some disadvantages; inasmuch as it places many articles of comfort and convenience, silver dishes, spoons, &c., beyond the reach of most private families; but there is no disadvantage in such increased value of the metal in its character of money; on the

---

* Ricardo and some other writers maintain, that the charges of obtaining the metal wholly determine its price or relative value in exchange for all other commodities. According to their notions, therefore, the want or demand nowise influences that price; a position in direct contradiction to daily and indisputable experience, which leads us invariably to the conclusion, that value is increased by increase of demand. Supposing that, by the discovery of new mines, silver were to become as common as copper, it would be subject to all the disqualifications of copper for the purposes of money, and gold would be more generally employed. The consequent increase of the demand for gold would increase the intensity of its value; and mines would be worked, that are now abandoned, because they do not defray the expense. It is true that the ore would then be obtained at a heavier rate; but will any one deny, that the increased value of the metal would be owing to the increased demand for it? It is the increased intensity of that demand, that determines the miner to incur the increased charge of production.

contrary, there is a greater convenience in the transfer of a less bulky commodity, on every change of residence, and every act of exchange.

The selection of any commodity, to act as money in but one part of the world, increases its value everywhere else. There is no doubt, that, if silver should cease to be current as money in Asia, the value of that metal in Europe would be affected, and more of it would be given in exchange for all other commodities; for one use of silver in Europe is, the possibility of exporting it to Asia.

The employment of the precious metals as money by no means renders their value stationary; they remain subject to local as well as temporary fluctuations of value, like every other object of commerce. In China, half an ounce of silver will purchase as many objects of use or pleasure as an ounce in France; and an ounce of silver in France will generally go much farther in the purchase of commodities, than it will in America. Silver is more valuable in China than in France, and in France than in America.

Thus money, or specie, as some people call it, is a commodity, whose value is determined by the same general laws, as that of all other commodities; that is to say, rises and falls in proportion to the relative demand and supply. And so intense is that demand, as to have sometimes been sufficient to make paper, employed as money, equal in value to gold of the same denomination; of which the money of Great Britain is a present example.

It must not be imagined, that the paper money of that country derives its value from the promise of payment in specie, which it purports to convey. That promise has been held out ever since the suspension of cash payments by the bank in 1797, without any attempt at performance, which many people consider impossible.*

---

* Before the Bank of England can pay off its notes in cash, the government, its principal debtor, must discharge its debts in specie; which it can not do unless it purchase the specie, either with its savings, or with the proceeds of further taxation. In doing so, it would, in effect, substitute a new and very costly engine of circulation, which must be purchased by the state, for the present one, which, although much out of order, and altogether destitute of intrinsic value, is yet made to do the business well enough. (1)

---

(1) The Bank of England, notwithstanding the opinion expressed by the author in this note, has long since resumed and continued the payment of its notes on demand in specie; and, it must be added, without any intention having been expressed, or attempt made, by the British government, to "discharge its debts in specie," which M. Say seemed here to think must be previously effected.

By an act of parliament, passed in July 1819, generally known as Mr. Peel's Act, the Bank of England was required, from the 1st of May, 1823, to pay its notes on demand, in the legal coins of the realm. The final resumption of cash payments by the Bank of England took place, however, at a still earlier period; for, finding itself in possession of sufficient gold to make payments in cash sooner than this law prescribed, the bank obtained the passage of another act, which made it imperative upon the institution to pay all demands in the legal coin of the realm on the 1st of May, 1822, since which time it has never ceased to "discharge its debts in specie" when required.

AMERICAN EDITOR.

Gold is only procurable piecemeal, and by payment of an agio or per centage; in other words, by giving a larger amount in paper for a smaller amount in gold. Yet the paper, though depreciated, is invested with value far exceeding that of its flimsy material. Whence, then, is that value derived? From the urgent want, in a very advanced stage of society and of industry, of some agent or medium of exchange. England, in its actual state, requires, for the effectuation of its sales and purchases, an agent or medium equal in value, say to 1,284,000 lbs. weight of gold; or, what is the same thing, to 1,200,000,000 lbs. weight of sugar; or, what is still the same thing, to 60,000,000l. sterling of paper, taking the Bank of England paper at 30 millions, and the paper of the country banks at as much more. (a) This is the reason, why the 60 millions of paper, though destitute of intrinsic value, are, by the mere want of a medium of exchange, made equal in value to 1,284,000 lbs. weight of gold, or 1,200,000,000 lbs. weight of sugar.

As a proof that this paper has a peculiar and inherent value, when its credit was the same as at present, and its volume or nominal amount was enlarged, its value fell in proportion to the enlargement, just like that of any other commodity. And, as all other commodities rose in price, in proportion to the depreciation of the paper, its total value never exceeded the same amount of 1,284,000 lbs. weight of gold, or, 1,200,000,000 lbs. weight of sugar. Why? Because the business of circulating all the values of England required no larger value. No government has the power of increasing the total national money otherwise than nominally. The increased quantity of the whole reduces the value of every part; and *vice versâ.**

Since the national money, whatever be its material, must have a peculiar and inherent value, originating in its employment in that character, it forms an item of national wealth, in the same manner as sugar, indigo, wheat, and all the other commodities that the nation may happen to possess.† It fluctuates in value like other commodi-

---

* For the consequence of an excessive issue of paper-money, *vide infrà*, Chap. XXII. sect. 4. where the subject of paper-money is discussed.

† The multiplication of paper-money, and its consequent depreciation, effects no augmentation of the wealth of the community, although it makes necessary a more liberal use of figures in the estimation; just in the same way as its valuation in wheat instead of silver would do. The total of national wealth might be 20,000,000,000 *kilogr.* of wheat, and but 25,000,000 *kilogr.* of silver, and yet the value precisely the same. If the value of the money be less intense, it will require more of it to express the same degree of value.

(a) It must not be supposed, that our author is ignorant of the wide difference between Bank of England and country bank paper, viz: that the one is paper-money, the principal; the other, its convertible representative. This position is perfectly correct. The credit, embodied, as it were, in the provincial paper, is equally an agent of circulation with the inconvertible principal, the paper-money; which, but for its presence and rivalry, would be required in double the quantity, to maintain the same scale of money-prices. Great confusion has hitherto prevailed on this subject for want of a clear conception of the concurrent operation of coin and its rival, credit. T.

ties; and like them, too, is consumed, though less rapidly than most of them. Wherefore, it would be wrong to subscribe to the opinion of Garnier, (a) who lays it down as a maxim, that, "so long as silver remains in the shape of money, it is not an item of actual wealth in the strict sense of the word; for it does not directly and immediately satisfy a want or procure an enjoyment." There are abundance of values incapable of satisfying a want, or procuring an enjoyment, in their present existing shape. A merchant may have his warehouse full of indigo, which is of no use in its actual state, either as food or as clothing; yet it is nevertheless an item of wealth, and one that can be converted, at will, into another value fit for immediate use. Silver, in the shape of crown pieces, is, therefore, equally an article of wealth with indigo in chests. Besides, is not the utility of money an object of desire in civilized society?

Indeed, the same writer elsewhere admits that, "specie in the coffers of an individual is real wealth, an integral part of his substance, which he may immediately devote to his personal enjoyment; although, in the eye of political economy, this same coin is a mere instrument of exchange, essentially differing from the wealth it helps to circulate."* I hope what I have said is quite sufficient to show the complete analogy of specie to all other items of wealth. Whatever is wealth to an individual, is wealth to the nation, which is but an aggregate of many individuals; and is wealth also in the eye of political economy, which must not be misled by the notion of imaginary value, or regard as value any thing, but what all the members of the community, individually, as well as jointly, treat as value, not nominal, but actual. And this is one proof more, that there are not two kinds of truth in this, more than in any other science. What is true in relation to an individual, is true in relation to the government, and to the community. Truth is uniform; in the application only can there be any variety.

Section IV.

Of the Utility of Coinage, and of the Charge of its Execution.

No mention has hitherto been made of the value that money derives from the impression and coinage. I have merely pointed out the various utility of gold and silver as articles of commerce, wherein originates their value; and considered their fitness to act as money, as part of that utility.

Wherever gold and silver act as money, they must of course be constantly passing from hand to hand. Most people buy or sell

---

* *Abregé des Principes d'Èconomie Publique*, 1re *partie*, c. 4, and the advertisement prefixed.

(a) *Garnier de Saintes*, translator of the *Wealth of Nations*.

several times a day; judge, then, what inconvenience must ensue, were it necessary to be always provided with scales to weigh the money paid or received; and what infinite blunders and disputes must arise from awkwardness or defective implements. Nor is this all; gold and silver can be compounded with other metals without any visible alteration. The degree of purity can not be exactly ascertained, without a delicate and complex chemical process. The transactions of exchange are wonderfully facilitated, when the weight and standard of each piece of money are denoted by an impression, that nobody can mistake.

Metals are reduced to an established standard, and divided into pieces of an established weight, by the art of coining.

The government of each state usually reserves to itself the exclusive exercise of this branch of manufacture; whether with a view of gaining somewhat more by the monopoly, than it could, if every body were at liberty to practise it, or to hold out to the subjects a more solid security, than any private manufacturer could offer, which is more frequently the motive. In fact, though governments have too often broken faith in this particular, their guarantee is still preferred by the people to that of individuals, both for the sake of uniformity in the coin, and because there would probably be more difficulty in detecting the frauds of private issuers.

The coinage unquestionably adds a value to the metal coined; that is to say, a lump of silver, wrought into a dollar, is better than an equal weight of bullion of like standard; and for a very simple reason. The fashion given to the metal saves the person, that takes it in course of exchange, all the charges of weighing and assaying, among which the loss of time and labour must be reckoned; just in the same manner as a coat ready made is worth more than the materials it is to be made of. Even if the business of coining were open to all the world, and government confined itself to fixing the standard, the weight, and the impression, that each piece should possess, still the holders of bullion would find it answer to pay a premium to the coiner, for coining their bullion into money; otherwise, they would have some difficulty in effecting an exchange, and would, perhaps, lose more on the exchange, than it would cost to have the bullion converted into coin.

But the additional value, thus communicated to the precious metals by the coinage, must not be confounded with that, which bullion, as an article of trade, receives from the circumstance of its employment as money. The latter value attaches to the whole stock of gold and silver in existence; a silver tankard is of greater value, because that metal is employed as money, whereas, the additional value accruing from the coinage is peculiar to the specific portion coined, exactly as its fashion is peculiar to the goblet; and is wholly independent of the value, that the commodity, silver, derives from its various utility.

In England, the whole expense of coinage is defrayed by the government; the same weight of guineas is delivered at the mint in return for a like weight of bullion of the legal standard. The nation, in quality of consumer of money, is gratuitously presented with the charges of coining, which are levied by taxation upon them in their other character of payers of taxes. Yet gold, in the shape of guineas, has an evident advantage over bullion; not that of being ready weighed, for people are often at the pains of re-weighing, but that of being ready assayed. Consequently, it has happened sometimes, that bullion has been carried to the mint, not to be converted into coin, but merely to have the standard ascertained, and certified to the foreign or domestic purchaser. (a) For guineas are a better article of export than bullion, inasmuch as bullion, bearing the certificate of assay, is preferable to bullion without any such certificate. On the contrary, for the purposes of importation into England, gold bullion answers every purpose of guineas ready coined, and is of just the same value, weight and standard being alike; for the mint makes no charge for converting the bullion into coin. Foreigners have, in fact, an object in keeping back the guineas, which have already received the certificate of assay, and remitting bullion to England to obtain a like gratuitous certificate. This system, therefore, makes it an object to export the coined metal, but holds out no encouragement to its reimportation.*

The mischief is somewhat palliated by an accidental circumstance, which never entered into the calculation of the legislature. There is no other mint in England, but that of the metropolis, which is so completely overloaded with business, that it can not re-deliver the

---

* It is hardly necessary to repeat, that the specie exported is not so much value lost to the community; for nobody will feel inclined to make a present of it to the foreigner. Its value is transmitted, for the purpose of obtaining a corresponding value in return; but the nation loses the value of the coinage in this operation. When guineas are exported from England, she receives in exchange the value of the metal only, and nothing for the impression it bears. (b)

(a) That is to say, to receive the certificate of coinage, for use, not in the character of money, but as an article of commerce. The assay is charged for at the English mint, upon bullion re-delivered without coinage. And, before the export of coin was made free, the risk was probably equal to the value of the certificate conferred by coinage. These remarks apply to the coinage of gold only, silver being now subject to a seignorage of 4s. in 66s. But silver is no longer the material of the metallic money, except for minute and fractional exchanges.
T.

(b) This is hardly true to the full extent. The Spanish dollars pass current in many countries at a considerable advance on bullion of equal weight and fineness, and constitute the legal currency of some communities, that have not undertaken the business of coinage themselves; as in Hayti, and elsewhere. The difference is the local value of the coinage, which is paid for sometimes very liberally. But to whom is it paid? to the Spanish individual or to the Spanish government. If to the former, it is an undue advantage to the individual at the expense of the community; if to the latter, it is the recompense of productive agency. Were the gold coinage of England subject to a seignorage like the silver, it would never be exported habitually, but to such nations as were content to pay the extra value of the coinage. Indeed, our author presently says in express terms, that the value of the coinage is not always lost on importation.
T.

metal coined till many weeks, and often months, after it is brought for coinage.* The consequence is, that the owner, who leaves his bullion to be coined, loses the interest of its value during the whole time it remains in the mint. This operates as a small tax on coinage, and raises the value of the coin somewhat above that of bullion. For it is manifest, that the value would be exactly the same, if bullion and guineas were taken without distinction, weight for weight.

So much for the effect of the English regulations on this head.

All the other governments of Europe, if I mistake not, derive from the coinage a revenue more than equal to the charges of the process.† The exclusive privilege of issuing money which they have most properly engrossed, together with the severe penalties denounced against private coiners, would enable them to raise the profit of the business very high by the limitation of their issues; for the value of money, like that of every thing else, is always in the direct ratio to the demand, and in the inverse ratio to the supply.

In fact when silver in the shape of coin is so rare and dear, that 18 dollars in coin will purchase the weight of 20 dollars of equal fineness in the shape of bullion, it is an indication that the public attaches the same value to 15 oz. 12 dwt. of coined, as to 17 oz. 6 dwt. 16 grs. of uncoined metal. Wherefore, the government can, by its coinage, in such case, give to 9 dollars, the value of 10 dollars, and make a profit of 10 per cent. But, if the coin become more abundant, and more of it be necessary in exchange for bullion, it may perhaps be necessary to give 95 dollars in coin for the weight of 100 dollars in bullion: in which latter case, the government can make a profit of no more than 5 per cent. upon the purchase and conversion of bullion into coin.

If, in the latter case, the government, with a view to increase the ratio of its profit, instead of purchasing bullion itself, were simply to charge a seignorage, say of 10 per cent. upon the bullion brought to the mint for coinage, none at all would be brought for that purpose by individuals, who would have to pay 10 per cent. for an operation, which added 5 per cent. only to the value of the metal. Thus the mint would have nothing to coin either on public or private account; and the government would find a high ratio of profit incompatible with an extended amount of coinage.

---

* *Wealth of Nations*, book i. c. 5.

† One of my German translators, the learned Professor *Morstadt*, of Heidelberg, has observed upon this passage, that since 1810, the Russian government has made no charge for the coinage. It might with equal reason execute gratuitously the business of letter-carriage, instead of charging for it to the individuals.

I am perhaps incorrect in saying, that most governments make a profit over and above the expense of execution. The French government charges a seignorage, equal at most to defray the expense of the mere process. But the interest and wear and tear of the capital vested in buildings, machinery, &c. and the charge of administration, &c. are so much dead loss to the government; and probably many other governments are in the same predicament.

Whence it may be concluded, that the duty or seignorage upon coinage, which has been so frequently discussed, is an absolute nullity; for that governments can not fix their own ratio of profit upon the execution of the coinage, but that it must depend upon the state of the bullion market, which again is regulated by the relative supplies of coined and uncoined metal, and the demand for them at the time being.

It is to be observed, that, to the public at large, in its capacity of consumer of coined bullion, it is a matter of perfect indifference, whether the coin be dear or cheap; for, so long as its value is not subject to sudden fluctuations, it will pass current for as much as it has been taken for.

When the coinage of money is not executed gratuitously, and especially when it is paid for at a monopoly-price, it is a matter of perfect indifference to the state, whether or not its coin be melted down or exported, for it can neither be melted down or exported, without having first paid the coinage in full, which is all that is lost by melting or exportation.* On the contrary, the export of such coin is quite as advantageous as that of any other manufactured commodity whatever. It is a branch of the bullion trade; and unquestionably, a coin, so well executed as to be difficult to counterfeit, accurate in the weight and assay, and charged with a moderate duty on the coinage, may acquire a currency in different parts of the world, and yield the government, that issues it, a profit of no contemptible amount.

Witness the gold ducats of Holland, which are in request throughout all the north of Europe, at a higher rate than their intrinsic value as bullion; and the dollars of Spain, which are all coined at Lima and Mexico, and have been executed with so much regularity and integrity, as to pass current as money not only all over Spanish America, but likewise in the United States and in several parts of Europe, Africa, and Asia.†

The Spanish dollar is a remarkable instance of the value attached to the metal by the process of coinage. When the Americans of the Union determined on a national coinage of dollars, they contented themselves with simply re-stamping those of the Spanish mint, without varying their weight or standard. But the piece thus re-stamped would not pass current with the Chinese, and other Asiatics, at the same rate; 100 dollars of the United States would not purchase so much of other commodities as 100 dollars of Spain. The American Executive, nevertheless, continued to deteriorate the coin by giving it a handsome impression, apparently wishing to avail

---

* The value of the coinage, or fashion of the metal, is not always lost in the export. The impression is, to a certain degree, a recommendation beyond the limits of the authority which executes it, and raises the value somewhat higher than that of bullion in bars.

† The 5 *fr.* pieces of France, have, by their invariable uniformity of weight and standard since their first issue, acquired a similar currency in many parts of the world.

itself of this method of checking the export of specie to Asia. For this purpose it was directed, that all exports of specie should be made in dollars of its own coinage, hoping in this way to make the exporters give a preference to the domestic products of its own territory. Thus, after wantonly depreciating the Spanish dollar, without prejudice, it is true, to the specie remaining current within the territory of the Union, it went on further to enjoin its use in the least profitable way, viz. in the commercial intercourse with those nations that set the least value on it. The natural course would have been, to suffer the value exported to go out of the country in the form that might offer the prospect of the largest returns. Self-interest might have been safely relied on in this particular. (1)

But what are we to think of the wisdom of the Spanish government, which was enabled by the confidence in its good faith in the execution of its coinage, to export dollars with a profit, and sell them abroad at an advance upon their intrinsic value; and yet thought fit to prohibit so advantageous a traffic, which would have furnished a vent to a product of the national soil, worked up by domestic industry for an ample recompense?

Though a government be the exclusive coiner of money, and is by no means bound to coin gratuitously, it can not with justice deduct the expense of coinage from its payments, in discharge of its own contracts. If it has engaged to pay a million, say for supplies advanced, it can not honestly say to the contractor : " We bargained to pay a million, but, we pay you in specie just coined; and therefore shall deduct 20,000 dollars, more or less, for the charges of coinage." In fact, all pecuniary engagements, contracted by government or individuals, virtually imply a promise to pay a given sum, not in bullion but in coin. The act of exchange, wherein the bargain originated, is effected with the implied condition, on behalf of one of the contracting parties, to give a commodity somewhat more valuable than silver bullion; namely, silver in crown pieces, or coin of some denomination or other. The virtual contract of a government is to pay in coined money; and, in consequence of that implied condition, it obtains a greater quantity of goods, than it will, if the bargain be to pay in bullion. In this instance, it offers the charge of coinage into the bargain at the time of concluding the contract, and thereby obtains better terms, than if it is in the habit of paying in bullion.

The charges of coinage should be deducted from the metal brought

---

(1) This paragraph contains three errors in relation to the coinage of dollars by the United States, and the exportation of specie, which it is of importance to point out : 1st. Spanish dollars *are not, and never have been*, simply restamped at our mint, *without* varying their weight or standard : 2d. A pound, troy, of Spanish dollars, contains 10 oz. 15 dwts. of fine silver : a pound, troy, of American dollars contains 10 oz. 14 dwts. 5 grains of fine silver : 3d. No law has ever been enacted by Congress, directing the exportation of specie to be made in dollars of our *own coinage;* nor has the executive the power to regulate, or in any manner interfere with the exportation of specie from the United States.

American Editor.

to the mint to be coined, at the time of its re-delivery in a coined
state.

These considerations lead us to the necessary conclusions,—that
the manufacture of bullion into coin increases the value of the
metal, in the ratio of the additional convenience resulting to the community, from the circumstance of coinage, and not an item further,
whatever charges or duties the state may attempt to saddle it with ;*
that a government, by monopolising the business of coining, may
make a profit to the whole extent of this accession of value; that it
can not possibly advance this profit any further, in its discharge of
engagements, fairly and freely entered into ; and that it can not do
so with regard to prior engagements, without committing an act of
partial bankruptcy.

Moreover, it is evident that, in all dealings between individuals,
the public authority has still less power, by means of the impression
of its die, to make the commodity, acting as money, pass for more
than its intrinsic value, *plus* the value added by the fashion it receives.
Vain will be any enactment, that the stamp impressed shall give to
an ounce of silver a specific or determinate value; it will never buy
more goods than an ounce of silver, bearing that impression, is worth
at the time being.

Section V.

Of Alterations of the Standard Money.

The first thing to be observed under this head is, that the public
authority has generally taken upon itself to fix arbitrarily the commodity, that shall serve as money. This assumption, on its part, has
little inconvenience in itself; for the interests of the nation and of
the ruling power happen to be exactly the same. Should a government attempt to force an ill-adapted medium into circulation, it would
sustain a loss itself on every bargain, and the people would, by
degrees, adopt some other medium. Thus, the first issue of coined
money among the Romans was by their King Numa, and his coinage was of copper, which at that time of day was the properest metal
for the purpose ; for, before the time of Numa, the Romans knew no
other money but copper in bars. On the same principle, modern
governments have made choice of gold and silver, which would
undoubtedly have been selected by the general accord of individuals
without the interference of their rulers.

But the sovereign power, being firmly persuaded that its mandate

---

* In Spanish America, a higher duty is charged, amounting, according to *Humboldt*, to 11½ per cent. on silver, and 3 per cent. on gold, over and above the
actual charges of coinage ; for the government allows no bullion to be exported
in an uncoined state. So that, in fact, this is not a seignorage, but a duty on
exportation, exacted at the time of converting the bullion into coin.

was necessary and compétent to invest any commodity whatever with the currency of money, succeeded in impressing its subjects with the same notion during the darker ages, and that too at the very time that individuals, with a view to personal interest, were acting upon principles diametrically opposite; for, whoever was dissatisfied with the authorised money, either abstained from selling altogether, or disposed of his goods in some other way.

This error led to another of much more serious mischief, that has overset all order whatever.

The public authority persuaded itself, that it could raise or depress the value of money at pleasure; and that on every exchange of goods for money, the value of the goods adjusted itself to the imaginary value, which it pleased authority to affix to it, and not to the value naturally attached to the agent of exchange, money, by the conflicting influence of demand and supply.

Thus, when Philip I. of France, adulterated the *livre* of Charlemagne, containing 12 oz. of fine silver,* and mixed with it a third part alloy, but still continued to call it a *livre*, though containing but 8 oz. of fine silver, he was nevertheless fully persuaded, that his adulterated *livre* was worth quite as much as the *livre* of his predecessors. Yet it was really worth 1-3 less than the *livre* of Charlemagne. A *livre* in coin would purchase but 2-3 of what it had done before. However, the creditors of the monarch, and of individuals, got paid but 2-3 of their just claims; land-owners received from their tenants but 2-3 of their former revenue, till the renewal of leases placed matters on a more equitable footing. Abundance of injustice was committed and authorised: but after all it was impossible to make 8 oz. of fine silver equal to 12.†

In the year 1113, the *livre*, as it was still called, contained no more than 6 oz. of fine silver. At the commencement of the reign of Louis VII. it had been reduced to 4 oz. St. Louis gave the name of *livre* to a quantity of silver weighing but 2 oz. or 6 gros. 6 grains.‡ At the era of the French revolution, the money bearing that name weighed only the 1-6 of an oz.; so that it had been reduced to 1.72 of its original standard of weight or quality in the days of Charlemagne.

I take no notice, at present, of the great fall experienced in the relative value of fine silver to commodities at large, which has been

---

* The measure of weight called a *livre* contained 12 oz. in the time of Charlemagne.

† According to the principles established *suprà*, sect. 3 of this chapter, there is reason to believe, that the value of the adulterated *livre* of 8 oz. of fine silver might have been kept up to that of the old *livre* of 12 oz., if the volume of the coin had not been augmented. But the rise of money prices, consequent upon the adulteration of the coin, is a ground of presumption, that the government, with a view to profit by this momentary operation, ordered a recoinage, and made 12 pieces out of 8, by the addition of alloy, so as to increase the total quantity proportionately to the reduction of the standard of quality.

‡ We find in the *Prolégomènes* of *Le Blanc*, 25, that the silver *sol* of St. Louis weighed 1 *gros*. 7½ *grains*, which, multiplied by 20, makes 2 oz. 6 *gros*. 6 *grains*, the *livre*.

reduced so low as 1-4 of its former amount; but this is foreign to the subject of the present section, and I shall take occasion to speak of it hereafter.

Thus the term, *livre tournois*, has at different times been applied to very different quantities of fine silver. The alteration has been effected, sometimes by reducing the size and weight of the coin bearing that denomination, sometimes by deteriorating the standard of quality, that is to say, mixing up a larger portion of alloy, and a smaller one of pure metal; and, sometimes, by raising the denomination of a specific coin; making, for instance, what was before a 2 *fr.* piece pass under the name of one of 3 *fr.* As no account is ever taken of any thing but the pure silver, which is the only valuable substance in silver coin, all these expedients have had a similar effect; for this reason; that they all, in fact, reduced the quantity of silver contained in what was called a *livre tournois.* And this is what all French writers, in compliment to the royal ordinances, have dignified by the term, raising the standard; on the ground, that the nominal value of the coin is raised by these operations; which might, with much more propriety, be said to lower the standard, since the metal, which alone constitutes the money, is thereby reduced in quantity.

Though the quantity of metal in the *livre* has been continually decreasing from the days of Charlemagne till the present period, many of our monarchs have, at different times, adopted a contrary course, and advanced the weight and standard of quality, particularly since the reign of St. Louis. The motives for deterioration are evident enough: it is extremely convenient to pay one's debts with less money than one borrowed. But kings are not only debtors; they are frequently creditors too. In the matter of taxation, they stand precisely in the same relative position to the subject, as landlords to their tenants. Now, if every body be enabled by law to pay their debts and discharge their contracts with a less amount of silver than bargained for, the subject, of course, can pay his taxes, and the tenant his rent, with a smaller quantity of that metal. And, although the king received less silver, yet he continued to spend as much as before; for the nominal price of commodities rose, in proportion to the diminution of metal in the coin. When what was before 3 *fr.* was declared by law to be 4 *fr.* the government was obliged to pay 4 *fr.* where it before paid but 3 *fr.*; so that it was necessary, either to increase the old, or to impose new taxes; in other words, the government, to obtain the same quantity of fine silver, was obliged to demand a greater number of *livrès* from the subject. This course, however, was always odious, even when it really made no difference in the real pressure of taxation, and was often quite impracticable. Recourse was, therefore, had to the restoration of the coin to the higher standard. The *livre* being made to contain a greater weight of silver, the nation really paid more silver in paying the same number of *livres.** Thus we find,

* The same expedient was resorted to by that monster of prodigality, the Roman emperor Heliogabalus. The taxes of the empire were payable in specific

that the ameliorations of the coin commence nearly about the same period as the establishment of permanent taxation. Before that innovation, the monarch had no personal motive for increasing the intrinsic value of the coin he issued.

It would be a great mistake to suppose that the frequent variations of standard alluded to, were effected in the same clear and intelligible manner which I have adopted to explain them. Sometimes the alteration, instead of being openly avowed, was kept secret as long as possible;* and this attempt at concealment gave occasion to the barbarous technical jargon used in this branch of manufacture. At other times, one denomination of coin was altered, while the rest were left untouched; so that, at a given period, a *livre*, paid in one denomination, contained more silver than if paid in another. Finally, to throw the matter in still greater obscurity, the subject was commonly forced to reckon up his accounts, sometimes in *livres* and *sous*, sometimes in crowns, and to pay in coin representing neither *livre*, *sol*, nor crown, but either fractions or multiples of these several denominations. Princes, that resort to such pettifogging expedients, can be viewed in no other light, than as counterfeiters armed with public authority.

The injurious effect of such measures upon credit, commercial integrity, industry, and all the sources of prosperity, may be easily conceived; indeed, it was so serious, that, at several periods of our history, the monetary operations of the state suspended all commerce whatever. Philip le Bel drove all foreigners out of the fairs of France, by compelling them to receive his discredited coin in payment, and prohibiting the making of bargains in a coin of better credit.† Philip de Valois did the same thing with respect to the gold coin, and with precisely the same result. A cotemporary chronicler‡ informs us, that almost all foreign merchants discontinued their dealings with France; that the French traders themselves, ruined by the frequent alterations of the coin, and the consequent uncertainty of values, withdrew to other countries; and that the rest of the king's subjects, both noble and *bourgeois*, were equally impoverished with the merchants; for which reason, the annalist adds simply enough, the king was not at all beloved.

The examples I have cited are taken from the monetary system

---

gold coin, called *aurei*, and not in gold by the tale: and the emperor, to enlarge his receipts, made a new issue of *aurei*, weighing as much as 24 oz. each. The virtuous Alexander Severus, actuated by an opposite motive, made a considerable reduction of the weight.

* Philip de Valois, in his official instructions to the officers of the mint, A. D. 1350, enjoins the utmost secrecy on the subject of the purposed adulteration, even with the sanction of an oath, for the express purpose of taking in the commercial classes; directing them "to put a good face upon the matter of the course of exchange of the mark of gold, so that the intended adulteration might not be discovered." Many similar instances are to be met with in the reign of King John. *Le Blanc, Traité Hist. des Monnaies*, p. 251.

† *Le Blanc, Traité Hist. des Monnaies*, p. 27.

‡ *Matthieu Villani.*

of France; but similar expedients have been practised in almost every nation, ancient or modern. Popular forms of government have been equally culpable with those of a despotic character. The Romans, during the most glorious periods of the republic, effected a national bankruptcy more than once, by deteriorating the intrinsic value of their coin. In the course of the first Punic war, the *as*, which was originally 12 oz. of copper, was reduced to 2 oz.; and, in the second Punic war, was again lowered to 1 oz.*

In the year 1722, the State of Pennsylvania, which acted, in this particular, as an independent government, even before the American war, passed a law, enacting, that 1*l.* sterling should pass for 1*l.* 5*s.*;† and the United States, and France also, after declaring themselves republics, have both gone still further.

"It would require a separate treatise," says Stewart, "to investigate all the artifices which have been contrived to make mankind lose sight of the principles of money, in order to palliate and make this power in the sovereign to change the value of the coin appear reasonable."‡ He might have added, that such a volume would be of little practical service, and by no means prevent the speedy adoption of some new device of the same kind. The only effectual preventive would be, the exposure of the corrupt system, that engenders such abuses; were that system rendered simple and intelligible, every abuse would be detected and extinguished in the outset.

And let no government imagine, that, to strip them of the power of defrauding their subjects, is to deprive them of a valuable privilege. A system of swindling can never be long-lived, and must infallibly in the end produce much more loss than profit. The feeling of personal interest is that which soonest awakens the intellectual faculties of mankind, and sharpens the dullest apprehensions. Wherefore, in matters affecting personal interest, a government has the least chance of outwitting its subjects. Individuals are not easily duped by measures tending to procure supplies to the state in an under-hand manner: and although they cannot guard against direct outrage, or breach of public faith, yet it can never long escape their penetration, however artfully disguised and concealed. The government will acquire a character for cunning as well as faithlessness, and will lose entirely the powerful engine of credit, which will operate with infinitely more efficacy, than the mere trifle that fraud can procure. Yet, even that trifle will often be wholly engrossed by the agents of government, who are sure to turn every act of injustice towards the subject, to their own private advantage. Thus, while the government loses its credit, its agents get all the profit; and the public authority is disgraced, for no other purpose, than to enrich its menials.

The real interest of a government is, to look not to fictitious, disgraceful, and destructive resources, but to such as are really prolific

---

* *Montesquieu, Esprit des Lois,* liv. xxii. c. 11.

† Smith's *Wealth of Nations,* book ii. c. 2.

‡ Stewart's *Inquiry into the Princ. Pol. Econ.* 8vo. 1805, vol. ii. p. 306.

and inexhaustible; and one can render it no better service, than to expose and render abortive those of the former kind, and point out to it those of the latter.

The immediate consequence of a deterioration of the coin is, a proportionate reduction of all debts and obligations payable in money; of all perpetual or redeemable rent-charges, whether upon the state or upon individuals; of all salaries, pensions, and rack-rents; in short, of all values previously expressed in money; by which reduction, the debtor gains what the creditor loses. It is a legal authorization of a partial bankruptcy, or compromise, by every money-debtor with his creditor, for a sum less than his fair claim, in the ratio of the diminution of precious metal in the same denomination of coin.

Thus, whatever government has recourse to this expedient, is not content with giving itself an illegitimate advantage, but urges all other debtors to do so likewise.

The kings of France, however, have not always allowed their subjects to reap the same advantage in their private concerns, which the monarch proposed to himself by the operation of increasing or diminishing the quantity of metal contained in a particular denomination of coin. Their personal motive was, on all such occasions, to pay less, or receive more silver or gold themselves, than in honesty they ought; but they sometimes compelled individuals, notwithstanding the alteration, to pay and receive in the old coin, or, if in the new, at the current rate of exchange between the two.*   This was a close copy of a Roman precedent. When that republic, in the second Punic war, reduced the *as* of copper from two oz. to one, the republic paid its creditors 1 *as* instead of two, that is to say, 50 per cent. on their claims. But private accounts were kept in *denarii;* and the *denarius,* which till then was worth 10 *asses,* was, by law, made to pass for 16 *asses;* so that individuals paid 16 *asses* or oz. of copper only for every *denarius,* instead of paying 20 as they should have done to fulfil their engagements: that is to say, 10 *asses* of 2 oz. or 20 of 1 oz. each, for every *denarius.* Thus, the republic paid a dividend of 50 per cent. only, but compelled private persons to pay one of 80 per cent.

A bankruptcy, effected by deterioration of the coin, has been sometimes considered in the light of a plain and simple bankruptcy, or mere reduction of the public debt. It has been thought less injurious to the public creditor to pay him in adulterated coin, that he again may pay over at the same rate as he receives it, than to curtail his claim by $\frac{1}{4}$, $\frac{1}{2}$, or in any other proportion. Let us see how the two methods differ.

In either case, the creditor is equally a loser in all his purchases posterior to the bankruptcy. Whether his income be abridged by one-half, or whether he find himself obliged to pay for every thing twice as dear as before, is to him precisely the same thing.

* *Vide* the several ordinances of Philip le Bel in 1303; of Philip de Valois in 1329 and 1343; of John in 1354; and of Charles VI. in 1421.

As to all his own existing debts, he may undoubtedly get rid of them on the same terms as the public has discharged his own claim; but what ground is there for supposing, that the public creditors are always in arrear in their private accounts with the rest of the community? They stand in the same relation to society as all other classes; and there is every reason to believe that the public creditors have as much owing to them by one set of individuals as they owe themselves to another; in short, that the accounts will square. Thus, the injustice they do to their private claimants is balanced by the injury they receive; and a bankruptcy, in the shape of a deterioration of the coin, is to them full as bad, as in any other shape.

But it is attended with other serious evils, destructive of national welfare and prosperity.

It occasions a violent dislocation of the money-prices of commodities, operating in a thousand different ways, according to the particular circumstances of each respectively, and thereby disconcerting the best planned and most useful speculations, and destroying all confidence between lender and borrower. Nobody will willingly lend when he runs the risk of receiving a less sum than he has advanced; nor will any one be in a hurry to borrow, if he is in danger of paying more than he gets. Capital is, consequently, diverted from productive investment, and the blow given to production by deterioration of the coin, is commonly followed up by the still more fatal ones of taxation upon commodities, and the establishment of a maximum of price.

Nor is the effect less serious in respect to national morality. People's ideas of value are kept in a state of confusion for a length of time, during which knavery has an advantage over honest simplicity, in the conduct of pecuniary matters. Moreover, robbery and spoliation are sanctioned by public practice and example; personal interest is set in opposition to integrity; and the voice of the law to the impulse of conscience.

Section VI.

Of the reason why Money is neither a Sign nor a Measure.

Money would be a mere *sign* or representative, had it no intrinsic value of its own; but, on the contrary, whenever it is employed in sale or purchase, its intrinsic value alone is considered. When an article is sold for a dollar piece, it is not the impression or the name that is given or taken in exchange, but the quantity of silver that is known to be contained in it. As a proof of the truth of this position, if the government were to issue crown pieces made of tin or pewter, they would not be worth so much as those of silver. Though declared by law to be of equal value, a great many more of them would be required in purchase of the same commodities; which would not happen if they were nothing but a mere sign.

Violence, ingenuity, or extraordinary political circumstances have sometimes kept up the current value of a money, after a reduction of its intrinsic value; but not for any length of time. Personal interest very soon finds out whether more value is paid than is received, and contrives some expedient to avoid the loss of an unequal and unfair exchange. Even when the absolute necessity of finding some medium of circulation of value obliges a government to invest with value an agent destitute either of intrinsic value or substantial guarantee, the value attached to the sign by this demand for a medium, is actual value, originating in utility, and makes it a substantive object of traffic. A Bank of England note, during the suspension of cash payments, was of no value whatever as a representative; for it then really represented nothing, and was a mere promise without security, given by the bank, which had advanced it to the government without any security; yet this note, by its mere utility, was possessed of positive value in England, as a piece of gold or silver.

But a bank-note, payable on demand, is the representative, the sign,(1) of the silver or specie, which may be had whenever it is wanted, on presenting the note. The money or specie, which the bank gives for it is not the representative, but the thing represented.

When a man sells any commodity, he exchanges it, not for a sign or representative, but for another commodity called money, which he supposes to possess a value equal to the value sold. When he buys, he does so, not with a sign or representative, but with a commodity of real, substantial value, equivalent to the value received.

A radical error, in this particular, has given rise to another of very general prevalence. Money having been pronounced to be the sign of all values whatever, it was boldly inferred, that, in every country, the total value of the money, bank and other notes, and credit paper, is equal to the total value of all other commodities. A position that derives some show of plausibility, from the circumstance, that the relative value of money declines when its quantity is increased, and advances when that quantity is diminished.

---

(1) The term, "representative," or "sign," of silver or specie, as applied to bank-notes, has no precise or definite meaning. A bank-note, with no sort of accuracy can be said to be "the representative of money;" and as such loose metaphorical expressions have given occasion to most of the vague and mystical notions respecting paper-money which have been too long current, and only serve to involve the subject in obscurity and confusion, they cannot too soon be discarded.

We have already seen, that coins are neither more nor less than commodities, which are bought and sold for their value, like other commodities. Bank-notes are not, any more than bills of exchange, or other transferable engagements for the payment of money, the representatives or symbols of these commodities; but are actual obligations for the payment, on demand, or at a stated time, of the quantity of the coins expressed on the face of them, and are themselves received in payment as readily as specie itself, only when it is perfectly understood, that the specie can be obtained for them, or when it is generally known, that they will be as readily received in the market as the coins which they specify.

AMERICAN EDITOR.

It is obvious, however, that the same fluctuation affects all other commodities whatever. If the vintage be twice as productive one year as it is another year, the price of wine falls to half what it was the year preceding. In like manner, one may readily concede, that, should the aggregate of circulating specie be doubled, the prices of all goods would be doubled also; in other words, twice the quantity of specie would go to the purchase of the same articles. But this consequence by no means proves, that the total value of the circulating medium is always equal to the sum total of all the other items of wealth, any more, than that the sum total of the produce of the vintage is equal to the totality of other values. The casual fluctuation in the value of silver and of wine, in the cases supposed, is the effect of a difference in quantity of these respective commodities at two different times, and has nothing to do with the quantity of other commodities.

It has been already remarked, that the total value of the money of any country, even with the addition to the value of all the precious metals contained in the nation under any other shape, is but an atom, compared with the gross amount of other values. Wherefore, the thing represented would exceed in value the representative; and the latter could not command the presence or possession of the former.*

Nor is the position of Montesquieu, that money-price depends upon the relative quantity of the total commodities to that of the total money of the nation† at all better founded. What do sellers and buyers know of the existence of any other commodities, but those that are the objects of their dealing? And what difference could such knowledge make in the demand and supply in respect to those particular commodities? These opinions have originated in the ignorance at once of fact and of principle.

Money or specie has with more plausibility, but in reality with no better ground of truth, been pronounced to be a *measure* of value. Value may be estimated in the way of price; but it can not be measured, that is to say, compared with a known and invariable measure of intensity, for no such measure has yet been discovered.

Authority, however absolute, can never succeed in fixing the general ratio of value. It may enact, that John, the owner of a sack of wheat, shall give it to Richard for 4 dollars; and so it may that John shall give his sack of wheat for nothing. This enactment will probably rob John to benefit Richard; but it can no more make 4

---

* If credit-paper be thrown into the scale, it will not help us over this difficulty. The agent of circulation, whether in form of specie or of paper, can never exceed in amount the total utility vested in it. The expansion of the volume of a national money, whether of metal or of paper, is sure to be followed by a proportionate dilution of its value, which disables the whole from being equal to the purchase of a greater portion of commodities at large: and the value, devoted to the business of circulation, is always a trifle, compared with the value it is employed to circulate. *Vide infrà*, under the head of Bank-notes.

† *Esprit des Lois*, liv. xxii. c. 7.

dollars the exact measure of the value of a sack of wheat, than it can make a sack of wheat worth nothing, by ordering it to be given for nothing.

A yard or a foot is a real measure of length; it always presents to the mind the idea of the self-same degree of length. No matter in what part of the world a man may be, he is quite sure, that a man of 6 feet high in one place is as tall as a man 6 feet high in another. When I am told that the great pyramid of Ghaize is 656 feet square at the base, I can measure a space of 656 feet square at Paris, or elsewhere, and form an exact notion of the space the pyramid will cover; but when I am told that a camel is at Cairo worth 50 *sequins*, that is to say, about 90 ounces of silver, or 100 dollars in coin, I can form no precise notion of the value of the camel; because, although I may have every reason to believe that 100 dollars are worth less at Paris than at Cairo, I can not tell what may be the difference of value.

The utmost, therefore, that can be done is, merely to estimate or reckon the *relative* value of commodities; in other words, to declare, that at a given time and place, one commodity is worth more or less than another; their *positive* value it is impossible to determine. A house may be said to be worth 4000 dollars; but what idea does that sum present to the mind? The idea of whatever I can purchase with it; which is, in fact, as much as to say, the idea of value equivalent to the house, and not of value of any fixed degree of intensity, or independent of comparison between one commodity and another.

When two objects of unequal value are both compared to different portions of one specific product, still it is a mere estimate of relative value. One house is said to be worth 4000 dollars, another 2000 dollars; which is simply saying, the former is worth two of the latter. It is true, that, when both are compared to a product capable of separation into equal portions, as money is, a more accurate idea can be formed of the relative value of one to the other; for the mind has no difficulty in conceiving the relation of 2 integers to 1, or 4000 to 2000. But any attempt to form an abstract notion of the value of one of these integers must be abortive.

If this be all that is meant by the term, *measure of value*, I admit that money is such a measure; but so, it should be observed, is every other divisible commodity, though not employed in the character of money. The ratio of the one house to the other will be equally intelligible, if one be said to be worth 1000, and the other only 500, quarters of wheat.

Nor will this measure of relative value, if we may so call it, convey an accurate idea of the ratio of two commodities one to the other, at any considerable distance of time or place. The 1000 quarters of wheat, or 4000 dollars, will not be of any use in the comparison of a house in former, with a house in the present times; for the value of silver coin and of wheat have both varied in the interim. A house at Paris, worth 10,000 crowns in the days of

Henry IV., would now be worth a great deal more, than another of
that value now-a-days. So, likewise, one in Lower Britany, worth
4000 dollars, is of much more value than one of that price at Paris;
for the same reason that an income of 2000 dollars is a much larger
one in Britany than at Paris.

Wherefore it is impossible to succeed in comparing the wealth of
different eras or different nations. This, in political economy, like
squaring the circle in mathematics, is impracticable, for want of a
common mean or measure to go by.

Silver, and coin too, whatever be its material, is a commodity,
whose value is arbitrary and variable, like that of commodities in
general, and is regulated in every bargain by the mutual accord of
the buyer and seller. Silver is more valuable when it will purchase
a large quantity of commodities, than when it will purchase a smaller
quantity. It can not, therefore, serve as a measure, the first requisite of which is invariability. Thus, in the assertion of Montesquieu, when speaking of money, that "what is the common measure of all things, should of all things be the least subject to change,"*
there are no less than three errors in two lines. For, in the first
place, it has never been pretended, that money is the measure of all
things, but merely that it is the measure of values; secondly, it is not
even the measure of values; and lastly, its value can not be made
invariable. If it was the object of Montesquieu to deter governments
from altering the standard of their coin, he should have laboured
to enforce those sound arguments, which the question would fairly
have supplied him with, instead of dealing in brilliant expressions,
which serve to mislead and give currency to error.

It would, however, often be a matter of curiosity, and sometimes
even of utility, to be able to compare two values at an interval of
time or place; as, for instance, when there is occasion to stipulate
for a payment at a distant place, or a rent for a long prospective
term.

Smith recommends the value of labour as a less variable, and,
consequently, more appropriate, measure of absent or distant value;
he reasons thus upon the matter: "Equal quantities of labour, at all
times and places, may be said to be of equal value to the labourer.
In his ordinary state of health, strength, and spirits, in the ordinary
degree of his skill and dexterity, he must always lay down the same
portion of his ease, his liberty, and his happiness. The price, which
he pays, must always be the same, whatever may be the quantity of
goods which he receives in return for it. Of them, indeed, it may
sometimes purchase a greater and sometimes a smaller quantity; but
it is their value which varies, not that of the labour which purchases
them. At all times and places, that is dear, which it is difficult to
come at, or which it costs much labour to acquire; and that cheap,
which is to be had easily, or with very little labour. Labour alone,
therefore, never varying in its own value, is alone the ultimate and

---

* *Esprit des Lois*, liv. xxii. c. 3.

real standard, by which the value of all commodities can at all times and places be estimated and compared."*

With great deference to so able a writer, it by no means follows, that, because labour in the same degree is always to the labourer himself of the same value, therefore it must always bear the same value as an object of exchange. Labour, like commodities, may vary in the supply and demand; and its value, like value in general, is determined by the mutual accord of the adverse interests of buyer and seller, and fluctuates accordingly.

The value of labour is affected materially by its quality. The labour of a strong and intelligent person is worth much more than that of a weak and ignorant one. Again, labour is more valuable in a thriving community, where there is a lively demand for it, than in a country overloaded with population. In the United States, the daily wages of an artificer amount in silver to three times as much as in France.† Are we to infer, that silver has then but ⅓ of its value in France? The artificer is there better fed, better clothed, and better lodged; which is a convincing proof, that he is really better paid. Labour is probably one of the most fluctuating of values, because at times it is in great request, and at others is offered with that distressing importunity occasionally witnessed in cities where industry is on the decline.

Its value has, therefore, no better title to act as a measure of two values at great distances of time or place, than that of any other commodity. There is, in fact, no such thing as a measure of value, because there is nothing possessed of the indispensable requisite, invariability of value.

In the absence of an exact measure, we must be content to approximate to accuracy; and, to this end, many commodities of well known value will serve to give a notion, more or less correct, of the value of any specific product. At the same point of time and place, there is little difficulty in the approximation: the value of any given article may be readily measured by almost all others. To ascertain

---

* *Wealth of Nations*, book i. c. 5. On this point, Smith observes, that " labour was the first price, the original purchase-money, that was paid for all things. It was not by gold or silver, but by labour, that all the wealth of the world was originally purchased." I think I have succeeded in proving that he is mistaken. Nature executes an essential part of the production of values; and her agency is in most cases paid for, and forms a portion of the value of the product. The profit of land, which is called rent, is paid to the proprietor, who does nothing himself, and stands in place of the original occupant; and it affects the value of the product, raised by the joint agency of nature and industry; the portion of value contributed by nature is not the product of human labour. Capital also, which is, for the most part, the accumulated product of labour, concurs, like nature, in the business of production, and receives in recompense a portion of the product; but the gains, accruing to the capitalist, are quite distinct from the accumulated labour vested in the capital itself, which can be expended or consumed *in toto*, by one set of persons; while its share in the product, in other words, the interest paid for its use, may be consumed by another.

† *Humboldt* reckons it at from 3 *fr.* 50 *cents* to 4 *fr.* of our money. *Essai Pol. sur la Nouvelle Espagne*, tom. iii. p. 105. oct. ed.

pretty nearly the value of an article amongst the ancients, we must
find out some article which there is reason to think has subsequently
undergone little change of value, and then compare the quantity of
that article given by the ancients and moderns respectively, in exchange for the article in question. Wherefore, silk would be a bad
object of comparison; because it was, in the time of Cæsar, procurable from China only, at a most extravagant expense, and, being then
nowhere produced in Europe, must of course have been much dearer
than at present. Is there any commodity that has varied less in the
intervening period? and, if there be any such, how much of it was
then given for an ounce of silk? These are the two points we must
inquire into. If any one article can be discovered, that was produced with equal ease and perfection at the two periods, and the
consumption of which had a natural tendency to keep pace with its
abundance, this article would probably have varied little in value,
and may be taken as a tolerable measure of other values.

Ever since the earliest times recorded in history, wheat has been
the staple food of the great mass of the population, in all the principal nations of Europe; consequently, their relative population must
have been influenced by the abundance or scarcity of this article of
food, more than of any other: the ratio of the demand to the supply
must have been, therefore, at all times nearly the same. There is,
besides, no product which I know of, that has undergone less alteration in the course of production. The agricultural skill of the ancients was in most respects equal, and in some, perhaps, superior to
our own. Capital, indeed, was dearer amongst them; but that difference was little felt; for, in ancient times, the proprietor was commonly both farmer and capitalist; and the capital embarked in agriculture yielded less return than other investments; because, as more
honour was attached to this, than to the other branches of industry,
commerce and manufacture, the influx of capital, as well as of labour,
into that channel, was greater than into the other two. And, during
the middle ages, in spite of the general declension of all the arts, the
tillage of arable land was prosecuted with a skill little inferior to that
of the present day.

Whence I infer, that the same quantity of wheat must have borne
nearly the same value among the ancients, during the middle ages
and at the present time. But, as there has all along been a vast difference in the produce of the harvest in one year and another, grain
being sometimes so abundant, as to sell extremely low, and at other
times so scarce, as to occasion famine, the value of grain must be
taken on an average of years, whenever it is made the basis of any
calculation.

So much for the estimation of values at distant periods of time.

There is equal difficulty in the estimation at great distances of
place. The staple articles of national food, which, as such, maintain
the greatest uniformity in the ratio of the demand and supply, are
very different in different climates. In Europe, wheat is the staple;
in Asia, it is rice: the relative value of neither the one nor the other

in Asia and Europe is tolerably steady; nor has the value of rice in Asia any relation to the value of wheat in Europe. Rice is beyond question less valuable in India, than wheat is in this part of the world; for, besides that the cultivation is less expensive, it yields two crops in the year. This is one reason, why labour is so cheap in India and China.

The article of food in most general use is, therefore, but a bad measure of value at great distances of place. Nor are the precious metals by any means a correct one: their value is indubitably not so great in North America and the West Indies, as in Europe, and much greater in every part of Asia, as the constant efflux of specie thither sufficiently proves. Yet the frequency of communication between these different parts of the world, and the facility of transport, give us reason to suppose them the least liable to fluctuation of value on their passage from one climate to another.

There is happily no necessity, for the purposes of commerce, to compare the relative value of goods and of metals in two distant parts of the world; it is quite enough to know their relation to other commodities in each country. When a merchant remits to China half an ounce of silver, it is of little importance to him, whether it has more relative value in China than in Europe. All he wants to know is, whether he can buy with it at Canton a pound of tea of a certain quality, which he can re-sell in Europe, say for two ounces of silver. With these *data*, and in expectation of receiving, at the close of the speculation, a gross profit of an ounce and a half of silver, he calculates whether that profit will leave him a sufficient net profit, after covering the charges and risk out and home; and this is all he cares about. If, instead of bullion, he remit goods, it is enough for him to know; 1. The relation between the value of these goods and silver in Europe; that is to say, how much they will cost; 2. The relation between their value and that of Chinese products at Canton; that is to say, what he can get in exchange for them; and, lastly, the relation between these latter and silver in Europe; that is to say, what they will be worth when imported. It is evident that every repetition of this operation brings into question nothing more than the relative value of two or more articles at the same time, and at the same place.

For the common purposes of life, or, in other words, when nothing more is requisite, than to compare the value of two objects, at no great distance of time or place, most commodities possessed of any value at all may serve as a measure; and if, in describing the value of an object, even where there is no question of either buying or selling, the estimation is more generally made in the precious metals, or in money, than in any other commodity; it is simply, because its value is more generally known, than that of other commodities.* But, in all bargains for a long prospective period, as for

---

* The difference of value in different objects has, throughout this work, been noted in money-price or what they will fetch in money; extreme correctness not

the reservation of a perpetual rent, it is more advisable to reckon in wheat : for the discovery of a single mine might perhaps greatly reduce the present value of silver ; whereas the tillage of all North America could not sensibly alter the value of wheat in Europe : for the number of mouths to be fed in America, would increase almost in the ratio of the improved cultivation. But long prospective stipulations regarding value must unavoidably, under any circumstances, be very precarious, and can never give any certain notion of the value that is likely to be received. Perhaps the most improvident course of all is, to stipulate for a particular denomination of money; for the same denomination may be fixed to any variation of weight or quality whatever ; and the contracting party may find he has bargained for a name, rather than a value, and that he runs the risk of paying, or being paid, in mere words.

I have dwelt thus long upon the refutation of incorrect expressions, because they appear to have acquired too general a circulation,* and because they often confirm people in false notions and ideas, which ideas sometimes serve as the basis of erroneous systems, that in their turn give birth to conduct equally erroneous.

Section VII.

Of a Peculiarity that should be attended to, in estimating the Sums mentioned in History.

In reducing the money of former ages into money of the present day, the best informed historians have contented themselves with converting the actual quantity of gold and silver, designated by the term made use of by the authority cited, into the current money of their own times. But this is not enough: the actual sum, the real amount of the metal, can give no correct notion of its then value, which is the very point we want to arrive at. It is, therefore, necessary to reckon, besides, the fluctuations of value that the metal itself has undergone.

A few examples will best explain my meaning :

Voltaire tells us, in his Essay on Universal History,† that Charles V. enacted, that the sons of France should have an annual revenue settled on them of 12,000 *livres :* and, as he reckons this sum to be equal to 100,000 *livres* of the present day, he naturally enough observes, that this was no great provision for the sons of the monarch. But let us examine the grounds for this calculation of Voltaire.

---

being necessary for illustration. Even in the exact science of geometry, the figures are given merely to make the demonstrations more intelligible; strict accuracy is necessary in the reasoning and conclusions only.

* After the appearance of three editions of this work, *Sismondi* published his *Nouveaux Principes d'Econ. Pol. ;* wherein amongst many excellent chapters, there is one entitled, " money, the sign, token, and measure of value." Liv. v. c. 1.

† Edit. de Kehl, oct. tom. xvii. p. 394.

First, he reckons that the mark of fine silver was, in the time of Charles V., worth about 6 *livres;* at this rate, 12,000 *livres* will make 2000 marks of silver, which, at their relative value at the date of Voltaire's writing, would in fact amount to 100,000 *livres,* or thereabouts. But 2000 marks of fine silver were worth in the reign of Charles V. much more than in the reign of Louis XV. Of this we shall be convinced, by a comparison of the relative average at the two different periods, of pure silver to wheat, which we will take as one of the least variable.

Dupre of St. Maur, whose book* is an ample repository of learned information upon the value of commodities, gives it as his opinion, that, from the reign of Philip Augustus, who died A. D. 1223, until about the year 1520, the *setier* of wheat (Paris measure) was worth, on the average, as much as 1-9 of a mark of fine silver; *i. e.* about 512 *grains* weight.

About the year 1536, when the mark of silver was of the value of 13 *livres tournois,* or rather passed under the denomination of 13 *livres tournois,* the ordinary price of a *setier* of wheat was about 3 *livres tournois, i. e.* 3-13 of a mark of fine silver, amounting to 1063 *grains* weight of that metal.

In 1602, under the reign of Henry IV., the mark of fine silver being at that time equal to 22 *livres,* the average price of the *setier* of wheat was 9 *liv.* 16 *s.* 9 *d.; i. e.* 2060 *grains* of fine silver.†

Since that period, the *setier* of wheat has, one year with another, been constantly worth about the same weight of silver. In 1789, when the mark was equivalent to 54 *liv.* 19 *s.* the average price of wheat was, according to Lavoisier, 24 *liv.* the *setier, i. e.* 2012 *grains* of fine silver. I have not reckoned the fractions of *grains,* for in these matters it is enough to approximate to accuracy; indeed the price of the *setier,* taken at the average of Paris and the environs, is itself but loosely calculated.

The result of this comparative statement is, that the *setier* of wheat, whose relative value to other commodities has varied little from 1520 down to the present time, has undergone great fluctuations, being worth,

> A. D. 1520　-　-　512 *gr.* of pure silver.
> 1536　-　-　1063 do.　　do.
> 1602　-　-　2060 do.　　do.
> 1789　-　-　2012 do.　　do.

which shows that the value of pure silver must have varied considerably since the first of these dates; inasmuch as on every act of exchange, four times as much of it must now be given for the same quantity of commodities, as was given three centuries ago. We shall see by-and-by,‡ why the discovery of the American mines, and

---

* *Rapport entre l'Argent et les Denrées,* p. 35.

† For these calculations I am indebted to the *Essai sur les Monnaies,* and the *Variations dans les Prix,* both by *Dupré de Saint Maur.*

‡ Book II. Chap. 4.

the influx into the market of about ten times as much silver as before, has operated to reduce its value only in the ratio of 4 to 1.

Now to the application of this information to the royal stipend in question: if pure silver was worth in the time of Charles V. four times as much as in the age of Voltaire, the settlement of 2000 marks upon the sons of France was equivalent to 8000 marks at the present, that is to say, more than 400,000 *fr.* of our present currency, or about 75,000 dollars; which makes the observations of Voltaire upon the inadequacy of the provision much less applicable.

Raynal, though he wrote avowedly upon commercial matters, has committed a similar error, in estimating the public revenue in the reign of Louis XII. at 36 millions of our present money (*francs*) on the ground, that it amounted to 7,650,000 *liv.* of 11 *liv.* to the mark of silver. The sum, indeed, was equal to 695,454 marks of silver: but it would not be enough merely to reduce the mark into *livres* of the present day; for the same quantity of silver was then worth four times as much as it is now; so that, before reducing them into modern money, they should be multiplied by four, which will swell the public revenue under Louis XII. to a sum of 144 millions of *francs* of present currency, or nearly 27 millions of dollars.

Again, we read in Suetonius, that Cæsar made Servilius a present of a pearl worth 6 millions of *sestertii*, which his translators, La Harpe and Levesque, estimate to be equal to 1,200,000 *fr.* present money. But a little lower down, we find, that Cæsar, on his return to Italy, disposed of the gold bullion, accruing from the plunder of Gaul, for coin, at the rate of 3000 *sestertii* to the pound of gold; which shows the pearl of Servilius to have been much under-rated. The Roman pound, according to Le Blanc, weighed $10\frac{3}{4}$ of our ounces; and $10\frac{3}{4}$ oz. of gold in Cæsar's time, were worth as much as 32 ounces of that metal at the present day, for it may reasonably be reckoned, that the value of gold has fallen in the ratio of 3 to 1.* Now 32 oz. of gold are worth nearly 3036 *fr.* which may therefore be looked upon as about the real value of 3000 *sestertii*; at which rate the pearl in question must have been worth 6,072,000 *fr.* (1,129,392 dollars,) and the Roman *sestertius*, somewhat more than a *franc* of our money; which is greatly beyond the ordinary estimate.†

---

* 12 oz. of silver were given for 1 oz. of gold, in Cæsar's time. Wherefore, silver having fallen in the ratio of 4 to 1, 1 oz. of gold was worth as much in his days, as 48 oz. of pure silver at the present period. But 48 oz. of silver are now worth 3 oz. of gold or thereabouts; so that gold must have fallen in the ratio of about 3 to 1.

† The same error of calculation has led these translators involuntarily to underrate the prodigality of the worst of the emperors. Thus we are told, that Caligula, in less than a year, squandered the whole of the treasure accumulated by Tiberius, amounting to 2700 millions of *sestertii*, which La Harpe translates into no more than 540 millions of *livres:* whereas, supposing the value of gold to have varied little between the days of Cæsar and of Caligula, which is probable enough, it will be found to amount to very nearly 3000 millions of livres.

When Cæsar laid hands upon the public treasures of Rome, in spite of the opposition of the tribune Metellus, he is stated to have found them to consist of 4130 lbs. of gold, and 80,000 lbs. of silver; which Vertot estimates to have amounted to 2,911,100 *liv. tourn.;* but upon what grounds I am at a loss to imagine. To form a tolerably correct notion of the treasure seized by Cæsar upon his usurpation, the 4130 lbs. of gold should be reduced into oz. of the French standard, at the rate of 10ᵢ oz. to the Roman lb.* which makes 44,052 oz. But, as the same weight of gold was then worth three times as much as at present, the value will appear to have been 132,156 oz. or 12,530,346 *fr.* (2,330,644 dollars,) supposing the standard of quality in the gold to have been the same as at present. The 80,000 lbs. weight of silver also were then worth as much as 320,000 lbs. at the present period, *i. e.* 20,915,735 *fr.*, (3,890,327 dollars,) reckoning the Roman lb. at 10⅔ oz. and taking the standard of quality to have been the same. Wherefore, the sum appropriated by the usurper amounted to 33,446,081 *fr.* (6,232,971 dollars,) of our money; which is greatly above Vertot's estimate of about 3 millions only.

From this specimen we may judge, how little reliance can be placed on the calculations of other historians, of less information and accuracy than those I have been quoting. Rollin, in his Ancient, and Fleury, in his Ecclesiastical History, have reckoned the *talentum, mina* and *sestertius,* according to the scale made out by some learned persons, under the administration of Colbert. This scale is liable to many objections: 1. It establishes upon very questionable *data,* the respective quantities of the precious metals contained in the coins of the ancients, which is a primary source of error: 2. The value of the precious metals has considerably varied, between the period of antiquity in question and the ministry of Colbert, which is another source of error: 3. The scale of reduction, drawn up under the direction of that minister, was calculated at the rate of 26 *liv.* 10 *sous,* to the mark of silver, being the then mint price of silver bullion; but this rate was altered before the days of Rollin, which is a third source of error. Lastly, since the date of his publication, that rate has been still further altered, and a *livres tournois,* conveys to us the idea of a smaller quantity of silver, than it did in his time;

Indeed, it seems hardly possible, that a less sum would have sufficed for the monstrous extravagancies recorded of him.

Horace, Epist. 2. lib. ii. speaks of an estate, that, from the context, must have been a considerable one, as being of the value of 300,000 *sestertii,* which, according to my view, amounted to 303,600 *fr.* (about 56,470 dollars) of our present money. His commentator, *Dacier,* perverts the meaning of the passage, by estimating the estate in question, at 22,500 *fr.* only, or 4185 dollars.

* *Le Blanc. Traité Monnaies,* p. 3. estimates the Roman lb. of 12 oz. at the actual weight of only 10⅔ oz. of our standard, taking as a guide, the weight of some of the coins of the emperors which are in a state of high preservation. The valuation I have here given of the oz. of gold, takes it at the mint standard; viz. with a proportion of $\frac{1}{12}$ alloy; for I take it for granted, that the gold, thus laid hands upon by Cæsar, was not pure gold, but coin with a mixture of alloy.

and this is a fourth source of error. Thus, whoever now takes up that work, relying on the calculations therein contained, will entertain a most erroneous idea of the income and expenditure of the states of antiquity, as well as of their commerce, their resources, and every part of their system and organization.

Not that I would be understood to say, that a writer of history can ever have sufficient *data*, to give his readers, in all cases, a correct notion of values in general; but, for the sake of a closer approximation to accuracy, than has hitherto been effected, in reducing the sums of ancient times, and even of the middle ages, into modern money, I would recommend, what indeed is generally done, first, to inquire from those learned in antiquity, the actual weight of precious metal contained in the coin in question: secondly, as far back as the Emperor Charles V., that is to say, about the year 1520, that quantity, if gold, must be multiplied by 3 only, and if silver, by 4 : * because the discovery of the American mines has occasioned a fall in nearly that proportion: and lastly, to reduce that quantity of gold or silver into the current money of the period, at which he may happen to be writing.

From the year 1520 downwards, the value of silver progressively declined until the latter end of the reign of Henry IV., that is to say, towards the beginning of the seventeenth century. We may judge of the depression of its value by the increasing price of any given commodity, in the manner explained in the preceding section. To acquire a correct notion of the value of the mark of silver during this period, it will be necessary to allow for a diminution in the ratio of the increased real, that is, metal, and not nominal or coin, price of commodities in general, or of any one, as wheat, for instance, in particular.

From the beginning of the seventeenth century, there will be no occasion for any further allowance, after having reduced the money of the time being into marks of silver; for there does not appear to have been any further sensible decline in the value of silver, since most commodities have been procurable for the same metal-price. It will be sufficient, therefore, to reduce them into the money current for the time being, according to the then current value of the mark of fine silver.†

---

* Until the period specified, the ratio of gold to silver in Europe was 1 to 12. At present, it is in most nations of Europe 1 to 14, or 1 to 15; so that taking the average ratio in ancient times at 1 to 11¼ and in modern times at 1 to 15, gold will have increased in relative value to silver in the proportion of 4 to 3. Wherefore, if gold be multiplied by 3, and silver by 4, the result will be equal.

† I am disposed to believe, that the value of both gold and silver began again to decline about the commencement of the present century; for more gold and silver are now given for most of the commodities least liable to vary in the costs of production. (1)

---

(1) In the very able and laborious " Historical Inquiry into the Production and Consumption of the Precious Metals, by William Jacobs, Esq. F. R. S. London, 1831," we are furnished with a chapter (xxv.) on the production of gold

By way of illustration, let us take the statement we find in the Memoirs de Sully, viz. that this minister accumulated, in the vaults of the Bastile, a sum of 36 millions of *livres tournois*, to further the designs of his master against the house of Austria. If we wish to know the actual value of that hoard, we must, in the first place, examine what weight of fine silver it amounted to. The mark of fine silver was then represented by 22 *livres tournois;* consequently 36 millions of *livres* make 1,636,363 marks, 5 oz. of silver. There has been no sensible variation in the value of that metal since the period in question; for the same quantity of metal would then buy the same quantity of wheat as at present. Now, at the present time, 1,636,363 marks 5 oz., or, in other terms, 399,588,018, 5 *grammes*

---

and silver from the end of the year 1809 to the end of 1829. The author remarks, "that it was at the first named period, 1809, when a great change took place in the production of the mines of gold and silver, in every part of the western continent, after a space of more than three centuries, during the whole of which there had been a constant increase of the quantities obtained; each succeeding decennial period yielding a larger portion than the similar number of years that preceded it; and though they have in some measure been restored, it has been by slow degrees, and they are yet very far from having approached the copious produce which they yielded before their general abruption from European government."

After then examining the productiveness of the mines of Mexico, Colombia, including New Grenada, Peru, Buenos Ayres, Chili, and Brazil, in gold and silver, and also after taking notice of the gold found in North and South Carolina and Georgia, from 1824 to 1830, he sums up the whole of the amount of the gold and silver supplied by the late Spanish dominions in America, during the twenty years, from the end of the year 1809 to the end of 1829, thus:—

Divisions.	Amount in dollars in twenty years.
Mexico, - - - - - - -	220,043,200
Guatimala, - - - - - -	2,893,710
Colombia, - - - - - -	33,564,267
Peru, - - - - - - - -	64,688,429
Buenos Ayres, - - - - -	30,000,000
Chili, - - - - - - - -	16,618,880
	367,808,486
Or in sterling, at 4s. 2d. the dollar,	l.76,626,768
To this may be added the produce of Brazil, - - - - - - - - -	4,110,000
Whole produce of America, - - -	l.80,736,768

"In Europe," he states, likewise, "the produce of gold and silver has declined, when the average of the last twenty years is compared with that of the one hundred and ten years which preceded it. The value of the gold produced in Europe, he estimates about 720,000l. and of the silver 530,000l., being together 1,250,000l. annually, or in the period of twenty years from 1810 to 1829, 23 millions; to this the supply from America, 80,736,768l., will make together, 103,736,768 pounds sterling." Mr. Jacobs estimates the diminution in the mass of metallic money, during the twenty years mentioned, at 13 per cent.

AMERICAN EDITOR.

of fine silver, coined into money, will make exactly 88,797,315 *fr.* or 16,516,300 dollars. A sum, indeed, that would go no great way in modern warfare; but it must be considered, that war is now conducted on a very different principle, and has become infinitely more wasteful, in reality as well as in name.

Section VIII.

Of the Absence of any fixed ratio of Value between one Metal and another.

The same error, which led public functionaries to believe, that they could fix the relative value of any metal to commodities, has also induced them to determine by act of law the relative value of the metals employed as money, one to the other. Thus, it has been arbitrarily enacted, that a given quantity of silver shall be worth 24 *liv.*, and that a given quantity of gold shall likewise be worth 24 *liv.* In this manner, the ratio of the nominal value of gold to that of silver came to be legally established.

The pretension of authority was in both cases equally vain and impotent; and what has been the consequence? The relative value of the two metals to other commodities has, in fact, been constantly fluctuating, as well as the relative value of the metals themselves, when exchanged one for the other. Before the re-coinage of gold, in pursuance of the *arret* of 13th October, 1785, the *louis d'or* was commonly sold for 25 *liv.* and some *sous* of the silver coin. Consequently, people took good care not to pay in gold coin the sums bargained for in silver; otherwise they would really have paid 25 *liv.* and 8 or 10 *sous*, for every 24 *liv.* of the sums stipulated.

Since the re-coinage in 1785, when the quantity of gold in the *louis d'or* was reduced by one-sixth, its value has nearly kept pace with that of 24 *liv.* in silver; so that gold and silver have been paid indifferently. However, it has still continued most customary to pay in silver, partly from long habit, and partly because the gold coin, being more liable to be clipped or counterfeited, was received with more caution and liable to more frequent cavils about the weight and quality.

In England a different arrangement has produced an effect directly contrary. In the year 1728, the natural course of exchange fixed the relative value of gold to silver as $15\frac{2}{11}$ to 1; say $15\frac{1}{14}$ to 1, for the sake of simplicity; 1 oz. of gold was sold for $15\frac{1}{14}$ oz. of silver, and *vice versâ*. Accordingly that ratio was established by law, 1 oz. of gold being coined into the nominal sum of 3*l.* 17*s.* 10½*d.* and $15\frac{1}{14}$ oz. of silver into the same sum. Thus, the government attempted permanently to fix a ratio, that is, in the nature of things, perpetually varying. The demand for silver gradually increased; its use for plate and other domestic purposes became more general; the India trade received an additional stimulus, and took off silver in preference to gold, for this reason, that the relative value of silver to gold is higher in the East than in Europe; so that, by the end of the last century, the ratio of these metals one to the other in England became about 14½ to 1 only; and the same quantity of silver, that was coined into 3*l.* 17*s.* 10½*d.*, would then sell in the market for 4*l.* in gold.   There was thus a profit on melting down the silver, and a loss on payments in that metal; for which reason, thenceforward, until the parliamentary suspension of specie payments by the Bank of England in 1797, payments of course were commonly made in gold.

Since 1797, all payments have been made in paper.   But, if England shall return to a metallic currency, framed upon the former monetary principles and regulations, it is probable that payments will be made in silver instead of gold, as before the suspension; for gold has risen in relative price to silver in the English market, probably in consequence of the large export of specie for commercial purposes, and greater difficulty of prevention in gold than in silver. Gold bullion in the English market is now to silver bullion in the ratio of about 1 to 15½, although the mint ratio is still 1 to 15$\frac{1}{14}$.   A payment in gold instead of silver would therefore be a gratuitous sacrifice of the difference between 15$\frac{1}{14}$ and 15½.

Hence may be drawn this conclusion; that it is impossible in practice to assign any fixed ratio of exchangeable value to commodities, whose ratio is for ever fluctuating, and, therefore, that gold and silver must be left to find their own mutual level, in the transactions in which mankind may think proper to employ them.*

The above remarks upon the relative value of gold and silver are equally applicable to silver and copper, as well as to all other metals whatever.   There is no more propriety in declaring, that the copper contained in twenty *sous* shall be worth the silver contained in a *livre tournois*, than in enacting, that the silver contained in 24 *liv. tournois* shall be worth the gold in a *louis d'or.*   However, little mischief has been occasioned by fixing the ratio of copper to the precious metals, because the law does not authorize the payment of sums stipulated in *livres tournois* and *francs* in either copper or the precious metals indifferently; so that, in reality, the only metal money recognised by law as legal tender, for sums above the value of the lowest denomination of silver coin, is silver or gold.

---

* The relative position of gold and silver, in respect to value, is by no means determined by the respective supply of each from the mines.   *Humboldt* states, in his *Essai Pol. sur la Nouvelle Espagne*, tom. iv. p. 222, oct., that silver is produced from the mines of America and Europe jointly, in the ratio to gold, of 45 to 1.   Now the ratio of their value, instead of being 45 to 1, is only,

In Mexico,	- - - - - 15⅗	- - - -	to 1
France,	- - - - - 15½	- - - - -	1
China, -	- - - from 12 to 13	- - - -	1
Japan, -	- - - - - - 8 to 9	- - - -	1

The difference is probably owing to the superior utility and demand of silver for the purposes of plate, &c. as well as of money.   It would seem, that this cause operates more forcibly in the East than in the West; for gold jewellery is relatively cheaper there than in our part of the world.

Of Money as it ought to be.

From all that has been said in the preceding sections may be inferred my opinion of what money ought to be.

The precious metals are so well adapted for the purposes of money, as to have gained a preference almost universal; and, as no other material has so many recommendations, no change in this particular is desirable.

So also of their division into equal and portable particles. They may very properly be coined into pieces of equal weight and quality as has heretofore been the practice among most civilized nations.

Nor can there be any better contrivance, than the giving them such an impression, as shall certify the weight and quality; or than the exclusive reservation to government of the right of impressing such certificate, and, consequently, of coining money; for the certificate of a number of coiners, all working together and in competition one with the other, could never give an equal security.

Thus far, then, and no further, should the public authority intermeddle with the business of money.

The value of a piece of silver is arbitrary, and is established by a kind of mutual accord on every act of dealing between one individual and another, or between the government and an individual. Why, therefore, attempt to fix its value beforehand? since, after all, the fixation must be imaginary, and can never answer any practical purpose, in the money transactions of mankind. Why give a denomination to this fixed, imaginary value, which money can never possess? For what is a dollar, a ducat, a florin, a pound sterling, or a franc; what, but a certain weight of gold or silver of a certain established standard of quality? And, if this be all, why give these respective portions of bullion any other name, than the natural one of their weight and quality?

Five *grammes* of silver, says the law, shall be equivalent to a *franc:* which is just as much as to say, 5 *grammes* of silver is equivalent to 5 *grammes* of silver. For the only idea presented to the mind by the word *franc,* is that of the 5 *grammes* of silver it contains. Do wheat, chocolate or wax, change their name by the mere act of apportioning their weight? A pound weight of bread, chocolate, or of wax candles, is still called a pound weight of bread, chocolate, or wax candles. Why, then, should not a piece of silver, weighing 5 *grammes*, go by its natural appellation? Why not call it simply 5 *grammes* of silver?

This slight alteration, verbal, critical, and nugatory as it may seem, is of immense practical consequence. Were it once admitted, it would be no longer possible to stipulate in nominal value; every bargain would be a barter of one substantial commodity for another, of a given quantity of silver for a given quantity of grain, or butcher's meat, of cloth, &c. &c. Whenever a contract for a long prospective period was entered into, its violation could not escape detection: a person taking an obligation to pay a given quantity of fine silver, at a day certain, would know precisely how much silver he would have to receive at the period assigned, provided his debtor continued solvent.

The whole monetary system would thenceforth fall to the ground; a system replete with fraud, injustice, and robbery, and moreover so complicated, as rarely to be thoroughly understood, even by those who make it their profession. It would ever after be impossible to effect an adulteration of the coin, except by issuing counterfeit money; or to compound with creditors, without an open, avowed bankruptcy. The coinage of money would become a matter of perfect simplicity, a mere branch of metallurgy.

The denominations of weight, in common use before the introduction into France of the metrical system, that is to say, the *once, gros, grain,* had the advantage of conveying the notion of portions of weight, that had remained stationary for many ages, and were applicable to all commodities whatever, without distinction: so that the *once* could not be altered for the precious metals, without altering it at the same time for sugar, honey, and all commodities sold by the weight: but, in this particular, the new metrical system is infinitely preferable. It is founded upon a basis provided by nature, which must remain invariable as long as our world shall last. The *gramme* is the weight of a cubic *centimetre* of water: the *centimetre* is the hundredth part of a metre, and the metre is $\frac{1}{10,000,000}$ part of the arc formed by the circumference of the earth, from the pole to the equator. The term *gramme* may be changed, but no human power can change that portion of weight actually designated by the term *gramme;* and whoever shall contract to pay at a future date a quantity of silver, equal to 100 *grammes* weight, can never pay a less quantity of silver, without a manifest breach of faith, whatever arbitrary measures of power may intervene.

The power of a government to facilitate the transactions of exchange and contract, wherein the commodity, money, is employed, consists in dividing the metal into different pieces of one or more *grammes* or *centigrammes,* in such a manner, as to admit of instant calculation of the number of *grammes* a given payment will require.

It has been ascertained by the experiments of the Academy of Sciences, that gold and silver resist friction better with a slight mixture of alloy, than in a pure state. People versed in these matters say, besides, that this complete purity cannot be obtained, without a very expensive chemical process, that would add greatly to the expense of coinage. There is no sort of objection to mixing alloy, provided the proportion be signified by the impression, which should be nothing more than a mere certificate of the weight and quality of the metal.

I make no mention of the terms *franc, decime, centime,* because those names should never have been given to the coin, being, in fact, names indicative of nothing whatever. The laws of France, instead of enacting that pieces called *francs*, shall be coined, having the weight of 5 *grammes* of silver, should have simply ordered a coinage of pieces of 5 *grammes*. In which case, a letter of credit or bill of exchange, instead of being drawn for, say 400 *fr.*, would be for 2000 *grammes* of silver of the standard of $\frac{9}{10}$ silver to $\frac{1}{10}$ alloy; or if preferred, for 130 *grammes* of gold of the same degree of purity; and the payment would be the most simple imaginable; for the pieces of coin, gold and silver, would be all fractions or multiples of the *gramme* of metal of that standard.

However, it would still be necessary to enact, that no sum stipulated in *grammes* of silver or gold should be payable otherwise than in coin, unless under a special proviso; else, the debtor might discharge all claims in bullion of somewhat less value than coin. This is obviously matter of practical arrangement; the principle requiring nothing, but that the obligation, after mentioning the metal and standard, should specify on the face of it, whether payable in national coin or bullion. The only object of such a law would be, to save the continual necessity of enumerating many particulars that would thenceforward be implied.

A government should never coin the bullion of private persons, without charging the profit, as well as the cost, of the operation. The monopoly of coinage will enable it to make this profit somewhat high: but it should be varied according to the state of metallurgic science, and the demand for circulation. Whenever the state has little to coin on its own account, it had better lower its charges, than let its machinery and workmen remain idle; and, on the other hand, raise its charges, when the influx of bullion is rapid and superabundant. And in this, it would but imitate other manufacturers. As to the bullion bought and coined by government on its own account, the coin issued would reimburse the charges; and yield a profit by its superior value in exchange; as I have endeavoured to prove above, in Section IV.

To the marks indicative of weight and quality, should of course be superadded every device to prevent counterfeits.

I have not occupied my reader's time with any observations on the relative proportion of gold to silver; nor was there any occasion to do so. Having avoided any specification of their value under any particular denomination, I shall pay no more attention to the alternating variations of that value, than to the fluctuations of the relative value of both to all other commodities. This must be left to regulate itself; for any attempt to fix it would be vain. With regard to obligations, they would be dischargeable in the terms of contract: an undertaking to pay 100 *grammes* of silver would be discharged by the transfer of 100 *grammes* of silver; unless, at the time of payment, by mutual consent of the contracting parties, any other metal, or goods at a rate agreed on, should be substituted in preference.

It would be difficult to calculate the advantage, that would accrue to industry in all its branches, from so simple an arrangement; but some notion of it may be obtained, by considering the mischiefs that have resulted from a contrary system. Not only has the relative pecuniary position of individuals been repeatedly overset, and the best planned and most beneficial productive enterprises altogether thwarted and rendered abortive; but the interests of the public, as well as of private persons, are, almost everywhere, subject to daily and hourly aggression.

A medium, composed entirely of either silver or gold, bearing a certificate, pretending to none but its real intrinsic value, and, consequently exempt from the caprice of legislation, would hold out such advantages to every department of commerce, and to every class of society, that it could not fail to obtain currency even in foreign countries. Thus, the nation, that should issue it, would become a general manufacturer of money for foreign consumption, and might derive from that branch of manufacture no inconsiderable revenue. We read in Le Blanc,* that a particular coin issued by St. Louis, and called *agnels d'or*, from the figure of a lamb impressed upon them, was in great request even among foreigners, and a favourite money in commercial dealings, for the sole reason that it invariably contained the same quantity of gold, from the reign of St. Louis to that of Charles VI.

Should France be so fortunate as to make this experiment, I hope none of those who do me the honour to read this work, will feel any regret at the drain of its money, to use the expression of certain persons, who neither know nor choose to learn any thing of the matter. It is quite clear, that neither silver nor gold coin will go out of the kingdom, without leaving behind a value fully equivalent to the metal and the fashion it bears. The trade and manufacture of jewellery for export are considered lucrative to the nation; yet they occasion an outgoing of the precious metals. The beauty of the form and pattern adds, to be sure, greatly to the price of the metal thus exported; but the accuracy of assay and weight, and, above all things, the maintenance of the coin at an invariable standard of weight and quality, would be an equal recommendation, and would undoubtedly be just as well paid for.

Should it be objected, that the same system was adopted by Charlemagne, when he called a pound of silver a *livre*, and that notwithstanding the coin has been since repeatedly deteriorated, until, at last, what was called a *livre*, contained, in fact, but 96 *gr.*, I answer:

1. That, neither in the time of Charlemagne, nor at any subsequent period, has there ever been a coin containing a pound of silver; that the *livre* has always been a money of account, an ideal measure. The silver coin of Charlemagne and his successors, consisted of *sols* of silver, the *sol* being a fractional part of the pound weight.

---

* *Traité Hist. des Monnaies de la France, Prolegom.* p. 4.

2. None of the coin has ever borne on the face of it the indication of the weight of metal it contained. There are extant in the collections of medals many pieces coined in the reign of Charlemagne. The impression was nothing more than the name of the monarch, with the occasional addition of the name of the town where the coin was struck, executed in very rude characters; which, indeed, is not to be wondered at, considering that the monarch, though an avowed patron of literature, was himself unable to write.

3. The coin was yet further from bearing any thing indicative of the standard quality of the metal, and this was the thing first encroached upon; for the *sol* in the reign of Philip I. still contained the same fractional weight of the *livre* as originally; but it was made up of 8 parts of silver to 4 copper, instead of containing, as under the second race of monarchs, 12 oz. of fine silver, which was the then weight of the *livre*.

The very singular state of the actual money of England, and the extraordinary circumstances, that have occurred in respect to it since the first editions of this work appeared, have given a decisive proof, that the mere want of an agent of circulation, or, of the commodity, money, is sufficient to support a paper-money absolutely destitute of security for its convertibility at a high rate of value, or even at a par with metal, provided it be limited in amount to the actual demand of circulation.* Whence some English writers of great intelligence in this branch of science have been led to conclude, that, since the purposes of money call into action none of the physical and metallic properties of its material, some substance less costly than the precious metals, paper, for instance, may be employed in them with good effect, if due attention be paid to keep the amount of the paper within the demands of circulation. The celebrated Ricardo, has, with this object, proposed an ingenious plan, making the Bank or corporate body, invested with the privilege of issuing the paper-money, liable to pay in bullion for its notes on demand. A note, actually convertible on demand into so much gold or silver bullion, cannot fall in value below the value of the bullion it purports to represent; and, on the other hand, so long as the issues of the paper do not exceed the wants of circulation, the holder will have no inducement to present it for conversion, because the bullion, when obtained, would not answer the purposes of circulation. If a casual interruption of confidence in the paper should bring it for conversion in too large quantity, the paper remaining in circulation must rise in value, in the absence of any other circulating medium, and there would be an inducement to bring bullion to the bank to be converted into paper.†

---

* *Vide* our author's pamphlet, entitled, *de l'Angleterre, et des Anglais*, 1815, 3d edition, p. 50, *et seq.*

† *Proposals for an economical and secure Currency*, by D. Ricardo, 1816. It seems, the British legislature has since adopted the expedient of that writer, in 1819. The experiment is yet in progress; and whatever be its ultimate result, it must needs advance the interests of the science.

Of a Copper and Base Metal* Coinage.

The copper coin and that of base metal, are not, strictly speaking, money; for debts cannot be legally tendered in this coin, except such fractional sums, as are too minute to be paid in gold or silver. Gold and silver are the only metal-money of almost all commercial nations. Copper coin is a kind of transferable security, a sign or representative of a quantity of silver too diminutive to be worth the coinage; and, as such, the government, that issues it, should always exchange it on demand for silver, when tendered to an amount equal to the smallest piece of silver coin. Otherwise, there is no security against the issue of an excess beyond the demand of circulation.

Whenever there is such an excess, the holders, finding the base metal less advantageous than the gold and silver it represents but does not equal in value, would strive to get rid of it in every way; whether by selling to a loss, or by employing it in preference to pay for low-priced articles, which would consequently rise in nominal price; or by proffering it to their creditors in larger quantity, than enough to make up the fractional part of sums in account. The government, having an interest in preventing its being at a discount, because that would reduce the profit upon all future issues, generally authorizes the latter expedient.

Before 1808, for instance, it was a legal tender at Paris to the extent of $\frac{1}{10}$ of every sum due; which had exactly the same effect, as a partial debasement of the national currency. Every body knew, when a bargain was concluded, that he was liable to be paid in proportion of $\frac{1}{10}$ copper or brass metal, to $\frac{10}{10}$ silver, and made his calculation accordingly, on terms proportionably higher, than if no such regulation had existed. It is with this particular, precisely as with the weight and standard of the silver coin; sellers do not stop to weigh and assay every piece they receive, but the dealers in gold and silver, and those connected with the trade, are perpetually on the watch to compare the intrinsic, with the current, value of the coin; and, whenever their values differ, they have an opportunity of gain; their operations to obtain which, have a constant tendency to put the current value of the coin on a level with its real value.

The obligation to receive copper in any considerable proportion, has, in like manner, an influence upon the exchange with foreigners. There is no question, that a letter of exchange on Paris payable in *francs* is sold cheaper at Amsterdam, in consequence of the liability to receive part payment in copper or base metal; just as it would

---

* *Billon*, a compound of copper and silver, containing $\frac{1}{4}$ or $\frac{1}{3}$ only of the latter, and the residue of the former. It is used in the fractional coinage of France, to supersede the employment of copper in large quantities.

be, if the *franc* were made to contain less of silver and more of alloy.

Yet, it is to be observed, that, on the whole, the value of money is not so much affected by this circumstance, as by the mixture of alloy; for the alloy has positively no value whatever, for the reasons above stated;* whereas, the copper money, payable in the ratio of $\frac{1}{10}$, had a small intrinsic value, though inferior to the sum in silver, it was made to pass for: had it been of equal value, there would have been no occasion for an express law to give it currency.

As long as a government gives silver on demand for the copper and base metal regularly presented, it can with little inconvenience give them very trifling intrinsic value; the demand for circulation will always absorb a very large quantity, and they will maintain their value as fully, as if really worth the fractional silver represented; on exactly the same principle, as a bank-note passes current, and that too for years together, without any intrinsic value, just as well as if really worth the sum it purports on the face of it to contain. In this manner, such a coinage can be made more profitable to the government than by any compulsion to receive it in part payment; and the value of the legal coin will suffer no depreciation. The only danger is that of counterfeits, which there is the strongest stimulus for avarice to fabricate, in proportion as the difference between the intrinsic, and the current value, grows wider.

The last King of Sardinia's predecessor, in attempting to withdraw from circulation a base currency, issued by his father in a period of calamity, had more than thrice the quantity originally issued by the government thrown upon his hands. The same thing happened to the king of Prussia, when, under the assumed name of the Jew Ephraim, he withdrew the base coin he had compelled the Saxons to receive, during his distresses in the seven years' war;† and for exactly the same reason. Counterfeits of the coin are usually executed beyond the national frontier. In England it was attempted to remedy this evil in the year 1799, by a coinage of half-pence with a very fine impression, and executed with an attention and perfection, that counterfeiters can rarely bestow.

Section XI.

Of the preferable Form of Coined Money.

The wear of the coin by friction is proportionate to the extent of its surface. Of two pieces of coin of equal weight and quality, that will suffer least from continual use, which offers the least surface to the friction.

The spherical or globular form is, consequently, preferable in this

---

* *Suprà*, p. 166.
† *Mongez, Consider. sur les Monnaies*, p. 31.

respect, as least liable to wear; but it has been rejected on account of its inconvenience.

Next to this form, the cylinder, of equal depth and breadth, is that, which exposes the smallest surface; but this is fully as inconvenient as the other; the form of a very flat cylinder has, consequently, been very generally adopted. However, from what has been already said, it will appear, that the less it is flattened the better; and that the coin should rather be made thick than broad.

With regard to the impression, the chief requisites are, 1. That it specify the weight and quality of the piece; 2. That it be very distinct, and intelligible to the meanest capacity; 3. That the die oppose all possible difficulties to the defacing or reducing of the coin; that is to say, that it be so contrived, that neither the ordinary wear nor fraudulent practices should be able to reduce the weight without destroying the impression. The last coined English half-pence have a cord, not projecting, but indented in the thickness of the circumference, and occupying the central part of the circumference only, so as to make it liable neither to clipping nor wear. This mode might be adopted in the silver and gold coinage with certainty and success; and it is of much more consequence to prevent their deterioration.

When the impression is in basso relievo, it should project but little, for the convenience of piling the pieces one upon another, as well as to reduce the friction. On the same account a projecting impression should not be too sharp on the surface, or it would wear away too rapidly. With a view to prevent this, experiments have been made of dies executed in alto relievo; but it was found that the coin was thereby too much weakened, and liable to be bent or broken. This plan, however, might possibly be practised with advantage, if the pieces were secured by greater thickness.

The same motive of giving to the coin the least possible surface, should induce the government to issue as large pieces as convenience will admit; for the more pieces there are, the greater is the surface exposed to friction. No more small pieces of coin should be issued, than just enough to transact exchanges of small amount, and to pay fractional sums. All large sums should be paid in large pieces of coin.

SECTION XII.

Of the Party, on whom the Loss of the Coin by Wear should properly fall.

It has been a question, who ought to defray the loss, consequent upon the friction or wear of the coin? In strict justice, the person who had made use of it, in like manner as the wearer of any other commodity. A man, that re-sells a coat after having worn it, sells it for less than he gave for it when new. So a man, that sells a crown-piece for some other commodity, should sell it for less than he gave; that is to say, should receive a smaller quantity of goods than he obtained it with.

But the portion of a specific coin, consumed in its passage through the hands of any one honest person, is less than almost any assignable value. It may circulate for many years together, without any sensible diminution of its weight; and, when the diminution is discovered, it may be impossible to tell, by which of the innumerable holders it was effected. I am aware, that each of them has imperceptibly shared the depreciation of its exchangeable value, occasioned by the wear; that the quantity of goods it would purchase has declined by an insensible gradation; that, although the depreciation has been imperceptibly progressive, it becomes at last very manifest; and that worn money will not be taken at par with new coin. Consequently, I think, that, if an entire class of coin were gradually so reduced as to make a re-coinage necessary, its holders could not in reason expect that their reduced coin should be exchanged for new at par, piece for piece. Their money should be received, even by the government, at no more than its real value; the silver it contains is less in quantity than at the first issue; and it has been received by the holders at a lower rate of value; they have given for it less goods than they would have done in the outset.

In fact, this is the course that rigid justice would prescribe; but there are two reasons, why it should not be strictly enforced.

1. Each individual piece of coin is not, if I may be allowed the expression, a substantive article of commerce. Its exchangeable value is calculated, not according to the weight and quality of the identical piece in question, but according to the average weight and quality of the coin in large quantities, as ascertained by common experience. A crown piece of an earlier date, and more worn, is yet freely received in exchange for one more new and perfect; the difference is sunk in the average. The mint issues new pieces every year of the full weight and standard, which prevents the coin from declining sensibly in value, in consequence of the friction, even for many years after its issue.

This circumstance is illustrated by the fact, of the French pieces of 12 and 24 *sous* passing current at par with the crown-pieces of 6 *livres* without any difficulty; although the same nominal sum, in the shape of the worn pieces of 12 and 24s., contained in reality about ¼ less silver than the crown-piece.

The subsequent law, which prohibited their being taken by the public receivers or private persons at more than 10 and 20 *sous*, rated them at their full intrinsic value, but below the rate, at which the then holders had taken them. For their value had been previously kept up to 12 and 24 *sous* in spite of the wear, by reason of their passing current at par with the crown-piece. Thus, the last holder was saddled with the entire loss of a friction, to which the innumerable hands they had passed through had all contributed.

2. The impression is equally effectual in giving currency at the

last as at the first, although it becomes in course of time scarcely, if at all visible; witness the shillings of England. The coin derives, as above explained, a certain degree of value from the mere impression, which value has been admitted and recognised throughout, until it reaches the ultimate holder, who has in consequence received it at a higher rate, than he would a piece of blank bullion of equal weight. To saddle him with the difference, would be to make him lose the whole value of the impression, although it has been equally serviceable to perhaps a million of others.

On these grounds, I am inclined to think, the loss by wear, and that of the impression, should be borne by the community at large; that is to say, by the public purse: for the whole society derives the benefit of the money; and it is impossible to tax each individual, in the precise proportion of the use he has made of it.

To conclude: every individual, that carries bullion to the mint to be coined may be fairly charged the expenses of the process, and, if thought advisable, the full monopoly-profit. Thus far there is no harm done: his bullion is increased in value to the full amount of what he has been charged by the mint; otherwise, he would never have carried it thither. At the same time, I am of opinion, that the mint should always give a new piece in exchange for an old one on demand: which need nowise interfere with the utmost possible precautions against the clipping and debasing of the coin. The mint should refuse such pieces as have lost certain parts of the impression, which are not liable to fair and unavoidable wear; and the loss in that case should fall on the individual, careless enough to take a piece thus palpably deficient. The promptitude, with which the public would take care to carry injured or suspicious pieces to the mint, would greatly facilitate the detection of fraudulent practices.

With diligence on the part of the executive, the loss arising from this source might be reduced to a mere trifle, and the system of national money would be materially improved, as well as the foreign exchange.

CHAPTER XXII.

OF SIGNS OR REPRESENTATIVES OF MONEY.

SECTION I.

Of Bills of Exchange and Letters of Credit.

A BILL of exchange, a promissory note or check, and a letter of credit, are written obligations to pay, or cause to be paid, a sum of money, either at a future time, or at a different place.

. The right conveyed by the assignment of these engagements, though not capable of being enforced immediately, or elsewhere than at the stipulated place, yet gives them an actual value, greater or less, according to circumstances. Thus a bill of exchange for 100 dollars, payable at Paris at two months' date, may be negotiated or sold, at pleasure, at the rate of, say 99 dollars, while a letter of credit of like amount, payable at Marseilles in the same space of time, will, perhaps, be worth at Paris but 98 dollars.

These engagements may be used as money in all transactions of purchase, as soon as they are invested with actual present value, by the prospect of their future value; indeed, most of the greater operations of commerce are effected through the medium of these securities.

Sometimes, the circumstance of a bill of exchange being payable at another place will increase, instead of diminishing its value; but this depends upon the state of commerce for the time being. If the merchants of Paris have large payments to make to those of London, they will readily give more money at Paris for a bill upon London, than it will produce to the holder at the latter place. Thus, although the pound sterling contain precisely as much silver as 24 *fr.* 74 *cents*, they will, perhaps, give at Paris 25 *fr.*, more or less, for every pound sterling payable in London.*

This is what is called the course of exchange, being, in fact, a mere specification of the quantity of precious metal people will consent to give, for the transfer of a right to receive a given quantity of the same metal at any other specified place. The particular locality of the metal reduces or increases its value, in relation to the same metal situated elsewhere.

The exchange is said to be in favour of any country, France, for example, whenever less of the precious metal is there given for, than will be produced by, a bill of exchange upon another country; or whenever in the foreign country more of the precious metal is given for a bill of exchange on France, than it will there produce to the holder. The difference is never very considerable, and cannot exceed the charge of transporting the precious metal itself; for, if a foreigner, who wants to make a payment at Paris, can remit the sum in specie at less expense than he could be put to by the existing course of exchange, he would undoubtedly remit in specie.†

It has been imagined by some people, that all debts to foreigners can be paid by bills of exchange; and measures have been frequently suggested, and sometimes adopted, for the encouragement of this fictitious mode of payment. But this is a mere delusion. A bill of exchange has no intrinsic value; it can only be drawn upon any

* If the credit on London be payable in paper-money *instead of* specie, the course of exchange with Paris of the pound sterling, may, perhaps, fall to 21 *fr.*, 18 *fr.*, or even less, in proportion to the discredit of the paper of England.

† In that expense I include the charge and risk of transport and of smuggling also, if the export of specie be prohibited; which latter is proportionate to the difficulty of the operation. The risks are estimated in the rate of insurance.

place for a sum actually due at that place; and no sum can be there actually due, unless an equal value, in some shape or other, has been remitted thither: the imports of a nation can only be paid by the national export; and *vice versâ*. Bills of exchange are a mere representative of sums due; in other words, the merchants of one country can draw bills on those of another for no more, than the full amount of the goods of every description, silver and gold included, which they may have sent thither directly or indirectly. If one country, say France, have remitted to another country, Germany perhaps, merchandise to the value of 2 millions of dollars, and the latter have remitted to the former to the amount of 3 millions of dollars, France can pay as much as 2 millions by the means of bills of exchange, representing the value of her export; but the remaining 1 million cannot be so discharged directly, although possibly they may by bills of exchange upon a third country, Italy, for instance, whither she may have exported goods to that extent.

There is, indeed, a species of bills, called by commercial men, accommodation-paper, which actually represents no value whatever. A merchant at Paris, in league with another of Hamburgh, draws bills upon his correspondent, which the latter pays or provides for, by re-drawing and negotiating or selling bills at Hamburgh upon his correspondent at Paris. So long as these bills are in possession of any third person, that third person has advanced their value. The negotiation of such accommodation-paper is an expedient for borrowing, and a very expensive one; for it entails the loss of the banker's commission, brokerage and other incidental charges, over and above the discount for the time the bills have to run. Paper of this description can never wipe out the debt, that one nation owes another; for the bills drawn on one side balance and extinguish those on the other. The Hamburgh bills will naturally counterpoise those of Paris, being in fact drawn to meet them; the second set destroys the first, and the result is absolute nullity.

Thus it is evident, that one nation cannot otherwise discharge its debts to another, than by remittance of actual value in goods or commodities, in which term I comprise the precious metals, amongst others, to the full amount of what it has received or owes. If the actual values directly remitted thither are insufficient to balance the receipts or imports thence, it may remit to a third nation, and thence transport produce enough to make up the deficit. How does France pay Russia for the hemp and timber for ship-building imported thence? By remittance of wines, brandies, silks, not merely to Russia, but, likewise to Hamburgh and Amsterdam, whence again a remittance of colonial and other commercial produce is forwarded to Russia.

Governments have commonly made it their object to contrive that the precious metals shall form the largest possible portion of the national import from, and the least possible portion of the national export to, foreign countries. I have already taken occasion to remark, with regard to what is improperly called the balance of trade, that, if the national merchant finds the precious metals a more profitable foreign remittance than another commodity, it is likewise the interest of the state to remit in that form; for the state can only gain and lose in the persons of its individual subjects; and, in the matter of foreign commerce, whatever is best for the individuals in the aggregate, is best for the state also.* Thus, when impediments are thrown in the way of the export of the precious metals by individuals, the effect is to compel an export in some other shape, less advantageous to the individual and the public too.

Section II.

Of Banks of Deposit.

The constant intercourse between a small state and its neighbours occasions a perpetual influx of foreign coin. For, although the small state may have a national coinage of its own, yet, the frequent necessity of taking the foreign instead of the national coin in payment, requires the fixation of the ratio of their relative value, in the current transactions of business.

There are many mischiefs attending the use of foreign coin, arising chiefly from the great variation of weight and quality. It is often extremely old, worn, and defaced; not having participated in the general re-coinage of the nation that issued it, where, perhaps, it is no longer current; all which circumstances, though considered in settling its current relative value to the local coin, yet, do not quite reduce it to the natural level of depreciation.

Bills drawn from abroad upon such a state, being payable in the coin thus rendered current, are, in consequence, negotiated abroad at some loss; and those drawn upon foreign countries, and, consequently, payable in coin of a more steady and intelligible value, are negotiated in a smaller state at a premium, because the holder of them must have purchased them in a depreciated currency. In short, the foreign coin is always exchanged for the local currency to a loss.

The remedy devised by states of this inferior class is the subject of the present section. They established banks,† where private merchants could lodge any amount of local national coin, of bullion, or of foreign coin, reckoned by the bank as bullion; and the amount,

---

* This position applies to foreign commerce only; the monopoly-profits of individuals in the home-market are not entirely national gains. In internal dealings, the sum of the utility obtained is all that is acquired by the community.

† Venice, Genoa, Amsterdam, and Hamburgh had each an establishment of this nature. All have been swept away by the torrent of the revolutionary war; but there may be some use in examining the nature of institutions that may some day or other be re-established. Besides, the investigation will throw light upon the history of the communities that established them, and of commerce in general. At any rate, it was necessary to enumerate all the various expedients that have been resorted to as substitutes for money.

so lodged, was entered as so much money of the legal national standard of weight and quality. At the same time, the bank opened an account with each merchant making such deposit, giving him credit for the amount of the deposit. Whenever a merchant wanted to make a payment, there was no occasion to touch the deposit at all; it was sufficient to transfer the sum required, from the credit of the party paying, to that of the party receiving. Thus values could be transferred continually by a mere transfer in the books of the bank. The whole operation was conducted without any actual transfer of specie; the original deposit, which was entered at the real intrinsic value at the time of making it, remained as security for the credit transferred from one person to another; and the specie, so lodged with the bank, was exempt from any reduction of value by wear, fraud, or even legislative enactment.

The money still remaining in circulation, wherever it was exchanged for the bank deposits, that is to say, for entries in the bank books, necessarily lost in proportion to the reduction of its intrinsic value. And this loss occasioned the difference of value, or agio at Amsterdam, between bank money and circulating money, which was on the average from 3 to 4 per cent. in favour of the former.

It will easily be imagined, that the bills of exchange, payable in a currency so little liable to injury or fluctuation, must be negotiable on better than ordinary terms. In fact, it was observable, that on the whole, the course of exchange was rather in favour of the countries that paid in bank, and unfavourable to those that paid in circulating money only.

The bank retained the deposites in perpetuity; for the re-issue would have been attended with serious loss; inasmuch as it would have been the same thing, as producing good money of the full original value, to be taken at par with the deteriorated circulating coin, which passes current for—not its intrinsic, but its average weight. The coin withdrawn from the bank would have been mixed up with the mass of circulation, and passed current at par with the rest. So that the withdrawing such deposits would have been a gratuitous sacrifice of the excess of value of bank above circulating money.

This is the nature of banks of deposit; most of which combined other operations with the primary object of their institution; but of them I shall speak elsewhere. They derived their profits, partly from a duty levied upon every transfer, and partly from operations incident to, and compatible with, their institution; as, for example, advances made upon a deposit of bullion.

It is evident, that the inviolability of the deposit, confided to them, is essential to the success of such establishments. At Amsterdam, the four burgomasters, or municipal magistrates, were trustees for the creditors. Annually, on leaving office, they handed over the trust to their successors, who, after inspecting the account, and verifying it by the registers of the bank, bound themselves by

23*

oath, to surrender their charge inviolate to their successors in office. This trust was scrupulously executed from the first establishment of the bank in 1609 until 1672, when the forces of Louis XIV. penetrated as far as Utrecht. The deposits were then faithfully restored to the individuals. It would seem to have been afterwards less scrupulously managed; for, when the French took possession of that capital, in 1794, and called for a statement of the concern, it was found to be in advance of no less a sum than 10,624,793 *florins* to the India company, and to the provinces of Holland and West-Friezeland, which were wholly unable to repay it. In a country governed by a power without control or responsibility, it may be expected, that such a deposit would have been still more exposed to violation. (*a*)

Section III.

Of Banks of Circulation or Discount, and of Bank-notes, or Convertible Paper.

There is another kind of bank, founded on totally different principles; consisting of associated capitalists, subscribing a capital in transferable shares, to be employed in various profitable ways, but chiefly in the discount of promissory notes and bills of exchange, that is to say, the advance of the value of commercial paper not yet due, with the deduction of interest for the time it has to run, which is called, the discount.

These companies, with a view to enlarge their capital and extend their business, commonly issue notes, purporting to bear a promise to pay to the bearer on demand, the gold or silver specified on the face of them. Their security for the due discharge of these engagements is, the commercial paper held by the bank, and subscribed by individuals in solvent circumstances; for the company gives its notes in discount, or, what is the same thing, in purchase of this paper.

The private commercial paper, indeed, having a term to run before it falls due, can not be available in discharge of notes payable on demand; for which reason, every well-conducted bank of circulation confines its advances of cash, or notes payable in cash on

---

(*a*) Public banks of deposit are now quite obsolete, and will probably never be revived. In fact they are clumsy expedients, suited only to the early stages of commercial prosperity, and are liable to many inconveniences. They hold out a strong temptation to internal fraud and violence, as well as to external rapacity; they withdraw from active utility a large portion of the precious metals, which might perhaps be turned to better account elsewhere; and they yield a degree of facility of circulation nowise superior to what may be afforded by the common process of banking, except perhaps in security, and infinitely more expensive to the public and to individuals. They have accordingly been everywhere supplanted by banks of circulation, or by the expedient of an inconvertible paper-money. T.

demand, to the discount of bills at very short dates, and is careful to have always in hand a considerable amount of specie, probably a third, or as much as the half of the total amount of their circulating notes ; and, even with all possible caution, it is at times greatly embarrassed, whenever a want of confidence in its solvency, or any untoward event, causes a sudden run upon the bank for cash.   The bank of England has been obliged, on an occasion of this kind, to scrape together as many sixpences as it possibly could find, to gain time by the delay inseparable from payments in such a diminutive coin, until a part of the paper in its possession had fallen due.   The discount bank of Paris, in the year 1788, being then under control of government, had recourse to similar paltry expedients.

The profits of banks of circulation are very considerable ; that portion of the notes, which is issued on the credit of private commercial paper, continues running at interest ; for the advances have been made with the deduction of the discount.   But the portion of the paper, issued on the credit of the specie in reserve, brings no profit ; the interest lying dormant in the specie thus withdrawn from circulation.

The banks of England and France make no advances to private persons, except on bills of exchange, and give no credit beyond the funds in hand.   They indemnify themselves for the trouble of receiving and paying on account of individuals by turning to account the floating balance left in their hands.   These two establishments have, besides, undertaken the business of paying the interest upon the respective national debts, receiving an allowance for their trouble : furthermore, they occasionally make advances to the governments.

From these various operations, they derive a great increase of their profits.   The one last mentioned, however, is completely at variance with the purposes of their establishment, as we shall presently find.   The advances made to the old government of France by the then bank of discount, and those of the bank of England to the English government, compelled those bodies to apply to the respective legislatures to give their notes a compulsory circulation ; thus destroying their fundamental requisites of convertibility.   The consequence has been, that the former of these banks went all to pieces.

The establishment of several banks, for the issue of convertible notes, is more beneficial than the investment of any single body with the exclusive privilege ; for the competition obliges each of them to court the public favour, by a rivalship of accommodation and solidity.

Banks of circulation issue their notes either in the discount of promissory notes or bills of exchange, that is to say, in giving their notes payable on demand, and circulating like cash, in exchange for private paper payable at a future date, upon which interest is deducted ; which is the course pursued by the present bank of France, and by all the English banks, public and private ; or else in lending at interest to solvent individuals, like those of Scotland. Merchants of good credit are, in the latter way, supplied with the sums necessary for their current expenses and payments, and each of them is thereby enabled to embark his whole capital in his commercial enterprises, without being obliged to reserve any part to meet the calls upon him in the course of business. The merchant of Paris or London must contrive matters, so as to have always on hand either in his private coffers or in the bank, a sum sufficient to face the demands upon him; whereas, the merchant of Edinburgh is relieved from this necessity, and at liberty to invest the whole of his funds, in the confidence that the bank will advance him the money he may happen to require. (*a*)

A bank of circulation affords the advantage of economizing capital, by reducing the amount of the sum, kept in reserve for the current and contingent expenses of the individuals it accommodates.

Bank bills or notes, payable on demand, and circulating as cash, play so important a part in the progress of national wealth, and have engendered such important errors in the brain of many writers of repute and information on other topics, that it will be worth while to examine their nature and consequences in a very particular manner.

I should premise, that the residue of this section applies exclusively to bank-notes, depending solely upon the credit of the bank for their currency, and convertible at pleasure into cash or specie.

It is a matter of no less curiosity than of importance, to inquire whether bank-notes, or paper destitute of intrinsic value, be any addition to the stock of national wealth, and what, if any, is the possible extent of that addition; for, were there no limits to it, there could be no end to the wealth, that a state might acquire in a short time by the mere fabrication of some reams of paper. The solution of this grand problem may be set down as one of Smith's happiest efforts; yet it is not every body that comprehends his reasoning; I will try to render it more generally intelligible.

The wants of a nation require a certain supply of such particular commodity, and the extent of that supply is determined by the relative prosperity of the nation for the time being. A surplus of each of those commodities beyond this demand is either not produced at all, or, if produced, must occasion a decline of relative local value: it, therefore, naturally finds its way out of the country, and goes in quest of a market, where it may be in higher estimation.

Money is, in this respect, like all other commodities; it is a con-

---

(*a*) The two methods resolve themselves practically into one; for merchants of good credit can always procure discountable paper; and the sole essential difference is, that, in one case, the credit is individual and unevidenced, in the other, evidenced, and, in most cases, joint also. The bank of England requires the names of more than one firm on the paper it discounts. Country bankers often content themselves with the security, or note of hand, of the borrower alone. T.

venient agent, and, therefore, employed as such in all operations of exchange; but the intensity of the demand for it is determined in each community, by the relative extent and activity of the exchanges negotiated within it. As soon as there is a supply of money sufficient to circulate all the commodities there are to be circulated, no more money is imported; or, if a surplus flow in, it emigrates again in quest of a market, where its value is greater, or where its utility is more desired. It is seldom or never that any body keeps in his purse or his coffers more specie than enough to meet the current demands of his business or consumption.* Every excess beyond these demands is rejected, as bearing neither utility nor interest; and the community at large is fully supplied with specie, as soon as each individual is possessed of the portion suitable to his condition and relative station in society.

It may be safely left to private interest, to make the best use of the excess of specie beyond the demand for circulation. The notion that every item of specie, that crosses the frontier, is so much dead loss to the community, is just as absurd as the supposition, that a manufacturer is so much the poorer, every time he parts with his money in the purchase of the ingredient or raw material of his manufacture; or that individuals, the aggregate of whom makes up the nation, present foreigners gratuitously with all the money they part with.

Taking it for granted, then, that the specie, remaining in circulation within the community, is limited by the national demand for circulating medium; if any expedient can be devised, for substituting bank-notes in place of half the specie or the commodity, money, there will evidently be a superabundance of metal-money, and that superabundance must be followed by a diminution of its relative value. But, as such diminution in one place by no means implies a contemporaneous diminution in other places, where the expedient of bank-notes is not resorted to, and where, consequently, no such superabundance of the commodity, money, exists, money naturally resorts thither, and is attracted to the spot where it bears the highest relative value, or is exchangeable for the largest quantity of other goods: in other words, it flows to the markets where commodities are the cheapest, and is replaced by goods, of value equal to the money exported.

The money that can emigrate in this manner, is that part only of the circulating medium, which has a value elsewhere than within the limits of the nation; that is to say, the specie or metal-money. Since, however, specie does not emigrate without an equivalent return; and, since its value, which before existed in the shape of specie, and was exclusively engaged in facilitating circulation, thenceforth assumes the form of a variety of commodities, all items of the reproductive national capital, there follows this remarkable consequence: that the national capital is enlarged to the full amount of all the spe-

* No account is here taken of the money hoarded, which, for the national interest, might just as well have remained in the mine.

cie exported upon the introduction of the substitute. Nor is the internal national circulation at all cramped for want of money by this export; for the functions of the specie, that has been withdrawn, are just as well performed by the paper substituted in its stead.

However valuable an acquisition the national capital may thus receive, it must not be rated above its real amount. I have supposed, for the sake of simplicity, that half the specie might be replaced by circulating notes: but this is a monstrous proportion; particularly if it be considered, that paper cannot retain its value as money any longer than while it is readily and instantly convertible into specie; I say, readily and instantly, because otherwise people would prefer specie, which is at all times, and without the least hesitation, taken for money. To insure this requisite convertibility, it is necessary, that, besides having at all times a fund in reserve, in private bills or securities, or in specie, sufficient to meet all the notes that may be presented, the bank itself should be at all times within the reach of the holders of its notes. Therefore, if the territory be of any extent, and the notes so generally circulated, as to form half of the circulating medium, the subordinate offices of the bank must be greatly multiplied to place them within reach of all the note-holders.

But, granting the possibility of such an arrangement, and admitting, that paper might supplant as much as half the requisite national currency of specie, let us see what would be the amount of the acquisition to the national capital.

No writer of repute has ventured to estimate the requisite circulating specie of any nation, higher than $\frac{1}{5}$ of the annual national product; some, indeed, have reckoned it as low as $\frac{1}{30}$. Taking the highest estimate, viz. $\frac{1}{5}$ of the annual product, which, for my own part, I consider greatly above the reality in any case; a nation, whose annual product should amount to 20 millions, would need but 4 millions of specie. Therefore, in case the half, or 2 millions, were supplanted by circulating paper, and employed in augmenting the national productive capital, that capital would be once for all augmented, by a value equal to $\frac{2}{20}$ or $\frac{1}{10}$ of the annual product of the nation.

Again, the annual product of a nation would, probably, be much overrated at $\frac{1}{10}$ of the gross national productive capital; but let it be set down at that rate, allowing 5 per cent. interest on productive capital, and 5 per cent. wages and profits of the industry it sets in motion. On this calculation, supposing the paper substitute to add to the national capital, in the ratio of $\frac{1}{10}$ of its annual product, this addition will not at the highest estimate exceed $\frac{1}{100}$ of the previous capital.

Although the practicable issue of bank-notes procures to a nation of moderate wealth an accession of capital, much less considerable than people may fondly imagine, this accession is, notwithstanding, of very great value; for, unless the productive energy of the nation be extremely great, as in Great Britain, or the national spirit of frugality very general and persevering, as in Holland, the annual savings withdrawn from unproductive consumption, to be added to productive capital, form, even in thriving states, a very inconsiderable portion of the gross annual revenue. Nations, whose production is stationary, as every body knows, make no addition to their productive capitals; and the consumption of those on the decline annually encroaches on their capitals.

Should the paper-issues of a bank at any time exceed the demands of circulation, and the credit enjoyed by the establishment, there follows a perpetual reflux of its notes, and it is put to the expense of collecting specie, which is absorbed as fast as collected. The Scotch banks, though productive of great benefit, have been obliged, upon such trying occasions, to keep agents in London constantly employed, in scraping specie together at a charge of two per cent., which specie was instantly absorbed. The bank of England, in similar circumstances, was under the necessity of buying gold bullion, and getting it coined; and this coin was melted again as fast as it was paid by the bank, in consequence of the high price of the metal, which was itself the effect of the constant purchases made by the bank, to meet the calls upon it for specie. In this manner, it sustained the annual loss of from $2\frac{1}{2}$ to 3 per cent., upon a sum of about 850,000*l.*,* more than 20 millions of our money. I say nothing of the situation of this bank of late years, since its notes have acquired a forced circulation, and, consequently, altered their nature entirely.

The notes issued by a bank of circulation, even if it have no funds of its own, are never issued gratuitously; and, therefore, of course, imply the existence, in the coffers of the bank, of a value of like amount, either in the shape of specie, or of securities, bearing interest; upon which latter only the whole real advance of the bank is made; and this advance can never be made upon securities that have a long time to run; for the securities are the fund, that is to provide for the discharge of another class of securities, in the hands of the public at large, payable at the shortest of all possible notice, namely, on demand. Strictly speaking, a bank can not be at all times in a condition to face the calls upon it, and deserve the entire confidence of the public, unless the private paper it has discounted, be all, like its own notes, payable on demand; but, as it is no easy matter to find substantial assets, that shall bear interest, and at the same time be redeemable at sight, the next best course is to confine its issues to bills of very short dates; and, indeed, well-conducted banks have always rigidly adhered to this principle.

From the preceding considerations may be deduced a conclusion, fatal to abundance of systems and projects, viz. that credit-paper can supplant, and that but partially, nothing more than that portion of the national capital performing the functions of money, which circulates from hand to hand, as an agent for the facility of transfer; consequently, that no bank of circulation, or credit-paper of any denomination whatever, can supply to agricultural, manufacturing, or

---

* Wealth of Nations, book ii. c. 2.

commercial enterprise, any funds for the construction of ships or machinery, for the digging of mines or canals, for the bringing of waste land into cultivation, or the commencement of long-winded speculations; any funds, in short, to be employed as vested capital. The indispensable requisite of credit-paper is, its instant convertibility into specie; when the sum total of the paper issued does not exist in the coffers of the bank, under the shape of specie, the deficit should at least be supplied by securities of very short dates; whereas, an establishment, that should lend its funds to be vested in enterprises, whence they could not be withdrawn at pleasure, could never be prepared with such securities. An example will illustrate this position. Suppose a bank of circulation to lend 6,000 dollars of its notes, circulating as cash, to a landholder on mortgage of his land, presenting the amplest security. This loan is destined by the landholder to the construction of necessary buildings, for the cultivation of the estate; for which purpose he contracts with a builder, and pays him the 6,000 dollars of notes advanced by the bank. Now, if the builder, after a short lapse of time, be desirous of turning the notes into specie, the bank can not pay him by a transfer of the mortgage. The only property the bank has to meet the 6,000 dollars of notes is a security, ample beyond doubt, but not available at the moment.

The securities in the hands of a bank, I hold to be a solid basis for the whole of its issues of notes, provided those securities be of solvent persons, and have not too long to run; for the securities will be redeemed either with specie, or with the notes of the bank itself. In the first case, the bank is supplied with the means of paying its notes; in the second, it is saved the trouble of providing for them.

If, by any circumstance, the notes be deprived of their power of circulating as specie, the task of replacing the metal for the paper-money does not devolve upon the bank; nor was it at the first saddled with the business of turning to account the metal-money its notes rendered superfluous. For, as we have already observed, the bank can extinguish the whole of its paper with the private securities it holds. The inconvenience falls upon the public, which is under the necessity of finding a new agent of circulation, either by a re-import of the metal-money, or by the substitution of private paper; but probably the public would, in such circumstances, apply again to a bank conducted on sound principles.*

---

* Since the first publication of this passage, this very circumstance has happened in respect to the bank of Paris, in 1814 and 1815, when that capital was besieged and occupied by the allied armies. The advances of the bank to the government, and to individuals, which could not be recalled immediately, did not exceed the capital of the establishment, for which the shareholders can not be called upon; and its paper-issues, payable to bearer, were all covered, either by specie in hand, or by commercial paper of short dates. By this means, notwithstanding the very critical circumstances of the moment, the merchants continued to employ its notes: which they could not well do without; and they were paid as usual in cash without interruption, during the whole of the hostile occupation: which shows at once the utility of a bank of circulation, and the advantage of leaving inviolate the convertibility of paper-issues.

This will serve to explain, why so many schemes of agricultural banks for the issue of circulating and convertible notes on ample landed security, and so many other schemes of a similar nature, have fallen to the ground in very little time, with more or less loss to the shareholders and the public.* Specie is equivalent to paper of perfect solidity, and payable at the moment; consequently it can only be supplanted by notes of unquestionable credit, and payable on demand; and such notes cannot be discharged by a bare security, even of the best possible kind.

For the same reason, bills of exchange in the nature of accommodation-paper, as it is called, can never be a sound basis for an issue of convertible paper. Such bills of exchange are paid when due by fresh bills, that have a further term to run, and are negotiated with the deduction of discount. When the latter fall due, they are met by a third set payable at a still later date, which are discounted in like manner. If the bank discounts such bills, the operation is no more than an expedient for borrowing of the bank in perpetuity; the first loan being paid with a second, the second with the third, and so on. And the bank experiences the evil of issuing more of its notes, than the circulation will naturally absorb, and the credit of the establishment will support; for the notes, borrowed upon such bills, do not help to circulate and diffuse real value, because they represent and contain no real value themselves; consequently, they continually recur to be exchanged for specie. It is on this account, that the discount-bank of Paris, while it continued to be well administered, did, as the present banks of France and England do still refuse, as far as it is able, to discount accommodation-paper.

The consequences are similar and equally mischievous, when a bank makes advances to government in perpetuity, or even for a very long period. (*a*) This was the cause of the failure of the bank of England. Not being able to obtain payment from government, it was unable to withdraw the notes in which the loan was made. From that moment its notes ceased to be convertible; and until the resumption of cash payments in 1822, enjoyed a forced circulation. The government, being itself unable to supply the bank with the means of payment, discharged that body from its liability to its own creditors.†

---

* In 1803, the land-bank of Paris was, for this reason, obliged to suspend the payment of its notes in cash; and to give notice, that they would be paid off by instalments out of the proceeds of its real securities.

† Thornton, in his tract on the *Paper Credit of Great Britain*, written expressly

---

(*a*) That is to say, advances its notes. A bank, like an individual, may advance its capital, which then becomes more or less vested and fixed. The whole capital of the bank of England has been thus advanced; and there would have been no danger, had it not advanced its notes also. When the advances of paper are made upon transferable securities, stock, exchequer bills, and the like, those securities may be sold for cash, or for the notes of the bank itself, so long as they retain their value, and thus the safety and solvency of the bank maintained. But this operation is unnecessarily complex; for the government might itself have sold, and thus have saved the brokerage or profit accruing upon the operation to the bank. T.

The holders of the notes of a bank issuing convertible money run little or no risk, so long as the bank is well administered, and independent of the government. Supposing a total failure of confidence to bring all its notes upon it at once for payment, the worst that can happen to the holders is, to be paid in good bills of exchange at short dates, with the benefit of discount; that is to say, to be paid with the same bills of exchange, whereon the bank has issued its notes. If the bank have a capital of its own, there is so much additional security; but, under a government subject to no control, or to nominal control only, neither the capital of the bank, nor the assets in its hands, offer any solid security whatever. The will of an arbitrary prince is all the holders have to depend upon: and every act of credit is an act of imprudence.

As far as I am capable of judging, such is the effect of banks of circulation and of their paper issues upon individuals and national wealth. This effect is described by Smith in a quaint and ingenious metaphor. The capital of a nation he likens to an extensive tract of country, whereupon the cultivated districts represent the productive capital, and the high roads the agent of circulation, that is to say, the money, that serves as the medium to distribute the produce among the several branches of society. He then supposes a machine to be invented, for transporting the produce of the land through the air; that machine would be the exact parallel of credit-paper. Thenceforward the high roads might be devoted to cultivation. 'The commerce and industry of the country, however,' he continues, 'though they may be somewhat augmented, cannot be altogether so secure, when they are thus, as it were, suspended upon the Dædalian wings of paper-money, as when they travel about upon the

---

with a view to justify the suspension of cash-payments by that establishment, has attacked the positions of Smith upon this subject. He tells us, that the extraordinary run upon the bank, which brought about the suspension, was occasioned, not by the excess of its issues, but, on the contrary, by their partial contraction. "An excessive limitation of bank-notes," he observes, "will produce failures, failures must cause consternation, and consternation must lead to a run upon the bank for guineas." By this reference to an extreme case, he endeavours to support his paradoxical opinions. When a convertible paper has succeeded in driving out of the country too large a portion of the metallic money, and the confidence in the paper happens suddenly to decline, great confusion and embarrassment will doubtless ensue, because the remaining agent of circulation is insufficient to effect the business; but it is a great mistake to suppose, that the deficiency can be remedied by the multiplication of a paper, not enjoying the confidence of the public. If the bank of England was able to survive the shock, it was because of the indispensable necessity of some agent of transfer, of some money or other, of paper in default of all others, in so commercial a country; because the government and the bankers of London, who were interested in the safety of the bank, unanimously agreed not to call upon it for cash, until it should be in a condition to pay; that is to say, until the government should have paid its advances in actual value. The bank had lent to the government more than its whole capital; for to that extent it might have gone with safety, its capital not being wanted for the discharge or convertibility of its paper; had it not so done, the short bills in its possession would have been sufficient for the extinction of its convertible paper.

solid ground of gold and silver.   Over and above the accidents, to which they are exposed from the unskilfulness of the conductors of this paper-money, they are liable to several others, from which no prudence or skill of those conductors can guard them.   An unsuccessful war, for example, in which the enemy get possession of the capital, and consequently of that treasure, which supported the credit of the paper-money, would occasion a much greater confusion in a country, where the whole circulation was carried on by paper, than in one, where the greater part of it was carried on by gold and silver. The usual instrument of commerce having lost its value, no exchanges could be made except by barter or upon credit.   All taxes having usually been paid in paper-money, the prince would not have wherewithal either to pay his troops, or to furnish his magazines; and the state of the country would be much more irretrievable, than if the greater part of its circulation had consisted in gold and silver. A prince, anxious to maintain his dominions at all times in the state in which he can most easily defend them, ought upon this account to guard, not only against that excessive multiplication of paper-money, which ruins the very banks which issue it, but even against that multiplication of it, which enables them to fill the greater part of the circulation of the country with it.' *

Forgery alone is enough to derange the affairs of the best conducted and most solid bank.   And forgery of notes is more to be apprehended, than counterfeits of specie.   The stimulus of gain is greater.   For there is more profit to be made by converting a sheet of paper into money, than by giving the appearance of precious metal to another metal, that has some though very little, intrinsic value, especially if it be compounded or covered with a small portion of the counterfeited metal; and perhaps, too, the materials for the former operation are less liable to discovery.   Besides, the counterfeits of specie can never reduce the value of the specie itself, because the latter has an intrinsic and independent value as a commodity; whereas, the mere belief that there are forged notes abroad, so well executed, as to be scarcely distinguishable from the genuine, is enough to bring both forged and genuine into discredit.   For which reason, banks have sometimes preferred the loss of paying notes they know to be forged, to the hazard of bringing the genuine ones into discredit, by the exposure of the fraud.

One method of checking the immoderate use of notes is, to limit them to a fixed and high denomination of value; so as to make them adapted to the circulation of goods from one merchant to another, but inconvenient for the circulation between the merchant and the consumer.   It has been questioned whether a government has any right to prohibit the issue of small notes, where the public is willing to take them; and whether such limitation be not a violation of that liberty of commerce, which it is the chief duty of a government to protect.   But the right undoubtedly is just as complete, as that of

* *Wealth of Nations*, book ii. chap. 2.

ordering a building to be pulled down, because it endangers the public safety.

<h2 style="text-align:center">SECTION IV.</h2>

Of Paper-Money.

The distinctive appellation of paper-money, I have reserved exclusively for those obligations, to which the ruling power may give a compulsory circulation in payment for all purchases, and discharge all debts and contracts, stipulating a delivery of money. I call them obligations, because, though the authority that issues, is not bound to redeem them, at least not immediately, yet they commonly express a promise of redemption at sight, which is absolutely nugatory; or of redemption at a date expressed, for which there is no sort of security; or of territorial indemnity, the value of which we shall presently inquire into.

Such obligations, whether subscribed by the government or by individuals, can be converted into paper-money by the public authority only, which alone can authorise the owners of money to pay in paper. The act is, indeed, an exertion, not of legitimate, but of arbitrary authority; being a deterioration of the national money in the extreme degree.

Upon the principles above established, it should seem, that a money destitute of all value as a commodity, ought to pass for none in all free dealing subsequent to its issue; and this is always the case in practice sooner or later. The notes of what was improperly called Law's Bank, and the *assignats* issued during the French revolution, were never regularly called in or cancelled; yet those of the highest denomination would not pass at present for a single *sol.* How then, came they ever to pass for more than their real value? Because there are many expedients of fraud and violence, which will always have a temporary efficacy.

In the first place, a paper, wherewith debts can be legally, though fraudulently, discharged, derives a kind of value from that single circumstance. Moreover, the paper-money may be made efficient to discharge the perpetually recurring claims of public taxation. Sometimes a *tariff* or *maximum* of price is established; which, indeed, soon extinguishes the production of the commodities affected by it, but gives to the paper-money a portion of the value of those actually in existence. Besides, the very creation of a paper-money with forced circulation occasions the disappearance of metallic money; for, as it is made to pass at par with paper, it naturally seeks a market, where it can find its true level of value. The paper-money is thus left in the exclusive possession of the business of circulation; and the absolute necessity of some agent of transfer, in every civilized community, will then operate to maintain its value.* So urgent

---

* Wherever a paper-money has been established, the difference between its

is this necessity, that the paper-money of England, consisting of the notes of the bank, has been kept at par with specie, simply by the limitation of the issues to the demands of circulation.

Nations precipitated into foreign wars, before they have had time previously to accumulate the requisite capital for carrying them on, and destitute of sufficient credit to borrow of their neighbours, have almost always had recourse to paper-money, or some similar expedient. The Dutch, in their struggle with the Spanish crown for independence, issued money of paper, of leather, and of many other materials. The United States of America, under similar circumstances, likewise had recourse to paper-money; and the expedient that enabled the French republic to foil the formidable attack of the first coalition, has immortalized the name of *assignats.*

Law has been unjustly charged with the whole blame of the calamities resulting from the scheme that bears his name. That he entertained just ideas respecting money, may be gathered from the perusal of a tract* he published in his native country, Scotland, to induce the Scotch government to establish a bank of circulation. The bank established in France, in 1716, was founded on the principles there set forth. Its notes were expressed in these words:

" The bank promises to pay the bearer at sight * * * * * * * *livres* in money of the same weight and standard as the money of this day. Value received at Paris," &c.

The bank, which was then but a private association, paid its notes regularly on demand: they were not yet metamorphosed into paper-money. Matters remained on this footing, and went on very well, till the year 1719;† at which period the king, or rather the regent, repaid the shareholders, and took the management into his own hands, calling it the Royal Bank. The notes were then altered to this form:

---

value in the home market, where it has utility, and its value in foreign markets, where it has no utility, has afforded a fruitful field for speculation, that has enriched many adventurers. In 1811, 100 guineas in gold would purchase at Paris a bill of exchange on London, for 140*l.* sterling, payable in the paper which was the only currency of England. Yet the difference between gold and paper in the London market at the same period, was only 15 per cent. It was in this way, that the paper was of higher value in England than abroad. Accordingly, I find from returns with which I have been favoured, that gold in guineas or bullion was smuggled into the ports of Dunkirk and Gravelines alone, in the years 1810, 11, 12, and 13, to the amount of 33,875,090 dollars. There was a similar speculation in other commodities at large; but it was attended with more risk and difficulty; the import into France being very hazardous, although the export from England was encouraged in every possible way. Yet this traffic would soon have found its level, for it must have produced bills on England in such quantity, as to have brought the exchange to par at least, had not the continental subsidies of England furnished a continual supply of bills on London without any return.

* This work was translated into French while Law continued in the office of Controller-General of France; and is entitled *Considerations on Commerce and Money.*

† *Vide Dutot.* tom. ii. p. 200, for a detail of the beneficial effects of the institution, as originally conducted.

" The bank promises to pay the bearer at sight * * * † * * *
livres in *silver* coin. Value received at Paris," &c.

This alteration, slight as it was in appearance, was a radical one
in substance. The first note stipulated to pay a fixed quantity of
silver, viz. the quantity contained in the *livres* current at the date
of issuing the notes. The second merely engaged to pay *livres*, and
so opened a door for whatever alterations an arbitrary power might
think proper to make in the real value expressed by the word *livre.*
And this was called fixing the rate of the paper-money; whereas, on
the contrary, it was unfixing, and making it a fluctuating value; and
the fluctuations were truly deplorable. Law strenuously opposed
the innovation; but principle was compelled to give way to power;
and the crimes of power, when the consequences began to be felt,
were confidently attributed to the fallacy of the principle.

The *assignats* issued by the revolutionary government were
worth even less than the paper-money of the regency. The latter
gave a promise, at least, of paying in silver: and, though the payment
might be greatly curtailed by a deterioration of the silver coin, yet
sooner or later the paper might have been redeemed, if the government had but been more moderate in its issues, and more scrupulous
in fulfilling its engagements. But the *assignats* conveyed no right
to call for silver; nothing but a right to purchase or obtain the national domains. Let us see what this right was really worth.

The original *assignats* purported to be payable at sight, at the
Caisse de l'Extraordinaire, where they were, in fact, never paid at
all. It is true, they were received in payment for the national
domains bought by individuals at a competition-price; but the value
of these domains could never give any determinate value to the
assignats, because their nominal value increased exactly in proportion as that of the *assignats* declined. The government was not
sorry to find the price of national domains advance, because it was
thereby enabled to withdraw a greater amount of *assignats*, and
consequently, to re-issue new ones, without enlarging the quantity
afloat. It was not aware, that, instead of the national domains
advancing in price, the *assignats* were undergoing a rapid depreciation, and that the further that depreciation was pushed, the more
assignats must be issued in payment of an equal quantity of
supplies.

The last *assignats* no longer purported to be payable at sight.
The alteration was little attended to, because neither first nor last
were, in fact, ever paid at all. But their vicious origin was made
more apparent. The paper contained these words:

" National domains—*Assignat* of one hundred *francs*," &c.
Now, what was the meaning of the term one hundred *francs?* What
value did they convey the notion of? Was it the value of the quantity of silver, heretofore known under the designation of one hundred
francs? No; for 100 *fr.* could not possibly be obtained with an
assignat to that amount. Did it convey the idea of as much land,
as might be purchased for 100 *fr.* in silver? Certainly not; for that

quantity of land could no more be obtained, even from the government, by an *assignat* of 100 *fr.* than 100 *fr.* in specie. The domains were disposed of at public auction for as many *assignats* as they would fetch; and the value of this paper had latterly so far declined, that one of 100 *fr.* would not buy an inch square of land.

In short, setting aside all consideration of the discredit attached to that government, the sum expressed in an *assignat* presented the idea of no definite value whatever; and those securities could not but have fallen to nothing, even had the government inspired all the confidence, of which it was so eminently destitute. The error was discovered in the end, when it was impossible any longer to purchase the most trifling article with any sum of *assignats*, whatever might be its amount. The next measure was to issue *mandats*, that is to say, papers purporting to be an order for the absolute transfer of the specific portion of the national domains expressed in the *mandat*: but, besides that it was then too late, the operation was infamously executed.

BOOK II.

OF THE DISTRIBUTION OF WEALTH.

CHAPTER I.

OF THE BASIS OF VALUE; AND OF SUPPLY AND DEMAND.

THE principal phenomena of production have been investigated in the first book; wherein I have shown how human industry, with the aid of capital and of natural agents and properties, creates every kind of utility, which is the primary source of value; and in what way social institutions and public authority operate to the benefit or the prejudice of production. This second book will be devoted to the consideration of the distribution of wealth: to which end it will be necessary, first, to analyze the nature of value, the object of distribution; secondly, to ascertain the laws, which regulate the distribution of value, when once created amongst the various members of society, so as to constitute individual revenue.

The valuation of an object is nothing more or less than the affirmation, that it is in a certain degree of comparative estimation with some other specified object; and any other object possessed of value may serve as the point of comparison. A house, for instance, may be valued in corn or in money. To say that it is worth 4000 dollars conveys a more accurate notion of its value, than to say that it is worth 4000 bushels of wheat, solely because the habit of reckoning the value of all commodities in coin makes it easier for the mind to form an idea of the value of 4000 dollars in other commodities, that is to say, of the quantity of other commodities obtainable for that sum, than of that obtainable for 4000 bushels of wheat. Yet, if wheat be 1 dollar a bushel, the degree of value expressed by each is the same.

In every act of valuation, the object valued is the fixed *datum*. In the instance first given, the house is the *datum*: it is a definite amount of materials, put together in a definite manner, upon a definite site. But the point of comparison is variable in amount, according to the degree of estimation in the mind of the valuer. If valued at 4000 dollars, the house is reckoned to be equivalent to so many pieces of silver coin of the weight of 416 grains, with a mixture of 179-1664 parts of alloy; if at 4500 dollars, or 3500 dollars, it is but a variation of the quantity of the commodity, that is the specific point of comparison. So likewise, if that point be wheat, the variable quantity of that commodity would express the degree of value.

Valuation is vague and arbitrary, when there is no assurance that it will be generally acquiesced in by others. The owner of the house may reckon it worth 4500 dollars, while an indifferent person would value it at no more than 3500 dollars, and probably neither would be right. But if another, or a dozen other persons be willing to give for it a specific amount of other commodities, say 4000 dollars, or 4000 bushels of wheat, we may conclude the estimate to be a correct one. A house that will fetch 4000 dollars in the market is worth that sum.* But if one bidder only will give that price, and he is unable to re-sell it without loss, he will give more than it is worth. The only fair criterion of the value of an object is, the quantity of other commodities at large, that can be readily obtained for it in exchange, whenever the owner wishes to part with it; and this, in all commercial dealings, and in all money valuations, is called the *current price.*†

What is it, then, that determines this current price of commodities?

The want or desire of any particular object depends upon the physical and moral constitution of man, the climate he may live in, the laws, customs, and manners of the particular society, in which he may happen to be enrolled. He has wants, both corporeal and intellectual, social and individual; wants for himself and for his family. His bear-skin and reindeer are articles of the first necessity to the Laplander; whilst their very name is unknown to the *lazzarone* of Naples, who cares for nothing in the world if he get but his meal of macaroni. In Europe, courts of justice are considered indispensable to the maintenance of social union; whereas the Indian of America, the Tartar, and the Arab, feel no want of such establishments. It is not our business here to inquire, wherein these wants originate; we must take them as existing *data*, and reason upon them accordingly.

---

* My brother, *Louis Say,* of Nantes, has attacked this position in a short tract entitled, *Principales Causes de la Richesse et de la Misère des Peuples et des Particuliers,* 8vo. *Paris. Déterville.* He lays down the maxim, that objects are items of wealth, solely in respect of their *actual* utility, and not of their *admitted* or *recognised* utility. In the eye of reason, his position is certainly correct; but in this science relative value is the only guide. Unless the degree of utility be measured by the scale of comparison, it is left quite indefinite and vague, and, even at the same time and place, at the mercy of individual caprice. The positive nature of value was to be established, before political economy could pretend to the character of a science, whose province it is to investigate its origin, and the consequences of its existence.

† In the earlier editions of this work, I had described the measure of value to be the *value* of the other product, that was the point of comparison, which was incorrect. The *quantity* and not the *value* of that other product, is the measure of value in the object of valuation. This mistake gave rise to much ambiguity of demonstration, which the severity of criticism, both fair and unfair, has taught me to correct. *Fas est et ab hoste doceri.*

Of these wants, some are satisfied by the gratuitous agency of natural objects; as of air, water, or solar light. These may be denominated *natural* wealth, because they are the spontaneous offering of nature; and, as such, mankind is not called upon to earn them by any sacrifice or exertion whatever; for which reason, they are never possessed of exchangeable value. Other wants there are, that can only be satisfied by the employment of objects possessed of an utility, which they could not have been invested with without some modification by human agency,—without having undergone some change of condition, and without some difficulty having been surmounted for the purpose. Of this kind are the products of agriculture, commerce, and manufacture, in all their infinite ramifications. To them alone is any value attached; and for a very obvious reason; because the very act of production implies an act of mutual exchange, in which the producer has given his personal agency for the product obtained by its exertion. Wherefore, he will hardly resign it without receiving what is, in his estimation, an equivalent. These may be called *social* wealth, both because an act of exchange is in itself a social act, and because exclusive property in the product obtained by personal exertion, or by an act of exchange, can only be secured by social institutions. Social wealth, it is to be observed, is the only part of human wealth, that can form the subject of scientific research. 1. Because it is the only part that is the object of human estimation, or at least of such estimation, as is not altogether arbitrary and mental. 2. Because it is the only one which is created, distributed, and destroyed, according to any rules that can be assigned by human science.

The knowledge of the ground-work of the quality, *value*, or rather *exchangeable value*, leads to the perception of its origin. The items of social wealth are invested with value by the necessity of giving something to obtain them; and that something is productive exertion. When once obtained, when this sacrifice has been made in the attainment, the party is really more wealthy; he has wherewithal to satisfy more wants; and, if the object obtained by this sacrifice be unsuited to the personal wants of the owner, he may make use of it for the attainment of some object of personal desire, by the way of exchange for some other product; which other product will itself be the result of similar productive exertion; so that, in fact, the exchange will be a mere mutual transfer of the productive exertion on either side, whereof the two products respectively are the result. When a bushel of wheat is given for seven pounds of coffee, there is a mere transfer of the productive agency exerted in creating the one, for that exerted in the creation of the other.*

---

* It is scarcely necessary to mention, that when commodities are exchanged, not for one another, but for money, the case is nowise varied. No seller ever takes money for his own consumption, or for any other purpose, than as an object of a second exchange; so that, in reality, the product sold is exchanged for the product bought with the price. When a bushel of wheat has been sold for a dollar, and 7 lbs. of coffee bought with that dollar, the wheat has actually been

Wherefore, there is a current value or price established for productive service as well as for products. For, if the agency exerted in the creation of a bushel of wheat can obtain, as its reward, in the way of exchange, either a bushel of wheat or seven pounds of coffee indifferently, what is there to prevent its obtaining in the same way any other equivalent product, say a yard of cotton cloth, 5 yards of ribbon, a dozen plates, or any thing else? Should the bushel of wheat be exchangeable for a less amount of any of these commodities respectively, the productive agency exerted in the creation of wheat would be proportionately less rewarded, than that exerted in the creation of the specific commodity; and a portion of the former would be attracted to the latter branch of production, until the recompense of labour in each department should find its fair level.

Each class of productive agency has a current price peculiar to itself. If the productive agency exerted in the production of a bushel of wheat can obtain for itself but 1-15 of its own product, it will be entitled to no more than 1-15 of the value of any other product obtainable by exchange for that quantity of wheat; for instance to 1-15 of a dollar: and so of other products.

Thus it is obvious, that the current value of productive exertion is founded upon the value of an infinity of products compared one with another:* that the value of products is not founded upon that of productive agency, as some authors have erroneously affirmed;† and that since the desire of an object, and consequently its value, originates in its utility, it is the ability to create the utility wherein originates that desire, that gives value to productive agency; which value is proportionate to the importance of its co-operation in the business of production, and forms, in respect to each product individually, what is called, the cost of its production.

The utility of a product is not confined to one human being, but applies to a whole class of society at the least, as in the case of particular articles of clothing; or to a whole community, as in that of most of the articles of food that are adapted to human consumption in general, without distinction of sex or age. For this reason, the demand for a specific object, or product, or act of productive exertion, has a certain degree of extent. The aggregate demand for sugar in France is said to exceed 500,000 *quintals* per annum. Even the individual demand of a specific product for individual consumption may be more or less urgent. Whatever be its intensity, it may be

---

bartered for the coffee, and the money that has intervened has withdrawn itself as completely, as if it had never appeared at all in the transaction. Wherefore it is quite correct to say, that relative value is determined by the relation of commodities one to another, and not solely by that of each commodity to money.

* It must not be inferred from this passage, that I mean to say, that the productive agency exerted in raising a product, whose charges of production have amounted to a dollar, although it is saleable for 75 cents only, is therefore worth but 75 cents. My position merely implies, that this amount of productive service has, in such case, raised a value of 75 cents only, though it might have raised a value of a dollar.

† Ricardo, *Prin. Pol. Econ. and Taxation.*

called by the general name of demand; and the quantity attainable at a given time, and ready for the satisfaction of those who are in want of the specific article, may be called the supply or amount in circulation.

But this must be understood with some limitation; for there is no object of pleasure or utility, whereof the mere desire may not be unlimited, since every body is always ready to receive whatever can contribute to his benefit or gratification. There must, therefore, be some bounds to demand; and the most effectual limitation is, the ability to give some other equivalent product for the object of desire. All the porters in a commercial city might desire to have a coach and six for the more comfortable execution of their business, without raising the price of horses and carriages a tittle. The objects, which each individual has to give as an equivalent for the object of his desire, are no other than the products of his own productive means, which are limited even in the case of the most wealthy member of society.

Wealth is, in all countries, distributed in every degree of gradation, from the populous level of mediocrity to the solitary pinnacle of extreme affluence. Accordingly, the products most generally desirable are really demanded by a limited number only, because they alone have wherewithal to obtain them; and even their ability may be more or less according to circumstances. Whence it may be further concluded, that the same product or products may be in greater demand at a lower scale of price, and when attainable by less productive exertion, although nowise increased in utility, merely because accessible to a greater number of consumers; and, on the contrary, less in demand at a higher scale of price, because accessible to a smaller number.

Suppose that, in a severe winter, a method should be hit upon of manufacturing knit-waistcoats of woollen at 2 dollars each; probably all who should have 2 dollars left, after satisfying more urgent wants, would provide themselves with these waistcoats; but those who should have but a dollar and a half left must still go without. If the same article could be produced at one dollar and a half, these latter also might all be provided and become consumers; and the consumption would be still further extended, if they should be produced at one dollar only. In this manner, products formerly within reach of the rich alone have been made accessible to almost every class of society, as in the case of stockings.

When a product is raised in price, whether by taxation or otherwise howsoever, the contrary effect is experienced; the number of its consumers is reduced; for it can only be obtained by such as can afford to pay for it; and the ability to purchase is not increased by the same causes, that operate to raise the price. Thus, in England, the great majority of the population is wholly precluded from the consumption of vinous liquors, and of many other articles; for their attainment involves so large a sacrifice of products, or of productive agency, that those only can attempt it, who have a great deal of either to spare. In such cases, not only is the number of consumers diminished, but the consumption of each consumer is reduced also. Though a consumer of coffee may not be compelled, by a rise of its price, to relinquish that beverage altogether, he must at all events curtail the amount of his consumption; which is then like that of two individuals, of whom one discontinues, and the other remains able and willing to continue the use of the article.

In commercial speculation, as the purchaser does not buy for his own consumption, he proportions his purchases to what he expects to sell. Since, then, the quantity he can sell depends upon the price he can afford to sell at, he will buy less according as the price rises, and more according as it falls.

In poor countries, objects of even the commonest use, and of inferior price, frequently exceed the means of a great proportion of the population. There are countries, where shoes, though cheap, are out of reach of most of the inhabitants. The price of this commodity does not fall to a level with the means of the people; because that level is still below the bare cost of production. But, shoes of leather not being absolutely necessary to existence, those who are unable to procure these, wear wooden shoes, (*sabots*) or go barefoot. When this is unhappily the case with an article of primary necessity, part of the population must perish, or at least cease to be renewed. These are the causes of a general nature, that limit the demand for each product, and for all products in general.

In respect to supply, it consists of the whole of any commodity which the owners for the time being are disposed to part with for an equivalent, in other words, to sell at the current rate, and not merely of what is actually on sale at the time. The whole of this is also called the circulating or floating stock. Yet, strictly speaking, no commodity is in circulation, except during the act of transit from the seller to the purchaser, which is almost instantaneous. But the bare act of transit has no influence on the terms of the bargain, to which it is commonly subsequent; it is a mere matter of executive detail. The point of real importance is, the inclination of the owner to part with the object of property. A commodity is in circulation, whenever it is in quest of a purchaser, which it may be in the most urgent need of, without altering its locality in the least. Thus, the stock in a shop or warehouse is in circulation; thus too, lands, rent-charges, houses, and the like, are said to be in circulation; and the expression is intelligible enough. Even industry is sometimes in circulation and sometimes not, according as it is either in quest of employment, or already employed.

For the same reason, an object ceases to be in circulation, the moment it is set apart, either for consumption or for export to another market, or accidentally destroyed, or withdrawn by the caprice of its owner, or held back at a price, which amounts to a refusal to sell.

Inasmuch as supply consists of those commodities only, which are to be had at the current price or ordinary rate of the market, a commodity raised by the cost of production above that level, will cease to be produced, or to form part of the supply. Wherefore, the supply will be more abundant, when the current price is high, and more scanty when that price has declined.

Besides these universal and permanent limitations of supply and demand, there are others of a casual and transient nature, which always operate concurrently with the former.

The prospect of an abundant vintage will lower the price of all the wine on hand, even before a single pipe of the expected vintage has been brought to market; for the supply is brisker, and the sale duller, in consequence of the anticipation. The dealers are anxious to dispose of their stock in hand, in fear of the competition of the new vintage; while the consumers, on the other hand, retard their fresh purchases, in the expectation of gaining in price by the delay. A large arrival and immediate sale of foreign articles all at once, lowers their price, by the relative excess of supply above demand. On the contrary, the expectation of a bad vintage, or the loss of many cargoes on the voyage, will raise prices above the cost of production.

Moreover, there are some particular products, which nature or human institutions have subjected to monopoly, and thus prevented from being supplied in equal abundance with those of a similar description. Of this kind are the wines of particular and celebrated vineyards, the soil of which cannot be extended by the extended demand. So the postage of letters is, in most countries, charged at a monopoly-price.

Finally, whatever be the general or particular causes, that operate to determine the relative intensity of supply and demand, it is that intensity, which is the ground-work of price on every act of exchange; for price, it will be remembered, is merely the current value estimated in money. The demand for all objects of pleasure, or utility, would be unlimited, did not the difficulty of attainment, or price, limit and circumscribe the supply. On the other hand, the supply would be infinite, were it not restricted by the same circumstance, the price, or difficulty of attainment: for there can be no doubt, that whatever is producible would then be produced in unlimited quantity, so long as it could find purchasers at any price at all. Demand and supply are the opposite extremes of the beam, whence depend the scales of dearness and cheapness; the price is the point of equilibrium, where the momentum of the one ceases, and that of the other begins.

This is the meaning of the assertion, that, at a given time and place, the price of a commodity rises in proportion to the increase of the demand and the decrease of the supply, and *vice versâ*; or in other words, that the rise of price is in direct ratio to the demand, and inverse ratio to the supply.

The utility of an object, or, what is the same thing, the desire to obtain it, may possibly be unable to raise its price to a level with its cost of production. In this case it is not produced, because its production would cost more than the product would be worth. Probably the price that *caviar** would fetch at Paris would hardly equal the charge of producing it there; for it is so little in request there, that it scarcely would bring the lowest price that it could be procured for, and consequently it is not produced; but elsewhere, it is both produced and consumed in great quantities.

When the price of any object is legally fixed below the charges of its production, the production of it is discontinued, because nobody is willing to labour for a loss: those, who before earned their livelihood by this branch of production, must die of hunger, if they find no other employment; and those, who could have purchased the product at its natural price, are obliged to go without it. The establishment of the fixed rate, or maximum, is a suppression of a portion of production and consumption; that is to say, a diminution of the prosperity of the community, which consists in production and consumption. Even the produce already existing is not so properly consumed as it should be. For, in the first place, the proprietor withholds it as much as possible from the market. In the next, it passes into the hands, not of those who want it most, but of those who have most avidity, cunning, and dishonesty; and often with the most flagrant disregard of natural equity and humanity. A scarcity of corn occurs; the price rises in consequence; yet still it is possible, that the labourer, by redoubling his exertions, or by an increase of wages, may earn wherewithal to buy it at the market price. In the mean time, the magistrate fixes corn at half its natural price: what is the consequence? Another consumer, who had already provided himself, and consequently would have bought no more corn had it remained at its natural price, gets the start of the labourer, and now, from mere superfluous precaution, and to take advantage of the forced cheapness, adds to his own store that portion, which should have gone to the labourer. The one has a double provision, the other none at all. The sale is no longer regulated by the wants and means, but by the superior activity of the purchasers. It is, therefore, not surprising, that a maximum of price on commodities should aggravate their scarcity.

A law, that simply fixes the price of commodities at the rate they would naturally obtain, is merely nugatory, or serves only to alarm producers and consumers, and consequently to derange the natural proportion between the production and the demand; which proportion, if left to itself, is invariably established in the manner most favourable to both.

Hope, fear, malevolence, benevolence, in short, every human passion or virtue may influence the scale of price. But it is the province of moral science to estimate the intensity of their effect upon actual price in every instance, which is the only thing we are here to attend to. Neither need we advert to the operation of the causes of a nature purely political, that may operate to raise the price of a

---

* A pickle made of the roe of sturgeons, a favourite condiment of Russian diet,

product above the degree of its real utility. For these are of the same class with actual robbery and spoliation, which come under the department of criminal jurisprudence, although they may intrude themselves into the business of the distribution of wealth. The functions of national government, which is a class of industry, whose result or product is consumed by the governed as fast as it is produced, may be too dearly paid for, when they get into the hands of usurpation and tyranny, and the people be compelled to contribute a larger sum than is necessary for the maintenance of good government. This is a parallel case to that of a producer without competitors, whether he have got rid of them by force, or by accidental circumstances. He may raise his product to what price he will, even to the extreme limit of the consumer's ability, if his monopoly be seconded by authority. But it is the province of the political philosopher, and not of the political economist, to teach us how this evil may be avoided. In like manner, although it be the province of ethics, or of the knowledge of the moral qualities of man, to teach the means of ensuring the good conduct of mankind, in their mutual relations, yet, whenever the intervention of a superhuman power appears necessary to effect this purpose, those who assume to be the interpreters of that power must be paid for their service. If their labour be useful, its utility is an immaterial product, which has a real value; but, if mankind be nowise improved by it, their labour, not being productive of utility, that portion of the revenues of society, devoted to their maintenance, is a total loss; a sacrifice without any return.

With the most earnest wish to confine myself within my subject, it is impossible to avoid sometimes touching upon the confines of policy and morality, were it only for the purpose of marking out their points of contact.

CHAPTER II.

THE SOURCES OF REVENUE.

It has been shown in Book I., that products are raised by the productive means at the command of mankind, that is to say, by human industry, capital, and natural powers and agents. The products thus raised, form the revenue of those possessed of these means of production, and enable them to procure such of the necessaries and comforts of existence, as are not furnished gratuitously, either by nature, or by their fellow-creatures.

The exclusive right to dispose of revenue is a consequence of the exclusive right, or property, in the means of production; and such of them, as are not the subject of human appropriation, are not either items of productive means, or sources of revenue; they form no part of human wealth, which implies appropriation and exclusive possession; for there is no such thing as wealth, unless where property is known and established, and where possession is both acknowledged and secured.

The origin or the justice of the right of property, it is unnecessary to investigate, in the study of the nature, and progress of human wealth. Whether the actual owner of the soil, or the person from whom he derived its possession, have obtained it by prior occupancy, by violence, or by fraud, can make no difference whatever in the business of the production and distribution of its product or revenue.

Perhaps it is scarcely necessary to remark, that property in that class of productive means, which has been called human industry, and in that distinguished by the general name of capital, is far more sacred and indisputable, than in the remaining class of natural powers and agents. The industrious faculties of man, his intelligence, muscular strength, and dexterity, are peculiar to himself and inherent in his nature. And capital, or accumulated produce, is the mere result of human frugality and forbearance to exercise the faculty of consuming, which, if fully exerted, would have destroyed products as fast as they were created, and these never could have been the existing property of any one; wherefore, no one else, but he who has practised this self-denial, can claim the result of it with any show of justice. Frugality is next of kin to the actual creation of products, which confers the most unquestionable of all titles to the property in them.

These several sources of production are some of them alienable, as land, implements of arts, &c.; and some inalienable, as personal faculties. Some also are consumable, as are all the items of floating capital; others, inconsumable, as land. Some, too, there are, that are neither alienable nor consumable, yet are capable of destruction; as the human faculties, intellectual and corporeal, which vanish with human existence.

Such as are capable of consumption, as, for instance, the floating values, whereon production expends its energies, may be consumed either in such manner as to occasion a re-production, in which case they will still constitute a part of the means of production; or in such manner as to yield no further production, in which case they cease to form any part of those means, and are devoted to pure destruction, more or less rapid.

Although revenue, as well as the sources of production, is a constituent part of individual wealth, yet no one is reputed to reduce his fortune by the consumption of his revenue only, provided that he does not encroach upon his productive means; because revenue is a regenerating product, whereas the means of production, so long as they continue to exist, are a constant and perpetual source of new products.

The current value of these appropriable sources of production is established on the same principles, as that of all other objects; that is to say, by the conflicting influence of supply and demand. The only remark that need be made upon it is, that the demand does not originate in the enjoyment anticipated from the immediate use of the particular source; for a field or an implement of trade yields to the owner no direct enjoyment, which is capable of estimation; their value has reference to the value of the product they are capable of raising, which itself originates in the utility of that product, or the satisfaction it may be capable of affording.

With regard to those sources, that are inalienable, as are the human faculties of mind and body, they can never be the subject of actual exchange, and their value is a matter of mere mental estimation, grounded upon the value they may be capable of producing. Thus the productive means of this description, which yield to an artisan the wages of 1 dollar a day, or of 365 dollars a year, may be reckoned equivalent to a vested capital yielding an equal annual revenue.

And now that we have taken this general and cursory view of the sources of production and of revenue in the abstract, we may enter upon a more minute analysis of their nature, which will lead us into the labyrinth of the science of political economy, and furnish us with a clue to some of its most intricate windings.

The immediate result of these sources is not, strictly speaking, a product, but a productive service that helps us to a product. Products should, therefore, be considered as the result of an interchange of productive service on the one hand, and the actual products on the other, subsequently to which, revenue appears for the first time in the shape of products; and these again may be exchanged for other products, into which latter form the same revenue will then be converted.

The conception of this matter will be rendered clearer by a practical illustration. A piece of arable land yields an annual product, say of 300 bushels of wheat, whereof 200 bushels more or less, may be considered as resulting from the agency of the capital and industry employed in its cultivation, and the remaining 100 bushels as resulting from the natural productive powers of the soil. The revenue, yielded by the land to the proprietor, will have appeared first in the way of concurring productive service afforded by the object of property, the land: which productive service will have been transferred or lent to the cultivator for the sum of 100 bushels of wheat, and this will be the first act of exchange. If these 100 bushels of wheat be converted into specie, either by the proprietor himself or by the cultivator on his behalf, and in consequence of a mutual arrangement, this specie will still be the same identical revenue, though under the secondary form of money.

This analysis will conduct us to a knowledge of the real value of revenue, which falls in with the general definition of value given in the preceding chapter, namely, the amount of other objects obtainable by exchange for the object of intended transfer. What,

then, is the object of transfer, for which revenue is given in exchange? why, the productive service of those means, that the receiver of revenue may be possessed of. And what is obtained by
the primary act of exchange, which we designate production? why,
products. Wherefore, the value of revenue is large in proportion,
not to the value, but to the quantity of the product obtained, to the
sum total of utility created.

Thus we find, that the ratio of national revenue, in the aggregate,
is determined by the amount of the product, and not by its value.*
It is not so with individual revenue; because a variation in the relative value of different products will operate to swell that of one
individual, or class, at the expense of another.

Could each member of society live on the primary products
whereof his revenue is composed, the relative degree of revenue
would, like that of nations, in the aggregate, depend upon the
amount of the product, upon the sum of utility created, and not
upon its exchangeable value. But, in a state of society at all
elevated above barbarism, this is impossible; each individual
consumes a much less quantity of his own peculiar product, than
of those of other people, which he buys with his own. The grand
point, therefore, of individual importance to the producer, is, the
quantity of product not of his own creation, which he may be able
to procure with his own productive means, or with the products
created by their agency. Suppose, for instance, the land, capital,
and personal faculties of a particular individual to be engaged in the
cultivation of saffron; as he will probably himself consume little or
no saffron, his revenue will consist of such other objects, as his
annual crop of saffron can be exchanged for; and the ratio of that
revenue will be elevated by a rise in the price of saffron; while that
of the consumers of that article will be proportionately reduced to
the full extent of the rise of its price. On the contrary, their revenue will be augmented in like manner by a fall of its price, to the
prejudice of the revenue of the grower.

Every saving in the charges of production, that is to say, every
saving in the productive agency exerted to raise the same product, is
an increase of the revenue of the community to an equal extent; as,
for example, the contrivance to raise as much upon one acre of land
as before upon two, or to effect with two days' labour, what before
required as much as four; for the productive agency thus released
may be directed to the increase of production. (a) And this acces-

---

* Hence the futility of any attempt to compare the wealth of different nations,
of France and England for instance, by comparison of the value of their respective
national products. Indeed, two values are not capable of comparison, when placed
at a distance from each other. The only fair way of comparing the wealth of
one nation with that of another, is, by a moral estimate of the individual welfare
in each respectively.

(a) And will be so for the most part, though not entirely, wherever the members of the community have no other hope of subsistence, than from the product

sion of revenue will accrue to the individual benefit of the contriver, so long as the contrivance can be confined to his own knowledge; but to that of consumers at large, as soon as the notoriety shall have awakened competition, and obliged him to limit his profits to the actual charges of production.

However revenue may be transformed by the various acts of exchange, commencing with the productive agency, which is the primitive exhibition of revenue, it remains the same in substance, until the moment of its ultimate consumption. The revenue yielded by an acre of arable land remains, in reality, the same, both after its primary exchange, by the act of production, into the form of wheat, and after its secondary transformation into silver coin, even although the wheat have been consumed by the purchasers. But, as soon as the revenued individual converts his silver coin into an object of consumption, and that object is simply consumed, the value of his revenue thenceforth ceases to exist, and is destroyed and lost, although the silver coin, whose form it once assumed, continue in existence. It must not be imagined still to exist in the hands of the temporary holder of the coin, although lost to the receiver of revenue; but is equally lost to mankind at large; for the actual holder of the coin must have obtained possession of it by the transfer of other revenue of his own, or of some source of revenue before in his own possession.

When revenue is added to capital, it thenceforth ceases to be revenue, or, as such, to be capable of satisfying the wants of the proprietor: it can only yield an increased revenue, being an item of productive capital, consumable in the manner of capital, that is to say, in such way as to yield a product in exchange and return for the value consumed.

When capital or land, or personal service, is let out to hire, its productive power is transferred to the renter or adventurer in production, in consideration of a given amount of products agreed upon beforehand. It is a sort of speculative bargain, wherein the renter takes the risk of profit and loss, according as the revenue he may realise, or the product obtained by the agency transferred, shall exceed or fall short of the rent or hire he is to pay. Yet one revenue only can be realised; and, though a borrowed capital may yield to

of their own productive means; for the whole surplus of revenue thus created, is sure to go, in the end, to the appropriators of the natural sources of production; leaving those, whose productive means are merely personal, to employ them upon some other object, or upon an enlarged production of the same object. And this is a complete answer to the position of *Sismondi* and Malthus, that economy of human productive exertion makes the multiplication of unproductive consumers, not only probable, but necessary. But where a poor-law or monastic establishment provides for the subsistence of the human agency thus rendered superfluous, there will probably be no increase of national revenue consequent upon a saving of productive agency; for the surplus labour is thereby released from the necessity of exertion in some other channel. With such institutions, the enlargement of productive power by machinery or otherwise may be very great, without any enlargement of national production, revenue, or wealth. T.

the adventurer an annual product of 10 per cent. instead of 5 per cent. which he pays in the shape of interest, yet the revenue of the capital, the productive service it affords, will not be 10 per cent.; for in that gross product is included the recompense of the productive agency, both of the capital and of the industry that has turned it to account.

The actual revenue of each individual is proportionate to the quantity of products at his disposal, being either the immediate fruit of his productive means, or the result of those transformations from its primitive state, which his revenue may have undergone, until it have assumed the shape of the ultimate object of his consumption. The ratio of that quantity, or of utility inherent in it, can only be estimated from its current price in the dealings of mankind. In this sense, the revenue of an individual is equal to the value derived from his productive means; which value, however, is the greater, in respect to the objects of his consumption, in proportion to the cheapness of those objects, which augments his command of other than his own immediate products.

In like manner, the revenue of a nation is the more considerable, in proportion to the intensity of the value whereof it consists, i. e. of the value of its aggregate productive powers, and to its high relative degree to the value of the objects of external attainment. The value of productive agency must be high, even where that of products is low; for it should be always recollected, that, since the intensity of value depends upon the quantity of objects obtainable in exchange, revenue, or, in other words, the agency of the national sources of production, is large, in proportion to the abundance and cheapness of the products derived from them.

CHAPTER III.

OF REAL AND RELATIVE VARIATION OF PRICE.

The price of an article is the quantity of money it may be worth; current price, the quantity it may be sure of obtaining at the particular place. Its locality is material, for the desire of a specific object varies in relation to the quantity procurable according to the locality.

The price obtained upon the sale of an article represents all other articles procurable with that price. To say, that the price of an ell of broad-cloth is 8 dollars, implies, that it is exchangeable either for so much coined silver, or for so much of any other product or products as may be procurable with that sum. Money-price is selected for the purposes of an illustration, in preference to price in commodities at large, merely for greater simplicity; but the real and ultimate object of exchange is, not money, but commodities.

Price, in this sense, may be divided into buying price and selling price; that is to say, the price given to obtain possession of an object, and the price obtainable for the relinquishment of its possession.

The price paid for every product, at the time of its original attainment or creation, is, the charge of the productive agency exerted, or the cost of its production.* Tracing upwards to this original price of a product, we unavoidably come to other products; for the charge of productive agency can only have been defrayed by other products. The daily wages of the weaver engaged in producing broad-cloth are products; they consist either of the articles of his daily subsistence, or of the money wherewith he may procure them: both which are equally products. Wherefore the production, as well as the subsequent interchange of products, may be said to resolve itself into a barter of one product for another, conducted upon a comparison of their respective current prices. But there is one important particular, that requires the most assiduous attention, the neglect or oversight of which has led to abundance of error and misrepresentation, and has made the works of many writers calculated only to mislead the students in this science.

An ell of broad-cloth, that has, in the production, required the purchase of productive agency at the price of 8 dollars, will have cost that sum in the manufacture; but if three-fourths only of that productive agency can be made to suffice for its production; if, supposing one kind of productive agency only to be requisite, 15 instead of 20 days' labour of a single workman be enabled to complete the product, the same ell of broad-cloth will cost 6 dollars to the producer, at the same rate of wages. In this case the current price of human productive agency will have remained the same, although the cost of production will have varied in the ratio of the difference between 6 dollars and 8 dollars. But, as this difference in the relation between the cost of production and the current price of the product holds out a prospect of larger profit than ordinary in this particular channel, it naturally attracts a larger proportion of productive agency, the exertion of which, by enlarging the supply, reduces again the current price to a level with the bare cost of production.†

This kind of variation in the price of a product I shall call *real* variation of price, because it is a positive variation, involving no equivalent variation in the object of exchange, and both may, and actually does occur, without any cotemporaneous variation of the price, either of productive agency, of the products wherewith it is recompensed, or of those, for which the specific object of this real variation is procurable.

* *Vide Wealth of Nations*, book i. c. 5.

† The cost of production is what Smith calls the natural price of products, as contrasted with their current or market price, as he terms it. But it results from what has been said above, that every act of barter or exchange, among the rest even that implied in the act of production, is conducted with reference to current price.

It is otherwise with regard to the variation of price of products already in existence one to another, without reference to their respective cost of production. When the wine of the last vintage, that a month before sold at 40 dollars the tun, will fetch no more than 30 dollars, money and all other objects of desire to the wine-vender have actually advanced in price to him; for the productive agency exerted in raising the wine, receives a recompense of but 30 dollars, instead of 40 dollars in money, and of commodities in a like proportion, which is an abatement of $\frac{1}{4}$; whereas, in the instance above cited, an equal amount of productive agency will receive an equal recompense in all other products; for a degree of agency, which has both cost and received 6 dollars, will be equally well paid with one that cost and received 8 dollars.

In the former case, then, of a *real* variation, the wealth of the community will have received an accession; in the latter, of *relative* variation, it will have remained stationary; and for this plain reason; because, in the one case all the purchasers of cloth, will be so much the richer, without the seller being any poorer; while in the other, the gain of the one class will be exactly equipoised by the corresponding loss of the other. In the former case, a larger amount of products will be procured with an equal charge of production, and without any alteration in the revenues of either buyers or sellers: there will be more actual wealth, more means of enjoyment, without any increased expenditure of productive means; the aggregate utility will be augmented; the quantum of products procurable for the same price will be enlarged; all which are but varied expressions of the same meaning.

But whence is derived this accession of enjoyment, this larger supply of wealth, that nobody pays for? From the increased command acquired by human intelligence over the productive powers and agents presented gratuitously by nature. A power has been rendered available for human purposes, that had before been not known, or not directed to any human object; as in the instance of wind, water, and steam-engines: or one before known and available is directed with superior skill and effect, as in the case of every improvement in mechanism, whereby human or animal power is assisted or expanded. The merit of the merchant, who contrives, by good management, to make the same capital suffice for an extended business, is precisely analogous to that of the engineer, who simplifies machinery, or renders it more productive.

The discovery of a new mineral, animal, or vegetable, possessed of the properties of utility in a novel form, or in a greater degree of abundance or perfection, is an acquisition of the same kind. The productive means of mankind were amplified, and a larger product rendered procurable by an equal degree of human exertion, when indigo was substituted for woad, sugar for honey, and cochineal for the Tyrian dye. In all these instances of improvement, and those of a similar nature that may be hereafter effected, it is observable, that, since the means of production placed at the disposal of mankind become in reality more powerful, the product raised always increases in quantity, in proportion as it diminishes in value. We shall presently see the consequences of this circumstance.*

A fall of price may be general and affect all commodities at once; or it may be partial and affect certain commodities only; as I shall endeavour to explain by example.

Suppose that, when stockings were made by knitting only, thread-stockings, of a given quality, amounted to the price of 1 dollar the pair. Hence, we should infer, that the rent of the land whereon the flax was grown, the profits upon the labour and capital of the cultivators, those of the flax-dresser and spinner, with those likewise of the stocking-knitter, amounted altogether to the sum of a dollar for each pair of stockings. Suppose that, in consequence of the invention of a stocking-machine, 1 dollar will buy two pair of stockings instead of one. As the competition has a tendency to bring the price to a level with the cost of production, we may infer from this reduced price, that the outlay in land, capital, and labour, necessary to produce two pair of stockings, is still no more than 1 dollar; thus, with equal means of production, the product raised is doubled in quantity. And what is a convincing proof that this fall is positive, is the fact, that every person, of what profession soever, may thenceforward obtain a pair of stockings with half the quantity of his own particular product. A capitalist, the holder of 5 per cent. stock, was before obliged to devote the annual interest of 20 dollars to the purchase of a pair of stockings; he now gives the interest of 10 dollars only. A tradesman selling his sugar at $33\frac{1}{3}$ cents per lb. must before have sold 3 lb. of sugar to buy a pair of stockings, now he need but sell $1\frac{1}{2}$ lb.: he therefore sacrifices in the pair of stockings only half the means of production he formerly devoted to the acquisition of the same object.

We have hitherto supposed this product alone to have fallen in price. Let us suppose two products to fall, stockings and sugar: that by an improvement of commerce, 1 lb. of sugar cost 22 cents instead of 33 cents. In this case all purchasers of sugar, including the stocking-maker, whose product has likewise fallen, will sacrifice, in the purchase of 1 lb. of sugar, but half the productive means, which they before allotted for that purpose.

The truth of this position may be easily ascertained. When sugar was at $33\frac{1}{3}$ cents per lb. and stockings at a dollar the pair, the stock-

---

* Within the last hundred years, the improvements of industry, effected by the advance of human knowledge, more especially in the department of natural science, have vastly abridged the business of production, but the slow progress in moral and political science, and particularly in the branch of social organisation, has hitherto prevented mankind from reaping the full benefit of those improvements. Yet it would be wrong to suppose they have reaped none at all. The pressure of taxation has indeed been doubled, tripled, or even quadrupled; yet population has increased in most countries of Europe; which is a sign, that a portion at least of the increase of products has fallen to the lot of the subject; and the population, besides being augmented, is likewise better lodged, clothed, and conditioned and I believe better fed too, than it was a century ago.

ing-maker was obliged to sell one pair of stockings, before he could buy 3 lbs. of sugar : and, as the charges of producing this pair of stockings were one dollar, he in reality bought 3 lbs. of sugar at the price of a dollar value in his own productive means; in like manner as the grocer bought a pair of stockings for 3 lbs. of sugar, that is to say, in his case also, for one dollar value of his peculiar productive means. But when both these commodities have fallen to half their price, one pair only, or productive means equivalent to 50 cents, would buy 3 lbs. of sugar; and 3 lbs. of sugar, procurable at a charge of production amounting to 50 cents, will suffice to purchase a pair of stockings. Wherefore, if two kinds of products, which we have set one against the other, and supposed to pass in exchange the one for the other, can both have fallen in price at the same time, are we not authorised to infer, that this fall is a positive fall, and has no reference or relation to the prices of commodities one to another? that commodities in general may fall at one and the same time, some more, some less, and yet that the diminution of price may be no loss to any body?

It is for this reason, that, in modern times, although wages stand in nearly the same relation to corn as they did four or five hundred years ago, yet the lower classes now enjoy many luxuries, that were then denied them; many articles of dress and household furniture, for instance, have suffered a real diminution of value; and that the same individuals are more scantily supplied with others, as with butcher's meat and game,* because they have sustained a real increase of value.

Every saving in the cost of production implies the procurement, either of an equal product by the exertion of a smaller amount of productive agency, or of a larger product by the exertion of equal agency, which are both the same thing; and it is sure to be followed by an enlargement of the product. It may be thought, perhaps, that this increase of production may possibly take place without any corresponding increase of demand; and, therefore, that the price

---

* I find in the *Recherches* of *Dupre de Saint Maur*, that in 1342, an ox was sold from 10 to 11 *livres tournois*. This sum then contained 7 oz. of fine silver, which was worth about 28 oz. of the present day ; and 28 oz. of our present money are coined into 171 *fr.* 30 *c.*, (32 dollars,) which is lower than the price of an ordinary ox. A lean ox bought in Poitou for 300 *fr.*, and afterwards fatted in Lower Normandy, will sell at Paris for from 450 to 500 *fr.* (84 to 93 dollars.) Butcher's meat has, therefore, more than doubled in price since the 14th century; and probably most other articles of food likewise; and, if the labouring classes had not at the same time been greatly benefited by the progress of industry, and put in possession of additional sources of revenue, they would be worse fed than in the time of Philip of Valois.

This may be easily explained. The growing revenues of the industrious classes have enabled them to multiply, and consequently to swell the demand for all objects of food. But their supply can not keep pace with the increasing demand, because, although the same surface of soil may be rendered more productive, it can not be so to an indefinite degree ; and the supply of food by the channel of external commerce, is more expensive than by that of internal agriculture, on account of the bulky nature of most of the articles of aliment.

current of the product may fall below the cost of its production, even on its reduced scale. But this is a groundless apprehension; for the fall of price tends so strongly to expand the sphere of consumption, that, in all the instances I have been able to meet with, the increase of demand has invariably outrun the increasing powers of an improved production, operating upon the same productive means; so that every enlargement of the power of productive agency has created a demand for more of that agency, in the preparation of the product cheapened by the improvement.

Of this a striking example has been afforded by the invention of the art of printing. By this expeditious method of multiplying the copies of a literary work, each copy costs but a twentieth part of what was before paid for manuscript; an equal intensity of total demand, would, therefore, take off only twenty times the number of copies; but probably it is within the mark to say, that a hundred times as many are now consumed. So that, where there was formerly one copy only of the value of 12 dollars of present money, there are now a hundred copies, the aggregate value of which is 60 dollars, though that of each single copy be reduced to 1-20. Thus the reduction of price, consequent upon a real variation, does not occasion even a nominal diminution of wealth.*

On the other hand, and by the rule of contraries, as a real advance of price must always proceed from a deficiency in the product raised by equal productive means, it is attended by a diminution in the general stock of wealth; for the rise of price upon each portion does not counterpoise the reduction that takes place in the total quantity of the commodity; to say nothing of the greater relative dearness of the object of consumption to the consumer, and of his consequent impoverishment in comparison.

Suppose a murrain, or a bad system of management, to cause a scarcity of any kind of live stock, of sheep for instance, the price will rise, but not in proportion to the reduction of the supply; because in proportion as they grow dearer, the demand will decrease. If there were but one-fifth of the present number of sheep, it is very probable their price would advance to no more than double; so, that in place of five sheep, which might together be worth 20 dollars at 4 dollars each, there would remain but one valued at 8 dollars. The diminution of wealth in the article of sheep, notwithstanding the increased price, must therefore be computed at 60 per cent., which is considerably more than a moiety.†

---

* Our *data* in relation to the products of former times are too few to enable us to deduce from them any precise result; but those at all acquainted with the subject will see, that, whether over or under-stated, will make no difference in the reasoning. The statistic researches of the present generation will provide future ages with more accurate means of calculation, but will add nothing to the solidity of the principles upon which it must be made.

† Of this nature are the evil effects of taxation, (especially if it be exorbitant,) upon the general wealth of the community, independently of its effects upon the individual assessed. The cost of production, and consequently the real price of commodities, are aggravated thereby, and their aggregate value diminished.

Thus, it may be affirmed, that every real reduction of price, instead of reducing the nominal value of produce raised, in point of fact, augments it; and that a real increase of price reduces, instead of adding to the general wealth; to say nothing of the quantum of human enjoyment, which in the former case is multiplied, and in the latter abridged. Besides it would be a capital error to imagine, that a real fall of price, or in other words, a reduction in the price paid to productive exertion, occasions as much loss to the producer as gain to the consumer. A real depreciation of commodities is a benefit to the consumer, without curtailing the profits of the producer. The stocking-maker, who for one dollar manufactures two pair of stockings instead of one, gains as much upon that sum as if it were the price of a single pair. The landed proprietor receives the same rent, although, by a better rotation of crops, the tenant should multiply and cheapen the produce of his land. Whenever, without additional fatigue to the labourer, means are devised to double the quantity of work he can perform, the ratio of his daily gains is not reduced, although his product is sold at a lower price.*

This will serve to confirm and explain a maxim, which has been hitherto imperfectly understood, and even disputed by many writers, and sects of political reasoners; namely, that a country is rich and plentiful, in proportion as the price of commodities is low.†

For argument's sake, I will put the matter in the most favourable light for those who dispute this maxim, and suppose them to urge an extreme case, namely, that, by successive economical reductions, the charges of production are at length reduced to nothing; in which case, it is evident there can no longer be rent for land, interest upon

---

* I have met with persons, who imagined themselves adding to national wealth, by favouring the production of expensive, in preference to that of cheaper articles. In their opinion, it is better to make a yard of rich brocade than one of common sarsenet. They do not consider, that, if the former costs four times as much as the latter, it is because it requires the exertion of four times as much productive agency, which could be made to produce four yards of the latter, as easily as one of the former. The total value is the same; but society derives less benefit; for a yard of brocade makes fewer dresses than four yards of sarsenet. It is the grand curse of luxury, that it ever presents meanness in company with magnificence.

† *Dupont de Nemours (Physiocratie.* p. 117.) says, that "it must not be supposed, that the cheapness of commodities is advantageous to the lower classes; for the reduction of prices lessens the wages of the labourer, curtails his comforts, and affords him less work and lucrative occupation." But theory and practice both controvert this position. A fall of wages, occasioned solely by a fall in the price of commodities, does not diminish the comforts of the labourer; and, inasmuch as the low price of wages enables the adventurer to produce at a less expense, it tends powerfully to promote the vent and demand for the produce of labour.

Melon, Forbonnais, and all the partisans of the exclusive system, or balance of trade, concur with the economists in this erroneous opinion; and it has been re-affirmed by *Sismondi,* in his *Nouveaux Prin. d'Econ. Pol.* liv. iv. c. 6.; where the lower price of products is treated as an advantage gained by the consumer upon the producer, in despite of the obvious impossibility of any loss to the labouring or other productive classes, by a reduction tantamount only to the saving in the cost of production.

capital, or wages on labour, and consequently, no longer any revenue to the productive classes. What then? Why then, I say, these classes would no longer exist. Every object of human want would stand in the same predicament as the air or the water, which are consumed without the necessity of being either produced or purchased. In like manner as every one is rich enough to provide himself with air, so would he be to provide himself with every other imaginable product. This would be the very *acme* of wealth. Political economy would no longer be a science; we should have no occasion to learn the mode of acquiring wealth; for we should find it ready made to our hands.

Although there be no instance of a product falling to nothing in price, and becoming worth no more than mere water, yet some kinds have undergone prodigious abatements; as fuel in those places where coal-pits have been discovered; and such abatements are so many approximations to that imaginary state of complete abundance, I have just been speaking of.

If different commodities have fallen in different ratios, some more, others less, it is plain they must have varied in relative value to each other. That which has fallen, stockings, for instance, has changed its value relatively to that which has not fallen, as butcher's meat; and such as have fallen in equal proportion, like stockings and sugar in our hypothesis, have varied in *real* though not in *relative* value.

There is this difference between a real and a relative variation of price: that the former is a change of value, arising from an alteration of the charges of production; the latter, a change, arising from an alteration of the ratio of value of one particular commodity to other commodities. Real variations are beneficial to buyers, without injury to sellers; and *vice versâ;* but in relative ones, what is gained by the seller is lost by the purchaser, and *vice versâ.* A dealer, having in his warehouse 100,000 lbs. of wool at 20 cents per lb., is *worth* 20,000 dollars; if, by reason of an extraordinary demand, wool should rise to 40 cents per lb., that portion of his capital will be doubled, but all goods brought to be exchanged for wool will lose as much in relative value as the wool will gain. A person in want of 100 lbs. of wool, who could before have obtained it by disposing, say of 20 bushels of wheat valued at 20 dollars, must now dispose of twice that quantity. He will lose the 20 dollars gained by the wool-dealer; and the nation be neither enriched nor impoverished.*

---

* The Earl of Lauderdale published in 1807, a work, entitled, " *Researches on the Nature and Origin of Public Wealth, and on the Causes which concur in its Increase;*" the whole reasoning of which is built on this erroneous proposition, that the scarcity of a commodity, though it diminish the wealth of society in the aggregate, augments that of individuals, by increasing the value of that commodity in the hands of its possessors. Whence the author deduces the unsound conclusion, that national, differs in principle from individual wealth. He has not perceived, that, whenever a purchaser is obliged to make the acquisition by the sacrifice of a greater value, he loses just as much as the seller gains; and

When sales of this kind take place between one nation and another, the nation, that sells the commodity, which has advanced in relative price, gains to the amount of the advance, and the purchasing nation loses precisely to the same extent. Such a rise of price adds nothing to the general stock of wealth, existing in the world, which can only be enlarged by the production of some new utility, that may become the object of price or estimation; whereas, in other cases, one always loses what another gains: and so it is with all kinds of jobbing transactions, founded upon the fluctuations of prices one upon another.

In all probability, the time is not very distant, when the European states, awake at length to their real interests, will renounce the costly rights of colonial dominion, and aim at the independent colonization of those tropical regions nearest to Europe; as of some parts of Africa. The vast cultivation of what are called colonial products, that would ensue, could not fail to supply Europe in the greatest abundance, and probably at most moderate prices. Such merchants as shall then have stock on hand, purchased at the old prices, certainly will make a loss upon that stock; but their loss will be a clear gain to the consumer, who will for a time enjoy this kind of produce, at a price inferior to the charge of production; the merchants will gradually replace their dear-bought produce, by other of equal quality, raised with superior intelligence; and the consumer will then reap the advantage of superior cheapness and multiplied enjoyment, with no loss to any body; for the merchant will both buy and sell cheaper; and human industry will have made a rapid stride, and opened a new road to affluence and abundance.*

that every operation, designed to procure this kind of benefit, must occasion to one party a loss, equivalent to the gain of another.

He likewise refers this imaginary difference between the principle of public and of private wealth to this circumstance; that the accumulation of capital, which is an advantage to individual, is detrimental to national wealth, by obstructing the consumption, which is the stimulus of industry. He has fallen into the very common error of supposing, that capital is, by accumulation, withdrawn from consumption; whereas, on the contrary, it is consumed, but in a re-productive way, and so as to afford the means of a perpetual recurrence of purchase, which can occur but once in the case of unproductive consumption. *Vide* Book III. *infrà.* Thus it is, that a single error in principle, vitiates a whole work. The one in question is built upon this unsound foundation; and, therefore, serves only to multiply, instead of reducing the intricacies of the subject. (*a*)

* The vast means at the disposal of Napoleon might have been successfully directed to this grand object, and then he would have left the reputation of having contributed to civilize, enrich, and people the world; and not of having been

(*a*) The error of Lauderdale is analogous to that of *Sismondi* and of Malthus; and arises from the notion, that an extension of productive power makes an extension of unproductive consumption necessary; whereas, it is thereby rendered possible, or at the utmost probable only. The state, as well as its subjects, may consume in a way conducive to the further extension of productive power, and the state, like an individual, is powerful and wealthy in proportion to the extent of the productive sources in its possession, and to the fertility of those sources.   T.

CHAPTER IV.

OF NOMINAL VARIATION OF PRICE, AND OF THE PECULIAR VALUE OF BULLION AND OF COIN.

In treating of the elevation and depression of the price of commodities, although value has been expressed in money, no notice has been taken of the value of money itself; which, to say the truth, plays no part in real, or even in relative variation of the price of other commodities. One product is always ultimately bought with another, even when paid for in the first instance in money. When the price of wool is doubled, it is purchased with twice the quantity of every other commodity, whether the exchange be made directly, or through the intermediate agency of money. The baker, who could have bought 1 lb. of wool with 6 lbs. of bread, or, with its price in money, say 20 cents, will be obliged to sacrifice 12 lbs. of bread to obtain the 40 cents necessary to purchase 1 lb. of wool at its advanced price. But, if it be proposed to compare together the relative value, not of stockings, meat, sugar, wool, bread, &c., but of any one of those articles with that of money itself, we shall find, that money, like all other commodities, may undergo, and often has, in fact, undergone a real variation; that is to say, a variation in the cost of its production; and a relative one, that is to say, a change of value, in comparison with other products.

Since the discovery of the American mines, silver, having fallen to about a fourth of its former value, has lost three-fourths of its relative value to all other products, whose price has, meanwhile, remained stationary; as to that of corn, for instance; consequently, one must give 4 oz. of silver for 1 *setier* (about 43 bushels) of wheat, which, in the year 1500, was to be had for 1 oz. or thereabout. A commodity, which, since that period, may have fallen to half its price, while silver was falling to one-quarter, will, therefore, have doubled its relative value to silver, for this commodity then cost 1 oz., and would now be worth 4 oz. of silver, had it not fallen itself in value; but having itself lost one-half its value, it is sold for but 2 oz.; that is to say, for twice as much silver as at the former period.

Such is the effect of real and of relative variation in the price of silver. But, independently of these variations, there have been vast alterations in the denomination given, at different periods during the interim, to the same quantity of pure metal, which should make us place very little reliance on the accuracy of our estimate of real and relative variation.

In 1514, an ounce of silver would purchase 1 *setier* of wheat,

---

its scourge and devastator. When the Barbary shore shall be lined with peaceful, industrious, and polished inhabitants, the Mediterranean will be an immense lake, furrowed by the commerce of the wealthy nations, peopling its shores on every side.

which is now worth 4 oz.; this was a relative variation of silver to wheat. This quantity of silver then was denominated 30 *sous ;** and, had the same quantity of silver still preserved the same denomination, 4 oz. would now be called 120*s.* or 6 *fr.* Thus, wheat at 6 *fr.* the *setier* would have risen in relation to silver, or silver have fallen in comparison with wheat. There would, however, have been no nominal variation. But 4 oz. of silver are now denominated 24 *fr.* instead of 6 *fr. ;* so that there has been a nominal as well as a relative variation,—a mere verbal alteration. The real and relative variation has been in the ratio of 4 to 1; but the nominal value of money has declined in the ratio of 16 to 1, since 1514.

It is obvious, therefore, that one cannot form an idea of the value of a commodity from its estimate of money price, except during a space of time, and within a space of territory, in which neither the denomination of the coin, nor the value of its material, has undergone any change; else the valuation will be merely nominal, and convey no fixed idea of value whatever. To say that the *setier* of wheat sold for 30 *sous* in 1514, without explaining the then value of 30 *sous,* is giving us a price, that conveys either no idea at all, or a fallacious one, if it be meant to affirm, that the *setier* of wheat was then worth 30 *sous* of present money. In comparing values, the denomination of coin is useful only inasmuch as it designates the quantity of pure metal contained in the sum specified. It may serve to denote the quantity of the metal; but never serve as an index of value at any distance of time, or of place.

It is scarcely necessary to point out the effects of an alteration in the quantity of metal, to which a fixed denomination is given, upon national and individual property. Such an expedient can neither increase nor diminish the real, or even the relative value, either of the metal or of any other commodity. If 1 oz. of silver be struck into two crowns instead of one, two crowns will be paid wherever one was given before; that is to say, 1 oz. of silver will be given in either case: so that the value of silver will not have varied. But when a sale has been made on credit for a given time, and payment stipulated in crowns, the seller may be liable to receive ½ oz. in each crown, instead of 1 oz. according to the intention of the contracting parties. This transfer of the old denomination to a different portion of metal will, therefore, unjustly benefit the one party, to the injury of the other. For every profit to one individual is a loss to another, unless it arise from actual production, or from greater economy in the charges of production, which is equivalent to actual production.

With regard to the peculiar and inherent value of bullion or of money, it originates, like that of all other commodities, in the uses to which it is applicable, as we have before observed. The degree of that value is greater or less, according as its use is more or less

---

* *Traité Historique, Leblanc :* and, *Essai sur les Monnaies,* by *Dupre de Saint Maur.*

extensive, its employment more or less necessary, and its supply more or less abundant.

Gold and silver, though the most common materials of money, can not act as such while in an uncoined state; they are then not money, but the raw material of money. In the present condition of society, every individual can not turn bullion into coin at his pleasure; and, therefore, coin may be of considerably higher value than bullion of the same standard of weight and quality, if the demand for coin be more urgent than the demand for bullion. But bullion can never be perceptibly higher in value than coin of equal weight and quality; because the latter may be readily converted into the former. The reason why coin so seldom much exceeds bullion in value is, that the avidity of governments, which are monopolists of the business of coinage, to profit by the difference between coin and bullion, has led them into the error of overstocking the market with their manufacture of coin. Thus it is, that coin is never depressed in value below, and rarely much elevated above bullion. Wherefore, the detail of the circumstances, that have hitherto been, or may hereafter be, the occasion of variations in the intrinsic value of gold or silver bullion, will serve at the same time to explain the variations of their value in the peculiar character of money.

It has already been noticed,* that the ten-fold supply of those metals, poured into the market in consequence of the discovery of America, did not effect a corresponding reduction of their value to $\frac{1}{10}$ of what it had before been. For, the demand for them was at the same period greatly enlarged by the contemporaneous increase of commerce, manufacture, and luxury. All the leading states of Europe had before been wholly destitute of industry : the circulation of products, whether as capital or for mere consumption, was very trifling in amount. Industry and productive energy made a sudden and simultaneous effort all over Europe ; and the commodity employed as the material of money, the agent of exchange, could not but come more in demand, upon the greater extent and frequency of mutual dealings. About the same time, the new route to the Eastern ocean, by rounding the Cape of Good Hope, was discovered, and drew abundance of adventurers into that direction; the products of the East obtained a more general consumption; but Europe, having no other products of her own to offer in exchange, was compelled to give the precious metals, of which India absorbed an immense quantity. Nevertheless, the multiplication of products tended to the increase and diffusion of wealth; mere higlers grew up into opulent merchants, and the fishing towns of Holland already reckoned amongst their citizens individuals worth 200,000 dollars. The costly objects, that none but princes could before aspire to possess, became attainable by the commercial classes ; and the increasing taste for plate and expensive furniture created a greater

---

* *Suprà*, book i. chap. 21. sect. 7.

demand for gold and silver to be employed on those objects. Beyond all question, the value of those metals would have prodigiously advanced, had not the mines of America been then opportunely discovered.

Their discovery completely turned the scales. The rapid increase of the use and demand for gold and silver was far more than counterbalanced by the increasing supply, which completely glutted the market. Hence the great reduction of their value, which has been before observed upon, and which would have been far greater still, but for the concurrence of the circumstances just stated, whereby the value of silver, or its price in commodities at large, was checked in its fall, and limited to one-fourth, instead of being depressed in equal ratio with the increased supply, that is to say, to one-tenth.

This counteracting force must have escaped the penetration of Locke, or he would not have said, that the tenfold increase of silver, since the year 1500, necessarily raised the price of commodities in a tenfold degree. The few instances he might have cited in support of his position, were by no means sufficient to establish its accuracy; for a far greater number and variety of products might be mentioned, for which, as well as for silver, the demand compared with the supply had increased in the ratio of $2\frac{1}{2}$ to 1, between 1500 and the date of the work of Locke in question.* But, although this may be true of some particular products, it may not be so of abundance of others, for some of which the demand has not advanced at all since 1500, while the supply of others has kept pace with the progressive demand, and consequently the ratio of their value remained stationary, with the exception of trifling temporary variations arising from causes of a nature wholly distinct; which, by the way, should teach us the necessity, in this science, of submitting insulated facts to the test of reasoning: for fact will not subvert theory, unless the whole of the facts applicable be taken into consideration, as well as the whole of the circumstances, that may vary the nature of those facts; which is hardly possible in any case.

---

* The increased intensity of the demand for silver compared with its supply, consequent upon the discovery of America, is stated at $2\frac{1}{2}$ to 1, because, but for this increase of demand, the tenfold supply would have reduced its value to one-tenth of what it had been previously to that event, and given to 100 oz. the value of 10 oz. only. But 100 oz. were only reduced to one-fourth of their former value, i. e. to the value of 25 oz.; which bears to 10 oz. the ratio of $2\frac{1}{2}$ to 1. This could not have been the case, unless the demand for silver, compared with the supply, had advanced in that proportion. But the supply having increased tenfold in the same interval, if we would find the ratio of the actual increase of the demand for silver, whether for the purposes of circulation, of luxury, or of manufacture, since the first discovery of the American mines, we must multiply $2\frac{1}{2}$ by 10, which will give 25. And probably this estimate will not exceed the truth, although 25 times may seem a prodigious advance. However, it would doubtless have been infinitely less considerable, but for the influx of supply from America; for the excessive dearness of silver would have greatly curtailed the use of it. Silver plate would probably be as rare as gold plate is now; and silver coin would be less abundant, because it would go further, and be of higher value.

The writers of the Encyclopedie have fallen into the same error, in stating,* that a household establishment, wherein the silver plate should not have varied in quantity or quality from the middle of the sixteenth century to the present time, would be but one-tenth as rich in plate now as at the former period. Whereas, its comparative wealth would be reduced to one-fourth only; since, although the increase of supply has depressed that value to $\frac{10}{100}$, the increase of demand, on the other hand, has raised it to $\frac{25}{100}$.†

It is deserving of attention, that the major part of the coin is in constant circulation, in the appropriate sense of the word, as defined above. In this respect it differs from most other commodities; for they are in circulation only so long as they are in the hands of the dealers, and retire from it as soon as transferred to the consumer. Money, even when employed as capital, is never desired as an object of consumption, but merely as one of barter; every act of purchase is an offer of money in barter, and a furtherance of its circulation. The only part withdrawn from circulation is what may be hoarded or concealed, which is always done with a view to its re-appearance.

Gold or silver, in the shape of plate, embroidery, or jewellery, is in circulation only while in quest of, or in readiness for a purchaser; which it ceases to be, when it reaches the possession of the consumer.

The general use of silver amongst all the civilized nations of the world, coupled with its great facility of transport, makes it a commodity of such extensive demand, that none but a very large influx of fresh supply can sensibly affect its value. Thus, when Xenophon, in his essay on the revenues of Athens, urges his countrymen to give more assiduous attention to the working of the mines of Attica, by the suggestion, that silver does not, like other commodities, decline in value with the increase in quantity, he must be understood to say, that it does not perceptibly decline. Indeed, the mines of Attica were too inconsiderable in their product, to influence the value of the stock of that metal then existing in the numerous and flourishing states upon the borders of the Mediterranean Sea, and in Persia and India; between all which and Greece the commercial intercourse was sufficiently active, to keep the value of silver stationary in the Grecian market. The driblet of silver, furnished by Attician metallurgy, was a mere rivulet trickling into an ocean of existing supply. It was impossible for Xenophon to foresee the influx of the American torrent, or to guess at the consequence of its irruption.

If silver were, like corn and other fruits of the earth, an object of human food and sustenance, the enlargement of the sources of its

---

* Art. *Monnaies.*

† If we are to believe Ricardo, the increase of demand has no effect upon value, which is determined solely by the cost of production. He seems not to have perceived, that it is demand that makes productive agency an object of appreciation. A diminution of the demand for silver bullion would throw all those mines out of work, of which the lower scale of price was not adequate to the charges of bringing the product to market.

supply would not have lowered its value; for the strong impulse of the human race, towards the multiplication of their species to a level with the means of subsistence, would have made the demand keep pace with the increase of supply. The tenfold multiplication of corn would be followed by a tenfold increase of the demand for it; inasmuch as it would engender new mouths to consume it; and corn would maintain nearly the same average of relative value to other commodities.

This will explain, why the variations of the value of silver are both slow in operation, and considerable in amount. Their slowness is owing to the universality of the demand, which prevents a moderate variation of supply from being sensibly felt; and their magnitude to the limited uses of the metal, which prevent the increase of demand from keeping pace with a rapid increase of supply.

Silver has utility for the purposes of plate, furniture, and ornament, as well as for those of money; and is the more copiously employed on those objects, in proportion to the degree of national wealth. Its use in the peculiar character of money is proportionate to the quantity of moveable and immoveable objects of property, that there may be to be circulated; wherefore, coin would be more abundantly required in richer than in poorer nations, were not the following circumstances to control this general rule.

1. The superior rapidity of circulation, both of money and commodities in a state of national opulence, which makes a smaller quantity of money requisite, in proportion to the total of commercial dealings. The same sum in a rich country will effect perhaps ten successive operations of exchange in the same space of time, as one in a poor country.* Wherefore, the multiplication of commodities to be circulated is not necessarily attended with a co-extensive increase of the demand for money. The business of circulation is extended; but the agent of circulation becomes more active and efficient.

2. In a state of national opulence, credit is a more frequent substitute for money. In Chap. XXII, of the preceding book, it has been shown how a portion of the national money may be dispensed with by the employment of convertible paper, without any resulting inconvenience.† By this expedient, the use of metal money, and, consequently, the demand for silver for the purposes of money, is considerably diminished. Nor is convertible paper the sole expe-

---

* In a poor country, after a dealer has disposed of his wares, he is sometimes a long while before he can provide himself with the returns he has in view; and, during the interval, the money-proceeds remain idle in his hands. Moreover, in a poor country, the investment of money is always difficult. Savings are slow and gradual, and are seldom turned to profitable account, until after a lapse of many years; so that a great deal of money is always lying by in a state of inaction.

† Ricardo, whom I look upon as the individual in Europe the best acquainted with the subject of money, both in theory and in practice, has shown, in his *Proposal for an economical and secure Currency*, that, when the good government of the state may be safely reckoned upon, paper may be substituted for the whole of a metallic money; and a material possessed of no intrinsic value, by

dient of substitution amongst an industrious and commercial people; every kind of private obligations and covenants, as well as sales on credit, transfers of money-credit, and even mere debtor and creditor accounts current, have an effect precisely analogous.

Thus the necessity, and consequently the demand, for metal money never advances in equal ratio with the progressive multiplication of other products; and it may be truly said, that the richer a nation is, the smaller is the amount of its coin, in comparison with other nations.

Were the quantum of the supply alone to determine the exchangeable value of a commodity, silver would stand to gold in the ratio of 1 to 45; for silver and gold are produced by metallurgy as 45 to 1.* But the demand for silver is greater than for gold; its uses are both far more general and far more various; and thus its relative value is prevented from falling lower than 1 to 15.

A portion of the demand for the precious metals is occasioned by their gradual destruction by use; for, although less subject to decay than most products, they are still perishable in a certain degree; and doubtless the wear, though slow, must be considerable upon the immense quantity of gold and silver in constant use, as well in the character of money, as in the various objects of spoons, forks, goblets, dishes, and jewellery of all sorts. There is likewise a large consumption in plating and gilding. Smith asserts, that the manufacturers of Birmingham alone, in his time, worked up annually, as much as the worth of 50,000*l.* in these ways.† A further allowance

skilful management, be made to supplant a dear and cumbrous one, whose metallic properties are never called into play by the functions of money.

* *Humboldt. Essai Pol. sur la Nouvelle Espagne,* 8vo. tom. iv. p. 222.

† *Wealth of Nations,* book i. c. 11. The manufacturing consumption of Birmingham and other towns has greatly increased since the date of that work.(1)

(1) Mr. Jacobs, in his work on the precious metals, to which we have already had occasion to refer, has shed much light on the consumption, as well as on the production, of gold and silver, both before and since the discovery of the American continent. His twenty-sixth chapter is devoted to an inquiry into the consumption of the precious metals from 1810 to 1830. This chapter abounds with highly instructive and curious details, which it would be here impossible to present, but which furnish the grounds of the following statements, also taken from the same chapter, and which fully demonstrate the great increase in the consumption of gold and silver, in what our author, in this note, calls "the manufacturing consumption," since the date of Dr. Adam Smith's work on the Wealth of Nations, to which he refers.

According, then, to Mr. Jacobs, the annual consumption of the precious metals, from 1810 to 1830, in their application to ornamental and luxurious purposes, he estimates as follows:

In Great Britain,	2,457,221*l.*
France,	1,200,000
Switzerland,	350,000
The rest of Europe,	1,605,490
America,	280,630

Making the whole amount, ... 5,893,341*l.* equal to 28,288,036 dollars.
AMERICAN EDITOR.

must be made for the consumption of embroidery, tissue, book-binding, &c., all which may be set down as finally lost to other purposes. Add to this the buried hoards, the knowledge of which dies with the possessor, and the quantity lost by shipwreck.

If the nations of the world go on increasing their wealth, as most of them certainly have done for the last three centuries, their want of the precious metals will progressively advance, as well in consequence of the gradual wear, which will be greater in proportion to their increasing use, as of the multiplication and increased aggregate value of other commodities, which will create a larger demand for the purposes of transfer and circulation. If the produce of the mines do not keep pace with the increasing demand, the precious metals will rise in value, and less of them be given in exchange for other products in general. If the progress of mining shall keep pace with the advances of human industry, their value will remain stationary, as it seems to have done for the last two centuries; during which the demand and supply have regularly advanced together.*

---

* We are assured by *Humboldt*, that the produce of the mines of Mexico has, in the last 100 years, been increased in the ratio of 110 to 25; also, that such is the abundance of silver ore, in the chain of the Andes, that, reckoning the number of veins either worked superficially, or not worked at all, one would be led to imagine, that Europe has hitherto had a mere sample of their incalculable stores. *Essai Pol. sur la N. Espagne*, 8vo. tom. iv. p. 149.

The very slight and gradual depreciation of gold and silver, effected by their immense and increasing annual supply, is one amongst many proofs of the rapid and general advance of human wealth, whereby the demand is made to keep pace with the supply. Yet I am inclined to think, that their value, after remaining nearly stationary for a century, has within the last thirty years begun again to decline. The *setier* of wheat, Paris measure, which was for a long time, on an average, sold for 4 oz. of silver, has now risen to $4\frac{1}{2}$ oz., and rents are raised upon every renewal of lease. All other things seem to be rising in the like proportion: which indicates, that silver is undergoing a depreciation of relative value. (1)

---

(1) In a former note we referred to the great decline, since the year 1809, in the productiveness of the whole mines, both in this and in the eastern continent, on the authorities which Mr. Jacobs has given, in his learned work on the precious metals. From the same work, we here extract his concluding observations of the twenty-sixth chapter, in relation to the stock of coin now in existence, by which it will appear, that during the twenty years from 1810 to 1830, the diminution of gold and silver coin amounted to nearly one-sixth part of the whole stock.

"We have estimated," says Mr. Jacobs, "the stock of coin in existence at the end of the year 1809 to have been 380 million pounds; and the additions made to it between that period and the year 1829, at the rate of 5,186,800 pounds annually, would make it 103,736,000 pounds.

From the 380,000,000 of coin left in 1809, we deduct for loss
by abrasion, at the rate of 1 part in 400 in each year, which
in the 20 years would amount to 18,095,220*l*., thus leaving
in 1829, ... 361,904,780*l*.
To which may be added the supply from the mines, ... 103,736,000

Thus showing . . . . 465,640,780*l*.

And, if the supply of those metals outrun the progress of general wealth, as it seems to be doing at this moment, they will fall in respect to other commodities at large. Metal-money will thereby be rendered more cumbrous; but the other uses of gold and silver will be more widely diffused.

It would be a long and tedious task to expose all the false reasoning and erroneous views, originating in the perpetual confusion of the different kinds of variation, that it has cost so much time to analyze and distinguish. It is enough to put the reader into a condition himself to discover their fallacy, and estimate the tendency of measures avowedly directed to influence public wealth, by operating upon the scale of value.

CHAPTER V.

OF THE MANNER IN WHICH REVENUE IS DISTRIBUTED AMONGST SOCIETY.

THE causes, which determine the value of things, and which operate in the way described in the preceding chapters, apply without exception to all things possessed of value, however perishable; amongst others, therefore, to the productive service yielded by industry, capital, and land, in a state of productive activity. Those, who have had at their disposal any one of these three sources of

From which must be deducted that converted
into utensils and ornaments, ... 5,612,611
And that transferred into Asia, . . . 2,000,000

7,612,611 annually.
Or in twenty years, ... 152,252,220

This would show the estimated amount at the end of 1829 to be, 313,388,560*l.*
Or less than at the end of 1809, ... 66,611,440*l.*
Or a diminution of nearly one-sixth part in the twenty years."

"During the period we have been considering, and indeed for many years before, the comparative value of gold to silver had scarcely experienced any alteration. According to the view here taken, the amount of gold applied to purposes of luxury had far exceeded that of silver, perhaps in the proportion of four to one; but, on the other hand, the treasure transferred to India and China has consisted chiefly of silver, and much more gold had been brought to Europe from those countries than had been conveyed to them. It has before (twenty-fifth chapter of this inquiry) been attempted to be shown that the durability of gold in coin is in the proportion of four to one greater than that of silver. It has, too, been shown that the recently increased produce of the mines of Russia has consisted chiefly of gold. These circumstances, on which our limits do not admit of enlargement, might be shown to be sufficient to account for the equable rate of value which has been preserved between the two metals during a long period."

AMERICAN EDITOR.

production, are the venders of what we shall here denominate productive agency; and the consumers of its product are the purchasers. Its relative value, like that of every other commodity, rises in direct ratio to the demand, and inverse ratio to the supply.

The wholesale employers of industry, or adventurers, as they have been called, are but a kind of brokers between the venders and the purchasers, who engage a quantum of productive agency upon a particular product, proportionate to the demand for that product.* The farmer, the manufacturer, the merchant, is constantly occupied in comparing the price, which the consumer of a given product will and can give for it, with the necessary charges of its production; if that comparison determine him to produce it, he is the organ of a demand for all the productive agency applicable to this object, and thus furnishes one of the bases of the value of that agency.

On the other hand, the agents of production, animate and inanimate, land, capital, and human labour, are supplied in larger or smaller quantity, according to the action of the various motives, that will be detailed in the succeeding chapters; thus forming the other bases of the value at which their agency is rated.†

Every product, when completed, repays by its value the whole amount of productive agency employed in its completion. A great part of this agency has been paid for before the entire completion of the product, and must have been advanced by somebody: other part has been remunerated on its completion; but the whole is always paid for ultimately out of the value of the product.

By way of exemplifying the mode, in which the value of a product is distributed amongst all that have concurred in its production, let us take a watch, and trace from the commencement, the manner in which its smallest parts have been procured, and in which their value has been paid to every one of the infinite number of concurring producers.

In the first place we find, that the gold, copper, and steel, used in its construction, have been purchased of the miner, who has received in exchange for these products, the wages of labour, interest of capital, and rent paid to the landed proprietor.

The dealers in metal, who buy of the original producer, re-sell to those engaged in watchmaking, and are thus reimbursed their advance, and paid the profits of their business into the bargain.

---

* It has been already seen, that the demand for every product is great, in proportion to the degree of its utility, and to the quantity of other products possessed by others, and capable of being given in exchange. In other words, the utility of an object, and the wealth of the purchasers, jointly determine the extent of the demand.

† In digesting the plan of this work, I hesitated for a long time, whether or no to place the analysis of value before that of production; to explain the nature of the quality produced, before entering upon the investigation of the mode of its production. But it appeared to me, that to make the foundation of value intelligible, it was necessary to have a previous knowledge of wherein the cost of production consists; and for that purpose to have a just and enlarged conception of the agents of production, and of the service they are capable of yielding.

The respective mechanics, who fashion the different parts whereof a watch is composed, sell them to the watchmaker, who, in paying them, refunds the advance of their previous value, together with the interest upon that advance; and pays, besides, the wages of labour hitherto incurred. This very complex operation of payment may be effected by a single sum, equal to the aggregate of those united values.   In the same way, the watchmaker deals with the mechanics that furnish the dial-plate, the glass, &c., and such ornaments as he may think fit to add,—diamonds, enamel, or any thing he pleases.

Last of all, the individual purchaser of the watch for his own use refunds to the watchmaker the whole of his advances, together with interest on each part respectively, and pays him besides, a profit on his personal skill and industry.

We find, then, that the total value of the watch has been shared amongst all its producers, perhaps long before it was finished; and those producers are much more numerous than I have described or than is generally imagined.   Among them, probably, may be found the unconscious purchaser himself, who has bought the watch, and wears it in his fob. For who knows but he may have advanced his own capital to a mining adventurer, or a dealer in metal; or to the director of a large factory; or to an individual who acts himself in none of these capacities, but has underlent to one or more such persons a part of the funds he has borrowed at interest from the identical consumer of the watch?

It has been observed, that it is by no means necessary for a product to be perfected for use, before the majority of its concurring producers can have been reimbursed that portion of value they have contributed to its completion; in a great many cases, these producers have even consumed their equivalent long before the product has arrived at perfection.   Each successive producer makes the advance to his precursor of the then value of the product, including the labour already expended upon it.   His successor in the order of production, reimburses him in turn, with the addition of such value as the product may have received in passing through his hands. Finally, the last producer, who is generally the retail dealer, is compensated by the consumer for the aggregate of all these advances, *plus* the concluding operation performed by himself upon the product.

The whole revenues of the community are distributed in one and the same manner.

That portion of the value produced, which accrues in this manner to the landed proprietor, is called the *profit of land;* which is sometimes transferred to the farmer, in consideration of a fixed *rent.*

The portion assigned to the capitalist, or person making the advances, however minute and for however short a period of time, is called the *profit of capital;* which capital is sometimes lent, and the profit relinquished on condition of a stipulated *interest.*

The portion assigned to the mere mechanic or labourer is called the *profit of labour;* which is sometimes relinquished for certain *wages.**

Thus, each class receives its respective share of the total value produced; and this share composes its revenue. Some classes receive their share piecemeal, and consume as fast as they receive it; and these are the most numerous, for they comprise most of the labouring classes. The land-holder and the capitalist, who do not themselves turn their means to account, receive their revenue periodically, once or twice, or perhaps four times a year, according to the terms of the contract with the transferee. But, in whatever manner a revenue may be derived, it is always analogous in its nature, and must originate in actual value produced. Whatever value an individual receives in satisfaction of his wants, without having either directly or indirectly concurred in production of some kind or other, must be wholly either a gratuitous gift or a spoliation; there is no other alternative.

It is in this way, that the total value of products is distributed amongst the members of the community; I say, the total value, because such part of the whole value produced, as does not go to one of the concurring producers, is received by the rest. The clothier buys wool of the farmer, pays his workmen in every department, and sells the cloth, the result of their united exertion, at a price that reimburses all his advances, and affords himself a profit. He never reckons as profit, or as the revenue of his own industry, any thing more than the net surplus, after deducting all charges and outgoing; but those outgoings are merely an advance of their respective revenues to the previous producers, which are refunded by the gross value of the cloth. The price paid to the farmer for his wool, is the compound of the several revenues of the cultivator, the shepherd, and the landlord. Although the farmer reckons as net produce only the surplus remaining after payment of his landlord and his servants in husbandry, yet to them these payments are items of revenue,— rent to the one, and wages to the other; to the one, the revenue of his land, to the other, the revenue of his industry. The aggregate of all these is defrayed out of the value of the cloth, the whole† of which forms the revenue of some one or other, and is entirely absorbed in that way.

---

* In the above instance of the watch, many of the artisans are themselves the adventurers in respect to their own industry; in which case their receipts are profits, not wages. If the maker exclusively of the chain himself, buys the steel in its rude state, works it up, and sells the chain on his own account, he is the adventurer in respect to this particular part of the manufacture. A flax-spinner buys a few penny-worth of flax, spins it, and converts her thread into money. Part of this money goes to the purchase of more flax; this is her capital; another portion is spent in satisfying her wants; this is the joint profit of her industry and her little capital, and forms her revenue.

† Even that portion of the gross value, which is absorbed in the maintenance or restoration of the vested capital or machinery. If his works need repairs, which are executed by the proper mechanic, the sum expended in them forms the revenue of that mechanic, and is to the clothier a simple advance, which is refunded, like any other, by the value of the product when completed.

Whence it appears, that the term *net* produce applies only to the individual revenue of each separate producer or adventurer in industry; but that the aggregate of individual revenue, the total revenue of the community, is equal to the *gross* produce of its land, capital, and industry. Which entirely subverts the system of the economists of the last century, who considered nothing but the net produce of the land as forming revenue, and therefore concluded that this net produce was all that the community had to consume; instead of admitting the obvious inference, that the whole of what has been created, may also be consumed by mankind.*

If national revenue consisted of the mere excess of value produced above value consumed, this most absurd consequence would be inevitable, namely, that, where a nation consumes in the year the total of its annual product, it will have no revenue whatever. Is a man possessed of an income of 2000 dollars a year, to be said to have no revenue, because he may think proper to spend the whole of it?

The whole amount of profit derived by an individual from his land, capital, and industry, within the year, is called his *annual revenue*. The aggregate of the revenues of all the individuals, whereof a nation consists, is its national revenue.† Its sum is the *gross* value of the national product, *minus* the portion exported; for the relation of one nation, is like that of one individual to another. The profits of an individual are limited to the excess of his income above his expenditure, which expenditure, indeed, forms the revenue of other persons, but, if those persons be foreigners, must be reckoned in the estimate of the revenue of the respective nations they may belong to. Thus, for instance, when a consignment of ribbons is made to Brazil to the amount of 2000 dollars, and the returns received in cotton, in estimating the resulting product to France from this act of dealing, the export made to Brazil in payment of the cotton must be deducted. Supposing the investment of ribbons to procure, say 40 bales of cotton, which, when they reach France, will fetch 2400 dollars, 400 dollars only of that sum will go to the revenue of France, and the residue to that of Brazil.

Did all mankind form but one vast nation or community, it would be equally true in respect to mankind at large, as to the internal product of each insulated nation, that the whole gross value of the product would be revenue. But so long as it shall be necessary to consider the human race as split into distinct communities, taking

---

* Part of the value created is due to natural agency, amongst which that of land is comprised. But, as stated above in Book I., land is treated as a machine or instrument, and its appropriator as the producer that sets it in motion; in like manner as the productive quality of capital is said to be the productive quality of the capitalist to whom it belongs. Mere verbal criticism is of little moment, when once the meaning is explained; it is the correctness of the idea, and not of the expression, that is material.

† The term national revenue, has been sometimes incorrectly applied to the financial receipts of the state. Individuals, indeed, pay their taxes out of their respective revenues; but the sum levied by taxation is not revenue, but rather a tax upon revenue, and sometimes unhappily upon capital too.

each an independent interest, this circumstance must be taken into the account. Wherefore, a nation, whose imports exceed its exports in value, gains in revenue to the extent of the excess; which excess constitutes the profit of its external commerce. A nation that should export to the value of 20,000 dollars, and import to the value of 24,000 dollars wholly in goods, without any money passing on either side, would make a profit of 4000 dollars, in direct contradiction to the theory of the partizans of the balance of trade.*

The voluminous head of perishable products consumed within the year, nay, often at the very moment of production, as in the case of all immaterial products, is nevertheless an item of national revenue. For what are they but so many values produced and consumed in the satisfaction of human wants, which are the sole characteristics of revenue?

The estimation of individual and of national revenue is made in the same way, as that of every collection of values, under whatever varieties of form; as of the estate of a deceased person. Each product is successively valued in money or coin. For instance, the revenues of France are said to amount to 1300 millions of dollars; which by no means implies, that the commerce of France produces a return of that amount in specie. Probably a very small amount of specie, or none at all, may have been imported. All that is meant by the assertion is, that the aggregate annual products of the nation, valued separately and successively in silver coin, make the total value above stated. The only reason of making the estimate in money is, the greater facility acquired by habit of forming an idea of the unchangeable value of a specific amount of money, than of other commodities. Were it not for that facility, it would be quite as well to make the estimate in corn; and to say, that the revenues of France amounted to 1,300,000,000 bushels of wheat, which at one dollar the bushel, would make precisely the same amount.

Money facilitates the circulation from hand to hand of the values composing both revenue and capital; but is itself not an item of annual revenue, not being an annual product, but a product of previous commerce or metallurgy, of a date more or less remote.

The same coin has effected the circulation of the former year, possibly of the former century, and has all the while remained the same in amount; nay, if the value of its material have declined in the interim, the nation will even have lost upon its capital existing under the form of money; just in the same way as a merchant would lose upon the fall of price of the goods in his warehouses.

Thus, although the greater part of revenue, that is to say, of value produced, is momentarily resolved into money, the money, the quantity of silver coin itself, is not what constitutes revence; revenue is value produced, wherewith that quantity of silver coin has

---

* Their profit arises from increase of value effected by the transport upon both the export and the import, by the time they have reached their destination respectively.

been bought; and, as that value assumes the form of money but for
a moment, the same identical pieces of money are made use of many
times in the course of a year, for the purpose of paying or receiving
specific portions of revenue. Indeed, some portions of revenue
never assume the form of money at all. The manufacturer, that
boards his workmen himself, pays part of their wages in food; so
that this far greater portion of the mechanic's revenue is paid,
received, and consumed, without having once taken the shape of
money, even for an instant. In the United States of America, and
in countries similarly circumstanced, it is not uncommon for the
colonist to derive from the produce of his own estate, food, lodging,
and raiment for the whole of his establishment; receiving and consuming his whole revenue in kind, without any intervention of
money whatsoever.

I think I have said enough to warn the reader against confounding the money, into which revenue may be converted, with revenue
itself; and to establish a conviction that the revenue of an individual, or of a nation, is not composed of the money received in lieu
of the products of his or their creation, but is the actual product or
its value, which, by a process of exchange, may undoubtedly arrive
at its destination in the shape of a bag of crown pieces, or in any
other shape whatsoever.

No value, whether received in the shape of money or otherwise,
can form a portion of annual revenue, unless it be the product, or
the price of a product, created within the year: all else is capital,—
is property passing from one hand to another, either in exchange, as
a gift, or by inheritance. For an item of capital, or one of revenue,
may be transferred or paid any how, whether in the shape of personal or real, of moveable or immoveable property, or of money.
But, no matter what shape it assume, revenue differs from capital
essentially in this, that it is the result or product of a pre-existing
source, whether land, capital, or industry.

It has with some been a matter of doubt, whether the same value,
which has already been received by one individual as the profit or
revenue of his land, capital, or industry, can constitute the revenue
of a second. For instance, a man receives 100 crowns in part of
his personal revenue, and lays it out in books; can this item of
revenue, thus converted into books, and in that shape destined to his
consumption, further contribute to form the revenue of the printer,
bookseller, and all the other concurring agents in the production of
the books, and be by them consumed a second time? The difficulty
may be solved thus. The value forming the revenue of the first
individual, derived from his land, capital, or industry, and by him
consumed in the shape of books, was not originally produced in that
form. There has been a double production: 1. Of corn perhaps by
the land and the industry of the farmer, which has been converted
into crown pieces, and paid as rent to the proprietor: 2. Of books by
the capital and industry of the bookseller. The two products have
been subsequently interchanged one for the other, and consumed

each by the producer of the other: having arrived at the particular form adapted to their respective wants.

So likewise of immaterial products. The opinion of the lawyer, the advice of the physician, is the product of their respective talents and knowledge, which are their peculiar productive means. If the merchant have occasion to purchase their assistance, he gives for it a commercial product of his own converted into money. Each of them ultimately consumes his own revenue respectively, transformed into the object best adapted to his peculiar occasions.

CHAPTER VI.

OF WHAT BRANCHES OF PRODUCTION YIELD THE MOST LIBERAL RECOMPENSE TO PRODUCTIVE AGENCY.

The aggregate value of a product, in the way just described, refunds to its different concurring producers the amount of their advances, with the addition in most cases, of a profit, that constitutes their revenue. But the profits of productive agency are not of equal amount in all its branches; some yielding but a very scanty revenue for the land, capital, or industry, embarked in them; while others give an exorbitant return. True it is, that productive agents always endeavour to direct their agency to those employments, in which the profits are the greatest, and thus, by their competition, have as much tendency to lower price, as demand has to raise it; but the effects of competition can not always so nicely proportion the supply to the demand, as in every case to ensure an equal remuneration. Some kinds of labour are scantily supplied, in countries where people are not accustomed to them; and capital is often so sunk in a particular channel of production, that it can never be transferred to any other from that wherein it was originally embarked. Besides, the land may stubbornly resist that kind of cultivation, whose products are in the greatest demand.

One cannot trace the fluctuation of profit on each particular occasion. A wonderful change may be effected by a new invention, a hostile invasion, or a siege. Such partial circumstances may influence or derange the operation of general causes, but can not destroy their general tendency. No dissertation, however voluminous, could be made to embrace every individual circumstance, that by possibility may influence the relative value of objects; but one may specify general causes, and such as have an uniform activity; thereby enabling every one, when the particular occasion may present itself, to estimate the effect produced by the operation of partial and transient circumstances.

It may appear extraordinary at first sight, but will on inquiry be found generally true, that the largest profit is made, not on the dearest commodities or upon those which are least indispensable, but rather on those, which are the most common and least to be dispensed with. In fact the demand for these latter is necessarily permanent; for it is stimulated by actual want, and grows with every increase of the means of production; inasmuch as nothing tends to increase population more, than providing the means of its subsistence. The demand for superfluities, on the contrary, does not expand with the increased power of producing them. An extraordinary run, which, by the way, can never take place but in large towns, may raise the current considerably above the natural price; that is to say, above the actual cost of production; or a change of fashion may again depress it infinitely below that point. Superfluities are, after all, but objects of secondary want even to the rich themselves; and the demand for them is limited to the very small number of persons that can indulge in them. When a casual calamity obliges individuals to reduce their expenditure, when their revenues are curtailed by the ravages of war, by taxation, or by natural scarcity, the first items of retrenchment are always the articles of least necessary consumption. And this may serve, perhaps, to explain, why the productive agency directed to the raising of superfluities, is generally worse paid than that otherwise employed.

I say generally, for it is possible enough that, in a great metropolis, where the demand for luxuries is more urgent than elsewhere, and the dictates of fashion, however absurd, more implicitly obeyed than the eternal laws of nature; where a man will, perhaps, be content to lose his dinner, so he may appear in the evening circle in embroidered ruffles, it is possible, that in such a place the price of the gewgaws may sometimes very liberally reward the labour and capital devoted to their production. But, except in such particular cases, balancing one year's profits with another, and allowing for contingent losses, it has been ascertained, that the adventurers in the production of superfluities make the most scanty profits, and that their workmen are the worst paid. The manufacturers of the finest laces in Normandy and Flanders are a very indigent set of people; and at Lyons, the workers of gold-embroidery are absolutely clothed in rags. Not but that very considerable profits have occasionally been derived from such articles. A hat-maker has been known to make a fortune by a fancy hat; but, taking all the profits made on superfluities, and deducting the value of goods remaining unsold, or, though sold, never paid for, we shall find that this class of products affords, on the whole, the scantiest profit. The most fashionable tradesmen are oftenest in the list of bankrupts.

Commodities of general use are attainable by a greater number of persons, and are in demand with almost every class of society. The chandelier is to be found only in the mansions of the rich; but the meanest cottage is furnished with the convenience of a candlestick:

the demand for candlesticks is, therefore, regular, and always more brisk than that for chandeliers; and, even in the most opulent country, the total value of the candlesticks is far greater than that of the chandeliers.

The articles of human food are unquestionably those of most indispensable use; the demand for them recurs daily; and no occupations are so regular as those which minister to human sustenance. Wherefore, it is they that yield the most certain profit, notwithstanding the effects of brisk competition.* The butchers, bakers, and porkmen, of Paris, are pretty sure to retire with a fortune sooner or later; indeed, I have it from pretty good authority in such matters, that half the houses and real property sold in Paris and the environs, is bought up by tradesmen in those lines.

It is on this account, that individuals and nations, who understand their true interest, unless they have very cogent reasons for acting otherwise, apply themselves in preference to the production of what tradesmen call current articles. Mr. Eden, who, in 1706, negotiated on the part of Great Britain the treaty of commerce concluded by M. de Vergennes, went upon this principle, in stipulating the free import of the common English earthenware into France. " The few dozens of plates we may sell you," said the English agent, " will be a poor set-off against the magnificent services of Sevres porcelain we shall take of you." This appeal to the vanity of the French agent was decisive. But, as soon as the English earthenware was admitted, its lightness, cheapness, convenience and simplicity of form, recommended it to the most moderate establishments; its regular import, in a short time, amounted to many millions, and continued increasing every year until the war. The exportation of Sevres china, was a mere trifle in comparison.

The scale for current articles, besides being more considerable, is likewise more steady. A tradesman is never long in disposing of common linen shirting.

The examples I have selected from the class of manufacture might easily be paralleled in the agricultural and commercial branches. A much larger value is consumed in lettuces than in pine-apples, throughout Europe at large; and the superb shawls of Cachemere are, in France, a very poor object in trade, in comparison with the plain cotton goods of Rouen.

Wherefore, it is a bad speculation for a nation to aim at the export of objects of luxury, and the import of objects of general utility. France supplies Germany with fashions and finery, which very few persons can make use of; and Germany makes the return in tapes

---

* I speak here of the adventurers, masters, or tradesmen; the mere labourer or journeyman benefits only, as it were, by re-action. The farmer, who is an adventurer in agriculture, employed in raising products for human sustenance, lies under disadvantages, that very much curtail his profits. His concerns are too much at the mercy of his landlord, and of the financial exactions of public authority, to say nothing of the vicissitudes of seasons, to be very gainful on the average.

and other merceries, in files, scythes, shovels, tongs, and other hard-ware of common use. But for the wines and oils of France, the annual product of a soil highly favoured by nature, together with a few products of superior execution, France would derive less advantage from Germany than Germany from France. The same may be said of the French trade with the north of Europe. (a)

CHAPTER VII.

OF THE REVENUE OF INDUSTRY.

Section I.

Of the Profits of Industry in general.

THE general motives, which stimulate the demand of products, have been above investigated.* When the demand for any product whatever, is very lively, the productive agency, through whose means alone it is obtainable, is likewise in brisk demand, which necessarily raises its ratio of value: this is true generally, of every kind of productive agency. Industry, capital, and land, all yield, *ceteris paribus*, the largest profits, when the general demand for products is most active, affluence most expanded, profits most widely diffused, and production most vigorous and prolific.

In the preceding chapter, we have seen that the demand for some products is always more steady and active than for others. Whence, we have inferred, that the agency directed to those particular products, receives the most ample remuneration.

Descending in our progress more and more into particular detail,

---

* Book I. c. 15.

(a) The reasoning of this whole chapter is superfluous and inconclusive. Where value is left to find its natural level, one class of productive agency will, in the long run, be equally recompensed with another, presenting an equipoise of facility or difficulty, of repute or disrepute, of enjoyment or suffering, in the general estimation of mankind; this he states fully in the next chapter. If our author means here to say merely, that a large class of productive agency will receive a larger portion of the general product as its recompense or revenue, or that agency in permanent employ will obtain a regular and permanent recompense, he has taken a very circuitous mode of expressing a position, which is, indeed, almost self-evident. The grand division of productive agency is into *corporeal* and *intellectual;* whereof the former is, on the average, the more amply rewarded by the rest of mankind, because the latter, in some measure, rewards itself. Thus, the profits of printing and bookselling are, on the whole, more liberal than those of authorship; because the latter is partly paid in self-gratification, in vanity, or conscious merit. T.

we shall examine in this, and some following chapters, in what cases the profits of industry bear a greater or a less proportion to those of capital and of land, and *vice versâ ;* together with the reasons why certain ways of employing industry, capital, or land, are more profitable than others.

To begin, then, with the comparison of the relative profits of industry, to those of capital and land, we shall find these bear the highest ratio, where abundance of capital creates a demand for a great mass of industrious agency; as it did in Holland before the revolution. Industrious agency was very dearly paid there ; as it still is in countries like the United States of America, where population, and consequently, the human agents of production, spite of their rapid increase, bear no proportion to the demands of an unlimited extent of land, and of the daily accumulation of capital by the prevalence of frugal habits.

In countries thus circumstanced, the condition of man is generally the most comfortable; because those, who live in idleness upon the profits of their capital and land, are better able to live on moderate profits, than those who live upon the profits of their own industry only; the former, besides the resource of living on their capital, can, when they please, add the profits of industry to their other revenue ; but the mere mechanic or labourer can not add at pleasure to the profits of his industry those of capital and land, of which he possesses none.

Proceeding next to compare the profits of different branches of industrious agency one with another, we shall find them greater or less in proportion, 1st, To the degree of danger, trouble, or fatigue, attending them, or to their being more or less agreeable ; 2dly, To the regularity or irregularity of the occupation ; 3dly, To the degree of skill or talent that may be requisite.

Every one of these causes tends to diminish the quantity of labour in circulation in each department, and consequently to vary its natural rate of profit. It is scarcely necessary to cite examples in support of propositions so very evident.

Among the agreeable or disagreeable circumstances attending an occupation, must be reckoned the consideration or contempt which it entails. Some professions are partly paid in honour. Of any given price, the more is paid in this coin, the less may be paid in any other, without deducing the ratio of price. Smith remarks, that the scholar, the poet, and the philosopher, are almost wholly paid in personal consideration.—Whether with reason or from prejudice, this is not entirely the case with the professions of a comic actor, a dancer, and innumerable others; they must, therefore, be paid in money what they are denied in estimation. "It seems absurd at first sight," says Smith, "that we should despise their persons, and yet reward their talents with the most profuse liberality. Whilst we do the one, however, we must of necessity do the other. Should the public opinion or prejudice ever alter with regard to such occupations, their pecuniary recompense would quickly diminish;

More people would apply to them, and the competition would
quickly reduce the price of their labour. ·Such talents, though far
from being common, are by no means so rare as is imagined. Many
people possess them in great perfection, who disdain to make this
use of them; and many more are capable of acquiring them, if any
thing could be honourably made by them."*

In some countries, the functions of national administration are
requited at the same time with high honour and large emolument;
but it is only so, where, instead of being open to free competition,
like other occupations and professions, they are in the disposal of
royal favour. A nation, awake to its true interest, is careful not to
lavish this double recompense upon official mediocrity; but to
husband its pecuniary bounty, where it is prodigal of distinction and
authority.

Every temporary occupation is dearly paid; for the labourer must
be indemnified as well for the time he is employed, as for that
during which he is waiting for employment. A job coachmaster
must charge more for the days he is employed, than may appear
sufficient for his trouble and capital embarked, because the busy
days must pay for the idle ones; any thing else would be ruin to
him. The hire of masquerade dresses is expensive for the same
reason; the receipts of the carnival must pay for the whole year.
Upon a cross road, an innkeeper must charge high for indifferent
entertainment; for he may be some days before the arrival of
another traveller.

However, the proneness of mankind to expect, that, if there be
a single lucky chance, it will be sure to fall to their peculiar lot,
attracts towards particular channels a portion of industry disproportionate to the profit they hold out. 'In a perfectly fair lottery,'
says the author of the Wealth of Nations, 'those who draw prizes
ought to gain all that is lost by those who draw blanks. In a profession, where twenty fail for one that succeeds, that one ought to
gain all that should have been gained by the unsuccessful twenty.'†
Now many occupations are far from being paid according to this
rate. The same author states his belief, that, how extravagant
soever the fees of counsellors at law of celebrity may appear, the
annual gains of all the counsellors of a large town bear but a very
small proportion to their annual expense; so that this profession,
must, in great part, derive its subsistence from some other independent source of revenue.

It is hardly necessary to state, that these several causes of difference in the ratio of profit may act all in the same, or each in an
opposite direction; or that, in the former case, the effect is more
intense; whereas, in the latter, the opposite action of one controls
and neutralizes the other. It would be a waste of time to prove,
that the agreeable circumstances of a profession may balance the
uncertainty of its product: or that a business that does not furnish

* *Wealth of Nations*, book i. c. 10.   † Ibid.

constant occupation, and is moreover attended with danger, must be indemnified by a double increase of salary.

The last, and perhaps the principal cause of inequality in the profits of industry in general is, the degree of skill it may require.

When the skill requisite to any calling, whether of a superior or subordinate character, is attainable only by long and expensive training, that training must every year have involved a certain expense, and the total outlay forms an accumulated capital. In such case, its remuneration includes, over and above the wages of labour, an interest upon the capital advanced in the training, and an interest higher than the ordinary rate; for the capital advanced has been actually sunk, and exists no longer than the life of the individual. It should, therefore, be calculated as an annuity.*

It is for this reason, that all employments of time and talents, which require a liberal education, are better paid than those, which require less education. Education is capital which ought to yield interest, independent of the ordinary profits of industry.

There are facts, it is true, that militate against this principle; but they are capable of explanation. The priesthood is sometimes very ill paid;† yet a religion, founded upon very complicated doctrines, and obscure historical facts, requires in its ministers a long course of study and probation, and such study and probation necessarily call for an advance of capital; it would seem requisite, therefore, for the continued existence of the clerical profession, that the salary of the minister should pay the interest on the capital expended, as well as the wages of his personal trouble, which the profits of the inferior clergy rarely exceed, particularly in Catholic countries. It must, however, be ascertained, whether the public have not themselves advanced this capital in the maintenance and education of clerical students at the public charge; in which case, the public advancing the capital, may find people enough to execute the duties for the mere wages of their labour, or a bare subsistence, especially where there is no family to be provided for.

---

* Nay, even more than annuity interest on the sums spent in the education of the person who receives the salary; strictly speaking, it should be annuity interest upon the total sum devoted to the same class of study, whether it have or have not been made productive in its kind. Thus the aggregate of the fees of a physician ought to replace not only what has been spent in their studies, but, in addition, all the sums expended in the instruction of the students, who may have died during their education, or whose success may not have repaid the care bestowed upon them; for the stock of medical industry in actual existence could never have been reared, without the loss of some part of the outlay devoted to medical instruction. However, there is little use in too minute attention to accuracy in the estimates of political economy, which are frequently found at variance with fact, on account of the influence of moral considerations in the matter of national wealth, an influence that does not admit of mathematical estimation. The forms of algebra are therefore inapplicable to this science, and serve only to introduce unnecessary perplexity. Smith has not once had recourse to them.

† I do not mean to include the superior orders of the clergy, whose benefices are extremely rich and well paid, though upon principles of state policy.

When, besides expensive training, peculiar natural talent is required for a particular branch of industry, the supply is still more limited in proportion to the demand, and must consequently be better paid. A great nation will probably contain but two or three artists capable of painting a superior picture, or modelling a beautiful statue; if such objects, then, be much in demand, those few can charge almost what they please; and, though much of the profit is but the return with interest of capital advanced in the acquisition of their art, yet the profit it brings leaves a very large surplus. (a) A celebrated painter, advocate, or physician, will have spent, of his own or relations' money, six or eight thousand dollars at most, in acquiring the ability from which his gains are derived; the interest of this sum calculated as an annuity, is but 800 dollars; so that, if he make 6000 dollars by his art, there remains an annual sum of 3000 dollars, which is wholly the salary of his skill and industry. If every thing affording revenue is to be set down as property, his fortune at ten years' purchase may be reckoned 50,000 dollars, even supposing him not to have inherited a *sol*.

Section II.

Of the Profits of the Man of Science.

The philosopher, the man who makes it his study to direct the laws of nature to the greatest possible benefit of mankind, receives a very small proportion of the products of that industry, which derives such prodigious advantage from the knowledge, whereof he is at the same time the depository and the promoter. The cause of his disproportionate payment seems to be, that, to speak technically, he throws into circulation, in a moment, an immense stock of his product, which is one that suffers very little by wear; so that it is long before operative industry is obliged to resort to him for a fresh supply.

The scientific acquirements, without which abundance of manufacturing processes could never have been executed, are probably the result of long study, intense reflection, and a course of experiments equally ingenious and delicate, that are the joint occupation of the highest degree of chemical, medical, and mathematical skill. But the knowledge, acquired with so much difficulty, is probably transmissible in a few pages; and, through the channel of public lec-

---

(a) From which, however, is to be deducted the average loss on the general balance of less successful competitors in the same line. It does not appear, that, in England at least, any allowance is to be made for personal consideration, which is seldom attached in a high ratio even to the greatest excellence in the department of pure art. There is no instance of a sculptor or a painter arriving at the honours of the peerage, which have been placed within the reach of successful commercial enterprise. T.

tures, or of the press, is circulated in much greater abundance, than is required for consumption; or, rather, it spreads of itself, and, being imperishable, there is never any necessity to recur to those, from whom it originally emanated.

Thus, according to the natural laws, whereby the price of things is determined, this superior class of knowledge will be very ill paid; that is to say, it will receive a very inadequate portion of the value of the product, to which it has contributed. It is from a sense of this injustice, that every nation, sufficiently enlightened to conceive the immense benefit of scientific pursuits, has endeavoured, by special favours and flattering distinctions, to indemnify the man of science, for the very trifling profit derivable from his professional occupations, and from the exertion of his natural or acquired faculties.

Sometimes a manufacturer discovers a process, calculated either to introduce a new product, to increase the beauty of an old one, or to produce with greater economy; and, by observance of strict secrecy, may make for many years, for his whole life perhaps, or even bequeath to his children, profits exceeding the ordinary ratio of his calling. In this particular case the manufacturer combines two different operations of industry: that of the man of science, whose profit he engrosses himself, and that of the adventurer too. But few such discoveries can long remain secret; which is a fortunate circumstance for the public, because this secrecy keeps the price of the particular product it applies to above, and the number of consumers enabled to enjoy it below, the natural level.*

It is obvious, that I am speaking only of the revenue a man of science derives from his calling. There is nothing to prevent his being at the same time a landed proprietor, capitalist or adventurer, and possessed of other revenue in these different capacities.

SECTION III.

Of the Profits of the Master-agent, or Adventurer, in Industry.

We shall, in this section, consider only that portion of the profits of the master-agent, or adventurer, which may be considered as the recompense of that peculiar character. If a master-manufacturer have a share in the capital embarked in his concern, he must be ranked *pro tanto* in the class of capitalists, and the benefits thence derived be set down as part of the profits of the capital so embarked.†

---

* Such of my readers as may imagine, that the sum of the production of a country is greater, when the scale of price is unnaturally high, are requested to refer to what has been said on the subject, *suprà*, Chap. 3, of this Book.

† Smith is greatly embarrassed by his neglect of the distinction between the profits of superintendency, and those of capital. He confounds them under the general head of profits of stock; and all his sagacity and acuteness have scarcely been sufficient to expound the causes, which influence their fluctuations. *Wealth*

It very seldom happens, that the party engaged in the management of any undertaking, is not at the same time in the receipt of interest upon some capital of his own. The manager of a concern rarely borrows from strangers the whole of the capital employed. If he have but purchased some of the implements with his own capital, or made advances from his own funds, he will then be entitled to one portion of his revenue in quality of manager, and another in that of capitalist. Mankind are so little inclined to sacrifice any particle of their self-interest, that even those, who have never analyzed these respective rights, know well enough how to enforce them to their full extent in practice.

Our present concern is, to distinguish the portion of revenue, which the adventurer receives as adventurer. We shall see by-and-by, what he, or somebody else, derives in the character of capitalist.

It may be remembered, that the occupation of adventurer is comprised in the second class of operations specified as necessary for the setting in motion of every class of industry whatever; that is to say, the application of acquired knowledge to the creation of a product for human consumption.* It will likewise be recollected, that such application is equally necessary in agricultural, manufacturing, and commercial industry; that the labour of the farmer or cultivator on his own account, of the master-manufacturer and of the merchant, all come under this description; they are the adventurers in each department of industry respectively. The nature of the profits of these three classes of men, is what we are now about to consider.

The price of their labour is regulated, like that of all other objects, by the ratio of the supply, or quantity of that labour thrown into circulation, to the demand or desire for it. There are two principal causes operating to limit the supply, which, consequently, maintain at a high rate the price of this superior kind of labour.

It is commonly requisite for the adventurer himself to provide the necessary funds. Not that he must be already rich; for he may work upon borrowed capital; but he must at least be solvent, and have the reputation of intelligence, prudence, probity, and regularity; and must be able, by the nature of his connexions, to procure the loan of capital he may happen himself not to possess. These requisites shut out a great many competitors.

In the second place, this kind of labour requires a combination of moral qualities, that are not often found together. Judgment, perseverance, and a knowledge of the world, as well as of business. He is called upon to estimate, with tolerable accuracy, the importance of the specific product, the probable amount of the demand, and the means of its production: at one time he must employ a great

---

of *Nations*, book i. c. 8. And no wonder he found himself thus perplexed; their value is regulated upon entirely different principles. The profits of labour depend upon the degree of skill, activity, judgment, &c. exerted: those of capital, on the abundance or scarcity of capital, the security of the investment, &c.

* *Vide suprà*, Book I. chap. 6.

number of hands; at another, buy or order the raw material, collect labourers, find consumers, and give at all times a rigid attention to order and economy; in a word, he must possess the art of superintendence and administration. He must have a ready knack of calculation, to compare the charges of production with the probable value of the product when completed and brought to market. In the course of such complex operations, there are abundance of obstacles to be surmounted, of anxieties to be repressed, of misfortunes to be repaired, and of expedients to be devised. Those who are not possessed of a combination of these necessary qualities, are unsuccessful in their undertakings; their concerns soon fall to the ground, and their labour is quickly withdrawn from the stock in circulation; leaving such only, as is successfully, that is to say, skilfully directed. Thus, the requisite capacity and talent limit the number of competitors for the business of adventurers. Nor is this all: there is always a degree of risk attending such undertakings; however well they may be conducted, there is a chance of failure; the adventurer may, without any fault of his own, sink his fortune, and in some measure his character; which is another check to the number of competitors, that also tends to make their agency so much the dearer.

All branches of industry do not require an equal degree of capacity and knowledge. A farmer who adventures in tillage, is not expected to have such extensive knowledge as a merchant, who adventures in trade with distant countries. The farmer may do well enough with a knowledge of the ordinary routine of two or three kinds of cultivation. But the science necessary for conducting a commerce with long returns is of a much higher order. It is necessary to be well versed, not only in the nature and quality of the merchandise in which the adventure is made, but likewise to have some notion of the extent of demand, and of the markets whither it is consigned for sale. For this purpose, the trader must be constantly informed of the price-current of every commodity in different parts of the world. To form a correct estimate of these prices, he must be acquainted with the different national currencies, and their relative value, or, as it is termed, the rate of exchange. He must know the means of transport, its risk and expense, the custom and laws of the people he corresponds with; in addition to all which, he must possess sufficient knowledge of mankind to preserve him from the dangers of misplaced confidence in his agents, correspondents, and connexions. If the science requisite to make a good farmer is more common than that which can make a good merchant, it is not surprising, that the labour of the former is but poorly paid, in comparison with that of the latter.

It is not meant by this to be understood, that commercial industry in every branch, requires a combination of rarer qualifications than agricultural. The retail dealers for the most part pursue the routine of their business quite as mechanically as the generality of farmers; and, in some kinds of cultivation, very uncommon care and sagacity are requisite. It is for the reader to make the application: the business of the teacher is, firmly to establish general principles; whence it will be easy to draw a multitude of inferences, varied and modified by circumstances, which are themselves the consequences of other principles laid down in other parts of the subject. Thus, in astronomy, when we are told, that all the planets describe equal areas in the same space of time, there is an implied reservation of such derangements, as arise from the proximity of other planets, whose attractive powers depend on another law of natural philosophy; and this must be attended to in the examination of the phenomena of each in particular. It is for him, who would apply general laws to particular and isolated cases, to make allowance for the influence of each of those laws or principles, whose existence is already recognised.

In reviewing presently the profit of mere manual labour, we shall see the peculiar advantage, which his character of master gives to the adventurer over the labourer; but it may be useful to observe by the way the other advantages within reach of an intelligent superior. He is the link of communication, as well between the various classes of producers, one with another, as between the producer and the consumer. He directs the business of production, and is the centre of many bearings and relations; he profits by the knowledge and by the ignorance of other people, and by every accidental advantage of production.

Thus, it is this class of producers, which accumulates the largest fortunes, whenever productive exertion is crowned by unusual success.

SECTION IV.

Of the Profits of the Operative Labourer.

Simple, or rude labour may be executed by any man possessed of life and health; wherefore, bare existence is all that is requisite to insure a supply of this description of industry. Consequently, its wages seldom rise in any country much above what is absolutely necessary to subsistence; and the quantum of supply always remains on a level with the demand; nay, often goes beyond it; for the difficulty lies not in acquiring existence, but in supporting it. Whenever the mere circumstance of existence is sufficient for the

---

* By the term labourer, I mean, the person who works on account of a master-agent, or adventurer, in industry ; for such as are masters of their own labour, like the cobbler in his stall, or the itinerant knife-grinder, unite the two characters of adventurer and labourer; their profits being in part governed by the circumstances detailed in the preceding section, and partly by those developed in this. It is necessary also to premise, that the labour spoken of in the present section is that, which requires little or no study or training ; the acquisition of any talent or personal skill entitles the possessor to a further profit, regulated upon the principles explained, *suprà*, sect. 1. of this chapter.

execution of any kind of work, and that work affords the means of supporting existence, the vacuum is speedily filled up.

There is, however, one thing to be observed. Man does not come into the world with the size and strength sufficient.to perform labour even of the rudest kind. He acquires this capability not till the age of fifteen or twenty, more or less, and may be regarded as an item of capital, formed of the growing annual accumulation of the sums spent in rearing him.* By whom, then, is this accumulation effected? In general by the parents of the labourer, by persons of his own calling, or of one akin to it. In this class of life, therefore, the wages are somewhat more than is necessary for bare personal existence; they must be sufficient to maintain the children of the labourer also.

If the wages of the lowest class of labour were insufficient to maintain a family, and bring up children, its supply would never be kept up to the complement; the demand would exceed the supply in circulation; and its wages would increase, until that class were again enabled to bring up children enough to supply the deficiency.

This would happen, if marriage were discouraged amongst the labouring class. A man without wife or children may afford his labour at a much cheaper rate, than one who is a husband and a father. If celibacy were to gain ground amongst the labouring class, that class would not only contribute nothing to recruit its own members, but would prevent others from supplying the deficiency. A temporary fall in the price of manual labour, arising from the cheaper rate, at which single men can afford to work, would soon be followed by a disproportionate rise; because the number of workmen would fall off. Thus, even were it not more to the interest of masters to employ married men, on account of their steadiness, they should do so, though at a greater charge, to avoid the higher price of labour, that must eventually recoil on them.

Every particular line or profession does not, indeed, recruit its own numbers with children nursed among its own members. The new generation is transferred from one class of life to another, and particularly from rural occupations to occupations of a similar cast in the towns; for this reason, that children are cheaper trained in the country: all I mean to say is, that the rudest and lowest class of labour necessarily derives from its product a portion sufficient, not merely for its present maintenance, but likewise for the recruiting of its numerical strength.†

When a country is on the decline, and contains less of the means

---

* A full-grown man is an accumulated capital; the sum spent in rearing him is indeed consumed, but consumed in a reproductive way, calculated to yield the product man.

† The evidence examined before a committee of the House of Commons of England, in 1815, leads to the conclusion, that the high price of food, at that period, had the effect of depressing, rather than elevating the scale of wages. I have myself remarked the similar effect of the scarcities in France, of the years 1811 and 1817. The difficulty of procuring subsistence either forced more

of production, and less of knowledge, activity, and capital, the demand for raw or simple labour diminishes by degrees; wages fall gradually below the rate necessary for recruiting the labouring class; its numbers consequently decrease, and the offspring of the other classes, whose employment diminishes in the same proportion, is degraded to the step immediately below. On the contrary, when prosperity is advancing, the inferior classes not only fill up their own complement with ease, but furnish a surplus and addition to the classes immediately above them: and some, by great good fortune or brilliancy of talent, arrive at a still loftier eminence, and reach even the highest stations in society.

The labour of persons not entirely dependent for subsistence on the fruits of labour can be afforded cheaper, than that of such as are labourers by occupation. Being fed from other sources, their wages are not settled by the price of subsistence. The female spinners in country villages probably do not earn the half of their necessary expenses, small as they are: one is perhaps the mother, another the daughter, sister, aunt, or mother-in-law of a labourer, who would probably support her, if she earned nothing for herself. Were she dependent for subsistence on her own earnings only, she must evidently double her prices, or die of want; in other words, her industry must be paid doubly, or would cease to exist.

The same may be said of most kinds of work performed by females. They are in general but poorly paid, because a large proportion of them are supported by other resources than those of their own industry, and can, therefore, supply the work they are capable of at a cheaper rate, than even the bare satisfaction of their wants. The work of the monastic order is similarly circumstanced. It is fortunate for the actual labourers in those countries where monachism abounds, that it manufactures little else but trumpery; for, if its industry were applied to works of current utility, the necessitous labourers in the same department, having families to support, would be unable to work at so low a rate, and must absolutely perish by want and starvation. The wages of manufacturing, are often higher than those of agricultural labour; but they are liable to the most calamitous oscillation. War or legislative prohibition will sometimes suddenly extinguish the demand for a particular product, and reduce the industry employed upon it to a state of utter destitution. The mere caprice of fashion is often fatal to whole classes. The substitution of shoe ribands for buckles was a severe temporary blow to the population of Sheffield and Birmingham.*

The smallest variations in the price of rude or simple labour have ever been justly considered as serious calamities. In classes of somewhat superior wealth and talents, which are, in fact, a species of personal wealth, a diminution in the rate of profits entails only a

---

labourers into the market, or exacted more exertion from those already engaged; thus occasioning a temporary glut of labour. But the necessary sufferings of the labouring class at the time must inevitably have thinned its ranks.

* Malthus, *Essay on Popul.* ed. 5. b. iii. c. 13.

reduction of expense, or, at most, but trenches, in some measure, upon the capital those classes generally have at their disposal. But to those, whose whole income is a bare subsistence, a fall of wages is an absolute death-warrant, if not to the labourer himself, to part of his family at least.

Wherefore, all governments, pretending to the smallest paternal solicitude for their subjects' welfare, have evinced a readiness to aid the indigent class, whenever any unexpected event has accidentally reduced the wages of common labour below the level of the labourer's subsistence. Yet the benevolent intentions of the government have too often failed in their efficacy, for want of judgment in the choice of a remedy. To render it effective, it is necessary first to explore the cause of depression in the price of labour. If that depression be of a permanent nature, pecuniary and temporary aid is of no possible avail, and merely defers the pressure of the mischief. Of this nature are the discovery of new processes, the introduction of new articles of import, or the emigration of a considerable number of consumers. (a) In such emergencies, a remedy must be sought in the discovery of some new and permanent occupation for the hands thrown out of employ, in the encouragement of new channels of industry, in the setting on foot of distant enterprises, the planting of colonies, &c.

If the depression be not of a permanent nature, if it be the mere result of good or bad crops, the temporary assistance should be limited to the unfortunate sufferers by the oscillation.

Governments or individuals, who attempt indiscriminate beneficence, will have the frequent mortification of finding their bounty unavailing. This may be more convincingly demonstrated by example than by argument.

Suppose in a vine district the quantity of casks to be so abundant, as to make it impossible to use them all. A war, or a statute levelled against the production of wine, may, perhaps, have caused many proprietors of vineyards to adopt a different cultivation of their lands; this is a permanent cause of surplus cooperage in the market. In ignorance of this cause, a general effort is made to assist the labouring coopers, either by purchasing their casks without wanting them, or by making up, in the shape of alms, the loss they have sustained in the diminution of their profits. Useless pur-

---

(a) The second and last of these circumstances are neither of them necessarily, universally, or permanently, followed by the depression of the rate of wages. When a new object of import does not supersede one of either home or foreign production, it must tend to raise the rate of wages, as it can only be procured by enlarged home production. The emigration of consumers, continuing to draw subsistence from the country they desert, leaves in activity an equal mass of human labour, though possibly with some variation of employment. Besides, it may be temporary only, as that of the English to the continent, and of the Irish both to England and to the continent; who possibly might be brought back by an improvement of domestic finances or of domestic security and comfort. T.

chases, or eleemosynary aid, however, can not last forever; and, the moment they cease, the poor coopers will find themselves precisely in the same distressful situation, from which it was attempted to extricate them. All the sacrifices and expense will have been incurred with no advantage, other than that of a little delay in the date of their hopeless sufferings and privations.

Suppose on the contrary, the cause of the superabundance of casks to be but temporary; to be nothing more than the failure of the annual crop. If, instead of affording temporary relief to the working coopers, they be encouraged to remove to other districts, or to enter upon some other branch of industry, it will follow, that the next year, when wine may be abundant, there will be a scarcity of casks to receive it; the price will become exorbitant, and be settled at the suggestion of avarice and speculation; which being unable themselves to manufacture casks, after the means of producing them have been thus destroyed, part of the wine will probably be spoiled for want of casks to hold it. It will require a second shock and derangement of the rate of wages, before the manufacture of the article can be brought again to a level with the demand.

Whence it is evident, that the remedy must be adapted to the particular cause of the mischief; consequently, the cause must be ascertained, before the remedy is devised.

Necessary subsistence, then, may be taken to be the standard of the wages of common raw labour; but this standard is itself extremely fluctuating; for habit has great influence upon the extent of human wants. It is by no means certain, that the labourers of some cantons of France could exist under a total privation of wine. In London, beer is considered indispensable; that beverage is there so much an article of necessity, that beggars ask for money to buy a pot of beer, as commonly as in France for the purchase of a morsel of bread; and this latter object of solicitation, which appears to us so very natural, may seem impertinent to foreigners just arrived from a country, where the poor subsist on potatoes, manioc, or other still coarser diet.

What is necessary subsistence, depends, therefore, partly on the habits of the nation, to which the labourer may happen to belong. In proportion as the value he consumes is small, his ordinary wages may be low, and the product of his labour cheap. If his condition be improved, and his wages raised, either his product becomes dearer to the consumer, or the share of his fellow producers is diminished.

The disadvantages of their position are an effectual barrier against any great extension of the consumption of the labouring classes. Humanity, indeed, would rejoice to see them and their families dressed in clothing suitable to the climate and season; houses in roomy, warm, airy, and healthy habitations, and fed with wholesome and plentiful diet, with perhaps occasional delicacy and variety; but there are very few countries, where wants, apparently so moderate, are not considered far beyond the limits of strict necessity, and therefore not to be gratified by the customary wages of the mere labouring class.

The limit of strict necessity varies, not only according to the more or less comfortable condition of the labourer, and his family, but likewise according to the several items of expense reputed unavoidable in the country he inhabits. Among these is the one we have just adverted to; namely, the rearing of children; there are others less urgent and imperative in their nature, though equally enforced by feeling and natural sentiments; such as the care of the aged, to which unhappily the labouring class are far too inattentive. Nature could entrust the perpetuation of the human species to no impulse less strong, than the vehemence of appetite and desire, and the anxiety of paternal love; but has abandoned the aged, whom she no longer wants, to the slow workings of filial gratitude, or, what is even less to be depended upon, to the providence of their younger years. Did the habitual practice of society imperatively subject every family to the obligation of laying by some provision for age, as it commonly does for infancy, our ideas of necessity would be somewhat enlarged, and the minimum of wages somewhat raised.

It must appear shocking to the eye of philanthropy, that such is not always the case. It is lamentable to think of the little providence of the labouring classes against the season of casual misfortune, infirmity, and sickness, as well as against the certain helplessness of old age. Such considerations afford most powerful reasons for forwarding and encouraging provident associations of the labouring class, for the daily deposit of a trifling saving, as a fund in reserve for that period, when age, or unexpected calamity, shall cut off the resource of their industry.* But such institutions can not be ex-

---

* Saving-banks have succeeded in several districts of England, Holland, and Germany; particularly where the government has been wise enough to withhold its interference. The Insurance Company of Paris has set one on foot, upon the most liberal principles and with the most substantial guarantee. It is to be hoped, that the labouring classes in general will see the wisdom of placing their little savings in such an establishment, in preference to the hazardous investments they have often been decoyed into. There is besides a further national advantage in such a practice, namely, that of augmenting the general mass of productive capital, and consequently extending the demand for human agency. (1)

---

(1) [In the principal cities of the United States, Saving-banks have also been established, and have been attended with so much benefit, that they are now spreading through every part of the Union. To the Friendly or Beneficial Societies there are strong objections, to which the Saving-banks are not liable. The Friendly Societies have, undoubtedly, done some good; but attended with a certain portion of evil. The following extract from a report of the Committee of the Highland Society, places these latter societies in a very proper light.

"During the last century, a number of Friendly Societies have been established by the labourers in different parts of Great Britain, to enable them to make provision against want. The principle of these societies usually is, that the members pay a certain stated sum periodically, from which an allowance is made to them upon sickness or old age, and to their families upon their death. These societies have done much good; but they are attended with some disadvantages. In particular, the frequent meetings of the members occasion the loss

pected to succeed, unless the labourer be taught to consider these means of precaution as a matter of duty and necessity, and hold to the obligation to carry his savings to such places of deposit, as equally indispensable with the payment of his rent or taxes: this new duty would doubtless tend in a slight degree to raise the scale of wages, so as to allow of such frugality, but for that very reason it is desirable. How can such establishments thrive in countries where habit and the interested views of the government conspire to make the labourer spend in the public-house not only what he might lay by, but frequently the very subsistence of his family, in which all his comforts and pleasures should be centred. The vain and costly amusements of the rich are not always justifiable in the eye of reason; but how much more disastrous is the senseless dissipation of the poor! The mirth of the indigent is invariably seasoned with tears; and the orgies of the populace are days of mourning to the philosopher.

Besides the reasons advanced in this and the preceding sections, to explain why the wages of the adventurer, even if he derive no profit as a capitalist, are generally higher than those of the mere labourer, there are others, not so solid or well founded indeed, but such as nevertheless must not be overlooked.

The wages of the labourer are a matter of adjustment and compact between the conflicting interests of master and workman; the latter endeavouring to get as much, the former to give as little, as he possibly can; but in a contest of this kind, there is on the side of the master an advantage, over and above what is given him by the nature of his occupation. The master and the workman are no doubt equally necessary to each other; for one gains nothing but with the other's assistance; the wants of the master are, however, of the two, less urgent and less immediate. There are few masters but what could exist several months or even years, without employing a single labourer; and few labourers that can remain out of work for many weeks, without being reduced to the extremity of distress. And this circumstance must have its weight in striking the bargain for wages between them.

Sismondi, in a late work* published since the appearance of my

___

of much time, and frequently of a good deal of money spent in entertainments. The stated payments must be regularly made; otherwise, after a certain time, the member (necessarily from its being in fact an insurance) loses the benefit of all that he has formerly paid. Nothing more than the stated payments can be made, however easily the member might be able at the moment to add a little to his store. Frequently the value of the chances on which the societies are formed, is ill calculated; in which case either the contributors do not receive an equivalent for their payments, or too large an allowance is given at first, which brings on the bankruptcy of the institution. Frequently the sums are embezzled by artful men, who, by imposing on the inexperience of the members, get themselves elected into offices of trust. The benefit is distant and contingent; each member not having benefit from his contributions in every case, but only in the case of his falling into the situations of distress provided for by the society. And the whole concern is so complicated, that many have hesitation in embarking in it their hard-earned savings."]　　　　　　　　AMERICAN EDITOR.

* *Nouveaux Prin. d'Econ. Pol.* liv. vii. c. 9.

third edition, has suggested some legislative provisions, for the
avowed purpose of bettering the condition of the labouring classes.
He sets out with the position, that the low rate of their wages accrues to the benefit of the adventurers and masters who employ
them; and thence infers, that in the moment of calamity, their claim
for relief is upon the masters, and not upon society at large. Wherefore, he proposes to make it obligatory upon the proprietors and
farmers of land at all times to feed the agricultural, and upon the
manufacturers to provide subsistence for the manufacturing labourer.
On the other hand, to prevent the probable excess of population,
consequent upon the certain prospect of subsistence to themselves
and their families, he would give to their respective masters the
right of preventing or permitting marriage amongst their people.

This scheme, however entitled to favourable consideration by the
motive of humanity in which it originated, seems to me altogether
impracticable. It would be a gross violation of the right of property,
to saddle one class of society with the compulsory maintenance of
another; and it would be a violation still more gross, to give one
set of men a personal control over another; for the freedom of personal action is the most sacred of all the objects of property. The
arbitrary prohibition of marriage to one class is a premium to the
procreation of all the rest. Besides, there is no truth in the position, that the low rate of wages redounds exclusively to the profit
of the master. Their reduction, followed up by the constant action
of competition, is sure to bring about a fall of the price of products;
so that it is the class of consumers, in other words, the whole community, that derives the profit. And if it be so great as to throw
the subsistence of the labourers upon the public at large, the public
is in a great measure indemnified by the reduced prices of the objects
of its consumption.

There are some evils incident to the imperfection of the human
species, and to the constitution of nature; and of this description is
the excess of population above the means of subsistence. On the
whole, this evil is quite as severely felt in a horde of savages, as in
a civilized community. It would be unjust to suppose it a creature
of social institutions, and a mere fallacy to hold out the prospect of
a complete remedy; and, however it may merit the thanks of mankind to study the means of palliation, we must be cautious not to
give a ready ear to expedients that can have no good effect, and
must prove worse than the disease itself. A government ought
doubtless to protect the interests of the labouring classes, as far as it
can do so without deranging the course of human affairs, or cramping the freedom of individual dealings; for those classes are less
advantageously placed than the masters, in the common course of
things; but a wise ruler will studiously avoid all interference
between individuals, lest it superadd the evils of administration to
those of natural position. Thus, he will equally protect the master
and the labourer from the effects of combination. The masters have
the advantage of smaller numbers and easier communication; where-

as, the labourers can scarcely combine, without assuming the air of revolt and disaffection, which the police is ever on the watch to repress.   Nay, the partisans of the exporting system have gone so far as to consider the combinations of the journeymen as injurious to national prosperity, because they tend to raise the price of the commodities destined for export, and thereby to injure their preference in the foreign market, which they look upon as so desirable.   But what must be the character of that policy, which aims at national prosperity through the impoverishment of a large proportion of the home producers, with a view to supply foreigners at a cheaper rate, and give them all the benefit of the national privation and self-denial?

One sometimes meets with masters, who, in their anxiety to justify their avaricious practices by argument, assert roundly, that the labourer would perform less work, if better paid, and that he must be stimulated by the impulse of want.   Smith, a writer of no small experience and singular penetration, is of a very different opinion.   Let us take his own words.   " The liberal reward of labour, as it encourages the propagation, so it increases the industry of the common people. The wages of labour are the encouragement of industry, which, like every other human quality, improves in proportion to the encouragement it receives.   A plentiful subsistence increases the bodily strength of the labourer, and the comfortable hope of bettering his condition, and of ending his days perhaps in ease and plenty, animates him to exert that strength to the utmost. Where wages are high, accordingly, we shall always find the workmen more active, diligent, and expeditious, than where they are low; in England, for example, than Scotland; in the neighbourhood of great towns, than in remote country places.   Some workmen, indeed, when they can earn in four days what will maintain them through the week, will be idle the other three.   This, however, is by no means the case with the greater part.   Workmen, on the contrary, when they are liberally paid by the piece, are very apt to overwork themselves, and to ruin their health and constitution in a few years."*

Section V.

Of the Independence accruing to the Moderns from the Advancement of Industry.

The maxims of political economy are immutable; ere yet observed or discovered, they were operating in the way above described; the same cause regularly producing the same effect; the wealth of Tyre and of Amsterdam originated in a common source.   It is society that has been subject to change, in the progressive advancement of industry.

---

* Wealth of Nations, book i. c. 8.

The ancients were not nearly so far behind the moderns in agriculture, as in the mechanical arts. Wherefore, since agricultural products are alone (1) essential to the multiplication of mankind, the unoccupied surplus of human labour was larger than in modern days. Those, who happened to have little or no land, unable to subsist upon the product of their own industry, unprovided with capital, and too proud to engage in those subordinate employments, which were commonly filled by slaves, had no resource but to borrow, without a prospect of the ability to repay, and were continually demanding that equal division of property, which was utterly impracticable. With a view to stifle their discontents, the leading men of the state were obliged to engage them in warlike enterprises, and, in the intervals of peace, to subsist them on the spoils of the enemy, or on their own private means. This was the grand source of the civil disorder and discord, which continually distracted the states of antiquity; of the frequency of their wars, of the corruption of their suffrages, and of the connexion of patron and client, which backed the ambition of a Marius and a Sylla, a Pompey and a Cæsar, an Antony and an Octavius, and which finally reduced the whole Roman people to the condition of servile attendants upon the court of a Caligula, a Heliogabalus, or some monster of equal enormity, whose grand condition of empire was the subsistence of the objects of his atrocious tyranny.

The industrious cities of Tyre, Corinth, and Carthage, were somewhat differently circumstanced; but they could not permanently resist the hostility of poorer and more warlike nations, impelled by the prospect of plunder. Industry and civilization were the continual prey of barbarism and penury; and Rome herself at length yielded to the attack of Gothic and Vandalic conquerors.

Thus re-plunged into a state of barbarism, the condition of Europe, during the middle ages, was but a revival of the earliest scenes of Grecian and Italian history, in an aggravated form. Each baron or great landholder, was surrounded by a circle of vassals or clients on his domain, ready to follow him in civil broils or foreign warfare.

---

(1) The "multiplication of mankind" is not, as is here asserted by our author, *alone* dependent upon "agricultural products;" but, likewise, upon every other description of commodities essential to human maintenance and support. Food, or subsistence, is unquestionably indispensable to the existence of man; but not more necessary to his prolonged being and health, than raiment, shelter, and fire. The position of Mr. Malthus, which limits population to subsistence only, and which is here taken for granted and adopted by our author, is not accurate or just; and by the more recent political economical inquirers has, therefore, either been modified or abandoned. Professor Senior, in his "Two Lectures on Population, delivered before the University of Oxford in Easter Term, 1828," in considering the general principles, adopts the following proposition, as what appears to him an outline of the laws of population: "That the population of a given district is limited only by moral or physical evil, or by the apprehension of a deficiency in the means of obtaining those articles of wealth; or, in other words, those necessaries, decencies and luxuries, which the habits of the individuals of each class of the inhabitants of that district lead them to require."

AMERICAN EDITOR.

I should trench upon the province of the historian, were I to attempt the delineation of the various causes that have aided the progress of industry since that period; but I may be allowed merely to note, by the way, the great change that has been effected, and the consequence of that change. Industry has become a means of subsistence to the bulk of the population, independent of the caprice of the large proprietors, and without being to them a constant source of alarm: it is nursed and supported by the capital accumulated by its own exertions. The relation of client and vassal has ceased to exist; and the poorest individual is his own master, and dependent upon his personal faculties alone. Nations can support themselves upon their internal resources; and governments derive from their subjects those supplies, which they were wont to dispense as a matter of favour.

The increasing prosperity of manufacture and commerce has raised them in the scale of estimation. The object of war is changed, from the spoliation and destruction of the sources of wealth, to their quiet and exclusive possession. For the last two centuries, where war has not been made to gratify the childish vanity of a nation or a monarch, the bone of contention has always been, either colonial sovereignty, or commercial monopoly. Instead of a contest of hungry barbarians against their wealthy and industrious neighbours, it has been one between civilized nations on either side; wherein the victor has shown the greatest anxiety to preserve the resources of the conquered territory. The invasion of Greece by the Turks, in the fifteenth century, appears to have been the final effort of pure barbarism arrayed against civilization. The present preponderance of industry and civilized habits amongst the general mass of mankind seems to exclude all probability of a recurrence of such calamitous events. Indeed, the improvement of military science takes away all fear of the result of such a conflict.

There is yet one step more to be made; and that can only be rendered practicable by the wider diffusion of the principles of political economy. They will some day have taught mankind that the sacrifice of their lives, in a contest for the acquisition or retention of colonial dominion or commercial monopoly, is a vain pursuit of a costly and delusive good; that external products, even those of the colonial dependencies of a nation, are only procurable with the products of domestic growth: that internal production is, therefore, the proper object of solicitude, and is best to be promoted by political tranquillity, moderate and equal laws, and facility of intercourse. The fate of nations will thenceforth hang no longer upon the precarious tenure of political pre-eminence, but upon the relative degree of information and intelligence. Public functionaries will grow more and more dependent upon the productive classes, to whom they must look for supplies; the people, retaining the right of taxation in their own hands, will always be well governed; and the struggles of power against the current of improvement will end in its own subversion; for it will vainly strive against the dispensations of nature.

CHAPTER VIII.

OF THE REVENUE OF CAPITAL.

The service, rendered by capital, in productive operations, establishes a demand for capital to be so employed, and enables the proprietors of it to charge more or less for that service.

Whether the capitalist thus employ his capital himself, or lend it to another for that purpose, it yields a profit, that is called the *profit of capital*, distinct from that of the industry employing it. In the former case, the profit obtained constitutes the *revenue* of his capital, which is added to that of his personal talent and industry, and often confounded with it.—In the latter, the revenue of capital is precisely the *interest* paid for its use, the proprietor abandoning to the borrower the profit derivable from his personal employment of the capital lent.

As the investigation of the interest of capital lent will help to throw light on the subject of the profit derivable from its personal employment, it may be as well, in the first instance, to acquire a just idea of the nature and variation of interest.

Section I.

Of Loans at Interest.

The interest of capital lent, improperly called the interest of money, was formerly denominated usury, that is to say, rent for its use and enjoyment; which, indeed, was the correct term; for interest is nothing more than the price, or rent, paid for the enjoyment of an object of value. But the word has acquired an odious meaning, and now presents to the mind the idea of illegal, exorbitant interest only, a milder but less expressive term having been substituted by common usage.

Before the functions and utility of capital were known, it is probable, that the demand of rent for it by lenders was considered an abuse and oppression,—an expedient to favour the rich and prejudice the poor; nay, further, that frugality, the sole means of amassing capital, was regarded as parsimony, and deemed a public mischief by the populace, in whose eyes the sums not spent by great proprietors were looked upon as lost to themselves. They could not comprehend, that money, laid by to be turned to account in some beneficial employment, must be equally spent; for, if it were buried, it could never be turned to account at all; that it is, in fact, spent in a manner a thousand times more profitable to the poor;* and that a

---

* *Vide infrà*, Book III. on the subject of re-productive consumption.

labouring man is never sure of earning a subsistence, except where there is a capital in reserve for him to work upon. This prejudice against rich individuals, who do not spend their whole income, still exists pretty generally; formerly it was universal; lenders themselves were not altogether free from it, but were so much ashamed of the part they were acting, as to employ the most disreputable agents in the collection of profits perfectly just, and highly advantageous to society.

It is, therefore, not surprising that the ecclesiastical, and at several periods, the civil codes, likewise, should have interdicted loans at interest; and that, during the whole of the middle ages, throughout the larger states of Europe, this traffic should have been reputed infamous, and abandoned to the Jews.—The little manufacturing or commercial industry of those days was kept alive by the scanty capital of the dealers and mechanics themselves: and agricultural industry, which was pursued with somewhat better success, was supported by the advances of the lords and great proprietors, who employed their serfs or retainers on their own account. Loans were contracted for, not with a view of profitably employing the money, but merely to satisfy some urgent want, so that the exactor of interest was profiting by a neighbour's distress; and it may easily be conceived, that a religion, founded on the principle of fraternal love, as the Christian religion is, must disapprove a calculating spirit, that even now is a stranger to generous bosoms, and repugnant to the common maxims of morality.—Montesquieu* attributes the decline of commerce to this proscription of loans at interest; which was undoubtedly one -cause, although, indeed, it was one amongst many.

The progressive advance of industry has taught us to view the loan of capital in a different light. In ordinary cases, it is no longer a resource in the hour of emergency, but an agent, an instrument, which may be turned to the great benefit, as well of society, as of the individual. Henceforward, it will be reckoned no more avaricious or immoral to take interest, than to receive rent for land, or wages for labour; it is an equitable compensation adjusted by mutual convenience; and the contract, fixing the terms between borrower and lender, is of precisely the same nature, as any other contract whatsoever.

In ordinary cases of exchange, however, the transaction is ended as soon as the exchange is completed; whereas, in the case of a loan, there remains to be calculated the risk the lender incurs of never recovering the whole, or at least a part, of his capital. The risk is practically estimated, and indemnified by some addition of interest, in the nature of a premium of insurance. Whenever there happens to be a question about the interest of advances, a careful distinction should be made between these, its two component parts; otherwise, there is always danger of error; and individuals, or even the agents

* *Esprit des Lois*, liv. xxi. c. 20.

of public authority, will be apt to involve themselves in useless and disastrous operations.

Thus, the practice of usury has been uniformly revived, whenever it has been attempted to limit the rate of interest, or abolish it altogether. The severer the penalties, and the more rigid their exaction, the higher the interest of money was sure to rise; and this is what might naturally have been expected; for the greater the risk, the greater premium of insurance did it require to tempt the lender. At Rome, while the republican form of government lasted, the interest of money was enormous, as it was natural to suppose, even if it were not a matter of history. The debtors, who are always the plebeians, were continually threatening their patrician creditors. The laws of Mahomet have prohibited loans at interest; and what is the consequence in the *Mussulman* dominions? Money is lent at interest, but the lender must be indemnified for the use of his capital, and, moreover, for the risk incurred in the contravention of the law. It was the same in Christian countries, so long as loans at interest were illegal: and where the necessity of borrowing enforced the toleration of the practice amongst the Jews, such were the humiliation, oppression, and extortion, to which, on one pretext or another, that nation was exposed on this score, that nothing short of a very heavy rate of interest could indemnify for such repeated loss and mortification. Leters patent of the French king John, bearing date in the year 1360, are now extant, which authorises the Jews to lend on pledges at the rate of four *deniers* per week for every *livre* of twenty *sous*, which is more than eighty-six per cent. per annum; but in the year following, the same monarch, though recorded as one of the most scrupulous performers of his royal word that our annals can boast of, caused the quantity of pure metal contained in the coin to be reduced; so that the lenders no longer received back a value equal to what they had lent.

This explanation will alone suffice to justify the very heavy interest demanded, without at all taking into calculation, that at a period, when loans were negotiated, not to forward industrious enterprises, but to support war, to feed extravagance, and to further the most hazardous projects; at a period when laws were powerless, and lenders unable legally to enforce their claims against their debtors, it required a very ample premium to cover the risk of non-payment. In fact, the premium of insurance absorbed the far greater part of what passed under the name of interest, or usury: and the actual *bona fide* interest, the rent for the use of capital lent, was reduced to a very trifle; for, though capital was scarce, there is reason to suppose, that productive employment was still more so. Of the 86 per cent. interest paid in the reign of king John, perhaps not more than 3 or 4 per cent. was the equivalent for the productive service of the capital advanced; for all productive labour is better paid now, than it was in those days; and even now-a-days the rent of capital can scarcely be reckoned higher than 5 per cent.; the excess is so much premium of insurance for the lender's indemnity.

Thus, the ratio of the premium of insurance, which frequently forms the greater portion of what is called interest, depends on the degree of security presented to the lender; which security consists chiefly in three circumstances :—1. The safety of the mode of employment; 2. The personal ability and character of the borrower, 3. The good government of the country he happens to reside in. We have just seen, how much the hazardous purposes, to which loans were applied in the middle ages, enhanced the premium of insurance necessarily paid to the lender.

It is the same with all perilous investments of capital, with a difference in degree only. The Athenians of old, made a distinction between marine interest, or interest of capital afloat, and land-interest, or interest on shore; the former was rated at 30 per cent. more or less per voyage, whether to the Euxine, or to any port in the Mediterranean.* As two such voyages were accomplished with ease in the year, the annual marine interest may be rated at about 60, while other interest was commonly not more than 12 per cent. Supposing that, of the 12 per cent. one half was assigned to cover the risk of the lender; we shall find, that the mere annual rent or hire of money at Athens, was 6 per cent. only, which I should still think above the mark; yet, supposing it to have been so high, the marine interest allowed 54 per cent. for insurance of the lender's risk. So enormous a premium must be attributed in part to the barbarous habits then prevalent among the nations with whom they traded; for different nations were then much greater strangers to each other, than they are at present, and commercial laws and customs much less respected; and in part to the imperfections of the art of navigation. There was more danger in a voyage from the Piræus to Trapezus, though but three hundred leagues distant, than there is now in one from L'Orient to China, which is a distance of seven thousand. Thus, the improvements of geography and navigation have contributed to lower the rate of interest, and ultimately to reduce the cost price of products. Loans are sometimes contracted not for a productive investment, but for mere barren consumption. Transactions of this kind should always awaken the suspicion of the lender, inasmuch as they engender no means of repayment of either principal or interest. If charged upon a growing revenue, they are, at all events, an anticipation of that revenue; and if charged upon any of the sources of revenue, they afford the means of dissipating the particular source itself. If there be the security neither of revenue nor of its source, they barely place the property of one person at the wanton disposition of another.

Among the circumstances incident to the nature of the employment, which influence the rate of interest, the duration of the loan must not be forgotten; *ceteris paribus*, interest is lower when the lender can withdraw his funds at pleasure, or at least in a very short period; and that both on account of the positive advantage of having capital readily at command, and because there is less dread of a risk,

* *Voyage d'Anacharsis,* tom. iv. p. 371.

which may probably be avoided by timely retreat. The facility of immediate negotiation presented by the transferable bills and notes of modern governments, is one principal cause of the low rate of interest, at which many of these governments are enabled to borrow. (a) This interest, in my opinion, hardly covers the risk of the lender; but he always reckons on the certainty of selling his securities before the moment of catastrophe, should any serious alarm be entertained. The public securities that are not negotiable, bear a much higher interest; such, for instance, as the old personal annuities in France, which the government generally sold at the rate of 10 per cent. a high average for young lives. Wherefore the Genevese acted with excellent judgment, in settling their annuities on thirty lives of well-known public characters. By this means, they made their annuities negotiable, and so contrived to get the rate of interest of securities not negotiable, upon securities that were negotiable.

About the vast influence of personal character and ability in the borrower, in determining the amount of the premium of insurance to the lender, there can be no doubt whatever: they are the basis of what is called *personal credit;* and it is hardly necessary to say, that a person in good credit borrows at a cheaper rate, than another who has none.

Next to approved integrity and probity, what most contributes to the credit of an individual or of a government, is past punctuality in performance of engagements; this is, in fact, the very corner-stone of credit, and one that seldom proves insecure. But why, it may be asked, may not a man who has never yet made default in his payment, fail the very next moment? There is very little probability that he will, especially if his punctuality be of long standing. For, to have been ever punctual in his payments, he must either have always been possessed of value in hand sufficient to meet demands upon him; that is to say, he must have been a man of property over and above his debts, which is the best possible ground of trust; or else he must have managed matters so well, and have speculated with so much judgment and safety, as always to have had his returns arrive before the calls became due; thus evincing a degree of ability and prudence, which afforded an excellent guarantee for his future punctuality. The converse of this is the reason, why a merchant, that has once failed or hesitated in the performance of his engagements, thenceforward loses his credit entirely.

Finally, the good government of the country, where the debtor resides, reduces the risk of the creditor, and consequently, the premium of insurance he is obliged to demand to cover that risk. Hence it is, that the rate of interest rises, whenever the laws and their administration do not insure the performance of engagements.

(a) This is strongly illustrated by the unfunded and the funded debt of Great Britain. The former, in the shape of exchequer and treasury bills, bears a rate of interest considerably lower than the latter in the shape of stock; because the bills are convertible readily at par; whereas, the usual rise and fall of the capital stock is much greater, than the interest upon it for short periods. T.

It is yet more aggravated, when they excite to the violation of them; as when they authorise non-payment, or do not acknowledge the validity of *bona fide* contracts.

The resort to personal restraint against insolvent debtors has been generally considered as injurious to the borrower; but is, on the contrary, much in his favour. Loans are made more willingly, and on better terms, where the rights of the lender are best secured by law. (*a*) Besides, the encouragement to accumulate capital is thereby nlarged; whenever individuals mistrust the mode of investing their savings, there is a strong inducement to every one to consume the whole of his income, and this consideration will, perhaps, help to explain a curious moral phenomenon; namely, that irresistible avidity for excessive enjoyment, which is a common symptom in times of political turbulence and confusion.*

However, while on the subject of the necessity of personal severity towards debtors, I cannot recommend the practice of imprisonment; to confine a debtor is to command him to discharge his debts, and at the same time deprive him of the means of so doing. There seems more reason in the Hindu institution, giving the creditor the option of seizing the person of his insolvent debtor, and confining him at the creditor's own home to compulsory labour, for the creditor's benefit.† But, whatever be the means, whereby the public authority enforces the payment of debts, they must always be ineffective, if law be partially or capriciously administered. The moment a debtor is, or hopes to be, out of his creditor's reach, there is a risk to be run by the creditor, which is of value, and must be indemnified.

After having thus detached from the rate of bare interest all that is paid as premium of insurance to the lender against the risk of total or partial loss of his capital, it remains to consider that part, which is purely and simply interest; that is to say, rent paid for the utility and the use of capital.

Now this portion of the gross sum called interest is larger in pro-

---

* See the description of the Plague at Florence, as given after *Boccaccio* by *Sismondi*, in his admirable *Histoire des Républiques d'Italie.* A similar effect was observed at several of the most dreadful epochs of the French revolution.

† *Raynal, Histoire Philosophique,* tom. i.

(*a*) The personal restraint of the debtor has nowhere been carried to such extreme length as in England. Not only was a debtor at one time liable to imprisonment *pendent lite*, and before the debt was legally established, and that for the smallest sum; but the term of his imprisonment in execution after judgment, was absolutely unlimited. The hardship, in both these particulars, was partially remedied before the erection of our insolvent code; and that code has still further alleviated the condition of the debtor. But the whole system is vitiated, and in a great measure, neutralised, by total neglect of all measures for the prevention of insolvency, *in limine*. The grand expedient is, publicity of property; which, in the first place, gives the creditor the means of estimating beforehand, and with more accuracy, the grounds and fair extent of his debtor's credit; and in the next, enables him, in case of default, to resort to those means, instead of endeavouring to discover or extort them by personal restraint. Thus it is, that one error of policy is sure to engender another. T

portion as the supply of capital available for loans is less; and as the demand of capital for that specific object is greater; and again, that demand is the greater in proportion to the more numerous and more lucrative employments of capital. Consequently, a rise in the rate of interest does not infallibly or universally denote, that capital is growing scarcer; for possibly, it may be a sign, that its uses are multiplied. Smith has remarked this consequence upon the close of the very successful war on the part of England, which terminated with the peace of 1763.* The rate of interest then advanced instead of declining; the important acquisitions of England had opened a new field for her commercial enterprise and speculation; capital was not diminished in quantity, but the demand for it was increased; and the rise of interest, which ensued, though in most cases a sign of impoverishment, was, in this, a consequence of the acquisition of new sources of wealth.

France, in 1812, experienced the opposite effect of a cause directly the reverse. A long and destructive war, which had annihilated almost all external communication; exorbitant taxation; the ruinous system of licenses; the commercial enterprises of the government itself; frequent and arbitrary alterations in the duties on import; confiscation, destruction, vexation; in fine, a system of administration uniformly avaricious and hostile to private interest, had rendered all enterprises of industry difficult, hazardous and ruinous in the extreme. The aggregate capital of the nation was probably on the decline; but the beneficial employment of it became still more rare as well as dangerous; so much so, that interest never fell so low in France as at that period; and, what is in general the sign of extreme prosperity, was then the effect of extreme distress.

These exceptions serve but to confirm the general and eternal law, that the more abundant is the disposable capital, in proportion to the multiplicity of its employments, the lower will the interest of borrowed capital fall. With regard to the supply of disposable capital, that must depend on the quantum of previous savings. On this head, I must refer to what I have before said upon the subject of the formation of capital.†

---

* *Wealth of Nations*, book i. c. 9.

† *Suprà*, Book I. chap. 11. It has been remarked that the rate of interest is usually somewhat lower in towns, than in country places. *Wealth of Nations*, book i. c. 9. The reason is plain. Capital is for the most part in the hands of the wealthy residents of the towns, or at least of persons who resort to them for their business, and carry with them the commodity they deal in, *i. e.* capital, which they do not like to employ at much distance from their own inspection. Towns, and particularly great cities, are the grand markets for capital, perhaps even more than for labour itself; accordingly, labour is there comparatively dearer than capital. In the country, where there is little unemployed capital, the contrary is observable. Thus, usury is more prevalent in country places; it would be less so, if the business of lending were more safe and in better repute. (*a*)

(*a*) These remarks are just in the main; but the advantage of town over country, in this particular, may be reduced to a very trifle, by the ease of internal communication. In England the difference is scarcely perceptible. T.

If it be desired, that capital in search of employment, and industry in search of capital, should both be satisfied in the fullest manner, entire liberty of dealing must be allowed in all matters touching loans at interest. Disposable capital, being thus left to itself, will seldom remain long unemployed; and there is every reason to believe, that as much industry will be called into activity, as the actual state of society will admit.

But it is essential to pay a strict attention to the meaning of the term, *supply of disposable capital;* for this alone can have any influence upon the rate of interest; it is only so much capital, as the owners have both the power and the will to dispose of, that can be said to be in circulation. A capital already vested and engaged in production or otherwise, is no longer in the market, and therefore no longer forms a part of the total circulating capital; its owner is no longer a competitor of other owners in the business of lending, unless the employment be one, from which capital may be easily disengaged and transferred to other objects. Thus, capital lent to a trader, and liable to be withdrawn from his hands at a short notice, and, *à fortiori,* capital employed in the discount of bills of exchange, which is one way of lending among commercial men, is capital, readily disposable and transferable to any other channel of employment, which the owner may judge convenient.

Capital employed by the owner on his own account, in a trade that may be soon wound up, in that of a grocer for instance, stands nearly in the same predicament. The articles he deals in find at all times a ready market, and the capital thus employed may be realized, repaid if lent, re-lent and re-employed in other trades, or applied to any other use. It is always either in actual circulation, or at least on the point of being so. Of all values, the one most immediately disposable is that of money. But capital embarked in the construction of a mill, or other fabric, or even in a movable of small dimensions, is fixed capital, which being no longer available for any other purpose, is withdrawn from the mass of circulating capital, and can no longer yield any other benefit than that of the product wherein it has been vested. Nor should it be lost sight of, that even though the mill or other fabric be sold, its value, as capital, is not by that means restored to circulation; it has merely passed from one proprietor to another. On the other hand, the disposable value, wherewith the buyer has made the purchase, is not thrown out of circulation, having merely passed from his into the seller's hands. The sale neither increases nor diminishes the mass of floating capital in the market. Attention to this circumstance is essential to the forming a correct estimate of the causes, that determine the rate, as well of interest on capital, as likewise of profit accruing from capital employed, which we are about to consider presently.

It has been sometimes supposed, that capital is multiplied by the operation of credit. This error, though frequently recurring in works professing to treat of political economy, can only arise from a total ignorance of the nature and functions of capital. Capital consists of positive value vested in material substance, and not of immaterial products, which are utterly incapable of being accumulated.   And a material product evidently cannot be in more places than one, or be employed by more persons than one, at the same identical moment.   The works, machinery, utensils, provisions, and stock in hand, composing the capital of a manufacturer, may possibly be wholly borrowed; in which case, he will be acting upon a hired capital, and not on one of his own; yet, beyond all question that capital can be made use of by no one else, so long as it remains within his control and management: the lender has parted with the power of otherwise disposing of it for the time.   A hundred others might have equal security and credit to offer; but their applications could not multiply the volume of disposable capital, and could have no other effect than to prevent other capital from remaining idle and out of employ.*

It is not to be expected, that I should here enter upon a computation of the motives of affection, consanguinity, generosity, or gratitude, which may occasionally give rise to the loan of capital, or influence the amount of interest demanded for it.   Every reader must take upon himself to appreciate the influence of moral causes upon the laws of political economy, which alone we profess to expound.

To limit capitalists to the lending at a certain fixed rate only, is to set an arbitrary value on their commodity, to impose a maximum of price upon it, and to exclude, from the mass of floating or circulating capital, all that portion, whose proprietors cannot, or will not, accept of the limited rate of interest.   Laws of this description are so mischievous, that it is well they are so little regarded as they almost always are, the wants of borrowers combining with those of lenders, for the purpose of evading them; which is easily managed, by stipulating for benefits to the lender, not indeed bearing the name of interest, although really the same thing in the end.   The only consequence of such enactments is, to raise the rate of interest, by adding to the risks, to which the lender is exposed, and against which he must be indemnified.   It is somewhat amusing to find that those governments, which have fixed the rate of interest, have

* *Vide suprà*, Book I. chap. 10, 11, on the mode of employing, and on the transformation and accumulation of capital.   What is here said does not militate against the positions laid down in Book I. chap. 22. on the representatives of money.   A bill of exchange, with good names upon it, is only an expedient for borrowing of a third person actual and positive value, in the interim between the negotiation and the maturity of the bill.   Bills and notes, payable on demand, or at sight, whether issued by the government, or by private banking-establishments, are a mere substitution of a cheap paper agent of circulation, in the place of a costly and metallic agent.   The monetary functions of the metal being executed by the paper, the former is set free for other objects; and, inasmuch as it is exchangeable for other commodities or implements of industry, a positive accession is made by the substitution to the natural capital; but no further.   The degree of the accession is limited strictly to the amount of value required for the business of circulation, and dispensed with by this expedient; which amount is a mere trifle, in comparison with the total value of the national capital.

almost invariably themselves set the example of breaking their own laws, by borrowing at higher than legal interest in their own case.

That interest should be fixed by law is highly proper and necessary; but it should be fixed only in cases, where there is no previous agreement about it; as in the case of a legal recovery of a sum with interest. And, in such case, I think the interest fixed by law should be estimated at the lowest rate that is usually paid by individuals; because the lowest rate is that paid by the safest investments. Now, it is quite consistent with justice, that the withholder of capital should restore it even with interest; but that is in the supposition, that it has remained all the while in his possession; which it cannot be supposed to have done, without his having invested it in the way the least hazardous, and consequently without his having drawn from it at least the lowest interest it would have afforded.

But this rate should not be denominated the legal interest, because the rate of interest ought no more to be restricted, or determined by law, than the rate of exchange, or the price of wine, linen, or any other commodity. And this is the proper place to expose a very prevalent error.

Capital, at the moment of lending, commonly assumes the form of money; whence it has been inferred, that abundance of money is the same thing as abundance of capital; and, consequently, that abundance of money is what lowers the rate of interest. Hence the erroneous expressions used by men of business, when they tell us, that money is scarce, or that money is plentiful; which, it must be confessed, are equally just and appropriate, as the very incorrect term, interest of money. The fact is, that abundance or scarcity of money, or of its substitute, whatever it may be, no more affects the rate of interest, than abundance or scarcity of cinnamon, of wheat, or of silk. The article lent is not any commodity in particular, or even money, which is itself but a commodity, like all others; but it is a value accumulated and destined to beneficial investment.

A man, who is about to lend, converts into money the aggregate value he means to devote to that particular purpose; and the borrower no sooner has it at command, than he exchanges it for something else; the money that has effected this operation, forthwith served to effect other similar or dissimilar operations; the payment of a tax perhaps, or the subsidy of an army. The value lent has but for a moment assumed the form of money, in the same manner, as we have traced revenue received and expended, passing through the same temporary form; the identical pieces of money serving perhaps a hundred times in the course of a year, to transfer equivalent portions of income. So, likewise, the same sum of money, that has served to transfer a value from the hands of one lender into those of a borrower, may, after infinite intervening transfers, perform the like office between a second borrower and lender, without stripping the former borrower of any part of the value he has received. In reality, then, it is value which has been borrowed, and not any particular sort of metal or of merchandise. All kinds of merchandise may be lent and borrowed, as well as money; nor does the rate of interest at all depend upon the quality of the object lent or borrowed. Nothing is more common in trade, than to lend and borrow other objects than money. When a manufacturer buys the raw material of his business at a certain credit, he, in fact, borrows the wool, or cotton, as the case may be, making use of the value of those materials in his concern; and their quality has no influence on the interest, with which he credits the seller.* The glut or scarcity of the commodity lent only affects its relative price to other commodities, and has no influence whatever on the rate of interest upon its advance or loan. Thus, when silver money lost three-fourths of its former relative value, although four times as much of it was necessary to pass a loan of the same extent of capital, the rate of interest remained unaltered. The quantity of specie or money in the market, might increase tenfold, without multiplying the quantity of disposable, or circulating capital.†

Wherefore, it is a great abuse of words, to talk of the interest of money; and probably this erroneous expression has led to the false inference, that the abundance or scarcity of money regulates the rate of interest.‡ Law, Montesquieu, nay, even the judicious Locke, in a work expressly treating of the means of lowering the interest of money, have all fallen into this mistake; and it is no wonder that others should have been misled by their authority. The theory of

---

* Many loans on interest are made without bearing that name, and without implying a transfer of money. When a retail dealer supplies his shop by buying of the manufacturer or wholesale dealer, he borrows at interest, and repays, either at a certain term, or before it, retaining the discount, which is but the return of the interest charged him in addition to the price of the goods. When a provincial dealer makes a remittance to a banker at Paris, and afterwards draws upon his banker, he lends to him, during the time that elapses between the arrival of the remittance and the payment of the draft. The interest of this advance is allowed in the interest account which the banker annexes to the merchant's account current. In the *Cours d'Economie Politique*, compiled by *Storch*, for the instruction of the young grand-dukes of Russia, and printed at Petersburgh, tom. vi. p. 103, we are informed, that the English merchants, or factors, settled in Russia, sell to their customers at a credit of twelve months, which enables the Russian purchaser of current articles, to realize long before the day of payment, and turn the proceeds to account in the interim; thereby operating with English capital, never intended to be so employed. It is to be presumed, that the English indemnify themselves for this loss of interest, by the additional price of their goods. But the average rate of profit upon capital in Russia is so high, that even this round-about way of borrowing is sufficiently profitable to the native dealers.

† This is no contradiction to the former position, that the precious metals form part of the capital of society. They form an item of capital, but not of *disposable*, or *lendable* capital; for they are already employed, and not in search of employment;—employed in the business of circulating value from one hand to another. If their supply exceed the demand for this object, they are sent to other parts, where their price continues higher; if their general abundance lower their price everywhere, the sum of their value is not increased, but a larger quantity of them is given in exchange for the same value in other commodities.

‡ If interest were always low in proportion to the greater supply of money, it would be lower in Portugal, Brazil, and the West Indies, than in Germany, Switzerland, &c., which is by no means the case.

interest was wrapped in utter obscurity, until Hume and Smith*
dispelled the vapour.   Nor will it ever be clearly comprehended,
except by such as shall have acquired a correct notion of what has,
throughout this work, been denominated capital, and shall proceed
in the conviction, that the object lent or borrowed, is not a particular
commodity or object of merchandise, but a portion of value,—of the
aggregate value of the capital available for that object; and that the
per centage paid for the use of this portion of capital, at all times
and places, depends on the relative supply and demand of capital to
be lent, and is wholly independent of the specific form or quality
of the commodity, wherein the loan is made, whether it be money,
or any other article whatever.

SECTION II.

Of the Profits of Capital.

We have now sufficiently considered the nature and motive of the
interest paid by the borrower to the lender of capital, and, though
it appears pretty plainly, that this interest is compounded of the rent
of the capital, and of the premium of insurance against the risk of
its partial or total loss, we have also seen enough, to comprehend
the extreme difficulty of severing and distinguishing these two
ingredients.

Let us then proceed, in the next place, to investigate the causes of
the profit derivable from the employment of capital, whether by a
borrower or by the proprietor himself: to which end it will be
necessary, in the outset, to sever it from the profit of the industry,
that turns it to account; and here again we shall meet with the
greatest difficulty, in drawing the line of distinction; though it is
easy to perceive, that these two classes of profit, generally speaking,
are combined in the recompense or portion of the adventurer. Smith,
and most of the English writers on this science, have omitted to
notice this distinction; they comprise under the general head of the
profit of capital, or stock, as they term it, many items, which evidently belong to the head of the profit of industry.†

---

* *Essays* of D. Hume, part ii. ess. 4.   *Wealth of Nations*, book ii. c. 4.   It
is well for the student in political economy, that Locke and *Montesquieu* have
not written more upon it; for the talent and ingenuity of a writer serve only to
perplex a subject he is not thoroughly acquainted with.   To say the truth, a
man of lively wit can not satisfy his own mind without a degree of speciousness
and plausibility, which is of all things the most dangerous to the generality of
readers, who are not sufficiently grounded in principle to discover an error at
first sight.   In those sciences, which consist in mere compilation and classification, as in botany or natural history, one can scarcely read too much; but in
those dependent upon the deduction of general laws from particular facts, the
better course is to read little, and select that little with judgment.

† This omission is justified by Smith, on the following grounds. " Let us
suppose," says he, " that in some particular place, where the common annual

Perhaps an approximation may be made to the accurate appreciation of that part of the aggregate profit, which appertains to the capital, and that, which appertains to the industry employing it, respectively, by comparing the mean ratio of total profit with the mean ratio of the difference of profit in the same line of business, which seems a fair index of the difference of the skill and labour engaged. We will suppose two houses, in the fur trade for example, to work each upon a capital of 100,000 dollars, and to make on the average, an annual profit, the one of 24,000 dollars, the other of 6000 dollars only; a difference of 18,000 dollars fairly referable to the different degree of skill and labour, the mean of which is 9000 dollars; this may be considered as the gains of industry, which, deducted from 15,000 dollars, the mean profit of the trade, will leave 6000 dollars for the profit of the capital embarked in it.

This example I could suggest as a means, rather of distinguishing those items of profit thus mixed up together, than of estimating their respective ratio with any tolerable certainty. But, without any index to the precise line of demarkation between the profits of capital and those of the industry employing it, we may take it for granted, that the former will always be proportionate to the risk of partial or total loss, and to the duration of the employment. In practice, adventurers, having capital at their command, always weigh beforehand the advantages and disadvantages of the different modes of investment, as specified above,* and naturally prefer, *ceteris paribus*, those presenting the smallest risk and the quickest return; so that there is less competition of capital for hazardous and longwinded adventurers; indeed, none whatever is embarked in them, unless they hold out a rate of profit so much above the average rate, as to tempt the capitalist to run the risk. Theory, therefore, leads to the presumption, which is confirmed by the test of experience, that the profit of capital is high, in proportion to the hazard of the adventure, and to the length of its duration.

When a particular employment of capital, the trade with China,

---

profits of a manufacturing stock are 10 per cent., there are two different manufactures, in one of which the coarse materials annually wrought up cost only 700*l.*, while the finer materials in the other cost 7000*l.* If the labour in each cost 300*l.* per annum, the capital employed in the one will amount only to 1000*l.*; whereas that employed in the other will amount to 7300*l.* At the rate of 10 per cent., therefore, the undertaker of the one will expect a yearly profit of 100*l.* only, and that of the other 730*l.*;" and he goes on to infer, "that the profit is in proportion to the capital, and not to the labour and skill of inspection and direction." But the instance put is altogether inconclusive; and it is equally easy to suppose the case of two manufactures, carried on in the same place, and in the same line, each with an equal capital of 1000*l.* the one under the conduct of an active, frugal, and intelligent manager, the other under that of an idle, ignorant, and extravagant one; the former yielding a profit of 150*l.* per annum, the latter one of 50*l.* only. The difference in this case will arise, not from any difference in the respective capitals employed, but from the difference in the skill and industry employing them; which latter qualities will be more productive in the one instance than in the other.

* Book II. chap. 7. sect. 3.

for instance, does not afford a profit proportionate, not only to the time of the detention, but likewise to the danger of loss, and the inconvenience of a long, perhaps a two years' duration of one single operation before the returns come to hand, a proportion of the capital is gradually withdrawn from that channel; the competition slackens, and the profits advance, until they rise high enough to attract fresh capital.*

This will serve also to explain, why the profits, derivable from a new mode of employment, are larger than those of common and ordinary employments, where the production and consumption have been well understood for years. In the former case, competition is deterred by the uncertainty of success; in the latter, allured by the security of the employment.

In short, in this matter, as in all others, where the interests of mankind clash one with another, the ratio is determined by the relative demand and supply for each mode of employment of capital respectively.

It is a maxim with Smith and those of his school, that human labour was the first price,—the original purchase-money, paid for all things. They have omitted to add, that for every object of purchase, there is, moreover, paid, the agency and co-operation of the capital employed in its production. Is not capital itself, they will say, composed of accumulated products,—of accumulated labour? Granted: but the value of capital, like that of land, is distinguishable from the value of its productive agency; the value of a field is quite different from that of its annual rent. When a capital of 1000 dollars is lent, or rather lent on hire, for a year, in consideration of 50 dollars more or less, its agency is transferred for that space of time, and for that consideration; besides the 50 dollars, the lender receives back the whole principal sum of 1000 dollars, which is applicable to the same objects as before. Thus, although the capital be itself a pre-existent product, the annual profit upon it is an entirely new one, and has no reference to the industry, wherein the capital originated.

Wherefore when a product is ultimately completed by the aid of capital, one portion of its value must go to recompense the agency of the capital, as well as another to reward that of the industry, that have concurred in its production. And the portion so applied is wholly distinct from the value of the capital itself, which is returned to the full amount, and emerges in a perfect state from its productive employment. Nor does this profit upon capital represent any part of the industry engaged in its original formation.

From all which it is impossible to avoid drawing this conclusion,

---

* To say nothing of the other motives, that attract industry towards any particular profession or repel it thence, which have been noticed in the preceding chapter. These motives sometimes operate all in the same direction, and then the profits of both industry and capital rise or fall together; when they act in opposite directions, the difference on the profit of capital balances that on the profit of industry; or *vice versâ*.

that the profit of capital, like that of land and the other natural sources, is the equivalent given for a productive service, which though distinct from that of human industry, is nevertheless its efficient ally in the production of wealth.

Of the Employments of Capital most beneficial to Society.

To the capitalist himself, the most advantageous employment of capital is that, which with equal risk yields the largest profit; but what is to him most beneficial, may perhaps not be so to the community at large; for capital has this peculiar faculty, that, besides being productive of a revenue peculiar to itself, it is, moreover, a means, whereby land and industry may generate a revenue likewise. This is an exception to the general principle, that what is the most productive to the individual, is so to the community at large. A capital lent to a foreign country, may very probably produce to the proprietors and the nation, the highest possible rate of interest; but can afford no assistance towards extending the revenue of the national territory, or for the national industry, as it would do, if employed within the pale of the nation.

The portion of capital embarked in domestic agriculture is employed best for the interests of a nation; it enhances the productive power of the land and of the labour of a country. It augments at once the profits of industry and those of real property. Capital employed under intelligent direction, may make barren rocks to bear increase. The Cevennes, the Pyrenees, and the Pays de Vaud, present on every side the view of mountains, once a scene of unvaried sterility, now covered with verdure and enriched by cultivation. Parts of these rocks have been blasted with gunpowder, and the shivered fragments employed in the construction of terraces one above another, supporting a thin stratum of earth carried thither by human labour. In this manner is the barren surface of the rock transformed into shelving platforms, richly furnished with verdure, and teeming with produce and population. The capital originally expended in these laborious improvements might, perhaps, have produced larger profits to the capitalist, if employed in external commerce; but probably the total revenue of the district would have been inferior in amount.

For a similar reason, capital cannot be more beneficially employed, than in strengthening and aiding the productive powers of nature. Well contrived and useful machinery produces more than the interest of its prime cost; and besides affording additional profit to the proprietor, benefits the consumer and the community at large, to the full extent of the saving effected by its means; for every thing saved is so much gain.

The productive employments, that rank next in point of national benefit, are those of manufacture and internal commerce; for the profits of the industry they set in motion are earned at home; whereas, capital embarked in foreign trade benefits the industry and natural resources of all nations indiscriminately.

The employment of capital, that tends least to the national advantage, is the carrying trade between one foreign country and another.

When a nation is possessed of an immense accumulation of capital, it will do well to embark it in all these different channels of industry; for they are all lucrative, and in nearly equal degree to the capitalist, though in very different degrees to the nation at large. What prejudice can arise to the lands of Holland, which are already in a high state of cultivation and management, and want neither clearing nor enclosing, or what injury be sustained by nations possessed of little territory, like the old states of Venice, Genoa, and Hamburg, from the large investments of national capital in the carrying trade? It flowed into that particular channel of employment, merely because there was no other open to it. But that class of trade, and generally all external commerce, is ill adapted to a nation deficient in capital, and having not enough to keep its agriculture and manufacture in activity; and it would be absurd for its government to give premature encouragement to those external branches of industry; for such a measure would but check the employment of capital in the manner best calculated to increase the national revenue. China, though it is the largest empire in the world, and must possess the greatest aggregate revenue, since it maintains the most numerous and dense population, abandons to foreigners almost all its external commerce. Undoubtedly, in her present condition, she would be a gainer by extending her external relations of commerce; but she affords a very striking example of the prosperity attainable without them.

It is very fortunate, that the natural course of things impels capital rather into those channels, which are the most beneficial to the community, than into those, which afford the largest ratio of profit. The investments generally preferred are those that are nearest home; whereof the first and foremost is the improvement of the soil, which is justly considered the most safe and permanent; the next, manufacture and internal commerce; and the last of all, external commerce, the trade of transport, and the commerce with distant nations. The owner of a capital, especially of a moderate one, will embark it rather under his own superintendence, than in distant and remote concerns. He is apt to think his risk too hazardous, when he loses sight of his property for any considerable length of time, when he consigns it to strangers, or can expect only tardy returns, or is exposed to the chances of litigation with fraudulent debtors, who may take advantage of their unsettled habits of life, or of the laws of foreign countries, with which he is himself unacquainted. Nothing, but the bait of exclusive privilege and monopoly-profit, or the violent derangement of internal industry, can induce an European nation, not possessed of a large surplus capital, to engage in the colonial or East India trade. (1)

CHAPTER IX.

OF THE REVENUE OF LAND.

Section I.

*Of the Profit of Landed Property.**

LAND has the faculty of transforming and adapting to the use of mankind an infinity of substances, which, without its intervention,

---

* In the preceding chapter, I have given the interest, precedence of the profit, of capital, because the former helps to render the latter more intelligible. I have here adopted a contrary arrangement, because the consideration of the profit of land elucidates the subject of rent.

---

(1) [The reasoning of this whole section appears to me to be unsound and inconclusive. There is no distinction in point of productiveness, between any of the various employments of capital. There can, in short, be no line drawn between the different productive channels, into which capital may be directed. Whatever occupations tend to supply the wants and increase the comforts and accommodations of life, are, in the strictest sense of the word, equally productive, and nearly in the same proportion augment the national wealth. The capital employed in the carrying-trade between one foreign country and another is as advantageous to the individual and nation to which it belongs, as the capital employed at home. For, as has been already remaked in relation to the profits of industry (vide note page 6) in the absence of all restraints, the profits of all the different employments of capital, will be on an equality or nearly approaching it, inasmuch as any material difference will cause its diversion to a more productive channel, and thus restore the equilibrium. In a word, capital flows into the carrying-trade only because it yields a greater profit than it otherwise would do, did it not take that direction.

Moreover, there is *no* exception to the general principle, that what is most productive to the individual is also so to the community at large. Notwithstanding the contrary assertion of our author, in the foregoing section, a capital lent to, or employed in, a foreign country, if it yield to the proprietors and nation the highest rate of interest, must necessarily afford the national revenue as much, and extend the same assistance to the national industry, as if it were employed within the pale of the nation. If, for example, a capital lent abroad, give employment to foreign industry and natural agents, it is because its productive service, when things, I must again repeat, are left to take their natural course, will yield a larger revenue to its owners. Were not this the case, this capital would not seek employment abroad, but remain at home. The revenue produced by capital employed abroad, if the proprietor does not himself at the same time emigrate there, must be the means of calling into activity, and giving a greater development to the productive faculties of the national industry and land, as this revenue must be consumed, either productively or unproductively at home.]

AMERICAN EDITOR.

would be to them of no service; it yields nutriment and vegetative juices to the grain, the fruits, and vegetables, whereon we subsist; as well as to the forests, whereof we construct our houses, ships, and furniture, and whence we derive fuel to keep us warm. Its agency in the production of all these commodities may be called, the productive service of land. And thence it is, that the profit of the proprietor originates.

He derives a further benefit from the useful substances to be extracted from its entrails; the stone, metal, coal, peat, &c. &c.

Land, as we have above remarked, is not the only natural agent possessing productive properties; but it is the only one, or almost the only one, which man has been able to appropriate, and turn to his own peculiar and exclusive benefit. The water of rivers and of the ocean has the power of giving motion to machinery, affords a means of navigation, and supply of fish; it is, therefore, undoubtedly possessed of productive power. The wind turns our mill; even the heat of the sun co-operates with human industry; but happily no man has yet been able to say, the wind and the sun's rays are mine, and I will be paid for their productive services. I would not be understood to insinuate, that land should be no more the object of property, than the rays of the sun, or blast of the wind. There is an essential difference between these sources of production; the power of the latter is inexhaustible; the benefit derived from them by one man does not hinder another from deriving equal advantage. The sea and the wind can at the same time convey my neighbour's vessel and my own. With land it is otherwise. Capital and industry will be expended upon it in vain, if all are equally privileged to make use of it; and no one will be fool enough to make the outlay, unless assured of reaping the benefit. Nay, paradoxical as it may seem at first sight, it is, nevertheless, perfectly true, that a man, who is himself no share-holder of land, is equally interested in its appropriation with the share-holder himself. The savage tribes of New Zealand, and of the north-western coast of America, where the land is unappropriated, have the greatest difficulty in procuring a precarious subsistence upon fish and game, and are often reduced to devour worms, caterpillars, and the most nauseous vermin:* not unfrequently even to wage war on one another, from absolute want, and to devour their prisoners as food; whereas, in Europe, where the appropriation is complete, the meanest individual, with bodily health, and inclination to work, is sure of shelter, clothing, and subsistence, at the least.

In preceding chapters, we have noticed the profit resulting from industry and capital, embarked in agriculture or other branches of industry. In the present, we are to inquire, wherein consists the peculiar profit of land itself, independent of that accruing from the industry and capital, devoted to its cultivation; and to consider the

---

* Malthus, in his *Essay on Population*, book i. c. 405, has given a detail of some of the revolting extremes, to which savage tribes have been reduced by the want of a regular supply of food.

profit of land in the abstract, and whence it originates, without any inquiry as to who may be the cultivator, whether the proprietor himself, or a tenant under him.

It is the declared opinion of many writers,* that the value of products is never more than the recompense of the human agency or surplus, that can be set apart as the peculiar profit of land, and constitute the rent paid for its use to the proprietor. The tenor of their argument is this: the proprietor of land lying waste or fallow, having also a capital to dispose of, may, at his pleasure, expend it, either in cultivation, or in some other way. If he reckons that the cultivation of his land will yield him as large a return as any other investment, he will give it the preference; and, indeed, it is found by experience, that this mode of investment is preferred, even though somewhat less advantageous than others, as being at all events more safe. Well: and what do they infer from this? Why, that cultivation yields no return whatever, beyond the interest of the capital engaged in it;† and if so, what is there left for the profit

---

* *Destutt de Tracy. Commentaire sur l'Esprit de Lois*, c. 13.　Ricardo (a) *Prin. of Pol. Econ. and Tax.* c. 2.

† According to these writers, even the interest of capital is not given as the recompense of its concurrence in the business of production. I have already exposed the fallacy of this opinion, *suprà*, chap. 8. sect. 2.

(a) This chapter of Ricardo is perhaps the least satisfactory and intelligible of his whole work. It goes upon the principle detailed by Malthus, in his *Essay on Rent;* viz. that the ratio of rent is determined by the difference in the product of land of different qualities, the worst land in cultivation yielding no rent at all.   But there is a great deal of land yielding rent without any cultivation; and, in a country where the whole of the land is appropriated, none is ever cultivated without paying some rent or other.   The downs of Wiltshire yield a rent, without any labour, or capital, being expended upon them; so likewise the forests of Norway; this rent is the natural product of the soil; it is paid for the perception of that natural product, between which, and the desire for it, an artificial difficulty is interposed by human appropriation.   The whole rent is, therefore, referable, not to the quality of the land only, but to the quality jointly with the appropriation; and so it is in all cases.   Wherever a difficulty is thus interposed, rent will be paid upon all land brought into cultivation; for why should the proprietor part with the temporary possession for nothing, any more than the capitalist with his capital?   And the ratio of rent is determined, not altogether by the quality of the soil, but by the intensity—1. Of the desire, or demand for its productive agency; 2. Of the artificial difficulty interposed by nature and human appropriation.   The quality of the soil may vary the intensity of the demand for it beyond all question; for the quality is the productive agency: but the supply of agricultural industry and capital in the market will also vary the proportion of its product, which industry and capital will expect for themselves. Why is rent highest, when a population is condensed on a limited territorial surface? because then the utility of its productive qualities is more strongly felt and desired, in consequence of their intense difficulty and attainment.   And why is rent still further raised by the prohibition of the import of products of external agriculture? because the natural difficulty of obtaining the benefit of the productive agency of foreign land is aggravated, by the artificial difficulty interposed by legislative enactments.   The degree of productive agency, of course, affects the amount of the product; but rent originates in the union of that agency, or utility, with difficulty of attainment, natural and artificial, and is regulated in its ratio by their combined intensity. T.

on the productive powers of the soil? Evidently nothing whatever. I have endeavoured to put the argument in the clearest and most intelligible light; and I have to observe upon it, that it proceeds upon a partial and imperfect view of the matter, and upon a total neglect of the influence of demand in the fixation of value. I will now endeavour to give a more complete view of the subject.

The productive power of the soil has no value, unless where its products are objects of demand. Travellers, who have explored the interior of America, and other desert parts of the globe, make repeated mention of tracts of the richest land, capable of every kind of culture, yet wholly destitute of any useful or valuable products. But no sooner is a colony established in the vicinity, or, by some means or other, a market found where the products of the soil will, in the way of exchange, pay the usual rate of interest upon the requisite advances, than cultivation begins immediately. Up to this point, there is no difference between us. But if any circumstance operate to aggravate the demand beyond this point, the value of agricultural products will exceed, and sometimes very greatly exceed, the ordinary rate of interest upon capital; and this excess it is, which constitutes the profit of land, and enables the actual cultivator, when not himself the proprietor, to pay a rent to the proprietor, after having first retained the full interest upon his own advances, and the full recompense of his own industry.

Land is an agent gratuitously furnished to mankind at large, by whom it is afterwards exclusively appropriated; but its appropriation does not begin to be profitable to the individual, in whose favour it is made, until its products are an object of demand, and until their supply ceases to be co-extensive with the desire for them, as it is with respect to some other natural objects, air, water, &c.

From those products of the soil only, thus raised in value by the demand, can there accrue that profit to the proprietor which has been called the profit of land; and which is paid in all civilized countries, and especially where manufacture and commerce multiply the objects of exchange. It may sometimes happen, that in a particular district of such a country, the rent of land may be very trifling; as in our own district of Sologne, where it is no more than 20 cents an acre; but this is owing to the want of roads, and particularly of water-carriage, which makes the charge of bringing its agricultural produce to market, added to the charge of cultivation, absorb nearly the whole value it will there sell for. In some countries, highly civilized and productive in the extreme, land pays no more than 3 or 4 per cent. upon its price or purchase-money. Yet, this is no proof of the poverty of the soil; it proves only, that it sells dear. A landed estate may yield 24 dollars the acre, and require very little expense of cultivation; as if it be laid down in pasture, for instance; in such case it must owe most of its value to its natural properties; yet, if it have cost the proprietor 800 dollars the acre, it will yield a return of 3 per cent. only. And herein consists the difference between the *profit* and the *rent* of land: profit is high or low, according to the quantum of the product; rent, according to the quantum of the purchase-money or price. An acre of land, yielding a profit of one dollar only, will bring as high a rent as an acre yielding a profit of 50 dollars, if 50 times as much has been paid for the one as for the other.

Whenever land is bought with capital, or capital with land, occasion is given for a comparison of the returns of the one species of property with the returns of the other. It is possible, that an estate, bought with a capital of 100,000 dollars, may produce but 3 or 4000 dollars per annum, whilst the same amount of capital would yield 5 or 6000 dollars. The lower rate of interest, which the proprietor is content to take on a purchase of land, may be attributed, in the first place, to the superior stability of the investment. Capital can seldom be made productive, without undergoing several changes both of form and of place, the risk of which is always more or less alarming to persons unaccustomed to the operations of industry; whereas, on the contrary, landed property produces without any change of either quality or position. The satisfaction and pleasure attached to territorial possession, the consideration, weight, and dignity it communicates, and the titles and privileges with which it is in some countries accompanied, contribute greatly to increase this natural preference.

It is true, that land is more exposed than other property to the burden of public taxation, and to the arbitrary exactions of power, precisely because it can neither be removed nor concealed. A floating capital may take any shape whatever, and be removed at will. It can escape tyranny and civil commotions more readily, than even the person of its proprietor. It is a safer object of property; for it is often impossible to attach it, or to make it specifically responsible for the debts of the proprietor. Moreover, it is much less exposed to litigation than landed property. Yet, it is clear, that all these advantages are more than counterpoised by the superior risk of investment; and, that landed property is still preferred to floating capital; since land is dearer, in proportion to its annual returns.

Whatever may be the exchangeable price of land and capital one to the other, it is proper to observe, that their interchange makes no variation in the supply of productive agency of land and capital respectively in circulation, and disposable for the purpose of production; consequently, that exchangeable price can nowise affect the real and positive profit of land and of capital. When Richard sells his estate to Thomas, the productive service of the land is at the disposal of Thomas instead of Richard; and that of the capital, given in exchange for it, is at the disposal of Richard instead of Thomas.

The only thing, which really varies the amount of productive agency of land in circulation, is the actual amelioration of the soil, by clearing and bringing new land into cultivation, or enlarging the productive power of old land, and thus increasing its product. Savings and accumulations of capital are, in the shape of agricultural improvements, transformed into landed property, and made to participate in all the peculiar advantages and disadvantages attached to it. The same may be said of houses, and generally of all capital invested in a fixed and permanent object; it thenceforth loses the character of capital, and assumes that of landed property.

Whence we may draw this invariable maxim; that the productive agency of land is possessed of value, which value, like value in general, increases in the direct ratio of the demand, and the inverse ratio of the supply; and that, since land differs as much in quality, as in site and position, there is a peculiar demand and supply for each peculiar quality. A demand for so much wine, more or less, whatever it arise from, creates a specific demand for as much productive agency of the soil, as may be requisite for its growth;* and the extent of surface, adapted to the culture of the grape, determines the supply of that productive service. If the soil, capable of growing good wine, be very limited in extent, and the demand for such wine very brisk, the profit of the soil itself will be extravagantly high.

It is worthy of remark, that all land, that yields any profit at all, however trifling the amount, even so little as 20 cents the acre, or even less, may be kept in a state of cultivation: and there have been many instances of its cultivation under such circumstances. Herein it differs from capital and industry. A labourer, if he finds himself settled in a place, where his labour does not yield him what he has reason to expect, can migrate to another. So, likewise, capital quickly flows from a channel, that affords a less, to one that affords a greater return. But land has not the same facilities: it is of necessity immoveable; consequently, out of its gross product, after the deduction in the first instance of all advances of capital, with interest, as well as of the profits of industry, without which there could be no product whatever, there still remains to be deducted the expense of carrying the product to the market, or place of exchange. When these several deductions absorb the whole product of the land, the land itself yields no profit at all, and the proprietor can never succeed in getting a rent from it. Even if he cultivate it himself, he can only gain a profit on his capital and industry, but will receive none whatever from the bare ownership of the land. In Scotland, there are tracts of unproductive land thus cultivated by the proprietors, which it would not answer for any one else to undertake. So, likewise, in the back settlements of the United States, there are tracts of great extent and fertility, whose revenue alone would not maintain the proprietors; yet they are, nevertheless, cultivated with success: but it is by the proprietors themselves, who consume the product at the place of growth, and are obliged to superadd to the profit of the land, which is little or nothing, the further profit of capital and personal industry, which afford a handsome competency.

It is obvious, that land, though in a state of cultivation, yields no profit, when no farmer will pay rent for it, which is a convincing proof that it gives no surplus, after allowing for the profit of the capital and industry requisite for its cultivation.

In the instance just mentioned, the effect is occasioned by the dis-

---

* As well as a demand for the capital and industry requisite for the cultivation.

tance of the market; the expense of transport swallows up the profit, which might otherwise be made of the land.   Other instances might be adduced, in which badness of seasons, war, or taxation, have produced the same effect, and partially or totally absorbed the profit of land, and thus thrown it out of cultivation.*

SECTION II.

Of Rent.

When a farmer takes a lease of land, he pays to the proprietor the profit accruing from its productive agency, and reserves to himself, besides the wages of his own industry the profit upon the capital he embarks in the concern; which capital consists in implements of husbandry, carts, cattle, &c.   He is an adventurer in the business of agricultural industry; and, amongst the means he has to work with, there is one that does not belong to him, and for which he pays rent, *i. e.* the land.

The preceding section was occupied in explaining the source of the profit of land.   Its rent is generally fixed at the highest rate of that profit, and for the following reason.

Agricultural adventure requires, on the average, a smaller capital,(*a*) in proportion, than other classes of industry, reckoning the land itself as no part of the capital of the adventurer.   Wherefore, there is a greater number of persons able, from their pecuniary circumstances, to embark in agricultural, than in any other speculations; consequently, a greater competition of bidders for land upon lease. On the other hand, the quantity of land fit for cultivation is limited in all countries; whereas the quantity of capital and the number of cultivators have no assignable limitation.   Landed proprietors, therefore, at least in those countries which have been long peopled and cultivated, are enabled to enforce a kind of monopoly against the farmers.   The demand for their commodity, land, may go on continually increasing; but the quantity of it can never be extended.

This circumstance is equally applicable to the nation at large, and to each particular province or district.   The number of acres to be rented in each province is incapable of extension; whilst the

---

* This catalogue of adverse circumstances, all bearing more strongly upon the profit of land, than upon that of other sources of revenue, explains the frequent and unavoidable remission of rent to the farmer, and proves the accuracy of M. de Sevigne's judgment, when she writes from the country:—"I wish my son could come here and convince himself of the fallacy of fancying oneself possessed of wealth, when one is only possessed of land." *Lettre* 224.

(*a*) This is not universally true.   In England, where agriculture has attained a high degree of perfection, arable farms require much larger capitals than formerly; and a farmer is commonly a much richer man, than the majority of the tradesmen in his neighbourhood.   T.

number of persons in a condition to rent them has no fixed and absolute limit.

Whenever this is the case, the bargain between the land-holder and the tenant must always be greatly in favour of the former; and, whenever there is any portion of the soil, which yields to the latter more than the interest of his capital and the wages of his industry, a higher bidder will soon offer himself. The liberality of a few proprietors, the distance at which they happen to reside, the ignorance of others, and even of the farmers themselves, and the imprudence of a few more, may sometimes operate to depress the ratio of rent below the maximum of profit; but these are accidental circumstances, which act for a season only, and can never prevent the regular and constant action of natural causes, which must in the end prevail.

Besides this advantage accruing to the land-holder, derived from the very nature of things, he has likewise in general the advantage of possessing, or being able to accumulate greater wealth, and sometimes credit, patronage and influence, into the bargain: but the first advantage is alone sufficient to insure him the sole benefit of any circumstances, that may happen to enhance the profit of land. The opening of a canal or road, the increase of population, wealth, and affluence in the province, always operate to raise his rent. He also benefits by every improvement in the cultivation; for a man can afford to pay dearer for the hire of an instrument, when he knows how to turn it to better account.

When the proprietor himself expends a capital in the improvement of his land, in draining, irrigation, fences, buildings, houses, or other erections, the rent then includes, in addition to the profit of the land, the interest likewise of the capital so expended.*

The farmer may sometimes undertake these expenses of amelioration himself; but he can only calculate on receiving interest on the outlay during the continuance of his lease: at the expiration of which, the benefit must devolve to the land-holder, being wholly incapable of removal: thenceforward the landlord derives the whole profit, without having made any of the advances: for he receives a proportionate increase of rent in consequence. The farmer should, therefore, engage only in those improvements, whose effects will last no longer than his lease; unless the lease be long enough, to allow the profit arising from his improvements to repay the whole outlay, together with the interest. It is in this way, that long leases operate to increase the product of the land; and it is evident the effect will be the greatest, when the land is farmed by the proprietor himself; for he is far less likely, than the farmer, to lose the benefit of such advances; every judicious improvement yields him a permanent profit, and the original outlay is amply repaid, when the land is finally disposed of. The farmer's certainty

---

* The capital, vested in improvements upon land, is sometimes of greater value than the land itself. This is the case with dwelling-houses.

of reaping the advantage till the end of his lease, is equally conducive to the improvement of landed property with the length of leases. On the contrary, such laws and customs, as authorize the cancelling of leases in specified cases, as in case of sale by the proprietor, are highly prejudicial to agriculture; since the farmer will hardly venture to undertake any considerable improvement, if kept in continual fear of seeing an intrusive successor appropriate the recompense of his ingenuity, labour, and capital. In fact, every improvement he should make would but increase the risk of that injustice; for land is far more saleable in good condition than otherwise.

Leases are nowhere more sacredly regarded than in England; and the privilege, enjoyed by leasees to the amount of 40s. (about 10 dollars) and upwards, of voting at Parliamentary elections, has, in some measure, restored the equipoise of power and influence between landlords and tenants, which seldom exists in practice. In no other country do we see tenants so confident of undisturbed possession, as to build upon ground held on lease. Such tenants improve the land, as if it were their own; and their landlords are punctually paid; which is less frequently the case elsewhere.

The land is sometimes cultivated by persons possessed of no capital whatever: the proprietor furnishes himself the requisite capital, as well as the land. They are called in France, *metayers*, and commonly pay to the landlord half the gross product. This arrangement is to be met with only in the infancy of agriculture, and is of all others the least conducive to improvement; for the party who bears the expense of amelioration, whether landlord or tenant, makes the other a gratuitous present of half the interest on his advances. This kind of tendency was more common in the feudal times, than it is at present. The lords were above tilling the land themselves, and their vassals had not the means. The largest incomes were then derived from the land, because the lords were large proprietors; but they bore no proportion to the extent of the land. Nor was this owing to the defect of agricultural skill, so much as to the scarcity of capital devoted to improvements. The lord felt little anxiety to improve his property, and expended, in a way more liberal than productive, an income that he might easily have tripled. He levied war, gave feasts and tournaments, and maintained a numerous retinue. If we look at the then degraded condition of commerce and manufacture, superadded to the insecurity of the agricultural interest, we need go no further for the explanation of the reason, why the bulk of the community was in the extreme of indigence; and why, independently of every political cause, the nation itself was weak and impotent. Five departments would now be able to repel attacks, which overwhelmed all France at that period: but happily for her, the other states of Europe were nowise in a better condition.

CHAPTER X.

OF THE EFFECT OF REVENUE DERIVED BY ONE NATION FROM ANOTHER.

ONE nation cannot take from another the revenues of its industry. A German tailor, establishing himself in France, there makes a profit, in which Germany had no participation. But, if this tailor contrive to amass a little capital, and after the lapse of several years carry it back with him to his native country, he injures France to the same extent as a French capitalist, who should emigrate with the same amount of fortune.* In a political view, the injury to the wealth of the nation is equal in both cases; but in a moral light, it is otherwise; for I reckon that a native Frenchman in quitting his country, robs it of an affectionate attachment, and a spirit of exclusive nationality, which it can never look for in a stranger born.

A nation, receiving a stray child into its bosom again, acquires a real treasure; inasmuch as in him it receives an addition to its population, an accession to the profits of national industry, and an acquisition of capital. It at the same time recovers a lost citizen, and the means for him to subsist upon. If the exile bring back his industry only, at any rate the profits of industry are added to the national stock. It is true, that a source of consumption is likewise superadded; but supposing it to counterbalance the advantage, there is no diminution of revenue, while the moral and political strength of the country is actually augmented. (a)

With regard to the capital lent by one nation to another, the effect upon their respective wealth is precisely analogous to that, resulting from every loan from one individual to another. If France borrow capital from Holland, and devote it to a productive purpose, she will gain the profit of industry and land accruing from the employment of that capital; and she will do so even though she pay interest; in like manner as a merchant or manufacturer borrows for the pur-

---

* If, however, this capital be the fruit of his personal frugality, he robs France of no part of her wealth existing previous to his arrival. Had he continued resident there, the aggregate of the capital of France would have been increased to the full extent of his accumulation; but, in taking the whole away with him, he takes no more than his own earnings, and no value but what is of his own creation; in so doing, he commits no individual, and, therefore, no national wrong.

(a) In the common course of things, such an addition is a national benefit, because it is an accession to the secondary source of production, i. e. industry. But defective human institutions may convert a benefit into a curse; as where a poor-law system gives gratuitous subsistence to a part of the population, capable of labour, but not incited by want. In such case, every additional human being may be a burthen instead of a prize; for he may be one more on the list of idle pensioners. T.

poses of his concern, and gains a residue of profit, even after paying the interest of the loan.

But, if one state borrow from another, not for productive purposes, but for those of mere expenditure, the capital borrowed will then yield no return, and the national revenue be saddled with the interest to the foreign creditor. Such was the condition of France, when she borrowed from the Genoese, the Dutch, and the Genevese, for the support of her wars, or to feed the prodigality of a court. Yet it was better to borrow from strangers than from natives, even for the purpose of dissipation; because, the amount so borrowed was not withdrawn from the national productive capital of France. In either case, the French people would have to pay the interest;* but had they likewise lent the capital, they would have had to pay the interest, and at the same time have lost the benefit, which their industry and land might have derived from its employment and agency.

With regard to such landed property, as may belong to foreigners residing abroad, the revenue arising from it is an item of foreign, and forms no part of the national revenue. But it is to be remembered, that the foreigner cannot have purchased it without a remittance of capital equal in value to the land; which capital is an equally valuable acquisition, particularly if the nation be possessed of improveable land in abundance, but of little capital to set industry in motion. In making his purchase of land, the foreigner exchanges a revenue of capital, which he leaves the nation to profit by, for a revenue of land; which he thenceforth receives: thus bartering interest of money for rent of land. If the national industry be active and skilfully directed, more benefit may be derived from the interest, than was before obtained from the rent; the purchaser, however, acquires a fixed and permanent property, in lieu of one more perishable, transferable, and destructible. Mismanagement may soon annihilate the capital the nation has acquired; but the land remains a permanent possession of the purchaser, and he may sell it and get back the value when he pleases. There is therefore nothing to be apprehended from the purchase of land by foreigners, provided there be wisdom enough, to employ in reproduction the value received in exchange.

The particular form, in which one nation may draw revenue from another, is of no importance whatever. It may be remitted in specie, in bullion, or in any other kind of merchandise: indeed it is of the greatest consequence to leave individuals to take it in the shape that best suits their convenience; for what suits them will infallibly be the best for both nations; in like manner as in the conduct of international trade, the commodity, which individuals export or import in preference, is that which best suits the mutual national interests.

The agents of the English East India Company drew from that

---

* It will be shown in Book III. that the interest is equally lost, whether spent internally or externally.

country, either an annual revenue, or an accumulated fortune, which they returned to England to enjoy and live upon: they took good care not to withdraw these remittances in the shape of gold or silver, because the precious metals were of more relative value in Asia than in Europe; they remitted in the shape of India goods and products, on which a fresh profit was made on arrival in Europe: every million they remitted, swelled, perhaps, to so much as 1,200,000, by the time it reached the place of destination. Thus, Europe gained to the amount of 1,200,000, while India lost only a million. If these despoilers of India*(a) insisted on transmitting this whole sum in specie, they must have robbed Hindostan, perhaps, of 1,500,000, or upwards, for every 1,200,000 that England received. The same sum may, perhaps, have been amassed originally in specie; but it was always remitted in the shape of that commodity, which, for the time being, answered best as an object of transport. As long as exportation of any kind is allowed, and exportation has always been regarded by statesmen with a favourable eye, it is easy to receive in one country, the revenue and capital derived from another. And the remittance cannot be prevented by the government, without the interdiction of all external commerce, which, after all, would leave the resource of smuggling and contraband. In the eyes of political economy, nothing is more absurd, than to see governments prohibit the export of the national specie, as a means of checking the emigration of wealth.†

* Raynal tells us, that, inasmuch as the East India Company derived a revenue from Bengal, to be consumed in Europe, it must infallibly drain it of specie in the end, since the company is the only merchant, and imports no specie itself. But Raynal is mistaken in this. In the first place, private merchants do carry the precious metals to India, because they are of more value there than in Europe; and that very reason also deters the servants of the company, who may have made fortunes in Asia, from remitting them in specie.

And if it were to be suggested, that a fortune, remitted to Europe, is less substantial and more speedily dissipated, when it arrives in the shape of goods, than when in that of specie, this again would be an error. The form, that property happens to assume, does not affect its substantiality; when once transferred to Europe, it may be converted into specie, or land, or what not. It is the amount of values, and not the temporary form they appear under, which, in this colonial connexion, as in that of international trade, is the essential circumstance.

† The complete interception of all export of objects of value would not help them towards the point of intent; because free communication occasions a much greater influx than efflux of wealth. Value, or wealth, is by nature fugitive and independent. Incapable of all restraint, it is sure to vanish from the fetters that are contrived to confine it, and to expand and flourish under the influence of liberty.

(a) This is a harsh word, yet probably justified by the history of the original acquisition. But the scene has now changed; the servants of the sovereign company no longer look to spoliation as a public or private resource, but are content with the liberal remuneration of laborious duties, civil, military, and financial. A slight examination of the connexion between Britain and her Asiatic dependencies will show, how small a balance is remitted to the former in any shape; and it should be remembered that part, even of this, is but the interest of loans raised in England, for the purposes of Indian administration, though not always of a wise or paternal character. T.

CHAPTER XI.

OF THE MODE IN WHICH THE QUANTITY OF THE PRODUCT AFFECTS POPULATION.

SECTION I.

Of Population, as connected with Political Economy.

HAVING, in Book I, investigated the production of the articles necessary to the satisfaction of human wants, and in the present Book, traced their distribution among the different members of the community, let us now further extend our observations to the influence those products exercise upon the number of individuals, of which the community is composed; that is to say, upon population.

In her treatment of all organic bodies, nature seems to neglect the individual, and afford protection only to the species. Natural history presents very curious examples of her extraordinary care to perpetuate the species; but the most powerful means she adopts for that purpose, is the multiplication of germs in such vast profusion, that notwithstanding the immense variety of accidents occurring to prevent their early development, or destroy them in the progress to maturity, there are always left more than sufficient to perpetuate the species. Did not accident, destruction, or failure of the means of development, check the multiplication of organic existence, there is no animal or plant that might not cover the face of the globe in a very few years.

This faculty of infinite increase is common to man, with all other organic bodies; and although his superior intelligence continually enlarges his own means of existence, he must sooner or later arrive at the ultimum.

Animal existence depends upon the gratification of one sole and immediate want, that of food and sustenance; but man is enabled, by the faculty of communication with his species, to barter one product for another, and to regard the value, rather than the nature, of the product. The producer and owner of a piece of furniture of twenty dollars value, may consider himself as possessing as much human food, as may be procurable for that price. And with respect to the relative price of products, it is in all cases determined by the intensity of the desire, the degree of utility in each product for the time being. We may safely take it for granted, that mankind in general will not barter an object of more, for one of less urgent necessity. In a season of agricultural scarcity, a larger quantity of furniture will be given for a smaller quantity of human aliment; but it is invariably true, that whenever barter takes place, the object given on one side is worth that given on the other, and that the one is procurable for the other.*

Trade and barter, as we have seen above, adapt the products to the general nature of the demand. The objects, whether of food or raiment, or of habitation, for which the strongest desire is felt, are of course the most in request; and the wants of each family or individual, are more or less fully satisfied, in proportion to the ability to purchase these objects; which ability depends upon the productive means and exertion of each respectively; in plain terms, upon the revenue of each respectively. Thus, in the end, if we sift this matter to the bottom, we shall find, that families, and nations, which are but aggregations of families, subsist wholly on their own products; and that the amount of product in each case necessarily limits the numbers of those who can subsist upon it.

Such animals as are incapable of providing for future exigencies, after they are engendered, if they do not fall a prey to man, or some of their fellow brutes, perish the moment they experience an imperative want, which they have not the means of gratifying. But man has so many future wants to provide for, that he could not answer the end of his creation, without a certain degree of providence and forethought; and this provident turn can alone preserve the human species from part of the evils it would necessarily endure, if its numbers were to be perpetually reduced by the process of destructive violence.†

Yet notwithstanding the forethought ascribed to man, and the restraints imposed on him by reason, legislation, and social habits, the increase of population is always evidently co-extensive, and even something more than co-extensive, with the means of subsistence. It is a melancholy but an undoubted fact, that, even in the most

---

* Although all products are necessary to the social existence of man, the necessity of food being of all others most urgent and unceasing, and of most frequent recurrence, objects of aliment are justly placed first in the catalogue of the means of human existence. They are not all, however, the produce of the national territorial surface; but are procurable by commerce as well as by internal agriculture; and many countries contain a greater number of inhabitants than could subsist upon the produce of their land. Nay, the importation of another commodity may be equivalent to an importation of an article of food. The export of wines and brandies to the north of Europe is almost equivalent to an export of bread; for wine and brandy, in great measure, supply the place of beer and spirits distilled from grain, and thus allow the grain, which would otherwise be employed in the preparation of beer or spirits, to be reserved for that of bread.

† The practice of infanticide in China proves, that the local prejudices of custom and of religion there counteract the foresight which tends to check the increase of population; and one can not but deplore such prejudices; for the human misery resulting from the destruction is great, in proportion as its object is more fully developed, and more capable of sensation. For this reason it would be still more barbarous and irrational policy to multiply wars, and other means of human destruction, in order to increase the enjoyments of the survivors; because the destructive scourge would affect human beings in a state more perfect, more susceptible of feeling and suffering, and arrived at a period of life when the mature display of his faculties renders man more valuable to himself and to others.

thriving countries, part of the population annually dies of mere want. Not that all who perish from want absolutely die of hunger; though this calamity is of more frequent occurrence than is generally supposed.* I mean only that they have not at command all the necessaries of life, and die for want of some part of those articles of necessity. A sick or disabled person may, perhaps, require nothing more than a little rest, or medical advice, together with, perhaps, some simple remedy, to set him up again; but the requisite rest, or advice, or remedy, is denied, or not afforded. A child may require the attentions of the mother, but the mother may perhaps be taken away to labour, by the imperious calls of necessity; and the child perish through accident, neglect, or disease. It is a fact well established by the researches of all who have turned their attention to statistics, that out of an equal number of children of wealthy and of indigent parents, at least twice as many of the latter die in infancy as of the former. In short, scanty or unwholesome diet, the insufficient change of linen, the want of warm and dry clothing, or of fuel, ruin the health, undermine the constitution, and sooner or later bring multitudes of human beings to an untimely end; and all, that perish in consequence of want beyond their means to supply, may be said to die of want.

Thus, to man, particularly in a forward state of civilization, a variety of products, some of them in the class of what have been denominated immaterial products, are necessaries of existence; these are multiplied in a degree proportionate to the desire for them, respectively, because its intensity causes a proportionate elevation

---

* The *Hospice de Bicetre*, near Paris, contains, on the average, five or six thousand poor. In the scarcity of the year 1795, the governors could not afford them food, either so good or so abundant as usual; and I am assured by the house-steward of the establishment, that at that period almost all the inmates died.

It would appear from the returns given in a tract entitled "*Observations on the Condition of the Labouring Classes,*" by J. Barton, that the average of deaths, in seven distinct manufacturing districts of England, has been proportionate to the dearness, or, in other words, to the scarcity of subsistence. I subjoin an extract from his statements.

Years.	Average price of Wheat per qr.		Deaths.
	s.	d.	
1801	118	3	55,965
1804	60	1	44,794
1807	73	3	48,108
1810	106	2	54,864

From the same returns it appears, that the scarcity occasioned less mortality in the agricultural districts. The reason is manifest: the labourer is there more commonly paid in kind, and the high sale-price of the product enabled the farmer to give a high purchase-price for labour. (*a*)

(*a*) The latter reason is not very satisfactory; for the total receipts of the corn-growers are probably not larger in years of scarcity, than in those of abundance. T.

of their price: and it may be laid down as a general maxim, that the population of a state is always proportionate to the sum of its production in every kind.* This is a truth acknowledged by most writers on political economy, however various and discordant their opinions on most other points.† (1)

It appears to me, however, that one very natural consequence, deducible from this maxim, has escaped their observation; which is, that nothing can permanently increase population, except the encouragement and advance of production; and that nothing can occasion its permanent diminution, but such circumstances as attack production in its sources.

The Romans were forever making regulations to repair the loss of population, occasioned by their state of perpetual external warfare. Their censors preached up matrimony; their laws offered premiums

---

* Not but that accidental causes may sometimes qualify these general rules. A country, where property is very unequally distributed, and where a few individuals consume produce enough for the maintenance of numbers, will doubtless subsist a smaller population, than a country of equal production, where wealth is more equally diffused. The very opulent are notoriously averse to the burthen of a family; and the very indigent are unable to rear one.

† Vide *Stewart, On Political Economy*, book i. c. 4. *Quesnay Encyclopédie.* art. *Grains. Montesquieu, Esprit des Lois*, liv. 18. c. 10. and liv. 23. c. 10. *Buffon*, ed. *de Bernard*, tom. iv. p. 266. *Forbonnais, Principes et Observations*, p. 39, 45. Hume, *Essays*, part 2. Ess. 2. *Œuvres de Poivre*, p. 145, 146. *Condillac, Le Commerce et le Gouvernement*, part 1. chap. 24, 25. *Verri, Reflexions sur l'Economie Politique*, c. 210. *Mirabeau, Ami des Hommes*, tom. i. p. 40. *Raynal, Histoire de l'Etablissement*, liv. 21. s. 23. *Chastellux, de la Félicité Publique*, tom. ii. p. 205. *Necker, Administration des Finances de France*, c. 9. and *Notes sur l'Eloge de Colbert. Condorcet, Notes sur Voltaire*, ed. *de Kepl.* tom. xlv. p. 60. Smith, *Wealth of Nations*, book i. c. 8, 11. *Garnier, Abrégé Elémentaire*, part 1. c. 3. and *Préface de sa Traduction de Smith. Canard, Principes d'Economie Politique*, p. 133. Godwin, *On Political Justice*, book viii. c. 3. *Clavière, De la France et des Etats Unis*, ed. 2. p. 60, 315. Brown-Duignan, *Essay on the Principles of National Economy*, p. 97. Lond. 1776. *Beccaria, Elementi di Economia Publica*, par. prim. c. 2, 3. *Gorani, Recherches sur la Science du Gouvernement*, tom. ii. c. 7. *Sismondi, Nouv. Prin. d'Econ. Pol.* liv. vii. c. 1. *et seq. Vide* also, more especially, Malthus, *Essay on Population*, a work of considerable research; the sound and powerful arguments of which would put this matter beyond dispute, if it indeed had been doubted.

---

(1) The simple laws of population, or their general principles, which are few and plain, are examined, discussed, and established with great ability by Professor Senior, of Oxford, as well in the two lectures on Population we have already referred to, as in his subsequent correspondence with Mr. Malthus, to which these lectures gave rise, and which Mr. Senior has subjoined to them, in an appendix. Full justice is done, by Mr. Senior, to the originality and depth of Mr. Malthus's views on Population, as well as to their great importance, at the *time* he first gave them to the public; the inaccuracy, nevertheless, in his statement of the general proposition, namely, the *tendency* of every people to increase in their numbers, more rapidly than in their wealth, is clearly pointed out, and the errors which flow from it satisfactorily exhibited. "If a single country," says Mr. Senior, "can be found in which there is now less poverty than is universal in a savage state, it must be true, that under the circumstances in which that country has been placed, the means of subsistence have a greater tendency to increase than the population." AMERICAN EDITOR.

and honours to plurality of children; but these measures were fruitless. There is no difficulty in getting children; the difficulty lies in maintaining them. They should have enlarged their internal production, instead of spreading devastation amongst their neighbours. All their boasted regulations did not prevent the effectual depopulation of Italy and Greece, even long before the inroads of the barbarous northern hordes.*

The edict of Louis XVI. in favour of marriage, awarding pensions to those parents who should have ten, and larger ones to those who should have twelve chidren, was attended with no better success. The premiums that monarch held out in a thousand ways to indolence and uselessness, were much more adverse, than such poor encouragements could be conducive, to the increase of population.

It is the fashion to assert, that the discovery of the new world has tended to depopulate old Spain; whereas her depopulation has resulted from the vicious institutions of her government, and the small amount of her internal product, in proportion to her territorial extent.† The most effectual encouragement to population is, the activity of industry, and the consequent multiplication of the national products. It abounds in all industrious districts, and, when a virgin soil happens to co-operate with the exertions of a community, whence idleness is altogether discarded, its rapid increase is truly astonishing. In the United States of America, population has been doubling in the course of twenty years.

For the same reasons, although temporary calamities may sweep off multitudes, yet, if they leave untainted the source of reproduction, they are sure to prove more afflicting to humanity, than fatal to population. It soon trenches again upon the limit, assigned by the aggregate of annual production. Messance has given some very curious calculations, whereby it appears, that after the ravages occasioned by the famous plague of Marseilles in 1720, marriages throughout Provence were more fruitful than before. The Abbé d'Expilly comes to the same conclusion. The same effect was observable in Prussia, after the plague of 1710. Although it had swept off a third of the population, the tables of Sussmilch ‡ show the number of births, which, before the plague, amounted annually to about 26,000, to have advanced in the year following, 1711, to no less than 32,000, It might have been supposed, that the number of marriages, after so terrible a mortality, would have been at least considerably reduced; on the contrary, it actually doubled; a strong indication of the tendency of population to keep always on a level with the national resources.

The loss of population is not the greatest calamity resulting from

---

* *Vide Livii Hist.* lib. vi.   *Plutarchi Moralia,* xxx.   *De defectu oraculorum.* *Strabonis,* lib. vii.

† *Ustariz* has remarked, that the most populous provinces of Spain are those, from which there has been the greatest emigration to America.

‡ Quoted by Malthus, in his *Essay on Popul.* vol. ii.

such temporary visitations; the first and greatest is, the misery they occasion to the human race. Great multitudes can not be swept from the land of the living by pestilence, famine or war, without the endurance of a vast deal of suffering and agony, by numbers of sentient beings; besides the pain, distress, and misery of the survivors; the destitution of widows, orphans, brothers, sisters, and parents. It is a subject of additional regret, if among the rest, there happen to fall one or two of those superior and enlightened men, whose single talents and virtues have more effect upon the happiness and wealth of nations, than the grovelling industry of a million of ordinary mortals.

Moreover, a great loss of human beings, arrived at maturity, is certainly a loss of so much acquired wealth or capital; for every grown person is an accumulated capital, representing all the advances expended during a course of many years, in training and making him what he is. A bantling a day old by no means replaces a man of twenty; and the well-known expression of the Prince de Condé, on the victorious field of Senef, was equally absurd and unfeeling.*

The destructive scourges of the human species, therefore, if not injurious to population, are at least an outrage on humanity; on which account alone, their authors are highly criminal.†

But though such temporary calamities are more afflicting to humanity than hurtful to the population of nations, far other is the effect of a vicious government, acting upon a bad system of political economy. This latter attacks the very principle of population, by drying up the sources of production; and since the numbers of mankind, as before seen, always approach nearly to the utmost

---

* *"Une nuit de Paris reparera tout cela."* It requires the care and expenditure of twenty successive years to replace the full-grown man, that a cannon-ball has destroyed in a moment. The destruction of the human race by war is far more extensive than is commonly imagined. The ravage of a cultivated district, the plunder of dwelling-houses, the demolition of establishments of industry, the consumption of capital, &c. &c. deprive numbers of the means of livelihood, and cause many more to perish, than are left on the field of battle.

† Upon this principle, no capital improvement of the medicinal or chirurgical art, like that of vaccination for instance, can permanently influence national population; yet its influence upon the lot of humanity may be very considerable; for it may operate powerfully to preserve beings already far advanced in age, in strength, and in knowledge: whom to replace, would cost fresh births and fresh advances; in other words, abundance of sacrifices, privations, and sufferings both to the parents and the children. When population must be kept up by additional births, there is always more of the suffering incident to the entrance and the exit of human existence; for they are both of more frequent occurrence. Population may be kept up with half the number of births and deaths, if the average term of life be advanced from forty to fifty years. There will, indeed, be a greater waste of the germs of existence; but the condition of mankind must be measured by the quantum of human suffering, whereof mere germs are not susceptible. The waste of them is so immense, in the ordinary course of nature, that the small addition can be of no consequence. Were the vegetable creation endowed with sensation, the best thing that could happen to it would be, that the seeds of all the vegetables, now rooted up and destroyed, should be decomposed before the vegetable faculties were awakened.

limits the annual revenue of the nation will admit of, if the government reduce that revenue by the pressure of intolerable taxation, forcing the subject to sacrifice part of his capital, and consequently diminishing the aggregate means of subsistence and reproduction possessed by the community, such a government not only imposes a preventive check on further procreation, but may be fairly said to commit downright murder; for nothing so effectually thins the effective ranks of mankind, as privation of the means of subsistence.

The evil effects of monastic establishments upon population, have been severely and justly inveighed against; but the mode, in which they operate, has been misunderstood; it is the idleness, not the celibacy, of the monastic orders, that ought to be censured. They put their lands into cultivation, it is true, but where is the merit of that? Would the lands remain untilled, if the monastic system were abolished? So far from that evil resulting from the abolition, wherever these establishments have been converted into manufactories, of which the French revolution has offered many examples, equal agricultural produce has continued to be raised, and the produce of the manufacturing industry has been all clear gain; while the increased total product, thus created, has been followed by an increase of population also.

From these premises, may likewise be drawn this further conclusion; that the inhabitants of a country are not more scantily supplied with the necessaries of life, because their number is on the increase; nor more plentifully, because it is on the decline. Their relative condition depends on the relative quantity of products they have at their disposal; and it is easy to conceive these products to be considerable, though the population be dense; and scanty, though the population be thinly spread. Famine was of more frequent occurrence in Europe during the middle ages, than it has been of late years, although Europe is evidently more thickly peopled at present. The product of England, during the reign of queen Elizabeth, was not nearly so abundant as it is now, although her population was then less by half; and the population of Spain, reduced to but eight millions, enjoys not nearly so much affluence, as when it amounted to twenty-four.*

Some writers† have considered a dense population as an index of national prosperity; and, doubtless, it is a certain sign of enlarged national production. But general prosperity implies the general diffusion and abundance of all the necessaries, and some of the superfluities of life amongst all classes of the population. Some parts of India and of China are oppressed with population, and with misery also; but their condition would be nowise improved by thinning its

---

* If population depends on the amount of product, the number of births is a very imperfect criterion, by which to measure it. When industry and produce are increasing, births are multiplied disproportionately to the existing population, so as to swell the estimate; on the contrary, in the declining state of national wealth, the actual population exceeds the average ratio to the births.

† Wallace, *Condorcet*, Godwin.

numbers, at least if it were brought about by a diminution of the aggregate product. Instead of reducing the numbers of the population, it were far more desirable to augment the gross product; which may always be effected by superior individual activity, industry, and frugality, and the better administration, that is to say, the less frequent interference of public authority.

But it will naturally be asked, if the population of a country regularly keeps pace with its means of subsistence, what will become of it in years of scarcity and famine?

Hear what Stewart* says on the subject: "There is a very great deception as to the difference between crops; a good year for one soil is bad for another." "It is far from being true," he continues, "that the same number of people consume always the same quantity of food. In years of plenty, every one is well fed;—food is not so frugally managed; a quantity of animals are fatted for use;—and people drink more largely, because all is cheap. A year of scarcity comes; the people are ill fed; and when the lower classes come to divide with their children, the portions are brought to be very small;" instead of saving, they consume their previous hoard; and after all, it is unhappily too true, that part of that class must suffer and perish.

This calamity is most common in countries overflowing with population, like Hindostan, or China, where there is little external or maritime commerce, and where the poorer classes have always been strictly limited to the mere necessaries of life. There, the produce of ordinary years is barely sufficient to allow this miserable pittance; consequently, the slightest failure of the crop leaves multitudes wholly destitute of common necessaries, to rot and perish by wholesale. All accounts agree in representing that famines are, for this reason, very frequent and destructive in China and many parts of Hindostan.

Commerce in general, and maritime commerce in particular, facilitates the interchange of products, even with the most remote countries, and thus renders it practicable to import articles of subsistence, in return for several other kinds of produce; but too great a dependence on this resource, leaves the nation at the mercy of every natural or political occurrence, which may happen to intercept or derange the intercourse with foreign countries. The intercourse must then be preserved at all events, no matter whether by force or fraud; competition must be got rid of by every means, however unjustifiable; a separate province, or weak ally, perhaps, is obliged to purchase the national products, under restrictions equally galling, as the exaction of actual tribute; and a commercial monopoly enforced, even at the hazard of a war; all which evils make the state of the nation extremely precarious indeed.

The produce of England, in articles of human subsistence, had undoubtedly increased largely towards the end of the 18th century;

* Sir James, of Coltness, book i. c. 17.

but its produce in articles of apparel and household furniture had probably increased still more rapidly. The consequence has been, that immensity of production, which enables her to multiply her population beyond what the produce of her soil can support,* and to bear up under the pressure of public burthens, to which there is no parallel nor even approximation. But England has suffered severely, whenever foreign markets have been shut against her produce; and she has sometimes been obliged to resort to violent means to preserve her external intercourse. She would act wisely, perhaps, in discontinuing those encouragements, that impel fresh capital into the channels of manufacture and external commerce, and directing it rather towards that of agricultural industry. It is probable, that in that case, several districts, which have not yet received the utmost cultivation of which they are susceptible, particularly many parts of Scotland and Ireland, would raise agricultural produce enough to purchase most part, if not the whole, of the surplus product of her manufactures and commerce beyond her present consumption.† Great Britain would thereby create for herself a domestic consumption, which is always the surest and the most advantageous. Her neighbours, no longer offended by the necessarily jealous and exclusive nature of her policy, would probably lay aside their hostile feelings, and become willing customers. But, after all, if her manufactured should still be disproportioned to her agricultural produce, what is there to prevent her from adopting a system of judicious colonization, and thus creating for herself fresh markets for the produce of her domestic industry in every part of the globe, whence she might derive, in return, a supply of food for her superfluous population?‡

In this particular, the position of France appears to be precisely opposite to that of Great Britain. It would seem, that her agricultural product is equal to the maintenance of a much larger manufacturing and commercial population. The face of the country pre-

---

* In a pamphlet entitled, *Considerations on British Agriculture*, published in 1814, by W. Jacob, a member of the Royal Society, and a well-informed writer upon agricultural topics, we are told, (p. 34,) that England ceased to be an exporter, and became an importer, of wheat, about the year 1800.

† The writer last cited enters into long details to show, that the soil of the British isles could be made to produce at least a third more than their present product, *ibid.* p. 115. *et seq.*

‡ By judicious colonization, I mean colonization formed on the principles of complete expatriation, of self-government without control of the mother-country, and of freedom of external relations; but with the enjoyment of protection only by the mother-country, while it should continue necessary. Why should not political bodies imitate in this particular the relation of parent and child? When arrived at the age of maturity, the personal independence of the child is both just and natural; the relation it engenders is, moreover, the most lasting and most beneficial to both parties. Great part of Africa might be peopled with European colonies formed on these principles. The world has yet room enough, and the cultivated land on the face of the globe is far inferior in extent to the fertile land remaining untilled. The earl of Selkirk has thrown much light on this matter, in his tract on *Emigration and the State of the Highlands.*

sents the picture of high and general cultivation; but the villages and country towns are, for the most part, surprisingly small, poor, ill-built, and ill-paved, the few shops scantily supplied, and the public houses neither neat nor comfortable. It is plain, the agricultural product must either be less than the appearance would indicate, or it must be consumed in a thriftless and unprofitable manner; probably both these causes are in operation.

In the first place, the production is far less than it might be; and that is chiefly owing to three causes:—1. The want of capital, particularly in enclosures, live stock, and amelioration:* 2. The indolence of the cultivators, and the too general neglect of weeding, trimming the hedges, clearing the trees of moss, destroying insects, &c. &c. 3. The neglect of a proper alternation of crops, and of the most approved methods of cultivation.

In the second place, the consumption is unthrifty and unprofitable; for a great part of it is mere waste, and yields no human gratification whatever. To speak of one article alone, that is, of firing, which is an object of great value in districts, where coal and wood are scarce; the waste of it is enormous in the huts of the peasantry, lighted as they often are by the door-way only, and admitting the rain down the chimney while the fire is burning. Unwholesome beverage or food, and the indulgence of the alehouse, are like injurious modes of consumption.

In fine, towns and villages would be more thickly spread, and would besides present an appearance of greater affluence, were the generality of the inhabitants more active and industrious, and actuated by the laudable emulation, tinctured perhaps with some little vanity, rather of possessing every object of real utility, and exhibiting in their domestic arrangements the utmost order and neatness, than of living in indolence upon the rent of a trifling patrimony, or the scanty salary of some useless public employ. The small proprietor, with an income of 3 or 400 dollars per annum, just sufficient to vegetate upon, might double or triple it perhaps by adding the revenue derivable from personal industry; and even those engaged in useful occupations do not push them to the full extent of their activity and intelligence. Moreover, the spirit of inquiry and improvement has probably been disheartened by the example of frequent ill success; although the failure has commonly been occasioned by the want of judgment, perseverance, and frugality.

National population is uniformly proportionate to the quantum of national production; but it may vary locally within the limits of each state, according to the favourable or unfavourable operation of local circumstances. A particular district will be rich, because its soil is fertile, its inhabitants industrious, and possessed of capi-

---

* The want of capital prevents the employment of machinery for expediting the operations, like the thrashing machine in common use in England. This makes a larger supply of human agency requisite in agriculture; and the more mouths there are to be fed, the smaller will be the surplus produce, which alone is disposable.

tal accumulated by their frugality; in like manner as a family will surpass its neighbours in wealth, because of its superior intelligence and activity. The boundaries and political constitutions of states affect population only, inasmuch as they affect the national production. The influence of religion and national habits upon population is precisely analogous. All travellers agree, that protestant are both richer and more populous than catholic countries; and the reason is, because the habits of the former are more conducive to production.

SECTION II.

Of the influence of the Quality of a national product upon the local distribution of the Population.

For the earth to be cultivated, it is necessary that population should be spread over its surface; for industry and commerce to flourish, it is desirable to collect together in those spots, where the arts may be exercised with the most advantage; that is to say, where there can be the greatest subdivision of labour. The dyer naturally establishes himself near the clothier; the druggist near the dyer; the agent, or owner, of a vessel employed in the transport of drugs will approximate in locality to the druggist; and so of other producers in general.

At the same time, all such as live without labour on the interest of capital, or the rent of landed property, are attracted to the towns, where they find brought to a focus, every luxury to feed their appetites, as well as a choice of society, and a variety of pleasure and amusement. The charms of a town life attract foreign visiters, and all such as live by their labour, but are free to exercise it wherever they like. Thus, towns become the abode of literary men and artizans, and likewise the seats of government, of courts of justice, and most other public establishments; and their population is enlarged by the addition of all the persons attached to such establishments, and all who are accidentally brought thither by business.

Not but what there is always a number of country residents, that are employed in manufacturing industry, exclusive of such as make it their abode in preference. Local convenience, running water, the contiguity of a forest or a mine, will draw a good deal of machinery, and a number of labourers, in manufacture, out of the precincts of towns. There are, likewise, some kinds of work, which must be performed in the neighbourhood of the consumers; that of the tailor, the shoemaker, or the farrier; but these are trifling compared with the manufacturing industry of all kinds executed in towns.

Writers on political economy have calculated, that a thriving country is capable of supporting in its towns, a population equal to that of the country. Some examples lead to an opinion, that it could support a still greater proportion, were its industry directed with greater skill and its agriculture conducted with more intelligence and less waste, even supposing its soil to be of very moderate fertility.* Thus much at least is certain, that, when the towns raise a product for foreign consumption, they are then enabled to draw from abroad provisions in return, and may sustain a population much larger in proportion to that of the country. Of this we have instances in the numerous petty states, whose territory alone is barely sufficient to afford subsistence to one of the suburbs of their capital.

Again, the cultivation of pasture land, requiring much less human labour than that of arable, it follows, that, in grazing countries, a greater proportion of the inhabitants can apply themselves to the arts of industry; which are therefore more attended to in pasture than in corn countries. Witness Flanders, Holland, and Normandy that was. (b)

---

* There is good reason to believe, that the total population of England is more than the double of that employed in her internal agriculture. From the returns laid before parliament, 1811, it appears there were in Great Britain, inclusive of Wales and Scotland, 895,998 families employed in agriculture; and that the total number of families amounted to 2,544,215, which would give but a third of the population to the purposes of agriculture.

According to Arthur Young, the country population of France, within her old limits, was 20,521,538
And that of the cities and towns 5,709,270

Making a total of 26,230,808
Supposing him to be correct, France, within her old boundary, could maintain, on this principle, a population of 41 millions, supposing her merely to double her agricultural population; and of 60 millions, supposing her industry were equally active with that of Great Britain. (a)
It is the general remark of travellers, that the traffic of the great roads of France is much less, than might be expected, in a country possessing so many natural advantages. This may be attributed chiefly to the small number and size of her towns; for it is the communication from town to town that peoples the great road; that of the rural population being principally from one part of the village or farm to another.

(a) Our author has here fallen into a palpaple error. The ratio of the agricultural, to the total population of Great Britain, has not been varied as above stated, solely, or even chiefly by the multiplication of the commercial and manufacturing classes; but by the transfer of the human labour spared in agriculture to the two other branches of industry. Agriculture might occupy one third only of the population of France, and yet the total population be decreased and not multiplied. T.

(b) This position is too general. A pastoral nation, devoting the whole of its territory to pasture, could spare a very small proportion of its population for commerce and manufacture; witness Tartary and the Pampas of South America. Where a dense manufacturing and commercial population makes it advantageous to the land-holder to devote his land to pasture, and look to foreigners for the supply of corn, as in Holland, a small proportion of the population may, indeed, be required for domestic, but a large proportion will be required for the animation of foreign agriculture. T.

From the period of the irruption of the barbarians into the Roman empire, down to the 17th century, that is to say, to a date almost within living memory, the towns made but little figure in the larger states of Europe. That portion of the population, which was thought to live upon the cultivators of the land, was not then, as now, composed principally of merchants and manufacturers, but consisted of a nobility, surrounded by numerous retainers, of churchmen and other idlers, the tenants of the *chateau*, the abbey, or the convent, with their several dependencies; very few of them living within the towns. The products of manufacture and commerce were very limited indeed; the manufacturers were the poor cottagers, and the merchants mere pedlars; a few rude implements of husbandry, and some very clumsy utensils and articles of furniture, answered all the purposes of cultivation and ordinary life. The fairs, held three or four times in the year, furnished commodities of a superior quality, which we should now look upon with contempt; and what rare household articles, stuffs, or jewels, of price, were from time to time imported from the commercial cities of Italy, or from the Greeks of Constantinople, were regarded as objects of uncommon luxury and magnificence, far too costly for any but the richest princes and nobles.

In this state of things, the towns of course made but a poor figure. Whatever magnificence they may possess in our time is of very modern date. In all the towns of France together, it would be impossible to point out a single handsome range of buildings, or fine street, of two hundred years' antiquity. There is nothing of anterior date, with the exception of a few Gothic churches, but clumsy tenements huddled together in dirty and crooked streets, utterly impassable to the swarm of carriages, cattle, and foot-passengers, that indicates the present population and opulence.

No country can yield the utmost agricultural produce it is equal to, until every part of its surface be studded with towns and cities. Few manufactures could arrive at perfection, without the conveniences they afford; and, without manufactures, what is there to give in exchange for agricultural products? A district whose agricultural products can find no market, feeds not half the number of inhabitants it is capable of supporting; and the condition, even of those it does support, is rude enough, and destitute both of comfort and refinement; they are in the lowest stage of civilization. But, if an industrious colony comes to establish itself in the district, and gradually forms a town, whose inhabitants increase till they equal the numbers of the original cultivators, the town will find subsistence on the agricultural product of the district, and the cultivators be enriched by the product of the industry of the town.

Moreover, towns offer indirect channels for the export of the agricultural values of the district to a distant market. The raw products of agriculture are not easy of transport, because the expense soon swallows up the total price of the commodity transported. Manufactured produce has greatly the advantage in this respect; for industry will frequently attach very considerable value to a substance of little bulk and weight. By the means of manufacture, the raw products of national agriculture are converted into manufactured goods of much more condensed value, which will defray the charge of a more distant transport, and bring a return of produce adapted to the wants of the exporting country.

There are many of the provinces of France, that are miserable enough at present, yet want nothing but towns to bring them into high cultivation. Their situation would, indeed, be hopeless, were we to adopt the system of that class of economists, which recommends the purchase of manufactures from foreign countries, with the raw produce of domestic agriculture. (1)

However, if towns owe their origin and increase to the concentration of a variety of manufactures, great and small, manufactures, again, are to be set in activity by nothing but productive capital; and productive capital is only to be accumulated by frugality of consumption. Wherefore, it is not enough to trace the plan of a town, and give it a name; before it can have real existence, it must be gradually supplied with industrious hands, mechanical skill, implements of trade, raw materials and the necessary subsistence of those engaged

---

(1) [The slow progress of agriculture in these provinces of France is not attributable to the want of towns in the midst of them; towns and cities are a consequence, not the cause of the general prosperity of a country. Nor would the adoption of a different policy from that which recommends the purchase of manufactures from foreign countries with the raw produce of domestic agriculture, improve the situation of these districts. A system of policy which should attempt by restraints or encouragements, to divert a portion of the capital and industry employed in agriculture or commerce from those channels towards the erection of a town, or the establishment of a manufactory, with a view to promote the better cultivation of the soil, would be subversive of this end.

To what causes then must the misery, said by our author to prevail in those provinces, be ascribed, or what has retarded their agricultural improvement? The prosperity of agriculture, as well as that of every other branch of industry, depends upon the unrestrained operation of individual interest; not only furnishing motives to exertion, but knowledge to direct that exertion. All that is necessary to enable a state to reach the highest pitch of opulence, is not to disturb the action of this important principle. The obstacles, it will accordingly be found, which have opposed the progress of improvement in the countries alluded to, may be traced to the interference by the public authorities with the salutary operation of this powerful motive of action, or, in other words, to their bad laws and political institutions. Sometimes imposing restraints on the cultivator, and exposing him to numberless oppressions, either by prescribing the mode in which the soil shall be cultivated, or the products it shall yield. And, when not thus directly interfering with the business of production, prohibiting the exportation of the raw produce of the soil, and thereby depriving it of the best market. At other times harassing the husbandman with taxation, the shameful inequalities of which, whilst they relieve the higher orders, permit the burden to fall, almost exclusively, on his shoulders, or depriving him of the freedom of trade from province to province within his own country; but, above all, by perpetuating the inheritance of landed property in particular bodies or families, without the power of alienation. These are a few of the corrupt and barbarous laws which have retarded the agriculture, not of these particular provinces of France only, but of many of the fairest portions of Europe.]

American Editor.

in industry, until the completion and sale of their products.   Other-wise, instead of founding a city, a mere scaffolding is run up, which must soon fall to the ground, because it rests upon no solid founda-tion.   This was the case with regard to Ecatherinoslaw, in the Crimea; and was, indeed, foreseen by the emperor Joseph II., who assisted at the ceremony of its foundation, and laid the second stone in due form: " The empress of Russia and myself," said he to his suite, " have completed a great work in a single day: she has laid the first stone of a city, and I have laid the finishing one."

Nor will capital alone suffice to set in motion the mass of industry and the productive energy necessary to the formation and aggran-dizement of a city, unless it present also the advantages of locality and of beneficent public institutions.   The local position of Washing-ton, it should seem, is adverse to its progress in size and opulence: for it has been outstripped by most of the other cities of the Union;(1) whereas, Palmyra, in ancient times, grew both wealthy and popu-lous, though in the midst of a sandy desert, solely because it had become the *entrepot* of commerce between Europe and eastern Asia. The same advantage gave importance and splendour to Alexandria, and, at a still more remote period, to Egyptian Thebes.   The mere will of a despot could never have made it a city of a hundred gates, and of the magnitude and populousness recorded by Herodotus.   Its grandeur must have been owing to its vicinity to the Red Sea and the channel of the Nile, and to its central position between India and Europe. (*a*)

If a city cannot be raised, neither does it seem, that its further aggrandizement can be arrested by the mere fiat of the monarch. Paris continued to increase, in defiance of abundance of regulations issued by the government of the day to limit its extension.   The only effectual barrier is that opposed by natural causes, which it would be very difficult to define with precision, for it consists rather of an aggregate of little inconveniences, than of any grand or posi-

---

(*a*) There is some stretch of imagination in this.   Probably the Egyptian Thebes was itself the centre of manufacture and commerce in its day, and not its *entrepot;* indeed, there is no reason to suppose a very active intercourse be-tween India and Europe to have existed at so early a period; and, if it had, Thebes would hardly have been the *entrepot*.   But central India furnishes itself instances of cities containing as large a population.   Nineveh and Babylon seem to have been quite as populous; each was probably the central point of an enormous domestic industry.   T.

---

(1) [The local position of Washington, perhaps, is not as advantageous as that of some of the other cities of the Union; it certainly, however, has not been adverse to its progress in population and wealth.   In the year 1800, when Washington became the seat of the general government, its whole population amounted to 3,210; according to the census, it contained in 1810, 8,208 inhabit-ants, in 1820, 13,247 inhabitants, and in 1830, 18,828 inhabitants.   In the year 1820 the whole number of buildings was 2,208, of which 925 were of brick. By the assessment valuation of the year 1830, the whole number of buildings was 3,125.   It cannot, therefore, be said to have been outstripped by most of the other cities in the progress of improvement.]   American Editor.

tive obstruction.   In overgrown cities, the municipal administration is never well attended to; a vast deal of valuable time is lost in going from one quarter to another: the crossing and jostling is immense in the central parts: and the narrow streets and passages, having been calculated for a much smaller population, are unequal to the vast increase of horses, carriages, passengers, and traffic of all sorts. This evil is felt most seriously at Paris, and accidents are growing more frequent every day; yet new streets are now building on the same defective plan, with a certain prospect of a like inconvenience in a very few years hence.

BOOK III.

OF THE CONSUMPTION OF WEALTH.

CHAPTER I.

OF THE DIFFERENT KINDS OF CONSUMPTION.

In the course of my work, I have frequently been obliged to anticipate the explanation of terms and notions which in the natural order should have been postponed to a later period of the investigation. Thus I was obliged in the first book to explain the sense, in which I used the term, *consumption*, because production cannot be effected without consumption.

My reader will have seen from the explanation there given, that, in like manner as by production is meant the creation, not of substance, but of utility, so by consumption is meant the destruction of utility, and not of substance, or matter. When once the utility of a thing is destroyed, there is an end of the source and basis of its value;—an extinction of that, which made it an object of desire and of demand. It thenceforward ceases to possess value, and is no longer an item of wealth.

Thus, the terms, to *consume*, to *destroy* the *utility*, to *annihilate* the *value* of any thing, are as strictly synonymous as the opposite terms to *produce*, to *communicate utility*, to *create value*, and convey to the mind precisely the same idea. Consumption, then, being the destruction of value, is commensurate, not with the bulk, the weight, or the number of the products consumed, but with their value. Large consumption is the destruction of large value, whatever form that value may happen to have assumed.

Every product is liable to be consumed; because the value, which can be added to, can likewise be subtracted from, any object. If it has been added by human exertion or industry, it may be subtracted by human use, or a variety of accidents. But it cannot be more than once consumed; value once destroyed cannot be destroyed a second time. Consumption is sometimes rapid, sometimes gradual. A house, a ship, an implement of iron, are equally consumable as a loaf, a joint of meat, or a coat. Consumption again may be but partial. A horse, an article of furniture, or a house when re-sold by the possessor, has been but partially consumed; there is still a residue of value, for which an equivalent is received in exchange on the re-sale. Sometimes consumption is involuntary, and either accidental, as when a house is burnt, or a vessel shipwrecked, or contrary to the consumer's intention, as when a cargo is thrown overboard, or stores set on fire to prevent their falling into enemies' hands.

Value may be consumed, either long after its production, or at the very moment, and in the very act of production, as in the case of the pleasure afforded by a concert, or theatrical exhibition. Time and labour may be consumed; for labour, applicable to an useful purpose, is an object of value, and when once consumed, can never be consumed again.

Whatever cannot possibly lose its value is not liable to consumption. A landed estate cannot be consumed; but its annual productive agency may; for when once that agency has been exerted, it cannot be exerted again. The improvements of an estate may be consumed, although their value may possibly exceed that of the estate itself; for these improvements are the effect of human exertion and industry; but the land itself is inconsumable.*

So likewise it is with any industrious faculty. One may consume a labourer's day's work, but not his faculty of working; which, however, is liable to destruction by the death of the person possessing it.

All products are consumed sooner or later; indeed they are produced solely for the purpose of consumption, and, whenever the consumption of a product is delayed after it has reached the point of absolute maturity, it is value inert and neutralized for the time. For as all value may be employed re-productively, and made to yield a profit to the possessor, the withholding a product from consumption is a loss of the possible profit, in other words, of the interest its value would have yielded, if usefully employed.†

---

* Some materials are capable of receiving and discharging the same kind of value many times over; as linen, which will undergo repeated washing. The cleanliness given it by the laundress, is a value wholly consumed on each occasion, along with a part of that of the linen itself.

† The values not consumed sooner or later in a useful way are of little moment; such are provisions spoiled by keeping, products lost accidentally, and those whose use has become obsolete, or which have never been used at all, owing to the failure of the demand for them, wherein value originates. Values buried, or concealed, are commonly withdrawn but for a time from consumption; when found, it is always the interest of the finder to turn them to account, which he cannot do without submitting them to consumption. In this case, the only loss is that of the profit derivable from them during the period of their disappearance, and may be reckoned equivalent to the interest for that time. The same observation applies to the minute savings, successively laid by until the moment of investment, the aggregate of which is, doubtless, considerable. The loss, resulting from this inertness of capital, may be partially remedied by moderating the duties on transfer, by extending to the utmost the facility of circulation, and by the establishment of banks of deposite, in which capital

But, products being universally destined for consumption, and that too in the quickest way, how, it may be asked, can there be ever an accumulation of capital, that is to say, of values produced?

I answer—that value may be accumulated, without being necessarily vested all the while in the same identical product, provided only it be perpetuated in some product or other. Now, values employed as capital are perpetuated by reproduction; the various products of which capital consists, are consumed like all other products: but their value is no sooner destroyed by consumption, than it re-appears in another, or a similar substance. A manufactory can not be kept up, without a consumption of victuals and clothes for the workmen, as well as of the raw material of manufacture; but, while value in those forms is undergoing consumption, new value is communicated to the object of manufacture. The items that composed the capital so expended, are consumed and gone; but the capital, the accumulated value, still exists and re-appears under a new form, applicable to a second course of consumption. Whereas, if consumed unproductively, it never re-appears at all.

The annual consumption of an individual, is, the aggregate of all the values consumed by that individual within the year. The annual consumption of a nation is, the aggregate of values consumed within the year by all the individuals and communities, whereof the nation consists.

In the estimate of individual or national consumption, must be included every kind of consumption, whatever be its motive or consequence, whether productive of new value or not; in like manner, as the estimate of the annual production of a nation comprises the total value of its products raised within the year. Thus, a soap manufactory is said to consume such or such a quantity or value of alkali in a year, although this value be re-produced from the manufactory in the shape of soap; on the other hand, it is said to produce annually such and such a quantity or value of soap, although the production may have cost the destruction of a great variety of values, which, if deducted, would vastly reduce the apparent product. By annual production, or consumption, national or individual, is therefore meant, the gross and not the net amount.*

Whence it naturally follows, that all the commodities, which a nation imports, must be reckoned as a part of its annual product, and all its exports as part of its annual consumption. The trade of France consumes the total value of the silk it exports to the United States; and produces, on the other hand, the total value of cotton received in return. And, in like manner, the manufacture of France con-

---

may be safely vested, and whence it may readily be withdrawn. In times of political confusion, and under an arbitrary government, many will prefer to keep their capital inactive, concealed, and unproductive, either of profit or gratification, rather than run the risk of its display. This latter evil is never felt under a good government.

* For the distinction between the *gross* and the *net* product, *vide suprà*, Book II. chap. 5.

sumes the valué of alkali employed by the soap-boiler, and produces the value of soap derived from the concern.

The total annual consumption of a nation, or an individual, is a very different thing from the aggregate of capital. A capital may be wholly or partially consumed several times a year. When a shoe-maker buys leather, and cuts and works it up into shoes, there is so much capital consumed and reproduced. Every time he repeats the operation, there is so much more capital consumed. Suppose the leather purchased to amount to 40 dollars, and the operation to be repeated 12 times in the year, there will have been an annual consumption of 480 dollars upon a capital of 40 dollars. On the other hand, there may be portions of his capital, implements of trade, for instance, which it may take several years to consume. Of this part of his capital he may consume annually but 1-4 or 1-10 perhaps.

In each country the wants of the consumer determine the quality of the product. The product most wanted is most in demand; and that which is most in demand yields the largest profit to industry, capital, and land, which are therefore employed in raising this particular product in preference; and, *vice versâ,* when a product becomes less in demand, there is a less profit to be got by its produc-tion; it is, therefore, no longer produced. All the stock on hand falls in price; the low price encourages the consumption, which soon absorbs the stock on hand.

The total national consumption may be divided into the heads of public consumption, and private consumption; the former is effected by the public, or in its service; the latter by individuals or families. Either class may be productive or unproductive.

In every community each member is a consumer; for no one can subsist, without the satisfaction of some necessary wants, however confined and limited; on the other hand, all, who do not live on mere charity, or gratuitous bounty, contribute somehow to produc-tion, by their industry, their capital, or their land; wherefore, the consumers may be said to be themselves the producers; and the great bulk of consumption takes place amongst the middling and poorer classes, whose numbers more than counterbalance the small-ness of the share allotted to each.*

---

* It is probable, that, in all countries, anywise advanced in industry, the reve-nues of industry exceed those of capital and land united, and, consequently, that the consumption of those deriving income solely from industry, and wholly de-pendent for subsistence upon their personal faculties, exceeds that of both capi-talists and landlords together. It is not uncommon to meet with a manufactory, that, with a capital, say of 120,000 dollars, will pay daily in wages to its people, 60 dollars, which, with the deduction of Sundays and holidays, makes 18,000 dollars per annum; if to this be added, 4000 dollars more for the net profits of personal superintendence and management, it will give a total of 22,000 dollars per annum, for the revenue of industry alone. The same capital, vested in land at but 20 years' purchase would yield a revenue of 6000 dollars only.

The cultivation by *métayers,* the very lowest description of farmers, gives to them, and their subordinate labourers' industry, a revenue equal to that of the land jointly with the capital, which is advanced by the proprietor.

Opulent, civilised, and industrious nations, are greater consumers than poor ones, because they are infinitely greater producers. They annually, and in some cases, several times in the course of the year, re-consume their productive capital, which is thus continually renovated; and consume unproductively, the greater part of their revenues, whether derived from industry, from capital, or from land.

It is not uncommon to find authors proposing, as the model for imitation, those nations whose wants are few; whereas, it is far preferable to have numerous wants, along with the power to gratify them. This is the way at once to multiply the human species, and to give to each a more enlarged existence.

Stewart * extols the Lacedæmonian policy, which consisted in practising the art of self-denial in the extreme, without aiming at progressive advancement in the art of production. But herein the Spartans were rivalled by the rudest tribes of savages, which are commonly neither numerous nor amply provided. Upon this principle, it would be the very *acme* of perfection to produce nothing and to have no wants; that is to say, to annihilate human existence.

CHAPTER II.

OF THE EFFECT OF CONSUMPTION IN GENERAL.

The immediate effect of consumption of every kind is, the loss of value, consequently, of wealth, to the owner of the article consumed. This is the invariable and inevitable consequence, and should never be lost sight of in reasoning on this matter. A product consumed is a value lost to all the world and to all eternity; but the further consequence, that may follow, will depend upon the circumstances and nature of the consumption.

If the consumption be unproductive, there usually results the gratification of some want, but no reproduction of value whatever; if productive, there results the satisfaction of no want, but a creation of new value, equal, inferior, or superior in amount to that consumed, and profitable or unprofitable to the adventurer accordingly.†

---

* Book II. chap. 14.

† This may be illustrated by the burning of fuel in a grate or furnace. The fuel burnt, serves either to give warmth, or to cook victuals, boil dyeing ingredients, and the like, and thereby to increase their value. There is no utility in the mere gratuitous act of burning, except inasmuch as it tends to satisfy some human want, that of warmth for instance; in which case, the consumption is unproductive; or inasmuch as it confers upon a substance submitted to its action, a value, that may replace the value of the fuel consumed; in which case the consumption is productive.

If the fuel, burnt for the sake of warmth, produce either no warmth at all, or very little; or that burnt to give value to a substance, give it no value, or a less value than the value consumed in fuel, the consumption will be ill-judged and improvident.

Thus, consumption may be regarded as an act of barter, wherein the owner of the value consumed gives up that value on the one hand, and receives in return, either the satisfaction of a personal want, or a fresh value, equivalent to the value consumed.

It may be proper here to remark, that consumption, productive of nothing beyond a present gratification, requires no skill or talent in the consumer. It requires neither labour nor ingenuity to eat a good dinner, or dress in fine clothes.* On the contrary, productive consumption, besides yielding no immediate or present gratification, requires an exertion of combined labour and skill, or, of what has all along been denominated, *industry.*

When the owner of a product ready for consumption has himself no industrious faculty, and wishes, but knows not how to consume it productively, he lends it to some one more industrious than himself, who commences by destroying it, but in such a way, as to reproduce another, and thereby enable himself to make a full restitution to the lender, after retaining the profit of his own skill and labour. The value returned consists of different objects from that lent, it is true; indeed, the condition of a loan is in substance this; to replace the value lent, of whatever amount, say 2000 dollars, at a time specified, by other value, equivalent to the same amount of silver coin of the like weight and quality at the time of repayment. An object, lent on condition of specific restitution, cannot be available for reproduction; because, by the terms of the loan, it is not to be consumed.

Sometimes a producer is the consumer of his own product; as when the farmer eats his own poultry or vegetables; or the clothier wears his own cloth. But, the objects of human consumption being far more varied and numerous, than the objects of each person's production respectively, most operations of consumption are preceded by a process of barter. He first turns into money, or receives in that shape, the values composing his individual revenue; and then changes again that money for the articles he purposes to consume. Wherefore, in common parlance, to spend and to consume have become nearly synonymous. Yet, by the mere act of buying, the value expended is not lost; for the article purchased has likewise a value, which may be parted with again for what it cost, if it has not been bought over-dear. The loss of value does not happen till the actual consumption, after which the value is destroyed; it then ceases to exist, and is not the object of a second consumption. For this reason it is, that in domestic life, the bad management of the wife soon runs through a moderate fortune; for she in general regulates the daily consumption of the family, which is the chief source of expense, and one that is always recurring.

---

* There is unquestionably a sort of talent requisite in the expenditure of a large income with credit to the proprietor, so as to gratify personal taste, without awakening the self-love of others; to oblige without the sense of humiliation; to labour for the public good, without alarming individual interests. But this kind of talent is referable rather to the head of practical, whilst its influence upon the rest of mankind falls within the province of theoretical, morality.

This will serve to expose the error of the notion, that where there is no loss of money, there can be no loss of wealth. It is the commonest thing in the world to hear it roundly asserted, that the money spent is not lost, but remains in the country; and, therefore, that the country cannot be impoverished by its internal expenditure. It is true, the value of the money remains as before; but the object, or the hundred objects, perhaps, that have been successively bought with the same money, have been consumed, and their value destroyed.

Wherefore, it is superfluous, I had almost said ridiculous, to confine at home the national money, for the purpose of preserving national wealth. Money by no means prevents the consumption of value, and the consequent diminution of wealth; on the contrary, it facilitates the arrival of consumable objects at their ultimate destination; which is a most beneficial act, when the end is well chosen, and the result satisfactory. Nor would it be correct even to maintain, that the export of specie is at all events a loss, although its presence in the country may be no hindrance to consumption or to the diminution of wealth. For unless it be made without any view to a return, which is rarely the case, it is in fact the same thing as productive consumption; being merely a sacrifice of one value, for the purpose of obtaining another. Where no return whatever is in view, there indeed is so much loss of national capital; but the loss would be quite as great, were goods, and not money, so exported.

CHAPTER III.

OF THE EFFECT OF PRODUCTIVE CONSUMPTION.

The nature of productive consumption has been explained above, in Book I. The value absorbed by it is what has been called Capital. The trader, manufacturer, and cultivator, purchase the raw material * and productive agency, which they consume in the preparation of new products; and the immediate effect is precisely the same as that of unproductive consumption, namely, to create a demand for the objects of their consumption, which operates upon their price, and upon their production; and to cause a destruction of value. But the ultimate effect is different; there is no satisfaction of a human want, and no resulting gratification, except that accruing to the adventurer from the possession of the fresh product,

---

* The raw materials of manufacture and commerce are, the products bought with a view to the communication to them of further value. Calicoes are raw material to the calico-printer, and printed calicoes to the dealer who buys them for re-sale or export. In commerce, every act of purchase is an act of consumption; and every act of re-sale, an act of production.

the value which replaces that of the products consumed, and commonly affords him a profit into the bargain.

To this position, that productive consumption does not immediately satisfy any human want, a cursory observer may possibly object, that the wages of labour, though a productive outlay, go to satisfy the wants of the labourer, in food, raiment, and amusement perhaps. But, in this operation, there is a double consumption; 1. Of the capital consumed productively in the purchase of productive agency, wherefrom results no human gratification: 2. Of the daily or weekly revenue of the labourer, *i. e.* of his productive agency, the recompense for which is consumed unproductively by himself and his family, in like manner as the rent of the manufactory, which forms the revenue of the landlord, is by him consumed unproductively. And this does not imply the consumption of the same value twice over, first productively, and afterwards unproductively; for the values consumed are two distinct values resting on bases altogether different. The first, the productive agency of the labourer, is the effect of his muscular power and skill, which is itself a positive product, bearing value like any other. The second is a portion of capital, given by the adventurer in exchange for that productive agency. After the act of exchange is once completed, the consumption of the value given on either side, is contemporaneous, but with a different object in view; the one being intended to create a new product, the other to satisfy the wants of the productive agent and his family. Thus, the object, expended and consumed by the adventurer, is the equivalent he receives for his capital; and that, consumed unproductively by the labourer, is the equivalent for his revenue. The interchange of these two values by no means makes them one and the same.

So likewise, the intellectual industry of superintendence is reproductively consumed in the concern; and the profits, accruing to the adventurer as its recompense, are consumed unproductively by himself and his family.

In short, this double consumption is precisely analogous to that of the raw material used in the concern. The clothier presents himself to the wool-dealer, with 1000 crowns in his hand; there are, at this moment, two values in existence, on the one side, that of the 1000 crowns, which is the result of previous production, and now forms a part of the capital of the clothier; on the other, the wool constituting a part of the annual product of a grazing farm. These products are interchanged, and each is separately consumed; the capital converted into wool, in a way to produce cloth; the product of the farm, converted into crown-pieces, in the satisfaction of the wants of the farmer, or his landlord.

Since every thing consumed is so much lost, the gain of reproductive consumption is equal, whether proceeding from reduced consumption, or from enlarged production. In China, they make a great saving, in the consumption of seed-corn, by following the drilling, in lieu of the broad-cast, method. The effect of this saving is precisely the same, as if the land were, in China, proportionately more productive than in Europe.*

In manufacture, when the raw material used is of no value whatever, it is not to be reckoned as forming any part of the requisite consumption of the concern; thus, the stone used by the lime-burner, and the sand employed by the glass-blower, are no part of their respective consumption, whenever they have cost them nothing.

A saving of productive agency, whether of industry, of land, or of capital, is equally real and effectual, as a saving of raw material; and it is practicable in two ways; either by making the same productive means yield more agency; or by obtaining the same result from a smaller quantity of productive means.

Such savings generally operate in a very short time to the benefit of the community at large; they reduce the charges of production; and in proportion as the economical process becomes better understood, and more generally practised, the competition of producers brings the price of the product gradually to a level with the charges of production. But for this very reason, all, who do not learn to economise like their neighbours, must necessarily lose, while others are gaining. Manufacturers have been ruined by hundreds, because they would go to work in a grand style with too costly and complex an apparatus, provided of course at an excessive expense of capital.

Fortunately, in the great majority of cases, self-interest is most sensibly and immediately affected by a loss of this kind; and in the concerns of business, like pain in the human frame, gives timely warning of injuries, that require care and reparation. If the rash or ignorant adventurer in production were not the first to suffer the punishment of his own errors or misconduct, we should find it far more common than it is to dash into improvident speculation; which is quite as fatal to public prosperity, as profusion and extravagance. A merchant, that spends 10,000 dollars in the acquisition of 6000 dollars, stands, in respect to his private concerns and to the general wealth of the community, upon exactly the same footing, as a man of fashion, who spends 4000 dollars in horses, mistresses, gluttony, or ostentation; except, perhaps, that the latter has more pleasure and personal gratification for his money.†

---

* One of the suite of Lord Macartney estimated the saving of grain in China, by this method alone, to be equal to the supply of the whole population of Great Britain.

† There is almost insuperable difficulty in estimating with precision the consumption and production of value; and individuals have no other means of knowing, whether their fortune be increased or diminished, except by keeping regular accounts of their receipt and expenditure; indeed, all prudent persons are careful to do so, and it is a duty imposed by law in the case of traders. An adventurer could otherwise scarcely know whether his concern were gainful or losing, and might be involving himself and his creditors in ruin. Besides keeping regular accounts, a prudent manager will make previous estimates of the value that will be absorbed in the concern, and of its probable proceeds; the use of which, like that of a plan or design in building, is to give an approximation, though it can afford no certainty.

What has been said on this subject in Book I, of this work, makes it needless to enlarge here on the head of productive consumption. I shall, therefore, henceforward direct my reader's attention to the subject of unproductive consumption, its motives, and consequences; premising, that in what I am about to say, the word *consumption*, used alone, will import unproductive consumption, as it does in common conversation.

CHAPTER IV.

OF THE EFFECT OF UNPRODUCTIVE CONSUMPTION IN GENERAL.

HAVING just considered the nature and effect of consumption in general, as well as the general effect of productive consumption in particular, it remains only to consider, in this and the following chapters, such consumption as is effected with no other end or object in view, than the mere satisfaction of a want, or the enjoyment of some pleasurable sensation.

Whoever has thoroughly comprehended the nature of consumption and production, as displayed in the preceding pages, will have arrived at the conviction, that no consumption of the class denominated unproductive, has any ulterior effect, beyond the satisfaction of a want by the destruction of existing value. It is a mere exchange of a portion of existing wealth on the one side, for human gratification on the other, and nothing more. Beyond this, what can be expected?—reproduction? how can the same identical utility be afforded a second time? Wine can not be both drunk and distilled into brandy too. Neither can the object consumed serve to establish a fresh demand, and thus indirectly to stimulate future productive exertion; for it has already been explained that the only effectual demand is created by the possession of wherewithal to purchase,—of something to give in exchange; and what can that be, except a product, which, before the act of exchange and consumption, must have been an item, either of revenue or of capital? The existence and intensity of the demand must invariably depend upon the amount of revenue and of capital: the bare existence of revenue and of capital is all that is necessary for the stimulus of production, which nothing else can stimulate. The choice of one object of consumption necessarily precludes that of another; what is consumed in the shape of silks cannot be consumed in the shape of linens or woollens; nor can what has once been devoted to pleasure or amusement, be made productive also of more positive or substantial utility.

Wherefore, the sole object of inquiry, with regard to unproductive consumption, is, the degree of gratification resulting from the act of consumption itself: and this inquiry will, in the remainder of this chapter, be pursued in respect of unproductive consumption in general, after which we shall give in the following chapters, a separate consideration to that of individuals, and that of the public, or community at large. The sole point is, to weigh the loss, occasioned to the consumer by his consumption, against the satisfaction it affords him. The degree of correctness, with which the balance of loss and gain is struck, will determine whether the consumption be judicious or otherwise; which is a point that next to the actual production of wealth, has the most powerful influence upon the well or ill-being of families and of nations.

In this point of view, the most judicious kinds of consumption seem to be:—

1. Such as conduce to the satisfaction of positive wants; by which term I mean those, upon the satisfaction of which depends the existence, the health, and the contentment of the generality of mankind; being the very reverse of such as are generated by refined sensuality, pride, and caprice. Thus, the national consumption will, on the whole, be judicious, if it absorb the articles rather of convenience than of display: the more linen and the less lace; the more plain and wholesome dishes, and the fewer dainties; the more warm clothing, and the less embroidery, the better. In a nation whose consumption is so directed, the public establishments will be remarkable rather for utility than splendour, its hospitals will be less magnificent than salutary and extensive; its roads well furnished with inns, rather than unnecessarily wide and spacious, and its towns well paved, though with few palaces to attract the gaze of strangers.

The luxury of ostentation affords a much less substantial and solid gratification, than the luxury of comfort, if I may be allowed the expression. Besides, the latter is less costly, that is to say, involves the necessity of a smaller consumption; whereas the former is insatiable; it spreads from one to another, from the mere proneness to imitation; and the extent to which it may reach, is as absolutely unlimited. (a) " Pride," says Franklin, " is a beggar quite as clamorous as want, but infinitely more insatiable."

Taking society in the aggregate, it will be found that, one with another, the gratification of real wants is more important to the community, than the gratification of artificial ones. The wants of the rich man occasion the production and consumption of an exquisite perfume, perhaps those of the poor man, the production and consumption of a good warm winter cloak; supposing the value to

---

(a) It is strange, that so acute a writer should not have perceived, that the mischief of pure individual vanity can never be very formidable, because the pleasure it affords loses in intensity, in proportion to its diffusion. Indeed, as far as individual consumption is concerned, attacks upon luxury are mere idle declamations; for the productive energies of mankind will always be directed towards an object, with a force and in a degree porportionate to the intensity of the want for it. It is the extravagance of public luxury alone that can ever be formidable; this, as well as public consumption of every kind, it is always the interest of the community at large to contract, and that of public functionaries to expand, to the utmost. T,

be equal, the diminution of the general wealth is the same in both cases; but the resulting gratification will, in the one case, be trifling, transient, and scarcely perceptible; in the other, solid, ample, and of long duration.*

2. Such as are the most gradual, and absorb products of the best quality. A nation or an individual, will do wisely to direct consumption chiefly to those articles, that are the longest time in wearing out, and the most frequently in use. Good houses and furniture are, therefore, objects of judicious preference; for there are few products that take longer time to consume than a house, or that are of more frequent utility; in fact, the best part of one's life is passed in it. Frequent changes of fashion are unwise; for fashion takes upon itself to throw things away long before they have lost their utility, and sometimes before they have lost even the freshness of novelty, thus multiplying consumption exceedingly, and rejecting as good for nothing what is perhaps still useful, convenient, or even elegant. So that a rapid succession of fashions impoverishes a state, as well by the consumption it occasions, as by that which it arrests.

There is an advantage in consuming articles of superior quality, although somewhat dearer, and for this reason: in every kind of manufacture, there are some charges that are always the same, whether the product be of good or bad quality. Coarse linen will have cost, in weaving, packing, storing, retailing, and carriage, before it comes to the ultimate consumer, quite as much trouble and labour, as linen of the finest quality, therefore in purchasing an inferior quality, the only saving is the cost of the raw material: the labour and trouble must always be paid in full, and at the same rate; yet the product of that labour and trouble are much quicker consumed, when the linen is of inferior, than when it is of superior quality.

This reasoning is applicable indifferently to every class of product; for in every one there are some kinds of productive agency, that are paid equally without reference to quality; and that agency is more profitably bestowed in the raising of products of good than of bad quality; therefore, it is generally more advantageous for a nation to consume the former. But this can not be done, unless the nation can discern between good and bad, and have acquired taste for the former; wherein again appears the necessity of knowledge† to the furtherance of national prosperity; and unless, besides, the bulk of the population be so far removed above penury, as not to be obliged to buy whatever is the cheapest in the first instance, although it be in the long-run the dearest to the consumer.

It is evident, that the interference of public authority in regu-

---

* The lending at interest what might have been spent in frivolity is of this latter class; for interest can not be paid, unless the loan be productively employed; in which case it will go in part to the maintenance of the labouring classes.

† By knowledge, I would always be understood to mean, acquaintance with the true state of things, or generally with truth in every branch.

lating the details of the manufacture, supposing it to succeed in making the manufacturer produce goods of the best quality, which is very problematical, must be quite ineffectual in promoting their consumption; for it can give the consumer, neither the taste of what is of the better quality, nor the ability to purchase. The difficulty lies, not in finding a producer, but in finding a consumer. It will be no hard matter to supply good and elegant commodities, if there be consumers both willing and able to purchase them. But such a demand can exist only in nations enjoying comparative affluence; it is affluence, that both furnishes the means of buying articles of good quality, and gives a taste for them. Now the interference of authority is not the road to affluence, which results from activity of production, seconded by the spirit of frugality;—from habits of industry pervading every channel of occupation, and of frugality tending to accumulation of capital. In a country, where these qualities are prevalent, and in no other, can individuals be at all nice or fastidious in what they consume. On the contrary, profusion and embarrassment are inseparable companions; there is no choice when necessity drives.

The pleasures of the table, of play, of pyrotechnic exhibitions, and the like, are to be reckoned amongst those of shortest duration. I have seen villages, that, although in want of good water, yet do not hesitate to spend in a wake or festival, that lasts but one day, as much money as would suffice to construct a conduit for the supply of that necessary of life, and a fountain or public cistern on the village green; the inhabitants preferring to get once drunk in honour of the squire or saint, and to go day after day with the greatest inconvenience, and bring muddy water from half a league distance. The filth and discomfort prevalent in rustic habitations are attributable, partly to poverty, and partly to injudicious consumption.

In most countries, if a part of what is squandered in frivolous and hazardous amusements, whether in town or country, were spent in the embellishment and convenience of the habitations, in suitable clothing, in neat and useful furniture, or in the instruction of the population, the whole community would soon assume an appearance of improvement, civilization, and affluence, infinitely more attractive to strangers, as well as more gratifying to the people themselves.

3. The collective consumption of numbers. There are some kinds of agency, that need not be multiplied in proportion to the increased consumption. One cook can dress dinner for ten as easily as for one; the same grate will roast a dozen joints as well as one; and this is the reason, why there is so much economy in the mess-table of a college, a monastery, a regiment, or a large manufactory, in the supply of great numbers from a common kettle or kitchen, and in the dispensaries of cheap soups.

4. And lastly, on grounds entirely different, those kinds of consumption are judicious, which are consistent with moral rectitude; and, on the contrary, those, which infringe its laws, generally end in public, as well as private calamity. But it would be too wide a

digression from my subject to attempt the illustration of this position.

. It is observable, that great inequality of private fortune is hostile to those kinds of consumption, that must be regarded as most judicious. In proportion as that inequality is more marked, the artificial wants of the population are more numerous, the real ones more scantily supplied, and the rapid consumption more common and destructive. The patrician spendthrifts and imperial gluttons of ancient Rome thought they never could squander enough. Besides, immoral kinds of consumption are infinitely more general, where the extremes of wealth and poverty are found blended together.' In such a state of society, there are few, who can indulge in the refinement of luxury, but a vast number, who look on their enjoyments with envy, and are ever impatient to imitate them. To get into the privileged class is the grand object, be the means ever so questionable; and those who are little scrupulous in the acquirement, are seldom more so in the employment of wealth. (a)

The government has, in all countries, a vast influence, in determining the character of the national consumption; not only because it absolutely directs the consumption of the state itself, but because a great proportion of the consumption of individuals is gained by its will and example. If the government indulge a taste for splendour and ostentation, splendour and ostentation will be the order of the day, with the whole host of imitators; and even those of better judgment and discretion must, in some measure, yield to the torrent. For, how seldom are they independent of that consideration and good opinion, which, under such circumstances, are to be earned, not by personal qualities, but by a course of extravagance they can not approve?

First and foremost in the list of injudicious kinds of consumption stand those which yield disgust and displeasure, in lieu of the gratification anticipated. Under this class may be ranged, excess and intemperance in private individuals; and, in the state, wars undertaken with the motive of pure vengeance, like that of Louis XIV. in revenge for the attacks of a Dutch newspaper, or with that of empty glory, which leads commonly to disgrace and odium. Yet such wars are even less to be deplored for the waste of national wealth and resources, than for the irremediable loss of personal virtue and talent sacrificed in the struggle; a loss which involves

(a) In a wholesome state of society, when public institutions are not needlessly multiplied, and all tend to the common purpose of public good, this very impatience and anxiety is conducive to the welfare, and not to the injury, of society. Indeed, great inequality of fortune seems to be a necessary accompaniment to social wealth and great national productive power. It is the prospect of great prizes only, that can stimulate to the extreme of intellectual and corporeal industry; and there is no instance on record of a nation far advanced in industry, in which great inequality of fortune has not existed. One bishopric of Durham will tempt more clerical adventurers, than five hundred moderate benefices; and the example of a single Arkwright or Peel will stimulate manufacturing science and activity more than a whole Manchester of moderate cotton-spinning concerns. T.

families in distress enough, when exacted by the public good, and by the pressure of inexorable necessity; but must be doubly shocking and afflicting, when it originates in the caprice, the wickedness, the folly, or the ungovernable passions of national rulers.

CHAPTER V.

OF INDIVIDUAL CONSUMPTION—ITS MOTIVES AND ITS EFFECTS.

THE consumption of individuals, as contrasted with that of the public or community at large, is such as is made with the object of satisfying the wants of families and individuals. These wants chiefly consist in those of food, raiment, lodging, and amusement. They are supplied with the necessary articles of consumption in each department, out of the respective revenue of each family or individual, whether derived from personal industry, from capital, or from land. The wealth of a family advances, declines, or remains stationary, according as its consumption equals, exceeds, or falls short of its revenue. The aggregate of the consumption of all the individuals, added to that of the government for public purposes, forms the grand total of national consumption.

A family, or indeed a community, or nation, may certainly consume the whole of its revenue, without being thereby impoverished; but it by no means follows, that it either must, or would act wisely, in so doing. Common prudence would counsel to provide against casualties. Who can say with certainty, that his income will not fall off, or that his fortune is exempt from the injustice, the fraud, or the violence of mankind? Lands may be confiscated; ships may be wrecked; litigation may involve him in its expenses and uncertainties. The richest merchant is liable to be ruined by one unlucky speculation, or by the failure of others. Were he to spend his whole income, his capital might, and in all probability would, be continually on the decline.

But, supposing it to remain stationary, should one be content with keeping it so? A fortune, however large, will seem little enough, when it comes to be divided amongst a number of children. And, even if there be no occasion to divide it, what harm is there in enlarging it; so it be done by honourable means? what else is it, but the desire of each individual to better his situation, that suggests the frugality that accumulates capital, and thereby assists the progress of industry, and leads to national opulence and civilisation? Had not previous generations been actuated by this stimulus, the present one would now be in the savage state; and it is impossible to say, how much farther it may yet be possible to carry civilization. It has never been proved to my satisfaction, that nine-tenths of the population must inevitably remain in that degree of misery and semi-barbarism, which they are found in at present in most countries of Europe.

The observance of the rules of private economy keeps the consumption of a family within reasonable bounds: that is to say, the bounds prescribed in each instance by a judicious comparison of the value sacrificed in consumption, with the satisfaction it affords. None but the individual himself, can fairly and correctly estimate the loss and gain, resulting to himself or family from each particular act of consumption; for the balance will depend upon the fortune, the rank, and the wants of himself and family; and, in some degree, perhaps, upon personal taste and feelings. To restrain consumption within too narrow limits, would involve the privation of gratification that fortune has placed within reach; and, on the other hand, a too profuse consumption might trench upon resources, that it might be but common prudence to husband.*

Individual consumption has constant reference to the character and passions of the consumer. It is influenced alternately by the noblest and the vilest propensities of our nature; at one time it is stimulated by sensuality; at another by vanity, by generosity, by revenge, or even by covetousness. It is checked by prudence or foresight, by groundless apprehension, by distrust, or by selfishness. As these various qualities happen in turn to predominate, they direct mankind in the use they make of their wealth. In this, as in every other action of life, the line of true wisdom is the most difficult to observe. Human infirmity is perpetually deviating to the one side or the other, and seldom steers altogether clear of excess.†

In respect to consumption, prodigality and avarice are the two faults to be avoided: both of them neutralize the benefits that wealth is calculated to confer on its possessor; prodigality by exhausting, avarice by not using, the means of enjoyment. Prodigality is, indeed, the more amiable of the two, because it is allied to many amiable and social qualities. It is regarded with more indulgence, because it imparts its pleasures to others; yet it is of the two the more mischievous to society; for it squanders and makes away with the capital that should be the support of industry; it destroys indus-

---

* On this ground sumptuary laws are superfluous and unjust. The indulgence proscribed is either within the means of the individual or not: in the former case, it is an act of oppression to prohibit a gratification involving no injury to others, equally unjustifiable as prohibition in any other particular; in the latter, it is at all events nugatory to do so; for there is no occasion for legal interference, where pecuniary circumstances alone are an effectual bar. Every irregularity of this kind works its own punishment. It has been said, that it is the duty of the government to check those habits, which have a tendency to lead people into expenses exceeding their means; but it will be found, that such habits can only be introduced by the example and encouragement of the public authorities themselves. In all other circumstances, neither custom nor fashion will ever lead the different classes of society into any expenses, but what are suitable to their respective means.

† The weaker sex is, from the very circumstance of inferiority in strength of mind, exposed to greater excess both of avarice and prodigality.

try, the grand agent of production, by the destruction of the other agent, capital. If, by expense and consumption, are meant those kinds only which minister to our pleasures and luxuries, it is a great mistake to say that money is good for nothing but to be spent, and that products are only raised to be consumed. Money may be employed in the work of re-production; when so employed, it must be productive of great benefit; and, every time that a fixed capital is squandered, a corresponding quantity of industry must be extinguished, in some quarter or other. The spendthrift, in running through his fortune, is at the same time exhausting, *pro tanto*, the source of the profits upon industry.

The miser, who, in the dread of losing his money, hesitates to turn it to account, does, indeed, nothing to promote the progress of industry; but at least he can not be said to reduce the means of production. His hoard is scraped together by the abridgment of his personal gratifications, not at the expense of the public, according to the vulgar notion; it has been withdrawn from no productive occupation, and will at any rate re-appear at his death, and be available for the purpose of extending the operations of industry, if it be not squandered by his heirs, or so effectually concealed, as to evade all search or recovery.

It is absurd in spendthrifts to boast of their prodigality, which is quite as unworthy the nobleness of our nature, as the sordid meanness of the opposite character. There is no merit in consuming all one can lay hands upon, and desisting only when one can get no more to consume; every animal can do as much; nay, there are some animals that set a better example of provident management. It is more becoming the character of a being gifted with reason and foresight, never to consume, in any instance, without some reasonable object in view. At least, this is the course that economy would prescribe.

In short, economy is nothing more than the direction of human consumption with judgment and discretion,—the knowledge of our means, and the best mode of employing them. There is no fixed rule of economy; it must be guided by a reference to the fortune, condition, and wants of the consumer. An expense, that may be authorized by the strictest economy in a person of moderate fortune, would, perhaps, be pitiful in a rich man, and absolute extravagance in a poor one. In a state of sickness, a man must allow himself indulgences, that he would not think of in health. An act of beneficence, that trenches on the personal enjoyments of the benefactor, is deserving of the highest praise; but it would be highly blamable, if done at the expense of his children's subsistence.

Economy is equally distant from avarice and profusion. Avarice hoards, not for the purpose of consuming or re-producing, but for the mere sake of hoarding; it is a kind of instinct, or mechanical impulse, much to the discredit of those in whom it is detected; whereas, true economy is the offspring of prudence and sound reason, and does not sacrifice necessaries to superfluities, like the miser, when he denies himself present comforts, in the view of luxury, ever prospective and never to be enjoyed. The most sumptuous enter tainment may be conducted with economy, without diminishing, but rather adding to its splendour, which the slightest appearance of avarice would tarnish and deface. The economical man balances his means against his present or future wants, and those of his family and friends, not forgetting the calls of humanity. The miser regards neither family nor friends; scarcely attends to his own personal wants, and is an utter stranger to those of mankind at large. Economy never consumes without an object; avarice never willingly consumes at all; the one is a sober and rational study, the only one that supplies the means of fulfilling our duties, and being at the same time just and generous; the other, a vile propensity to sacrifice every thing to the sordid consideration of self.

Economy has not unreasonably been ranked among the virtues of mankind; for, like the other virtues, it implies self-command and control; and is productive of the happiest consequences; the good education of children, physical and moral; the careful attendance of old age; the calmness of mind, so necessary to the good conduct of middle life; and that independence of circumstances which alone can secure against mercenary motives, are all referable to this quality. Without it there can be no liberality, none at least of a permanent and wholesome kind; for, when it degenerates into prodigality, it is an indiscriminate largess, alike to deserving and unde- serving; stinting those who have claims in favour of those who have none. It is common to see the spendthrift reduced to beg a favour from people that he has loaded with his bounty; for what he gives now, one expects a return will some day be called for; whereas, the gifts of the economical man are purely gratuitous; for he never gives except from his superfluities. The latter is rich with a mode- rate fortune; but the miser and the prodigal are poor, though in possession of the largest resources.

Economy is inconsistent with disorder, which stumbles blindfold over wealth, sometimes missing what it most desires, although close within its reach, and sometimes seizing and devouring what it is most interested in preserving; ever impelled by the occurrences of the moment, which it either can not foresee, or can not emancipate itself from; and always unconscious of its own position, and utterly incapable of choosing the proper course for the future. A house- hold, conducted without order, is preyed upon by all the world: neither the fidelity of the servants, nor even the parsimony of the master, can save it from ultimate ruin. For it is exposed to the perpetual recurrence of a variety of little outgoings, on every occa- sion, however trivial.*

---

* I remember being once in the country a witness of the numberless minute losses that neglectful housekeeping entails. For want of a trumpery latch, the gate of the poultry-yard was forever open: there being no means of closing it externally, it was on the swing every time a person went out; and many of the

Among the motives that operate to determine the consumption of individuals, the most prominent is luxury, that frequent theme of declamation, which, however, I should probably not have dwelt upon, could I expect that every body would take the trouble of applying the principles I have been labouring to establish; and were it not always useful to substitute reason for declamation.

Luxury has been defined to be, the use of superfluities.* For my own part, I am at a loss to draw the line between superfluities and necessaries; the shades of difference are as indistinct and completely blended as the colours of the rainbow.

Taste, education, temperament, bodily health, make the degrees of utility and necessity infinitely variable, and render it impossible to employ in an absolute sense, terms, which always of necessity convey an idea of relation and comparison.

The line of demarcation between necessaries and superfluities shifts with the fluctuating condition of society. Strictly speaking, mankind might exist upon roots and herbs, with a sheepskin for clothing, and a wigwam for lodging; yet, in the present state of European society, we cannot look upon bread or butcher's meat, woollen-clothes or houses of masonry, as luxuries. For the same reason, the line varies also according to the varying circumstances of individual fortune; what is a necessary in a large town, or in a particular line of life, may, in another line of life, or in the country, be a mere superfluity. Wherefore, it is impossible exactly to define the boundary between the one and the other. Smith has fixed it a little in advance of Stewart; including in the rank of necessaries, besides natural wants, such as the established rules of decency and propriety have made necessary in the lower classes of society. But Smith was wrong in attempting to fix at all what must, in the nature of things, be ever varying.

Luxury may be said, in a general way, to be, the use or consump-

---

poultry were lost in consequence. One day a fine young porker made his escape into the woods, and the whole family, gardener, cook, milk-maid, &c., presently turned out in quest of the fugitive. The gardener was the first to discover the object of pursuit, and in leaping a ditch to cut off his further escape, got a sprain that confined him to his bed for the next fortnight: the cook found the linen burnt that she had left hung up before the fire to dry; and the milkmaid, having forgotten in her haste to tie up the cattle properly in the cow-house, one of the loose cows had broken the leg of a colt that happened to be kept in the same shed. The linen burnt and the gardener's work lost, were worth full twenty crowns; and the colt about as much more: so that here was a loss in a few minutes of forty crowns, purely for want of a latch that might have cost a few *sous* at the utmost; and this in a household where the strictest economy was necessary, to say nothing of the suffering of the poor man, or the anxiety and other troublesome incidents. The misfortune was to be sure not very serious, nor the loss very heavy; yet when it is considered, that similar neglect was the occasion of repeated disasters of the same kind, and ultimately of the ruin of a worthy family, it was deserving of some little attention.

* Stewart, *Essay on Pol. Econ.* book ii. c. 20. The same writer has in another passage observed, that every thing not absolutely necessary to bare existence is a superfluity.

tion of dear articles; for the term dear is one of relation, and therefore may be properly enough applied in the definition of another term, whose sense is likewise relative. Luxury* with us in France conveys the idea rather of ostentation than of sensuality; applied to dress, it denotes rather the superior beauty and impression upon the beholder, than superior convenience and comfort to the wearer; applied to the table, it means rather the splendour of a sumptuous banquet, than the exquisite farce of the solitary epicure. The grand aim of luxury in this sense is to attract admiration by the rarity, the costliness, and the magnificence of the objects displayed, recommended probably neither by utility, nor convenience, nor pleasurable qualities, but merely by their dazzling exterior and effect upon the opinions of mankind at large. Luxury conveys the idea of ostentation; but ostentation has itself a far more extensive meaning, and comprehends every quality assumed for the purpose of display. A man may be ostentatiously virtuous, but is never luxuriously so; for luxury implies expense. Thus, luxury of wit or genius is a metaphorical expression, implying a profuse display or expenditure, if it may be so called, of those qualities of the intellect, which it is the characteristic of good taste to deal out with a sparing hand.

Although, with us in France, what we term luxury is chiefly directed to ostentatious indulgence, the excess and refinement of sensuality are equally unjustifiable, and of precisely similar effect: that is to say, of a frivolous and inconsiderable enjoyment or satisfaction, obtained by a large consumption, calculated to satisfy more urgent and extensive wants. But I should not stigmatise as luxury that degree of variety or abundance, which a prudent and well-informed person in a civilised community would like to see upon his table upon domestic and common occasions, or aim at in his dress and abode, when under no compulsion to keep up an appearance. I should call this degree of indulgence judicious and suitable to his condition, but not an instance of luxury.

Having thus defined the term luxury, we may go on to investigate its effect upon the well-ordering or economy of nations.

Under the head of unproductive consumption is comprised the satisfaction of many actual and urgent wants, which is a purpose of sufficient consequence to outweigh the mischief, that must ensue from the destruction of values. But what is there to compensate that mischief, where such consumption has not for its object the satisfaction of such wants? where money is spent for the mere sake of spending, and the value destroyed without any object beyond its destruction?

It is supposed to be beneficial, at all events, to the producers of the articles consumed. But it is to be considered, that the same expenditure must take place, though not, perhaps, upon objects quite

---

* The English term luxury has a much more sensual meaning than the French *luxe*, and seems to comprise both *luxe* and *luxure*, the *luxus*, or *luxuria*, and *luxuries* of the Latin writers.

so frivolous; for the money withheld from luxurious indulgences is not absolutely thrown into the sea; it is sure to be spent either upon more judicious gratifications or upon reproduction. In one way or other, all the revenue, not absolutely sunk or buried, is consumed by the receiver of it, or by some one in his stead; and in all cases whatever, the encouragement held out by consumption to the producer is co-extensive with the total amount of revenue to be expended. Whence it follows:

1. That the encouragement which ostentatious extravagance affords to one class of production is necessarily withdrawn from another.

2. That the encouragement resulting from this kind of consumption cannot increase, except in the event of an increase in the revenue of the consumers: which revenue, as we can not but know by this time, is not to be increased by luxurious, but solely by reproductive consumption.

How great, then, must be the mistake of those, who, on observing the obvious fact, that the production always equals the consumption, as it must necessarily do, since a thing can not be consumed before it is produced, have confounded the cause with the effect, and laid it down as a maxim, that consumption originates production; therefore that frugality is directly adverse to public prosperity, and that the most useful citizen is the one who spends the most.

The partisans of the two opposite systems above adverted to, the economists, and the advocates of exclusive commerce, or the balance of trade, have made this maxim a fundamental article of their creed. The merchants and manufacturers, who seldom look beyond the actual sale of their products, or inquire into the causes which may operate to extend their sale, have warmly supported a position, apparently so consistent with their interests; the poets, who are ever apt to be seduced by appearances, and do not consider themselves bound to be wiser than politicians and men of business, have been loud in the praise of luxury;* and the rich have not been backward

---

* Though it is not every subject that allows equal scope to poetical genius, it does not seem, that error affords a finer field than truth. The lines of *Voltaire* on the system of the world, and on the discoveries of Newton regarding the properties of light, are strictly conformable to the rules of science, and nowise inferior in beauty to those of Lucretius on the fanciful dogmas of the Epicurean school. But if *Voltaire* had been better acquainted with the principles of political economy, he would never have given utterance to such sentiments as the following:

> *Sachez surtout que le luxe enrichit*
> *Un grand état, s'il en perd un petit.*
> *Cette splendeur, cette pompe mondaine,*
> *D'un regne heureux est la marque certain.*
> *Le riche est né pour beaucoup dépenser* . . . .

The progress of science compels those who covet literary fame, to make themselves acquainted with general principles at the least; without a close adherence to truth and nature, there is little chance of permanent reputation, even in the poetical department.

in adopting principles, that exalt their ostentation into a virtue. and
their self-gratification into benevolence.*

This prejudice, however, must vanish as the increasing knowledge
of political economy begins to reveal the real sources of wealth, the
means of production, and the effect of consumption. Vanity may
take pride in idle expense, but will ever be held in no less contempt
by the wise, on account of its pernicious effects, than it has been all
along, for the motives by which it is actuated.

These conclusions of theory have been confirmed by experience.
Misery is the inseparable companion of luxury. The man of wealth
and ostentation squanders upon costly trinkets, sumptuous repasts,
magnificent mansions, dogs, horses, and mistresses, a portion of
value, which, vested in productive occupation, would enable a multitude of willing labourers, whom his extravagance now consigns to
idleness and misery, to provide themselves with warm clothing
nourishing food, and household conveniences. The gold buckles
of the rich man leave the poor one without shoes to his feet; and
the labourer will want a shirt to his back, while his rich neighbour
glitters in velvet and embroidery.

It is vain to resist the nature of things. Magnificence may do
what it will to keep poverty out of sight, yet it will cross it at every
turn, still haunting, as if to reproach it for its excesses. This contrast was to be met with at Versailles, at Rome, at Madrid, and in
every seat of royal residence. In a recent instance, it occurred in
France in an afflicting degree, after a long series of extravagant and
ostentatious administration; yet the principle is so undeniable, that
one would not suppose it had required so terrible an illustration.†

------

* *La République a bien affaire*
   De Gens, qui ne dépensent rien ;
   Je ne sais d'homme nécessaire,
   Que celui dont le luxe épand beaucoup de bien.
           La Fontaine, Avantage de la Science.

"Were the rich not to spend their money freely," says *Montesquieu,* "the
poor would starve." *Esprit des Lois,* liv. vii. c. 4.

† There are other circumstances that contribute to veil the residence of the
court in an atmosphere of human misery. It is there, that personal service is
consumed by wholesale; and that is of all things the most rapidly consumed,
being, indeed, consumed as fast as produced. Under this denomination, is to be
comprised, the agency of the soldiery, of menial servants, of public functionaries, whether useful or not, of clerks, lawyers, judges, civilians, ecclesiastics,
actors, musicians, drolls, and numerous other hangers-on, who all crowd towards
the focus of power and occupation, civil, judicial, military, or religious. It is
there also, that material products seem to be more wantonly consumed. The
choicest viands, the most beautiful and costly stuffs, the rarest works of art and
fashion, all seem emulous to reach this general sink, whence little or nothing
ever emerges.

Yet, if the accumulated values, that are drained from every quarter of the
national territory to feed the consumption of the seat of royalty, were distributed
with any regard to equity, they would probably suffice to maintain all classes in
comfort and plenty. Though such drains must always be calamitous, because
they absorb value, and yield no return, at any rate the local population might be
pretty well off; but it is notorious that wealth is nowhere less equally diffused.

Those who are little in the habit of looking through the appearance to the reality of things, are apt to be seduced by the glitter and the bustle of ostentatious luxury. They take the display of consumption as conclusive evidence of national prosperity. If they could open their eyes, they would see, that a nation verging towards decline will for some time continue to preserve a show of opulence; like the establishment of a spendthrift on the high road to ruin. But this false glare can not last long; the effort dries up the sources of reproduction, and, therefore, must infallibly be followed by a state of apathy and exhaustion of the political frame, which is only to be remedied by slow degrees, and by the adoption of a regimen the very reverse of that, by which it has thus been reduced.

It is distressing to see the fatal habits and customs of the nation one is attached to by birth, fortune, and social affection, extending their influence over the wisest individuals, and those best able to appreciate this danger and foresee its disastrous consequences. The number of persons, who have sufficient spirit and independence of fortune to act up to their principles, and set themselves forward as an example, is extremely small. Most men yield to the torrent, and rush on ruin with their eyes open, in search of happiness; although it requires a very small share of philosophy to see the madness of this course, and to perceive, that, when once the common wants of nature are satisfied, happiness is to be found, not in the frivolous enjoyments of luxurious vanity, but in the moderate exercise of our physical and moral faculties.

Wherefore, those, who abuse great power, or talent, by exerting it in diffusing a taste for luxury, are the worst enemies of social happiness. If there is one habit, that deserves more encouragement than another, in monarchies as well as republics, in great as well as small, it is this of economy. Yet, after all, no encouragement is wanted; it is quite enough to withdraw favour and honour from habits of profusion; to afford inviolable security to all savings and acquirements; to give perfect freedom to their investment and occupation in every branch of industry, that is not absolutely criminal.

It is alleged, that, to excite mankind to spend or consume, is to excite them to produce, inasmuch as they can only spend what they may acquire. This fallacy is grounded on the assumption, that production is equally within the ability of mankind as consumption; that it is as easy to augment as to expend one's revenue. But, supposing it were so, nay further, that the desire to spend, begets a

---

The prince, the favourite, a mistress, or a bloated peculator, takes the lion's share, leaving to the subordinate drones the pittance assigned to them by the generosity or caprice of their superiors.

The residence of an overgrown proprietor upon his estate then only tends to diffuse abundance and cheerfulness around him, when his expenditure is directed to objects of utility, rather than of pomp; in which case he is really an adventurer in agriculture, and an accumulator of capital in the shape of improvements and ameliorations.

liking for labour, although experience by no means warrants such a conclusion, yet there can be no enlargement of production, without an augmentation of capital, which is one of the necessary elements of production; but it is clear, that capital can only be accumulated by frugality; and how can that be expected from those, whose only stimulus to production is the desire of enjoyment.

Moreover, when the desire of acquirement is stimulated by the love of display, how can the slow and limited progress of real production keep pace with the ardour of that motive? Will it not find a shorter road to its object, in the rapid and disreputable profits of jobbing and intrigue, classes of industry most fatal to national welfare, because they produce nothing themselves, but only aim at appropriating a share of the produce of other people? It is this motive, that sets in motion the despicable art and cunning of the knave, leads the pettifogger to speculate on the obscurity of the laws, and the man of authority to sell to folly and wickedness that patronage which it is his duty to dispense gratuitously to merit and to right. Pliny mentions having seen Paulina at a supper, dressed in a network of pearls and emeralds, that cost 40 millions of *sestertii*, (1) as she was ready to prove by her jeweller's bills. It was bought with the fruit of her ancestor's speculations. "Thus," says the Roman writer, "it was to dress out his grand-daughter in jewels at an entertainment, that Lollius forgot himself so far, as to lay waste whole provinces, to become the object of detestation to the Asiatics he governed, to forfeit the favour of Cæsar, and end his life by poison."

This is the kind of industry generated by love of display.

If it be pretended, that a system, which encourages profusion, operates only upon the wealthy, and thus tends to a beneficial end, inasmuch as it reduces the evil of the inequality of fortune, there can be little difficulty in showing, that profusion in the higher, begets a similar spirit in the middling and lower classes of society, which last must, of course, the soonest arrive at the limits of their income; so that, in fact, the universal profusion has the effect of increasing, instead of reducing, that inequality. Besides, the profusion of the wealthier class is always preceded, or followed, by that of the government, which must be fed and supplied by taxation, that is always sure to fall more heavily upon small incomes than on large ones.*

---

* In favour of luxury, the following paradoxical argument has been advanced; for what is too ridiculous to be hazarded in such a cause? "That since luxury consumes superfluities only, the objects it destroys are of little real utility, and therefore the loss to society can be but small." There is this ready answer: the value of the objects consumed by luxury must have been reduced by the competition of producers to a level with the charges of production, wherein are comprised the profits of the producers. Objects of luxury are equally the product of land, capital, and industry, which might have been employed in raising objects of real utility, had the demand taken that direction; for production invariably accommodates itself to the taste of the consumers.

---

(1) [About 140,000 dollars. Some English ladies wear jewels of greater

The apologists of luxury have sometimes gone so far as to cry up the advantages of misery and indigence; on the ground, that, without the stimulus of want, the lower classes of mankind could never be impelled to labour, so that neither the upper classes, nor society at large, could have the benefit of their exertions.

Happily, this position is as false in principle as it would be cruel in practice. Were nakedness a sufficient motive of exertion, the savage would be the most diligent and laborious, for he is the nearest to nakedness, of his species. Yet his indolence is equally notorious and incurable. Savages will often fret themselves to death, if compelled to work. It is observable throughout Europe, that the laziest nations are those nearest approaching to the savage state; a mechanic in good circumstances, at London or Paris, would execute twice as much work in a given time, as the rude mechanic of a poor district. Wants multiply as fast as they are satisfied; a man who has a jacket is for having a coat; and, when he has his coat, he must have a greatcoat too. The artisan, that is lodged in an apartment by himself, extends his views to a second; if he has two shirts, he soon wants a dozen, for the comforts of more frequent change of linen; whereas, if he has none at all, he never feels the want of it. No man feels any disinclination to make a further acquisition, in consequence of having made one already.

The comforts of the lower classes are, therefore, by no means incompatible with the existence of society, as too many have maintained. The shoemaker will make quite as good shoes in a warm room, with a good coat to his back, and wholesome food for himself and his family, as when perishing with cold in an open stall; he is not less skilful or inclined to work, because he has the reasonable conveniences of life. Linen is washed as well in England, where washing is carried on comfortably within doors, as where it is executed in the nearest stream in the neighbourhood.

It is time for the rich to abandon the puerile apprehension of losing the objects of their sensuality, if the poor man's comforts be promoted. On the contrary, reason and experience concur in teaching, that the greatest variety, abundance, and refinement of enjoyment are to be found in those countries, where wealth abounds most, and is the most widely diffused.

---

value; but some read the passage in Pliny *Quadringenties*, instead of *Quadragies Sestertium*. This would make the jewels of Paulina worth 1,400,000 dollars; the more probable sum.] AMERICAN EDITOR.

CHAPTER VI.

ON PUBLIC CONSUMPTION

Section I.

Of the Nature and general Effect of Public Consumption.

Besides the wants of individuals and of families which it is the object of private consumption to satisfy, the collection of many individuals into a community gives rise to a new class of wants, the wants of the society in its aggregate capacity, the satisfaction of which is the object of public consumption. The public buys and consumes the personal service of the minister, that directs its affairs, the soldier, that protects it from external violence, the civil or criminal judge, that protects the rights and interests of each member against the aggression of the rest. All these different vocations have their use, although they may often be unnecessarily multiplied or overpaid; but that arises from a defective political organization, which it does not fall within the scope of this work to investigate.

We shall see presently whence it is, that the public derives all the values, wherewith it purchases the services of its agents, as well as the articles its wants require. All we have to consider in this chapter is, the mode in which its consumption is effected, and the consequences resulting from it.

If I have made myself understood in the commencement of this third book, my readers will have no difficulty in comprehending, that public consumption, or that which takes place for the general utility of the whole community, is precisely analogous to that consumption, which goes to satisfy the wants of individuals or families. In either case, there is a destruction of values, and a loss of wealth; although, perhaps, not a shilling of specie goes out of the country.

By way of insuring conviction of the truth of this position, let us trace from first to last the passage of a product towards ultimate consumption on the public account.

The government exacts from a tax-payer the payment of a given tax in the shape of money. To meet this demand, the tax-payer exchanges part of the products at his disposal for coin, which he pays to the tax-gatherer:* a second set of government agents is

---

* Although the capitalist and landholder receive their interest and rent originally in the shape of money, and have, therefore, no occasion to go through any previous act of exchange, to obtain wherewithal to pay the tax, yet such a previous exchange must have been effected by the adventurer, who turns the land or capital to account. The effect is precisely the same, as if the rent or interest had been paid in kind; that is, in the immediate products of the land or capital; and the landholder or capitalist had paid the tax either by the direct transfer of

busied in buying with that coin, cloth and other necessaries for
the soldiery. Up to this point, there is no value lost or consumed:
there has only been a gratuitous transfer of value, and a subsequent
act of barter: but the value contributed by the subject still exists in
the shape of stores and supplies in the military depôt. In the end,
however, this value is consumed; and then the portion of wealth,
which passes from the hands of the tax-payer into those of the tax-
gatherer, is destroyed and annihilated.

Yet it is not the sum of money that is destroyed: that has only
passed from one hand to another, either without any return, as when
it passed from the tax-payer to the tax-gatherer; or in exchange for
an equivalent, as when it passed from the government agent to the
contractor for clothing and supplies. The value of the money sur-
vives the whole operation, and goes through three, four, or a dozen
hands, without any sensible alteration; it is the value of the clothing
and necessaries that disappears, with precisely the same effect, as if
the tax-payer had, with the same money, purchased clothing and
necessaries for his own private consumption. The sole difference
is, that the individual in the one case, and the state in the other,
enjoys the satisfaction resulting from that consumption.

The same reasoning may be easily applied to all other kinds of
public consumption. When the money of the tax-payer goes to
pay the salary of a public officer, that officer sells his time, his talents, and his exertions, to the public, all of which are consumed for
public purposes. On the other hand, that officer consumes, instead
of the tax-payer, the value he receives in lieu of his services; in
the same manner as any clerk or person in the private employ of
the tax-payer would do.

There has been long a prevalent notion, that the values, paid by
the community for the public service, return to it again in some
shape or other; in the vulgar phrase, that what government and its
agents receive, is refunded again by their expenditure. This is a
gross fallacy; but one that has been productive of infinite mischief, inasmuch as it has been the pretext for a great deal of shame-
less waste and dilapidation. The value paid to government by the
tax-payer is given without equivalent or return: it is expended by
the government in the purchase of personal service, of objects of
consumption; in one word, of products of equivalent value, which
are actually transferred. Purchase or exchange is a very different
thing from restitution.*

---

part of those products, or by first selling them, and afterwards paying over the
proceeds. On this subject, *vide suprà*, Book II. chap. 5, for the mode in which
revenue is distributed amongst the community.

* Dr. Hamilton, in his valuable tract upon *The National Debt of Great Britain*, illustrates the absurdity of the position here attacked, by comparing it to
the "forcible entry of a robber into a merchant's house, who should take away
his money, and tell him he did him no injury, for the money, or part of it, would
be employed in purchasing the commodities he dealt in, upon which he would
receive a profit." The encouragement afforded by the public expenditure is precisely analogous.

Turn it which way you will, this operation, though often very complex in the execution, must always be reducible by analysis to this plain statement. A product consumed must always be a product lost, be the consumer who he may; lost without return, whenever no value or advantage is received in return; but, to the taxpayer, the advantage derived from the services of the public functionary, or from the consumption effected in the prosecution of public objects, is a positive return.

If, then, public and private expenditure affect social wealth in the same manner, the principles of economy, by which it should be regulated, must be the same in both cases. There are not two kinds of economy, any more than two kinds of honesty, or of morality. If a government or an individual consume in such a way, as to give birth to a product larger than that consumed, a successful effort of productive industry will be made. If no product result from the act of consumption, there is a loss of value, whether to the state or to the individual; yet, probably, that loss of value may have been productive of all the good anticipated. Military stores and supplies, and the time and labour of civil and military functionaries, engaged in the effectual defence of the state, are well bestowed, though consumed and annihilated; it is the same with them, as with the commodities and personal service, that have been consumed in a private establishment. The sole benefit resulting in the latter case is, the satisfaction of a want; if the want had no existence, the expense or consumption is a positive mischief, incurred without an object. So likewise of the public consumption; consumption for the mere purpose of consumption, systematic profusion, the creation of an office for the sole purpose of giving a salary, the destruction of an article for the mere pleasure of paying for it, are acts of extravagance either in a government or an individual, in a small state or a large one, a republic or a monarchy. Nay, there is more criminality in public, than in private extravagance and profusion; inasmuch as the individual squanders only what belongs to him; but the government has nothing of its own to squander, being, in fact, a mere trustee of the public treasure.*

What, then, are we to think of the principles laid down by those writers, who have laboured to draw an essential distinction between public and private wealth; to show, that economy is the way to increase private fortune, but, on the contrary, that public wealth increases with the increase of public consumption: inferring thence this false and dangerous conclusion, that the rules of conduct in the management of private fortune and of public treasure, are not only different, but in direct opposition?

If such principles were to be found only in books, and had never crept into practice, one might suffer them without care or regret to

---

* It is mere usurpation in a government, to pretend to a right over the property of individuals, or to act as if possessing such a right; and usurpation can never constitute right; although it may confer possession. Were it otherwise, a thief, who had once, by force or fraud, obtained possession of another man's property, could never be called upon to make restitution, when overpowered and taken prisoner, for he might set up the plea of legitimate ownership.

swell the monstrous heap of printed absurdity; but it must excite
our compassion and indignation to hear them professed by men of
eminent rank, talents, and intelligence; and still more to see them
reduced into practice by the agents of public authority, who can
enforce error and absurdity at the point of the bayonet or mouth of
the cannon.*

Madame de Maintenon mentions in a letter to the Cardinal de
Noailles, that, when she one day urged Louis XIV. to be more
liberal in charitable donations, he replied, that royalty dispenses
charity by its profuse expenditure; a truly alarming dogma, and one
that shows the ruin of France to have been reduced to principle.†
False principles are more fatal than even intentional misconduct;
because they are followed up with erroneous notions of self-interest,
and are long persevered in without remorse or reserve. If Louis
XIV. had believed his extravagant ostentation to have been a mere
gratification of his personal vanity, and his conquests the satisfaction
of personal ambition alone, his good sense and proper feeling would
probably, in a short time, have made it a matter of conscience to
desist, or at any rate, he would have stopped short for his own sake;
but he was firmly persuaded, that his prodigality was for the public
good as well as his own; so that nothing could stop him, but misfortune and humiliation.‡

---

* The reader will readily perceive, that this and many other passages, were
written under the pressure of a military despotism, which had assumed the absolute disposal of the national resources, and suffered no one to express a doubt
of the justice and policy of its acts.

† *Fenelon, Vauban,* and a very few more, of the most distinguished talent, had
a confused idea of the ruinous tendency of this system; but they failed in impressing the rest of the world with the same conviction; for want of just notions
on the subject of the production and consumption of wealth. Thus *Vauban,* in
his *Dixme royale,* says, 'the present misery of France is attributable, not to the
rigour of the climate, the character of the inhabitants, or the barrenness of the
soil: for the climate is most favourable, the people active, diligent, dexterous, and
numerous: but to the frequency and long continuance of war, and the ignorance
and neglect of economy.' *Fenelon* had expressed the same sentiments in several admirable passages of his *Telemaque,* but they passed for mere declamation,
as well they might; for he was not qualified to prove their truth and accuracy.

‡ When *Voltaire* tells us, speaking of the superb edifices of Louis XIV., that
they were by no means burthensome to the nation, but served to circulate money
in the community, he gives a decisive proof of the utter ignorance of the most
celebrated French writers of his day upon these matters. He looked no further
than the money employed on the occasion; and, when the view is limited to that
alone, the extreme of prodigality exhibits no appearance of loss; for money is, in
fact, an item, neither of revenue, nor of annual consumption. But a little closer
attention will convince us of the fallacy of this position, which would lead us to
the absurd inference, that no consumption whatever has occurred within the
year, whenever the amount of specie at the end of it is found to be nowise diminished. The vigilance of the historian should have traced the 167 millions of
dollars expended on the chateau of Versailles alone, from the original production by the laborious efforts of the productive classes of the nation, to the first
exchange into money, wherewith to pay the taxes, through the second exchange
into building materials, painting, gilding, &c. to the ultimate consumption in
that shape, for the personal gratification of the vanity of the monarch. The
money acted as a mere means of facilitating the transfers of value in the course

So little were the true principles of political economy understood, even by men of the greatest science, so late as the 18th century, that Frederick II. of Prussia, with all his anxiety in search of truth, his sagacity, and his merit, writes thus to D'Alembert, in justification of his wars: "My numerous armies promote the circulation of money, and disburse impartially amongst the provinces the taxes paid by the people to the state." Again I repeat, this is not the fact; the taxes paid to the government by the subject are not refunded by its expenditure. Whether paid in money or in kind, they are converted into provisions and supplies, and in that shape consumed and destroyed by persons, that never can replace the value, because they produce no value whatever.* It was well for Prussia that Frederick II. did not square his conduct to his principles. The good he did to his people, by the economy of his internal administration, more than compensated for the mischief of his wars.

Since the consumption of nations or the governments which represent them, occasions a loss of value, and consequently, of wealth, it is only so far justifiable, as there results from it some national advantage, equivalent to the sacrifice of value. The whole skill of government, therefore, consists in the continual and judicious comparison of the sacrifice about to be incurred, with the expected benefit to the community; for I have no hesitation in pronouncing every instance, where the benefit is not equivalent to the loss, to be an instance of folly, or of criminality, in the government.

It is yet more monstrous, then, to see how frequently governments, not content with squandering the substance of the people†

---

of the transaction; and the winding up of the account will show, a destruction of value to the amount of 167 millions of dollars, balanced by the production of a palace, in need of constant repair, and of the splendid promenade of the gardens.

Even land, though imperishable, may be consumed in the shape of the value received for it. It has been asserted, that France lost nothing by the sale of her national domains after the revolution, because they were all sold and transferred to French subjects; but what became of the capital paid in the shape of purchase-money, when it left the pockets of the purchasers? Was it not consumed and lost?

* In the execution of the national military enterprise, two different values pass through the hands of the government or its agents: 1. The value paid in taxes by the public at large: 2. The value received in supplies and services from the parties affording them. For the first of these no return whatever is made; for the second, an equivalent is paid in wages or purchase-money. Wherefore, there it has no ground for saying that the government refunds with one hand what is received with the other; that the whole transaction is a mere circulation of value, and causes no loss to the nation; for the government returns but one, where it receives two; the loss of the other half falls upon the community at large. Thus, the national, being but the aggregate of individual wealth, is diminished to the extent of the total consumption of the government, *minus* the product of the public establishment; as we shall presently see more in detail.

† It has been seen in the concluding chapter of Book II. that, inasmuch as population is always commensurate with production, the obstruction of the progressive multiplication of products is a preventive check to the further multiplication of the human race; and that the waste of capital, the extinction of industry, and the exhaustion of the sources of production, amount to positive decimation of those in actual existence. A wicked or ignorant administration may, in this way, be a far more destructive scourge, than war with all its atrocities.

in folly and absurdity, instead of aiming at any return of value, actually spend that substance in bringing down upon the nation calamities innumerable; practise exactions the most cruel and arbitrary, to forward schemes the most extravagant and wicked; first rifle the pockets of the subject, to enable them afterwards to urge him to the further sacrifice of his blood. Nothing, but the obstinacy of human passion and weakness, could induce me again and again to repeat these unpalatable truths, at the risk of incurring the charge of declamation.

The consumption effected by the government* forms so large a portion of the total national consumption, amounting sometimes to a sixth, a fifth, or even a fourth part† of the total consumption of the

---

* By government, I mean, the ruling power in all its branches, and under whatever constitutional form; it would be wrong to limit the term to the executive branch alone; the first enactment of a law is as much an act of authority, as its subsequent enforcement.

† The consumption of a nation may undoubtedly exceed its aggregate annual revenue; but we can hardly suppose that of Great Britain to have done so; for she has evidently been advancing in opulence, up to the present time, whence it may be inferred, that her consumption, at the very utmost, only equals her revenue. *Gentz*, who will hardly be accused of underrating the financial resources of that country, estimated her total annual revenue at no more than two hundred millions sterling; Dr. Beeke at two hundred and eighteen millions, inclusive of one hundred millions for the revenues of industry. Granting her to have made some further progress since those estimates were made, and that her total revenue in 1813 had advanced to two hundred and twenty-four millions, we are told by Colquhoun, in his *Wealth, Power, and Resources of the British Empire*, that her public expenditure in that year amounted to one hundred and twelve millions. By this statement it should seem, that her public expenditure then amounted to the half of the total expenditure of the nation! Moreover, the expenses of her central government do not include all her public charges; there are to be added, county and parish rates, poor rates, &c. &c. The business of government might be conducted, even in extensive empires, at a charge of not more than one per cent. upon the aggregate of individual revenue; but, to attain this degree of perfection, a vast improvement is still requisite in the department of practical policy. (1)

---

(1) We copy from a Treatise on the Taxation of the British Empire, by R. Montgomery Martin, published in London, in 1833, the following note:—"Lord Liverpool said, in 1822, that the *annual* income of Great Britain, after making allowances for the reduction of rents, and the diminution of the profits of trade since the war, may be stated to be from 250,000,000*l*. to 280,000,000*l*. sterling. Now if the population of Great Britain in 1833 be taken in round numbers at 16 millions, and the average expenditure for each individual be so low as *one shilling per day*, or 18*l*. 5*s*. a-year, the annual income would be 452,000,000*l*. and double that sum if the average expenditure of each individual were taken at *two* shillings per day, which would not be an unreasonable calculation: applying the same rule to Ireland, but giving the average expenditure of each individual so low as *sixpence* a-day, on a population of eight millions, the annual income of Ireland would be 73,000,000*l*. Thus the annual income of the United Kingdom in 1833, is upwards of 500,000,000*l*. sterling on the lowest computation."

Estimating, on such authority, the annual income of Great Britain and Ireland at 500 millions sterling, we perceive that this income, even after the payment of the taxes, enormous as they have been, is much greater now than at any former period of her history; and there therefore can be no doubt that a continued

community, that the system acted upon by the government, must needs have a vast influence upon the advance or decline of the national prosperity. Should an individual take it into his head, that the more he spends the more he gets, or that his profusion is a virtue; or should he yield to the powerful attractions of pleasure, or the suggestions of perhaps a reasonable resentment, he will in all probability be ruined, and his example will operate upon a very small circle of his neighbours. But a mistake of this kind in the government, will entail misery upon millions, and possibly end in the national downfal or degradation. It is doubtless very desirable, that private persons should have a correct knowledge of their personal interests; but it must be infinitely more so, that governments should possess that knowledge. Economy and order are virtues in a private station; but, in a public station, their influence upon national happiness is so immense, that one hardly knows how sufficiently to extol and honour them in the guides and rulers of national conduct.

An individual is fully sensible of the value of the article he is consuming; it has probably cost him a world of labour, perseverance, and economy; he can easily balance the satisfaction he derives from its consumption against the loss it will involve. But a government is not so immediately interested in regularity and economy, nor does it so soon feel the ill consequences of the opposite qualities. Besides, private persons have a further motive than even self-interest; their feelings are concerned; their economy may be a benefit to the objects of their affection; whereas, the economy of a ruler accrues to the benefit of those he knows very little of; and perhaps he is but husbanding for an extravagant and rival successor.

Nor is this evil remedied, by adopting the principle of hereditary rule. The monarch has little of the feelings common to other men in this respect. He is taught to consider the fortune of his descendants as secure, if they have ever so little assurance of the succession. Besides, the far greater part of the public consumption is not personally directed by himself; contracts are not made by himself, but by his generals and ministers; the experience of the world hitherto all tends to show, that aristocratical republics are more economical, than either monarchies or democracies.

Neither are we to suppose, that the genius which prompts and excites great national undertakings, is incompatible with the spirit of public order and economy. The name of Charlemagne stands among the foremost in the records of renown; he achieved the conquest of Italy, Hungary, and Austria; repulsed the Saracens; broke the Saxon confederacy; and obtained at length the honours of the purple. Yet Montesquieu has thought it not derogatory to say of

---

augmentation of the national capital must take place, even in defiance of many obstructions. The public expenditure, too, of the same kingdom, is in course of gradual reduction. During the late war, as has been observed by our author, on the authority of Colquhoun, the public expenditure of the year 1813 amounted to 112 millions, whereas in 1830 it was about 34 millions, in 1831, 33 millions, and in 1832 not so much by 100,000l. sterling. AMERICAN EDITOR.

him, that "the father of a family might take a lesson of good house-keeping from the ordinances of Charlemagne. His expenditure was conducted with admirable system; he had his demesnes valued with care, skill, and minuteness. We find detailed in his capitularies, the pure and legitimate sources of his wealth. In a word, such were his regularity and thrift, that he gave orders for the eggs of his poultry-yards, and the surplus vegetables of his garden, to be brought to market."* The celebrated Prince Eugene, who displayed equal talent in negotiation and administration as in the field, advised the Emperor Charles VI. to take the advice of merchants and men of business, in matters of finance.† Leopold, when Grand Duke of Tuscany, towards the close of the 18th century, gave an eminent example of the resources, to be derived from a rigid adherence to the principles of private economy, in the administration of a state of very limited extent. In a few years, he made Tuscany one of the most flourishing states of Europe.

The most successful financiers of France, Suger, Abbé de St. Dennis, the Cardinal D'Amboise, Sully, Colbert, and Necker, have all acted on the same principle. All found means of carrying into effect the grandest operations by adhering to the dictates of private economy. The Abbé de St. Dennis furnished the outfit of the second crusade; a scheme that required very large supplies, although one I am far from approving. The Cardinal furnished Louis XII. with the means of making his conquest of the Milanese. Sully accumulated the resources, that afterwards humbled the house of Austria.—Colbert supplied the splendid operations of Louis XIV. Necker provided the ways and means of the only successful war waged by France in the 18th century.‡

Those governments, on the contrary, that have been perpetually pressed with the want of money, have been obliged, like individuals, to have recourse to the most ruinous, and sometimes the most disgraceful, expedients to extricate themselves. Charles the Bald put his titles and safe-conducts up to sale. Thus, too, Charles II. of England sold Dunkirk to the French king, and took a bribe of 80,000*l.* from the Dutch, to delay the sailing of the English expedition to the East Indies, 1680, intended to protect their settlements in that quarter, which, in consequence, fell into the hands of the Dutchmen.§ Thus, too, have governments committed frequent acts

---

* *Esprit des Lois*, liv. xxxi. c. 18.

† *Memoires du Prince Eugene par luimême*, p. 187. The authenticity of this work has been contested, as well as the *Testament Politique* of Richelieu. If not themselves the authors, they must at least have been men of equal capacity, of which there is still less probability.

‡ He contrived to meet the charges of the American war, without the imposition of any additional taxes. He has been reproached, indeed, with having incurred heavy loans; but it is obvious, that, so long as he found means to pay the interest upon them without fresh taxation, they were nowise burthensome upon the nation; and that the interest must have been defrayed by retrenchment of the expenditure.

§ *Raynal. Histoire des Etab. des Europ. dans les Indes*, tom. ii. p. 36.

of ban ruptcy, sometimes in the shape of adulteration of their coin, and sometimes by open breach of their engagements.

Louis XIV. towards the close of his reign, having utterly exhausted the resources of a noble territory, was reduced to the paltry shift of creating the most ridiculous offices, making his counsellors of state, one an inspector of fagots, another a licenser of barber-wig-makers, another, visiting inspector of fresh, or taster of salt, butter, and the like. Such paltry and mischievous expedients can never long defer the hour of calamities, that must sooner or later befal the extravagant and spendthrift governments. "When a man will not listen to reason," says Franklin, " she is sure to make herself felt."

Fortunately, an economical administration soon repairs the mischiefs of one of an opposite character. Sound health can not be restored all at once; but there is a gradual and perceptible improvement; every day some cause of complaint disappears, and some new faculty comes again into play. Half the remaining resources of a nation, impoverished by an extravagant administration, are neutralized by alarm and uncertainty; whereas, credit* doubles those of a nation, blessed with one of a frugal character. It would seem, that there exists in the politic, to a stronger degree than even in the natural, body a principle of vitality and elasticity, which can not be extinguished without the most violent pressure. One can not look into the pages of history, without being struck with the rapidity, with which this principle has operated. It has nowhere been more strikingly exemplified, than in the frequent vicissitudes that our own France has experienced since the commencement of the revolution. Prussia has afforded another illustration in our time. The successor of Frederick the Great squandered the accumulations of that monarch, which were estimated at no less a sum than 42 millions of dollars, and left behind him, besides, a debt of 27 millions. In less than eight years, Frederick William III. had not only paid off his father's debts, but actually began a fresh accumulation; such is the power of economy, even in a country of limited extent and resources.

---

* The expressions, *credit* is *declining*, *credit* is *reviving*, are common in the mouths of the generality, who are, for the most part, ignorant of the precise meaning of *credit*. It does not imply confidence in the government exclusively; for the bulk of the community have no concern with government, in respect to their private affairs. Neither is it exclusively applied to the mutual confidence of individuals; for a person in good repute and circumstances, does not forfeit them all at once; and, even in times of general distress, the forfeiture of individual character is by no means so universal, as to justify the assertion, that credit is at an end. It would rather seem to imply, confidence in future events. The temporary dread of taxation, arbitrary exaction, or violence, will deter numbers from exposing their persons or their property; undertakings, however promising and well-planned, become too hazardous; new ones are altogether discouraged, old ones feel a diminution of profit; merchants contract their operations; and consumption in general falls off, in consequence of the decline and the uncertainty of individual revenue. There can be no confidence in future events, either under an enterprising, ambitious, or unjust government, or under one, that is wanting in strength, decision, or method. Credit, like crystallization, can only take place in a state of quiescence.

Section II.

Of the principal Objects of National Expenditure.

In the preceding section, it has been endeavoured to show, that, since all consumption by the public is in itself a sacrifice of value, an evil balanced only by such benefit, as may result to the community from the satisfaction of any of its wants, a good administration will never spend for the mere sake of spending, but take care to ascertain that the public benefit, resulting, in such instance, from the satisfaction of a public want, shall exceed the sacrifice incurred in its acquirement.

A comprehensive view of the principal public wants of a civilized community, can alone qualify us to estimate with tolerable accuracy the sacrifice it is worth while for the community to make for their gratification.*

The public consumes little else, but what have been denominated *Immaterial* products, that is to say, products destroyed as soon as created; in other words, the services or agency, either of human beings, or of other objects, animate or inanimate.†

It consumes the personal service of all its functionaries, civil, judicial, military, or ecclesiastical. It consumes the agency of land and capital. The navigation of rivers and seas, utility of roads and ground open to the public, are so much agency derived by the public from land, of which either the absolute property, or the beneficial enjoyment, is vested in the public. Where capital has been vested in the land, in the shape of buildings, bridges, artificial harbours, causeways, dikes, canals, &c. the public then consumes the agency, or the rent of the land, *plus* the agency, or the interest, of the capital so vested.

Sometimes the public maintains establishments of productive industry; for instance, the porcelain manufacture of Sevres, the Gobelin tapestry, the salt-works of Lorraine and of the Jura, &c., in France. When concerns of this kind bring more than their expenditure, which is but rarely the case, they furnish part of the national revenue, and must by no means be classed among the items of national charge.

Of the Charge of Civil and Judicial Administration.

The charge of civil and judicial administration is made up, partly of the specific allowances of magistrates and other officers,

---

* A mere sketch is all that can be expected in a work like the present: a complete treatise on government would be equally appropriate with a survey of the arts, when it became incidentally necessary to touch upon the processes of manufacture. Yet, either would be a valuable addition to literary wealth.

† This rule must be taken with some qualification. The habitual largesses of corn, distributed by the emperors to the people of ancient Rome, were material objects of public consumption. So likewise the provisions of all kinds consumed in hospitals and prisons, and the fireworks used on occasions of public display or rejoicing, for the amusement of the people at large.

and partly of such degree of pomp and parade, as may be deemed necessary in the execution of their duties. Even if the burthen of that pomp and parade be thrown wholly or partially upon the public functionary, it must ultimately fall upon the shoulders of the public, for the salary of the functionary must be raised, in proportion to the appearance he is expected to make. This observation applies to every description of functionary, from the prince to the constable inclusive; consequently, a nation, which reverences its prince only when surrounded with the externals of greatness, with guards, horse and foot, laced liveries, and such costly trappings of royalty, must pay dearly for its taste. If, on the contrary, it can be content, to respect simplicity rather than pageantry, and obey the laws, though unaided by the attributes of pomp and ceremony, it will save in proportion. This is what made the charges of government so light in many of the Swiss cantons, before the revolution, and in the North American colonies before their emancipation. It is well known, that those colonies, though under the dominion of England, had separate governments, of which they respectively defrayed the charge; yet the whole annual expenditure all together amounted to no more than 64,700*l.* sterling. " An ever memorable example," observes Smith, " at how small an expense three millions of people may not only be governed, but well governed."*

---

* It should be recollected, however, that they were at no charge of defence from external attack, except in respect to the savage tribes of the interior.

From the official account of the receipts and disbursements of the United States, in the year 1806, presented by Mr. Gallatin, then Secretary of the Treasury, it appears that the total expenditure fell short of twelve millions of dollars, of which eight millions went to pay the interest of the public debt; leaving a sum of four millions only for the charge of government, that is to say, the civil, judicial, military, and other public functions of a population of twelve millions: which is wholly defrayed by taxes on imports. (1)

(1) At the period to which our author here refers, namely, the year 1806, the actual expenditure by the government of the United States, for that year, according to the report of the Secretary of the Treasury, was 15,070,093 dollars 97 cents, and of this amount, according to the same authority, 8,989,884 dollars 61 cents, was on account of the extinguishment of the principal and interest of the public debt. The population of the United States, for the same year, was only about 6 millions; for, according to the official enumerations, the population, in the year 1800, was 5,305,925, and in the year 1810, was 7,239,814. Now the charges of the government, exclusive of the payment of the public debt, it will be seen, amounted then to 6,080,209 dollars 36 cents, or an expenditure equal to more than treble the amount given by our author.

The whole public expenditure of the people of the United States necessarily embraces the local disbursements of the different states, as well as the expenditure of the general government. Of the former, we have, as yet, no means of presenting our readers with any accurate or official account, and we will not venture to indulge in any loose estimates. Of the latter, however, we are enabled to furnish a tabular view, extracted from the letter of the Secretary of the Treasury to the Chairman of the Committee of the House of Representatives on Retrenchment, April 9, 1830, and from the subsequent annual Treasury Reports, which will exhibit an authentic and accurate view of the receipts and expenditures of the Federal Government, from the 4th of March, 1789, the period of its commencement, to the 31st of December, 1832, the last date to which the accounts have been all made up.

Causes entirely of a political nature as well as the form of government which they help to determine, have an influence in apportioning the salaries of public officers, civil and judicial, the charge of public display, and those likewise of public institutions and establish-

We also subjoin the last official revision of the population returns of the several states and territories, according to the five enumerations of the years 1790, 1800, 1810, 1820, and 1830.

RECEIPTS		
From March 4, 1789, to December 31, 1833.		
YEARS.	CUSTOMS.	TOTAL.
From March 4, 1789, to		
Dec. 31, 1791	$4,399,473 09	$10,210,025 75
" " 1792	3,443,070 85	8,740,766 77
" " 1793	4,255,606 56	5,720,624 28
" " 1794	4,801,065 28	10,041,101 65
" " 1795	5,588,461 26	9,419,802 79
" " 1796	6,567,987 94	8,740,329 65
" " 1797	7,549,649 65	8,758,916 40
" " 1798	7,106,061 93	8,209,070 07
" " 1799	6,610,449 31	12,621,459 84
" " 1800	9,080,932 73	12,451,184 14
" " 1801	10,750,778 93	12,945,455 95
" " 1802	12,438,235 74	15,001,391 31
" " 1803	10,479,417 61	11,064,097 63
" " 1804	11,098,565 33	11,835,840 02
" " 1805	12,936,487 04	13,689,508 14
" " 1806	14,667,698 17	15,608,823 78
" " 1807	15,845,521 61	16,398,019 26
" " 1808	16,363,550 58	17,062,544 09
" " 1809	7,296,020 58	7,773,473 12
" " 1810	8,583,309 31	12,144,206 53
" " 1811	13,313,222 73	14,431,838 14
" " 1812	8,958,777 53	22,639,032 76
" " 1813	13,224,623 25	40,524,844 95
" " 1814	5,998,772 08	34,559,536 95
" " 1815	7,282,942 22	50,961,237 60
" " 1816	36,306,874 88	57,171,421 82
" " 1817	26,283,348 49	33,833,592 33
" " 1818	17,176,385 00	21,593,936 66
" " 1819	20,283,608 76	24,605,665 37
" " 1820	15,005,612 15	20,881,493 68
" " 1821	13,004,447 15	19,573,703 72
" " 1822	17,589,761 94	20,232,427 94
" " 1823	19,088,433 44	20,540,666 26
" " 1824	17,878,325 71	24,381,212 79
" " 1825	20,098,713 45	26,840,858 02
" " 1826	23,341,331 77	25,260,434 21
" " 1827	19,712,283 29	22,966,363 96
" " 1828	23,205,523 64	24,763,629 23
" " 1829	22,681,965 91	24,767,122 22
" " 1830	21,922,391 39	24,844,116 51
" " 1831	24,224,441 97	28,526,820 82
" " 1832	28,465,237 21	31,865,561 16
" " 1833	29,032,508 91	33,948,426 25
	$623,941,576 17	$878,150,589 52

ments. Thus, in a despotic government, where the subject holds his property at the will of the sovereign, who fixes himself the charge of his household, that is to say, the amount of the public money which he chooses to spend on his personal necessities and pleasures, and the keeping up of the royal establishment, that charge will probably be fixed at a higher rate, than where it is arranged and

EXPENDITURES From March 4, 1789, to December 31, 1833.		
YEARS.	PUBLIC DEBT.	TOTAL.
From March 4, 1789, to Dec. 31, 1791	$5,287,949 50	$7,207,539 08
" " 1792	7,263,665 99	9,141,569 67
" " 1793	5,819,505 29	7,529,575 55
" " 1794	5,801,578 09	9,302,124 74
" " 1795	6,084,411 61	10,435,069 65
" " 1796	5,835,846 44	8,367,776 84
" " 1797	5,792,421 82	8,626,012 78
" " 1798	3,990,294 14	8,613,517 68
" " 1799	4,596,876 78	11,077,043 50
" " 1800	4,578,369 95	11,989,739 92
" " 1801	7,291,707 04	12,273,376 94
" " 1802	9,539,004 76	13,276,084 67
" " 1803	7,256,159 43	11,258,983 67
" " 1804	8,171,787 45	12,624,646 36
" " 1805	7,369,889 79	13,727,124 41
" " 1806	8,989,884 61	15,070,093 97
" " 1807	6,307,720 10	11,292,292 99
" " 1808	10,260,245 35	16,764,584 20
" " 1809	6,452,554 16	13,867,226 30
" " 1810	8,008,904 46	13,319,986 74
" " 1811	8,009,204 05	13,601,808 91
" " 1812	4,449,622 45	22,279,121 15
" " 1813	11,108,128 44	39,190,520 36
" " 1814	7,900,543 94	38,028,230 32
" " 1815	12,628,922 35	39,582,493 35
" " 1816	24,871,062 93	48,244,495 51
" " 1817	25,423,036 12	40,877,646 04
" " 1818	21,296,201 62	35,104,875 40
" " 1819	7,703,926 29	24,004,199 73
" " 1820	8,628,494 28	21,763,024 85
" " 1821	8,367,093 62	19,090,572 69
" " 1822	7,848,949 12	17,676,592 63
" " 1823	5,530,016 41	15,314,171 00
" " 1824	16,568,393 76	31,898,538 47
" " 1825	12,095,344 78	23,585,804 72
" " 1826	11,041,032 19	24,103,398 46
" " 1827	10,003,668 39	22,656,765 04
" " 1828	12,163,438 07	25,459,479 52
" " 1829	12,383,800 77	25,071,017 59
" " 1830	11,355,748 22	24,585,281 55
" " 1831	16,174,378 22	30,038,446 12
" " 1832	17,840,309 29	34,356,698 06
" " 1833	1,543,543 38	24,257,298 49
	$409,633,680 45	$866,534,848 56

contested between the representatives of the prince and of the tax-payers respectively.

The salaries of inferior public officers in like manner depend, partly upon their individual importance, and partly upon the general plan of government. Their services are dear or cheap to the public, not merely in proportion to what they actually cost, but likewise in proportion as they are well or ill executed. A duty ill performed is dearly bought, however little be paid for it; it is dear too, if it be superfluous, or unnecessary; resembling in this respect an article of furniture, that, if it do not answer its purpose, or be not wanted, is merely useless lumber. Of this description, under the old *régime* of France, were the officers of high-admiral, high-steward of the household, the king's cup-bearer, the master of his hounds, and a variety of others, which added nothing even to the splendour of royalty, and were merely so many means of dispensing personal favour and emolument.

For the same reason, whenever the officers of government are

POPULATION OF THE UNITED STATES, *According to Five Enumerations; from the Official Revision.*					
States.	1790.	1800.	1810.	1820.	1830.
Maine	96,540	151,719	228,705	298,335	399,955
New Hampshire . .	141,899	183,762	214,360	244,161	269,328
Vermont	85,416	154,465	217,713	235,764	280,652
Massachusetts . . .	378,717	423,245	472,040	523,287	610,408
Rhode Island . . .	69,110	69,122	77,031	83,059	97,199
Connecticut	238,141	251,002	262,042	275,202	297,665
New York	340,120	586,756	959,949	1,372,812	1,918,608
New Jersey	184,139	211,949	249,555	277,575	320,823
Pennsylvania . . .	434,373	602,365	810,091	1,049,458	1,348,233
Delaware	59,096	64,273	72,674	72,749	76,748
Maryland	319,728	341,548	380,546	407,350	447,040
Virginia	748,308	880,200	974,622	1,065,379	1,211,405
North Carolina . .	393,751	478,103	555,500	638,829	737,987
South Carolina . .	249,073	345,591	415,115	502,741	581,185
Georgia	82,548	162,101	252,433	340,987	516,823
Alabama	. .	. .	20,845	127,901	309,527
Mississippi	. .	8,850	40,352	75,448	136,621
Louisiana	. .	. .	76,556	153,407	215,739
Tennessee	35,791	105,602	261,727	422,813	681,904
Kentucky	73,077	220,955	406,511	564,317	687,917
Ohio	. .	45,365	230,760	581,434	937,903
Indiana	. .	4,875	24,520	147,178	343,031
Illinois	. .	. .	12,282	55,211	157,455
Missouri	. .	. .	20,845	66,586	140,445
District of Columbia	. .	14,093	24,023	33,039	39,834
Florida Territory .	. .	. .	. .	. .	34,730
Michigan Territory	. .	. .	4,762	8,896	31,639
Arkansas Territory	. .	. .	. .	14,273	30,388
Total	3,929,827	5,305,925	7,239,814	9,638,131	12,866,020

AMERICAN EDITOR.

needlessly multiplied, the people are saddled with charges, which are not necessary to the maintenance of public order. It is only giving an unnecessary form to that benefit, or product, which is not at all the better of it, if indeed it be not worse.* A bad government, that can not support its violence, injustice, and exaction, without a multitude of mercenaries, satellites, and spies, and gaols innumerable, makes its subjects pay for its prisons, spies, and soldiers, which nowise contribute to the public happiness.

On the other hand, a public duty may be cheap, although very liberally paid. A low salary is wholly thrown away upon an incapable and inefficient officer; his ignorance will probably cost the public ten times the amount of his salary; but the knowledge and activity of a man of ability are fully equivalent to the pay he receives; the losses he saves to the public, and the benefits derived from his exertions, greatly outweigh his personal emolument, even if settled on the most liberal scale.

There is real economy in procuring the best of every thing, even at a larger price. Merit can seldom be engaged at a low rate, because it is applicable to more occupations than one. The talent, that makes an able minister, would, in another profession, make a good advocate, physician, farmer, or merchant; and merit will find both employment and emolument in all these departments. If the public service offer no adequate reward for its exertion, it will choose some other more promising occupation.

Integrity is like talent; it can not be had without paying for it, which is not at all wonderful; for the honest man can not resort to those discreditable shifts and contrivances, which dishonesty looks to as a supplemental resource.

The power, which commonly accompanies the exercise of public functions, is a kind of salary, that often far exceeds the pecuniary emolument attached to them. It is true, that in a well ordered state, where law is supreme, and little is left to the arbitrary control of the ruler, there is little opportunity of indulging the caprice and love of domination implanted in the human breast. Yet the discretion, which the law must inevitably vest in those who are to enforce it, and particularly in the ministerial department, together with the honour commonly attendant on the higher offices of the state, have a real value, which makes them eagerly sought for, even in countries where they are by no means lucrative.

The rules of strict economy would probably make it advisable to abridge all pecuniary allowance, wherever there are other sufficient attractions to excite a competition for office, and to confer it on none but the wealthy, were there not a risk of losing, by the incapacity of the officer, more than would be gained by the

---

* An example occurs to me of a city of France, whose municipal administration was both mildly and efficiently conducted before 1789, at a charge of 1000 crowns per annum only, but under the imperial government, though it cost 30,000 *fr.* (5,580 dollars) afforded no security against the caprice and arbitrary will of the sovereign.

abridgment of his salary. This, as Plato well observes in his Republic, would be like entrusting the helm to the richest man on board. Besides, there is some danger, that a man, who gives his services for nothing, will make his authority a matter of gain, however rich he may be. The wealth of a public functionary is no security against his venality: for ample fortune is commonly accompanied with desires as ample, and probably even more ample, especially if he have to keep up an appearance, both as a man of wealth and a magistrate. Moreover, supposing what is not altogether impossible, namely, that one can meet with wealth united with probity, and with, besides, the activity requisite to the due performance of public duty, is it wise to run the risk of adding the preponderance of authority to that of wealth, which is already but too manifest? With what grace could his employers call to account an agent, who could assume the merit of generosity, both with the people and with the government? There are, however, some ways, in which the gratuitous services of the rich may be employed with advantage; particularly in those departments, that confer more honour than power: as in the administration of institutions of public charity, or of public correction or punishment.

In France under the old *régime*, the government, when harassed with the want of money, was in the habit of putting up its offices to sale. This is the very worst of all expedients; it introduces all the mischiefs of gratuitous service; for the emolument is then no more, than the interest of the capital expended in the purchase of the office; and has the additional evil of costing to the state as much as if the service were not gratuitously performed; for the public remains charged with the interest of a capital, that has been consumed and lost.

It has been sometimes the practice to consign certain civil functions, such as the registry of births, marriages, and deaths, to the ecclesiastical body, whose emoluments, arising from their clerical duties, may be supposed to enable them to execute these without pay. But there is always danger in confiding the execution of civil duties to a class of men, that pretend to a commission from a still higher than a national authority.*

In spite of every precaution, the public or the monarch will never be served so well or so cheaply as individuals. Inferior public

---

* Several times during the last century the Molinist priesthood refused to execute their clerical duties in favour of the Jansenists, in spite of all the government could do; on the pretence, that it was better to obey the divine command as conveyed by the voice of the Pope, than that of any human authority. (*a*)

(*a*) This inconvenience can arise only in countries, where there is an exclusive national church, subjected, in matters of doctrine and discipline, to an independent or external superior: as in countries embracing the faith of Rome. But there is another inconvenience, that has been much dwelt upon by an eminent divine of the Scottish church; viz. the inconvenience of directing the attention of the priesthood from its clerical to civil functions, and, by a confusion of such different duties, abridging the benefit of division of labour. T.

agents can not be so narrowly watched by their superiors, as private ones; nor have the superiors themselves an equal interest in vigilant superintendence. Besides, it is easy enough for underlings to impose on a superior, who has many to look after, is perhaps placed at a distance, and can give but little attention to each individually; and whose vanity makes him more alive to the officious zeal of his inferior, than to the real service and utility, that the public good requires. As to the monarch and the nation, who are the parties most interested in good public administration, because it consolidates the power of the one and enlarges the happiness of the other, it is next to impossible for them to exert a perpetual and effectual control. In most cases, this duty must of necessity devolve on agents, who will deceive them when it is their interest to do so, as is proved by abundance of examples. "Public services," says Smith, "are never better performed than when their reward comes only in consequence of their being performed, and is proportioned to the diligence employed in performing them." Accordingly, he recommends, that the salaries of judges should be paid at the final determination of each suit, and the share of each judge proportioned to their respective trouble in the progress of it. This would be some encouragement to the diligence of each particular judge, as well as to that of the court, in bringing litigation to an end. There would be some difficulty in applying this method to all the branches of the public service; and it would probably introduce as great abuses in the opposite way; but it would at least be productive of one good; viz. preventing the needless multiplication of offices. It would likewise give the public the same advantage of competition as is enjoyed by individuals, in respect to the services they call for.

Not only are the time and labour of public men in general better paid for than those of other persons, besides being often wasted by their own mismanagement, without the possibility of an efficient check; but there is often a further enormous waste, occasioned by compliance with the customs of the country, and court etiquette. It would be curious to calculate the time wasted in the toilet, or to estimate, if possible, the many dearly-paid hours lost, in the course of the last century, on the road between Paris and Versailles.

Thus, in the governments of Asia, there is an immense waste of the time of the superior public servants in tedious and ceremonious observances. The monarch, after allowing for the hours of customary parade, and those of personal pleasure, has little time left to look after his own affairs, which, consequently, soon go to ruin. Frederick II. of Prussia, by adopting a contrary line of conduct, and by the judicious distribution and apportionment of his time, contrived to get through a great deal of business himself. By this means, he really lived longer than older men than himself, and succeeded in raising his kingdom to a first-rate power. His other great qualities, doubtless, contributed to his success; but they would not have been sufficient, without a methodical arrangement of his time.

Of Charges, Military and Naval.

When a nation has made any considerable progress in commerce, manufacture, and the arts, and its products have, consequently, become various and abundant, it would be an immense inconvenience, if every citizen were liable to be dragged from a productive employment, which has become necessary to society, for the purposes of national defence. The cultivator of the soil works no longer for the sustenance of himself and family only, but also for that of many other families, who are either owners of the soil, and share in its produce, or traders and manufacturers, that supply him with articles he cannot do without. He must, therefore, cultivate a larger extent of surface, must vary his tillage, keep a larger stock of cattle, and follow a complex mode of cultivation that will fully occupy his leisure between seed-time and harvest.*

Still less can the trader and manufacturer afford thus to sacrifice time and talents, whereof the constant occupation, except during the intervals of rest, is necessary to the production, from which they are to derive their subsistence.

The owners of land let out to farm may, undoubtedly, serve as soldiers without pay; as, indeed, the nobility and gentry do, in some measure, in monarchical states; but they are, for the most part, so much accustomed to the sweets of social existence, so little goaded by necessity towards the conception and achievement of great enterprises, and feel so little of the enthusiasm of emulation and *esprit de corps*, that they commonly prefer a pecuniary sacrifice to that of comfort, and possibly of life. And these motives operate equally with the owners of capital.

All these reasons have led individuals, in most modern states, to consent to a taxation, that may enable the monarch or the republic to defend the country against external violence with a hired and professional soldiery, who are, however, too apt to become the tools of their leader's ambition or tyranny.

When war has become a trade, it benefits, like all other trades, from the division of labour. Every branch of human science is pressed into its service. Distinction or excellence, whether in the capacity of general, engineer, subaltern, or even private soldier, can not be obtained without long training, perhaps, and constant practice. The nation, which should act upon a different principle, would lie under the disadvantage of opposing the imperfection, to the perfection, of art. Thus, excepting the cases, in which the enthusiasm of a whole nation has been roused to action, the advantage has uni-

---

* The Greeks, until the second Persian war, and the Romans, until the siege of Veii, regularly made their military campaigns in that interval. Nations of hunters or shepherds, that pay little attention to the arts, and none to agriculture, like the Tartars and Arabs, are less circumscribed in time, and can prosecute their warlike enterprises in any quarter, that promises booty, and furnishes pasturage. Hence the vast area of the conquests of Attila, Genghis Khan, and Tamerlane, and of the Moors and the Turks.

formly been on the side of a disciplined and professional soldiery.
The Turks, although professing the utmost contempt for the arts of
their Christian neighbours, are compelled by the dread of extermi-
nation, to be their scholars in the art of war. The European powers
were all forced to adopt the military tactics of the Prussians; and,
when the violent agitation of the French revolution pressed every
resource of science to the aid of the armies of the republic, the enemies of France were obliged to follow the example.

This extensive application of science, and adaptation of fresh
means and more ample resources to military purposes, have made
war far more expensive now than in former times. It is necessary
now-a-days, to provide an army beforehand, with supplies of arms,
ammunition, magazines of provision, ordnance, &c., equal to the consumption of one campaign at the least. The invention of gunpowder
has introduced the use of weapons more complex and expensive, and
very chargeable in the transport, especially the field and battering
trains. Moreover, the wonderful improvement of naval tactics, the
variety of vessels of every class and construction, all requiring the
utmost exertion of human genius and industry; the yards, docks,
machinery, store-houses, &c. have entailed upon nations addicted to
war almost as heavy an expense in peace, as in times of actual hostility; and obliged them not only to expend a great portion of their
income, but to vest a great amount of capital likewise in military
establishments. In addition to which, it is to be observed, that the
modern colonial system, that is to say, the system of retaining the
sovereignty of towns and provinces in distant parts of the world,
has made the European states open to attack and aggression in the
most remote quarters of the globe, and the whole world the theatre
of warfare, when any of the leading powers are the belligerents.*

Wealth has, consequently, become as indispensable as valour to
the prosecution of modern warfare; and a poor nation can no longer
withstand a rich one. Wherefore, since wealth can be acquired
only by industry and frugality, it may safely be predicted, that
every nation, whose agriculture, manufacture, and commerce, shall
be ruined by bad government, or exorbitant taxation, must infallibly
fall under the yoke of its more provident neighbours. We may
further conclude, that henceforward national strength will accompany national science and civilization; for none but civilized nations
can maintain considerable standing armies; so that there is no reason
to apprehend the future recurrence of those sudden overthrows of
civilized empires by the influx of barbarous tribes, of which history
affords many examples.

War costs a nation more than its actual expense; it costs besides,
all that would have been gained, but for its occurrence.

When Louis XIV. in 1672, resolved in a fit of passion, to chas-

---

* It has been calculated that every soldier, brought into the field by Great
Britain, during her last war with America, cost her twice as much as one on the
continent of Europe. And the other charges of warfare must of course be aggravated by the distance in an equal ratio.

tise the Dutch for the insolence of their newspaper writers, Boreel, the Dutch ambassador, laid before him a memorial showing that France through the medium of Holland, sold produce annually to foreign nations, to the amount of sixty millions *fr.* at the then scale of price; which will fall little short of 120 millions (22,000,000 of dollars) at the present. But the court treated his representations as the mere empty bravado of an ambassador.

To conclude: the charges of war would be very incorrectly estimated, were we to take no account of the havoc and destruction it occasions; for that one at least of the belligerents, whose territory happens to be the scene of operations, must be exposed to its ravages. The more industrious the nation, the more does it suffer from warfare. When it penetrates into a district abounding in agricultural, manufacturing, and commercial establishments, it is like a fire in a place full of combustibles; its fury is aggravated, and the devastation prodigious. Smith calls the soldier an unproductive labourer; would to God he were nothing more, and not a destructive one into the bargain! he not only adds no product of his own (*a*) to the general stock of wealth, in return for the necessary subsistence he consumes, but is often set to work to destroy the fruits of other people's labour and toil, without doing himself any benefit.

The tardy, but irresistible expansion of intelligence will probably operate a still further change in external political relations, and with it a prodigious saving of expenditure for the purposes of war. Nations will be taught to know that they have really no interest in fighting one another; that they are sure to suffer all the calamities incident to defeat, while the advantages of success are altogether illusory. According to the international policy of the present day, the vanquished are sure to be taxed by the victor, and the victor by domestic authority: for the interest of loans must be raised by taxation. There is no instance on record, of any diminution of national expenditure being effected by the most successful issue of hostilities. And, what is the glory it can confer more than a mere toy of the most extravagant price, that can never even amuse rational minds for any length of time? Dominion by land or sea will appear equally destitute of attraction, when it comes to be generally understood, that all its advantages rest with the rulers, and that the subjects at large derive no benefit whatever. To private individuals, the greatest possible benefit is entire freedom of intercourse, which can hardly be enjoyed except in peace. Nature prompts nations to mutual amity; and, if their governments take upon themselves to interrupt it, and engage them in hostility, they are equally inimical to their own people, and to those they war against. If their subjects are weak enough to second the ruinous vanity or ambition of their rulers in this propensity, I know not

(*a*) This is too generally expressed. Where security from external attack is only to be had by means of a professional soldiery, the soldier is a productive agent—productive of the immaterial product, security from external attack, than which, under certain circumstances, none can be more valuable. T.

how to distinguish such egregious folly and absurdity, from that of the brutes that are trained to fight and tear each other to pieces, for the mere amusement of their savage masters.

But human intelligence will not stand still; the same impulse that has hitherto borne it onwards, will continue to advance it yet further.* The very circumstance of the vast increase of expense attending national warfare has made it impossible for governments henceforth to engage in it, without the public assent, express or implied; and that assent will be obtained with the more difficulty, in proportion as the public shall become more generally acquainted with their real interest. The national military establishment will be reduced to what is barely sufficient to repel external attack; for which purpose little more is necessary, than a small body of such kinds of troops as can not be had without long training and exercise; as of cavalry and artillery. For the rest, nations will rely on their militia, and on the excellence of their internal polity: for it is next to impossible to conquer a people unanimous in their attachment to their national institutions; and their attachment will always be proportionate to the loss they will incur by a change of domination.†

Of the Charges of Public Instruction.

Two questions have been raised in political economy; 1. Whether the public be interested in the cultivation of science in all its branches? 2. Whether it be necessary, that the public should be at the expense of teaching those branches, it has an interest in cultivating?

Whatever be the position of man in society, he is in constant dependence upon the three kingdoms of nature. His food, his clothing, his medicines, every object either of business or of pleasure, is subject to fixed laws; and the better those laws are understood, the more benefit will accrue to society. Every individual, from the common mechanic, that works in wood or clay, to the prime minister that regulates with the dash of his pen the agriculture, the breeding of cattle, the mining, or the commerce of a nation, will perform his business the better, the better he understands the nature of things, and the more his understanding is enlightened.

For this reason, every advance of science is followed by an in-

---

* Those who deny the progressive influence of human reason must have studied history to very little purpose. The perfidy and cruelty of war have considerably abated, in Europe, more than in Asia or America, and most of all amongst the most polished of the European nations. The ungenerous character of some recent military enterprises roused so much public indignation, as to make them recoil upon the projectors with ruinous violence.

† I am here speaking of the only sure reliance in an enlightened age. A people, that has nothing to lose by a change of domination, may defend itself with the most determined gallantry. The Mussulman will rush on certain destruction, in defence of a prince and a faith, that are neither of them worth defending. But political and religious prejudice will sooner or later fall to the ground; and leave mankind to seek for some more reasonable object of devotion.

crease of social happiness. A new application of the lever, or of the power of wind or water, or even a method of reducing the friction of bodies, will, perhaps, have an influence on twenty different arts. An uniformity of weights and measures, arranged upon mathematical principles, would be a benefit to the whole commercial world, if it were wise enough to adopt such an expedient. An important discovery in astronomy or geology may possibly afford the means of ascertaining the longitude at sea with precision, which would be an immense advantage to navigation all over the world. The naturalisation in Europe of a new botanical genus or species might possibly influence the comfort of many millions of individuals.*

Among the numerous classes of science, theoretical and practical, which it is the interest of the public to advance and promote, there are fortunately many, that individuals have a personal interest in pursuing, and which the public, therefore, is not called upon to pay the expense of teaching. Every adventurer in any branch of industry is urged most strongly by self-interest to learn his business and whatever concerns it. The journeyman gains in his apprenticeship, besides manual dexterity, a variety of notions and ideas only to be learnt in the work-shop, and which can be no otherwise recompensed, than by the wages he will receive.

But it is not every degree or class of knowledge, that yields a benefit to the individual, equivalent to that accruing to the public. In treating above† of the profits of the man of science, I have shown the reason, why his talents are not adequately remunerated; yet theoretical is quite as useful to society as practical knowledge; for how could science ever be applied to the practical utility of mankind, unless it were discovered and preserved by the theorist? It would rapidly degenerate into mere mechanical habit, which must soon decline; and the downfall of the arts would pave the way for the return of ignorance and barbarism.

In every country that can at all appreciate the benefits to be derived from the enlargement of human faculties, it has been deemed by no means a piece of extravagance, to support academies and learned institutions, and a limited number of very superior schools, intended not as mere repositories of science, and of the most approved mode of instruction, but as a means of its still further extension. But it requires some skill in the management, to prevent such establishments from operating as an impediment, instead of a furtherance, to the progress of knowledge, and as an obstruction rather than as an avenue to the improvement of education. Long before the revolution, it had become notorious, that most of our French universities had been thus perverted from the intention of their founders.

---

* Should the expected success attend the attempt to naturalise in Europe the flax of New Zealand, which is greatly superior to that of Europe in the length and delicacy of the fibre, as well as in the abundance of the crop, it is possible that fine linen may be produced at the rate now paid for the coarsest quality; which would greatly improve the cleanliness and health of the lower classes.

† Book II. chap. 7. sect. 2.

All the principal discoveries were made elsewhere; and most of them had to encounter the weight of their influence over the rising generation and credit with men in power.*(1)

From this example, we may see how dangerous it is, to entrust them with any discretionary control. If a candidate presents himself for examination, he must not be referred to teachers, who are at the same time judges and interested parties, sure to think well of their own scholars, and ill of those of every body else. The merit of the candidate should alone decide, and not the place where he happens to have studied, nor the length of his probation; for to oblige a student in any science, medicine for instance, to learn it at a particular place, is, possibly, to prevent his learning it better elsewhere; and, to prescribe any fixed routine of study, is, possibly, to prevent his fixing a shorter road. Moreover, in deciding upon comparative merit, there is much unfairness to be apprehended from the *esprit de corps* of such communities.

Encouragement may, with perfect safety, be held out to a mode of instruction of no small efficacy; I mean, the composition of good elementary† works. The reputation and profit of a good book in

---

*What was denominated an University, under the reign of Napoleon, was a still more mischievous institution; being, in fact, but a most expensive and vexatious contrivance, for depraving the intellectual faculties of the rising generation, by substituting, in the place of just and correct notions of things, opinions calculated to perpetuate the political slavery of their country.

† Under this head, I would include, the fundamental parts of knowledge in every department, and the familiar instruction adapted to each specific calling, respectively; such as would impart at a cheap rate to the hatter, the metalfounder, the potter, the dyer, &c., the general principles of their respective arts. Works of this kind keep up a constant channel of communication between the practical and theoretical branches, and enable them to profit mutually by each other's experience.

---

(1) ["It is chiefly," observes DUGALD STEWART, "in judging of questions coming home to their business and bosoms, that casual associations lead mankind astray; and of such associations, how incalculable is the number arising from false systems of religion, oppressive forms of government, and absurd plans of education. The consequence is, that while the physical and mathematical discoveries of former ages present themselves to the hand of the historian, like masses of pure and native gold, the truths which we are here in quest of may be compared to *iron*, which although at once the most necessary and the most widely diffused of all the metals, commonly requires a discriminating eye to detect its existence, and a tedious as well as nice process, to extract it from the ore."

"To the same circumstance it is owing, that improvements in Moral and in Political Science do not strike the imagination with nearly so great force as the discoveries of the Mathematician or of the Chemist. When an inveterate prejudice is destroyed by extirpating the casual associations on which it was grafted, how powerful is the new impulse given to the intellectual faculties of man! Yet how slow and silent the process by which the effect is accomplished! Were it not, indeed, for a certain class of learned authors, who, from time to time, heave the log into the deep, we should hardly believe that the reason of the species is progressive. In this respect, the religious and academical establishments in some parts of Europe are not without their use to the historian of the human mind. Immovably moored to the same station by the strength of

this class do not indemnify the labour, science, and skill, requisite to its composition. (a) A man must be a fool to serve the public in this line where the natural profit is so little proportioned to the benefit derived to the public. The want of good elementary books will never be thoroughly supplied, until the public shall hold out temptations, sufficiently ample to engage first-rate talents in their composition. It does not answer to employ particular individuals for the express purpose; for the man of most talents will not always succeed the best: nor to offer specific premiums; for they are often bestowed on very imperfect productions, and the encouragement ceases the moment the premium is awarded. But merit in this kind should be paid proportionately to its degree, and always liberally. A good work will thus be sure to be superseded by a better, till perfection is at last attained in each class. And I must observe, by the way, that there is no great expense incurred by liberally rewarding excellence; for it must always be extremely rare; and what is a great sum to an individual, is a small matter to the pockets of a nation.

These are the kinds of instruction most calculated to promote national wealth, and most likely to retrograde, if not in some measure supported by the public. There are others, which are essential to the softening of national manners, and stand yet more in need of that support.

When the useful arts have arrived at a high degree of perfection, and labour has been very generally and minutely subdivided, the occupation of the lowest classes of labourers is reduced to one or two operations, for the most part simple in themselves, and continually repeated: to these their whole thought and attention are directed; and from them they are seldom diverted by any novel or unforeseen occurrence: their intellectual faculties, being rarely or never called into play, must of course be degraded and brutified, and themselves rendered incapable of uttering two words of common sense out of their peculiar line of business, and utterly devoid of any generous ideas or elevated notions. Elevation of mind is generated by enlarged views of men and things, and can never exist in a being incapable of conceiving the general bearings and connexions of objects. A plodding mechanic can conceive no connexion between the inviolability of property and public prosperity, or how he can be more interested in that prosperity, than his more wealthy neighbour; but is apt to consider all these important benefits as so many encroachments on his rights and happiness. A certain degree of education,

---

(a) This can only be true where the demand for such works is limited. In England, works of instruction are probably amongst the most profitable to the authors. T.

---

their cables, and the weight of their anchors, they enable him to measure the rapidity of the current by which the rest of the world are borne along."
Vide Preface to Stewart's Dissertations, p. 28, *Boston edition.*]

AMERICAN EDITOR.

of reading, of reflection while at work, and of intercourse with persons of his own condition, will open his mind to these conceptions, as well as introduce a little more delicacy of feeling into his conduct, as a father, a husband, a brother, or a citizen.

But, in the vast machinery of national production, the mere manual labourer is so placed, as to earn little or nothing more than a bare subsistence. The most he can do is, to rear his young family, and bring them up to some occupation: he cannot be expected to give them that education, which we have supposed the well-being of society to require. If the community wish to have the benefit of more knowledge and intelligence in the labouring classes, it must dispense it at the public charge.

This object may be obtained by the establishment of primary schools, of reading, writing, and arithmetic. These are the groundwork of all knowledge, and are quite sufficient for the civilization of the lower classes. In fact, one can not call a nation civilized, nor consequently possessed of the benefits of civilization, until the people at large be instructed in these three particulars: till then it will be but partially reclaimed from barbarism. With the help of these advantages alone, it may safely be affirmed, that no transcendent genius or superior mind will long remain in obscurity, or be prevented from displaying itself to the infinite benefit of the community. The faculty of reading alone, will, for a few dollars, put a man in possession of all that eminent men have said or done, in the line to which the bent of genius impels. Nor should the female part of the creation be shut out from this elementary education; for the public is equally interested in their civilization; and they are indeed the first, and often the only teachers of the rising generation.

It would be the more unpardonable in governments to neglect the business of education, and abandon to their present ignorance the great majority of the population in those nations of Europe, that pretend to the character of refinement and civilization, now that the improved methods of mutual instruction, that have been tried with such complete success, afford a ready and most economical means of universally diffusing knowledge amongst the inferior classes.*

---

* According to the new method, introduced by Lancaster, and perfected by subsequent teachers, a single master with very little aid of books, pens, or paper, can rapidly and effectually teach reading, writing, and vulgar arithmetic, to five or six hundred scholars at a time. This truly economical result is produced, by taking advantage of the slightest superiority of intelligence of one above another, and directing the motive of emulation, natural to the human breast, towards an useful object. A large school is commonly divided into forms, consisting each of eight children, as nearly equal in advancement as possible, and instructed by a child somewhat more advanced, called the Monitor. These forms again are divided into eight classes; of which the lowest learns to pronounce the letters of the alphabet, and to trace their figures rudely with the finger upon sand spread out upon a flat board; and the highest is able to write upon paper, and to practise the four rules of arithmetic. The children of each form are ranged according to their progress; and whoever cannot give the answer, is immediately superseded by a more apt scholar. As soon as a child is perfected in one class, he is transferred to the next in degree. The lessons are received,

Thus, none but elementary and abstract science,—the highest and the lowest branches of knowledge, are so much less favoured in the natural course of things, and so little stimulated by the competition of demand, as to require the aid of that authority, which is created purposely to watch over the public interests. Not that individuals have no interest in the support and promotion of these, as well as of the other, branches of knowledge; but they have not so direct an interest,—the loss occasioned by their disappearance is neither so immediate nor so perceptible; a flourishing empire might retrograde, until it reached the confines of barbarism, before individuals had observed the operating cause of its decline.

I would not be understood to find fault with public establishments for purposes of education, in other branches than those I have been describing. I am only endeavouring to show, in what branches a nation may wisely, and with due regard to its own interest, defray the charge out of the public purse. Every diffusion of such knowledge, as is founded upon fact and experience, and does not proceed upon dogmatical opinions and assertions, every kind of instruction, that tends to improve the taste and understanding, is a positive good; and, consequently, an institution calculated to diffuse it must be beneficial. But care must be taken, that encouragement of one branch shall not operate to discourage another. This is the general mischief of premiums awarded by the public; a private teacher or institution will not be adequately paid, where the same kind of instruction is to be had for nothing, though, perhaps, from inferior teachers. There is, therefore, some danger, that talent may be superseded by mediocrity; and a check be given to private exertions, from which the resources of the state might expect incalculable benefit.

The only important science, which seems to me not susceptible of being taught at the public charge, is that of moral philosophy, which may be considered as either experimental or doctrinal. The former consists in the knowledge of moral qualities, and of the chain of connexion between events dependent upon human will; and forms indeed a part of the study of man, which is best pursued by social converse and intercourse. The latter is a series of maxims and precepts, possessing very little influence upon human conduct, which is best guided in the relations of public and of private life, by the operation of good laws, of good education, and of good example.*

---

sometimes in a sitting posture, and sometimes upright, with slates affixed to the walls. The instruction is thus always accommodated to the age and faculties of the child; it necessarily arrests and rewards his attention; and involves that personal activity, essential to the infant frame. The whole is conducted in a single apartment, and usually under the superintendence of a single master or mistress. The general adoption of this method will probably be for some time opposed by custom and prejudice; but its utility and conformity to the order of nature will ensure its ultimate and universal prevalence.

* I am strongly disposed to say the same of logic. Were nothing taught, but what is consistent with truth and good sense, logic would follow of itself as a

The sole encouragement to virtue and good conduct, that can be relied on, is, the interest that every body has in discovering and employing no persons but those of good character. Men the most independent in their circumstances want something more to make them happy; that is to say, the general esteem and good opinion of their fellow-creatures; and these can only be acquired by putting on the appearance at least of estimable qualities, which it is much easier to acquire than to simulate. The influence of the sovereign or ruling body, upon the manners of the nation, is very extensive, because it employs a vast number of people; but it operates less beneficially than that of individuals, because it is less interested in employing none but persons of integrity. If to its lukewarmness in this particular be added, the example of immorality and contempt for honesty and economy too frequently held out to people by their rulers, the corruption of national morals will be wonderfully accelerated.* But a nation may be rescued from moral degradation by the re-action of opposite causes. Colonies are, for the most part, composed of by no means the most estimable classes of the mother-country: in a very short time, however, when the hopes of return are wholly abandoned, and the settlers have made up their minds to pass the rest of their lives in their new abode, they gradually feel the necessity of conciliating the esteem of their fellow-citizens, and the morals of the colony improve rapidly. By morals, I mean the general course of human conduct and behaviour.

These are the causes, that have a positive influence upon national morality. To these must be added, the effect of education in general, in opening the eyes of mankind to their real interests, and softening the temper and disposition.

Religious instruction ought, strictly speaking, to be defrayed by the respective religious communions and societies, each of which regards the opinions of the rest as heretical, and naturally revolts at the injustice of contributing to the propagation of what it deems erroneous, if not criminal.

Of the Charges of Public Benevolent Institutions.

It has been much debated, whether individual distress has any title to public relief. I should say none, except inasmuch as it is an unavoidable consequence of existing social institutions. If infir-

---

matter of course: all the teaching in the world will never make a man a good reasoner, whose notions and ideas of things are unsound and erroneous; and, with the foundation of just notions, he will require no teaching to make him reason well. Just ideas of things are only to be acquired by attentive examination; by taking account of every particular concerning them, and of nothing but what concerns them; which is the object of all knowledge in general, and by no means of logic alone.

* The bad example of a vicious prince is of the most fatal tendency; it is notorious to all the world, and protected and abetted by public authority; and it is sure to be reflected by the subservience of courtiers to the extreme point of imitative servility.

mity and want be the effect of the social system, they have a title to public relief: provided always, that it be shown, that the same system affords no means of prevention or cure.   But it would be foreign to the matter to discuss the question of right in this place. All we need do is, to consider benevolent institutions with regard to their nature and consequences.

When a community establishes at the public charge any institution for benevolent purposes, it forms a kind of saving-bank, to which every member contributes a portion of his revenue, to entitle him to claim a benefit, in the event of accident or misfortune.   The wealthy are generally impressed with an idea, that they shall never stand in need of public charitable relief; but a little less confidence would become them better.   No man can reckon in his own case upon the continuance of good fortune, with as much certainty as upon the permanence of wants and infirmities; the former may desert him; but the latter are inseparable companions.   It is enough to know, that good fortune is not inexhaustible, to infuse an apprehension that it may some day or other be exhausted: one has but to look round, and this apprehension will be confirmed by the experience of numbers, whose misfortunes were to themselves quite unexpected.

Hospitals for the sick, almshouses and asylums for old age and infancy, inasmuch as they partially relieve the poorer classes from the charge of maintaining those who are naturally dependent on them, and thereby to allow population to advance somewhat more rapidly, have a natural tendency a little to depress the wages of labour.   That depression would be greater still, if such establishments should be so multiplied, as to take in all the sick, aged, and infants of those classes, who would then have none but themselves to provide for out of their wages. If they were entirely done away, there would be some rise of wages, although not sufficient to maintain so large a labouring population, as may be kept up with their help; for the demand for their labour would be somewhat reduced by the advance of its price.

From these two extreme suppositions, we may judge of the effect of those efforts to relieve indigence, which all nations have made in some degree or other; and see the reason, why the distress and relief go on increasing together, although not exactly in the same ratio.

Most nations preserve a middle course between the two extremes, affording public relief to a part only of those, who are helpless from age, infancy, or casual sickness.   Of the rest they endeavour to rid themselves in one of two ways; either by requiring certain qualifications in the applicants, whether of age, of specific disease, or, perhaps, of mere interest and favouritism; or by limiting narrowly the extent of the relief, giving it upon hard terms to the applicants, or attaching some degree of shame to the acceptance.*

* At Paris, the limitation of relief afforded by the *Hospice des Incurables*, and those of *Petites Maisons*, of *St. Louis*, of *Charite*, and many others, is of the

It is a distressing reflection, that there are no other methods of confining the number of applicants for relief within the means available to the community, except the offer of hard conditions, or the want of a patron. It were to be desired, that asylums of the more comfortable class, instead of favouritism, should be open to unmerited misfortune only; and that, to prevent improper nominations, the pretensions of the candidate should be ascertained by the inquest of a jury. The rest can probably be protected from too great an influx of indigence, by no other means consistent with humanity, except the observance of severe, though impartial, discipline, sufficient to invest them with some degree of terror.

This evil does not apply to the asylums devoted to invalid soldiers and sailors. The qualification is so plain and intelligible, that the doors ought to be shut against none who are possessed of it; and the comforts of the institution can never increase the number of applicants. Their being nursed in the public asylums with the same domestic care and comfort, as are to be found in the homes of persons in the same class of life, and indulged in repose, and some even of the whims of old age, will undoubtedly somewhat enhance the charge, that is to say, so far as it might prolong lives, that otherwise might fall a sacrifice to wretchedness; but this is the utmost increase of charge; and it is one, that neither patriotism nor humanity will grudge.*

The houses of industry, that are multiplying so rapidly in America, Holland, Germany, and France, are noble and excellent institutions of public benevolence. They are designed to provide all persons of sound health with work according to their respective capacities; some of them are open to any workman out of employ, that chooses to apply; others are a kind of houses of correction, where vagrants, beggars, and offenders, are kept to work for fixed periods. Convicts have sometimes been set to hard labour in their respective vocations, during their confinement; whereby the public has been wholly or partially relieved from the charge of keeping up gaols, and a method contrived for reforming the morals of the criminals, and rendering them a blessing, instead of a curse, to society.

Indeed, such establishments can hardly be reckoned among the items of public charge; for, the moment their production equals their consumption, they are no longer an incumbrance to any body. They are of immense benefit in a dense population, where, amidst

---

former kind; the admissions to the *Hotel-Dieu*, *Bicêtre*, *Saltpétrière*, and *Enfans-Trouvés*, are subject to a limitation of the latter kind. As the number of applicants duly qualified for admission in the establishment first mentioned always exceeds their capacity, the choice must ultimately be decided by favour or interest.

* Yet it is well worth consideration, whether it be not more to the advantage, both of the state and of its pensioners, to maintain them at their own homes upon a fixed income, or to board them out with individuals. The *Abbé de St. Pierre*, whose mind was ever actively at work for the public good, has estimated the charge of maintaining the invalids in their sumptuous establishment at Paris, to be three times as much as that of their maintenance at their respective homes. *Annales Polit.* p. 209.

the vast variety of occupations, some must unavoidably be in a state of temporary inaction.   The perpetual shiftings of commerce, the introduction of new processes, the withdrawing of capital from a productive concern, accidental fire, or other calamity, may throw numbers out of employment; and the most deserving individual may, without any fault of his own, be reduced to the extreme of want.   In these institutions, he is sure of earning at least a subsistence, if not in his own line, in one of a similar description.

The grand obstacle to such establishments is, the great outlay of capital they require.   They are adventures of industry, and as such must be provided with a variety of tools, implements, and machines, besides raw material of different kinds to work upon.   Before they can be said to maintain themselves, they must earn enough to pay the interest of the capital embarked, as well as their current expenses.

The favour shown them by the public authority, in the gratuitous supply of the capital and buildings, and in many other particulars, would make them interfere with private undertakings, were they not subject, on the other hand, to some peculiar disadvantages.   They are obliged to confine their operations to such kinds of work, as sort with the feebleness and general inferiority in skill of the inmates, and can not direct them to such as may be most in demand.   Moreover, it is in most of them a matter of regulation and police, to lay by always the third or fourth part of the labourer's wages or earnings, as a capital to set him up, on his quitting the establishment: this is an excellent precaution, but prevents their working at such cheap rates, as to drive all competition out of the market.

Although the honour, attached to the direction and management of institutions of public benevolence, will generally attract the gratuitous service of the affluent and respectable part of the community, yet, when the duties become numerous and laborious, they are commonly discharged by gratuitous administrators with the most unfeeling negligence.   It was probably by no means wise, to subject all the hospitals of Paris to a general superintendence.   At London, each hospital is separately administered; and the whole are managed with more economy and attention in consequence.   A laudable emulation is thereby excited amongst the managers of rival establishments; which affords an additional proof of the practicability and benefit of competition in the business of public administration.

Of the Charges of Public Edifices and Works.

I shall not here attempt to enumerate the great variety of works requisite for the use of the public; but merely lay down some general rules, for calculating their cost to the nation.   It is often impossible to estimate with any tolerable accuracy the public benefit derived from them.   How is one to calculate the utility, that is to say, the pleasure, which the inhabitants of a city derive from a public terrace or promenade? It is a positive benefit to have, within an easy distance of the close and crowded streets of a populous town, some place where the population can breathe a pure and wholesome atmosphere, and take health and exercise, under the shade of a grove, or with a verdant prospect before the eye; and where school-boys can spend their hours of recreation; yet this advantage it would be impossible to set a precise value upon.

The amount of its cost, however, may be ascertained or estimated. The cost of every public work or construction consists:—

1. Of the rent of the surface whereon it is erected; which rent amounts to what a tenant would give to the proprietor.

2. Of the interest of the capital expended in the erection.

3. Of the annual charge of maintenance.

Sometimes, one or more of these items may be curtailed. When the soil, whereon a public work is erected, will fetch nothing from either a purchaser, or a tenant, the public will be charged with nothing in the nature of rent; for no rent could be got if the spot had never been built on. A bridge, for instance, costs nothing but the interest of the capital expended in its construction, and the annual charge of keeping it in repair. If it be suffered to fall into decay, the public consumes, annually, the agency of the capital vested, reckoned in the shape of interest on the sum expended, and, gradually, the capital itself, into the bargain; for, as soon as the bridge ceases to be passable, not only is the agency or rent of the capital lost, but the capital is gone likewise.

Supposing one of the dikes in Holland to have cost in the outset, 20,000 dollars; the annual charge on the score of interest, at 5 per cent., will be 1000 dollars; and, if it cost 600 dollars more in the keeping it up, the total annual charge will be 1600 dollars.

The same mode of reckoning may be applied to roads and canals. If a road be broader than necessary, there is annually a loss of the rent of all the superfluous land it occupies, and, besides, of all the additional charge of repair. Many of the roads out of Paris are 180 feet wide, including the unpaved part on each side; whereas, a breadth of 60 feet would be full wide for all useful purposes, and would be quite magnificent enough, even for the approaches to a great metropolis. The surplus is only so much useless splendour; indeed, I hardly know how to call it so; for the narrow pavement in the centre of a broad road, the two sides of which are impassable the greater part of the year, is an equal imputation upon the liberality, and upon the good sense and taste of the nation. It gives a disagreeable sensation, to see so much loss of space, more particularly if it be badly kept. It appears like a wish to have magnificent roads, without having the means of keeping them uniform and in good condition; like the palaces of the Italian nobles, that never feel the effects of the broom.

Be it as it may, on the sides of the road I am speaking of, there is a space of 120 feet, that might be restored to cultivation; that is to say, 48 acres to the ordinary league. Add together the rent of the surplus land, the interest of the sum expended in the first cost and preparation, and the annual charge of keeping up the unnecessary space, which is something, badly as it is kept up; you will then ascertain the sum France pays annually for the very questionable honour of having roads too wide, by more than the half, leading to streets too narrow, by three-fourths.*

Roads and canals are costly public works, even in countries where they are under judicious and economical management. Yet, probably, in most cases, the benefits they afford to the community far exceed the charges. Of this the reader may be convinced, on reference to what has been said above of the value generated by the mere commercial operation of transfer from one spot to another,† and of the general rule, that every saving in the charges of production is so much gain to the consumer.‡ Were we to calculate what would be the charge of carriage upon all the articles and commodities, that now pass along any road in the course of a year, if the road did not exist, and compare it with the utmost charge under present circumstances, the whole difference, that would appear, will be so much gain to the consumers of all those articles, and so much positive and clear net profit to the community.§

Canals are still more beneficial; for in them the saving of carriage is still more considerable.‖

Public works of no utility, such as palaces, triumphal arches, monumental columns, and the like, are items of national luxury. They are equally indefensible, with instances of private prodigality. The unsatisfactory gratification afforded by them to the vanity of the prince or the people, by no means balances the cost, and often the misery, they have occasioned.

---

* With all this waste of space in the great roads of France, there are in none of them either paved or gravelled foot-ways, passable at all seasons, or stone seats, for the travellers to rest upon, or places of temporary shelter from the weather, or cisterns to quench the thirst; all which might be added with a very trifling expense.

† Book I. chap. 9.   ‡ Book II. chap. 3.

§ To say, that, if the road were not in existence, the charge of transport could never be so enormous as here suggested, because the transport would never take place at all, and people would contrive to do without the objects of transport, would be a strange way of eluding the argument. Self-denial of this kind, enforced by the want of means to purchase, is an instance of poverty, not of wealth. The poverty of the consumer is extreme, in respect to every object he is thus made too poor to purchase; and he becomes richer in respect to it, in proportion as its price or value declines.

‖ In lieu of canals, iron rail-roads from one town to another, will probably be one day constructed. The saving in the costs of transport would probably exceed the interest of the very heavy expense in the outset. Besides the additional facility of movement, roads of this kind would remedy the violent jolting of passengers and goods. Undertakings of such magnitude can only be prosecuted in countries where capital is very abundant, and where the government inspires the adventurers with the firm assurance of reaping themselves the profit of the adventure.

CHAPTER VII.

OF THE ACTUAL CONTRIBUTORS TO PUBLIC CONSUMPTION.

A PORTION of the objects of public consumption have, in some very rare instances, been provided by a private individual. We see occasional acts of private munificence, in the erection of a hospital, the laying out of a road, or of public gardens upon the land, and at the cost, of an individual. In ancient times, examples of this kind were more frequent, though much less meritorious. The private opulence of the ancients was commonly the fruit of domestic, or provincial, plunder and peculation, or perhaps the spoil of a hostile nation, purchased with the blood of fellow-citizens. Among the moderns, though such excesses do sometimes occur, individual wealth is, in the great majority of cases, the fruit of personal industry and economy. In England, where there are so many institutions founded and supported by private funds, most of the fortunes of the founders and supporters have been acquired in industrious occupations. It requires a greater exertion of generosity to sacrifice wealth, acquired by a long course of toil and self-denial, than to give away what has been obtained by a stroke of good fortune, or even by an act of lucky temerity.

Among the Romans, a further portion of the public consumption was supplied directly by the vanquished nations who were subjected to a tribute, which the victors consumed.

In most modern states, there is some territorial property vested, either in the nation at large, or in the subordinate communities, cities, towns, and villages, which is leased out, or occupied directly by the public. In France, most of the public lands of tillage and pasturage, with their appurtenances, are let out on lease; the government reserving only the national forests under the direct administration of its agents. The produce of the whole forms a considerable item in the catalogue of public resources.

But these resources consist, for the most part, of the produce of taxes levied upon the subjects or citizens. These taxes are sometimes national, that is, levied upon the whole nation, and paid into the general treasury of the state, whence the public national expenditure is defrayed; and sometimes local, or provincial, that is, levied upon the inhabitants of a separate canton or province only, and paid into the local treasury, whence are defrayed the local expenses.

It is a principle of equity, that consumption should be charged to those who derive gratification from it; consequently, those countries must be pronounced to be the best governed, in respect of taxation, where each class of inhabitants contributes in taxation proportionately to the benefit derived by it from the expenditure.

Every individual and class in the community is benefited by the central administration, or, in other words, the general government:

so likewise of the security afforded by the national military establishment; for the provinces can hardly be secure from external attack, if the enemy have possession of the metropolis, and can thence overawe and control them; imposing laws upon districts where his force has not penetrated, and disposing of the lives and property even of such as have not seen the face of an enemy. For the same reason the charge of fortresses, arsenals, and diplomatic agents is properly thrown upon the whole community.

It would seem, that the administration of justice should be classed among the general charges, although the security and advantage it affords have more of a local character. When the magistracy of Bordeaux arrests and tries an offender, the public internal security of France is unquestionably promoted. The charge of gaols and court-houses necessarily follows that of the magistracy. Smith has expressed an opinion, that civil justice should be defrayed by the litigating parties; which would be more practicable than at present, were the judges in the appointment of the parties in each particular case, and no otherwise in the nomination of the public authority, than inasmuch as the choice might be limited to specified persons of approved knowledge and integrity. They would then be arbitrators, and a sort of equitable jurors, and might be paid proportionately to the matter in dispute without regard to the length of the suit; and would thus have an obvious interest in simplifying the process, and sparing their own time and trouble, as well as in attracting business by the general equity of their decisions. (a)

But local administration and local institutions of utility, pleasure, instruction, or beneficence, appear to yield a benefit exclusively to the place or district where they are situated. Wherefore, it should seem, that their expenses ought to fall, as in most countries they do, upon the local population. Not but that the nation at large derives some benefit from good provincial administration, or institutions. A stranger has access to the public places, libraries, schools, walks, and hospitals of the district; but the principal benefit unquestionably results to the immediate neighbourhood.

It is good economy to leave the administration of the local receipts and disbursements to the local authorities; particularly where

(a) Our author seems in this passage to have become a convert to the opinion of Smith, in respect to the civil tribunals of a nation, from which he had expressed his dissent, in former editions. Though arbitration may be a very good mode of settling civil suits, where the parties are both anxious to come to a settlement, and indeed is frequently resorted to, and should always be encouraged; yet it is manifest, that there must be a compulsory tribunal for the obstinate, or refractory. And, since security of person and property is the main object of social institutions, it is but just, that invasion in a particular instance should be repelled and deterred at the public charge. In strict justice, the invader should be held to make good the whole damage; and so he is or ought to be, in the shape of costs, fine, damages, or otherwise. But it is not consistent with equity that the sufferer should be deterred from pursuing his claim, by superadding a proportion of the outlay upon the judicial establishments to the charge of witnesses and agents, which he must necessarily advance, and to the risk of inability in the delinquent, even in the event of ultimate success. T.

they are appointed by those, whose funds they administer. There is much less waste, when the money is spent under the eye of those who contribute it, and who are to reap the benefit; besides, the expense is better proportioned to the advantage expected. When one passes through a city or town badly paved and ill-conditioned, or sees a canal or harbour in a state of dilapidation, one may conclude, in nine cases out of ten, that the authorities, who are to administer the funds appropriated to those objects, do not reside on the spot.

In this particular, small states have an advantage over more extensive ones. They have more enjoyment from a less expenditure upon objects of public utility or amusement; because they are at hand to see that the funds, destined to the object, are faithfully applied.

CHAPTER VIII.

OF TAXATION.

Section I.

Of the Effect of all kinds of Taxation in general.

Taxation is the transfer of a portion of the national products from the hands of individuals to those of the government, for the purpose of meeting the public consumption or expenditure. Whatever be the denomination it bears, whether tax, contribution, duty, excise, custom, aid, subsidy,* grant, or free gift, it is virtually a burthen imposed upon individuals, either in a separate or corporate character, by the ruling power for the time being, for the purpose of supplying the consumption it may think proper to make at their expense; in short, an impost, in the literal sense.

It would be foreign to the plan of this work, to inquire in whom the right of taxation is or ought to be vested. In the science of political economy, taxation must be considered as matter of fact, and not of right; and nothing further is to be regarded, than its nature,

---

* What avails it, for instance, that taxation is imposed by consent of the people or their representatives, if there exists in the state a power, that by its acts can leave the people no alternative but consent? *De Lolme*, in his *Essay on the English Constitution*, says that the right of the Crown to make war is nugatory, while the people have the right of refusing the supplies for carrying it on. May it not be said, with much more truth, that the right of the people to deny the supplies is nugatory, when the crown has involved them in a predicament that makes consent a matter of necessity? The liberties of Great Britain have no real security, except in the freedom of the press; which rests itself, rather upon the habits and opinions of the nation, than upon legal enactments or judicial decisions. A nation is free, when it is bent on freedom; and the most formidable obstacle to the establishment of civil liberty is the absence of the desire for it.

the source whence it derives the values it absorbs, and its effect upon national and individual interests. The province of this science extends no further.

The object of taxation is, not the actual commodity, but the value of the commodity, given by the tax-payer to the tax-gatherer. Its being paid in silver, in goods, or in personal service, is a mere accidental circumstance, which may be more or less advantageous to the subject or to the sovereign. The essential point is, the value of the silver, the goods, or the service. The moment that value is parted with by the tax-payer, it is positively lost to him; the moment it is consumed by the government or its agents, it is lost to all the world, and never reverts to, or re-exists in society. This, I apprehend, has already been demonstrated, when the general effect of public consumption was under consideration. It was there shown, that however the money levied by taxation may be refunded to the nation, its value is never refunded; because it is never returned gratuitously, or refunded by the public functionaries, without receiving an equivalent in the way of barter or exchange.

The same causes, that we have found to make unproductive consumption nowise favourable to reproduction, prevent taxation from at all promoting it. Taxation deprives the producer of a product, which he would otherwise have the option of deriving a personal gratification from, if consumed unproductively, or of turning to profit, if he preferred to devote it to an useful employment. One product is a means of raising another; and, therefore, the subtraction of a product must needs diminish, instead of augmenting, productive power.

It may be urged, that the pressure of taxation impels the productive classes to redouble their exertions, and thus tends to enlarge the national production. I answer, that, in the first place, mere exertion can not alone produce, there must be capital for it to work upon, and capital is but an accumulation of the very products, that taxation takes from the subject: that, in the second place, it is evident, that the values, which industry creates expressly to satisfy the demands of taxation, are no increase of wealth; for they are seized on and devoured by taxation. It is a glaring absurdity to pretend, that taxation contributes to national wealth, by engrossing part of the national produce, and enriches the nation by consuming part of its wealth. Indeed, it would be trifling with my reader's time, to notice such a fallacy, did not most governments act upon this principle, and had not well-intentioned and scientific writers endeavoured to support and establish it.*

---

* By the same reasoning it has been attempted to prove, that luxury and barren consumption operate as a stimulus to production. Yet they are less mischievous than taxation; inasmuch as they redound to the personal gratification of the party himself: whereas, to use the expedient of taxation as a stimulative to increased production, is to redouble the exertions of the community, for the sole purpose of multiplying its privations, rather than its enjoyments. For, if increased taxation be applied to the support of a complex, overgrown, and ostentatious internal administration, or of a superfluous and disproportionate military establishment, that may act as a drain of individual wealth, and of the flower

If, from the circumstance, that the nations most grievously taxed are those most abounding in wealth, as Great Britain, for example, we are desired to infer, that their superior wealth arises from their heavier taxation, it would be a manifest inversion of cause and effect. A man is not rich, because he pays largely; but he is able to pay largely, because he is rich.' It would be not a little ridiculous, if a man should think to enrich himself by spending largely, because he sees a rich neighbour doing so. It must be clear, that the rich man spends, because he is rich; but never can enrich himself by the act of spending.

Cause and effect are easily distinguished, when they occur in succession; but are often confounded, when the operation is continuous and simultaneous.

Hence, it is manifest, that, although taxation may be, and often is, productive of good, when the sums it absorbs are properly applied, yet, the act of levying is always attended with mischief in the outset. And this mischief good princes and governments have always endeavoured to render as inconsiderable to their subjects as possible, by the practice of economy, and by levying, not to the full extent of the people's ability, but to such extent only as is absolutely unavoidable. That rigid economy is the rarest of princely virtues, is owing to the circumstance of the throne being constantly beset with individuals, who are interested in the absence of it; and who are always endeavouring, by the most specious reasoning, to impress the conviction, that magnificence is conducive to public prosperity, and that profuse public expenditure is beneficial to the state. It is the object of this third book to expose the absurdities of such representations.

Others there are, who are not impudent enough to pretend, that public profusion is a public benefit; yet undertake to show by arithmetical deduction, that the people are scarcely burthened at all, and are equal to a much higher scale of taxation. As Sully tells us in his Memoirs, " The ear of the prince is assailed by a set of flattering advisers, who think to make their court to him by perpetually suggesting new ways of raising money; discharged functionaries, for the most part, whose experience of the sweets of office has left no other impression, than the tincture of the baneful art of fiscal extortion; and who seek to recommend themselves to power and favour, by commending it to the lips of royalty."*

Others suggest financial projects, and ways and means for filling the coffers of the prince, as they assert, without fleecing the subject. But no plan of finance can give to the government, without taking either from the people, or from the government itself in some other way; unless it be a downright adventure of industry. Something can not be produced out of nothing by a mere touch of the wand. However an operation may be cloaked in mystery, however often

---

of the national youth, and an aggressor upon the peace and happiness of domestic life, will not this be paying as dearly for a grievous public nuisance, as if it were a benefit of the first magnitude?

* *Memoires*, liv. xx.

we may twist and turn and transform values, there are but two ways of obtaining them, namely, creating oneself, or taking from others. The best scheme of finance is, to spend as little as possible; and the best tax is always the lightest.

Admitting these premises, that taxation is the taking from individuals a part of their property* for public purposes; that the value levied by taxation never reverts to the members of the community, after it has once been taken from them; and that taxation is not itself a means of reproduction; it is impossible to deny the conclusion, that the best taxes, or, rather those that are least bad, are

1. Such as are the most moderate in their ratio.

2. Such as are least attended with those vexatious circumstances, that harass the tax-payer without bringing any thing into the public exchequer.

3. Such as press impartially on all classes.

4. Such as are least injurious to reproduction.

5. Such as are rather favourable than otherwise to the national morality; that is to say, to the prevalence of habits, useful and beneficial to society.

These positions are almost self-evident; yet I shall proceed to illustrate them successively, with some few observations.

1. Of such as are most moderate in their ratio.

Since taxation does, in point of fact, deprive the tax-payer of a product, which is to him, either a means of personal gratification, or a means of reproduction, the lighter the tax is, the less must be the privation.

Taxation, pushed to the extreme, has the lamentable effect of impoverishing the individual, without enriching the state. We may readily conceive how this can happen, if we recall to our attention the former position; viz. that each tax-payer's consumption, whether productive or not, is always limited to the amount of his revenue. No part of his revenue, therefore, can be taken from him without necessarily curtailing his consumption in the same ratio. This must needs reduce the demand for all those objects he can no longer consume, and particularly those affected by taxation. The diminution of demand must be followed by diminution of the supply of production; and, consequently, of the articles liable to taxation. Thus, the tax-payer is abridged of his enjoyments, the producer of his profits, and the public exchequer of its receipts.†

---

* It is hardly necessary to controvert an opinion, entertained by sovereigns in times past, respecting the property of their subjects. We find Louis XIV. writing in these terms, professedly for the instruction of his son in matters of government: "Kings are absolute lords naturally possessing the entire and uncontrolled disposal of all property, whether belonging to the church or to the laity, to be exercised at all times with due regard to economy, and to the general interests of the state." *Œuvres de Louis* XIV., *Mémoires Hist. A. D.* 1666.

† In France, before 1789, the average annual consumption of salt was estimated at 9 lbs. per head in the districts subject to the *gabelle*, and at 18 lbs. per head in those exempt from that impost. *De Monthieu, Influence des divers Impots*, p. 141. Thus, taxation in this form obstructed the production of ½

This is the reason why a tax is not productive to the public exchequer, in proportion to its ratio; and why it has become a sort of apophthegm, that two and two do not make four in the arithmetic of finance. Excessive taxation is a kind of suicide, whether laid upon objects of necessity, or upon those of luxury; but there is this distinction, that, in the latter case, it extinguishes only a portion of the products on which it falls, together with the gratification they are calculated to afford; while, in the former, it extinguishes both production and consumption, and the tax-payer into the bargain.

Were it not almost self-evident, this principle might be illustrated, by abundant examples of the profit the state derives from a moderate scale of taxation, where it is sufficiently awake to its real interests.

When Turgot, in 1775, reduced to $\frac{1}{2}$ the market-dues and duties of entry upon fresh sea-fish sold in Paris, their product was nowise diminished. The consumption of that article must, therefore, have doubled, the fishermen and dealers must have doubled their concerns and their profits; and, since population always increases with increasing production, the number of consumers must have been enlarged; and that of producers must have been enlarged likewise; for an increase of profits, that is to say of individual revenue, multiplies savings, and thus generates the multiplication of capital and of families; and that very increase of production will, beyond all doubt, augment the product of taxation in other branches; to say nothing of the popularity accruing to the government from the alleviation of the national burthens.

The government agents, who farm or administer the collection of the taxes, very often abuse their interest and authority, to construe

of this article in the districts subjected to it, and reduced to $\frac{1}{4}$ the enjoyment it was capable of affording; to say nothing of the other mischiefs resulting from it; the injury to tillage, to the feeding of cattle, and to the preparation of salted goods; the popular animosity against the collectors of tax, the consequent increase of crime and conviction, and the consignment to the galleys of numerous individuals, whose industry and courage might have been made available to the increase of national opulence.

In 1804, the English government raised the duties on sugar 20 per cent. It might have been expected, that their average product to the public exchequer would have been advanced in the same ratio; i. e. from 2,778,000l. the former amount, to 3,330,000l.: instead of which the increased duties produced but 2,537,000l.; exhibiting an absolute deficit. Speech of Henry Brougham, Esq., M. P., March 13, 1817.

The people of Great Britain might consume French wines at a very little advance upon the prices of France, and have the enjoyment of an unadulterated, wholesome, and exhilarating beverage, costing perhaps a shilling a bottle. But the exorbitant duty upon this article has reduced its import and the product of the duty to a very trifle; and thus, the sole benefit resulting from the tax to the British nation is, the total privation of a cheap and wholesome object of consumption.

The two last examples are a sufficient answer to the objection taken by Ricardo to this passage of my text; on the ground that taxation is not injurious to production in the aggregate, inasmuch as the consumption of the state itself replaces that of individuals, which is annihilated by the tax. A tax, that robs the individual, without benefit to the exchequer, substitutes no public consumption whatever, in place of the private consumption it extinguishes.

all doubtful points of fiscal law in their own favour, and sometimes
to create obscurity for the purpose of profiting by it.   The effect is
precisely the same, as if the scale of taxation were raised *pro tanto.* *
Turgot adopted a contrary course, and made it a rule to lean
always to the side of the tax-payer.   The public contractors made
a great outcry at this innovation, declaring that it was impossible
for them to fulfil their engagements, and offering to collect on the
government account and risk.   The event, however, falsified their
predictions by an actual increase of the receipts.   The greater lenity
in the collection proved so advantageous to production, and the consumption, consequent upon it, that the profits, which had before not
exceeded 10,550,000 *liv.*, rose to 60,000,000 *liv.;* an advance which
could hardly be credited, if it were not attested by unquestionable
evidence.†

We are told by Humboldt,‡ to whom we are indebted for a variety
of valuable information, that in thirteen years from 1778, during
which time Spain adopted a somewhat more liberal system of
government in regard to her American dependencies, the increase
of the revenue in Mexico alone amounted to no less a sum than 100
millions of dollars; and that she drew from that country, during the
same period, an addition in the single article of silver, to the amount
of 14,500,000 dollars.   We may naturally suppose, that, in those
years of prosperity, there was a corresponding, and rather greater
increase of individual profits; for that is the source, whence all
public revenue is derived.

A similar course of conduct has invariably been followed by a
similar effect;§ and it is a great satisfaction to a writer of liberal

---

* Of this, a striking instance is given in a work entitled, *Diverses Idées sur la
Legislation et l'Administration, par M. C. St. Paul.* One of the principal
bankers of Paris having died in 1817, the duty on legacies and inheritance was
levied upon the aggregate of his credit-account, and not upon the balance, after
deducting the debits; and this by virtue of a proviso in the revenue laws, which
charges the duty upon the gross estate of a defunct, and not upon the residue
after the discharge of the outstanding claims.   The danger of fraud upon the
revenue in stating the account, is not sufficient to justify the exaction of more
than is fairly due.

The same department is in the habit of giving no notice to the executors or
other parties, of the payments falling due, until after the legal time has expired,
in the hope of incurring the penalty of default.   The revolution had abolished
this official and fiscal severity; but it was revived by the imperial government,
and has been acted upon ever since.   A clerk or officer has no chance of promotion, unless he shows a disposition on all occasions to postpone the interests of
the public to those of the exchequer.

† *Œuvres de Turgot,* tom. i. p. 170.   The accounts of the farmers-general
were minutely stated, and rigidly investigated, because the crown participated
in their profits.

‡ *Essai Pol. sur la Nouvelle Espagne,* liv. v. c. 12.

§ This position is further confirmed by an instance mentioned in a letter, addressed in 1785, by the then Marquis of Lansdowne to the *Abbé Morellet,* stating,
'that in respect to the article of tea, the good effect of the reduction of duty had
surpassed all expectation.   The amount of sale had advanced from 5,000,000
lbs. to 12,000,000 lbs., in spite of many unfavourable circumstances; besides

principles to be able to prove by experience, that moderation is the best policy.*

Upon the same principles, it will be easy to demonstrate in the next place, that the taxes least mischievous are:

2. Such as are least attended with those vexatious circumstances, that harass the tax-payer, without bringing any thing into the public exchequer. .

It has been held by many, that the costs of collection are no very great evil, inasmuch as they are refunded to the community in some other shape. On this head, I must refer my readers to what has been already observed.† These costs are no more refunded, than the net proceeds of the taxes themselves; because both the one and the other consists in reality, not of the money, wherein the taxes are paid, but of the value, wherewith the tax-payer produces that money, and the value which the government again procures with it; which latter is destroyed and consumed outright.

The necessities of princes have operated far more effectually than their regard to the public good, to introduce the practice of better order and economy in the financial departments of most European states during the two last centuries, than in former times. The people are generally made to bear as much as they can well stand under; so that every saving in the charge of collection has gone to swell the receipts of the exchequer.

Sully tells us in his Memoirs,‡ that, for about 6 millions of dollars brought into the royal treasury, in 1598, by means of taxation, individuals were out of pocket about 30 millions of dollars, and assures us, that he had with great pains ascertained the fact, however incredible it might appear. Under the administration of Necker, upon a

---

which, smuggling had been so much crippled, that the public revenue had been increased to a degree that astonished every body.'

* This doctrine has been combated by Ricardo, in his *Principles of Political Economy and Taxation*. That writer maintains, that since the amount and the product of industry are always proportionate to the quantum of the capital engaged in it, the extinction of one branch by taxation must needs be compensated by the product of some other, towards which the industry and capital, thrown out of employ, will naturally be diverted. I answer, that whenever taxation diverts capital from one mode of employment to another, it annihilates the profits of all who are thrown out of employ by the change, and diminishes those of the rest of the community; for industry may be presumed to have chosen the most profitable channel. I will go further, and say, that a forcible diversion of the current of production annihilates many additional sources of profit to industry. Besides, it makes a vast difference to the public prosperity, whether the individual or the state be the consumer. A thriving and lucrative branch of industry promotes the creation and accumulation of new capital; whereas, under the pressure of taxation, and accumulation of new capital, it ceases to be lucrative; capital diminishes gradually instead of increasing; wealth and production decline in consequence, and prosperity vanishes, leaving behind the pressure of unremitting taxation. Ricardo has endeavoured to introduce the unbending maxims of geometrical demonstration; in the science of political economy, there is no method less worthy of reliance.

† Chap. V. sect. I.   ‡ Liv. xx.

revenue of about 110 millions of dollars, the charges of collection
amounted to no more than 10 millions of dollars; yet, under his
management, there were 250,000 persons employed in the collection:
most of them, however, had other collateral occupations. The charge
was, therefore, about 10⅔ per cent.; yet this is much higher than the
rate at which the business is done in England.*

Besides the charge of collection, there are other circumstances,
that are burthensome to the people without being productive of gain
to the public revenue. Law-suits, imprisonment and other preventive
measures, entail additional expense, without procuring the smallest
increase of revenue. And this addition is sure to fall on the most
necessitous class of tax-payers; for the other classes pay without
litigation or constraint. Such odious means of enforcing the payment of taxes are precisely the same as demanding of a man 12
dollars because he has not wherewithal to pay 10 dollars. Rigour
is never necessary to enforce taxation where it presses lightly on the
resources of individuals; but when a state is so unfortunate, as to be
obliged to impose heavy burthens, of two evils, the process of levy
by distress is preferable to that of personal constraint. For at any
rate, by seizing and selling the tax-payer's goods, and thereby raising
the arrears of his taxes, he is compelled to pay no more than is due;
and the whole of what he does pay goes into the public purse.

On this account it is, that works executed by the public requisition of labour, as the roads were in France under the old *régime*,
are always a mischievous kind of taxation. The time lost by the
labourers put in requisition in coming three or four leagues, perhaps,
to their work, and that which is always wasted by people who get
no pay, and work against their inclination, is all a dead loss to the
public, with no return of revenue. Even supposing the work to be
well executed, there is often more loss incurred by the interruption
of the regular agricultural pursuits, than gain made from the compulsory employment that has been substituted. Turgot called upon
the surveyors and engineers of the respective provinces for an estimate of the average expense, one year with another, of keeping up
old roads, and constructing the usual number of new ones, directing
them to make their calculations on the most liberal scale. The estimate of the annual expense, made in compliance with his orders,
amounted to 2 millions of dollars for the whole kingdom: whereas,
according to the calculations of Turgot, the old *corvée* system involved a sacrifice to the nation of 8 millions of dollars.†

Days of rest, enjoined either by law, or by custom and usage too
powerful to be infringed upon, are another kind of taxation, productive of nothing to the public purse.

---

* Under the system of Napoleon, which made civilization retrograde to this,
as well as in most other particulars, the charges of collection in which must be
included the charge of privation and the irrecoverable arrears, were much more
considerable; but the full extent of the mischief he caused is not yet ascertained.

† Necker reckons the *corvée* at four millions of dollars only; but probably he
takes account of nothing, but the value the day-labour exacted; and does not
notice the injury resulting from this method of supplying the public necessities.

3. Such as press impartially on all classes.

Taxation being a burthen, must needs weigh lightest on each individual, when it bears upon all alike. When it presses inequitably upon one individual or branch of industry, it is an indirect, as well as a direct, incumbrance; for it prevents the particular branch or the individual from competing on even terms with the rest. An exemption, granted to one manufacture, has often been the ruin of several others. Favour to one is most commonly injustice to all others.

The partial assessment of taxation is no less prejudicial to the public revenue, than unjust to individual interests. Those who are too lightly taxed, are not likely to cry out for an increase; and those who are too heavily taxed, are seldom regular in their payments. The public revenue suffers in both ways.

It has been questioned whether it be just to tax that portion of revenues, which is spent on luxuries, more heavily than that spent on objects of necessity. It seems but reasonable to do so; for taxation is a sacrifice to the preservation of society and of social organization, which ought not to be purchased by the destruction of individuals. Yet, the privation of absolute necessaries implies the extinction of existence. It would be somewhat bold to maintain, that a parent is bound in justice to stint the food or clothing of his child, to furnish his contingent to the ostentatious splendour of a court, or the needless magnificence of public edifices. Where is the benefit of social institutions to an individual, whom they rob of an object of positive enjoyment or necessity in actual possession, and offer nothing in return, but the participation in a remote and contingent good, which any man in his senses would reject with disdain?

But how is the line to be drawn between necessaries and superfluities? In this discrimination, there is the greatest difficulty, for the terms, necessaries and superfluities, convey no determinate or absolute notion, but always have reference to the time, the place, the age, and the condition of the party; so that, were it laid down as a general rule, to tax none but superfluities, there would be no knowing where to begin and where to stop. All that we certainly know is, that the income of a person or a family may be so confined, as barely to suffice for existence; and may be augmented from that minimum upwards by imperceptible gradation, till it embrace every gratification of sense, of luxury, or of vanity; each successive gratification being one step further removed from the limits of strict necessity, till at last the extreme of frivolity and caprice is arrived at; so that, if it be desired to tax individual income, in such manner as to press lighter, in proportion as that income approaches to the confines of bare necessity, taxation must not only be equitably apportioned, but must press on revenue with progressive gravity.

In fact, supposing taxation to be exactly proportionate to individual income, a tax of ten per cent. for instance, a family possessed of 60,000 dollars per annum would pay 6000 dollars in taxes, leave ing a clear residue of 54,000 dollars for the family expenditure. With such an expenditure, the family could not only live in abundance, but could still enjoy a vast number of gratifications by no means essential to happiness. Whereas another family, with an income of 60 dollars, reduced by taxation to 54 dollars per annum, would, with our present habits of life, and ways of thinking, be stinted in the bare necessaries of subsistence. Thus, a tax merely proportionate to individual income would be far from equitable; and this is probably what Smith meant, by declaring it reasonable, that the rich man should contribute to the public expenses, not merely in proportion to the amount of his revenue, but even somewhat more. For my part, I have no hesitation in going further, and saying, that taxation can not be equitable, unless its ratio is progressive.*

4. Such as are least injurious to reproduction.

Of the values, whereof taxation deprives individuals, a great part would, undoubtedly, if left at the disposal of the individuals themselves, have gone to the satisfaction of their wants and appetites; but some part would have been laid by, and have gone to the further accumulation of productive capital. Thus, all taxation may be said to injure reproduction, inasmuch as it prevents the accumulation of productive capital.

This effect is more direct and serious, whenever the tax-payer is obliged to withdraw a part of the capital already embarked, for the purpose of enabling him to pay the tax; which case, as Sismondi has shrewdly observed, resembles the exaction of a tithe upon grain at seed-time, instead of harvest-time. Of this kind is the tax on legacies and successions. An heir, succeeding to a property of 20,000 dollars, and called upon for a tax of 5 per cent. upon it, will pay it, not out of his ordinary income, burthened as it is already with the ordinary taxes, but out of the inheritance, which is thereby reduced to 19,000 dollars. Wherefore, if it happen to be a vested capital of 20,000 dollars and be reduced by the tax to 19,000 dollars, the national capital will be diminished to the amount of the 1000 dollars thus diverted into the public exchequer.

It is the same with all taxes upon the transfer of property. The owner of land worth 20,000 dollars, will get but 19,000 dollars for it, if the purchaser be saddled with a tax of 5 per cent. The seller will have a disposable capital of 19,000 dollars only, in lieu of land worth 20,000 dollars; and the national capital will sustain a loss of the difference. Should the purchaser be so bad an arithmetician, as

---

* *Wealth of Nations*, book v. c. 2. It has been objected, that a progressive scale of taxation presents the disadvantage of operating as a penalty to deter activity and frugality from the accumulation of capital. But it must be obvious, that taxation of all kinds subtracts a portion only, and generally a very moderate portion, of the addition made to the fortune of an individual; so that every one has a much stronger inducement to invite, than penalty to deter, accumulation. If a person had to pay 40 dollars more in taxes, upon every addition of 200 dollars to his revenue, still he would multiply his enjoyments in a larger ratio than his sacrifices. *Vide* what is said in Sect. 4. of the same Chapter, on the subject of the land-tax of England. *Ibid.*

to pay the full value of the land, without allowing for the tax, he will sacrifice a capital of 21,000 dollars in the purchase of value to the amount of but 20,000 dollars. In either case, the loss to the national capital will be the same; although in the latter, it will fall upon the purchaser instead of the seller.

Taxes, upon transfer, besides the mischief of pressing upon capital, are a clog to the circulation of property. But, has the public any interest in its free circulation? So long as the object is in existence, is it not as well placed in one hand as in another? Certainly not. The public has a perpetual interest in the utmost possible freedom of its circulation; because by that means it is most likely to get into the hands of those, who can make the most of it. Why does one man sell his land? but because he thinks he can lay out the value to more advantage in some channel of productive industry. And why does another buy it? but because he wishes to invest a capital, that is lying idle, or less productively vested; or because he thinks it capable of improvement. The transfer tends to augment the national income, because it tends to augment the income of the two contracting parties. If they be deterred by the expenses of the transfer, those expenses will have prevented this probable increase of the national income.

Such taxes, however, as encroach upon the productive capital of the community, and consequently abridge the demand for labour and the profits of industry within the community, possess, in a very high degree, one quality, which that distinguished political economist, Arthur Young, has pronounced to be an essential requisite in taxation, namely, the facility and cheapness of collection.* Since taxation presents at best but a choice of evils, a nation, heavily burthened, will probably do well, in submitting to a moderate impost upon capital.

Taxes upon law-proceedings, and, generally, all that is paid to law-officers and agents, are taxes upon capital. (1) For litigation is

---

*This is the reason, why it has been found practicable to raise the duty on registration to its present high scale. Were it reduced, the product to the exchequer would probably be equally great; and the nation would enjoy the benefit of greater freedom of circulation, besides experiencing less encroachment upon its capital.

---

(1) Taxes upon law proceedings are the most grievous and oppressive that have ever been resorted to, and since the appearance of Mr. Bentham's work on Law taxes, no one, who has read it, can doubt their impolicy. It is said in the Edinburgh Review (vol. 27, page 358.), "that one day Mr. Rose, in Mr. Pitt's presence, took Mr. Bentham aside, and informed him that they had read the pamphlet—that its reasoning was unanswerable—and that it was resolved there should be no more such taxes." "Yet Budget after Budget," remarks the reviewer, "has since been formed, in which those duties have made a part; and Mr. Pitt himself was found to patronize them upon his return to office in 1804." All the arguments ever brought forward in support of this objectionable impost, have been triumphantly refuted by Mr. Bentham, in this work, which it is said in the same Review, "for closeness of reasoning, has not perhaps been equalled, and for excellence of style, has certainly never been surpassed."

AMERICAN EDITOR.

not proportionate to the income of the suitors, but to accident, to the complexity of family interests, and to the imperfections of the law itself.

Forfeitures are equally a tax on capital.

The influence of taxation upon production is not confined to the circumstance of diminishing one of its sources, that is to say, capital; it operates besides in the nature of a penalty, inflicted upon certain branches of production and consumption. Patents, licenses to follow any specified calling, and, generally, all taxes, that bear directly upon industry, are liable to this objection; but, when moderate in their ratio, industry will contrive to surmount such obstacles without much difficulty.

Nor is industry affected only by taxes bearing directly upon it; it is indirectly affected by such also, as bear upon the consumption of the articles it has to work upon.

The products consumed in reproduction are, for the most part, those of primary necessity; and taxes, that discourage such products, must be injurious to reproduction. This is more especially the case in respect to those raw materials of manufacture, which can only be consumed reproductively. An excessive duty upon cotton, checks the production of all articles, wherein that substance is worked up.*

Brazil is a country abounding in animal productions, that might be cured and exported, if they were allowed to be salted. Its fisheries are very productive, and cattle so abundant, that they are killed merely for the sake of the hide. Indeed, it is thence that our tanneries in Europe are in a great measure supplied. But the salt duties prevent the export of either fish or meat; and thus, for the sake of a revenue of about 200,000 dollars perhaps, incalculable mischief is done to the productive powers of the country, as well as to the public revenue, which they might be made to yield.

In like manner, as taxation operates in the nature of a penalty, to discourage reproductive consumption, it may be employed to check consumption of an unproductive kind; in which case it has the two-fold advantage, of subtracting no value from reproductive investment, and of rescuing values from unproductive consumption, to be employed in a manner more beneficial to the community. This is the advantage of all taxes upon luxuries.†

---

* In both England and France, premiums are given upon the importation of specific raw materials, with a view to encourage manufacture. This is an error on the opposite side. Upon this principle, instead of a tax on the product of land, a bounty should be given to all who would take the trouble to cultivate; for domestic agriculture furnishes the raw material of most manufactures; as grain in particular, which is transformed, through the mediation of human exertion, into value of various kinds, exceeding that consumed in the process. Customs or duties of import upon any article whatever are equally equitable with direct taxes upon land; both are positive evils; but the lighter the tax, the smaller the injury.

† When it is absolutely necessary to lay a tax upon a particular kind of consumption or industry, which it is desirable not to extinguish altogether, the burthen must be light in the commencement, and increased gradually and cau-

When sums, levied by taxation upon capital, instead of being simply expended by the government, are laid out upon productive objects; or, when individuals contrive to make good the deficiency out of their private savings, the positive mischief of taxation is then balanced by a counteracting benefit. The proceeds of taxation are reproductively vested, when laid out in improving the internal communications, constructing harbours, or other such works of utility. Governments sometimes employ a part of the revenue thus realised in adventures of industry. Colbert did so, when he made advances to the manufacturers of Lyons. The governments of Hamburgh, and of some other places in Germany, were in the habit of embarking their revenues in productive undertakings; and it is said, that the authorities of Berne were in the habit of so employing a part of its revenues every year: but such instances are of very rare occurrence.

5. Such as are rather favourable than otherwise to the national morality; that is to say, to the prevalence of habits, useful and beneficial to society.

Taxation influences the habits of a nation, in the same way as it operates upon its production and consumption, that is, by imposing a pecuniary penalty upon specified acts; and it is, moreover, possessed of the grand requisites to render punishment effectual; namely, moderation and difficulty of evasion.* Without reference, therefore, to the purposes of finance and revenue, it is a powerful engine in the hands of government, for either corrupting or reforming the national morals, and may be directed to the promotion of idleness or industry, extravagance or economy.

The tax of five per cent. upon all lands devoted to productive husbandry, and the exemption of pleasure-grounds, which existed in France before the revolution, operated, of course, as a premium upon luxury, and a penalty upon agricultural enterprise.

The tax of one per cent. upon the redemption of ground-rents and rent-charges was virtually a penalty upon an act, equally advantageous to the parties and to the community at large; a fine upon the meritorious exertions of prudent land-owners to pay off their incumbrances.

The law of Napoleon, exacting from each scholar, educated in a private academy, a specified payment into the chests of the public universities, operated as a penalty upon that mode of education, which alone can soften national manners and fully develope the faculties of the human mind.†

---

tiously. But if it be desired to repress or annihilate a mischievous class of consumption or industry, the full weight of the tax should be thrown upon it at once.

* The efficacy of the characteristics of punishment has been placed beyond all doubt by Beccaria, in his tract, *Dei delitti e delle pene.*

† This species of tax is still more iniquitous, because it must fall either upon orphans, or upon parents, who are disposed to submit to personal privations, for the purpose of rearing valuable citizens; because it is heavier in proportion to the number of children, and the degree of privation of the parent; and because it is disproportionate to the means of the individual, poor and rich being taxed alike.

When a government derives a profit from the licensing of lotteries and gambling-houses, what does it else but offer a premium to a vice most fatal to domestic happiness, and destructive of national prosperity? How disgraceful is it, to see a government thus acting as the pander of irregular desires, and imitating the fraudulent conduct it punishes in others, by holding out to want and avarice the bait of hollow and deceitful chance!*

On the contrary, taxes, that check and confine the excesses of vanity and vice, besides yielding a revenue to the state, operate as a means of prevention. Humboldt mentions a tax upon cock-fighting, which yields to the Mexican government 45,000 dollars per annum, and has the further advantage of checking that cruel and barbarous diversion.

Exorbitant or inequitable taxation promotes fraud, falsehood, and perjury. Well-meaning persons are presented with the distressing alternative, of violating truth, or sacrificing their interests in favour of less scrupulous fellow-citizens. They can not but feel involuntary disgust, at seeing acts, in themselves innocent, and sometimes even useful and meritorious, branded with the name, and subjected to all the consequences, of criminality.

These are the principal rules, by which present or future taxation must be weighed, with a view to the public prosperity. After these general remarks, which are applicable to taxation in all its

---

A parent of moderate fortune, with one son only, pays as much to the university as all the rest of his taxes together: if he have more sons than one, he is still worse off. Thus was this institution converted by the usurper into an instrument of fiscal extortion, sufficient of itself to have insured the relapse into barbarism, even had it never been made the medium of instilling false ideas or habits of servility. The pretext, of making the profits of private establishments contribute to the expense of compulsory tuition, is by no means satisfactory. Supposing the tuition of the public *Lycées* to be, of all others, the best calculated to train up useful citizens; and, admitting the justice of compelling a father, or a teacher to his choice, to bring his pupil to the lectures of the authorized professors, still the parties, least in need of this instruction, are those already placed in private establishments of education, and entrusted to teachers of their own selection. It may be for the interest of the community at large, to dispense particular classes of learning gratuitously; but it is the greatest oppression to force learning upon individuals, and make them pay dear for it into the bargain. If any one class in particular ought to defray the charge of moderate gratuitous tuition, it is that, which has no children of its own, and is in the reception of all the benefits of social life, without being subject to all its burthens.

* Lotteries and games of hazard, besides occupying capital unprofitably, involve the waste of a vast deal of time, that might be turned to useful account; and this item of expenditure can never redound to the profit of the exchequer. They have the further mischievous effect of accustoming mankind to look to chance alone for what their own talents or enterprise might attain; and to seek for personal gain, rather in the loss of others, than in the original sources of wealth. The reward of active energy appears paltry beside the bait of a capital prize. Moreover, lotteries are a sort of tax, that, however voluntarily incurred, falls almost wholly upon the necessitous; for nothing, but the pressure of want can drive mankind to adventure, with the chances manifestly against them. The sums thus embarked are, for the most part, the portion of misery; or, what is worse, the fruit of actual crime.

branches, it may be useful to examine the various modes of assessment; in other words, the methods adopted for procuring money
from the subject; as well as to inquire, upon what classes of the
community the burthen principally falls.

*Of the different Modes of Assessment, and the Classes they press upon
respectively.*

Taxation, as we have seen above, is a requisition by the government upon its subjects for a portion of their products, or of their
value.   It is the business of the political economist to explain the
effects resulting from the nature of the products put in requisition,
and from the mode of apportioning the burthen, as well as upon
whom the burthen of the charge really falls, since it must inevitably
fall upon some one or other. The application of the above principles
in a few specific instances will show, how they may be applied in
all others.

The public authority levies the values taken in the way of taxation, sometimes in the shape of money, sometimes in kind, according to its own wants, or the ability of the tax-payer. In whatever
shape it is paid, the actual contribution of the tax-payer is always
of the value of the article he gives. If the government, wanting or
pretending to want corn, or leather, or woollens, makes a requisition of those articles upon the tax-payer, and obliges him to furnish
them in kind, the tax paid amounts exactly to what the payer has
expended in procuring those articles, or what he could have sold
them for, if the government had not taken them from him. This
is the only way of ascertaining the amount of the tax, whatever
price or rate the government may set upon it in the plenitude of its
power.

So, likewise, the charges of collection, in whatever shape they
may appear, are always an aggravation of the assessment, whether
they accrue to the profit of the state or not. If the tax-payer be
obliged to lose his time, or transport his goods, for the purpose of
paying the tax, the whole of the time lost, or expense of transport,
is an aggravation of the tax.

Among the contributions, that a government exacts from its subjects, should likewise be comprised, all the expenses which its political conduct may bring upon the nation. Thus, in estimating the
expenses of war, we must include the value of equipment and
pocket-money, with which the military are supplied by themselves or their families; the value of the time lost by the militia;
the sums paid for exemption and substitutes; the full charge of
quarters for the troops; the pillage and destruction they may be
guilty of; the presents and attentions lavished on them by friends
or countrymen on their return; to all which must be added, the

alms extorted from pity and compassion by the misery consequent upon such misrule. For, in fact, none of these values need have been taken from the members of the community under a better system of government. And, although none of them have gone into the treasury of the monarch, yet have they been paid by the people, and their amount is as completely lost, as if they had contributed to the happiness of the human species.

Hence, we may form some notion of the extent of the national sacrifices. But, from what source are they drawn?—Doubtless, either from the annual product of the national industry, land, and capital; that is to say, from the national revenue; or from the values previously saved and accumulated; that is to say, from the national capital.

When taxation is moderate, the subject can not only pay his taxes wholly out of his revenue, but will not be altogether disabled from besides saving some part of that revenue: and although some of the tax-payers may be obliged to trench upon their capital for the payment of their taxes, the loss to the general stock is amply reimbursed by the savings, which this happy state of affairs allows others to effect.

But it is far otherwise, when military despotism or usurped authority extorts excessive contributions. Great part of the taxes is then taken from the vested and accumulated capital; and, if the country be long subjected to its domination, the revenues of each successive year are progressively reduced, and the ruin and depopulation of the country, will recoil upon its rulers, unless their downfall be accelerated by their own folly and excesses.

Under the protecting influence of just and regular government, on the contrary, there is a progressive annual enlargement of the profits and revenues, on which taxation is to be levied; and that taxation, without any alteration of its ratio, gradually becomes more productive by the mere multiplication of taxable products.

Nor is the government more deeply interested in moderating the ratio of taxation, than its impartial assessment upon every class of individual revenue, and its equal pressure upon all. In fact, when revenue is partially affected, taxation sooner reaches the extreme limits of the ability of some classes, while others are scarcely touched at all: it becomes vexatious and destructive, before it arrives at the highest practical ratio. The burthen is galling, not because of its weight, but because it does not rest upon all shoulders alike.

The different methods employed to reach individual revenues, may be classed under two grand divisions—direct, and indirect, taxation; the former is the absolute demand of a specific portion of an individual's real or supposed revenue; the latter, a demand of a specific sum on each act of consumption of certain specified objects, to which that income may be applied.

In neither case, is the real subject of taxation that commodity, on which the estimate is made, and which forms the ground-work of the demand for the tax; or of necessity that value, whereof a part is taken by the state; individual revenue is the only real subject of taxation; and the specific commodity is selected only as a more or less effective means of discovering and attacking that revenue. If individual honesty could in every case be relied on, the matter would be simple enough; all that would be requisite would be, to ask each person the amount of his annual profits, that is to say, his annual revenue. The contingent of each would be readily settled, and one tax only necessary, which would be at the same time the most equitable, and the cheapest in the collection. This was the method adopted at Hamburgh, before that city fell into misfortune; but it can never be practised, except in a republic of small extent, and very moderately taxed.

As a means of assessing direct taxation proportionately to the respective revenues of the tax-payers, governments sometimes compel the production of leases by landlords, or, where there is no lease, set a value on the land, and demand a certain proportion of that value from the proprietor; this is called a land-tax.* Sometimes they estimate the revenue by the rent of the habitation, and the number of servants, horses, and carriages kept, and make the assessment accordingly. This is called in France, the tax on moveables.† Sometimes they calculate the profits of each person's profession or calling, by the extent of the population and district where it is followed. This is called in France, the license-tax.‡ All these different modes of assessment are expedients of direct taxation.

In the assessment of indirect taxation, and such as is intended to bear upon specific classes of consumption, the object itself is alone attended to, without regard to the party who may incur the charge. Sometimes a portion of the value of the specific product is demanded at the time of production; as in France, in the article of salt. Sometimes the demand is made on entry, either into the state, as in the duties of import; § or into the towns only, as in the duties of entry.|| Sometimes a tax is demanded of the consumer at the moment of transfer to him from the last producer; as in the case of the stamp duty in England, and the duty on theatrical tickets in France. Sometimes the government requires a commodity to bear a particular mark, for which it makes a charge, as in the case of the assay-mark of silver, and stamp on newspapers. Sometimes it monopolizes the manufacture of a particular article, or the performance of a particular kind of business; as in the monopoly of tobacco, and the postage of letters. Sometimes, instead of charging the commodity itself, it charges the payment of its price; as in the case of stamps on receipts and mercantile paper. All these are different ways of raising a revenue by indirect taxation; for the demand is not made on any person in particular, but attaches upon the product or article taxed.¶

---

* *Contribution-foncière.* † *Mobilière.*

‡ *Les Patentes.* § *Douanes.* || *Octroi.*

¶ Not because they affect the tax-payer indirectly; for this circumstance is equally applicable to many items of direct taxation; as, for instance, to the license-tax (*patentes*,) part of which falls indirectly upon the consumer, who buys of the licensed dealer.

It may easily be conceived, that a class of revenue, which may escape'one of these taxes, will be affected by another; and that the multiplicity of the forms of taxation gives a great approximation to its equal distribution; provided always, that all are kept within the bounds of moderation.

Every one of these modes of assessment has peculiar advantages and peculiar disadvantages, besides the general evil of all taxation, to wit, that of appropriating a part of the products of the community to purposes little conducive to its happiness and reproductive powers. Direct taxation, for instance, is cheap in the collection; but, on the other hand, it is paid with reluctance, and must be enforced with considerable harshness and rigour. Besides, it bears very inequitably upon the individual. A rich merchant, charged only 120 dollars for his license, makes an annual profit, perhaps, of 20,000 dollars; while the retailer, who can scarcely be supposed to make more than 300 dollars, is charged for his license 20 dollars, which is the lowest rate. The revenue of the landholder is already affected by the land-tax, before it is further reduced by the tax on moveables; while the capitalist is subjected to the latter burthen only.

Indirect taxation has the recommendation of being levyable with more ease, and with less apparent vexation or hardship. All taxes are paid with reluctance, because the equivalent to be expected for them, that is, the security afforded by good order and government, is a negative benefit, which does not immediately interest individuals; for the benefit afforded consists rather in prevention of ill, than in the diffusion of good. But the buyer of the taxed commodity does not suspect himself to be paying for the protection of government, which probably he cares very little about; but merely for the commodity itself, which is an object of his urgent desire, although, in fact, that price is aggravated by the tax. The inducement to consume is strong enough to include the demand of the government; and he readily parts with a value, that procures an immediate gratification.

It is this circumstance, that makes such taxes appear to be voluntary. And, indeed, so much so were they considered by the United States before their emancipation, that, although the right of the British Parliament to tax America without her consent was stoutly denied, yet she was ready to acknowledge the right of imposing taxes upon consumption, which every body could evade if he pleased, by abstaining from the articles taxed.* Personal taxes are

---

* *Vide* Examination of B. Franklin, at the bar of the House of Commons, 1767. *Memoirs*, vol. i. Appendix 6. (*a*)

(*a*) The denial went to the whole of what is called *internal* taxation; the admission, which appears on the part of the American agents to have been a concession for the sake of peace, went no farther than to *external* taxes for the regulation of trade. And even this concession on the part of some of the agents was very soon retracted, and the right of taxation denied *in toto*. *Ibid.* vol. i. *passim.* T.

viewed in a different light, and have more of the character of ostensible spoliation.

Indirect taxation is levied piecemeal, and paid by individuals according to their respective ability at the moment. It involves none of the perplexity of separate assessments on each province, department, or individual; or of the inquisitorial inspection into private circumstances; nor does it make one person suffer for the default of another. The inconvenience of appeals and private animosities, as well as of levy by distress or imprisonment, is avoided altogether.

Another advantage of indirect taxation is, that it enables the government to bias the different classes of consumption; favouring such as promote the public prosperity, as does reproductive consumption of all kinds; and checking such as tend to public impoverishment, as do all kinds of unproductive consumption; discouraging the costly and insipid indulgences of the wealthy, and promoting the simpler and cheaper enjoyments of the poor and industrious.

It has been objected to indirect taxation, that it entails a heavy expense of collection and management, and a large establishment of clerks, officers, directors, and subordinate agents; but it is observable, that these charges may be vastly reduced by good administration. The excise and stamp-duties in England cost but $3\frac{1}{4}$ per cent. in the collection, in the year 1799.* There are few classes of direct taxation, that are managed so economically in France.

It has been further objected, that its product is uncertain and fluctuating; whereas, the public exigencies require a regular and certain supply: but there has never been any lack of bidders, whenever such taxes have been let out to farm; and experience has shown, that the product of every class of taxation may always be nearly estimated and safely reckoned upon, except in very rare and extraordinary emergencies. Besides, taxes on consumption are necessarily various; so that, the deficit of one is covered by the surplus of another.

Indirect taxation is, however, an incentive to fraud, and obliges governments to brand with the character of guilt, actions that are innocent in their nature; and, consequently, to resort to a distressing severity of punishment. But this mischief is never considerable, until taxation has grown excessive, so as to make the temptation to fraud counterbalance the danger incurred. All excess of taxation is attended with this evil; that, without enlarging the receipts of the public purse, it multiplies the sufferings of the population.

It may be observed, that consumption, and, consequently, individual revenue, are unequally affected by indirect, as well as by direct, taxation: for the private consumption of many articles is not pro-

---

* *Garnier, Traduction de Smith,* tom. iv. p. 438. According to Arthur Young, the stamp-duties in his time cost but 5,691*l.* in the collection, upon the receipt of 1,330,000*l.*; which is less than ½ per cent.

portionate to the revenue of the consumer. The possessor of an annual revenue of 20,000 dollars does not consume in the year an hundred times as much salt, as the possessor of a revenue of 200 dollars only. But this inequality may be obviated by the variety of taxes on consumption. Moreover, it is to be recollected, that such taxes fall upon incomes already charged with the taxes on land and on moveables. A person, whose whole income is derived from land, in respect to which he is taxed in the first instance, pays on the same income a second tax under the head of moveables; and a third on every taxed article, that he buys and consumes.

Although all these kinds of taxes be paid in the outset, by the persons of whom they are demanded by the public authority, it would be wrong to suppose, that they always ultimately fall on the original payers, who, in many instances, are not the parties really charged, but merely advance the tax in the first instance, and contrive to get indemnified wholly or partially by the consumers of their own peculiar products. But the rate of indemnity is infinitely diversified by the respective circumstances of the individuals.

Of this diversity, we may form some notion, by the consideration of the following general facts:

When the taxation of the producers of a specific commodity operates to raise its price, part of the tax is paid by the consumers of the commodity. If its price be nowise raised, it falls wholly upon the producers. If the commodity, instead of being thereby advanced in price, is deteriorated in quality, a portion of the tax at least must fall upon the consumer; for a purchase of inferior quality at equal price is equivalent to a purchase of equal quality and superior price.

Every addition to price must needs reduce the number of those possessed of the ability to purchase; or, at any rate, must diminish the extent of that ability.* There is much less salt consumed, when it sells for three cents, than when it sells for one cent per lb. Now, the ratio of the demand to the means of production being lowered, productive agency in this department is worse paid; that is to say, the master-manufacturer of salt, and all the subordinate agents and labourers, together with the capitalist that supplies the funds, and the landlord of the premises where the concern is carried on, must be content with smaller profits, because their product is less in demand.† The productive classes, indeed, naturally strive to indemnify

---

* *Suprà*, Book II. chap. I.

† The position, that the interest of the capitalist and the rent of the landlord are thereby lowered, however paradoxical it may appear, is nevertheless quite true. It may be asked, why should the capitalist, who makes the advance to the manufacturer, or the landlord, whose land he occupies, lower their demands, in consequence of a portion of the product being subtracted by taxation? But is no allowance to be made for consequent delay of payment, claims of allowances, failures, and legal expenses? All, or at least a portion, of which must fall upon the landlord and capitalist: and often without any suspicion on their part, that they are thus made to participate in the burthen. In a complex social organization the pressure of taxation is often imperceptible.

themselves to the amount of the tax; but, they can never succeed to the full extent, because the intrinsic value of the commodity, that, I mean, which goes to pay the charges of production, is really diminished. So that, in fact, the tax upon an article never raises its total price by the full amount of the tax; because, to do so, the total demand must remain the same; which it never can do. Wherefore, in such cases, the tax falls, partly upon those, who still continue to consume, notwithstanding the increase of price, and partly upon the producers, who raise a less product, and find that, in consequence of the reduced demand, they really obtain less on the sale, when the tax comes to be deducted. The public revenue gains the whole excess of price to the consumer, and the whole of the profit, which the produce is thus compelled to resign. The effect is analogous to that of gunpowder, which at the same time propels the bullet, and makes the piece recoil.

By laying a tax upon the consumption of woollens, their consumption is reduced, and the revenue of the wool-grower suffers in consequence. It is true, he may take to a different kind of cultivation, but we may fairly suppose, that, under all the circumstances of soil and situation, the rearing of sheep was the most profitable kind of culture; otherwise, he would not have chosen it. A change in the mode of cultivation must, therefore, involve a loss of revenue. But the clothier and the capitalist will each be subjected to a portion of the loss resulting from the tax.

Each concurrent producer is affected by a tax on an article of consumption, in proportion only to the share he may have in raising the product taxed.

When the owner of the soil furnishes the greatest part of the value of a product, as he does in respect to products consumed nearly in the primary state, he it is that bears the greatest part of that portion of the tax, which falls on the producers. A duty of entry upon the wine imported into the towns, falls heavily upon the wine-grower; but an exorbitant excise upon lace will affect the flax-grower in a degree hardly perceptible; whereas, all the other producers, the dealers, the operative and speculative manufacturers, who create the far greater proportion of the value of the lace, will suffer very severely.

When the value of a product is partly of foreign, and partly of domestic creation, the domestic producers bear nearly the whole burthen of the tax. A tax upon cottons in France will reduce the earnings of her cotton manufacturers, by lowering the demand for their product; thus, part of the tax will fall on them. But the wages of the productive agency of the cotton-growers in America will be very little affected indeed, unless there be a concurrence of other circumstances. In fact, the tax would reduce the consumption in

---

This shows the danger of adherence to invariable principle; and of abandoning the experimental method of Smith, and constructing a system of theoretical deduction, as some recent English writers have done, in imitation of the economists of the last century.

France 10 per cent. perhaps, and demand in America 1 per cent. only, if the demand from France were but one-tenth of the general demand upon America.

The taxation of an object of consumption, if it be one of primary necessity, operates upon the price of almost all other products, and consequently falls upon the revenues of all the other consumers. An *octroi* upon meat, corn, and fuel, at their entry into a town, enhances the price of every thing manufactured in it; while a tax upon the tobacco there consumed makes no other commodity dearer; the producers and consumers of tobacco alone are affected; and for a very plain reason; the producer who indulges in superfluities has to maintain a competition with another, who abstains from them; but, if he pays a tax upon necessaries, he need fear no competition; for his neighbours will be all in the same predicament.

The direct taxation of the productive classes must, *à fortiori*, affect the consumers of their products, but can never raise the prices of those products so much, as completely to indemnify the producer; because, as I have repeatedly explained, the increased price abridges the demand, and the contraction of the demand reduces the profits of all the productive agency, that has been exerted in the supply.

Of the concurrent producers of a specific product, some can more easily evade the effect of the tax than others. The capitalist, whose capital is not absolutely vested and sunk in a particular business, may withdraw it and transfer it elsewhere, from a concern that yields him a reduced interest, or has become more hazardous. The adventurer or master-manufacturer may, in many cases, liquidate his account, and transfer his labour and intelligence to some other quarter. Not so the land-owner and proprietor of fixed capital.* An acre of vineyard or corn-land will only produce a given quantity of corn or wine, whatever be the ratio of taxation; which may take the $\frac{1}{2}$ or even $\frac{3}{4}$ of the net produce, or rent as it is called, and yet the land be tilled for the sake of the remaining $\frac{1}{2}$ or $\frac{1}{4}$.† The rent, that is to say, the portion assigned to the proprietor, will be reduced, and that is all. The reason will be manifest to any one, who considers, that in the case supposed, the land continues to raise and supply the market with the same amount of produce as before; while on the other hand, the motives in which the demand originates remain just as they were.‡ If, then, the intensity of supply and

---

* *Vide Supra*, Book I. chap. 4. for the explanation of the mode, in which the land-holder concurs in production by the advance of his land; and must, therefore, be included amongst the productive classes.

† The cultivation need never be abandoned altogether, until taxation takes more than the whole surplus product applicable to the payment of rent; it is then worth nobody's while to cultivate at all; for not only could the proprietor receive nothing, the whole being appropriated by the state; but the farmer would be compelled to pay to the state a higher rent, than he could afford.

‡ There is this peculiarity attending the products of agricultural industry, viz. that their average price is not raised by growing scarcity, because population is sure to decline co-extensively with the declining supply of human aliment; so that the demand necessarily diminishes equally with the supply. Thus it is not

demand must both remain the same, in spite of any increase or diminution of the ratio of the direct taxation upon the land, the price of the product supplied will likewise remain unchanged, and nothing but a change of price can saddle the consumer with any portion whatever of that taxation.*

Nor can the proprietor evade the tax even by the sale of the estate; for the price or purchase-money will be calculated according to the revenue which may be left him by taxation. The purchaser makes his estimate according to the net revenue, charges and taxes deducted. If the ordinary interest on such investments of capital be five per cent., an estate that before would have sold for 20,000 dollars, will fetch but 16,000 dollars when it comes to be charged with an annual tax of 200 dollars; for its actual product to the proprietor will not exceed 800 dollars. The effect is precisely the same, as if government were to appropriate to itself 1-5 of the land in the country; which would make no difference at all to the consumers of its produce.†

But property in dwelling-houses is otherwise circumstanced; a tax upon the ownership raises the rents; for a house, or rather the satisfaction it yields to the occupier, is a product of manufacture and not of land; and the high rate of house-rent reduces the production and consumption of houses, in the like manner as of cloth or any other manufactured commodity. Builders, finding their profits reduced, will build less; and consumers, finding the accommodation dearer, will content themselves with inferior lodging.

From all those circumstances, we may judge of the temerity of asserting as a general maxim, that taxation falls exclusively upon any specific class or classes of the community. It always falls upon those who can find no means of evasion; for every one naturally tries to shift the burthen off his own shoulders if possible; but the ability to evade it is infinitely varied, according to the various forms

---

found, that wheat is dearer in those countries where great part of the land is thrown out of tillage, than where it is all in a high state of cultivation. In Spain, wheat is not now dearer, than in the time of Ferdinand and Isabella, though it is there produced in much less abundance; for the number of mouths to be fed is also much less. On the contrary, the lands of both England and France were less cultivated in the middle ages than at the present day; and their product of grain less abundant; yet it does not appear, from a comparison of other values, that it was then much dearer than at present. The product and the population were both greatly inferior; and the slackness of demand counterbalanced the slackness of supply.

* It is a mistake to suppose, that the tax must bear equally upon the proprietor and the farmer, who finds the requisite capital and industry; for taxation can have no effect, either in reducing the quantity of land capable of cultivation, or in multiplying the number of farmers, able and willing to undertake it; and, if neither supply nor demand in this branch be varied, the ratio of the rent must needs remain unaltered likewise.

† The economists were quite correct in their position, that a land or territorial tax falls wholly upon the net product, and consequently, upon the proprietors; but they were wrong in extending the doctrine so far as to assert, that all other taxes were defrayed out of the same fund.

of assessment, and the position of each individual in the social system. Nay, more; it varies at different times even in the same, channel of production. When a commodity is in great request, the holder will not part with the possession, unless indemnified for all his advances, of which the tax he has paid is a part: he will take nothing short of a full and complete indemnity. But, if any unlooked-for occurrence should happen to lower the demand for his product, he will be glad enough to take the tax upon himself, for the sake of quickening the sale. There are few things so unsteady and variable, as the ratio of the pressure of taxation upon each respective class of the community. Those writers, who have maintained, that it bears upon any one or more classes in particular, or in any fixed or certain proportion, have found their theory contradicted by experience at every turn.

Furthermore, the effects I have been describing, and which are equally consonant to experience and to reason, are uniform in their operation and of equal duration with the causes in which they originate. The owner of land will never be able to saddle the consumers of its produce with any part of his land-tax; not so the manufacturer. A manufactured commodity will invariably feel a diminution in its consumption, in consequence of the price being raised by taxation, supposing other circumstances to be stationary; and its production will be a less profitable occupation. A person, who is neither producer nor consumer of an object of luxury, will never bear any portion whatever of the tax that may be laid upon it.—What, then, must we think of a proposition, unfortunately sanctioned by the approbation of an illustrious body,* that has too much neglected this branch of science, namely, that it is of little importance whether a tax press upon one branch of revenue or another, provided it be of long standing; because every tax in the end affects every class of revenue, in like manner, as bleeding in the arm reduces the circulating blood of the whole human frame. The object of comparison has no analogy whatever with taxation. Social wealth is not a fluid, tending constantly to find a level. It rather resembles the vegetable creation, which admits of the loss of a limb without the destruction of the trunk, and in which the loss is more to be lamented, if the branch be productive, than if it be barren.—But the tree will bear cutting and hacking in every part, before it becomes barren all over, or necessarily falls into decay. This is a far more apposite case; but neither will do to reason upon. Comparisons are not proofs, but mere illustrations, tending to make that intelligible, which can be made out in proof without their assistance.

When speaking of taxes upon products, which I have sometimes called taxes upon consumption, although not paid entirely in all cases by the consumer, I have hitherto made no mention of the particular stage of production, at which the tax may be demanded,

---

* The French institute, which awarded the prize of merit to an Essay of *M. Canard,* in support of this doctrine.

or of the consequence of this particular circumstance, which deserves a little of our attention.

Products increase in value progressively, as they pass through the hands of the different concurrent producers: and even the most simple undergo a variety of modifications, before they arrive at a fit state for consumption. Wherefore, a tax does not take the proportion of the value of a product which it professes, unless it be levied at the precise moment, when it has arrived at the full value, and has undergone all the productive modifications. If a tax be imposed on the raw material in the outset, proportioned, not to its then value, but to the value it is about to receive, the producer, in whose hands it happens to be, is obliged to advance a tax out of proportion to the value in hand; which advance, besides being highly inconvenient to himself, is refunded with equal inconvenience by every successive producer, till it reach the hands of the last, who is in turn but partially indemnified by the consumer. And there is this further mischief in such an advance of tax; that it prevents the class of industry, which is called upon to make it, from being originally set in motion, without a larger capital than the nature of the business requires; and that the additional interest of the capital, which must be paid, part by the consumers, and part by the producers, is so much additional taxation, without any addition of public revenue.*

Thus, both theory and experience lead to the conclusion precisely opposite to that drawn by the sect of economists; and show that portion of the tax, which presses upon the consumer's revenue, to be always the more burthensome, the earlier it is levied in the process of production.

Direct and personal taxes, which operate to raise the price of necessaries, or such as fall immediately upon necessaries, are liable to this inconvenience in the highest degree: for they oblige each producer to advance the personal tax on all the producers that have preceded him: so that the same amount of capital will set in motion a smaller amount of industry; and the tax-payers pay the tax, *plus* a compound interest upon it, yielding no benefit to the exchequer.

Nor is this mere theory: the neglect of these principles has occasioned may serious practical errors; like that of the Constituent

---

* The duty on the import of cotton into France was, in 1812, as high as 200 dollars per bale, one bale with another. There were several manufactories averaging a consumption of two bales per day; and as the amount of duty was a dead outlay, during the whole interval between the purchase of the raw material and the realization of the manufactured product, which may be taken at twelve months, they must each have required an additional capital of 120,000 dollars more than would have been requisite but for the tax; the interest of which they must have charged to the consumer, or have paid out of their own profits. The whole of it was so much addition of price to the French consumer, and aggravation of the pressure of taxation, unproductive of a single additional dollar to the public revenue. The heaviest of the national burthens of that period were those that made the least figure in the annual budget of the ministry: the people suffered, in very many instances, without knowing the nature of the grievance, as in the example, just cited.

Assembly of France, which carried to excess the system of direct taxation, especially upon land; being misled by the prevailing and fashionable doctrine of the economists;—that land is the source of all wealth, the agriculturist the only productive labourer, and France naturally and essentially an agricultural country.

It seems to me that, in the present stage of political economy, the principles of taxation will be more correctly laid down as follows:

Taxation is the taking a portion of the general product of the community, which never returns to the community in the channel of consumption.

It takes from the community over and above the values actually brought into the exchequer, the charges of collection, and the personal trouble it entails; together with all those values, of which it obstructs the creation.

The privation resulting from taxation, whether voluntary or compulsory, affects the tax-payer in his quality of producer, whenever it operates to curtail his profits; that is to say, his income or revenue; and affects him in his character of consumer, whenever it increases his expenditure, by raising the prices of products.

And, since an increase of expenditure is precisely the same thing as a diminution of revenue, whatever is taken by taxation may be said to be so much deducted from the revenues of the community.

In a great majority of cases, the tax-payer is affected by taxation in both his characters, of producer and consumer; and, when he can not manage to pay the public burthens out of his revenue, along with his personal consumption, he must encroach upon his capital. When this encroachment of one person is not counterbalanced by the savings of another, the wealth of the community must gradually decline.

The individual actually paying the tax to the tax-gatherer is not always the party really charged with it, at least, not the party charged with the whole that is paid. He frequently does no more than advance the tax, either wholly or partially; being afterwards reimbursed by the other classes of the community, in a very complicated way, and perhaps after a vast variety of intermediate operations; so that a great many persons are paying portions of the tax, at a time when probably they least suspect it, either in the shape of the advanced price of commodities, or of personal loss, which they feel but can not account for.

The individuals, on whose revenues the tax ultimately falls, are the real tax-payers, and contribute value greatly exceeding the sum that is brought into the exchequer, even with the addition of the charges of collection. The misconduct of the government in the matter of taxation, is proportioned to this excess of the payment above the receipt.

A country heavily taxed may be considered in the same light as one labouring under natural impediments to production. With a heavy charge of production, it raises a very small product. Personal exertion, capital, and the productive agency of land, are all but poorly recompensed: and more is expended in earning a less profit.

It is worth while on this head to recur to the principles explained in the preceding book,* when describing the difference between positive and relative dearness. High price resulting from taxation is positive dearness: it indicates a smaller product raised by the efforts of a larger amount of productive agency. Besides which, taxation generally occasions a cotemporary advance of commodities in comparison with silver; that is to say, raises their money price: and for this reason; because specie is not an annual, regenerative product, like those that are swallowed up by taxation. Government is not a consumer of specie, except when it happens to export it for the payment of its armies, or foreign subsidies: it refunds in the purchases it makes all the specie it obtains by taxation: but the value levied is never refunded.† Wherefore, since taxation paralyzes one part of the sources of production, and effects the rapid destruction of the product of the other, when its ratio is excessive, it must gradually render products more scarce in proportion to the specie, which is not varied in quantity by the operation. Now, whenever the commodities to be circulated become fewer in proportion to the specie that is to circulate them, their relative value to the specie must rise; the same money will purchase a smaller quantity of products.

It might be supposed, that such a superabundance of gold and silver specie ought to operate in exoneration of the public: yet it can not have that effect; for, however plentiful it may be in proportion to other commodities, still individuals can only obtain it by giving their own products in exchange, and the raising of those products has become more difficult and more costly.

Besides, when money-prices grow high, and specie is consequently reduced in relative value, it gradually takes its departure, and becomes scarcer, like all other commodities: and thus a country, burthened with a taxation too heavy for its productive powers, is first drained of its commodities, and next of its specie; till it gradually reaches the extreme of penury and depopulation.

The careful study of these principles will give some insight into the mode, in which the annual and really monstrous expenditure of national governments, in modern times, has habituated the subject to severer toil and exertion, without which it would be impossible that, after providing for the subsistence, comfort, and pleasures of himself and family, according to the habits of the time and place, he should be able to meet the consumption of the state, and the collateral waste and destruction it occasions, the amount of which it is impossible to ascertain, though in the larger states it is confessedly enormous.

---

* Book II. chap. 3.

† For the reason already stated, viz. that purchases, made with the proceeds of taxation, are acts of exchange, and not of restitution.

This very profusion, though it proves the vices and defects of the political system and organization, has been attended with one advantage at any rate; it has operated to stimulate the approximation to perfection in the art of production, by obliging mankind to turn the natural agents to better account. In this point of view, taxation has certainly helped to develope and enlarge the human faculties; so that, when the progress of political science shall limit taxation to the supply of real public wants only, the improvements in the art of production will prove a vast accession to human happiness. But, should the abuses and complexity of the political system lead to the prevalence, extension, increase, and consolidation of oppressive and disproportionate taxation, it is much to be feared, that it may plunge again into barbarism those nations, whose productive powers are now the most astonishing; and the condition of the labouring classes, who are always the bulk of the community, may in such nations present a picture of drudgery so incessant and toilsome, as to make them cast a wistful eye upon the liberty of savage existence; which, though it offer no prospect of domestic comfort, at least promises emancipation from perpetual exertion to supply the prodigality of a public expenditure, yielding to them no satisfaction, and, perhaps even operating to their prejudice. (a)

SECTION III.

Of Taxation in Kind.

Taxation in kind is the specific and immediate appropriation of a portion of the gross product to the public service.

It has this advantage, of calling on the producer only for what he

---

(a) This ground of apprehension is certainly just. It has been doubted by many political theorists, whether the total remission of taxation would operate to improve the condition of the inferior productive classes: inasmuch, as all that is now paid into the public exchequer, would quickly be appropriated by the classes, who should happen to be in possession of those sources and means of production, which are capable of exclusive appropriation; and the owners of mere personal agency would nowise benefit. But it should be observed, that private persons have an immediate personal interest in making the most of their property; and will, on their own account, so conduct themselves, as to promote their own advantage, which is the advantage of the public also, where equality of personal right prevails. Wherefore, the strongest impulse of private cupidity can never operate to retard the advance of productive power and national wealth, or to make them retrograde; but just the contrary. Thus, although the present condition of the mere labourer might not be improved, his means of bettering his condition would be enlarged, by the growing increase of wealth, and by greater freedom of personal agency. The extortion of private cupidity, unaided by authority, must, for its own sake, regulate itself by the ability of the object of it: but that of public authority is inexorable, and is restrained by no consideration of immediate personal interest. Besides, personal suffering, occasioned by the hard-heartedness of primate task-masters, is not so strong an incentive of odium against public authority, as where that authority is itself the ostensible task-master. T.

has actually in hand, in the identical shape which it happens to be under. Belgium, after its conquest by France, found itself at times unable to pay its taxes, in spite of abundant crops; the war, and the prohibition of exportation, obstructed the sale of its produce, which the government enforced by demanding payment in money; whereas, the taxes might have been collected without difficulty, had the government been content to take payment in kind.

It has the further advantage of making it equally the interest of government and of the farmer to obtain plentiful crops, and improve the national agriculture. The levying of taxes in kind in China, was probably the origin of the peculiar encouragement, bestowed by its government upon the agricultural branch of production. But, why favour one branch, when all are equally entitled to protection, because all contribute to bear the public burthens? And, why has not government an equal interest in supporting the other branches, which it takes the trouble of extinguishing?

It has likewise the advantage of excluding all exaction and injustice in the collection; the individual, when he gathers in his harvest, knows exactly what he has to pay; and the state knows what it has to receive.

This tax, which might appear at first sight to be of all others the most equitable, is nevertheless of all others the most inequitable; for it makes no allowance for the advances made in the course of production, but is taken upon the gross, instead of the net, product. Take two farmers in different branches of cultivation; the one farming tillage-land of moderate quality; his expenses of cultivation, amounting, one year with another, say to 1600 dollars, and the gross product of his farm, say to 2400 dollars, so as to yield him a net product of 800 dollars only; the other farming pasturage or wood-land, yielding a gross product of precisely the same amount of 2400 dollars: with an expense of cultivation, amounting, perhaps, to but 400 dollars, leaving him a net product, one year with another, of 2000 dollars. Suppose a tax in kind to be imposed in the ratio of 1-12 of the annual product of land of all descriptions indiscriminately. The former will have to pay in sheaves of corn to the amount of 200 dollars; the latter will pay, in cattle or in wood, an equal value of 200 dollars. What is the result? The one will have paid the fourth part of a net revenue of 800 dollars; the other but a tenth part of a net revenue of 2000 dollars.

The revenue, that each person has for his own share, is the net residue only after replacing the capital he has embarked, whatever may be its amount. Is the gross amount of the sales he effects in the year the annual income of the merchant? Certainly not; all the income he gets is the surplus of his receipts above his advances; on this surplus alone can he pay taxes, without ruin to his concerns.

The ecclesiastical tithe levied in France under the old system was liable to this inconvenience in part only. It attached neither upon meadow, nor wood-land, nor kitchen-ground, nor many other kinds of cultivation; and in some places was 1-18, in others 1-15 or 1-10 of the gross product; so that the real, was corrected by the apparent inequality.

The marechal de Vauban, in his work entitled, *Dixime Royale*, a book replete with just views, and well worth the study of those who manage national finances, proposes a tax of 1-20 of the product of the land, which, in times of great emergency, might be raised to 1-10. But this proposition was made as a substitute for a still more inequitable system: namely, the saddling of the lands of the commonalty with the whole tax, and altogether exempting the lands of the nobles and clergy. The public-spirited writer, who had occasion, in his character of engineer, to become personally acquainted with every part of France, speaks most feelingly of the hardships resulting from the land-tax(a) of those days. And there is no doubt, that the adoption of his plan at that time would have been a vast relief to the country. But it was disregarded. Why? Because every courtier had an interest to resist it: and this fine country was left to flounder through its distresses. The consequence was, a heavier loss of population from famine, than from the sword, in the war of the Spanish succession.

The difficulty and expense of collection, together with the abuses to which it is liable, are another objection to taxation in kind. The immense number of agents must open a fine field for peculation. The government may be imposed upon, in respect to the amount collected, upon the subsequent sale and disposal, in respect to the quantity damaged, as well as in the charges of storing, preservation and carriage. If the tax be farmed to contractors, the profits and expenses of numberless farmers and contractors must all fall upon the public. The prosecution of the farmers and contractors would require the active vigilance of administration. 'A gentleman of great fortune,' says Smith, 'who lived in the capital, would be in danger of suffering much by the neglect, and more by the fraud, of his factors and agents, if the rents of an estate in a distant province were to be paid to him in this manner. The loss of the sovereign, from the abuse and depredation of his tax-gatherers, would necessarily be much greater.'*

Various other objections have been urged against taxation in kind, which it would be useless and tedious to enumerate. I shall only take the liberty of remarking the violent operation upon relative price, which must follow from so vast a quantity of produce being thrown upon the market by the agents of the public revenue, who are notoriously equally improvident as buyers and as sellers. The necessity of clearing the storehouses to make room for the fresh crop, and the ever urgent demands upon the public purse, would oblige them to sell below the level, to which the price would

---

* *Wealth of Nations*, book v. c. 2. art. I.

(a) *Taille* ; for the explanation of this tax, *vide Wealth of Nations*, book v. c 2. art. 2. T.

naturally be brought by the rent of the land, the wages of labour, and the interest of the capital, engaged in agriculture; and private dealers would be unable to maintain the competition. Such taxation not only takes from the cultivator a portion of his product, but prevents his turning the residue to good account.

SECTION IV.

Of the Territorial or Land-Tax of England.

In the year 1692, which was four years after the happy revolution, that placed the prince of Orange upon the British throne, a general valuation was made of the income of all the land in the country; and, upon that valuation, the land-tax continues to be levied to this day; so that the tax of four shillings in the pound, upon the rents of land, is a fifth of its rent in 1692, and not of the actual rent at the present day.

It may easily be conceived how much this tax must operate to encourage improvements of the land. An estate that has been improved so as to double the rent, does not pay double the original tax; neither does it pay a less tax if it be suffered to fall into neglect and impoverishment; thus, it operates as a penalty upon negligence.

To this fixation of the tax, many writers attribute the high state of the cultivation of the land in England: and doubtless it may have done much to promote improvement. But, what would be thought of a government that should say to a tradesman in a small way of business, "You are trading in a small way upon a small capital, and consequently pay very little in direct taxes. Borrow, and enlarge your capital, extend your dealings, and increase your profits as much as you can, and we will not charge you with any increase of taxes. Nay, further, when your heirs succeed to the business, and have still further extended it, they shall be assessed at precisely the same rate, and shall continue subject to the same taxes only." All this might be a vast encouragement to trade and manufacture; but would there be any equity in such a proceeding? and might they not advance without such assistance? Has not England herself presented the example of a still more rapid improvement in commercial and manufacturing industry, without any such unjust partiality? A land-owner, by attention, economy, and intelligence, improves his annual income to the amount, say of 1000 dollars: if the state claim a fifth of this advance, there will still be a bonus of 800 dollars to stimulate and reward his exertions.

It would be easy to put cases, in which the tax, becoming by its fixation disproportionate to the means of the tax-payers and the condition of the soil, might be productive of as much mischief, as it has done good in other instances: where it would operate to throw out of cultivation a class of land, that, by one cause or other, had become incompetent to pay the same ratio of taxation. We have seen an example of this in Tuscany. There, a census or terrier was made in 1496, wherein the plains and valleys were rated very low, on account of the frequent floods and inundations, which prevented any regular and profitable cultivation; while the uplands, that were then the only cultivated spots, were rated very high. Since then, the torrents and inundations have been confined by drainage and embankment, and the plains reduced to fertility; their produce, being comparatively exempt from tax, came to market cheaper than that of the uplands, which, consequently, were unable to maintain the competition, under the pressure of disproportionate taxation, and have gradually been abandoned and deserted.* Whereas, had the tax been adjusted to the change of circumstances, both might have been cultivated together.

In speaking of a tax, peculiar to a particular nation, I have used it merely in illustration of general and universal principles.

CHAPTER IX.

OF NATIONAL DEBT.

SECTION I.

Of the Contracting Debt by National Authority, and of its general Effect.

THERE is this grand distinction between an individual borrower and a borrowing government, that, in general, the former borrows capital for the purpose of beneficial employment, the latter for the purpose of barren consumption and expenditure. A nation borrows, either to satisfy an unlooked-for demand, or to meet an extraordinary emergency; to which ends, the loan may prove effectual or ineffectual: but, in either case, the whole sum borrowed is so much value consumed and lost, and the public revenue remains burthened with the interest upon it.

Melon maintains, that a national debt is no more than a debt from the right hand to the left, which nowise enfeebles the body politic. But he is mistaken; the state is enfeebled, inasmuch as the capital lent to its government, having been destroyed in the consumption of it by the government, can no longer yield any body the profit, or in other words, the interest, it might earn, in the character of a productive means. Wherewith, then, is the government to pay the interest of its debt? Why, with a portion of the revenue arising

---

* *Forbonnois, Principes et Observ.* &c. tom. ii. p. 247.

from some other source, which it must transfer from the tax-payer
to the public creditor for the purpose.

Before the act of borrowing, there will have been in existence
two productive capitals, each of them yielding, or capable of yielding, revenue; that is to say, a capital about to be lent to government,
and a capital whereon the future tax-payers derive that revenue,
which is about to be applied in satisfaction of the interest upon the
capital lent. After the act of borrowing, there will remain but one
of these capitals; viz. the latter of the two, whereof the revenue is
thenceforward no longer at the disposal of its former possessors,
the present tax-payers, since it must be taken in some form of taxation or other by the government, for the sake of providing the
payment of interest to its creditors. The lender loses no part of
his revenue: the only loser is the payer of taxes.

People are apt to suppose, that, because national loans do not
necessarily occasion any diminution of the national money or specie,
therefore, they occasion, not a loss but merely a transfer, of national
wealth. With a view to the more ready exposure of this fallacy, I
have subjoined a synoptical table, showing what becomes of the sum
borrowed, and whence the public creditor's interest is satisfied.*

When a government borrows, it either does or does not engage
to repay the principal. In the latter case, it grants what is called
a perpetual annuity. Redeemable loans are capable of infinite
variety in the terms. The principal is contracted to be repaid,
sometimes gradually, and in the way of lottery; sometimes by instalments payable together with the interest, sometimes in the way of
increased interest, with condition to expire on the death of the
lender; as in the case of tontines and life-annuities, whereof the
latter determine on the death of the individual lender; whereas, in
tontines, the full interest continues to be divided amongst the survivors, until the whole of the lives have expired.

Tontines and life-annuities are very improvident modes of borrowing; for the borrower remains throughout liable to the full rate
of interest, although he annually repays a part of the principal.
Besides, they savour of immorality; offering a premium to egotism,
and a stimulus to the dilapidation of capital, by enabling the lender
to consume both principal and interest without fear of personal
beggary.

The governments best acquainted with the business of borrowing
and lending have not, of late years at least, given any engagement
to repay the principal of the loan. Thus, public creditors have no
other way of altering the investment of their capital, except by
selling their transferable security, which they can do with more or
less advantage to themselves, according to the buyer's opinion of
the solidity of the debtor government, that has granted the perpetual
annuity.† Despotic governments have always found a great diffi-

---

* *Vide* App. A.

† In the next section it will be explained how an unredeemable debt may be
extinguished by purchase at the market price.

culty in negotiating such loans. Where the sovereign is powerful enough to violate his contracts at pleasure, or where there is a mere personal contract with the reigning monarch, with a risk of disavowal by the successor, lenders are loth to advance their money, without a near and definite period of payment.

The appointment to posts and offices, under condition of an annual payment, or of deposit for which the government engages to pay interest, is a mode of borrowing in perpetuity, in which the loan is compulsory. When once this paltry expedient is resorted to, it requires very little ingenuity to find plausible grounds, for converting almost every occupation, down to the dust-man and street-porter, into patent and saleable offices.

Another mode of borrowing is, by the anticipation of revenue; by which is meant, the assignment by a government of revenues not yet due, with allowance in the nature of discount, the taking up money in advance from lenders, who charge a discount proportionate to the risk they run from the instability of the government and possible deficiency of the revenue. Engagements of this kind contracted by a government, and satisfied either out of the revenue when collected, or by the issue of fresh bills upon the public treasury, constitute what bears the uncouth English denomination of *floating* debt; the consolidated debt being that, whereon the creditor can demand the interest only, and not the principal.

National loans of every kind are attended with the universal disadvantage of withdrawing capital from productive employment, and diverting it into the channel of barren consumption; and, in countries where the credit of the government is at a low ebb, with the further and particular disadvantage, of raising the interest of capital. Who can be expected to lend at 5 per cent. to the farmer, the manufacturer, or the merchant, while he can readily get an offer of 7 or 8 per cent. from the government? That class of revenue which has been called, profit of capital, is thereby advanced in its ratio, at the expense of the consumer: the consumption falls off, in consequence of the advance in the real price of products; the productive agency of the other sources of production are less in demand, and consequently worse paid; and the whole community is the sufferer, with the sole exception of the capitalist.

The ability to borrow affords one main advantage to the state, namely, the power of apportioning the burthen entailed by a sudden emergency among a great number of successive years. In the present state of public affairs, and on the present scale of international warfare, no country could support the enormous expense from its ordinary annual revenue. The larger states pay in taxation nearly as much as they are able; for economy is by no means the order of the day with them; and their ordinary expenditure seldom falls much short of the income. If the expenditure must be doubled to save the nation from ruin, borrowing is usually the only resource · unless it can make up its mind to violate all subsisting engagements, and be guilty of spoliation of its own subjects and foreigners too

The faculty of borrowing is a more powerful agent, than even gunpowder; but probably the gross abuse that is made of it, will soon destroy its efficacy.

Great pains have been taken, to find in the system of borrowing, as well as in taxation, some inherent advantage beyond that of supplying the public consumption. But a close examination will expose the hopelessness of such an attempt.

It has been maintained, for instance, that the debentures and securities, which form a national debt, become real and substantial values, existing within the community; that the capital, of which they are the evidence or representative, is so much positive wealth, and must be reckoned as an item of the total substance of the nation.*

But it is not so; a written contract or security is a mere evidence, that such or such property belongs to such an individual. But wealth consists in the property itself, and not in the parchment, by which its ownership is evidenced; therefore à fortiori, a security is not even an evidence of wealth, where it does not represent an actual existing value, and when it operates as a mere power of attorney from the government to its creditor, enabling him to receive annually a specified portion of the revenue expected to be levied upon the tax-payers at large. Supposing the security to be cancelled, as it might be by a national bankruptcy, would there be any the least diminution of wealth in the community? Undoubtedly not. The only difference would be, that the revenue, which before went to the public creditor, would now be at the disposal of the tax-payer, from whom it used to be taken.

Those who tell us, that the annual circulation is increased by the whole amount of the annual disbursements of the government,† forget that these disbursements are made out of the annual products, and are a portion of the annual revenue, taken from the tax-payer, which would have been brought into the general circulation just the same, although no such thing as national debt had existed. The tax-payer would have spent what is now spent by the public creditor; that is all.

The sale or purchase of debentures or securities is not a productive circulation, but a mere substitution of one public creditor in place of another. When these transfers degenerate into stock-jobbing, that is to say, the making of a profit by the rise and fall of their price, they are productive of much mischief; in the first place, by the unproductive employment on this object of the agent of circulation, money, which is an item of the national capital; and, in the

---

* Considerations sur les Avantages de l'Existence d'une Dette publique, p. 8.

† The transferable nature of these securities does not invest them with the properties of money, since they do not act in that capacity. But the use of convertible paper, as money, operates to create a positive addition to the total national capital; because, but for their agency in the transfer of value in general, it must be executed by specie, or some equally substantial item of capital. Government debentures of stock require money to circulate them, instead of acting themselves as money.

next, by procuring a gain to one person by the loss of another; which is the characteristic of all gaming. The occupation of the stock-jobber yields no new or useful product; consequently having no product of his own to give in exchange, he has no revenue to subsist upon, but what he contrives to make out of the unskilfulness or ill-fortune of gamesters like himself.

A national debt has been said to bind the public creditors more firmly to the government, and make them its natural supporters by a sense of common interest; and so it does, beyond all doubt. But, as this common interest may attach equally to a bad or a good government, there is just as much chance of its being an injury, as a benefit to a nation. If we look at England, we shall see a vast number of well-meaning persons, induced by this motive to uphold the abuses and misgovernment of a wretched administration.

It has been further urged, that a national debt is an index of the public opinion, respecting the degree of credit which the government deserves, and operates as a motive to its good conduct, and endeavours to preserve the public opinion, of which such a debt furnishes the index. This can not be admitted without some qualification. The good conduct of government in the eyes of the public creditors, consists in the regular payment of their own dividends; but in the eyes of the tax-payers, it consists in spending as little as possible. The market-price of stock does, indeed, furnish a tolerable index of the former kind of good conduct, but not of the latter. Perhaps it would be no exaggeration to say, that the punctual payments of the dividends, instead of being a sign of good, is in numberless instances a cloak to bad, government; and, in some countries, a boon for the toleration of frequent and glaring abuses.

Another argument in favour of national debt is, that it affords a prompt investment to capital, which can find no ready and profitable employment, and thus must, at any rate, prevent its emigration. If it do, so much the worse: it is a bait to tempt capital towards its destruction, leaving the nation burthened with the annual interest, which government must provide. It is far better that the capital should emigrate, as it would probably return sooner or later: and then its interest for the mean time will be chargeable to foreigners. A national debt of moderate amount, the capital of which should have been well and judiciously expended in useful works, might indeed be attended with the advantage of providing an investment for minute portions of capital, in the hands of persons incapable of turning them to account, who would probably keep them locked up, or spend them by driblets, but for the convenience of such an investment. This is perhaps the sole benefit of a national debt; and even this is attended with some danger ; inasmuch as it enables a government to squander the national savings. For, unless the principal be spent upon objects of permanent public benefit, as on roads, canals, or the like, it were better for the public, that the capital should remain inactive, or concealed ; since, if the public lost the use of it, at least it would not have to pay the interest.

Thus, it may be expedient to borrow, when capital must be spent by a government, having nothing but the usufruct at its command: but we are not to imagine, that, by the act of borrowing, the public prosperity can be advanced. The borrower, whether a sovereign, or an individual, incurs an annual charge upon his revenue, besides impoverishing himself to the full amount of the principal, if it be consumed; and nations never borrow but with a view to consume outright.

<h2 style="text-align:center">Section II.</h2>

Of public Credit, its Basis, and the Circumstances that endanger its Solidity.

Public credit is the confidence of individuals in the engagements of the ruling power, or government. This credit is at the extreme point of elevation, when the public creditor gets no higher interest, than he would by lending on the best private securities; which is a clear proof, that the lenders require no premium of insurance to cover the extra risk they incur, and that in their estimation there is no such extra risk. Public credit never reaches this elevation, except where the government is so constituted, as to find great difficulty in breaking its engagements, and where, moreover, its resources are known to be equal to its wants; for which latter reason, public credit is never very high, unless where the financial accounts of the nation are subject to general publicity.

Where the public authority is vested in a single individual, it is next to impossible, that public credit should be very extensive: for there is no security, beyond the pleasure and good faith of the monarch. When the authority resides in the people, or its representatives, there is the further security of a personal interest in the people themselves, who are creditors in their individual, and debtors in their aggregate character; and therefore, can not receive in the former, without paying in the latter. This circumstance alone would lead us to presume, that now, when great undertakings are so costly as to be effected by borrowing alone, representative governments will acquire a marked preponderance in the scale of national power, simply on account of their superior financial resources, without reference to any other circumstance.

In one light, the obligations of government inspire more confidence than those of individuals, that is to say, by the greater solidity of its resources. The resources of the most responsible individual may fail suddenly and totally, or at least to such an extent, as to disable him from performing his engagements.

Numerous commercial failures, political or national calamities, litigation, fraud or violence, may ruin him entirely; but the supplies of a government are derived from such various quarters, that the individual calamities of its subjects can operate but partially upon the revenue of the state. There is also another thing, that facilitates the borrowing of government even more than the credit it is fairly entitled to; and that is, the great facility of transfer presented to the stockholder. Public creditors always reckon upon the possibility of withdrawing by the sale of their debentures, before the occurrence of embarrassment or bankruptcy; and, even where they contemplate such a risk, generally consider some advance of the rate of interest a sufficient premium of insurance against it.

Moreover, it is observable, that the sentiments of lenders and indeed of mankind upon all occasions, are more powerfully operated upon by the impressions of the moment, than by any other motive; experience of the past must be very recent, and the prospect of the future very near, to have any sensible effect. The monstrous breach of faith on the part of the French government in 1721, in regard to its paper-money and the Mississippi share-holders, did not prevent the ready negotiation of a loan of 200,000,000 *liv.* in 1759; nor did the bankrupt measures of the Abbé Terrai in 1772 prevent the negotiation of fresh loans in 1778 and every subsequent year.

In other points of view, the credit of individuals is better founded than that of the government. There is no compulsory process against the latter, for the breach of its engagements; nor do governments ever husband the national resources with nearly the care and attention of individuals. Besides, in the event of external or internal subversion, individuals may withdraw their property from the wreck much better than governments can.

Public credit affords such facilities to public prodigality, that many political writers have regarded it as fatal to national prosperity. For, say they, when governments feel themselves strong in the ability to borrow, they are too apt to intermeddle in every political arrangement, and to conceive gigantic projects, that lead sometimes to disgrace, sometimes to glory, but always to a state of financial exhaustion; to make war themselves, and stir up others to do the like; to subsidize every mercenary agent, and deal in the blood and the consciences of mankind; making capital, which should be the fruit of industry and virtue, the prize of ambition, pride, and wickedness.

A nation, which has the power to borrow, and yet is in a state of political feebleness, will be exposed to the requisitions of its more powerful neighbours. It must subsidize them in its defence; must purchase peace; must pay for the toleration of its independence, which it generally loses after all; or perhaps must lend, with the certain prospect of never being repaid.

These are by no means hypothetical cases: but the reader is left to make the application himself.

By the establishment of sinking-funds, well-ordered governments have found means to extinguish and discharge their redeemable debt. The constant operation of this contrivance contributes more than any thing else to the consolidation of public credit. The mode of proceeding is simply this:

Suppose that the state borrows 100 millions of dollars at an interest of 5 per cent.; to pay that interest, it must appropriate a portion of the national revenue to the amount of 5 millions of dollars. For this purpose, it usually imposes a tax calculated to produce this sum annually. If the tax be made to produce somewhat more, say 5,462,400 dollars, and the surplus of 462,400 dollars be thrown into a particular fund, and laid out annually, in the purchase of government debentures to that amount in the market, and if, moreover, in addition to this surplus, the interest likewise upon the debt thus extinguished, be annually employed in such purchases, the whole principal debt will be extinguished at the end of fifty years. This is the mode in which a sinking-fund operates. The efficacy of this expedient depends upon the progressive power of compound interest; that is to say, the gradual augmentation of the interest of capital, by the addition of interest upon the arrears of interest, reckoned from certain stated periods.

It is obvious, that, by an annual instalment of not more than 10 per cent. upon its own interest, the principal of a debt bearing an interest of 5 per cent. may be extinguished in less than 50 years. However, the sale of the debentures being voluntary, if the holders will not sell at par, that is to say, at 20 years purchase, the redemption, in this way, will take somewhat longer time; but this very state of the market will be a convincing proof of the high ratio of national credit. On the other hand, if the credit decline, so that the same sum will purchase a larger amount of debentures, the extinction of the debt will be effected in a shorter period. So that the lower public credit falls, the more powerful is the operation of a sinking-fund to revive it; and that fund grows less efficient, exactly in proportion as it becomes less requisite.

To the establishment of such a fund, has the long-continued public credit of Great Britain been attributed, and her ability still to go on borrowing, in spite of a debt of more than 800 millions sterling. (1)

---

(1) In a note, here subjoined, the author stated the amount of the British national debt, in the year 1815, on the authority of a speech made in parliament in February, of that year, by the chancellor of the exchequer, Mr. Vansittart. We now have it in our power, in place of the note in question, to furnish the reader with an exact statement of the British national debt, from its commencement, at the revolution of 1688, to the 5th of January, 1832. The abstract we give is extracted from the Tables to Part II. of "Pebrer on the Taxation, Debt, Capital, Resources, &c. of the whole British Empire," a work which we before had occasion to refer to, and of the highest statistical authority.

	Pounds sterling.
National debt at the revolution, 1688, - - - - - - - -	664,263
Increase during the reign of William and Mary, - - - -	15,730,439
Debt at accession of Anne, 1702, - - - - - - - - -	16,394,702
Increase during reign of Anne, - - - - - - - - -	37,750,661
Debt at accession of George I., 1714, - - - - - - - -	54,145,363
Decrease during reign of George I., - - - - - - - -	2,053,128

And doubtless this it is, that has made Smith declare sinking-funds, which were contrived expressly to reduce national debt, the main instruments of their increase. Had not governments the happy knack of abusing resources of every kind, they would soon grow too rich and powerful.

A sinking-fund is a complete delusion, whenever a government continues borrowing on one hand, as much as it redeems on the other; and à fortiori, when it borrows more than it redeems, as England has constantly done, since the year 1793 to the present time. Whencesoever the amount of the sinking-fund be derived, whether it be merely the product of a fresh tax, or that product, augmented by the interest on the extinguished debt, if the government borrow a million for every million of debt that it pays off, it creates an annual charge of precisely the same amount as that extinguished: it is precisely the same thing, as lending to itself the million devoted to the purpose of redemption. Indeed, the latter course would save the expense of the operation. This position has been fully established in an excellent work, by professor Hamilton,* which is quite conclusive upon the subject. The enormous burthens

---

* On the National Debt of Great Britain. 8vo., Edinburgh, 1813.

Debt at accession of George II., 1727, - - - - - - - -	52,092,235
Decrease during the peace, - - - - - - - - - -	5,137,612
Debt at commencement of Spanish war, 1739, - - - -	46,954,623
Increase during the war, - - - - - - - - - - -	31,338,689
Debt at end of Spanish war, 1748, - - - - - - - -	78,293,312
Decrease during the peace, - - - - - - - - - -	3,721,472
Debt at commencement of war, 1755, - - - - - - -	74,571,840
Increase during the war, - - - - - - - - - - -	72,111,004
Debt at conclusion of the peace, 1762, - - - - - - -	146,682,844
Decrease during the peace, - - - - - - - - - -	10,739,793
Debt at commencement of American war, 1776, - - - -	135,943,051
Increase during the war, - - - - - - - - - - -	102,541,819
Debt at conclusion of American war, 1783, - - - - -	238,484,870
Decrease during the peace, - - - - - - - - - -	4,751,261
Debt at commencement of French revolutionary war, 1793,	233,733,609
Increase during the war, - - - - - - - - - - -	295,105,668
Debt at peace of Amiens, 1st February, 1801, - - - - -	528,839,277
Increase during the second war, - - - - - - - -	335,983,164
Debt at peace of Paris, 1st February, 1816, - - - - -	864,822,441
Decrease since the peace, - - - - - - - - - -	82,155,207
Debt on 5th January, 1832, - - - - - - - - -	£782,667,234
Equal to 3,756,802,723 dollars.	

AMERICAN EDITOR.

of the people of England, the scandalous abuse its government has made of the power of borrowing, and her substitution of paper-money in place of specie, will have produced some benefit at least; inasmuch as they have assisted the solution of many problems, highly interesting to the happiness of nations, and given warning to all future generations, to beware of the like excesses.

It must be evident, that the grand requisite to the efficiency of a sinking-fund is, the punctual and inviolable application of the sums appropriated to the purpose of redemption. Yet this has never been rigidly adhered to, even in England, where consistency and good faith to the creditors are a point of honour with the government. So that English writers put no faith in the extinction of the debt by the operation of the sinking-fund: nay, Smith makes no scruple of declaring, that national debts have never been extinguished except by national bankruptcy.

It has been sometimes a matter of speculation, to inquire into the effect of a national bankruptcy upon the relative condition of individuals, and the internal economy of the nation. In ordinary cases, when a government commits an act of bankruptcy, it adds to the revenues of the tax-payers the whole amount that it discontinues paying to the public creditors.—Nay, it goes somewhat further: for it remits likewise the charges of collection and management of the revenue and the debt. A nation burthened with 100 millions of annual interest on its debt, whereon the charges above mentioned should amount to 30 per cent.* more, might by a bankruptcy remit to the tax-payers 130 millions, while it stript its creditors of 100 millions only.

In England the effect would be more complicated; because she does not pay the dividends on her debt wholly out of the annual proceeds of taxation; at least, not at the moment of my writing; but annually borrows a sum nearly equal to the interest of her debt.† Were she to commit an act of bankruptcy, the annual loans of 40 millions sterling, more or less, would be withdrawn from unproductive consumption by the public creditors, and be applicable to the purposes of re-productive consumption: for it may fairly be supposed, that the capitalists who accumulate and lend to the state, would look out for some profitable investment. In this point of view, the operation would tend vastly to the increase of the national capital and revenue: but the execution would be attended with very disastrous immediate consequences: for this annual amount of 40 millions would be withdrawn from the class of consumers, who have no other means of subsistence, and would be utterly unable to make

---

* In England and the United States they are not nearly so high in proportion: but the ratio is even higher in some states that shall be nameless.

† Colquhoun, *Wealth, Power, and Resources of the British Empire*, 4to. London, 1814. Stokes, *Revenue and Expenditure of Great Britain*, London, 1815. Should a continuance of peace enable her to square her income with her annual expenditure, inclusive of the interest of her debt, it would still afford no relief, but merely arrest the further progress of the evil.

good their losses in any other way, for want of both personal indus‧ try, and of the command of capital.

A bankruptcy would probably obviate the necessity of fresh loans; but would not release an atom of the former taxation, where the interest of the debt is habitually paid, not with the proceeds of taxation, but with new loans. Thus, the burthens of the people would not be alleviated,* nor the charges of production reduced: consequently there would be no sensible reduction in the price of commodities; nor would British products find a readier market either at home or abroad.

The classes liable to taxation would be diminished in numerical strength, by the whole of the suppressed stockholders; and taxation less productive, although not lower in ratio. The 40 millions of revenue, withdrawn from the public creditors, would pay taxes only upon the annual profit or revenue, they might yield in the character of productive capital. The ruin of the public creditors would be attended with abundance of collateral distress; with private failures and insolvency without end; with the loss of employment to all their tradesmen and servants, and the utter destitution of all their dependants.

On the other hand, if she persevere in borrowing to pay the interest of the former loans, that interest and with it taxation also, must go on increasing to infinity. It is impossible to avoid a precipice, when one follows a road that leads nowhere else.

The potentates of Asia, and all sovereigns, who have no hopes of establishing a credit, have recourse to the accumulation of treasure. Treasure is the reserve of past, whereas a loan is the anticipation of future revenue. They are both serviceable expedients in case of emergency.

A treasure does not always contribute to the political security of its possessors. It rather invites attack, and very seldom is faithfully applied to the purpose for which it was destined. The accumulation of Charles V. of France fell into the hands of his brother, the duke of Anjou; those which pope Paul II. destined to oppose the Turkish arms, and drive them out of Europe, supplied the extravagancies of Sixtus IV. and his nephews. The treasures amassed by Henry IV., for the humiliation of the house of Austria, were lavished upon the favourites of the queen-mother: and, at a later period, we have seen the political power of Prussia brought into imminent hazard by those very savings, which were destined by Frederick III. to its consolidation.

The command of a large sum is a dangerous temptation to a national administration. Though accumulated at their expense, the people rarely, if ever profit by it: yet in point of fact, all value, and consequently, all wealth, originates with the people.

---

* Economy in the national expenditure is the only thing that can mitigate the pressure of taxation upon the British nation; yet were economy enforced, how is that system of corruption to be upheld, through which the interest of the minister of the day regularly prevails over that of the nation?

APPENDIX A.

A TABLE, SHOWING THE RESULT OF VALUE LENT TO THE STATE.

		These three portions yield but two of revenue; portion II. being absolutely extinct.
I. yielding	revenue	consumable by the proprietor himself.
II. yielding	nothing; being lent to, and consumed by the state	revenue.
III. yielding	revenue	transferred to, and consumable by, the lenders of Portion II.
IV. yielding	revenue	applicable to any purpose.

General Fund, whence all Revenue is derivable; consisting of the Total Natural Agency, Capital and Industry, at the command of the Nation, divided into four equal portions, whereof respectively each Individual is supposed to possess a share, proportionate to his Wealth. Of this stock, the only part applicable to the purpose of a National Loan, is the transferable or floating value, capable of acting as capital.

APPENDIX B.

A table, showing the comparative condition of France, Great Britain and Ireland, and the United States of America, in respect to Population, Debt, and Taxation, at the close of the year 1831.

	Population.	Debt.	Revenue.
France....	32,560,000	$1,035,800,000	$187,200,000
Britain and Ireland ...	24,304,000	3,756,802,723	247,075,200
United States	13,200,000	24,322,235*	28,526,820*

*These two sums only include the public debt and revenue of the Federal Government, at the period referred to, and not the debts and revenue of the different States of the Union. To show the comparative condition of the *people* of the United States, with those of France and Britain, in respect to debt and taxation, at the time mentioned, it would be necessary to add the debts and revenue of the respective States, which, however, at this time, we have no means of doing.

AMERICAN EDITOR.

THE END.